Computer and network organization
An introduction

Maarten van Steen
Vrije Universiteit, Amsterdam

Henk Sips
Delft University of Technology
University of Amsterdam

Prentice Hall

London   New York   Toronto   Sydney   Tokyo   Singapore
Madrid   Mexico City   Munich

First published 1995 by
Prentice Hall Europe
Campus 400, Maylands Avenue
Hemel Hempstead
Hertfordshire, HP2 7EZ
A division of
Simon & Schuster International Group

© Prentice Hall Europe 1995

Printed and bound in Great Britain by
Redwood Books, Trowbridge, Wiltshire.

Library of Congress Cataloging-in-Publication Data

Steen, Maarten van.
       Computer and network organization: an introduction/Maarten van
Steen, Henk Sips.
              p.   cm.
       Includes bibliographical references and index.
       ISBN 0-13-382425-X (alk. paper)
       1. Computer organization. 2. Computer networks. I. Sips, Henk.
II. Title.
QA76.9.C643S74   1995
004.2'2-dc20   95-16926
                                                           CIP

British Library Cataloguing in Publication Data

A catalogue record for this book is available
from the British Library

ISBN 0-13-382425-X
---
2   3   4   5   99 98 97

4004, 8008, 8086, 8088, 80286, 80386, 80586, Pentium are trademarks of Intel Corporation
68000 is a trademark of Motorola Corporation
Ada is a trademark of the US Department of Defense Ada Joint Program Office
IBM, 360 are trademarks of International Business Machines Corporation
MS-DOS is a trademark of Microsoft Corporation
PDP-11 is a trademark of Digital Equipment Corporation
UNIX is a trademark of UNIX Systems Laboratories

To Mariëlle and Annette

Contents

Foreword

This book solves the *Three Bears Problem*. As you may recall, when Goldilocks visited the three bears, some things were too big, and some things were too small, but she wanted something that was "just right."

Many scientists, engineers, and technical managers face the same problem. It is important for them to have a good grasp of modern computer technologies, including computer architecture, operating systems, and networks. All of these are complex and rapidly changing subjects.

Until now, these people have had two choices. On the one hand, there are many detailed computer science textbooks available for each subject separately. These books offer a comprehensive view of the subject, but require the reader to plow through 500–800 pages of material. Mastering computer architecture, operating systems, and networking might require absorbing 2000 pages of highly technical material.

On the other hand, bookstores are full of gee-whiz books telling how wonderful computers are and what they can do for you. Many are about specific systems, and are full of advice of the sort "To make X happen, click on icon Y." These books are written for readers with a casual interest in science and technology, but do not explain how computers and systems actually work inside.

For technically-oriented people in physics, chemistry, engineering, and management, neither of these choices is appropriate. What they need is a single volume that discusses the fundamentals of computer systems (architecture, operating systems, and networks) in considerable technical detail, but in a single well-integrated book. This is their book. In a little over 500 pages, it covers hardware, architecture, operating systems, communication, LANs, and WANs in a surprising amount of detail, with numerous algorithms given as actual programs in an Ada-like language.

At universities, this book can be used for a second computer course for non-computer science majors. It is also self contained, and makes fine reading for practicing professionals who want to keep up-to-date on three different subareas of computer science, but without having to read three different books. I recommend this book most highly for these audiences.

Andrew S. Tanenbaum

Preface

Why we have written this book

This book was written out of necessity. A few years ago, both of us were engaged in giving a course on the technical principles of computer systems for an audience with only a modest background in computer science. The goals set out for that course where quite challenging. First, undergraduate students were to be provided with a general insight into the actual working of computer systems, which covered the three main themes: computer organization, operating systems, and computer networks. Second, there was only room for 15 two-hour lectures, to be given in a single semester. Indeed, not an easy task to accomplish, especially when it turned out that hardly any single textbook existed that covered these three themes at an adequate introductory level.

The result was that an initial course text was written, comprising about 200 pages, which roughly explained the working of computer systems. The material was more or less equally divided between computer organization, operating systems, and computer networks. This course text, combined with the actual lectures given, proved at least one thing: explaining the technicalities of computer systems in a single semester was not only feasible, the students actually enjoyed it. Doing a complete rewrite and ending with a 550-page book is just one of those things that can happen when the two of us start having "good" ideas.

The main questions that are addressed

As mentioned, in this book we have made an attempt to explain the working of computer systems, but in such a way that it should be possible to go through almost the entire material in just a single one-semester course. The book roughly addresses, in order, the following questions:

- **What does a computer look like from the inside?** In particular, we explain the essence of chips, processors, memory, peripheral devices such as hard disks and keyboards, and how these various components are connected to each other so that they can operate together.

- **What is actually meant by a computer program?** This question (which to some may seem so simple that they will have a hard time giving a right answer) is addressed in two ways. First, we explain how we can use a computer's so-called instruction set to develop programs. Second, we shall demonstrate that computer programs can be more easily written in a high-level programming language for which no real processor exists, but which can nevertheless be executed.

- **What is an operating system, and how does it work?** This is an important question as it addresses the way that modern computers appear to users. We will explain that an operating system is a special program that allows you to work conveniently and efficiently with a computer. Above all, we will emphasize the role of operating systems as a mechanism to abstract matters that are specific to hardware, and in particular that they provide an important means for communication by computers.

- **How can computers be linked together?** This is the first topic of computer networks. Our attention will initially focus on various hardware aspects, i.e. the physical appearance of computer networks. Also, we shall present the basics of how computer programs are to be constructed by which information between two or several computers can be exchanged. In a sense, the answer to this question is treated very much at the same level as the first question posed above.

- **How does communication across a computer network take place?** This is an important question that will also be addressed. We shall explain how messages can be transferred from one user to another, possibly crossing a network that spans the world, or alternatively, one that is used in conjunction with, for example, printers. Central to answering this question is the concept of communication protocols: what are they, and how are they realized?

These questions are not addressed in isolation. Instead, we follow an approach by which the working of computer systems is gradually exposed. This approach not only allows the reader to understand the essentials, but above all, will provide an *overall view* on the technical principles of computer systems.

A book such as this probably cannot do otherwise than present the essentials. And indeed, this is as far as we go. But in doing so, we have sought to provide an understanding of the subjects in such a way that the reader will see the big picture, but at the same time will have a feeling for the details that are involved. For example, we have found it important to explain *how* the interaction between hardware and software takes place, in particular when discussing operating systems. Strangely enough, this topic is often hardly discussed explicitly in books on either computer organization or operating systems. Likewise, we provide simplified examples of programs that illustrate how layering of software can be achieved. Layering is an important concept when explaining computer networks. We have been surprised by the fact that again only relatively few books explain how the concept can be made concrete. And although our approach only permits us to give a glimpse of how layering works in practice, we feel that not doing this would have been a serious omission.

Intended readership

With these things in mind, we have written our text for people that are somewhat familiar with computers. This means that we expect that the reader already has a basic feeling of what computers are, and what you can do with them. Having followed an introductory course in computer science will give an understanding of the material presented here. Most of all, it will make it much easier to comprehend concepts such as processors and programs, which are of vital importance to understanding computer systems. Having a reading knowledge of computer programs, for example written in Pascal, will help.

The material is, by its nature, technical. As such, undergraduate students in engineering disciplines and natural sciences will perhaps find the book easier to understand than others. However, we emphasize that the material has also been classroom tested for students in business information sciences. As we have said above, a basic interest in computer science as experienced during a first introductory course should be sufficient for a successful understanding of this book.

The book can also serve as an alternative for courses in computer organization, with less emphasis on architecture and more on modern subjects as concurrency and communication. To our opinion this change in material coverage will inevitably take place, since computers and communication will be increasingly integrated.

But apart from a being a textbook to be used as part of a course, the material is also intended for those who would wish to know more about the various general technical principles, but find existing textbooks simply too overwhelming to start with. In that case, this book may well form a good starting point, and may even be sufficient. If the latter is not the case, then enough knowledge and terminology will have been introduced to make the transition to more specialized textbooks.

We have made an attempt to organize the material in such a way that different types of readers will feel equally comfortable. First, we have included so-called elaboration sections, which are distinguished from the main text as follows:

▷ This is an example of an elaboration section, and can be skipped at first reading.

Elaboration sections often contain additional material that may be either too technical or too detailed to be discussed initially. In all cases, these sections may be skipped if so required: they do not interfere with the main text but are pure extensions of it.

Each chapter concludes with a summary or discussion, as well as references for further reading. Where explicitly noted, the reader is particularly encouraged to consult the referenced material as it will generally provide further insight into the material as we have presented it. Finally, each chapter, except the first one, has been augmented with a number of exercises. Starred exercises generally require reading the elaboration sections.

More information

We find it important to keep the reader informed about additional material related to this book. Therefore, we have constructed a Web page at http://www.cs.vu.nl/~steen/cno.html. At present, the page contains links to problem solutions and Postscript versions of (nearly) all figures. Additional material will be made available through this Web page. You can also find out how and where we can be reached if you wish to contact us. Suggestions on how the book can be improved are most welcome, as well as any reports on errors and omissions.

Acknowledgments

Writing a book is definitely something you cannot do without having the support from many others. In order to get this project started, it was necessary to install a UNIX-based support environment on a rather unwilling personal computer. Paul Kranenburg, Eelco van Asperen, and Reino de Boer helped to get the software where it was needed. Reino deserves special credit for additionally helping with many of the intricacies related to LATEX and TEX.

Others helped us get the manuscript right by reading portions of the material, and pointing out the sections that needed improvement. In this respect, we owe much to Theun Bruins, Leendert van Doorn, Jaap Gordijn, Tom Hoeksma, Philip Homburg, Mark Polman, Kees van Reeuwijk, Ron Roozendaal, Andy Tanenbaum, Louis Tinzelboer, Joachim Trescher, and Hans de Vreught. Special thanks go particularly to Marcel Beemster and Wim Stut who both managed to read the entire manuscript at a level of detail that often not only surprised us but above all proved to be invaluable.

But perhaps in the end, much of the support comes from those that will presumably never read the book, but who have nonetheless undergone the entire project from the very beginning. Mariëlle and Annette get all the credit for their support.

Maarten van Steen
Henk Sips

Chapter 1

Introduction

The field of computer and network organization is large, but an exciting one. The number of problems that have been tackled and are still being studied is so large that it is often difficult to obtain an overview of the subject without being swamped by all kinds of details. In order to avoid losing the way while studying the material in the chapters yet to follow, we start with giving some rough guidelines on what computer and network organization is mainly about. This introductory chapter is centered around Section 1.2 which outlines the essence of computers, and Section 1.3 in which we concentrate on computer networks.

1.1 To start with

In order to understand the material presented in this book it is necessary to look at problems of computer and network organization from the right perspective. Let's start by explaining how we plan to tackle the problems by telling what *our* perspective is.

1.1.1 The *what* versus the *how*

It is hard to imagine what our daily lives would be without having computers. We have become so familiar with their existence that they hardly surprise us any more. For example, we expect that much of the administration that we are confronted with is handled one way or the other by means of a computer. That the inventory of supermarkets is kept up to date by simply coupling the cash registers to the computer is something we tend to consider as normal. Using credit cards that are electronically processed is also something we are accustomed to. We have grown used to producing documents through advanced word processing systems rather than using typewriters. These are only a few examples. Computers have indeed simply become a fact of life.

But this is just one side of computers. To date, many people have a fairly good idea of *what* can be done with computers. But knowing *how* computer engineers attained their remarkable achievements is a completely different story. As we have all become so acquainted with using computers, it also seems that we are willing to accept that it is necessary to be an expert to understand what's going on under the hood. And that is really unfortunate, for it is our belief that if someone knows more about *how* computers work, it becomes a lot easier to understand *what* they can do, and above all, what they cannot do.

In this book we will make a serious attempt to guide you through the principles that underlie computer systems. The term "computer systems" is to be taken in its broadest sense. It covers the field of relatively small personal computers, as well as that of worldwide networks consisting of millions of computers connected together to allow information to be easily communicated around the world.

1.1.2   Architecture versus organization

The approach that we have adopted is that of focusing on the **organization** of computers and networks. What does that mean? To make an easy comparison, suppose we had decided to write a book on the principles underlying cars. We could then roughly follow two approaches.

In the first approach, we could start by explaining that a car has an engine, and also explain what an engine consists of. We would be saying something about fan belts, cylinders, spark plugs, etc. And likewise, other necessary components that make up a car would be presented, together with an explanation of what they stand for. Putting it differently, we would follow an approach in which a car is successively decomposed into a number of **functional** components. In the end, you would be able to name all the necessary components and explain exactly what they stand for, and why they are needed. In that case, you would have a pretty good idea about the **architecture** of a car.

An alternative approach is the following. Rather than merely explaining that an engine is needed, we could choose to explain how that engine actually works. In that case, we would explain that an engine may have four cylinders, possibly arranged in a row, and that each cylinder is connected to a crankshaft. By pushing cylinders alternately downwards using compressed gas, we would show how an engine rotates the crankshaft that can then be subsequently used to rotate the wheels. Rather than just looking at *what* kind of components a car is made of, we would explain the principal working of each component, and the way that they are connected to each other. We would then be focusing on the **organization** of a car.

Admittedly, the distinction between architecture and organization is not a clear cut one. What should be clear, however, is that we are not going to focus on merely describing computer systems. Instead, our attention is focused on showing how the various components work, and how they are connected to each other. The main drawback of this approach is that we cannot tell what every computer looks like on the inside, and indeed, very many different organizations exist. In terms of our example above, we explain how a 4-cylinder engine works, and leave that of a 16-cylinder version to your own imagination.

At this point, let's start by gently introducing the various concepts that we will meet in succeeding chapters. In the next two sections we first concentrate on the concept of computers, followed by an introduction to computer networks.

1.2   Computers

The first part of this book, which consists roughly of Chapters 2 through 6, deals with explaining what computers actually are. An outline of our approach is explained in Section 1.2.1. Then, a structured approach to organizing computers is given in Section 1.2.2.

1.2.1   The essence of computing devices

The nomenclature applied to computers is illustrative of the way that they are conceived today. For example, it is not uncommon to blame the computer for not doing its job right, nor do we find it strange when someone says that the computer had a hard time getting calculations done. In the case of factory automation, as another example, computers are said to take over jobs that people previously did by hand. To take it one step further, computers are even said to be capable of *learning*. Many more examples can be thought of in which computers are not merely treated as appliances, but are perceived as autonomous entities having some kind of intelligence. The gap between our perception of what computers appear to be and what they really are is sometimes astonishing. Although it does make sense, for the sake of simplicity, to talk about computers as autonomous entities, it does not make sense to treat them as intelligent beings with a will of their own. Computers are not intelligent, and they cannot do anything that has not been put into them. They are just sometimes complex, that's all. In particular, they can be so complex that it is hard for one person to comprehend fully what computers really do. In this book we are going to explain some of the essentials of computers that will allow a person to get a grasp of how they work. We are convinced that this will help you put computers in the right perspective, namely that of useful appliances.

On simulation and interpretation

Let's start with saying something that might be surprising: computers have no concept of 0's and 1's. When giving the matter some thought, it is indeed hard to imagine that an electronic device can have any concepts. The essence of the matter is that computers are devices that *simulate* the way that we handle things. And they are doing such a good job at that, it is indeed sometimes hard to differentiate between simulation and what is really happening. Let's look at an example to illustrate this.

Suppose we had a box with five light bulbs and two switches as shown in Figure 1.1. The box hides an implementation of a simple calculator, capable of adding any combination of 0, 1, and 2. For example, if we set the first switch $S1$ to "0" and the second switch $S2$ to "2", then the third bulb marked "2" would light up. This would also be the case when $S1$ is set to "1" and $S2$ to "1" or, when $S1$ is set to "2" and $S2$" is set to "0".

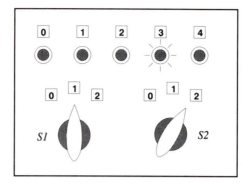

Figure 1.1 A simple calculating device.

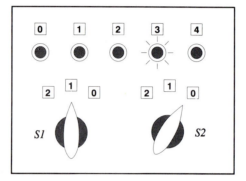

Figure 1.2 The effect of changing the labels: rubbish.

Now, the question that we want to raise here is whether or not our device can actually calculate.

Giving a straight answer to this question is really not easy. For one thing, it *appears* as if our device does have some calculation capabilities: no matter what combination of *S*1 and *S*2 we choose, it always gives the right answer. So, from that perspective, we would indeed say that we have a true calculator at our disposal.

But suppose we changed the labels at both switches. Labels "0" are replaced by "2", and labels "2" are replaced by "0" respectively, as shown in Figure 1.2. In that case, the fact that a bulb starts to light really does not make any sense. Putting it differently, there is no sensible **interpretation** of what comes out of the box when we turn the switches. For one thing, our device is difficult to recognize as some kind of calculator. The crux of the matter lies, of course, in the way that we interpret the setting of the switches in combination with which bulb starts to glow. As a last experiment, you will see that everything works properly again if we also replace the label at each bulb as shown in Figure 1.3.

So what does our device actually do? First, it is important to realize that our calculator can only be perceived as such if we can interpret the setting of the switches in combina-

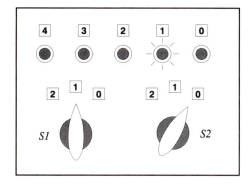

Figure 1.3 A working calculator again.

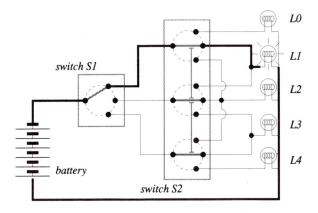

Figure 1.4 An implementation of our simple calculator.

tion with the light bulbs in a manner that makes sense to us. But there is more. It should be clear that the device itself has no "knowledge" built-in concerning arithmetic operations. Instead, what it does is merely **simulate** operations that have meaning to us. The combination of having the device properly simulate a part of our own world, and our own interpretation of its outcomes, puts us in a position to state that we indeed have a calculator at hand.

▷ Some of you might ask what our calculator looks like on the inside. An **implementation** is shown in Figure 1.4. Switch *S1* is rather simple. It is just a switch that allows a person to choose to connect the input with precisely one of the three outputs. In the figure, the input is connected to the first output, in our case, meaning that switch *S1* has been set to "0".

Switch *S2* consists of three sub-switches, each sub-switch enabling the input to be connected to one of the three outputs. However, we assume that these three sub-switches are mechanically constructed in such a way that turning the knob always implies turning the three switches at the same time. Consequently, if the first sub-switch connects its input to

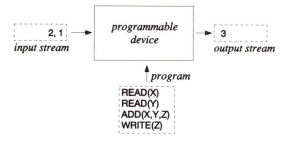

Figure 1.5 The principle of a programmable device.

its second output pin as shown in the figure, the other two sub-switches will do precisely the same in their case. What we have shown, therefore, is the state of affairs when switch $S2$ has been set to "1". And indeed, the light bulb marked $L1$ will now be fully connected to the battery, through which it then lights up.

Computers are in essence not very different from our simple calculator. They are constructed of electrical components that act as switches, such that if we feed them with the right electrical values (i.e. values to which we attach some useful interpretation) they will produce a set of output values in such a way that if we also interpret those values in some sensible manner it will appear as if our computer has really computed something worth while. The big difference with our calculator lies in the fact that real computers can be **programmed**.

Programmable devices

What do we mean exactly by a program? Following *Webster's Dictionary*, a **program** is "a plan or sequence of things to be done". For programmable devices, this can be reformulated as

>   *A program is a sequence of instructions that are to be executed.*

The keywords here are *instructions* and *execution*. For example, using our simple calculator for adding 1 and 2 could be done by executing the following two instructions:

>   *set switch $S1$ to "1"*
>   *set switch $S2$ to "2"*

In this case, the user of the calculator would be responsible for the execution of these instructions; in computers, the execution mechanism is part of them. In that case, we need only construct a program and feed it into the device.

The principle is shown in Figure 1.5. What we see there is an *input stream* of numbers, and a *program* consisting of a series of instructions that the computer is to perform. The *output stream* consists of the results produced by executing the instructions on the given input. In our highly simplified example, we basically distinguish three types of instructions:

- The instruction READ(X) by which the *next* input value is read from the input stream and *internally stored* as the variable X.

- The instruction WRITE(X) of which the execution yields that the value of the internally stored variable X is written to the output stream.

- A collection of simple arithmetic operations that generally require three internally stored variables. For example, the instruction ADD(X,Y,Z) assigns the value of the operation X + Y to Z.

Using these three types of instructions, we can then, for example, construct the following general *program* that does the same as our calculator for an arbitrary input stream consisting of just two numbers:

```
READ(X)
READ(Y)
ADD(X,Y,Z)
WRITE(Z)
```

Programs are referred to as **software** to distinguish them from the hardware components of which computers are made.

Already we can see an important difference from our simple calculator. Where we first merely needed to turn the knobs of the two switches *S*1 and *S*2 in order to get the result instantaneously, we now have the situation that the input values are first *stored* internally in the form of the variables X and Y, respectively. Also, instead of immediately getting a result, we explicitly instruct the computer to do an addition, and again separately store this result as the variable Z. The result is made available to us by writing it to the output stream. We have thus assumed two extra components: an internal store, and some processing unit that operates on values kept in that store.

Figure 1.5 is a very simple way of representing computers, and is in fact the way that the first computers worked. The point to realize, however, is that in this architecture, each instruction is separately fed into the computer and subsequently executed. In particular, it requires a separate mechanism to read the program instruction by instruction in order to have it executed. An important improvement was made when it was recognized that programs need essentially not be treated differently from the input data that they worked on. The idea is revolutionary and simple at the same time. What we do is treat the instructions that make up a program as ordinary values that can be stored internally. In that case, our computer design can be made a lot simpler. What it means is that we need a powerful, **central processing unit** that is connected to a large **main store**. This central processing unit, or processor as it is called, essentially has just two operations built into it:

- An operation FETCH that reads the next instruction from the main store and stores it locally in a special variable INSTRUCTION.

- An operation EXECUTE that does precisely what its name suggests. It executes the instruction currently stored as the variable INSTRUCTION, and in turn internally stores the result in a special variable RESULT.

(We shall see in Chapter 3 that the variable RESULT is actually not needed. It is introduced here for the sake of illustration.) As we have said, the processor itself is a computer in its own right. It has some storage capacity and is capable of performing just two operations. That designing computers now becomes a lot simpler is not difficult to see. Essentially, we need to implement a device that *continuously* executes the alternating sequence of only the two operations FETCH and EXECUTE. Expressing this as a program yields something like:

```
forever loop
    FETCH
    EXECUTE
end loop
```

There are two important things that need to be kept in mind when organizing computers in this way. First, we need to make a distinction between two distinctive levels. At the lowest level we have the two operations FETCH and EXECUTE; one level higher we have instructions such as READ, WRITE, and ADD that are fetched from the main store and subsequently fed into the central processing unit, which in turn is responsible for their actual execution. In principle, you never see the two low-level operations: they have been directly implemented in the form of a processor.

Second, we will have to assume that the EXECUTE operation is capable of handling only a restricted number of instructions. In other words, we may not expect that every possible high-level instruction that we can think of can be executed by the EXECUTE operation. Putting it differently, we say that EXECUTE **implements** a fixed set of instructions, also known as the processor's **instruction set**. Programming a computer then consists of telling it what to do by constructing valid sequences of instructions taken from this instruction set.

Using this approach, we can now show how computers are generally organized. In Figure 1.6 we have a distinction between two types of stores. One type is for storing values that come from the input stream as well as those for the output stream, and one type is for storing programs. We shall see later that these two stores can be taken together. Figure 1.6(a) shows what happens when the instruction ADD(X,Y,Z) is fetched; Figure 1.6(b) what happens when this instruction is executed by the processor.

1.2.2   The concept of a multi-level machine

Making a distinction between the two levels as discussed above simplified computer design considerably. The important issue was that designers need now concentrate mostly on just the implementation of the two operations FETCH and EXECUTE. The result would be a processor that could subsequently execute any instruction that EXECUTE could handle. But as you may imagine, implementing EXECUTE in itself is not an easy task to accomplish. In particular, in order to keep the complexity of the processor manageable, the set of instructions that can be handled generally consists of instructions that are still rather primitive. And in that respect, nothing much has changed over the years.

Having to use only primitive instructions is awkward when constructing large pro-

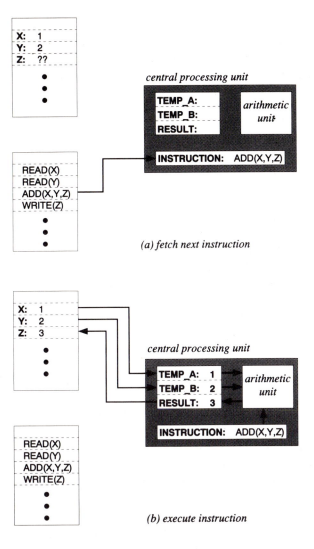

Figure 1.6 The organization of a computer in which an instruction is fetched (a) and subsequently executed (b).

grams. What effectively happens is that although the complexity of computer design can be greatly reduced if only primitive instructions are supported, the complexity of programs (that can only make use of these instructions) increases. This is comparable to some domestic appliances, most notably perhaps video recorders. What we see there is that the cheaper ones provide you with just simple buttons to operate the recorder. Programming the recorder can then indeed be a rather frustrating undertaking especially if a mistake is made somewhere. In that case, it will generally be necessary to start all over again. Modern recorders avoid this by sometimes providing just a single instruction that you have to execute, namely scanning the bar code as it appears in TV guides. And although it does make things simpler, the additional price paid for this facility reflects that the underlying technology can indeed be relatively difficult to realize.

Programming computers is not much different in this respect. Constructing programs that are built from primitive instruction sets is generally a cumbersome and error prone process. Two complementary solutions have been sought to alleviate these problems: high-level programming languages and operating systems.

High-level programming languages

There are various high-level programming languages. In this book our primary focus is on the use of a "conventional" high-level language which will be presented in Chapter 4. Conventional high-level programming languages allow us to arrange programs as a collection of **statements**, embedded in relatively small program units, of which the **procedure** is probably the best known. Consider the following example.

Suppose we want to write a program by which we can multiply two (positive integer) numbers M and N, and store the result in a variable P. This would be a simple task as all popular high-level programming languages support a multiplication operation. For example, we can simply use the language's **assignment statement** such as

   P := M * N;

of which the execution will show that the result of the multiplication M * N is assigned to the variable P.

Now, as it may seem obvious that there is a multiplication operation available, this becomes less obvious if you know exactly how multiplication is to be performed. For example, some computer designers have deliberately omitted a multiplication instruction to keep their computers as simple as possible. This means that we have to write our own multiplication program if necessary. To illustrate how this could be achieved by means of a high-level language, let's also assume that there is no multiplication facility at *that* level as well. In that case, we can calculate M * N through repeated addition, i.e.

$$P := \underbrace{M + \cdots + M}_{N \text{ times}}$$

which can easily be expressed in a high-level programming language as follows:

```
(1)   R := 0;
(2)   P := 0;
(3)   while R < N loop
(4)       P := P + M;
(5)       R := R + 1;
(6)   end loop
```

In the first line, we are initializing an additional variable R that is going to act as a *counter*. It counts how many times we have already added M to P. The latter is initialized in the second line. Lines (3)–(6) are an example of a so-called **while** statement that is supported

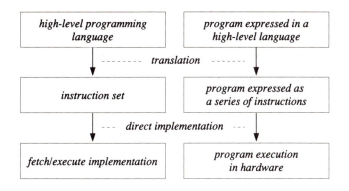

Figure 1.7 Viewing a computer as consisting of three distinct levels of instructions.

by almost every high-level language. In our case, we have simply stated that as long as we have not added M a sufficient number of times to P, we have to do another addition. The latter is done through the assignment statement in (4), whereas in line (5) we increment our counter by one.

It is not difficult to see that our small program is correct, and indeed fairly easy to understand. We will have much more to say about programs such as the one above, and we shall also illustrate that using high-level programming languages is much simpler to do than using rather primitive instruction sets. There is, however, a problem. There is no processor that can execute any program written in a high-level language. The only thing that a processor can do is handle programs that use instructions from its instruction set. The solution to this problem is found in *language translation*. What we can do is translate programs written in a high-level programming language into equivalent programs, but now expressed as a series of instructions that a processor can handle. Taking into account that instruction sets are in turn implemented through a fetch/execute mechanism, we can then show a computer as a multi-level machine as shown in Figure 1.7.

There are some intricacies related to translating programs expressed in a high-level language to a lower-level instruction set, but we shall postpone further discussion on this subject until Chapter 4. The important point to note now is that we are gradually making a computing device more easy to use by allowing more powerful programming constructs, even if we do not immediately have an implementation of these constructs at hand. Instead, we provide a translation mechanism from one language to another where needed. The advantage is that from a user's perspective the only thing that matters is what the programming language looks like, as this is the only interface to a computer that allows one to set it to work. And taking it from that perspective, a high-level programming language makes a computer look like a powerful and easy device to use. We return to this issue below after having introduced yet another concept that eases the use of computers.

Operating systems

Using high-level languages is not the only way to ease the construction of computer programs. In particular, it is not hard to imagine that having just a bare computer requires that parts of any program will have to be devoted to handling all kinds of input and output operations for transferring data between a peripheral device and the computer. For example, when using a disk, you would need a way to retrieve data from that disk, and also be able to store data on it. This would involve *controlling* the device by setting its read/write heads, doing the actual data transfer, etc. The whole point is that these parts of a program in essence have little to do with the main purpose of using the computer. But no matter what program is being developed, we will probably have to control input and output of data in any case. In that sense, it would be a lot easier if we could make use of a **service program** that handles disk manipulations. Such a service program would have to be constructed only once and could be subsequently used as part of the various other programs that are constructed. And things would be even better if someone else had constructed such a service program for us, preferably an expert in the field of writing programs that allowed us easily to make use of the hardware facilities of a computer.

From a certain perspective, this is exactly what so-called **operating systems** are made of: a large collection of general-purpose service programs for controlling the computer and its peripheral devices. Operating systems roughly establish two things. First, they make the life of programmers a lot easier by means of their service programs. Effectively, a service program establishes that you need no longer be concerned about how some of the computer's facilities such as disks are actually to be used, as this is completely taken care of. In other words, a service program provides an *easy* way of programming a computer. Second, service programs can be highly optimized once and for all so that these facilities are also used *efficiently*. Operating systems can thus be viewed as *resource managers*.

An important side-effect of operating systems is that from a programming perspective, you never see how this control of resources takes place. Putting it differently, service programs shield all kinds of intricacies that are related to controlling the hardware. As a consequence, the computer appears to the programmer only by means of the service programs that are part of the operating system. The service programs form a layer over the hardware. This principle is illustrated in Figure 1.8.

But if service programs hide all kinds of hardware details, and by doing so ease program construction, have we not then constructed an abstract view of what a computer actually is? Indeed, this is the case and you might say that an operating system combined with the underlying hardware is a realization of a **virtual machine**: a device that appears to be something different from its hardware components. This is, in principle, not much different from using a high-level programming language as discussed above. A high-level programming language provides a view of a computer's programming capabilities which are more extensive than actually provided. Operating systems establish similar goals, but in a different way. In both cases, the computer appears to be a more powerful device than is reflected by the hardware.

A question that comes to mind, is how operating systems and high-level languages are

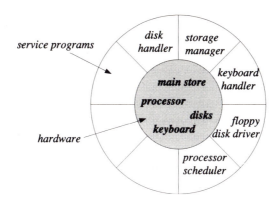

Figure 1.8   An operating system viewed as a collection of service programs shielding the hardware.

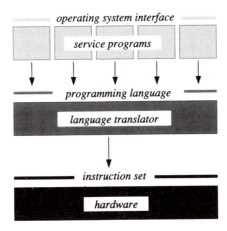

Figure 1.9 The construction of a virtual, multi-layered computing machine.

related to each other. There are different ways of viewing this relationship, but the one we shall take in this book is the following. The essence of the matter lies in how we construct service programs. In this book we shall demonstrate that this can be done by means of a high-level programming language. Consequently, we will be constructing service programs that are aimed at controlling a computer's resources, but will use the programming facilities as provided by some high-level programming language. This leads to further enhancement of our concept of a multi-level machine, as is shown in Figure 1.9.

And this is about as far as we shall go. It is not hard to imagine, however, that we can easily continue our line of reasoning by constructing yet another layer on top of an operating system. Typically, such a layer will further extend our view of what a computer can actually do, but at the same time will probably narrow our view as well in the sense that the presented capabilities will be more focused towards a particular *application domain*.

To illustrate, consider a modern word processing system such as those that are used for personal computers. The main purpose of such a system is to provide its users with all kinds of facilities for making documents. The instructions that are entered either through commands (such as combinations of keystrokes) or by means of a mouse (if a more advanced graphical interface is supported) allow you to move the cursor, display a specific portion of a document on the screen, generate a table of contents, etc. At the same time, word processing systems do a lot more. For example, they allow us to manage the storage of documents into files and directories. Also, they provide all kinds of ways for handling printing devices, help organize the screen, or even allow us to completely redefine the meaning of the keys on a keyboard. The last facilities are traditionally provided by operating systems. And if making documents is the only thing that is done with a computer, there may be no reason why someone should ever use another program. Indeed, in such cases the computer appears to its user as nothing but an advanced word processing device, again yet another virtual multi-level machine.

1.3   Computer networks

However, explaining how word processing systems and the like are constructed is not what we are interested in here. Instead, rather than building layers of software on top of each other, we will primarily be concerned with extending layers in such a way that *communication* between computers and their users becomes possible. We will thus enter the realm of **computer networks** which forms the topic of the second part of this book. Let's first consider why computer networks are so convenient to have.

1.3.1   The demand for computer networks

Linking computers to each other is attractive for a number of reasons, of which three important ones immediately come to mind:

- **Resource sharing.** This is a phenomenon with which most of us who have ever worked with computers connected in a network are already familiar. The most notable shared resources are perhaps printers. To date, good high-quality printers are still costly, especially if the combination of speed and quality is a major concern. But although a printer is typically something that is generally needed, it is not something that is needed all the time. This makes them ideal for sharing among several users, which in turn requires that those users can all have easy access. Hooking a printer into a network is a solution to that problem. But there are many other shared resources as well, although not always as visible to users as printers. An important type of shared resource is software. For example, it is a lot cheaper for an organization to buy just a single copy of some advanced word processing system, and keep that copy at one location. If someone wants to do word processing, they must collect the software from that single location and have it executed on his or her own computer. Getting the word processing system onto a computer is a lot easier if this can be done via a network.

- **Shared information.** This is an extremely important reason for linking computers together. Sharing information by having a database system as part of a computer network allows remote users located at different sites, all to have access to the same data. Typical examples of computer networks set up for sharing information are (electronic) banking systems, airline reservation systems, stock inventory systems used in e.g. supermarkets, and online library catalogs. Many more will come to mind. Sharing information through a computer network is practical for a number of reasons. First, it is a relatively easy way to allow users located at completely different sites to have easy access to a single source of information. Another important reason is that this construction allows the information to remain consistent (although this is not always an easy task to accomplish). If one user performs an update, then this change will be visible to all other users as well.

- **Information exchange.** This is going to be a main focus for us when discussing computer networks – communication between users and programmers. We shall see that computer networks offer important opportunities for users to exchange information, often much better than is currently possible via hand-delivered mail, telephones, faxes, etc. Computerized forms of standard communication facilities are becoming increasingly popular. For example, electronic mailing facilities have shown to be extremely useful: not only is it easy to get in touch with someone, it is also very efficient (it often just takes a few seconds, or at worst, a few minutes to get electronic mail to the other side of the world). As another example, exchanging documents over a computer network allows users to collaborate without having to be located at the same site. In the same way, it can be anticipated that participating in a so-called *video conference* with participants from all over a country or even the world will enhance ease of communication.

Just as we have become used to computers, we now also find it natural that computers are linked together into a network. The most dominant growth of computer networks has no doubt taken place in offices, factories, and of course, in universities and research institutes. Especially in the last two cases great efforts are seen in expanding networks to cover larger areas, and to improve the quality of the connections. These efforts are now gradually finding their spin-offs in the construction of networks that are commercially attractive to larger groups. For example, many banks today offer various services that allow people to perform parts of their financial administration through a personal computer. The French Minitel project that connects millions of homes to centralized information servers is another example of bringing computer network technology into our homes. The exponential growth of the worldwide Internet (which is discussed in Chapter 9) is sometimes beyond imagination, and as of today, services available on the Internet are readily available to many. Finally, as a last example, we may expect that in the near future the telephone companies will provide us with integrated services for communicating voice, data, and pictures through ISDN or related full digital networks.

1.3.2   Some fundamental problems

Having grasped the essentials of what a computer is all about, it becomes a lot easier to conceive how we can subsequently link computers together. Again, starting from first principles helps in understanding what the problems and their solutions are, and this is the approach that we have adopted in the second part of this book. In particular, as we gradually expose the workings of computers, we shall also present computer networks by discussing problems as they surface with the growth of a network in terms of its number of computers and geographical coverage.

The first type of computer network that we shall consider is a simple one. It consists of two computers that are linked together through some kind of **transmission medium**. There are various transmission media. Roughly, a distinction is made between guided and unguided media. Guided media are, for example, wires through which an electrical or optical signal is sent that represents the data we want to transmit. Unguided media are, for example, radio transmission and satellite connections. In that case, data is sent in the form of radio signals.

In order to transmit data from one computer to another, we encode it as some kind of signal that is subsequently sent across the transmission medium. In general, such a signal represents a so-called **bit string**, which in turn represents the data we want to transmit. A bit string is a series of *ones* and *zeroes*. Again, we emphasize that it is not the bit string that is being sent, but rather a signal representing that bit string. Nevertheless, when talking about data communication, it is a lot easier to think of it in terms of bit strings rather than signals, and we shall adopt this convention here.

Transmission errors

Now, sending bit strings from one computer to another seems a straightforward thing to do. However, this statement is not entirely true. The first problem that we are confronted with when we link two computers together is that our transmission medium will have some bounded quality with respect to its transmission capabilities. In particular, in many cases there is a low but non-negligible probability that transmission errors may occur. The effect of a transmission error is that a bit string b which is sent at one end of the transmission medium may arrive as a *different* bit string $\hat{b}$ at the other end. This problem is caused by many factors, but above all, it becomes more apparent as the length of the transmission medium increases. For this reason alone, transmission errors occur less frequently in a single computer as the connections between the various components in that case are relatively short.

One way or the other, we have to account for the fact that a bit string that arrives at a receiver may contain errors in the sense that it is different from the bit string that was originally sent. Devising schemes by which we can *detect* that a received bit string can never correspond to what was originally sent is an important subject when developing computer networks. There are all kinds of ways that errors can be detected, and some of the important ones will be discussed in Chapter 7. To give you a flavor of how error detection schemes work, consider the following.

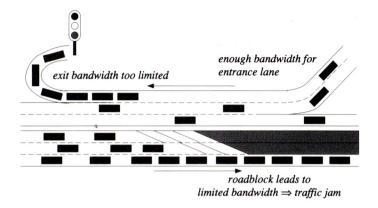

Figure 1.10 The phenomenon of limited bandwidth illustrated by road traffic.

To simplify matters, suppose we wish to transmit the series of decimal numbers $\mathbf{d} = \langle 2,3,4,5 \rangle$. In that case, we can choose to extend this series with an additional number by summing its values, leading to the series $\mathbf{e} = \langle 2,3,4,5,14 \rangle$. It is this series $\mathbf{e}$ that we then transmit. Now, suppose that the receiver eventually picks up the series $\hat{\mathbf{e}} = \langle 2,4,4,5,14 \rangle$. In that case it can conclude that something went wrong for the simple reason that $2 + 4 + 4 + 5 \neq 14$, which it would have expected in the first place. That this scheme does not always work is easily seen when considering that the receiver cannot detect that the series $\langle 1,4,4,5,14 \rangle$ also contains errors.

Limited bandwidth

Perhaps more serious when communicating between two computers is the fact that there is an upper bound to the amount of data that can be sent per time unit. This is generally expressed by the number of transmitted **bits per second** (bps). The two limiting factors here are the type of transmission medium and the computers themselves. There is an easy comparison to this phenomenon by considering road traffic. A highway is comparable to the transmission medium. The amount of traffic that can pass per hour depends on the number of lanes that are available. Likewise, the entrance and exit lanes determine how many cars can actually get on and off the highway, and as such are comparable to the transmission capabilities of the sending and receiving computer, respectively. This is illustrated in Figure 1.10.

What we see here are three potential bottlenecks that may cause **congestion**. First, an entrance lane may not be capable of handling all the traffic, despite the fact that the road itself at that point has enough capacity. In our example, we have shown an entrance lane that will presumably not lead to these kind of congestion problems. A second potential bottleneck is shown at the point where the three lanes are merged into one. In that case, it is the road that causes a traffic jam. Finally, our example also shows that an exit may also lead to traffic jams if not properly designed.

Figure 1.11 The effect of not properly balancing the work on a conveyor belt.

At present, computers as well as the transmission media that connect them may impose serious problems with respect to communication. With the introduction of new transmission technology, such as optical fiber, the problem is gradually shifting towards computers. What it means is that we have to find a way such that (1) computers can work at a pace that meets our needs for transmitting large amounts of data, and (2) that computers can adjust to each other's pace with respect to communication. We will return to the first issue on several occasions in later chapters. The second issue is the problem of **flow control** which we illustrate next.

The producer–consumer problem

Assume that two computers are connected through an ideal transmission medium (that such a medium does not exist is something we are not concerned about here). In that case, there is at least one issue that we will have to deal with, namely the difference in transmission speeds between the sender and the receiver, respectively. What do we mean by this? The problem is easily illustrated by comparing what happens if we put two workers on one end of a conveyor belt and only one person on the other end, as illustrated in Figure 1.11. For the sake of argument, assume that each box contains priceless chinaware.

The problem is that the two workers that put boxes onto the belt jointly operate at such a speed that it is almost impossible for the person on the other end to catch all the boxes and stack them. Consequently, a large number of the boxes will simply drop off the belt and their contents will be lost.

The same problem happens with computers. If a receiver is not capable of processing incoming data at the same speed at which a sender is transmitting it, data will simply be lost. To a certain extent, the problem can be solved through the use of **buffers**, as shown in Figure 1.12. What is seen there is that if a box is not immediately removed from the belt it will be stored automatically in a special area. But as soon as that area is full, boxes will start dropping off the belt again.

The whole idea of using buffers is to smooth the discrepancies in transmission speed between a sender and a receiver. If the sender stops sending for a while, the receiver can at least make up time by processing the data that has been stored temporarily in its buffers. Obviously, this scheme will only work if the sender does eventually stop transmission before the receiver's buffers are all full, or at least temporarily reduces the speed at which

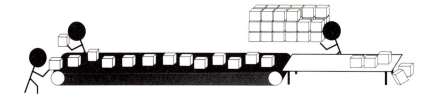

Figure 1.12 Using a buffering area to assist removal of boxes.

it transmits data. But as soon as buffers are full, we fall back into the situation described above: incoming data simply has to be discarded by the receiver.

The ultimate solution to this problem is that a sender and receiver agree on the rate at which data is transmitted. In that case, problems such as those described above can be avoided. But finding the right transmission rate is not always easy, and in the case of large networks sometimes almost impossible. The consequence of this is that despite the use of buffers, we will have to face the situation that data can still sometimes be lost. More precisely, incoming data will sometimes simply be discarded by a receiver because it has no capacity to store it temporarily. From a user's point of view, the situation that we then have created is that of an **unreliable** network: there can be no guarantee that transmitted data will actually reach the receiver. In practice, what happens is that a sender and receiver agree to acknowledge the successful receipt of data. In that way, a sender will at least know when data needs to be retransmitted. Alternatively, a receiver can explicitly request retransmission of data when it finds out that something has gone wrong. We will return to these problems in Chapter 9.

1.3.3 Expanding networks

The fundamental problems we have discussed so far have been illustrated by means of a simple network consisting of just two computers. But computer networks in practice are, of course, much larger. In general, there are two ways of constructing computer networks, which we discuss next.

Sharing a single transmission medium

Just as highways are used by many people at the same time, we would also like to use one transmission medium for the transfer of data between several computers. There are many reasons for wanting this, but, above all, sharing a transmission medium is simply cost-effective, and in many cases, it also makes the construction of computer networks much simpler. One particular scheme for sharing a transmission medium, and which is generally employed in relatively small networks, is the following.

The basic idea is simply to connect several computers to the same medium. The consequence of this is that if one computer starts sending some data, all other computers connected to the medium will be able to receive that data. This is comparable to connecting

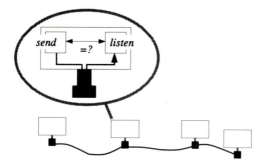

Figure 1.13 The principle of detecting message collisions.

several telephones to the same wall socket. As soon as someone phones, all telephones will start ringing. Likewise, we can also connect several radios or TV sets to one outlet. The incoming signal will just be propagated to all the devices at the same time. Depending on whether or not you tune into a station determines the actual receipt. In the case of the type of computer networks we are considering here, the same principle applies. By specifying exactly for which computers the transmitted data is intended, each computer can determine if it should receive the data, or otherwise ignore it.

The main problem with this scheme is that we have to prevent two or more computers from transmitting data at the same time. What it means is that if two bit strings are simultaneously transmitted over a shared medium, the result may be a bit string that makes no sense at all. In that case, we say that a **message collision** has occurred. Basically, there are two ways of avoiding collisions.

Collision detection.   A straightforward scheme is simply to let collisions happen. Because every computer connected to a shared medium is capable of receiving what is being transmitted, we have the situation that the sending computers can detect whether their transmitted data is being garbled by some other computer that is also transmitting data. This principle is illustrated in Figure 1.13.

There are various strategies that can be followed when a collision is detected, but the one most widely applied is to have the sending computer immediately stop transmission, and wait until the line is free again. Of course, there are some subtleties involved, such as when to decide to start transmitting again. These details will be explained in Chapter 8 when we describe so-called Ethernet networks.

Token-based solutions.   An alternative solution is to use a special data item, known as a **token**, and have it continuously circulate from computer to computer. In this case, the computers that share the medium are either physically or logically organized into a ring, as illustrated in Figure 1.14. The figure shows a network in which the computers are *logically* organized as a ring, but that are *physically* connected to the same transmission medium.

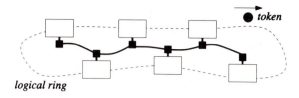

Figure 1.14 Using a token to avoid message collisions.

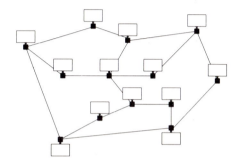

Figure 1.15 A computer network based on point-to-point links.

In this case, a computer is only allowed to transmit data just after it has received the token. And after the computer has finished its data transmission, the token is again sent across the transmission medium, but is allowed to be picked up only by the logically next computer. So, if computer #5 had transmitted the token, then it may be picked up only by computer #6. If a computer has no data to transmit, it immediately forwards the token to the next computer. Token-based computer networks will also be further discussed in Chapter 8.

Sharing the transmission medium is a technique that characterizes most **local area networks**, which, as their name suggests, cover a relatively small geographical area such as a department floor or a building. The number of computers is restricted from some tens to a few thousand computers, where in the latter case the overall network has been constructed by connecting several local networks. We return to local area networks in detail in Chapter 8.

Networks based on routing

A second type of scheme that is employed for the construction of computer networks is simply providing point-to-point links between a set of computers, resulting in a *graph* as shown in Figure 1.15. The main advantage of this scheme is that very large areas can be covered, and it is in this way that so-called **wide area networks** are constructed.

The point about this type of computer networks is that sending and receiving data requires that data be **routed** through the network. In other words, in order to get data across the network, we have to select a specific route that it has to travel. Route-based computer networks are thus seen to have an immediate analogy with, for example, road and railway networks. Note also that having to select a route is something that did not occur in the case of local area networks as discussed above. In other words, we have to provide an *additional* functionality.

Routing data through networks is a major and relatively difficult subject. The reason for this lies not so much in finding the appropriate route, but rather in the fact that the routing decisions have to made locally at the intermediate nodes through which the data passes. Let's take a look at what we mean by this.

Suppose you wish to make a fairly long trip by rail and that there are alternative routes to choose in order to get to your destination. Normally, what you would do is consult a railway map and decide how to travel. Or, perhaps more conveniently, the railway organization will suggest a route. The main issue here is that the railway network is known in advance and we can trust that this network will not undergo major changes during a trip. With computer networks, however, the situation is somewhat different.

As a sender of data, we generally do not have a very good idea of what the network actually looks like. Moreover, there is a considerable chance that while transmitting data through the network, this data may need to be rerouted once or several times, simply because computers can crash, or because some links have to cope with more traffic than they can handle adequately. In other words, in the case of computer networks we are faced with the problem that the network may change with respect to its physical structure, or otherwise with respect to its traffic load such that determining a complete route in advance is not always a good strategy to follow.

It becomes necessary to adopt an **adaptive routing strategy**. This means that each time data arrives at an intermediate node, it makes sense to re-evaluate where exactly that data should be forwarded. And it is the intermediate node that is responsible for making that decision. Indeed, an intermediate node becomes a true **routing device**. But if traffic in networks and networks themselves change so much, this means that an intermediate node will have to be informed of the overall status of the network. And this is precisely what makes routing so difficult. Where should this information come from? Surely, if we are dealing with a network that spans the world, it makes little sense to appoint a central routing information center that keeps track of this information. If this center malfunctioned the complete network would go down. Instead, what happens is that each intermediate node has to pass on its *local* information, i.e. information on the status of the links attached to it, to every other computer in the network. This is not an easy job to do when you think about it. How each intermediate node can keep informed about the overall status of the network and subsequently make routing decisions is a major topic of Chapter 9.

Connecting networks

So far, we have made a distinction between networks based on sharing a transmission medium, as in the case of local area networks, and those based on point-to-point connections as applied in wide area networks. There is also an important third type of network which is formed by connecting numerous local and smaller wide area networks into a single, very large **internetwork**. This is in fact the way that most large-scale computer networks are constructed. This type of wide area network is receiving a lot of attention as it allows worldwide communication between computers. Worldwide computer networks are still very much in their infancy. The major problem that has to be solved is providing the right technology in order to allow for large amounts of data to be transferred across such networks. In particular, a mixture of routing strategies has to be applied in order to distinguish local traffic from global traffic.

Also, we have to face the problem that an internetwork is built from different constituent networks in which each constituent network has its demands with respect to what message traffic should look like. To illustrate, just as zip codes vary from country to country, you can also expect networks to differ in the way that senders and receivers are identified. Another problem is that networks may vary with respect to the maximum size of a message. This means that if a message has a size of N bits, and is to be transferred across a network that can support messages only up to $M < N$ bits the communication will fail if no special measures are taken.

Constructing internetworks is a difficult task to accomplish, but at present it is the only way to achieve a worldwide computer network. In this context, the information superhighway that some people are so enthusiastically talking about today is still non-existent. A more appropriate term in that sense would perhaps be the information dirt road. Internetworks are discussed in Chapter 9, where we pay special attention to the world's largest computer network, the Internet.

1.3.4   Towards communication systems

At this point it can already be seen that the construction of computer networks is indeed something quite different from explaining how computers actually work. For one thing, the approach that can be followed in the case of computers is the one by which we gradually lift the level of abstraction, and each time we do that, we merely need to explain how such a higher level can be implemented on top of what we already have. With computer networks, expansion of a network only introduces new problems that need to be solved. The number of problems may even seem to grow faster than the number of solutions we can provide. And from a certain perspective, there is actually some truth in this statement. Fortunately, there is a large body of experience in constructing computer networks and although network technology is by no means a mature area of technology, there is a consensus on how networks can be built in a structured way. Again, the solution is found in adopting a *layered* approach.

Tackling computer network problems

So far, we have made a distinction between several types of computer networks:

- The simplest form we have addressed is the one in which only two computers are linked together. This is hardly to be considered as a network, but already here we see that our attention is drawn to the problem of choosing an appropriate transmission medium, and getting a bit string from one computer to another.

- Local area networks form a next step in the construction of computer networks. In this case, we use a single transmission medium to link several computers together and our focus of attention is directed towards the means for sharing that medium.

- Wide area networks form a next step. In this case, we construct a network by linking pairs of computers together having the advantage that geographically large areas can be covered. It does impose another problem: that of routing data from sender to receiver.

- Internetworks, constructed by connecting several local and wide area networks together forms a next step. The additional problem is how data is to be handled so that it can travel through different networks with varying demands on what messages should look like.

We have ordered these network types in such a way that with the increasing size and complexity of the network type, new problems are introduced for which functionality has to be added on top of what we already have. In other words, we are forcing a *layered organization* of network types. This approach has been widely adopted in the world of computer networks and has been formalized in the form of several so-called **reference models**. An important model that we shall roughly follow in this book is the one developed by the International Standards Organization (ISO) who produced the **Open Systems Interconnection** reference model, abbreviated to the OSI model. This model consists of seven layers, shown in Figure 1.16.

Without going into too many details, the four lower layers roughly cover the following functionalities:

- The **physical layer** specifies the functions that implement most of the aspects of getting data in the form of a bit string from a sender to a receiver.

- The **data link layer** covers the functions for accessing a transmission medium. As we shall see, the data link layer is a major concern when considering local area networks.

- The **network layer** covers the functions that deal with routing data through a network. As such, it is an important layer in wide area networks and internetworks.

- The **transport layer** deals mainly with the functions that are required for building a reliable computer network, regardless of the underlying technology.

Understanding what these layers mean in practice can be difficult. In fact, knowing what layering actually stands for and how it affects implementations can be difficult enough. Throughout this book we explicitly provide examples to illustrate the concept and once the end of Chapter 9 has been reached, you should have a good idea of these matters. The point to keep in mind for now is that organizing systems as layers provides you with the right means for gradually enhancing the functionality of a system, without having to affect the things that have been constructed so far.

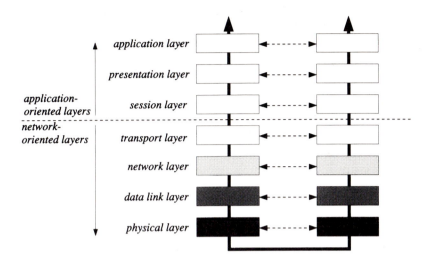

Figure 1.16 Outline of the OSI reference model.

Away from technology: communication systems

This book deals with technology, and in particular, we concentrate on how computers and networks are organized by describing how they work. In particular, with respect to networks this means that we concentrate primarily on the four lower layers of the OSI model. The systems we shall describe will only allow us to send a message from one side of the world to another. Not very spectacular, it may seem. But with some exaggeration, we can state that there is not much more needed to build worldwide communication systems. Nevertheless, to put things into better context, we shall also pay some attention to the way that actual communication systems are constructed. In particular, in the final chapter we shall outline the architecture of communications systems that provide services directly oriented towards the construction of applications that allow *users* to communicate. This is, in fact, a brief story about the upper layers of the OSI model. By the time you have reached Chapter 10, understanding communication systems will be a lot easier for the simple reason that you will then have developed a better understanding of the underlying technology.

1.4   Further reading

Introductory textbooks that explain computers *and* networks at a basic level are hard to find. Traditionally, the material covered in this book is more or less subdivided into three fields:

- Computer architecture and organization,
- Operating systems,
- Computer networks.

This subdivision often makes it difficult to understand what these fields have in common. In particular, the role of operating systems in computer networks is generally not easy to comprehend by the novice. The lack of a general textbook covering the material above in an integrated way, was a prime motivation to write this book. On the other hand, this does mean that many details have been omitted. It is hard for us to imagine that the answers found in this book will be more than the questions that will come to mind after having studied the material. And if this is indeed the case, the reader is encouraged to delve into the various subjects further. To that end, each chapter contains references for further reading.

Nevertheless, there are a number of general introductory textbooks worth mentioning at this point. Tanenbaum (1990a) focuses primarily on computer organization, but also pays attention to the role of operating systems. Likewise, Stallings (1990) will show to be a good introduction to these subjects, although with a stronger emphasis on computer organization.

In Tanenbaum (1992) the author explains the principles of traditional operating systems and of those that are distributed across a computer network. Distributed operating systems are more extensively discussed in Tanenbaum (1995). A somewhat different approach is followed by Silberschatz and Galvin (1994) but in which many aspects of distribution and computer networks can be found. An excellent treatise on distributed systems in general can be found in Coulouris *et al.* (1994).

A brief introduction to the hardware aspects of computer organization *and* computer networks can be found in Goupille (1993). However, we feel that the omission of discussing the important role of software prohibits a good general understanding of communication using computers.

There are numerous introductory books on computer networks. A thorough and in-depth presentation is given in Tanenbaum (1988) of which a revised and updated edition is to appear (Tanenbaum, 1996). An excellent treatise can also be found in Stallings (1994). A bottom-up approach starting with the basic principles of computer networks at the hardware level, and ending with discussing the software components of networks can be found in Shay (1995). As the author follows the same approach that we have taken, the book may show to be good additional reading to the material presented in Chapters 7–10.

Chapter 2

On data, operations, and storage

In this chapter we start with taking a look at the basic elements of computer systems: the representation of data and operations, and the means to store data values. To that end, we first pay attention to how we can represent data and operations in terms of so-called finite bit strings, and subsequently show how these representations can be implemented using digital circuits. The basic elements introduced up to that point will then be used to show how we can build devices which can store data values.

2.1 Introduction: information processing

Throughout this book we are concerned with finding an answer to the following question:

> *How does a computer system (1) process information, and (2) how can it communicate that information to other computers?*

In this chapter we start with taking a look at the basics of processing information. To be able to process information, we essentially need two things: data and a set of operations allowed on that data. When working with paper and pencil, information processing is mostly trivial for us. For example, suppose you were asked to write down a shopping list with an estimate of the total costs. In that case, you would use the symbols "0" ... "9" to represent the digits in our decimal system, and apply the mathematical operations for adding, and possibly also multiplying numbers in order to arrive at a total sum. But the most important part of this information processing is the person composing the list: he or she performs the actual processing.

This example at least illustrates one important issue. In order to process information we need to make use of **symbols** that represent the data we have in our heads. When processing information by means of a machine we have to find a means to represent data as well. In other words, we have to come to an agreement on a suitable set of symbols. But there is more. Our simple example also illustrates that we apply operations on data in order to arrive at a final result. These operations manifest themselves through **symbol**

manipulation: we arrange our numbers in such a way that in the end our shopping list also includes an estimate of the total costs. This manipulation of numbers is a reflection of applying mathematical rules. Clearly, automated information processing will require that we can represent these rules and their application to symbols as well.

The first important choice we have to make, therefore, is which symbols to choose for representing data. To make things as simple as possible, let's concentrate only on information that we can express in terms of ordinary text and numbers. In other words, we exclude illustrations and sound. It would then seem to make sense to simply choose our alphabet augmented with the ten decimal digits, punctuation marks, quotes, etc. This adds up to a mere one hundred symbols or so, not that much, it would seem. Unfortunately, it *is* rather much. The problem that we need to take into account is that each symbol needs to have a unique *physical* counterpart in the machine that we are going to use for our information processing. And although having to represent many symbols can be done, it turns out that building machines becomes a lot easier and cheaper if the number of symbols that it needs to represent is as low as possible. Taking this into account, an obvious choice is then to take the absolute minimum: *two* symbols. And in computer systems, the choice was made for the two symbols "0" and "1".

Having just "0" and "1" at our disposal then brings us to another problem: how can we represent real-world data which we normally express through our one hundred symbols or so in terms of just these two symbols? In the following section we first discuss how we can merely represent data in terms "0" and "1". In Section 2.3, we continue by concentrating on the representation of operations on data. This will put us in a position to concentrate on an extremely important issue: how can we *implement* the notions introduced so far in terms of devices? This is the main subject of Section 2.4. Our last topic is formed by taking our approach one step further. In Section 2.5, we take the devices used for implementing our representations, and construct a *storage device* that will allow us to store data temporarily.

2.2   Data representation

In this section we concentrate on representing just two kinds of data: numbers and plain text. The reason for restricting ourselves to these kinds of data is twofold. The first reason is that of simplicity. As we shall see, representing either numbers or text in computer systems is relatively straightforward, although there are a few snags that need to be considered. As such, numbers and text are excellent candidates to illustrate representational issues. Second, they stand for two slightly different kinds of information processing. One kind is primarily focused towards doing calculations: weather forecasting, analysis of economic models, building constructions, etc. The other kind of information processing is primarily concentrated around manipulating text-based data, encompassing areas such as office automation, business management, and administrative information processing.

We first concentrate on representing numbers, followed by a brief discussion on the representation of text. But before doing so, we need to introduce some terminology. In order to speak sensibly about manipulating symbols, it is common practice to use the notion of variables. In our case, two kinds of variables are relevant. First, we shall make use of so-called **binary digits** which are variables that can take on only two values, namely the symbols "0" and "1". A binary digit is commonly referred to as a **bit**.

The second kind of variable we shall come across is that of a **bit string**, which is nothing but a series of consecutive bits. A bit string of length 8 is usually called a **byte**. Throughout this book we denote bit strings by enclosing them between the brackets "⟨" and "⟩" as in, for example, ⟨10010111⟩.

2.2.1 Numbers

Let's start by taking a look at how we can represent numbers in the form of bit strings. In this subsection we concentrate mainly on so-called integer numbers, i.e. numbers such as $\pm 1, \pm 2$, etc. Although other kinds of numbers can also be represented as bit strings, their representation is often more intricate, and also less important for the material presented in this book. We therefore discuss them only briefly.

From decimal to binary numbers

Human beings generally use *decimal arithmetic* to represent numbers. For example, when we mention the number 1625, we actually mean a number that is calculated as

$$1625 = 1 \cdot 1000 + 6 \cdot 100 + 2 \cdot 10 + 5 \cdot 1$$

or, more systematically

$$1625 = 1 \cdot 10^3 + 6 \cdot 10^2 + 2 \cdot 10^1 + 5 \cdot 10^0$$

In the case of decimal arithmetic, 10 is called the **base number** or **radix**. But, of course, it is also possible to use another radix. For example, if we use 8 as our radix, the number 1625_8 is equal to:[1]

$$1625_8 = 1 \cdot 8^3 + 6 \cdot 8^2 + 2 \cdot 8^1 + 1 \cdot 8^0 = 917_{10} \tag{2.1}$$

Likewise, we can express 917_{10} in radix 2:

$$
\begin{aligned}
917_{10} &= 1 \cdot 2^9 + 1 \cdot 2^8 + 1 \cdot 2^7 + 0 \cdot 2^6 + 0 \cdot 2^5 + \\
&\quad 1 \cdot 2^4 + 0 \cdot 2^3 + 1 \cdot 2^2 + 0 \cdot 2^1 + 1 \cdot 2^0 \\
&= 1110010101_2
\end{aligned}
$$

That humans tend to think in terms of decimal arithmetic is even illustrated by our conversion (2.1). All the symbols after the first equation sign are expressed in decimals.

Coming to this point we need to make a clear distinction between numbers and symbols. For example, where a number such as 917 makes perfect sense to us, a computer

---

[1] We use the subscript *8* to indicate the base number of the arithmetic currently being used.

can deal with only two symbols: "0" and "1". Rather than having to place these two symbols between quotes each time, we adopt the convention that a number is always written in conjunction with its radix, i.e. we write 917_{10} rather than just 917. The latter, in turn, represents a sequence of three symbols: 9, 1, and 7. We omit the radix in those cases that this will not lead to confusion.

Now, how do we represent numbers if our computer can only deal with the symbols 0 and 1? As we have illustrated above, it is not hard to represent a decimal number such as 917_{10} by an equivalent **binary representation**, i.e. one that uses radix 2. In other words, if we interpret the *symbols* 0 and 1 as the *numbers* 0_2 and 1_2, respectively, it would seem that we would already be in a pretty good shape. As a clarification, what we are proposing is to take a bit string, say $\langle 10011 \rangle$, and consider it as a direct representation of a binary number, in this case the number 10011_2. The thing you have to realize here is that a bit string such as $\langle 10011 \rangle$ is nothing but a consecutive series of our basic symbols 0 and 1, whereas 10011_2 is a specific binary number. In order to represent a number from our decimal system, we thus first convert it to a binary number, and simply represent that number as a bit string where 0 or 1 stands for 0_2 or 1_2, respectively.

▷ Arithmetic operations on binary numbers such as addition, subtraction, multiplication, and division, work exactly the same as those on decimal numbers. The only thing you have to realize is that the set of digits now consists of 0 and 1, instead of 0 to 9.

Example 2.1. As an example, review how we actually add 42_{10} and 19_{10}:

$$
\begin{array}{rcc}
 & \downarrow add & \downarrow add \\
carry: & & \boxed{1} \\
first\ number: & 4\,\boxed{2} & \Rightarrow \quad \boxed{4}\,2 \\
second\ number: & 1\,\boxed{9} & \boxed{1}\,9 \quad + \\
\hline
result: & 1 & 6\ \ 1
\end{array}
$$

Note how we first add 2 and 9 and *carry a 1* to the next two digits 4 and 1. In binary arithmetic this is done exactly the same. If we add 1 and 1 the result will be 0 and a 1 is carried to the next two digits to add. So, adding $101010_2 = 42_{10}$ and $010011_2 = 19_{10}$ will then result in

$$
\begin{array}{rl}
carry: & 000100 \\
first\ number: & 101010 \\
second\ number: & 010011 \quad + \\
\hline
result: & 111101
\end{array}
$$

□

It is thus seen that our usual way of adding two numbers can be exactly the same as in binary arithmetic. And as you may suspect, binary subtraction is indeed quite similar as well as is illustrated in the following example.

Example 2.2. In order to subtract 9_{10} from 30_{10} we normally proceed as follows:

$$\downarrow sub \qquad \downarrow sub$$

effect of borrow: $\qquad\qquad\qquad\qquad \boxed{2}$

first number: $\qquad 3\boxed{0} \quad \Rightarrow \quad \boxed{\cancel{3}}\,0$

second number: $\qquad\quad \boxed{9} \qquad\quad \boxed{}\,9 \quad -$

result: $\qquad\qquad\qquad 1 \qquad\qquad 2 \ 1$

In this case, we have to *borrow a 1* from the next digit if necessary. We do the same in the case of binary subtraction:

$$
\begin{array}{rl}
\textit{effect of borrow:} & \text{- - -0-} \\
\textit{first number:} & 111\cancel{1}0 \\
\textit{second number:} & \underline{\quad 1001} \quad - \\
\textit{result:} & \overline{10101}
\end{array}
$$

$\square$

We leave it as an exercise for the reader to verify that binary multiplication and division can be performed likewise.

The problem of finite bit strings

Binary systems so far work fine and just as well as the decimal system we are used to. Unfortunately, there is a small problem which severely affects the representation of (binary) numbers as bit strings. In practice, there is an upper limit to the number of consecutive bits that can be used to represent numbers in a computer. In other words, when considering implementations of binary systems, one is faced with the fact that operations are only defined for bit strings up to a certain length. For instance, most modern personal computers only support binary operations for strings up to 16 or 32 bits. The consequence of this limitation is that we have to decide how a number is actually going to be represented as a bit string of a *finite* and *fixed* length.

There are two situations where this may lead to problems. In the first case, assume that our computer can only accept bit strings of length 8. This means that the largest positive number we could represent as a bit string would be $11111111_2 = 255_{10}$. Indeed, not a very large number. The only solution to this problem is that we will have to represent large numbers as a series of bit strings. For example, the number 917_{10} could be represented by two consecutive bit strings of length 8 as follows:

$$917_{10} = 1110010101_2 = \langle 00000011 \rangle \langle 10010101 \rangle$$

The drawback of this is that because (in this case) our computer supports only operations on bit strings of length 8, we will have to explicitly instruct the computer how it is to operate on *series* of bit strings. In practice, this is not something we want, but which simply cannot be avoided. Fortunately, most modern computers allow operations on bit strings of length 32, or sometimes even 64, which is adequate for most calculations.

The second problem that arises from having to deal with bit strings having a maximum length is a representation for negative numbers. An obvious representation of such numbers is using the first bit to indicate if the remainder of the string represents either a negative or a positive number. This representation is generally referred to as the **sign-magnitude** notation. So, for example, we would have[2]

$$\langle 011011 \rangle_{sm} = +11011_2 = +27_{10}$$
$$\langle 111011 \rangle_{sm} = -11011_2 = -27_{10}$$

Unfortunately, this does mean that we have a "special" bit which turns out to be rather awkward from an implementation point of view. Therefore, two other notations are more commonly used.

In the **one's complement** notation, positive binary numbers are represented in the usual way. So, for example, assuming the maximum bit string length is 8, 27_{10} is represented as the bit string $\langle 00011011 \rangle_{1\bar{c}}$. Negative binary numbers are represented by taking their positive counterpart, and subsequently inverting all bits. To illustrate, -27_{10} is obtained by considering the one's complement notation for 27_{10} and then changing each 0 to a 1 and vice versa. Consequently, using bit strings of length 8, we have that

$$-27_{10} = invert(\langle 00011011 \rangle_{1\bar{c}}) = \langle 11100100 \rangle_{1\bar{c}}$$

The approach followed by the one's complement notation for representing negative numbers does have one peculiar aspect. The number 0 can be represented by either the bit string $\langle 0 \ldots 0 \rangle_{1\bar{c}}$ or by the bit string $\langle 1 \ldots 1 \rangle_{1\bar{c}}$.

▷ To see how the one's complement notation works in practice, consider the subtraction $a - b$ of two positive numbers represented as bit strings of length N. In a one's complement system, this is done by taking the one's complement notation $\bar{b}$ of $-b$ and adding this to a. If a carry emerges from the most significant bit (i.e. the leftmost one), implying that $a + \bar{b} \geq 2^N$, the correct result is simply obtained by adding a one to the result found so far as is illustrated in the next example. We leave it as an exercise for the reader to verify that this correction actually works.

Example 2.3. Assume we need to calculate $42_{10} - 19_{10}$. In a one's complement system using bit strings of length 8 this is done as follows:

decimal	binary		1's compl.
42_{10}	00101010_2	$\rightarrow$	$00101010_{1\bar{c}}$
-19_{10}	-00010011_2	$\rightarrow$	$11101100_{1\bar{c}}$ +
	carry	$\longrightarrow$	$\boxed{1}\,00010110_2$
			$\rightarrow 1$ +
23_{10}			$00010111_{1\bar{c}}$

□

---

[2]Analogous to using the radix as a suffix to indicate the current arithmetic, we use the suffix *sm* to indicate that a bit string is represented in the sign-magnitude notation. Similarly, we use the suffices *$1\bar{c}$* and *$2\bar{c}$* for respectively the one's complement and two's complement notations, which are yet to be discussed.

The example illustrates what happens when $|a| > |b|$. Obviously, when $|a| < |b|$ we have that $a - b < 0$. Let's see how such a calculation is performed.

Example 2.4. Assume we want to calculate $19_{10} - 42_{10}$. In a one's complement system using bit strings of length 8 this is done as follows:

decimal	binary		1's compl.
19_{10}	00010011_2	$\rightarrow$	$00010011_{1\bar{c}}$
-42_{10}	00101010_2	$\rightarrow$	$11010101_{1\bar{c}}$ +
-23_{10}	*no carry*	$\longrightarrow$	$11101000_{1\bar{c}}$

What we see here is that no carry is generated and, indeed, the bit string $\langle 11101000 \rangle$ in one's complement notation represents the correct decimal number -23_{10}.

□

The disadvantage of the one's complement notation is illustrated by Example 2.3. We need to perform an additional operation in the case of subtracting a number b from a with $a - b > 0$. This can be avoided when using a slightly different representation, as is discussed next.

An alternative to the one's complement notation is the so-called **two's complement** notation. In this notation positive binary numbers are represented as normal, and negative numbers are represented by taking the one's complement representation, and adding 1 to it. So, for example, -27_{10} is represented as

$$-27_{10} = (invert(\langle 00011011 \rangle_{1\bar{c}})_2 + 00000001_2 = \langle 11100101 \rangle_{2\bar{c}}$$

Because no extra addition of 00000001_2 is needed, the two's complement notation is easier to use when representing the subtraction of two binary numbers.

Yet another representation is the so-called **excess n** or **biased n** notation. In this case, a number p with $-n \leq p \leq n - 1$ is represented by the binary number $\hat{p} = p + n$, which of course lies in the set $\{0, 1, \ldots, 2n - 1\}$. In other words, we simply add a value of n. The main advantage of this notation is that we need not be concerned about signs as each number is non-negative.

Table 2.1 shows these four widely used interpretations for the case of having to deal with bit strings of length 4. Note how the first bit in each representation is used to indicate whether the string represents a positive or negative number. These notations can easily be extended for larger bit strings. For example, each bit string starting with a 0 is simply interpreted as a positive binary number, except for the excess n notation where it is interpreted as a negative number. We leave it to the reader to verify that the bit string $\langle 10110101 \rangle$ corresponds to the numbers shown in Table 2.2.

▷ **Real numbers**

Most scientific calculations are based on *real numbers*, and their representation in computers has always been an important topic. Before going into details, it is not difficult to imagine

Table 2.1 Interpretation of bit strings as decimal numbers

Vector	Two's complement	One's complement	Sign magnitude	Excess 8
$\langle 0000 \rangle$	0	0	0	-8
$\langle 0001 \rangle$	1	1	1	-7
$\langle 0010 \rangle$	2	2	2	-6
$\langle 0011 \rangle$	3	3	3	-5
$\langle 0100 \rangle$	4	4	4	-4
$\langle 0101 \rangle$	5	5	5	-3
$\langle 0110 \rangle$	6	6	6	-2
$\langle 0111 \rangle$	7	7	7	-1
$\langle 1000 \rangle$	-8	-7	0	0
$\langle 1001 \rangle$	-7	-6	-1	1
$\langle 1010 \rangle$	-6	-5	-2	2
$\langle 1011 \rangle$	-5	-4	-3	3
$\langle 1100 \rangle$	-4	-3	-4	4
$\langle 1101 \rangle$	-3	-2	-5	5
$\langle 1110 \rangle$	-2	-1	-6	6
$\langle 1111 \rangle$	-1	0	-7	7

Table 2.2 The interpretation of the bit string $\langle 10110101 \rangle$

Bit string	Two's complement	One's complement	Sign magnitude	Excess 2^7
$\langle 10110101 \rangle$	-75_{10}	-74_{10}	-53_{10}	53_{10}

how we can actually represent binary *fractions*. It is done in the same way as decimal fractions. For example, the binary fraction 110.11_2 is equal to 6.75_{10}:

$$110.11_2 = 1 \cdot 2^2 + 1 \cdot 2^1 + 0 \cdot 2^0 + 1 \cdot 2^{-1} + 1 \cdot 2^{-2} = 6.75_{10} \tag{2.2}$$

The problems start when representations have to be devised that fit into a *fixed* number of bits. Note that in the case of natural numbers we can always perform calculations *exactly* (within a range defined by the number of digits we are using, and with exception of division). Natural numbers (being expressed in decimal or binary notation) always have a *finite* number of digits. The same holds for fractions that can be expressed as in equation (2.2). But difficulties are encountered when realizing that not every decimal fraction can be expressed by a binary fraction with a finite number of digits. Consider, for example, the decimal fraction $0,2_{10}$. It is not difficult to see that its binary counterpart is equal to:

$$0.2_{10} = 0.0011001100110011001100\ldots_2$$

thus having an infinite number of digits. But apart from this, there are real numbers such as π, $\sqrt{2}$, e^3, etc. which simply can never be written as fractions with a finite number of digits, regardless of the base number of the arithmetic used (which is always a positive natural number). Consequently, if only bit strings of finite length can be used, we are forced to resort to *approximations*. An alternative solution would then seem to use fractions for this purpose. So, for example, we might choose to represent $5\sqrt{2}$ as:

$$5\sqrt{2} \approx 7.0715332033_{10} = 111.000100100101_2 \tag{2.3}$$

Unfortunately, this is not going to work. This is caused by the two conflicting demands that are put on the notation for real numbers:

1. The notation should allow for very *large* (positive and negative) numbers to be represented, and
2. The notation should allow for a *precise* approximation of real numbers.

When only a finite number of bits can be used it is not hard to imagine that these two requirements are indeed conflicting. To this end, many solutions have been proposed, but a representation that has been generally accepted as a reasonable compromise is the **floating-point** notation.

Floating-point notations have a *base* β and a *precision* p such that each floating-point number can be represented as

$$\pm d_0.d_1 \ldots d_{p-1} \times \beta^{exp}$$

where $d_0.d_1 \ldots d_{p-1}$ is called the **mantissa** or **significand**, and *exp* the **exponent**. Of course, for each digit d_i we have that $0 \leq d_i < \beta$.

Example 2.5. To illustrate, if we take $\beta = 2$ and $p = 10$, the representation for $5\sqrt{2}$ as given by equation (2.3) would then become the floating-point number:

$$5\sqrt{2} \approx 1.110001001_2 \times \beta^2 \tag{2.4}$$

In this case, the exponent is equal to 2. Note how we have derived equation (2.4) from (2.3) by first dividing the latter by the exponent 2 (which means shifting all the bits 2 positions to the right), and subsequently discarding all the bits after the 10th position.

□

Two parameters associated with a floating-point notation are important: e_{min} and e_{max} representing the smallest and largest allowable exponent, respectively. It is important to note that the number of floating-point numbers for a given base, precision, and exponent range is *fixed*. There are β^p possible significands, and $e_{max} - e_{min} + 1$ exponents.

In general, floating-point numbers are *normalized*, meaning that the leading digit is non-zero ($d_0 \neq 0$). Demanding that floating-point numbers are normalized leads to a unique representation, but note that it does become impossible to represent 0! The latter problem is generally overcome by representing 0 as $1.0 \times \beta^{e_{min}-1}$. In other words, we use a representation that lies outside the set of valid floating-point numbers. By making use of the parameters e_{min} and e_{max} we are also capable of representing other non-valid but useful numbers, generally referred to as **NaN**s ("Not a Number"). For example, two useful *NaN*s are $\pm\infty$ which are available in most floating-point notations.

2.2.2 Representing text

Now that we have shown how numbers can be represented by finite bit strings, let's concentrate on the representation of text.

Character coding

As you might suspect, we need to devise a scheme by which text can also be represented in the form of bit strings. The approach that is taken in this case is straightforward. As text is ultimately nothing but a consecutive series of characters, our problem reduces to the question of how we can represent individual characters. To that aim, there are two widely used *codes*: **ASCII** ("American Standard Code for Information Interchange") and **EBCDIC** ("Extended Binary Code Decimal Interchange Code"). EBCDIC is used on large IBM mainframes; almost any other computer represents characters using ASCII code. Table 2.3 shows the standard ASCII codes, represented in decimals.

Two things are important here. First, note that the first 32 characters are "special". They represent characters for line feeds, carriage returns, etc., characters which no one enters other than by means of special keystrokes (such as e.g. the RETURN or BACKSPACE key). Second, there are exactly 128 codes. This means that when using ASCII we can represent each character by 7 bits. In practice, however, most computers represent the ASCII character set by means of 8-bit bit strings as this is more in line with the fact that computers generally store data in units of 8 bits. We shall return to this aspect in Section 2.5.

A word on text processing

It would seem that just having the ASCII coding is not enough to represent every kind of text that we come across. For example, the coding makes no distinction between different types of fonts (boldface, italic), nor does it account for aspects like subscripts. Furthermore, it also seems impossible to add new characters, or perhaps to use characters that are specific to a particular language (e.g. "Æ" or "ŏ"). These additional features are typically embedded into so-called **text processors**.

What a calculator is to numbers, so is a text processor with documents: a device that assists in producing results in an automated fashion. An important aspect of each text

Table 2.3 The ASCII codes

Dec.	Char.	Interpretation	Dec.	Char.	Dec.	Char.	Dec.	Char.
0	NUL	null	32	space	64	@	96	'
1	SOH	start of header	33	!	65	A	97	a
2	STX	start of text	34	"	66	B	98	b
3	ETX	end of text	35	#	67	C	99	c
4	EOT	end of transm.	36	$	68	D	100	d
5	ENQ	enquiry	37	%	69	E	101	e
6	ACK	acknowledge	38	&	70	F	102	f
7	BEL	bell	39	'	71	G	103	g
8	BS	backspace	40	(	72	H	104	h
9	HT	horizontal tabs	41	)	73	I	105	i
10	LF	linefeed	42	*	74	J	106	j
11	VT	vertical tabs	43	+	75	K	107	k
12	FF	formfeed	44	,	76	L	108	l
13	CR	carriage return	45	-	77	M	109	m
14	SO	shift out	46	.	78	N	110	n
15	SI	shift in	47	/	79	O	111	o
16	DLE	data link escape	48	0	80	P	112	p
17	DC1	device ctrl. 1	49	1	81	Q	113	q
18	DC2	device ctrl. 2	50	2	82	R	114	r
19	DC3	device ctrl. 3	51	3	83	S	115	s
20	DC4	device ctrl. 4	52	4	84	T	116	t
21	NAK	neg. acknowledge	53	5	85	U	117	u
22	SYN	synchronous idle	54	6	86	V	118	v
23	ETB	end of trans. block	55	7	87	W	119	w
24	CAN	cancel	56	8	88	X	120	x
25	EM	end of medium	57	9	89	Y	121	y
26	SUB	substitute	58	:	90	Z	122	z
27	ESC	escape	59	;	91	[	123	{
28	FS	file separator	60	<	92	\	124		
29	GS	group separator	61	=	93	]	125	}
30	RS	record separator	62	>	94	^	126	~
31	US	unit separator	63	?	95	_	127	DEL

processor is its support for a specific **markup language,** i.e. a set of commands that is used to mark parts of your document for special processing. For example, this book has been written using the LaTeX markup language. Using only the ASCII character set, it is possible to still produce documents having a wealth of variations concerning the presentation of text. To illustrate, consider the following LaTeX command and its result:

LᴬTᴇX *fragment*	*result*
`Using \textbf{boldface}` `is really simple.`	Using **boldface** is really simple.

If you are used to working with a personal computer, you will probably be using a text processor that hides most of these commands for you. Instead, you can select fragments of text and instruct the processor to process that fragment, for example, in boldface. Internally, the processor adds a command like the one used in LᴬTᴇX.

The problem with representing text using markup commands is that standardization in this area is still rather poor. This means that if you want to have your document processed by another text processor, you may have to take great pains to do the proper conversion.[3] Another problem is that most popular markup languages, especially used on personal computers, do *not* strictly adhere to the printable ASCII coding, but instead use many non-printable characters as well. Consequently, the text, including its markup commands as produced with such text processors, cannot be displayed directly on a screen. Moreover, as many high-level services in communication systems expect communicated data to use only printable ASCII characters, communication may become a problem as well.

2.3   Operations

So far, we have discussed only how our daily representations for numbers and other text can be transformed into finite bit strings. We have said nothing about operations: how can we describe operations that have meaning in our daily lives in such a way that when performed on bit strings still yield something meaningful? In this section, we introduce Boolean algebra which is a mathematical system in which operations on bit strings are described in terms of functions and expressions.

There are several reasons for introducing such a notation. The first point to realize is that we are now entering a world in which all things that we imagine in our daily lives are expressed in terms of bit strings. But to do things right, this also means that data manipulations that make sense to us in reality have to be converted to operations that act on bit strings. For example, adding two numbers is something we are accustomed to. But if numbers are to be represented as bit strings, then we also have to describe operations on bit strings that will allow us to manipulate our bit string representations in such a way that the result can be sensibly interpreted as an addition of numbers. This principle is shown in Figure 2.1.

Devising a scheme by which we can express operations on bit strings is thus something that we need. But such a scheme must prove to be beneficial in a number of ways. First, it should be as straightforward as possible. In other words, it should preferably correspond to something that we are more or less already used to. In the second place, as we are

---

[3] And if you really believe that popular text processors for personal computers are capable of converting a document to the format of their competitor, beware. In practice, they might produce something that *seems* converted, but which is now internally mismatched with a very large number of commands that can drive you crazy if you have to continue working with the converted document.

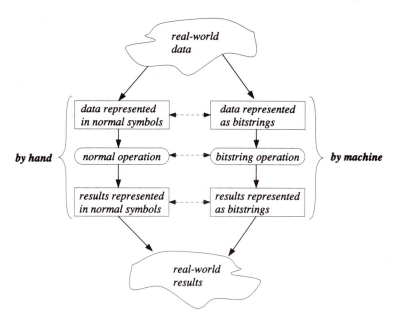

Figure 2.1 The relation between normal operations and the world of bit string operations.

dealing with computers, our scheme should also be easy to implement. That is, we have to invent a scheme that can easily be simulated through electrical or mechanical devices. Boolean algebra is such a scheme. In this section, we shall concentrate on the notational issues. Implementation aspects are discussed in Section 2.4.

2.3.1 Boolean functions

Boolean algebra is, as we have said, a mathematical notation. The basis of this notation is formed by treating bits as variables that can have only two possible values: the symbols 0 and 1. This property has an important consequence. Assume we have a Boolean function f with n input bits, for which we can use the normal notation:

$$y = f(x_1, x_2, \ldots, x_n)$$

Note that each bit $y, x_1, \ldots, x_n$ is considered as a Boolean variable so that it can be either 0 or 1. The important issue here is that there are precisely 2^n combinations of input values for f. This means that we can simply resort to constructing a table with 2^n rows and $n+1$ columns, where each row describes a unique combination of the values for the bits $x_1, \ldots, x_n$, together with the value for $f(x_1, \ldots, x_n)$. Such a table is denoted a **function table**. For example, look at the three function tables shown in Table 2.4. What is seen there is that each function *not*, *and*, and *or* is completely specified by listing all the possible combinations of values for their input bits.

Table 2.4 The three basic function tables

x	not(x)
0	1
1	0

x	y	and(x,y)
0	0	0
0	1	0
1	0	0
1	1	1

x	y	or(x,y)
0	0	0
0	1	1
1	0	1
1	1	1

But there is more. If we consider a 0 as the representation of the *logical* value FALSE, and 1 as the representation of the value TRUE, it is seen that we can also speak about *truth* tables. For example, the function *and* is now a representation of the logical AND operation. Using natural language

$$and(x,y) \quad :: \quad \text{"TRUE if and only if both } x \text{ and } y \text{ are TRUE."}$$

Likewise, *or* represents the logical OR operation and *not* the logical NOT operation:

$$or(x,y) \quad :: \quad \text{"TRUE if and only if either } x \text{ or } y \text{ is TRUE."}$$

$$not(x) \quad :: \quad \text{"TRUE if and only if } x \text{ is not TRUE, i.e. FALSE."}$$

Let's take a look at another example. Consider the Boolean function *xor* with two input bits that takes on the value 1 (TRUE) if and only if the two input values are different. This function, also known as the *exclusive-or* (XOR) function, can be specified as shown in Table 2.5. The question that comes to mind is if we can write down *xor* in terms of the three basic functions from Table 2.4. And indeed, this is the case. To that end, recall again from high-school algebra the concept of **function composition**. For example, suppose we had the following two functions:

$$f(x) = x^2$$
$$g(x) = 1 - x$$

Table 2.5 The specification of the exclusive-or (XOR) function

x	y	xor(x,y)
0	0	0
0	1	1
1	0	1
1	1	0

In this case, the composed functions $f(g(x))$ and $g(f(x))$ take the following form:

$$
\begin{aligned}
f(g(x)) &= [g(x)]^2 = (1-x)^2 = 1 - 2x + x^2 \\
g(f(x)) &= 1 - f(x) = 1 - x^2
\end{aligned}
$$

We can do the same in the case of *xor*, for it can be readily verified that[4]

$$
xor(x,y) = or(and(not(x),y), and(x,not(y)))
$$

The important thing to note here is that it can be shown that *any* Boolean function can be expressed as a combination of just the three functions *not*, *and*, and *or*. (In fact, it even turns out that using only a combination of the *not* function and either of the *and* or *or* functions is sufficient.) In turn, this implies that if we can devise implementations for just those three basic functions, we will be able to implement any Boolean function. A powerful result indeed.

2.3.2 Boolean algebra

But admittedly, writing functions such as *xor* in terms of function composition is rather awkward and it is not hard to imagine that this notation can easily lead to descriptions which are barely comprehensible by human beings. To solve this problem, we adopt a *symbolic notation* to deal with *expressions* that take a value of either 0 or 1. This notation was introduced by George Boole in 1854 and has come to be known as **Boolean algebra**.[5] Later, it was adopted for computer science and has since then also been known as **switching algebra**.

Notational issues

Boolean algebra is in fact a *formal language* that allows us to express function compositions in a convenient way. Being a language means that there will be certain syntactical rules, just as there are rules in its grammar. Its basis is formed by the three functions *not*, *and*, and *or* from Table 2.4 which are more conveniently written using the following notation:

$$
\begin{aligned}
not(x) &\Rightarrow \overline{x} \\
and(x,y) &\Rightarrow x \bullet y \\
or(x,y) &\Rightarrow x + y
\end{aligned}
$$

---

[4]Below we shall explain how we can derive function compositions in a systematic way.

[5]More precisely, Boole showed that logic could be expressed in terms of an algebraic system.

In other words, each of these functions is now specified in the form of an **operation** on either a single bit (the NOT operation) or as an operation between two bits (the AND and the OR operation). Note that we are only introducing some convenient syntax here: the notations above are just a way of writing down the basic functions in a more readable form. There is nothing special about it in any sense.

Using this notation makes it much easier to express function compositions. For example, the function *xor* given above can now be written as:

$$xor(x,y) \equiv (\bar{x} \bullet y) + (x \bullet \bar{y})$$

which is indeed easier to read.

But just as there are syntactical conventions, so there are also some grammatical rules that we should adhere to. And it is here where the mathematical nature of Boolean algebra is found. Before we elaborate on this issue, note that grammatical rules are something we are already used to. In effect, many of them are simply *rewriting* expressions. Consider the following examples:

expression		*can be rewritten as . . .*
8×1	$\Rightarrow$	8
$8 + 0$	$\Rightarrow$	8
$10 + 3$	$\Rightarrow$	$3 + 10$
$45 \times (3 + 26)$	$\Rightarrow$	$(45 \times 3) + (45 \times 26)$
$12 + (34 + 9)$	$\Rightarrow$	$(12 + 34) + 9$

In Boolean algebra, there are really not that many differences from the things we are already used to. For example, the following rules apply equally well in our case (where x, y, and z are bits):

expression		*can be rewritten as . . .*
$x \bullet 1$	$\Rightarrow$	x
$x + 0$	$\Rightarrow$	x
$x \bullet y$	$\Rightarrow$	$y \bullet x$
$x + y$	$\Rightarrow$	$y + x$
$x \bullet (y \bullet z)$	$\Rightarrow$	$(x \bullet y) \bullet z$
$x + (y + z)$	$\Rightarrow$	$(x + y) + z$
$x \bullet (y + z)$	$\Rightarrow$	$(x \bullet y) + (x \bullet z)$

We have more or less deliberately used the symbols "+" and "$\bullet$" to indicate that many of the properties of ordinary addition and multiplication that we are used to apply equally well in the case of Boolean algebra. There is, however, only one exception that does not immediately have its counterpart in ordinary arithmetic. It can be shown that

$$\text{for all } x :: x + x = x$$

We shall not go into any further details here on Boolean algebra, as most properties, except for the ones we have mentioned, are really not important for the remainder of this chapter. References to textbooks on Boolean algebra can be found at the end of this chapter.

Constructing Boolean expressions

At this point, the only thing we have done is to have introduced a notation that seems to be more readable than making use of function compositions. As we shall see later, our notation is in fact so convenient that it becomes relatively easy to derive implementations for Boolean expressions. But that leaves us with one more issue to solve, namely how to derive a Boolean expression for a function. This is best explained by means of an example. Let's reconsider our original specification of the exclusive-or function which was given by means of the following function table:

x	y	$xor(x,y)$
0	0	0
0	1	1
1	0	1
1	1	0

In order to derive a Boolean expression for *xor*, we consider only those rows from the table for which $xor(x,y) = 1$. This is true for the following two cases:

$$xor(x,y) = 1 \Leftrightarrow \quad (1) \quad x = 0 \quad \text{and} \quad y = 1$$
$$(2) \quad x = 1 \quad \text{and} \quad y = 0$$

For each row for which the function yields 1, we construct a separate Boolean expression as follows. If $x = 0$, we represent this fact in our expression by writing the term "$\overline{x}$". On the other hand, if $x = 1$, we write down "x". The same goes for the input y. All these terms are then subsequently brought together by using the AND operator:

$$(1) \quad x = 0 \quad \text{and} \quad y = 1 \quad \Rightarrow \quad \overline{x} \bullet y$$
$$(2) \quad x = 1 \quad \text{and} \quad y = 0 \quad \Rightarrow \quad x \bullet \overline{y}$$

The final expression is obtained by combining these expressions into a single expression by using the OR operator:

$$xor(x,y) = (\overline{x} \bullet y) + (x \bullet \overline{y}).$$

2.3.3 Some examples

Let's take a look at a few examples of how we can describe operations on bit strings using the notations above. The operations we consider here will be used in the following section as building blocks of a simple calculating device.

Table 2.6 The specification of the majority operation on bit strings of length 3

inputs			output
x	y	z	major3
0	0	0	0
0	0	1	0
0	1	0	0
0	1	1	1
1	0	0	0
1	0	1	1
1	1	0	1
1	1	1	1

The majority operation

Consider the following operation. Suppose we have a bit string $\langle xyz \rangle$ of length 3, and we wish to determine if the majority of the number of bits is 1. In other words, we wish to determine whether the bit string contains at least two bits that are 1. The operation, which we denote as *major3*, is specified in Table 2.6. In order to determine the corresponding Boolean expression, we proceed as follows. First, we consider only those rows for which the operation yields 1:

$$major3 = 1 \Leftrightarrow \quad \begin{array}{llll} (1) & x = 0 & \text{and} \quad y = 1 & \text{and} \quad z = 1 \\ (2) & x = 1 & \text{and} \quad y = 0 & \text{and} \quad z = 1 \\ (3) & x = 1 & \text{and} \quad y = 1 & \text{and} \quad z = 0 \\ (2) & x = 1 & \text{and} \quad y = 1 & \text{and} \quad z = 1 \end{array}$$

which results in four expressions, one per row:

$$\begin{array}{lllll} (1) & x = 0 & \text{and} \quad y = 1 & \text{and} \quad z = 1 & \Rightarrow \quad \bar{x} \bullet y \bullet z \\ (2) & x = 1 & \text{and} \quad y = 0 & \text{and} \quad z = 1 & \Rightarrow \quad x \bullet \bar{y} \bullet z \\ (3) & x = 1 & \text{and} \quad y = 1 & \text{and} \quad z = 0 & \Rightarrow \quad x \bullet y \bullet \bar{z} \\ (4) & x = 1 & \text{and} \quad y = 1 & \text{and} \quad z = 1 & \Rightarrow \quad x \bullet y \bullet z \end{array}$$

so that we obtain

$$major3 \quad = \quad (\bar{x} \bullet y \bullet z) + (x \bullet \bar{y} \bullet z) + (x \bullet y \bullet \bar{z}) + (x \bullet y \bullet z)$$

What we have achieved is a simple way of describing an operation on a bit string of length 3. As we shall see later, subsequently deriving an implementation from the expression for *major3* is straightforward.

Table 2.7 The specification of the oddbits operation on bit strings of length 3

inputs			output
x	y	z	odd3
0	0	0	0
0	0	1	1
0	1	0	1
0	1	1	0
1	0	0	1
1	0	1	0
1	1	0	0
1	1	1	1

The oddbits operation

Our next example concerns an operation by which we can determine if a bit string $\langle xyz \rangle$ of length 3 contains an odd number of bits being 1. In other words, the operation should yield 1, if and only if the number of bits that are 1 is either 1 or 3. The operation, which we denote as *odd3*, is given in Table 2.7.

Following the same procedure as in the case of the majority operation, we first consider only those rows for which the operation yields 1 as its result:

$$odd3 = 1 \Leftrightarrow \begin{array}{llll} (1) & x = 0 & \text{and} & y = 0 & \text{and} & z = 1 \\ (2) & x = 0 & \text{and} & y = 1 & \text{and} & z = 0 \\ (3) & x = 1 & \text{and} & y = 0 & \text{and} & z = 0 \\ (2) & x = 1 & \text{and} & y = 1 & \text{and} & z = 1 \end{array}$$

which results in four expressions, one per row:

$$\begin{array}{llllll} (1) & x = 0 & \text{and} & y = 0 & \text{and} & z = 1 & \Rightarrow & \bar{x} \bullet \bar{y} \bullet z \\ (2) & x = 0 & \text{and} & y = 1 & \text{and} & z = 0 & \Rightarrow & \bar{x} \bullet y \bullet \bar{z} \\ (3) & x = 1 & \text{and} & y = 0 & \text{and} & z = 0 & \Rightarrow & x \bullet \bar{y} \bullet \bar{z} \\ (4) & x = 1 & \text{and} & y = 1 & \text{and} & z = 1 & \Rightarrow & x \bullet y \bullet z \end{array}$$

so that we obtain

$$odd3 = (\bar{x} \bullet \bar{y} \bullet z) + (\bar{x} \bullet y \bullet \bar{z}) + (x \bullet \bar{y} \bullet \bar{z}) + (x \bullet y \bullet z)$$

A half adder

For the first time, let's make a link between the world of bit strings and that of binary arithmetic. Consider the operation *halfadd* shown in Table 2.8. We assume this operation takes two bits x and y as input, and likewise, has two bits z and c_{out} as output.

Table 2.8 The specification of the operation *halfadd*

inputs		outputs	
x	y	z	c_{out}
0	0	0	0
0	1	1	0
1	0	1	0
1	1	0	1

When dealing with multiple outputs, as in this case, it is convenient to write a Boolean expression per output variable. Following the same procedure as described in the two previous examples, it is not hard to see that

$$z = (\bar{x} \bullet y) + (x \bullet \bar{y})$$
$$c_{\text{out}} = x \bullet y$$

The special thing about our operation *halfadd* is that it behaves the same as mathematical addition in the case of binary numbers. To see this, first note that in binary arithmetic the following rules apply:

$$0_2 + 0_2 = 0_2$$
$$0_2 + 1_2 = 1_2$$
$$1_2 + 0_2 = 1_2$$
$$1_2 + 1_2 = 0_2, \text{ with an } \textit{overflow} \text{ of } 1_2$$

These rules are completely analogous to decimal arithmetic. For example, recall that if we perform the addition $43_{10} + 9_{10}$, we first write down a 2_{10}, and note that we had an *overflow* of 1_{10} which we *carry* to the next digit. This leads to our final result 52_{10}. In the case of binary arithmetic, we do exactly the same. By adding $1_2 + 1_2$, the final result will be 0_2, but with an additional overflow of 1_2. Now, if you look at z in Table 2.8 you will find that if we neglect possible overflows we have that $z = x + y$, where z, x, and y are now considered as binary numbers, and "$+$" denotes the usual add operation. A possible overflow is recorded in c_{out}, which, of course, only happens when $x = y = 1$. The operation *halfadd* is called a **half adder** for reasons we explain below.

This example illustrates an important point. What we have done is construct a *Boolean function* that behaves as an ordinary adder for *binary numbers*. In other words, we can apparently represent operations such as adding two numbers in terms of operations that make sense only in the world of bit strings. We shall return to this important observation below.

Table 2.9 Specification of the operation *fulladd*

inputs			outputs	
c_{in}	x	y	z	c_{out}
0	0	0	0	0
0	0	1	1	0
0	1	0	1	0
0	1	1	0	1
1	0	0	1	0
1	0	1	0	1
1	1	0	0	1
1	1	1	1	1

A full adder

You might suspect that the existence of a half adder implies that there will also be something as a **full adder**. And indeed, this is the case. This full adder operation, which we refer to here as *fulladd*, is closely related to the majority and oddbits operation given previously. The operation takes three bits c_{in}, x, and y as input, and produces two bits z and c_{out} as output according to Table 2.9. As we shall explain below, the special point about this operation is that it does a *full* addition on its input. But before we go into any details, let's first see how we can express this operation using our Boolean notations.

Again, using the procedure as described above, it should not be too hard to verify that we have:

$$z = (\overline{c}_{in} \bullet \overline{x} \bullet y) + (\overline{c}_{in} \bullet x \bullet \overline{y}) + (c_{in} \bullet \overline{x} \bullet \overline{y}) + (c_{in} \bullet x \bullet y)$$
$$c_{out} = (\overline{c}_{in} \bullet x \bullet y) + (c_{in} \bullet \overline{x} \bullet y) + (c_{in} \bullet x \bullet \overline{y}) + (c_{in} \bullet x \bullet y)$$

What is seen here is that our *fulladd* operation is nothing but a combination of the majority and oddbits operation discussed above. In fact, it can be immediately observed that

$$z = odd3 \quad \text{and} \quad c_{out} = major3$$

The distinction with the half adder operation is that we now take a possible overflow from a *previous* application of the operation *fulladd* into account as well. It is for this reason that the adder described here is called a full adder. A previous overflow is recorded in the additional bit c_{in}.

An overflow will again occur when at least two of the three bits x, y, and c_{in}, interpreted as binary numbers, have the value 1. Again, this is completely analogous to decimal arithmetic. For example, when adding $56_{10} + 49_{10}$, we first add $6_{10} + 9_{10}$ which leads to the digit 5_{10}, and second, record an overflow of 1_{10} which is carried to the next digit.

After that, we add $1_{10} + 5_{10} + 4_{10}$ which leads to the digit 0_{10} and, again, an overflow of 1_{10}. The final result is the number 105_{10}.

In the case of our full adder, the overflow as the result of the addition is again recorded in c_{out}. Full adders are important. As we shall see in the next section, it is possible to combine N full adders into an adder that can operate on bit strings of length N. In this sense, we are indeed using Boolean algebra to represent operations on binary numbers.

2.3.4   Towards the next step

Let's take a look at what we have accomplished so far:

1. We started out by making an attempt to represent our world of decimals, letters, etc. by a world consisting only of finite bit strings. Although we have skipped many details, we have demonstrated that merely *representing* data through bit strings is feasible.

2. Our next step consisted in the construction of Boolean functions: functions that can accept only variables that take on the values 0 and 1, values to which the function itself is also restricted. We have shown how we can describe these functions in terms of Boolean expressions. We are now capable of describing *operations* on finite bit strings.

3. Our example above is a crucial link. First, by using a suitable representation for our decimal numbers in terms of finite bit strings, and second by specifying a Boolean function that produces bit strings that can be sensibly interpreted as numbers, we have constructed an operation in terms of Boolean algebra and finite bit strings that makes sense to us in the world of binary and decimal numbers.

So where does this bring us? Up to this point we have merely concentrated on theoretical issues. It is time that we put things into practice. Suppose that we could *simulate* the world of finite bit strings and Boolean functions. In other words, suppose we could build a device that is capable of:

*   Representing the symbols 0 and 1 in a unique way, and

*   Simulating behavior of Boolean functions exactly according to the rules of Boolean algebra.

In that case, we would have a machine at our disposal that we could readily use as a *computing device*. How such a device is built is the subject of the succeeding sections.

2.4   Digital circuits

We now have the mechanisms to mold our world of decimals and letters into the world of finite bit strings. Also, we have shown by example how Boolean functions can be

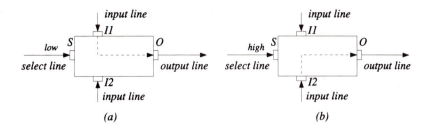

Figure 2.2 A binary switch viewed from the outside.

used to construct operations that are useful to us, such as, for example, addition of binary numbers. We now take a closer look at the actual implementation of these functions into hardware. Our main concern in this section is to show how we can construct devices out of electrical components that are capable of *simulating* the behavior of Boolean functions. These devices can then be used for doing computations in an automated way. We first present in Section 2.4.1 the basic building blocks for the construction of computers: gates. Then, we show in Section 2.4.2 how gates can be used to implement operations on bit strings, using Boolean expressions as our starting point. Finally, we consider the integration of several implementations into a single so-called chip in Section 2.4.3.

2.4.1 Gates

The question we want to answer here is if we can produce an electrical or mechanical device that is capable of *simulating* operations on bit strings. As we have mentioned above, all Boolean operations can be constructed from the three basic operations: NOT, AND, and OR. So, clearly, what we are seeking is a simple device that can simulate precisely these three operations. Such a device, which is denoted here as a **binary switch**, is shown in Figure 2.2. (We emphasize that our binary switch is just an example. In reality other kinds of binary switches are used.)

A binary switch operates on the basis of just two possible values of signals: a **low** value, and a **high** value. For most computers a high value corresponds to something between 2 and 5 volts, whereas a low value typically lies somewhere between 0 and 1 volt. On the outside, our switch has four pins. Two pins are used as *input lines*, one pin as an *output line*, and one as a *select line*, respectively. The whole idea is that based on the value of the signal put on the select line, either one of the two input lines is selected. In particular, we have:

value at select line is *low*   ⇒   select input line *I*1
value at select line is *high*   ⇒   select input line *I*2

The value of the signal at the selected input line is subsequently propagated to the output

Table 2.10   The relationship between the values of the input, output and select signals in a binary switch

	input lines		select	output
	I1	*I2*	*line S*	*line O*
1:	low	low	low	low
2:	low	low	high	low
3:	low	high	low	low
4:	low	high	high	high
5:	high	low	low	high
6:	high	low	high	low
7:	high	high	low	high
8:	high	high	high	high

line.[6] This gives rise to a number of possible output values, depending on the values of the signals at respectively the select line, and the two input lines. Table 2.10 shows this dependency.

Binary switches become interesting when we manipulate the signals at the input lines. Let's look at three particular schemes.

Making an inverter.   First, assume we permanently put a high-valued signal on $I1$ and a low-valued signal on $I2$. This corresponds to considering only rows #5 and #6 in Table 2.10. In that case, we get the following relationship between the select signal and the output signal:

$$\text{value at } S \text{ is } low \quad \Rightarrow \quad \text{value at } O \text{ is } high$$
$$\text{value at } S \text{ is } high \quad \Rightarrow \quad \text{value at } O \text{ is } low$$

In other words, we have made the switch act as an *inverter* for its select signal. What does this mean? If we consider the select signal as our actual input and *interpret* a low signal value as 0 and a high signal value as 1, it should be clear that our binary switch simulates the behavior of the Boolean NOT operation.

Making an AND switch.   In a similar way, we can construct a switch that simulates the Boolean AND operation. To that end, we directly connect input line $I1$ to the input line, and consider what happens to the value of the output line. This corresponds to considering rows #1, #3, #6, and #8 in Table 2.10. In that case, we obtain the following:

---

[6]How this is done in practice is beyond the scope of this book. This is typically something what concerns only electrical engineers.

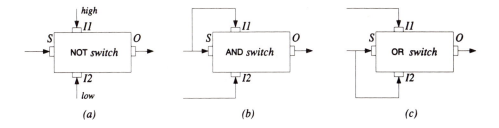

Figure 2.3 Wiring switches for construction of gates.

inputs		output
S	*I2*	*0*
low	*low*	*low*
low	*high*	*low*
high	*low*	*low*
high	*high*	*high*

Again, by interpreting a low signal value as 0 and a high signal value as 1 it is seen that our switch simulates the Boolean AND operation.

Making an OR switch.   Finally, we can wire the switch in such a way that it simulates the Boolean OR operation. To that end, we merely connect input line *I2* to the select line. This corresponds to considering only rows #1, #4, #5, and #8 in Table 2.10, leading to:

inputs		output
S	*I1*	*0*
low	*low*	*low*
low	*high*	*high*
high	*low*	*high*
high	*high*	*high*

These three different schemes are summarized in Figure 2.3. The relation to Boolean algebra is now evident. By *interpreting* a high signal value as a 1, and a low signal value as a 0, we have actually made **implementations** of the three basic operations into switches. In other words, by using binary switches we can *simulate* the behavior of our three basic Boolean functions *not*, *and*, and *or*. And because these three operations are all that is needed for constructing an arbitrary Boolean expression, the development of a machine that can actually do computations can now commence. As we shall see below, the only thing we have to do is to correctly wire a number of these switches together in order to simulate the behavior of a Boolean expression. The three switches are generally known as **gates** and their conventional graphical representation is shown in Figure 2.4.

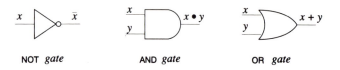

NOT *gate*   AND *gate*   OR *gate*

Figure 2.4 The graphical representation of the three basic gates.

2.4.2   Implementing arbitrary Boolean functions

Having shown how we can simulate the three basic operations NOT, AND, and OR through binary switches, it should now also be possible to simulate arbitrary Boolean functions by connecting gates to each other. In this section, we shall pay attention to how we can derive an implementation of a Boolean function in a systematic way. Let's first start with a few simple examples.

A multiple AND operation

As a first example of a more complicated Boolean function, consider the function *and5* specified as

$$and5(a,b,c,d,e) = a \bullet b \bullet c \bullet d \bullet e$$

In order to derive an implementation for this function, our first concern is to specify *add5* in terms of the basic functions *not*, *and*, and *or*. The point to note is that these functions take, at most, two variables as their input. Because Boolean algebra is similar to ordinary algebra, we can also place a few brackets here and there. In particular, we may choose to write *add5* as the following expression:

$$and5(a,b,c,d,e) = ((a \bullet b) \bullet (c \bullet d)) \bullet e$$

We can now easily implement the function *and5* using the basic AND gates, as shown in Figure 2.5(a). For each term "$y \bullet z$" we use a single AND gate and associate with its input lines "y" and "z," respectively, and with its output line the result "$y \bullet z$". To further illustrate, Figure 2.5(b) shows an implementation of *and5* after having rewritten it as the expression

$$and5(a,b,c,d,e) = (a \bullet b) \bullet (c \bullet (d \bullet e))$$

It should be clear how we can derive implementations of the AND or OR operations that can take any given number of bits as input. We leave this as an exercise for the reader.

The exclusive-or operation

As an another example, consider the XOR operation which was specified by the Boolean expression

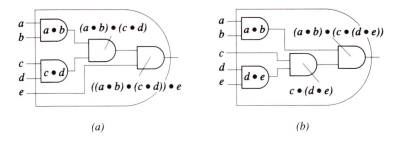

Figure 2.5 The construction of an AND gate with five input lines.

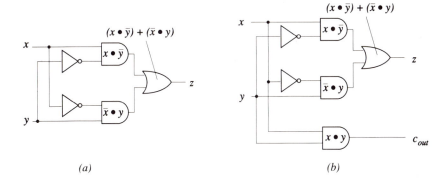

Figure 2.6 An implementation for the exclusive-or function (a) and a half adder (b).

$$xor(x, y) = (\overline{x} \bullet y) + (x \bullet \overline{y})$$

In this case, we start with deriving an implementation for the subexpression $(\overline{x} \bullet y)$ which requires a NOT gate, combined with an AND gate. Likewise, the subexpression $(x \bullet \overline{y})$ also requires a NOT gate and an AND gate. The implementation of the full expression is finally achieved by using an additional OR gate. The result is shown in Figure 2.6(a).

But, in fact, we can do even better than this. Recall that our half adder operation specified in Table 2.8 took two bits x and y as input, and had two output bits z and c_{out}, which could be specified as:

$$z = (\overline{x} \bullet y) + (x \bullet \overline{y})$$
$$c_{\text{out}} = x \bullet y$$

Clearly, z corresponds to the XOR operation. By adding just one single gate to Figure 2.6(a), we obtain a combined implementation for the exclusive-or function and our half adder,

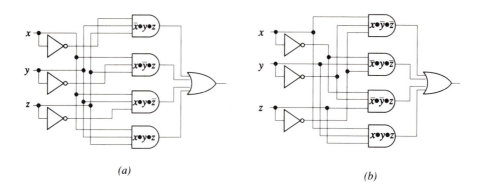

(a)   *(b)*

Figure 2.7   An implementation for the majority function *major3* (a), and the oddbits function *odd3* (b).

as shown in Figure 2.6(b). Combining several implementations into one is something we shall meet often.

The majority and oddbits operation

Using the conventions introduced in the previous two examples, it is now not too difficult to derive implementations for the majority and oddbits operations discussed in the previous section. These two operations could be specified as the following Boolean expressions:

$$major3 = (\bar{x} \bullet y \bullet z) + (x \bullet \bar{y} \bullet z) + (x \bullet y \bullet \bar{z}) + (x \bullet y \bullet z)$$
$$odd3 = (\bar{x} \bullet \bar{y} \bullet z) + (\bar{x} \bullet y \bullet \bar{z}) + (x \bullet \bar{y} \bullet \bar{z}) + (x \bullet y \bullet z)$$

We have already shown how to construct an implementation for the AND operation having five instead of two input bits. Here, we assume that there is also an implementation available for the three-bit case, as well as an implementation for the OR operation with four bits as input. Assuming this, deriving the implementations for *major3* and *odd3* is not too difficult; they are shown in Figure 2.7

A full adder

As a last example, let's consider an implementation of the full adder as specified in the previous section (Table 2.9). As we have mentioned, our full adder actually consists of two components: the majority and oddbits function. It would therefore seem reasonable that we can derive an implementation by simply merging the implementation of these two functions together, similar to the way that we combined the implementation of the exclusive-or operation and our half adder. And indeed, this can be done. Moreover, we

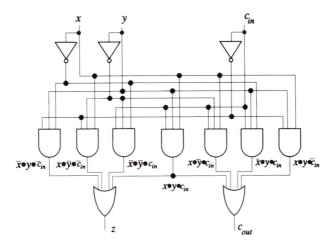

Figure 2.8 An implementation for the full adder operation.

can in fact have one gate less. Recall that the full adder was specified as an operation taking three input bits x, y, and c_{in}, and which had as output two bits z and c_{out}:

$$z = (\overline{c}_{in} \bullet \overline{x} \bullet y) + (\overline{c}_{in} \bullet x \bullet \overline{y}) + (c_{in} \bullet \overline{x} \bullet \overline{y}) + (c_{in} \bullet x \bullet y)$$
$$c_{out} = (\overline{c}_{in} \bullet x \bullet y) + (c_{in} \bullet \overline{x} \bullet y) + (c_{in} \bullet x \bullet \overline{y}) + (c_{in} \bullet x \bullet y)$$

What is seen here is that the subexpression $(c_{in} \bullet x \bullet y)$ appears for both output bits. This means that we can have just one AND gate for this expression in our implementation. This leads to the circuit shown in Figure 2.8.

Discussion

The functions discussed so far are rather simple and one may justifiably argue that their complexity is certainly not representative of most functions performed by computers. Nevertheless, even complex Boolean functions can be implemented by electrical circuits that combine only NOT, AND, and OR gates. But clearly, if complex functions are to be implemented we need to raise the level of abstraction, i.e. group functionality into more complex components that in turn can be combined to implement more complex functions. In the next subsection, we shall discuss how several gates can be integrated into so-called *integrated circuits*.

2.4.3   Integrated circuits

Gates form the basic building block in constructing computers. But manufacturing computers by starting to connect gates into the kind of circuits discussed so far is not very efficient. Instead, it seems more practical to make use of existing circuits, and preferably circuits that can be tailored to specific needs. In addition, and more important, the level of abstraction when considering only gates is simply not adequate if we are to construct such complex machines as computers. In this section, we take a closer look at the concept of an **integrated circuit** (**IC**), commonly referred to as a **chip**. An integrated circuit is a collection of gates and their interconnections grouped together into a single package with a number of pins that are connected to the input and output lines of some gates.[7] Integrated circuits will be seen to be useful in a number of ways. In the first place, they allow us to introduce a more convenient level of abstraction: rather than talking about circuits in terms of gates, we are able to consider circuits constructed by wiring chips together. In the second place, and the starting point for our discussion in this section, integrated circuits often combine several functions into a single chip which can each be selected through a separate mechanism.

Integrating and selecting implementations

An important feature of many chips is that they integrate functionality: several Boolean operations are implemented on the same chip. Doing so has several benefits. For example, by integrating several operations it becomes possible to optimize the overall implementation by minimizing the number of gates that are needed. We have briefly come meet this issue in the previous section when discussing our implementation of a full adder. Our solution was based on combining the implementation for the majority and oddbits operation, which each consisted of four AND gates. We observed that rather than having to use a total of eight AND gates, it would suffice to use only seven.

Another benefit of integration is that of convenience. Rather than having to buy a separate chip for each required operation, it suffices to purchase just a single chip, and select the operation needed. In turn, this reduces the overall complexity of constructing computers, of which the net effect is that costs can be kept relatively low. How operations can be integrated and subsequently selected is our main concern in this section.

Let's start by illustrating integrated implementations through a simple example. Suppose we wish to construct a circuit that accepts two input bits x and y and that offers implementations for calculating two different results: $(x + y)$ and $(x \bullet y)$. Now, rather than having two different output pins, we require that there be only a single output pin and additionally some selection mechanism to choose one of the two possible operations. An outline of such a chip is shown in Figure 2.9.

What we need at this point is to devise an implementation for our selection mechanism. To that end, first note that we can specify our result z more generally as:

$$z \;=\; (x + y) \bullet sel + (x \bullet y) \bullet \overline{sel}$$

---

[7]We note that in order to simplify our discussion we do not make an explicit distinction between integrated circuits and functional units, the latter being part of a chip. Instead, we focus only on the issues of abstraction and combining circuits. How things are actually packaged into chips is less important for our discussion.

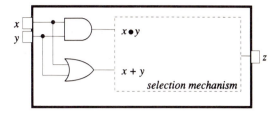

Figure 2.9 Outline of an implementation integrating two different operations.

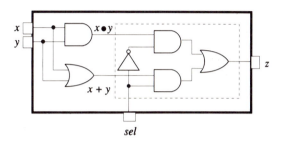

Figure 2.10 A complete integrated implementation and selection mechanism.

where *sel* is a so-called **selection bit** that either *enables* or *disables* an operation. If *sel* = 1, only the result of the operation $(x+y)$ is propagated to z, so that the operation $(x \bullet y)$ is effectively disabled. The converse holds for the case that *sel* = 0. The general expression for z also suggests how we can implement our selection mechanism by using two AND gates, a single OR gate, and an inverter. Our final implementation is shown in Figure 2.10.

We have shown so far that by using only one bit it is possible to select between two possible alternatives. This mechanism can easily be generalized as follows. Assume that we want to design an implementation of a selection mechanism using K selection bits. Because each selection bit can be either 0 or 1, it is not hard to see that this will allow us to select between 2^K input bits. For example, suppose that we have two selection bits sel_1 and sel_2. In that case, we can design an implementation that will allow us to select between four input bits $x_1, \ldots, x_4$ according to the following expression:

$$y = x_1 \bullet (\overline{sel_1} \bullet \overline{sel_2}) + x_2 \bullet (\overline{sel_1} \bullet sel_2) + x_3 \bullet (sel_1 \bullet \overline{sel_2}) + x_4 \bullet (sel_1 \bullet sel_2)$$

An implementation of this selection mechanism is shown in Figure 2.11(a). An application of the selector is found in Figure 2.11(b), which shows an implementation of an integrated circuit providing four operations:

$$z = \begin{cases} x \bullet y & \text{if } sel_1 = 0, sel_2 = 0 \\ x + y & \text{if } sel_1 = 0, sel_2 = 1 \\ \overline{x \bullet y} & \text{if } sel_1 = 1, sel_2 = 0 \\ \overline{x + y} & \text{if } sel_1 = 1, sel_2 = 1 \end{cases}$$

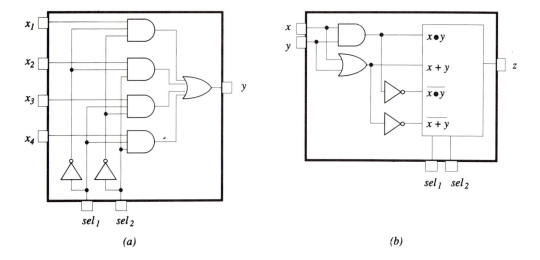

Figure 2.11   An implementation of a selection mechanism for four inputs (a), and its application in an integrated circuit (b).

In a similar way, we can derive implementations that allow us to use three selection bits to select between eight alternative input bits, etc. These implementations are also called **multiplexers**. We return to selection mechanisms when discussing memory chips in the next section. But before doing so, we first take a look at a useful and in fact indispensable integrated circuit.

Integrating arithmetic and logic

An important type of integrated circuit is a so-called **arithmetic and logic unit**, generally abbreviated to ALU. As its name suggests, an ALU integrates arithmetic and logical operations into a single circuit. In particular, one can expect that an ALU having two input bits x and y provides the following operations:

- The Boolean NOT operation for at least one input, say x: $\bar{x}$
- The Boolean AND operation: $x \bullet y$
- The Boolean OR operation: $x + y$
- The operation for doing *binary addition* on x and y.

With the implementations introduced so far, we are capable of constructing an integrated circuit that provides these operations. The simplest part is formed by the collection of three Boolean operations; for the binary arithmetic operation, we can use our full adder implementation from the previous section. This leads to a so-called **1-bit ALU** shown in Figure 2.12.

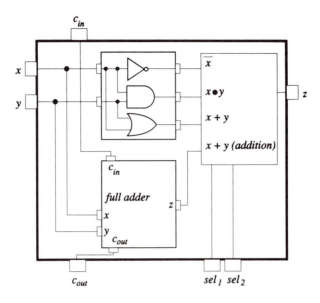

Figure 2.12 An implementation of a 1-bit ALU by integration of several circuits.

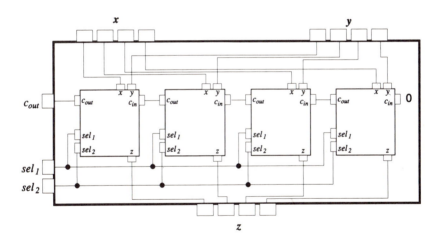

Figure 2.13 An implementation of a 4-bit ALU.

Our 1-bit ALU is a simple device, and certainly a lot simpler than it appears in practice. However, it can be used to build a more useful integrated circuit by *concatenating* several units as shown in Figure 2.13. What we have constructed there is an integrated implementation of four operations that each take two bit strings $\mathbf{x} = \langle x_4 x_3 x_2 x_1 \rangle$ and $\mathbf{y} = \langle y_4 y_3 y_2 y_1 \rangle$ as input, and produce a bit string $\mathbf{z} = \langle z_4 z_3 z_2 z_1 \rangle$ as output. The following four operations are implemented, and selected through the two selection bits sel_1 and sel_2:

selection		operation
sel₁	*sel₂*	
0	0	invert all the bits of **x**
0	1	perform a *bitwise* AND on **x** and **y**
1	0	perform a *bitwise* OR on **x** and **y**
1	1	perform a *binary addition* on **x** and **y**, where both input strings are interpreted as binary 4-bit numbers

To illustrate, if $\mathbf{x} = \langle 1011 \rangle$, and $\mathbf{y} = \langle 0110 \rangle$, we obtain the following results:

sel₁	*sel₂*	*operation*			*result*	
0	0	$\overline{\langle 1011 \rangle}$			$\langle 0100 \rangle$	
0	1	$\langle 1011 \rangle$	•	$\langle 0110 \rangle$	$\langle 0010 \rangle$	
1	0	$\langle 1011 \rangle$	+	$\langle 0110 \rangle$	$\langle 1111 \rangle$	
1	1	1011_2	+	0110_2	0001_2	overflow: 1

It is important to note that for the first time, we have constructed an implementation of an operation that can add binary numbers consisting of more than one bit. Moreover, we have embedded this implementation into a more generally applicable circuit. As we have said, in practice more sophisticated ALUs exist than we have demonstrated here. However, the principle of how such circuits can be constructed from simpler ones remains the same.

2.5 Storing data

In the previous sections we have concentrated on the implementation of Boolean operations. These operations have one thing in common: a result is only dependent on the specified operation and the input values. When building machines, this property is sometimes too restrictive. What we often want to do is temporarily *store* a value. Unfortunately, it is impossible to describe the process of storage in terms of Boolean operations. In this last section, we focus on how we can build storage devices. Quite surprisingly, we need not introduce any additional components other than the ones used so far. We demonstrate in Section 2.5.1 that it suffices to use only basic components such as NOT, AND, and OR gates. Then we construct in Section 2.5.2 a simple integrated circuit that acts as a so-called counter, a device which we shall meet a number of times in the next chapter. Our last concern is the development of storage devices that will allow us to store millions of bits in a so-called memory chip. These are treated in Section 2.5.3.

2.5.1 1-bit memories

We start by taking a look at a device that permits us to store precisely one bit. First, we consider only the underlying principle of how to store a single value. Then, we concentrate on how we can control *when* a value is either to be stored or retrieved.

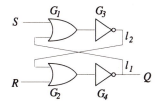

Figure 2.14 An SR latch.

The basic principle

Consider the circuit shown in Figure 2.14, which is also known as a **SET/RESET latch** or simply an **SR latch**. Unlike the circuits we have seen so far, the values of the output line are not determined by the input alone. For example, assume we put a low signal value on both input lines S and R. The output of gate G_1 can only be low if the value of the signal on line l_1 is low as well. Let's assume this is the case. Then clearly, the value of the signal on line l_2 will be high due to the NOT gate G_3. Effectively, this means that the output of gate G_2 is high, so that the value of the signal on line l_1 should be low. In other words, if we *assume* that line l_1 carries a low signal value (implying that Q is low as well), everything seems to be in order.

What happens if we assume l_1 carries a high signal value? Then, clearly, gate G_1 will produce a high signal value as well, which is inverted by gate G_3, so that l_2 will carry a low value. This in turn, implies that gate G_2 produces a low signal value which is inverted by gate G_4 to a high one on line l_1. In other words, if we *assume* l_1 carries a high signal value, then everything seems to be in order as well.

This is a rather peculiar situation. If we *assume* l_1 is either high or low, then the circuit seems to be consistent. We conclude that if we assume *nothing*, we cannot say anything sensible about the values on lines l_1 and l_2, and consequently, also nothing about the value on output line Q. Note, as a matter of fact, that if we assume line l_1 to carry a high signal value, then l_2 *must* carry a low signal value, and vice versa.

Let's continue our line of thought and assume that l_1 carries a low signal value (implying that Q is low as well). If we *change* the value of the signal on line S from low to high, gate G_1 will then produce a high signal value, which is inverted by gate G_3 into a low value. Gate G_2 will now still produce a low signal value which is inverted by gate G_4 so that the value of the signal on line l_1 and consequently also Q *changes* to high. It is not difficult to see that having a high signal value on S, a low value on R, and a high value on l_1 is perfectly acceptable. The circuit is said to be *stable*.

It can be verified that changing the value on line S back to low will not affect the value on l_1. In other words:

> *If the value of the signal on line Q is low, and we temporarily change the value of the signal on S from low to high, the value at Q becomes high, and remains high.*

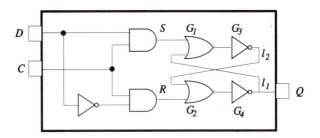

Figure 2.15 A clocked D-latch as a 1-bit memory.

This is an important observation. Apparently, by merely changing the value of the signal on S from low to high for a short period we can *permanently* change the value at Q from low to high. But this means that we can *store* a high signal value on line Q. A similar reasoning shows that if we temporarily change the value of the signal on line R from low to high while Q is high, this causes Q to switch *permanently* from high to low.

We conclude that the circuit shown in Figure 2.14 can be used for storing a single value, to be *set* to high by temporarily switching the value of the signal on S from low to high, and that can be *reset* to low by temporarily switching the value of the signal on R from low to high. However, we are not there yet. What we need is a *controlled* storage of a single value, i.e. the value is only to be stored when a control signal indicates so. This can be realized by a slightly extended circuit using the SR latch as described above. This so-called **1-bit memory** can be built as shown in Figure 2.15. The control line C is used to control the sampling on input line D (which is discussed below). Note that due to the two AND gates, only if the value at C is high is it possible to propagate the value of the signal on D to (the now internal) S and R lines.

Clocks and storage

Figure 2.15 shows the logical design of a so-called **clocked D-latch**. A characteristic feature of this circuit is that an external **control signal** is used to determine *when* a possible change of the contents of the memory can be made. To be more specific, note that if there is a low value at C, then the values at both S and R will be low as well. On the other hand, if C carries a high signal value, then the value at S will be the same as the value at D, while the value of the signal at R will be the opposite of that on D. Consequently, if during the time that C carries a high signal value the value of the signal at D will be high as well, then a high value will be stored in the 1-bit memory. On the other hand, if the value of the signal on D is low, a low value will be stored. In other words, we have that:

> *During the time that C carries a high signal value, and only during this time, the value of the signal at D will be stored in the 1-bit memory.*

The control signal at C itself is generated by a so-called **clock** (which is only another electrical device), and which is therefore referred to as a **clock signal**. A clock signal

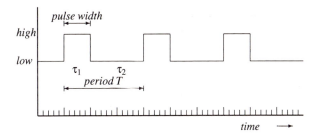

Figure 2.16 A characteristic clock signal.

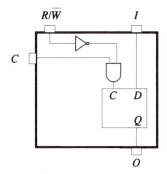

Figure 2.17 A 1-bit memory word.

is generated on a periodic basis as shown in Figure 2.16. Each T time unit the signal is repeated, consisting of a high value during the first τ_1 time units (called the *pulse width*), and followed by a low value during the remaining $T - \tau_1$ time units.

By now, we have introduced a powerful concept that enables us to deal with *changes* that occur in the course of time. Let's see how we can exploit the notion of a clock to describe the behavior of this circuit. To this end, we first construct the 1-bit memory shown in Figure 2.17 which we refer to as a **1-bit (memory) word**. Our 1-bit word is constructed from a clocked D-latch with some additional gates. Storing or retrieving a value from this circuit is controlled by the control line designated as "$R/\overline{W}$". If a high signal value is put on this line it will be inverted by the NOT gate to a low value, which is then propagated through the AND gate, thus effectively disabling the C control line of the D-latch. In other words, if a high signal value is put on the $R/\overline{W}$ line, no changes can be made to the value of the signal currently stored in the D-latch. On the other hand, it is seen that this stored value will be propagated to the output line O whenever the value of the signal at $R/\overline{W}$ is high. Following a similar reasoning, it can be seen that putting a low signal value on the $R/\overline{W}$ line will allow the value of the signal on the input line I to be stored in the D-latch, *during the time that the value of the signal on the C line of the word is high*.

What we have effectively accomplished by means of a 1-bit word is a digital circuit from which we can *read* the currently stored value (by setting a high signal value on $R/\overline{W}$), but to which we can also *write* a new value (by setting a low signal value on $R/\overline{W}$).

▷ We have shown that a circuit capable of storing information, such as that shown in Figure 2.17, can be implemented using the same basic components, namely gates, that we have used for implementing Boolean operations. However, Boolean algebra cannot be used to describe the function of a memory element. The reason for this is that a Boolean function only maps its input values to its output values according to a function prescription. Only the *current* input values determine the output. However, in a memory component the output is also dependent on input values of the *past*. In other words, the output value of a memory component is **history-sensitive**.

Closely related to this is the concept of **state**. We say that the state of a memory component is made up of the values of all history-sensitive signals in that component. Hence, the state of our 1-bit word W from Figure 2.17 can be defined as:

$$state_W(t) \quad = \quad q \quad if\ and\ only\ if\ t \in \tau_2$$

where q denotes the value of the signal at line Q, i.e. the value currently stored in W. Note that if $t \in \tau_1$ there is no state: during that time the value at the C line at the word will be high so that the component behaves as an ordinary Boolean function in the sense that the value at O is completely determined by the values of the signals at $R/\overline{W}$ and I.

Since a bit can have only two possible values, the state of a word can also have only two values: 0 and 1. This implies that there can only be four possible changes in the state of a 1-bit word:

$$0 \rightarrow 0, \quad 0 \rightarrow 1, \quad 1 \rightarrow 0, \quad 1 \rightarrow 1$$

A change of state, even if it means storing the same value as before, is called a **state transition**. State transitions occur at each clock cycle. To that end, denote by $state_W[k]$ the state of the 1-bit word W after k clock pulses have been generated, and let $state_W[0]$ denote the initial value stored in word W. Denoting by $I[k]$ the value of the signal on the input line I during the kth clock pulse, and using a similar notation for the control line $R/\overline{W}$, it can be seen that we have

$$state_W[k] = \begin{cases} state_W[k-1] & \text{if } R/\overline{W}[k] = 1 \\ I[k] & \text{if } R/\overline{W}[k] = 0 \end{cases}$$

Note that, by definition, a state transition occurs *at each clock pulse*.

However, a comment is in order at this point. Recall that our memory circuit has no state if $t \in \tau_1$. If we provided the same clock to every memory element in the system, then during the period τ_1 all these memory elements would simultaneously lose their state information. Clearly, this cannot be our intention. There are several solutions to this problem. One that is adopted in most circuits is to design memory circuits which only respond to *changes* in the clock pulse, i.e. the state is changed at the rising or falling edge of the clock pulse, in a finite, but very small time period. This period is so small that no memory information is lost. What it implies is that the state is *always* defined. Without going into further details, this will be an important assumption in the remainder of this chapter and in those that follow.

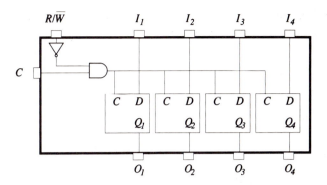

Figure 2.18 The layout of a 4-bit word integrated on a single chip.

2.5.2 Storing bit strings

Now that we have explained how a single value can be stored in a 1-bit memory, we describe how we can store entire bit strings. Also, we consider an example of a circuit in which two bit string memories are connected in such a way that they jointly act as a counting device. Such counters, as they are called, will be used in the next chapter where we explain automated selection of program instructions.

N-bit words

A 1-bit word is capable of storing just a single value, and it is not hard to imagine how we can group a collection of 1-bit memories such as D-latches onto a single chip in order to store *groups* of words. Consider the design of a 4-bit word as shown in Figure 2.18. In this case, the $R/\overline{W}$ control line has the same function as the $R/\overline{W}$ control line of the 1-bit word shown in Figure 2.17. Similarly, the C line is assumed to be connected to an external clock as previously.

The main difference with our 1-bit word is that input and output signals are now only considered in units of four. In other words, if we want to write to a 4-bit word, we can only do this by simultaneously providing four values at the respective input lines $I_1, \ldots, I_4$. These four values are simply denoted as a **bit string**. Similarly, reading signals can only be done by simultaneously reading the four values at the output lines $O_1, \ldots, O_4$. To illustrate, assume a 4-bit word contains the bit string $\langle 0011 \rangle$ and that we wish to change the second bit from 0 (low) to 1 (high). In that case, we have to set a low signal value on $R/\overline{W}$, and provide the bit string $\langle 0111 \rangle$ as input. Merely setting a high signal value on the second input line I_2 is thus not sufficient.

▷ In order to describe the behavior of this circuit we have to adapt our idea of a state. This is quite simple. Instead of considering only the output line of a single D-latch, we take all four output lines into account at the same time. If W is the 4-bit word shown in Figure 2.18, then the state of W at time t is defined as

$$state_W(t) \;=\; \langle q_1, q_2, q_3, q_4 \rangle$$

where $\langle q_1, q_2, q_3, q_4 \rangle$ denotes the bit string that is currently stored in W. Alternatively, we use the notation $state_W[k]$ to denote the state of W after k clock pulses have been generated, where again, $state_W[0]$ denotes the *initial* state. State transitions can be defined analogously. To that end, denote by $\mathbf{I}[k]$ the bit string $\langle I_1[k], I_2[k], I_3[k], I_4[k] \rangle$ where $I_j[k]$ denotes the value of the signal on input line I_j during the kth clock pulse. We then have

$$state_W[k] = \begin{cases} state_W[k-1] & \text{if } R/\overline{W}[k] = 1 \\ \mathbf{I}[k] & \text{if } R/\overline{W}[k] = 0 \end{cases}$$

In the case of a 4-bit word it is not difficult to see that there are $2^4 \times 2^4 = 256$ possible state transitions.

A counter

Before we continue with explaining how large storage circuits are constructed, we first look at a useful application of the technology introduced so far. In the following chapter we shall meet a special kind of storage circuit called a **counter**. A counter has the property that whenever its stored value is read, this value is automatically incremented by one. This means that the *next* read operation will yield an incremented value, and so forth. A counter can be *initialized* by explicitly storing some initial value in it. We stress at this point that the implementation of a counting mechanism as introduced here is slightly different from the way counters appear in practice. However, our implementation does provide insight into their principles, and more important, the implementation makes it easier to understand the mechanisms we introduce in the next chapter. We shall return to this issue below.

In order to construct a counter, we first introduce a mechanism that we shall also meet a number of times in the following chapter. A **(binary) timer** is a device that produces a signal that alternates between high and low as shown in Figure 2.19. In other words, it produces the infinite bit string $\langle 0101010101\ldots \rangle$. This signal will be used to control various components and the way that values that are stored in memory circuits are propagated to and manipulated by other circuits. Anticipating our further discussion, let's see how we can use a timer to construct our counter.

Assume we wish to implement a 4-bit counter which, of course, can store only 16 different values ranging from 0_2 to $1111_2 = 15_{10}$. To that end, we need at least three components:

- A 4-bit memory word, which we denote as VAL, that is used to store the *current* value of the counter. Reading the counter means that the bit string stored in VAL is propagated to the counter's output pins.

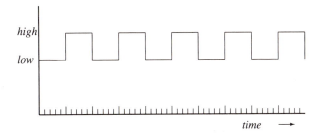

Figure 2.19 The signal produced by a timer.

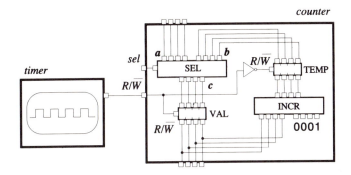

Figure 2.20 An implementation of a 4-bit counter.

- A 4-bit full adder, denoted as INCR, which is used to increment the current value stored in VAL whenever the counter is read. This full adder can be implemented by concatenating four 1-bit full adders in a similar way as the construction of a 4-bit ALU from four 1-bit ALUs.

- An additional 4-bit word TEMP which is used to store temporarily the *incremented* value from VAL whenever the counter is being read. After reading the counter, the value stored in TEMP is to be propagated back to VAL.

Using an additional selection mechanism to either reinitialize the counter or to increment its current value leads to an organization as shown in Figure 2.20. We assume that whenever the *sel* pin carries a high-valued signal, the component SEL propagates the values at the input lines marked **a** to the selector's output lines (marked **c**); otherwise, when $sel = 0$, the values at **b** are propagated to **c**.

Whenever we put a high-valued signal on the $R/\overline{W}$ pin of the counter the value stored in VAL is propagated not only to the output pins of the counter but also to the adder INCR where it is incremented by 1_2, and subsequently *stored* in the 4-bit word TEMP. Note that because we have inserted an inverter, whenever the value at the $R/\overline{W}$ pin of the counter is high, the value at the $R/\overline{W}$ pin of TEMP will be low. In other words, while *reading* the value from VAL we simultaneously *store* the incremented value in TEMP. But as soon as the value at the $R/\overline{W}$ pin of the counter becomes low, the opposite happens. VAL will store either the value at the input pins of the counter (when $sel = 1$) or the incremented value as found in TEMP (when $sel = 0$).

It should now be clear that if we connect our timer to the $R/\overline{W}$ pin of the counter and set *sel* to 0, each time we read a next value from the counter's output pins it will have been incremented by one compared to the previously read value. We leave it as an exercise for the reader to verify that after the counter has stored the bit string $\langle 1111 \rangle$ its next bit string will be $\langle 0000 \rangle$ which corresponds to the binary number 0_2.

▷ But as we have said, counters in practice are constructed in a slightly different way. Rather than using a timer device, counters are incremented at each clock pulse. As we have mentioned earlier, this clock pulse in turn actually corresponds to the falling or rising edge of the clock signal. This fact permits counters to be constructed in such a way that the additional 1-bit word TEMP that we have used in our implementation above can be removed. Instead, at each clock pulse, the value at the input lines of VAL are immediately stored. Then, before these signals are propagated to the output lines and even get a chance to make it back to the input lines, the clock pulse will already be "over". Consequently, it is seen that at each clock pulse the values at the input lines are stored in VAL, and *kept there*, until the next clock pulse.

The reason we have deviated from this implementation is that by using a separate timer we have an easier way of controlling exactly *when* a counter is incremented. In effect, it is the timer signal that accomplishes this. It is only each time that it produces a high-valued signal that the counter can be incremented. The timer device itself we have discussed here can, in turn, be constructed with this adaptation of counters. This is left as an exercise for the reader.

2.5.3 Large storage circuits

In practice, computers make use of large amounts of storage which are grouped together into a single integrated circuit called a **memory chip**. Memory chips are generally organized into units of 8-bit, 16-bit, or 32-bit words, similar to our extension of a 1-bit to a 4-bit word illustrated above. Technology to date allows for the development of a single chip containing more than 250 000 16-bit words, adding up to over 4 million 1-bit memories.

But additional measures need to be taken to avoid running into problems. The main issue is that of selecting a specific word from the memory chip. This can best be illustrated by means of an example. To that end, consider a simple circuit with three 4-bit words as shown in Figure 2.21. We first explain the additional circuitry for each word consisting of a NOT, an OR, and an AND gate, as also shown in Figure 2.22.

To start with, note that the $R/\overline{W}$ input line of this component is connected to the $R/\overline{W}$ pin of the memory chip shown in Figure 2.21, and that the output line $R/\overline{W}_i$ is connected to the $R/\overline{W}$ line of the component's associated word (shown as $R/\overline{W}_i$ in Figure 2.22). In other words, the $R/\overline{W}$ input line is used to indicate that the contents of the associated word should either be read (when $R/\overline{W} = 1$) or changed (when $R/\overline{W} = 0$). The point to note, however, is that reading or writing should only occur if the associated word has

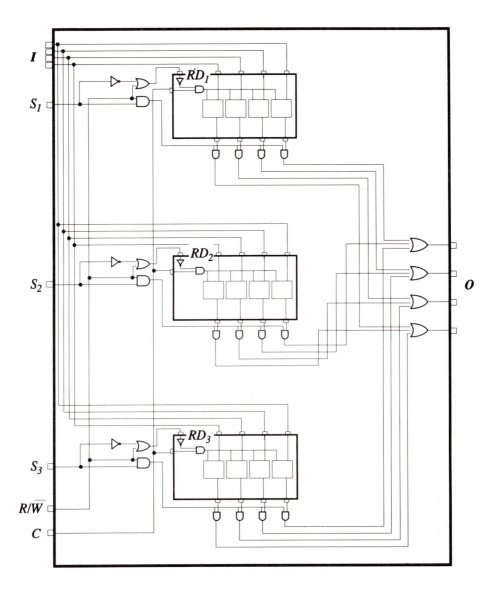

Figure 2.21 A naive construction of a three 4-bit word memory chip.

been selected by means of the input line S_i. Now, suppose we put a high signal value on the line S_i. In that case, we see that $R/\overline{W}_i = R/\overline{W}$. In other words, the value of the signal at $R/\overline{W}$ is propagated to the $R/\overline{W}_i$ control line of the associated word. This seems to be in order. And indeed, if $R/\overline{W} = 1$ and $S_i = 1$, i.e. we have selected to read the bit string currently stored in the word, this bit string is propagated to the output lines of the memory

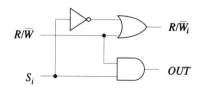

$R/\overline{W}$	S_i	$R/\overline{W}_i$	OUT
0	0	1	0
0	1	0	0
1	0	1	0
1	1	1	1

Figure 2.22 The basic digital circuit for selecting a word and its associated function table.

chip. Likewise, if $R/\overline{W} = 0$ and $S_i = 1$, it is seen that the bit string at the input lines of the memory chip is propagated to the input lines of the selected word and subsequently stored, while at the same time the output lines of the word are set to 0.

Now, suppose that $S_i = 0$. In that case, the bit string in the word will never be propagated to the output lines of the memory chip because the value at line OUT will always be 0 as well. Consequently, we have disabled reading the word's current contents. Furthermore, it can easily be seen that the value of the signal at $R/\overline{W}_i$ will always be 1 (high) when $S_i = 0$. In other words, it is not possible to store any new bit string in the word as long as $S_i = 0$. It can thus be concluded that if $S_i = 0$, the contents of the associated word can be neither read nor changed. And this is precisely what we wanted to achieve.

So what we see here is that by introducing an additional control line *per word* we are capable of selecting where we want to store a bit string in a memory chip, or which bit string we want to read. There is, however, a problem with this organization. If we simply grouped the 4-bit words together without too much thinking as we have done in Figure 2.21, we would need two groups of 4 pins for respectively the input lines and output lines, 1 pin for the clock signal, 1 pin to indicate if storage or retrieval should take place, and finally 3 pins (shown as S_1, S_2, and S_3) to select the proper word. This adds up to a total of 13 pins. In general, if we were to construct a chip with N M-bit words, we would need a total of $2M + N + 2$ pins. With $M = 16$ and $N = 65\,536$ this means that, one way or the other, we would have to find space for 65 570 pins! Indeed, this is not possible.

Clearly, it is the number of words that determine the number of pins we need. Fortunately, there is way to reduce this number. Observing that at any time precisely one word will be selected, implying that precisely one of the input lines $S_1, \ldots, S_N$ will carry a high signal value, while all the others carry a low value, we can devise an efficient *decoding* function that can easily be implemented as a Boolean function. To that end, assume that our memory chip contains a total of N words, identified as $W_0, W_1, \ldots, W_{N-1}$. With each word W_i we associate a unique **memory address** $addr(W_i)$ defined as:

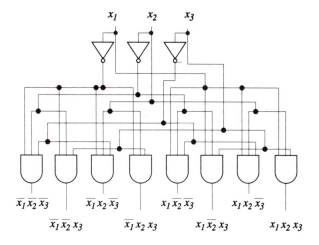

Figure 2.23 A 3-to-8 decoder circuit.

$$addr(W_i) = i$$

The next step is to write each memory address as a binary number, and use the corresponding bit string as the means to select a word. To illustrate, suppose that we have a memory chip with 256 words. In that case, each memory address can be written as a binary number using no more than 8 bits, and each address could then be encoded as a bit string of length 8. For example, in order to select word W_{27}, we encode its address as

$$addr(W_{27}) = 27_{10} = 11011_2 \mapsto \langle 00011011 \rangle$$

The only thing we have to do now is decode the bit string of length 8 into a bit string of length 256, where the 28th bit is 1, and all the others are 0. In other words, we have to implement a Boolean function $decode(i)$ specified as:

$$decode(i) \quad = \quad \langle \underbrace{00\ldots0}_{i} 1 \underbrace{00\ldots0}_{N-i-1} \rangle$$

where N is again the number of words contained in the memory chip.

This scheme should look familiar. What we are stating here is that we can use K bits to select among $N = 2^K$ alternatives. We came across this mechanism when discussing a general means for selecting one out of several inputs. It will therefore come as no surprise that an implementation of our decoder is similar to that of the selector implementations discussed in Section 2.4.3. As an example, Figure 2.23 shows an implementation of a so-called **3-to-8 decoder**. In this case, N is assumed to be 8, so that we can encode each memory address by using, at most, 3 bits. In general, if we assume that a memory chip contains a total of $N = 2^K$ M-bit words, we construct a K-to-N decoder as part of the chip, and effectively reduce the number of pins to $2M + K + 2$. So, with $M = 16$, and $N = 65\,536 = 2^{16}$ we would then need only 50 pins instead of the 65 570 required by our initial naive implementation.

2.6   Summary and further reading

In this chapter we have concentrated on binary computing systems, our main aim being to show that our world of computations can (to a certain extent) be *simulated* by electrical devices. In particular, attention has focused on four subjects:

1. The *representation* of data in a world consisting of finite bit strings

2. The *representation* of operations on such data in the form of Boolean expressions

3. The *implementation* of these operations by means of digital circuits

4. The *storage* of data also using digital circuits.

Representing data.   To some it may seem strange at first to start with a section on data representation. However, from the point of view that computing devices are only capable of manipulating electrical signals, it is obvious that we need a clearly defined mapping of our commonly used data objects to ones in the world of computers. The important aspect of data representation is that we always have to realize that only by properly *interpreting* electrical signals are we capable of constructing computers that can do something that seems sensible to us. In this sense, Section 2.2 has been a description of what such a mapping could look like.

Most of the material discussed in Section 2.2 can be found in introductory texts on computer architecture and design. A practical introduction to computer arithmetic with many exercises can be found in Goupille (1993). As we have mentioned, we have hardly paid any attention to the representation of real numbers. An excellent survey on these matters can be found in Goldberg (1991). For computer arithmetic in general, Knuth's (1981) book is generally considered a standard reference on the subject.

Representing operations.   Section 2.3 presented a mathematical basis that allows us to describe operations as Boolean functions. The point to note here is that by specifying a Boolean function in the form of a function table we can systematically derive equivalent expressions which are relatively easy to comprehend – and as we have illustrated – can be implemented straightforwardly as digital circuits. It should be clear that Boolean algebra lies at the basis of computer design, and, indeed, is far more extensive than we have presented here. There is much more to say concerning Boolean algebra and its relationship to computer design. The mathematical implications are severe and often difficult to comprehend by the novice. For those readers with a mathematical background, we refer to Birkhoff and Bartee (1970) for a thorough and in-depth discussion on applied algebra. A general introduction to switching algebra is given in Givone (1970).

An important topic that we have skipped almost entirely is the *minimization* of complex Boolean expressions: a systematic approach towards simplifying such expressions. If we use Boolean expressions to derive implementations in the form of gates, it should be clear that if we can reduce the complexity of an expression, i.e. reduce the number of operations occurring in an expression, our implementation will also be simpler. On the other hand, an expression with a minimal number of operations is not always desired because it may not be the *fastest* one that can be implemented. The speed of a circuit is generally determined by the maximum number of gates to be passed from any input to any output of a circuit. When implementing arithmetic operations, intricate designs have been developed which cannot simply be derived by applying some mathematical minimization procedure (Hwang, 1979).

Digital circuits. In Section 2.4 we discussed how electrical switches could be used to construct the fundamental building block of computers: gates. Combining switches to gates, and successively combining gates, we showed how Boolean functions can be implemented by electrical devices. The impact of being able to *implement* functions in actual devices should not be underestimated. What we have illustrated is that mathematical concepts which exist only in our minds can be *simulated* by *machines* in our daily lives. The basis for constructing machines that can do things has now been laid down, and, indeed, this basis is considered by us as being fundamental to all the topics yet to be discussed.

Some comments concerning Section 2.4 are in order. First, the electrical switches presented in Figure 2.2 exist only on paper. In the early days of computing these switches were made out of tubes, called *triodes*. Later, they were replaced by what can be considered as a revolution in technology: the *transistor*. How triodes and transistors actually work is outside the scope of this book and is a topic for electrical engineers and physicists. And just as we have simplified our presentation of electrical switches, this is also the case concerning integrated circuits.

Much of the material presented in Section 2.4 can also be found in Tanenbaum's textbook (1990a) on computer organization. Also, the material as presented in Shiva (1985) will show to be of value to the interested reader. A more thorough introduction to digital design is presented in Mano (1984) and Garrod and Borns (1991) where the latter is more suited for readers with a background in electrical engineering.

Storing data. Our last subject was that of storing data. The remarkable thing we have demonstrated in Section 2.5 is that by using the basic components we used for implementing Boolean functions, we could also construct circuits that were capable of storing a value. This is a functionality that cannot be described in terms of Boolean functions. Together with the introduction of memory words for storing values, we have introduced other components of importance: a clock, and what we have called a timer. A clock is used to control exactly *when* values can be retrieved from and stored into memory units.

A timer as we shall use it in this book is used to control several storage units in such a way that values are propagated from one storage unit to another in a controlled way. We will have more to say about timers in the next chapter. Most of the material of Section 2.5 can also be found in Tanenbaum (1990a) and Shiva (1985), to which we refer the interested reader.

Exercises

1. Find the binary representations for the following numbers: 23_{10}, 56_{10}, 10_{10}, 100_{10}, and $32\,765_{10}$.

2. Find the decimal representations for 100111_2, 10110_2, 110011_2, 1111_2, and 01100_2.

3. *Show how binary multiplication is done for $23_{10} \times 56_{10}$.

4. *If we have two bit strings of length n, denoting positive binary numbers, what is then the maximum length of the result in case of addition and multiplication, respectively.

5. Given the bit string $\langle 1001011 \rangle$, calculate its base 10 interpretation in one's complement, two's complement, and sign magnitude representation, respectively.

6. Determine the largest positive value that can be represented by a bit string of length 8, using two's complement, one's complement, and sign magnitude, respectively.

7. Explain how characters like 'ö', 'ň', 'Æ', etc. can be represented.

8. Show that $x \bullet x \bullet x \bullet x = x$ in Boolean algebra.

9. Show, by using function tables, that $x + (y \bullet z) = (x+y) \bullet (x+z)$.

10. Show, by using function tables, that $\overline{x \bullet y} = \overline{x} + \overline{y}$. Likewise, show that for any two bits x and y, $\overline{x+y} = \overline{x} \bullet \overline{y}$.

11. Show that by only using the function $nor(x,y) \equiv \overline{x+y}$, we can readily construct the functions *not*, *and*, and *or*. Hint: use the results from the previous exercise.

12. Construct a Boolean expression for the following function f:

x	y	$f(x,y)$
0	0	0
0	1	1
1	0	0
1	1	1

13. Construct a Boolean expression for the following function f:

x	y	z	$f(x,y,z)$
0	0	0	1
0	0	1	0
0	1	0	0
0	1	1	1
1	0	0	0
1	0	1	1
1	1	0	1
1	1	1	0

14. Show how the function $z \bullet \overline{y} \bullet x + \overline{z} \bullet \overline{y} \bullet x$ can be implemented using the three gates OR, NOT, and AND.

15. Derive an implementation for the selection mechanism of a 4-bit counter as used in Figure 2.20.

16. Explain the difference between a clock and a timer as introduced in this chapter.

17. *Consider the following digital circuit with input x and output y:

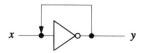

Assuming it takes δ time units for a signal to propagate from the input of the inverter to its output, what can be said about the value at y in terms of the value of the signal at x?

18. Suppose we have devised a memory chip containing 200 16-bit words. How many pins do we need for selecting a single word?

Chapter 3

Computers

In this chapter we explore how the basic components described in Chapter 2 can be used to build computing devices in which computations are performed as the execution of a sequence of instructions. To that end, we continue where we left off, by combining computational units and memories into a so-called microcalculator. We shall see that by adding a timer mechanism, and storing information on execution sequences, a microcalculator is capable of automatically executing a series of instructions. A next and important step is formed by copying the architecture of a calculator to a higher level of abstraction, leading to a processor. We conclude by briefly discussing peripheral devices.

3.1   Microcomputing

In this section we start by taking a look at how we can do simple calculations as a sequence of basic computational steps, where each step produces an intermediate result. Such a result is then to be temporarily stored so that it can be used in a following step. We shall demonstrate that executing such a sequence of steps can be fully automated using the components introduced in the previous chapter. At that point, we will have outlined the basic architecture of a simple, *programmable* calculator, which is a device that we can explicitly instruct to do specific calculations expressed as a series of basic computations.

3.1.1   Stepwise execution

Before starting our discussion on how we can build programmable computing devices, let's first illustrate how we can construct a device that is capable of performing a task as a *sequence* of smaller subtasks. To that end, consider the following example.[1] Suppose we have three bit strings $\mathbf{x}, \mathbf{y}$ and $\mathbf{z}$, each bit string having a length 8, and that we are to calculate a bit string $\mathbf{r}$ (also of length 8), such that

---

[1]In this section, a bit string $\mathbf{a}$ of length n is assumed to be written as $\mathbf{a} = \langle a_1 a_2 \ldots a_n \rangle$.

$$\mathbf{r} = \overline{(\mathbf{x}+\mathbf{y}) \bullet \mathbf{z}}, \tag{3.1}$$

where all operations are to be taken element-wise, i.e.

$$r_i \;=\; \overline{(x_i + y_i) \bullet z_i} \quad \text{for } i = 1\ldots 8.$$

Normally, in order to calculate $\mathbf{r}$ we would proceed by means of the following three steps:

- **Step 1 (S1):** Calculate the intermediate result $\mathbf{t1} = \mathbf{x} + \mathbf{y}$.
- **Step 2 (S2):** Calculate the second intermediate result $\mathbf{t2} = \mathbf{t1} \bullet \mathbf{z}$.
- **Step 3 (S3):** Calculate the final result $\mathbf{r} = \overline{\mathbf{t2}}$.

Considering the simplicity of this computation, it would seem that implementing computation (3.1) by means of digital circuits should not be that difficult. To that end, assume we have a single integrated circuit LOGUNIT8 at our disposal as shown in Figure 3.1. This circuit accepts two bit strings $\mathbf{a}$ and $\mathbf{b}$ (each of length 8) as input, and produces a result $\mathbf{c}$ as output (also of length 8), dependent on the control lines F_0 and F_1. In particular, LOGUNIT8 implements the following Boolean functions:

F_0	F_1	$\mathbf{c}$
0	0	$\mathbf{a} \bullet \mathbf{b}$
0	1	$\mathbf{a} + \mathbf{b}$
1	0	$\overline{\mathbf{a} \bullet \mathbf{b}}$
1	1	$\overline{\mathbf{a} + \mathbf{b}}$

where, again, all operations are performed element-wise. So, for example, if we set $F_0 = 0, F_1 = 1$, LOGUNIT8 implements the Boolean function

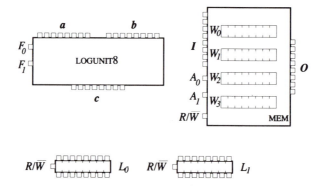

Figure 3.1　The available components: the IC LOGUNIT8, a four 8-bit word memory MEM, and two 8-bit words L_0 and L_1.

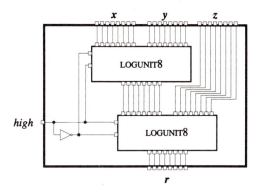

Figure 3.2 Cascading two circuits LOGUNIT8 in order to directly implement computation (3.1).

$$f(\mathbf{a}, \mathbf{b}) = \mathbf{a} + \mathbf{b}$$

Clearly, we can use LOGUNIT8 for implementing computation (3.1). In fact, we can reduce our original three steps to just two in the following way. First, consider Step 1 (S1) which is rewritten as

$$\mathbf{t} = \mathbf{x} + \mathbf{y}$$

yielding the intermediate result **t**. This calculation can be immediately implemented by means of LOGUNIT8 by setting the control lines $F_0 = 0, F_1 = 1$ and using **x** and **y** for its input. The second and third steps (S2 and S3), which yields the final result

$$\mathbf{r} = \overline{\mathbf{t} \bullet \mathbf{z}}$$

can be implemented as a single step by also making use of LOGUNIT8. To that end, we simply set the control lines to $F_0 = 1, F_1 = 0$ and use the intermediate result **t** and the bit string **z** as its input.

It should be clear how our computation can be implemented if we had *two* circuits LOGUNIT8 at our disposal. In that case, we would merely have to cascade the two as shown in Figure 3.2. However, the situation becomes rather more complicated if we assume that there is only *one* LOGUNIT8 available. In that case, it would still seem possible that we can implement our calculation, although some special measures will have to be taken. First, after performing the first step (S1), the intermediate result **t** will need to be temporarily *stored*, so that it can be used for the second step. Second, we will have to *change* the signals at the control lines F_0 and F_1 in order to continue with the second step.

Let's first concentrate on storing the intermediate result. In fact, what we can do is assume the existence of a memory containing four 8-bit words in which we can store all the

Table 3.1 Specification of the memory chip MEM

A_0	A_1	$R/\overline{W}$	effect
0	0	0	$W_0 \leftarrow \mathbf{I}$
0	0	1	$\mathbf{O} \leftarrow W_0$
0	1	0	$W_1 \leftarrow \mathbf{I}$
0	1	1	$\mathbf{O} \leftarrow W_1$
1	0	0	$W_2 \leftarrow \mathbf{I}$
1	0	1	$\mathbf{O} \leftarrow W_2$
1	1	0	$W_3 \leftarrow \mathbf{I}$
1	1	1	$\mathbf{O} \leftarrow W_3$

relevant bit strings: three to contain the bit strings $\mathbf{x}, \mathbf{y}$, and $\mathbf{z}$, and one to store the intermediate result $\mathbf{t}$. As we shall see, this is also enough to arrive at a final implementation of computation (3.1). To this end, we take a memory chip MEM also shown in Figure 3.1 of which the functionality is specified in Table 3.1. Note that because the chip contains four words, it will make use of a 2-to-4 memory address decoder as explained in Section 2.5.3. This explains the two address pins A_0 and A_1.

Using MEM is fine, but we have to realize that we can only read or write a single value from or to the chip at a time. Because LOGUNIT8 requires two input values, we can choose to first extract these two input bit strings from MEM, temporarily store them into separate 8-bit words, and then let LOGUNIT8 do its work. Therefore, we make use of two additional 8-bit storage units, which we refer to as L_0 and L_1 respectively, also shown in Figure 3.1. The result produced by LOGUNIT8 (which is $\mathbf{t}$ after the first step, and $\mathbf{r}$ after the second) can immediately be stored back into MEM as we shall see. We are now in a position to connect our four components together as shown in Figure 3.3.

Now let's see how we can actually do our original calculation by means of this implementation. We assume that initially word W_0 of the memory chip already contains the bit string $\mathbf{x}$. Likewise, W_1 is assumed to contain $\mathbf{y}$ and W_2 the bit string $\mathbf{z}$. The only thing that remains is reading these bit strings from MEM in the right order, storing them in the 8-bit words L_0 and L_1, doing a calculation by setting the control lines F_0 and F_1, and storing the result back into MEM. More precisely, if we perform the following six consecutive steps, we will have implemented our original calculation (3.1):

1. Read the value stored in W_0 (i.e. $\mathbf{x}$) and store this in L_0.

2. Read the value stored in W_1 (i.e. $\mathbf{y}$) and store it in L_1.

3. Input both bit strings stored in respectively L_0 and L_1 into LOGUNIT8, and save the result in word W_3. After this step, our device has calculated $\mathbf{t} = \mathbf{x} + \mathbf{y}$, which is stored in W_3.

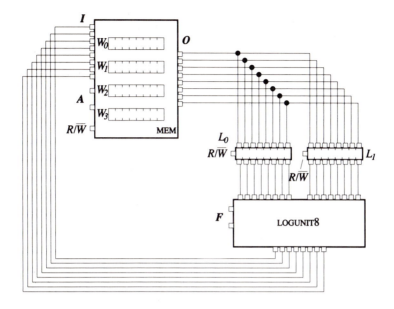

Figure 3.3 A simple, dedicated calculator.

Table 3.2 The setting of the control lines to realize the third step

component	control		comment
MEM :	A_0	$\leftarrow$ 1	*select word* W_3
	A_1	$\leftarrow$ 1	
	$R/\overline{W}$	$\leftarrow$ 0	*ensure that* MEM *can be written to*
L_0 :	$R/\overline{W}$	$\leftarrow$ 1	*read the first variable into* LOGUNIT8
L_1 :	$R/\overline{W}$	$\leftarrow$ 1	*read the second variable into* LOGUNIT8
LOGUNIT8 :	F_0	$\leftarrow$ 0	*select the right computation*
	F_1	$\leftarrow$ 1	*for* LOGUNIT8

4. Continue with reading the bit string **z** from word W_2 and store it in L_0.

5. Read the intermediate result **t** from word W_3 and store it in L_1.

6. Finally, input the bit strings stored in L_0 and L_1 respectively, into LOGUNIT8, and write the result to either word W_0 or W_1.

Assuming that the result of Step 6 is stored in word W_0, it is seen that after performing these six steps the final result of computation (3.1) is now stored in W_0 of MEM.

In order to perform each of these steps, it is not difficult to see that we only need to

Table 3.3 The setting of control lines for the dedicated calculator

| step | MEM | | | L_0 | L_1 | LOGUNIT8 | |
	A_0	A_1	$R/\overline{W}_{\mathrm{mem}}$	$R/\overline{W}_{L_0}$	$R/\overline{W}_{L_1}$	F_0	F_1
1 :	0	0	1	0	1	x	x
2 :	0	1	1	1	0	x	x
3 :	1	1	0	1	1	0	1
4 :	1	0	1	0	1	x	x
5 :	1	1	1	1	0	x	x
6 :	0	0	0	1	1	1	0

properly set the various control lines of each of the four components LOGUNIT8, L_0, L_1, and MEM, respectively. For example, Step 3 is realized by setting the values according to Table 3.2. In particular, for each step it can be verified that the proper setting is as shown in Table 3.3. Because the memory chip will not accept any new values (i.e. we cannot store a value) when performing steps 1, 2, 4, or 5, the setting of the control lines F_0 and F_1 for LOGUNIT8 is immaterial in these cases. We have expressed this by writing an "x" in the corresponding entries of Table 3.3. The six steps are shown in Figure 3.4.

3.1.2 Automated stepwise execution

So far, everything seems to be in order. We have constructed a device that, in principle, can be used to implement the calculation

$$\mathbf{r} = \overline{(\mathbf{x} + \mathbf{y}) \bullet \mathbf{z}}$$

provided we properly set the various control lines in six consecutive steps. But obviously, our device does not work in an automated way. We are still forced to set the control lines manually. The question that immediately comes to mind is how we can avoid this. And it is here that we arrive at a simple, yet extremely powerful and important conceptualization that is fundamental to programming computers. We *store* the consecutive values of the various control lines.

The whole idea is that if we want to automate the execution of our six steps, we will have to make the settings of the control lines per step available in some way. The point to note is that each of these settings is just a group of a total of 7 high and low signal values. In other words, each step requires a bit string of length 7. And as we have seen in Section 2.5.3, storing bit strings can be done by means of memory words. For example, we could choose to store the settings for the first step as the string

$$\mu I_1 = \langle 00101xx \rangle$$

where, again, x indicates that it does not matter if we store a 1 or a 0. The other control settings are stored in a similar way, leading to a total of six bit strings, one for each step, and in which each string has the general form

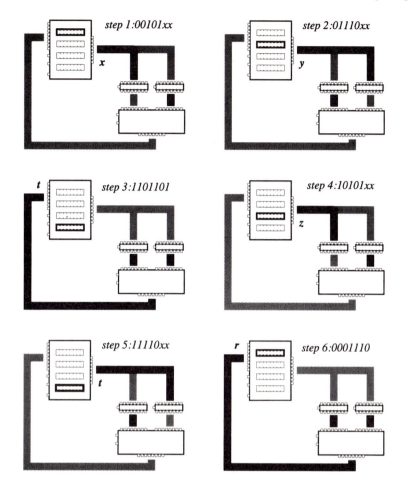

Figure 3.4 Six sequentially executed steps for calculating $\overline{(x+y)\bullet z}$.

$$\mathbf{C} \equiv \langle c_1, c_2, c_3, c_4, c_5, c_6, c_7\rangle \equiv \langle A_0, A_1, R/\overline{W}_{\text{mem}}, R/\overline{W}_{L_0}, R/\overline{W}_{L_1}, F_0, F_1\rangle$$

To store the complete set of these control settings, we need an additional memory chip consisting of six 7-bit words. Two comments about this chip are in order here. First, as this chip needs to contain six words, we will need to decode at least six memory addresses as explained in Section 2.5.3. This, in turn requires that each address should be represented by a bit string having at least length 3. Consequently, our memory chip will have at least 3 additional address pins (shown as $\mathbf{A}^*$ in Figure 3.5).

Second, we have no intention of *modifying* any values stored in this memory chip; we use it only to read its contents. In other words, we can take a so-called **read-only memory**, or **ROM** for our purposes, which is characterized by the omission of input pins (and

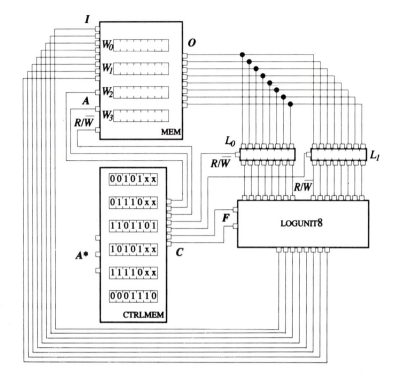

Figure 3.5 Adding a memory chip for storing settings of control lines.

also the $R/\overline{W}$ pin). This special memory chip, which we refer to here as CTRLMEM, can now be added to the other components as shown in Figure 3.5. Note how we have connected the output pins of this memory chip to the control pins of the other four components. The first two are used to select a word from MEM, the third is used to either read from, or write to MEM, the fourth and fifth are used to control L_0 and L_1, and the last two control the actual calculation performed by LOGUNIT8. Each bit string stored in CTRLMEM is generally referred to as a **microinstruction**.[2] The memory chip itself is called a **microstore**. Each time a specific microinstruction is used to set the control lines of the other components, we say that the **instruction is executed**.

Notice that we have stored the six microinstructions in the order in which they are to be executed. By doing so, we now need only to start with selecting the microinstruction stored at the first address and subsequently select the microinstruction stored at the *next* address at each execution step. If we can automate this selection of successive microinstructions, then we may justifiably state that we have constructed a *computing machine*.

So how do we produce such a mechanism? To answer this question, we first observe that selecting a microinstruction from CTRLMEM requires that we provide a 3-bit address. Therefore, we start by adding a digital circuit that can store bit strings of length 3, and

---

[2]The use of the adjective "micro" will become clear when we discuss instructions in Section 3.2.

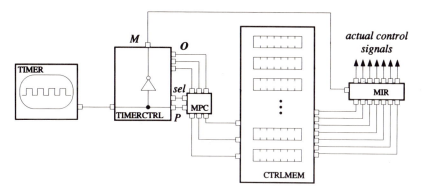

Figure 3.6 The outline of a mechanism for controlling the automated execution of micro-instructions.

which will always contain this address. This special digital circuit is generally referred to as a **microprogram counter**, or MPC for short. As its name suggests, it is indeed a counter in the sense as explained in Section 2.5.2: its stored value is automatically incremented by one each time it is read. In other words, when the contents of the counter is read, the *next* time it is read its contents will have been incremented. As we have explained in Section 2.5.2, it is also possible to initialize a counter by explicitly *setting* its contents by means of an additional selection pin. Like other storage units, we can thus explicitly store a bit string into a counter.

In the general case that a microstore contains more than eight microinstructions, it is obvious that we have to increase the size of this counter. A next observation is that during the time the address of the required microinstruction is stored in the MPC, nothing should change with respect to the setting of the control lines for the other components. In other words, the *previous* microinstruction should still be in execution. To do this, we use an additional 7-bit word in which a microinstruction is stored while it is being executed. What it means is that this so-called **microinstruction register** (MIR) is *read* during execution of the instruction it contains. The additional components MPC and MIR are now attached to CTRLMEM as shown in Figure 3.6. The component TIMERCTRL is discussed below. The component TIMER is a so-called **timer**, as was also discussed in Section 2.5.2. It continuously produces the alternating bit string ⟨01010101...⟩ and is used to provide the basic control in the course of time for the other components.

Now the whole idea is that MPC and MIR are read from, and written to, at the right time. For example, while MPC is updated with the address of the *next* microinstruction to be executed, MIR should contain the microinstruction that is presently executed. After that, the address stored in MPC is to be used to update the contents of MIR with the next microinstruction. This behavior is repeated many times, and is therefore referred to as the **micro fetch-execute cycle**. The component TIMERCTRL is responsible for producing this cycle. It controls the setting of the $R/\overline{W}$ control lines of MPC and MIR, respectively, by means of the two control lines marked as P and M. TIMERCTRL is also responsible for storing the appropriate address in MPC and it is connected to MPC via the output lines marked as **O**. More specifically, we have that TIMERCTRL implements the following algorithm:

Algorithm 3.1. The **micro fetch-execute cycle**: Consider the components as shown in Figure 3.6. The following two steps are repeatedly executed:

1. **Fetch microinstruction:** The next microinstruction is stored in MIR by taking the address found in MPC, and selecting the associated instruction from CTRLMEM. To this end, $P = 1$ and $M = 0$.

2. **Execute microinstruction:** The address of the next microinstruction is stored in MPC. At the same time, the microinstruction stored in MIR is executed. Therefore, we have $P = 0$ and $M = 1$.

□

In order to repeat these two steps, we connect TIMERCTRL to the component TIMER. What effectively happens is that each time the timer produces a high signal value, TIMER-CTRL sets its control lines such that the first step is executed. As soon as the value changes to low, the second step is executed. This scheme can be realized by the circuit for TIMER-CTRL shown in Figure 3.6.

3.1.3   Executing multiple microinstructions

Let's summarize what we have done so far. First, we showed that by using a single integrated circuit LOGUNIT8, a memory chip MEM, and two additional 8-bit words we could implement the calculation

$$\mathbf{r} = \overline{(\mathbf{x} + \mathbf{y}) \bullet \mathbf{z}}$$

by specifying a sequence of six steps. Each step was then represented by a bit string of length 7, called a **microinstruction**, in which each bit was used for a specific control line for one of the four components. These six microinstructions were then stored in a separate memory chip, called a **microstore**. By arranging the microinstructions in their consecutive order in the microstore, we then demonstrated that by making use of a timer and some additional circuitry, the six steps could be executed automatically.

Now let's first reconsider our set of six microinstructions, which were given as:

instruction	value
μI_1 :	00101xx
μI_2 :	01110xx
μI_3 :	1101101
μI_4 :	10101xx
μI_5 :	11110xx
μI_6 :	0001110

Clearly, this set falls naturally into two parts. The first three ($\mu I_1, \mu I_2, \mu I_3$) establish the partial computation

$$\mathbf{t} = \mathbf{x} + \mathbf{y}$$

yielding an intermediate result $\mathbf{t}$. Similarly, the last three ($\mu I_4, \mu I_5, \mu I_6$) also belong together. They jointly perform the second part of our computation:

$$\mathbf{r} = \overline{\mathbf{t} \bullet \mathbf{z}}$$

Let's refer to each of these two sets of microinstructions as a **microroutine**. The important thing to note is that execution of each of the two microroutines *changes one or more values stored in the memory chip* MEM. Moreover, these changes are *predictable*. If we know what the contents are of MEM before execution of a microroutine, we can unambiguously determine what the contents will be after its execution.

For now, let's denote the microroutine consisting of the sequence of microinstructions $\mu I_1, \mu I_2$ and μI_3 as OR01TO3 as it ORs the contents of words W_0 and W_1, and places the result in word W_3. The microroutine made up from the microinstructions $\mu I_4, \mu I_5$ and μI_6 will be referred to as NAND23TO0 as it places the complement of the contents of word W_2 and W_3, after having ANDing them, into word W_0.

The idea of grouping a number of microinstructions into a single microroutine can easily be generalized. For example, one could imagine that we use a larger microstore that would also contain an additional microroutine consisting of the following sequence of microinstructions:

μI_7 :	0	1	1	0	1	x	x
μI_8 :	1	0	1	1	0	x	x
μI_9 :	1	1	0	1	1	0	1

If we were to execute this sequence, it can be readily verified that this would yield that the value

$$\mathbf{t} = \mathbf{y} + \mathbf{z}$$

would be stored in word W_3 of MEM (assuming that $\mathbf{y}$ and $\mathbf{z}$ are stored in the second and third words of MEM, respectively). We refer to this microroutine as OR12TO3 for obvious reasons. Likewise, the microroutine AND03TO1 given by the set of microinstructions

μI_{10} :	0	0	1	0	1	x	x
μI_{11} :	1	1	1	1	0	x	x
μI_{12} :	0	1	0	1	1	0	0

can also be contained in the microstore, yielding that the result of the calculation

$$\mathbf{r} = \mathbf{x} \bullet \mathbf{t}$$

is stored in word W_1, where we now additionally assume that $\mathbf{t}$ is stored in word W_3.

Now assume that we have stored several such microroutines in a microstore, and that we had a mechanism for *selecting* which microroutine we wanted to be executed. In that case, we would have an extremely powerful device. We would merely indicate the microroutine it should execute, and by combining several of these microroutines we could actually *program* the device to perform a calculation as a number of consecutive *microroutines*.

For example, assuming that $\mathbf{x}$, $\mathbf{y}$, and $\mathbf{z}$ are already stored in respectively words W_0, W_1, and W_2 of MEM, our calculation

$$\mathbf{r} = \overline{(\mathbf{x} + \mathbf{y}) \bullet \mathbf{z}}$$

could be *implemented* by a program consisting of just two microroutines:

```
begin
    or01to3
    nand23to0
end
```

Similarly, the calculation

$$\mathbf{r} = \mathbf{x} \bullet (\mathbf{y} + \mathbf{z})$$

could be implemented by the program

```
begin
    or12to3
    and03to1
end
```

A question that needs to be addressed is how we can store several microinstructions as microroutines in a single microstore, such that it is possible to select individual microroutines. In fact, it turns out that this is not too difficult. Two points need to be considered: (1) how we identify a microroutine, and (2) how we know when to stop, i.e. how we can identify the last microinstruction to be executed.

(1) Identifying a microroutine in a microstore is actually quite straightforward. We simply take the address of the microinstruction that is the first one to be executed of that microroutine. So, for example, if a microroutine μR consists of the sequence of microinstructions $\mu I_1, \ldots, \mu I_N$, we simply take $addr(\mu I_1)$ as the identifier for μR. This is also denoted as the **address of the microroutine**.

(2) Identifying the last microinstruction to execute can be implemented rather straightforwardly as well. For example, we can choose to add a single bit to each microinstruction which is set to 1 for each but the last microinstruction of each microroutine. Then, if we find that the last bit of a microinstruction is 0, it is known that this is the last microinstruction of the current microroutine. ·

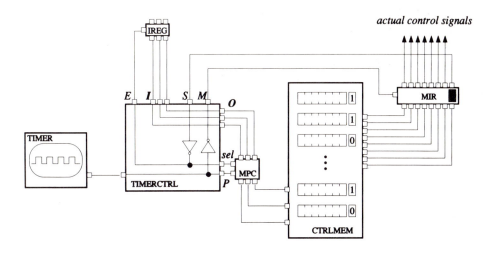

Figure 3.7 The actual control mechanism for the execution of microroutines.

Our micro fetch-execute cycle can now be refined so that an arbitrary microroutine can be executed. First, we assume that the identification of the microroutine that is to be executed, i.e. the address of its first microinstruction, is stored in a separate memory word IREG as shown in Figure 3.7, and which is controlled by the line marked E. In addition, we adapt the organization of our microstore by adding a bit to each microinstruction as discussed above. We shall denote this bit as MIR[0] and use it as input to TIMERCTRL. Using the notation CTRLMEM[k] to indicate the microinstruction at address k, we then come to the following specification of the behavior of TIMERCTRL:

Algorithm 3.2. Modified **micro fetch-execute cycle**:

1. **Fetch microinstruction:** Store the microinstruction identified by MPC in MIR, i.e. MIR ← CTRLMEM[MPC], by setting $P \leftarrow 1$ and $M \leftarrow 0$.

2. **Execute microinstruction:** Execute the microinstruction by setting $M \leftarrow 1$, and update MPC by setting $P \leftarrow 0$, $sel \leftarrow \overline{\text{MIR}[0]}$, and $E \leftarrow 1$.

The correctness of setting $sel \leftarrow \overline{\text{MIR}[0]}$ in the second step is not difficult to verify. If MIR[0] is equal to 0, then a new microroutine should be started implying that MPC should be re-initialized. This is done by setting $sel \leftarrow 1$ and $E \leftarrow 1$. Otherwise, if MIR[0] is equal to 1, MPC should be updated with the address of the next microinstruction of the current microroutine, i.e. MPC ← MPC + 1, which is done by setting $sel \leftarrow 0$. Meanwhile we can safely set $E \leftarrow 0$.

□

An implementation of TIMERCTRL is shown in Figure 3.7. Note that the second step of our fetch-execute cycle is executed when the value of the timer's signal is low. In that case, depending on whether or not MIR[0] is equal to 0, either MPC will store the valued contained in IREG or simply increment its present value.

▷ Storing microinstructions in a separate microstore and devising a component by which micro-instructions are fetched and executed at the right time is certainly not a bad choice. However, the question that may come to mind is if this solution is the only feasible one. The fact is, it is not. The solution presented here is one that tends to become increasingly out of date. The point is that fetching a microinstruction simply takes too much time to justify the use of a microstore. The alternative solution is to directly implement the sequence of micro-instructions into digital logic. This is generally referred to as **hardwired control**. Let's look at how this could be accomplished.

Suppose we want to execute the sequence of microinstructions corresponding to the OR01TO3 microroutine. This sequence was specified as follows:

step	OR01TO3
1 :	$\langle 00101xx \rangle$
2 :	$\langle 01110xx \rangle$
3 :	$\langle 1101101 \rangle$

Now the idea is that we can specify this microroutine in the form of a function table, which in turn corresponds to an ordinary Boolean function. In our case, we refer to this function as *or01to3*. The input for *or01to3* is a bit string of length 2, specifying the current step. The output is a bit string of length 9, consisting of 7 bits that specify the settings of the various control lines, and 2 bits specifying the *next* step that is to be taken. For simplicity, we assume that OR01TO3 is to be executed repeatedly, so that after the third step has been executed we simply continue with the first one. This then leads to the following function table:

input	*output*	
(step)	(control)	(next step)
01	0010100	10
10	0111000	11
11	1101101	01

(Note that we have chosen to set a low signal value for those control settings during steps 1 and 2 for which the setting actually did not matter.) Implementing *or01to3* as a digital circuit is straightforward. The interesting part is how we can use the last two bits that specify the next step in order to *change* the control settings. But this is not too difficult either. Consider the circuit shown in Figure 3.8.

The implementation of *or01to3* is shown as the integrated circuit OR01TO3. The crux of our implementation is formed by the two 2-bit words CR0 and CR1, of which the respective $R/\overline{W}$ control lines are connected to a timer. In particular, notice that whenever the $R/\overline{W}$ control line of CR0 is high (low) that at the same time, the $R/\overline{W}$ control line of CR1 will carry a low (high) signal value due to the inverter. Consequently, whenever the contents of CR0 is read, then CR1 is set to to be written to, and vice versa.

Now assume that CR0 initially contains the bit string $\langle 01 \rangle$, which corresponds to step 1. Then, when the signal generated by the timer is high, CR0 is read so that this bit string will

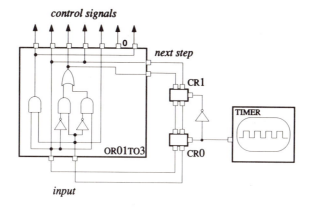

Figure 3.8 A hardwired control of three execution steps.

be passed to OR01TO3 leading to the setting of the control signals associated with step 1. At the same time, the last two bits produced by OR01TO3 are *stored* in CR1. In other words, the identification of the next step (which is the bit string $\langle 10 \rangle$) is written to CR1. Then, when the timer signal becomes low again, the contents of CR1 is passed on to CR0 where it is now stored. It should be clear by now that the *next* time the timer sets the signal high, the bit string $\langle 10 \rangle$ is passed to OR01TO3, leading to the control setting corresponding to step 2, while at the same time $\langle 11 \rangle$ is stored in CR1. This behavior is repeated many times.

Although our implementation is rather simple, the point to note is that we have actually realized the execution of a sequence of microinstructions without the need for explicitly storing them in a separate microstore. Therefore, when the total number of microroutines is not too large, and their sequencing not too complex, replacing a microstore by hardwired control will generally lead to a much faster implementation. The price to be paid is a much more complex, and less flexible implementation. The complexity is caused by the fact that implementing *all* microroutines by means of digital circuits is not that simple. The decrease in flexibility should be obvious. Once a series of microinstructions have been implemented by means of digital circuits, there is no way we can change them. We shall return briefly to this subject in our discussion at the end of this chapter.

3.1.4   A general architecture

We have demonstrated in the previous sections how we could automate the execution of computational steps by storing a sequence of microinstructions (called a microroutine) in a microstore, and adding a timer mechanism that ensures that such a microroutine is selected and executed. Furthermore, we have illustrated that we could even store several microroutines in a single microstore, and by providing a selection mechanism we could choose the microroutine to be executed.

The approach we have followed to implement these mechanisms can easily be generalized. Figure 3.9 shows the architecture of what we shall call a **microcalculator** and which is a great simplification of the ones that are found in many *personal computers*

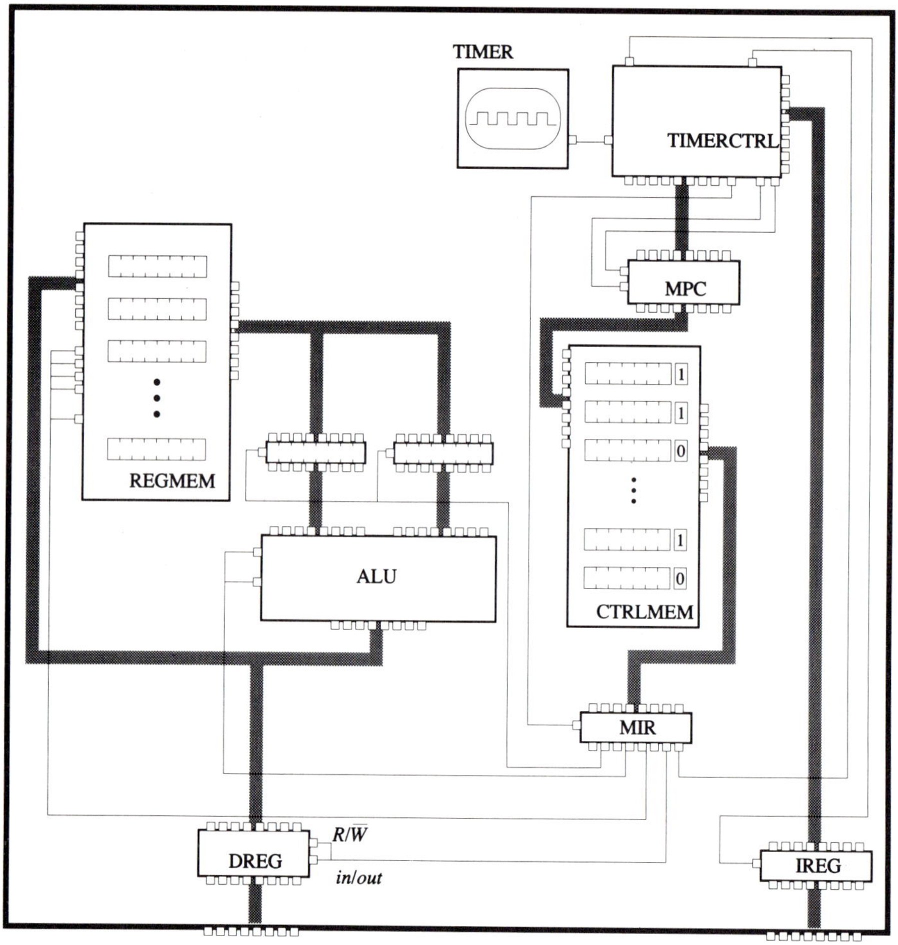

Figure 3.9 The architecture of a simplified microcalculator.

and *workstations*. For clarity, we have represented the connections between the various components as thick, gray lines. Also, control lines are not always drawn separately, but, instead, we have occasionally grouped several lines into one. A few comments about this architecture are in order.

First, we have added a special storage unit DREG which serves a similar purpose as IREG: it acts as an *interface* between the calculator and the outside world. In this case, DREG is intended to be used to hold both operands *and* results of the computations to be performed by the microcalculator. This means that it can be used to store incoming as well as outgoing data for the microcalculator. Second, note that we have used the same representation for MPC, MIR, DREG, and IREG in the sense that each storage unit can contain a bit string of length 8. However, in practice, the size of these units can vary between architectures. Obviously, depending on the size of the microstore, the microprogram counter MPC may vary in width as well. Finally, we have replaced our LOG-UNIT8 component by a more general ALU. ALUs have been discussed in Section 2.4.3.

A special comment should be made regarding the memory REGMEM. In practice, this memory is implemented through advanced technology in order to ensure that manipulation of its contents is *fast*. Each word of this memory is referred to as a **register**, and normally a number of these registers are dedicated to special purposes as we shall see below.

3.2   General processing

The previous section has put many components in place to make a simple microcalculator. By starting from a simple computation in Section 3.1.1 we have gradually shown how we could construct and use digital circuits to produce a microcalculator. We have now come to a point that if the register IREG contains the *identification* of a microroutine and the registers in REGMEM contain the necessary input bit strings, our microcalculator can work. What we have not addressed is *how* we can tell the calculator what to do, i.e. how we can load input bit strings into registers and indicate which operation it should perform. In this section, we shall take a closer look at these issues. In particular, we generalize our architecture of a microcalculator to that of a computer consisting of a so-called processor which is attached to a main memory module.

3.2.1   Instructions

Let's start with reconsidering our original computational example from Section 3.1.1, in which we needed to calculate

$$\mathbf{r} = \overline{(\mathbf{x} + \mathbf{y}) \bullet \mathbf{z}} \tag{3.2}$$

where $\mathbf{r}, \mathbf{x}, \mathbf{y}$, and $\mathbf{z}$ were bit strings of length 8. We showed that if we had four registers and an ALU that could perform an OR-operation and a NAND-operation, then we could implement computation (3.2), provided we had stored the bit strings in the appropriate registers.

So where do $\mathbf{x}, \mathbf{y}$ and $\mathbf{z}$ come from? And how can we tell which operation is to be performed? When you think of the microcalculator as part of a pocket calculator, the answer is quite simple. We provide the information manually. And indeed, this is how most pocket calculators work. We would be able to enter operands one by one, indicate the operation that we want to be performed (by pressing one of the special-purpose keys, e.g. "+" or "LOG"), and see the result on a small display. Generally, these simple pocket calculators also offer the possibility of storing a single intermediate result.

But this approach is hardly useful for complex operations that consist of many computational steps. In that case, we would want to provide just the initial operands and additionally provide a *series* of instructions that the microcalculator should then execute *automatically*. This approach is particularly useful if some of the computational steps were to be repeated many times. What we would need then is a means of storing the initial operands, as well as the series of instructions that make up the calculation. To that end, we simply connect a large memory module to our microcalculator. This memory module will contain data that is to be operated on, and, for now, series of *start addresses* of microroutines as stored in the microstore that the calculator should perform.

But simply connecting a memory module to our microcalculator is not enough. When giving the matter some thought, at least three questions come to mind:

1. How can we get information into and out of this memory module?

2. How can we exchange information (i.e. data and instructions) between the memory and microcalculator?

3. How we can automate the execution of a series of instructions?

An answer to the first question is postponed until Section 3.4 where we discuss peripheral devices. The third question will be addressed below, where we discuss the extension of our micro fetch-execute cycle. For now, we concentrate on answering the second question. We first need to reconsider our notion of microroutines as these simply do not support the kind of flexibility we need for telling a microcalculator what to do.

From microroutines to instructions

Until now, the only way that we can let a microcalculator do something is by giving it the address (of the first microinstruction) of a microroutine. Each microroutine is nothing but a series of microinstructions that successively set the various control lines within the calculator. Now suppose we have a microcalculator with four registers REG0 ... REG3 and that implements the following microroutines:

microroutine	meaning
ADD01TO3	REG3 ← REG0 + REG1
ADD02TO3	REG3 ← REG0 + REG2
ADD12TO3	REG3 ← REG1 + REG2

What we have here is a collection of similar microroutines that add the contents of two registers and always store the result in register REG3. These three microroutines thus represent the same **operation** but each acts on different (input) registers. Unfortunately, there is no relationship between these microroutines when we consider what each actually represents, namely the address of the first microinstruction that is to be executed. In other words, there is no or hardly any *logical coherence* between similar microroutines. This is a situation that needs to be corrected if we are to provide a convenient way to *program* a microprocessor (we shall discuss other and more important reasons for reconsidering

Table 3.4 Seven possible operations with associated 3-bit opcodes

operation	opcode	meaning
MIN	$\langle 000 \rangle$	subtract two binary numbers
ADD	$\langle 001 \rangle$	add two binary numbers
OR	$\langle 010 \rangle$	the bitwise operation $\mathbf{x} + \mathbf{y}$
AND	$\langle 011 \rangle$	the bitwise operation $\mathbf{x} \bullet \mathbf{y}$
XOR	$\langle 100 \rangle$	the bitwise operation $(\overline{\mathbf{x}} \bullet \mathbf{y}) + (\mathbf{x} \bullet \overline{\mathbf{y}})$
NOR	$\langle 101 \rangle$	the bitwise operation $\overline{\mathbf{x} + \mathbf{y}}$
NAND	$\langle 110 \rangle$	the bitwise operation $\overline{\mathbf{x} \bullet \mathbf{y}}$

microroutines in their present form below). This problem can be alleviated by properly grouping several microroutines into a so-called **instruction**. This is best illustrated by means of a simple example.

Imagine that our microcalculator supports a total of seven different types of operations, each taking two operands and producing a single result. These seven different kinds of operations can be represented by a 3-bit **operation code**, or **opcode** for short. For example, we may assume that we have the seven kinds of operations and associated encoding as shown in Table 3.4.

Likewise, the four registers can be represented by bit strings of length two as follows:

code		register
$\langle 00 \rangle$	$\mapsto$	REG0
$\langle 01 \rangle$	$\mapsto$	REG1
$\langle 10 \rangle$	$\mapsto$	REG2
$\langle 11 \rangle$	$\mapsto$	REG3

Using these coding schemes, it becomes much easier (for humans) to tell the calculator exactly what to do. We need merely supply (1) an opcode, (2) two operands specifying the registers that should be read, and (3) the register in which the result should be stored. This information can be grouped into a bit string of length 9 as follows:

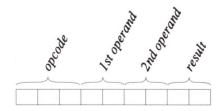

Consequently, in order to have the microroutine ADD01TO3 executed, we need to provide the bit string $\langle 001\ 00\ 01\ 11 \rangle$. This bit string then needs to be *interpreted* by the microcalculator as an ADD microroutine, operating on the contents of registers REG0 and REG1, and of which the result is to be stored in REG3. In other words, this instruction would have to be **decoded** into the microroutine ADD01TO3. As we shall see, decoding instructions will turn out to be an additional function that needs to be carried out by the control unit TIMERCTRL of a microcalculator.

▷ An issue that we have not addressed is that although our encoding scheme may be perfectly in order, it may also be possible to construct instructions that have no meaning. For example, suppose we provide the instruction ⟨111 00 01 10⟩, assuming that only the operations shown in Table 3.4 are available. Clearly, because the opcode ⟨111⟩ has no associated operation, this instruction makes no sense at all. It is therefore referred to as an **illegal instruction**. In that case, one thing the microcalculator can do is stop altogether, or, alternatively, ignore the instruction.

Load and store instructions

So far, we have only discussed instructions that manipulate the internal registers of the microcalculator. However, in order to communicate with the outside world, two other types of instructions are needed: one by which we can transfer data from an external memory module to an internal register, and one by which we can do the reverse. Let's briefly take a look at these so-called **load** and **store** operations.

In order to transfer data from external memory to a register, a microcalculator will generally have a **LOAD instruction**. This is an instruction that tells the calculator to *fill* or *load* one of its registers with data that can be found in the memory module connected to the microprocessor. For example, we might have the instruction

        LOAD   addr, reg0

that tells the calculator to *copy* the data stored at location addr in the memory module into register REG0. But apart from transferring data from memory to registers, it may also be possible to directly copy a bit string into a register by means of another type of LOAD instruction, such as

        LOAD   #00001001, reg0

by which the bit string ⟨00001001⟩ is written to register REG0. It is important to note that our notation for instructions given so far is just *symbolic*. In the end, all instructions are merely bit strings.

The counterpart of a LOAD instruction is a **STORE instruction**. This type of instruction specifies that data is to be copied *from* a register *to* a place in the memory connected to the calculator. For example, the instruction

        STORE reg0, addr

is a symbolic representation of a STORE instruction that tells the microcalculator to copy the contents of register REG0 into memory at address addr. The important thing to note is that LOAD and STORE instructions do more than just manipulate internal registers. In particular, a LOAD instruction leads to control signals to *read* a specified word of memory. Similarly, a STORE instruction leads to control signals to *write* data to a specified location in memory. What this implies is that our example microcalculator will need additional control pins to control the interaction with an external memory module. We shall return to this issue in Section 3.3 in more detail.

So where has this brought us? At this point, we have merely introduced the concept of an instruction. An instruction is a bit string containing information on the type of operation that is to be performed, and where the data that is associated with that operation can be found. An instruction that is to be executed is usually stored separately in a so-called **instruction register**, which is the analog of the microinstruction register MIR.

But just as we could store series of microinstructions in a microstore, we can also store series of instructions in a memory module. We now come to an important point. Suppose we have stored data and a series of associated instructions into a memory module. Moreover, let's assume that the instructions are stored in a series of consecutive memory locations that corresponds to the order in which the instructions are to be executed. The whole idea then is that the microcalculator should *automatically* execute these instructions, one by one, by fetching an instruction from, say, location addr, execute it, and then fetch and execute the instruction at location addr + 1, etc. How this is done is discussed next.

3.2.2   Processors

Let's see what we need in order to execute instructions in an automated way.

Organizing the basic components

First, we have to store instructions and the data they operate on. Completely analogous to our microprocessor architecture, we can use two separate memory modules for this purpose. One module, referred to as the data memory, will contain all the data that needs to be manipulated. The data memory is analogous to the set of registers REGMEM of Figure 3.9. The second memory module, called the instruction memory, is used to store the instructions that are to be executed. As in the ordering of microinstructions in a microstore, we shall organize the instructions in their order of required execution, as this will allow us to keep track of the *next* instruction to be executed. To that end, we use a special-purpose register, called the **program counter**, that will always contain the address in the instruction memory of the next instruction to execute. Finally, as indicated above, we shall make use of an **instruction register** to temporarily store the instruction to be executed. Now look at Figure 3.10, which shows an architecture of a small computer based on a single microcalculator.[3]

When comparing this architecture to that of the microcalculator shown in Figure 3.9, it is seen that the two more or less coincide. In fact, one might say that we have more or less *copied* the architecture of a microcalculator to a higher level of abstraction. And indeed, as we shall see, the behavior of our example computer is similar to that of a single microcalculator. We start with taking a closer look at each of the components of Figure 3.10.

---

[3]It should be noted that our architecture is not complete. For clarity, we shall not strive for completeness here, but instead focus on the basic principles.

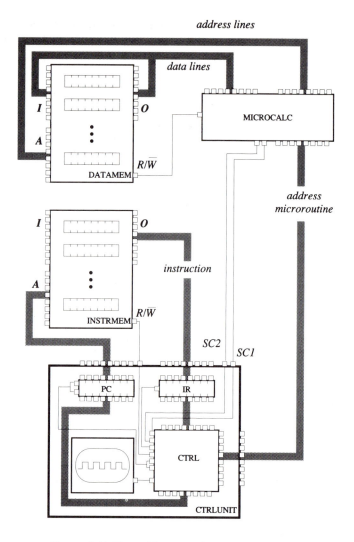

Figure 3.10 The architecture of a simple computer.

The data and instruction memories mentioned above return as the components DATA-
MEM and INSTRMEM, respectively. Now, because instructions are never modified, INSTR-
MEM could at first thought have been replaced by a read-only memory unit. But this
would have been too restrictive as it would not allow us to replace a series of instructions by another. Anticipating our discussion on loading and executing programs, we
have therefore used a normal memory module to store instructions. For our purposes
here, however, we shall simply assume that the current set of instructions contained in
INSTRMEM is not modified.

At the heart of our example architecture we have a microcalculator MICROCALC which has a similar role to that of an ALU. Comparing the interface of this microcalculator to that of Figure 3.9, it is seen that we have added a number of pins. There are pins connected to a collection of so-called **address lines** that connect the calculator to the memory module DATAMEM. What we have assumed here is that, in order to load and store data between its internal registers and the data memory, the microcalculator will separately address *which* data is to be transferred. These address lines are thus analogous to the address control lines of Figure 3.9 that connect the microinstruction register MIR to the address pins of the set of registers REGMEM. In order to facilitate this additional feature, we assume MICROCALC has a separate address register, analogous to its data register DREG.

Also, in order to indicate whether data should either be read from data memory (when a LOAD instruction is executed) or that data is to be written to it (in the case of a STORE instruction), a separate control line between the microcalculator and the data memory is used. The microcalculator thus controls whether data is either read from or written to DATAMEM. The pins connecting the microcalculator to the collection of **data lines** are used to transfer data between DATAMEM and the internal registers of MICROCALC. These pins thus correspond to the ones attached to the register DREG of Figure 3.9. Finally, the micro-routine that is actually to be executed is passed on to the microcalculator through th microroutine lines. These lines are connected to the internal register IREG of Figure 3.9. The additional control lines between MICROCALC and CTRLUNIT are explained below.

The last component we need to discuss is the **control unit** CTRLUNIT, which, as its name suggests, is responsible for controlling the execution of instructions. How does this unit work? We see that it contains a **program counter** and **instruction register** shown as the registers PC and IR, respectively. The register IR always contains the instruction that is *currently* being executed, whereas PC contains the address in the instruction memory of the *next* instruction to be executed. Both PC and IR are connected to CTRL, which has a similar functionality to the TIMERCTRL unit of our example microcalculator architecture. In particular, it updates the program counter each time an instruction has been executed by incrementing its contents by one. Additionally, it *decodes* the instruction contained in IR into the address of the appropriate microroutine, as mentioned in the previous section.

The fetch-decode-execute cycle

The interesting part of the control unit is its ability to enable execution of instructions *automatically* by attaching a timer to the CTRL circuit. And this is where the analogy with our example microcalculator architecture is almost complete. The control unit, namely, is responsible for execution of the so-called **fetch-decode-execute cycle** of the computer. In particular, the following algorithm is executed.

Algorithm 3.3. The **fetch-decode-execute** cycle. Assume that the register PC contains the address in the instruction memory of the next instruction to execute.

1. **Fetch instruction.** The address stored in PC is propagated to INSTRMEM, resulting in the selection of the next instruction to be executed. This instruction is then

loaded into the register IR. In other words, the control lines of PC and INSTRMEM are set to *read* signals, whereas the control line of IR is set to a *write* signal.

2. **Decode instruction.** The next time the timer generates a high value, the instruction stored in IR is propagated to CTRL and decoded into the address of the microroutine that is to be executed by the microcalculator. At the same time, the address stored in PC is incremented by one. Consequently, the control lines of IR and PC are set to respectively a *read* and a *write* signal.

   At this point, the address of the microroutine should be propagated to the microcalculator. In order to inform the latter that it should take the proper measures (in particular, by setting the register IREG open for writing), we assume the control unit sets a high signal on the *SC1* line. This control line is thus used to *synchronize* the control unit and the microprocessor.

3. **Execute instruction.** In this step, control is passed to the microcalculator which then executes the associated microroutine. In effect, this means that steps 1 and 2 of the micro execution cycle (Algorithm 3.1 on page 86) are repeatedly executed until the last microinstruction has completed. At that point, we assume the microcalculator synchronizes with the control unit by setting a high value on the *SC2* line. The control unit then continues with step 1.

$\square$

The third step, executing an instruction, is the most intricate. Depending on the type of instruction, this step may involve getting data from memory and loading it into the registers. Conversely, it may also involve copying data stored in the registers to specific locations in the data memory. The important point to note, however, is that during this step we effectively execute steps 1 and 2 of the micro execution cycle until the microroutine has been completed.

The von Neumann computer

So what have we accomplished at this point? We have discussed how a microcalculator can be connected to memory modules in such a way that it can automatically fetch and execute instructions. We have assumed that these instructions either manipulate the internal registers of the calculator or transfer data between the memory and these internal registers. The combination of these instructions and the extension of our control mechanism provide us with the right means for what we now refer to as **processing**. Whereas at the level of a microcalculator we had devised a means for organizing a series of microinstructions into a microroutine that could subsequently be executed automatically, we have now accomplished the same thing for a series of microroutines. In practice, a series of instructions, combined with the data that is to be manipulated, is generally referred to as a **program**. It should be clear that because we have shown how we can automatically execute a complete program, we have indeed more or less *copied* the architecture of a microcalculator to a higher level of conception.

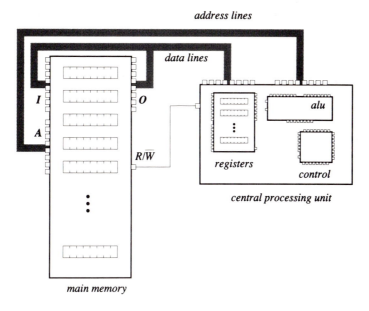

Figure 3.11 General architecture of a von Neumann-based computer.

But a few comments on computer design in practice are in order. Although we have placed the control unit as a separate component of our example computer, it is normally integrated as another part of the microcalculator. In particular, the control mechanism of our microcalculator and the one attached to the control unit are normally integrated into a single circuit called a **processor**. Moreover, most computer systems use only a single processor, also denoted as the **central processing unit**, or **CPU** for short. Another issue is that there is generally no *physical* distinction between a data memory and an instruction memory. Instead, both memories are amalgamated into a single **main memory unit**. Although this may seem a simple step, its implications cannot be underestimated. By taking the two memory types together, we are actually *unifying* data and instructions. In particular, instructions can be treated as *modifiable* data items. We shall return to this subject in the next chapter. Taking a single microprocessor and a main memory leads to an organization shown in Figure 3.11. This organization is generally referred to as a *von Neumann* computer, named after the mathematician John von Neumann who laid down the fundamental principles of digital computation.

3.2.3   On instruction sets

We are now in a much better position to take a closer look at instructions. In particular, we first consider why designing a set of instructions is such an important task. After that, we briefly discuss so-called addressing modes, which specify precisely to which memory locations an instruction is referring.

Designing instructions

Using instructions instead of microroutines not only makes a processor easier to program. More important is the fact that an instruction hides details concerning the way an operation is actually implemented. To illustrate, recall our instruction for adding the contents of two registers REG0 and REG1, and storing the result in REG3, which was encoded as the bit string

$$001 \quad 00 \quad 01 \quad 11$$
$$\uparrow \qquad \uparrow \qquad \uparrow \qquad \uparrow$$
$$\text{ADD} \quad \text{REG0} \quad \text{REG1} \quad \text{REG3}$$

This instruction was decoded into the microroutine ADD01TO3 which in turn is merely a reference to a specific location in the microstore, namely that of the first microinstruction that needs to be executed. Now the whole point is that in order to have the instruction above executed, we simply need not know that it is decoded into ADD01TO3. The fact that it is, is just an implementation issue that should be of no concern to us.

To see why this hiding of an implementation is so important, imagine that a manufacturer decides to upgrade a processor by *adding* a number of microroutines. For efficiency reasons, it may turn out that the original microstore may need to be reorganized. In particular, we assume that the start addresses of the original microroutines need to be changed as well. From a programming point of view, this really does not matter at all as long as the original set of instructions is still maintained. As long as the manufacturer takes care of that, we can still have our programs executed as before, but by a possibly better processor. This idea of upgrading a processor has been put into practice for many years. In fact, what generally happens is that an existing set of instructions is extended with some new ones, along with an improvement of the implementation of all instructions. In this way **families** of processors came to exist.

A well-known example of such a family of processors is the Intel 80x86 series. Originally starting in the late 1970s with the 8086 processor which formed the heart of most personal computers, it was soon followed by the 80186, and later by the 80286 processor. An important issue was that all programs that had been developed for the 8086 processor could still be executed by a 80286 processor. From a commercial point of view, this upward compatibility is extremely important. The 80286 was succeeded by the 80386 and 80486, the latter currently being used for most personal computers. The 80586, better known as the Pentium processor, is at present the most powerful processor of this Intel family.[4]

▷ But designing an instruction set is not as simple as it may seem at first. And certainly, it will not come as an afterthought in the way we have introduced instructions in this chapter. When constructing a processor, determining what the computer should be able to do, i.e. which instructions are to be implemented, is one of the first activities to be undertaken. Let's take a brief look at some of the more important issues involved.

---

[4]For completeness, it should be mentioned that the 8086 was based on the 8008, which in turn was preceded by Intel's 4004 processor. The 8088 was a popular, slower version of the 8086.

Number of instructions.   If we really wanted to accommodate a programmer with a processor that is easy to program it would seem desirable to provide a rich set of instructions, i.e. a set containing many different types of instructions. As computer engineers gradually obtained an increasing hold on the complexity of how to construct (micro)processors, it also became a lot easier to add functionality to instructions. This trend has resulted in processors that at first were extremely powerful in the sense that they were relatively easy to program. To date, these processors are referred to as **complex instruction set computers**, or simply **CISC** machines. Almost without exception, the instruction set of these processors is (primarily) implemented by means of microstore technology.

However, there is a price to be paid. As the complexity of an implementation increases, the speed by which a single (powerful) instruction can be executed is much harder to maintain at a satisfactory level. But practice has shown that, despite the availability of extremely powerful instructions, programmers tend to use only those instructions which they know can be executed quickly.[5] In effect, this meant that only a relatively small number of instructions were being used. A tradeoff was thus being made in favor of speed instead of programming flexibility. Therefore, the trend nowadays is to keep an instruction set as small as possible. Only instructions which it is known in advance can be implemented efficiently are supported. This has led to a new generation of processors referred to as **reduced instruction set computers** (**RISC machines**). It will come as no surprise that the implementation technique underlying these processors is that of hardwired control.

Instruction length.   Another important design criterion is the length, i.e. the number of bits, of an instruction. What it means is that the shorter the instruction, the faster the machine. How can this be? To see this, reconsider the fetch-decode-execute cycle. This cycle can be effectively broken down into two major steps: (1) fetching an instruction from main memory and loading it into the instruction register, and (2) decoding and executing the instruction. Each step takes time. In particular, the execution of the first step is determined by the time it takes to transfer bits from main memory to the instruction register. As instructions are longer, the more time this step will consume (at least if we assume that an instruction is several words in length). As we have mentioned, the second step generally dominates the total execution time. But this statement will not hold if the instruction mostly involves manipulating registers. By carefully programming the processor, for example by first ensuring that all the necessary data is contained in registers, we see that fetching an instruction becomes the predominant factor when determining the overall execution time. In practice, therefore, the trend is to keep instruction lengths as small as possible.

Word size and address length.   As discussed in Section 2.5.3, each word in memory has a unique address associated with it. Also, if we wish to read from or write to main memory then this can only be done in units determined by the size of a single word. Consequently, if we decide to group 16 bits into a single word, we can transfer data between memory and registers only in units of 16 bits. Now suppose at the same time that we had decided to choose a (fixed) instruction length of 32 bits. In that case, each instruction would not only require 2 words of memory, but more important is that *fetching* an instruction would require

---

[5]More precisely, it is not only programmers that take this approach, but also compiler developers. Compilers are discussed in Chapter 4.

two separate data transfers from main memory to the instruction register. From this point of view, it would have been better to have chosen a word size of 32 bits.

But equally important is deciding on the maximum amount of words that can be contained in memory. To date, it is not uncommon to assume that as much as 2^{30} words can be supported. Assuming that each word consists of 4 bytes (i.e. 32 bits), the maximum memory capacity would then be $2^{30} \times 4 = 4$ gigabyte. In effect, this means that in order to address a word, 30 bits need to be reserved within an instruction. In practice, this is not possible as we also need to reserve bits to identify the kind of operation that is to be performed, as well as possible additional operands. Therefore, special measures need to be taken of which some will be discussed below.

Addressing modes

Instructions are only useful if they allow us to manipulate data. But in order to do so, it is important to know exactly where data can be found. Although identifying the location where data resides may seem straightforward at first it is in fact not so. This is caused by a number of problems. Some of them are directly related to implementation restrictions, such as the length of instructions; others stem from the way we would like to refer to data in general. Here, we shall leave the reasons for having different ways of referencing data for what they are. Instead, we will just briefly discuss some of the more conventional ways of identifying memory locations, or **addressing modes** as they are called. In the following we shall adopt an informal notation for instructions when making a distinction between the different type of addressing modes. This notation will be further explained in the next chapter.

Immediate addressing.   Probably the simplest way of referring to data is by means of immediate addressing. In this case, the data that is to be operated on is immediately contained in the instruction itself. To illustrate, the instruction

        LOAD   #12, reg0

is an example showing how the decimal number 12 is directly written to register REG0. The prefix "#" is used explicitly to distinguish the fact that this LOAD instruction employs immediate addressing.

▷ Executing an instruction that uses immediate addressing is very efficient. The point to note is that the instruction itself does not refer to the memory module at all as the data is already contained in the instruction. Consequently, the execution step of the fetch-decode-execute cycle can be resolved entirely by transferring data *within* the processor. No data need thus be transferred across the data lines as shown in Figure 3.11.

Register addressing.   Another form of addressing occurs when no reference to memory is involved, but rather only to another register. This mode, called register addressing, takes the form

        LOAD   reg1, reg0

and, in this case, has the effect that the contents of register REG1 is copied to register REG0.

▷ Again, when we look at the execution of this instruction with respect to the fetch-decode-execute cycle, it is seen that no data transfer between the memory module and the processor needs to take place, other than loading the instruction into the instruction register. In effect, it can be expected that the efficiency of the execution of this instruction is of the same order as when employing immediate addressing.

Direct addressing. In the case of direct addressing, the instruction contains a reference to where the required data can be found in main memory. In practice this means that a memory address needs to be provided as in

    LOAD   1000, reg0

In this case, the data that is stored at memory location with address 1000 is copied, and written to register REG0.

▷ When employing direct addressing the execution of the instruction becomes more complicated. After having fetched and decoded the instruction, the processor will then need to read the contents at memory location 1000. Consequently, the complete fetch-decode-execute cycle requires *two* data transfers between main memory and the processor. One in order to fetch the instruction and store it in the instruction register, and one to get the data to which the instruction refers. In effect, it is seen that this instruction is less efficient than when either immediate or register addressing is employed.

Indirect addressing. A more complex form of addressing is that by which the reference to data is indirect. In that case, the reference contained in an instruction specifies not *where* the data can be found, but merely where the *reference* to that data is. To illustrate, consider the instruction

    LOAD   (reg1), reg0

In this case, the notation "(reg1)" is used to denote that the actual data can be found at the memory location of which the address is stored in register REG1. So, if we had stored 1000 in REG1, and memory location 1000 contains value 4520, then execution of the instruction above will show that 4520 is loaded into register REG0.

▷ When considering efficiency, it is not hard to imagine that this addressing mode will cost approximately as much as direct addressing. In particular, it is not difficult to see that two data transfers across the data lines of Figure 3.11 need to take place: (1) the instruction needs to be fetched from main memory and stored in the instruction register; and (2) the data contained at an indicated memory location (location 1000 in our example) needs to be transferred to the processor.

Indexed addressing.   Our last example at present is that of indexed addressing. In this case, the addressing scheme consists of a combination of a **base address** and an **offset**. To illustrate, consider the instruction

LOAD   12(reg1), reg0

If we assume that REG1 contains the value 1000, then in this case, the data that is to be LOADed into register REG0 can be found at memory location $1000 + 12 = 1012$. Address 1000 is called the base address; 12 is denoted as the offset relative to the base address. Indexed addressing is primarily used to access a series of data elements that are consecutively stored in main memory. For example, suppose we have stored the values $x_0, x_1, \ldots, x_{N-1}$ in main memory, starting at address 1000. In other words, the value x_0 is stored at location $1000, x_1$ at 1001, etc. The LOAD instruction above would then have the effect that the value x_{12} is copied to register REG0. Again, we shall see more examples of indexed addressing in the next chapter.

▷ Using a similar approach to that presented above, it should now be clear that indexed addressing requires two data transfers between main memory and the processor. The first, as usual, constitutes the transfer of the instruction into the instruction register. Decoding the instruction will ensure that the actual address (i.e. base address + offset) is calculated, after which the actual data transfer takes place.

In practice, some additional addressing modes are used as well, most notably those involving a so-called **stack**. Discussion of these additional addressing modes is deferred until we present an example instruction set in the next chapter.

3.3   Interfacing processors and memories

So far, we have discussed the design of only a simple computer consisting of a single processor-memory pair. But there should be more than just this. For example, almost every computer allows you to add components such as a graphics processor or a floating-point processor. Obviously, there should be a way of attaching peripheral devices (disks, keyboards, etc.) to the computer in such a way that they can interact with the other components. In this section, we shall consider the more general problem of connecting a *collection* of processors, memories, and other devices, allowing them to exchange data or, in other words, to *communicate*.

3.3.1   General bus architectures

An interconnection system between processors, memories, and other devices is generally referred to as a **bus**. In its simplest form, a bus is a set of wires with some additional control circuitry that directly connect processors and memories. A distinction is often made between three types of wires: control lines, data lines, and address lines.

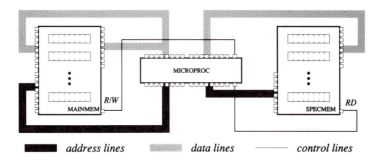

address lines   data lines   control lines

Figure 3.12 The implementation of a bus by direct wiring.

- **Control lines** are used to *synchronize* two communicating components. For example, if a processor wants to *send* data to a memory it must ascertain that the memory is capable of *receiving* that data. In other words, it must ensure that a high signal value is set on the memory's $R/\overline{W}$ control pin. This is done by means of one of the control lines of the bus. In addition to synchronization signals, control lines are also used to pass signals from I/O devices, clocks, etc.

- **Data lines** carry the data that is exchanged between two communicating components. For example, the result of a computation performed by a processor will be sent across the data lines of a bus connecting the processor to a memory.

- **Address lines**, finally, are used to select a word from memory by passing its address to the main memory module.

To illustrate, suppose we were to design an architecture consisting of a single processor, a large main memory module, and a special memory module containing a number of non-modifiable programs.[6] What we would need to do then is make sure that the processor can access both memory modules. Two approaches can be followed. First, we may choose for a processor that can be directly connected to the two modules as illustrated in Figure 3.12. This is a form of implementation that we refer to as **direct wiring**. It should be clear that this approach can only be followed if the processor is suited for it, i.e. it has separate pins to connect all data, address, and control lines.

Directly connecting processors and memories is fine, but does have a serious drawback which becomes apparent when considering how computer systems are actually built. In many cases, a manufacturer *assembles* a computer by taking various off-the-shelf components. For example, a personal computer may be based on memory chips, a processor, and various processors for peripheral devices, all from different manufacturers. It is not realistic to expect that these components can be directly wired together, i.e. that we can literally *solder* wires to the pins of the various chips and simply switch the system on.

---

[6]For example, such a module may contain a collection of basic I/O programs, as is the case with the so-called BIOS component of many IBM-compatible personal computers running the MS-DOS operating system.

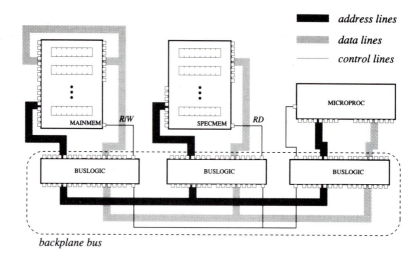

Figure 3.13 Connecting components by means of a backplane bus.

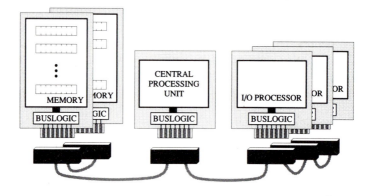

Figure 3.14 A general interconnection scheme by means of a single backplane bus.

What we need in this case is a *common* agreement on how the processors and memories are to communicate.

To this end, a so-called **backplane bus** can be used. A backplane bus consists of a number of integrated circuits that are simply wired together and which provide a means of interconnecting various memories and processors. For each component that is to be connected to the bus there will generally be a separate integrated circuit that implements an appropriate **interface**. Such an interface ensures that communication across the bus is the same for each connected component. Figure 3.13 illustrates the use of a backplane bus, using the same components of our previous configuration.

It is not hard to imagine that we can take our approach even further by attaching several processors and memory modules to the same bus. One particular scheme, and which we shall assume for the remainder of this chapter, employs a single **central processing unit** (CPU), one **main memory** constructed out of one or several memory modules, and a number of special **I/O processors**, as shown in Figure 3.14. The figure shows how the various digital components have been located on separate boards, which are to be plugged into slots. The bus, again, is formed by the wired slots and the circuits BUSLOGIC. The memories and processors are thus attached to a single backplane bus. I/O processors, which are discussed in Section 3.4, are special processors for handling communication with peripheral devices. The CPU acts as the main processor and is responsible for executing programs stored in main memory. The I/O processors handle all the communication with the outside world, to which end they will need to communicate with the CPU, and also access data stored in main memory.

However, when giving the matter some thought there are going to be problems with this scheme. First, what happens if two processors want to transfer data over the bus at the same time? For example, the CPU may want to execute a program while one of the I/O processors wants to transfer data to a peripheral device such as a printer. In general, this cannot be allowed and special measures have to be taken in order to serialize bus access. Second, it may be easy to transfer data between a processor and memory, but what about communication between processors? These two issues are addressed next.

3.3.2   Bus arbitration

In order to manage communication over a bus, a distinction is made between those processors that want to *initiate* a bus transfer, called **masters**, and those processors or memories that are *waiting for requests*, called **slaves**. For example, assume a processor wants to store a computed value in memory. The processor instructs the bus to set its control lines so that the value stored in one of the processor's internal registers will be transported to a specific word in the memory module (possibly via internal registers of one of the bus interfaces). In this case, the processor acts as a master, whereas the memory acts as a slave. The first activity involved in managing bus transfers is the selection of a master. If there is only one possible master, then selection is not a problem. When there is more than one candidate, we have to resort to **bus arbitration**. There exist several arbitration schemes that can roughly be divided into two classes: centralized and decentralized arbitration. Here, we shall discuss only centralized arbitration. Decentralized arbitration techniques will be discussed in a later chapter, when we consider networks.

In the case of **centralized bus arbitration** a separate component, called the **bus arbiter**, handles all bus requests. One particular form of centralized bus arbitration is illustrated in Figure 3.15. The principle is extremely simple: all processors are ordered one after the other in a so-called **daisy chain**. Now, if a processor wants to use the bus it first issues a request at the bus arbiter. The bus arbiter, in turn, responds by passing a grant to the first processor in the chain. The grant is forwarded from processor to processor, where each processor checks to see if it had requested the bus. If so, it picks up the grant signal; otherwise, the signal is passed on to its neighbor. As soon as the processor is finished using the bus, it signals the arbiter by means of the bus release line.

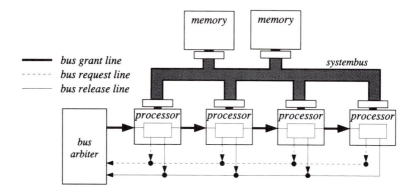

Figure 3.15   Requesting bus transfers by several masters through centralized daisy chain arbitration.

▷ As logical as this daisy chain scheme may seem, there are a few things that can easily be overlooked. Let's first see what we need in order to let a processor claim, and subsequently use the bus. Denote by req_i the value of the request signal that is set by the ith processor. In particular, if processor P_i wants to use the bus, we will have that $req_i = 1$. Similarly, let rel_i denote that processor P_i has released the bus. Obviously, the bus is not being used by any processor if all of them have released it. In other words

$$\text{the bus is free} \quad \Leftrightarrow \quad (rel_1 \bullet \cdots \bullet rel_N) = 1$$

Let $grant_i$ denote the value of the grant signal as observed by the ith processor. The general behavior of a processor that wants to use the bus can then initially be expressed by the following steps:

1. **Request:** set $req_i \leftarrow 1$.
2. **Acquire:** if $grant_i = 1$, then set $rel_i \leftarrow 0$ and $req_i \leftarrow 0$. The processor can now use the bus.
3. **Release:** set $rel_i \leftarrow 1$.

For the arbiter, it is important to know when to pass a grant signal to the first processor in the chain, and when to lower this signal again. It is not difficult to see that whenever there is a request from a processor, and the bus has also been released by every processor, it is time to pass the grant signal. As soon as the arbiter notices that the bus is in use, the grant signal should be lowered again. In other words, if we denote by $grant$ the value of the grant signal as produced by the arbiter, we have:

$$grant = (req_1 + \cdots + req_N) \bullet (rel_1 \bullet \cdots \bullet rel_N)$$

Unfortunately, this simple scheme is not going to work, for suppose that processor P_i had just passed the grant signal to a processor P_j further down the chain. This can only happen if P_i had not requested the use of the bus, i.e. $req_i = 0$. Now imagine what happens when P_i decides to issue a request just after it passed the grant signal to P_j, and before the arbiter had a chance to lower the grant signal again (i.e. before P_j could claim the use of the bus by setting $rel_j \leftarrow 0$). In that case, because we will still have $grant_i = 1$, P_i will inadvertently assume that it can claim the bus as well. Consequently, we will then have two processors starting to send signals across the bus simultaneously, leading to confusion.

The problem can be solved by letting P_i keep track of the fact that it had passed the grant signal to another processor down the chain. If this is the case, P_i will first have to wait until the grant signal is lowered again (indicating that the bus is now being used by P_j). At that moment, it can pass its request to the arbiter by setting $req_i \leftarrow 1$. As soon as it receives the grant signal again, it can then claim the bus for its own use.

The main disadvantage of daisy chaining is that the processors at the end of the chain may have a hard time attaining the bus. Their predecessors have a much better chance of claiming the grant signal for the simple reason that it arrives there earlier. An alternative approach that is fair to each processor is to let the arbiter select which processor is actually going to get the bus. To that end, each processor communicates separately with the bus arbiter through separate grant and request lines.

3.3.3 Interprocessor communication

Another issue that we mentioned was **interprocessor communication**. Typically, communication between processor and memory involves transferring instructions and data between the internal registers of the processor and the memory module. But interprocessor communication may actually involve transferring instructions and data from one processor to another as well. In particular, there should be a mechanism to let the CPU instruct an I/O processor to start transferring data from main memory to a peripheral device, and likewise, to let an I/O processor inform the CPU about the status of the data transfer. So how does one processor actually supply another processor with data or an instruction? In order to answer this question, the first point to realize is that (practically) all communication takes place by propagating bit strings stored in some internal register of the sending processor to some internal register of the receiving processor. So, if we can uniquely identify registers in processors, we have a way of communicating data and instructions between processors. Here, the notion of **address spaces** is needed.

Conceptually, an address space is merely a collection of storage locations, linearly ordered from address 0 and upwards. An address space is *implemented* by taking one or several memory units, and assigning to each storage location a unique number, starting at 0. In this sense, it is very much comparable to the address decoding scheme discussed in Section 2.5.3. Two different methods for identifying registers (and thus the processors they belong to) are generally employed in computer design. These methods are illustrated in Figure 3.16.

In the first scheme, *all* storage units, except for the internal registers of the CPU, are assigned a unique address from a single address space. For example, assume we have a computer with a single CPU and two I/O processors IOPROC1 and IOPROC2, each I/O

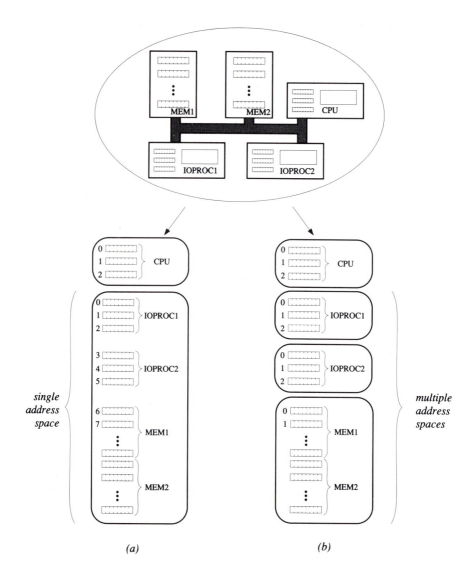

Figure 3.16 Mapping memory and registers into a single address space (a), or into different address spaces (b).

processor having three registers. Furthermore, assume there are two memory modules MEM1 and MEM2. Then, we might organize the address space as shown in Figure 3.16(a), in which the first six addresses are assigned to the registers belonging to the two I/O processors, whereas the remaining addresses are assigned to words from MEM1 and MEM2. The registers of the CPU are always assigned to a different address space. Consequently, communication between the CPU and an I/O processor is now accomplished by simply transferring data between two different memory locations. This mapping scheme is called **memory-mapped I/O** for obvious reasons.

▷ Memory-mapped I/O is in fact, an extremely simple and elegant way of controlling I/O processors. Anticipating our discussion on peripheral devices in the next section, suppose that we have an I/O processor that is responsible for data transfers between a floppy disk and the CPU. In order to transfer data, a floppy disk unit needs to be explicitly activated, i.e. it is the CPU's responsibility to either start or stop the rotating of the disk. To that end, assume we have a single address space as shown in Figure 3.16(a), and that the floppy disk unit is controlled by IOPROC2 having a special 8-bit register CTRLDISK mapped to address 5. If the last bit of this register contains a 1, then the I/O processor of the floppy disk unit will start the motor in order to rotate the disk. Otherwise, when it is 0, the motor is to be stopped. We can then let the CPU instruct the floppy disk's I/O processor to start the motor by means of the two instructions

```
LOAD   #00000001, reg0
STORE  reg0, 5
```

The LOAD instruction uses immediate addressing, and puts the bit string into the CPU's internal register REG0. The STORE instruction which employs direct addressing then writes this value to memory location 5, which is equivalent to storing ⟨00000001⟩ into register CTRLDISK of the floppy disk unit. At that point, the I/O processor (which is assumed to continuously read register CTRLDISK), will start the disk's motor.

In the second scheme, a distinction is made between distinct address spaces for the registers of the I/O processors and main memory, as shown in Figure 3.16(b). In particular, words from the memory module are mapped into one address space, whereas the registers of the CPU and each I/O processor are mapped into a different address space. The problem with this scheme is that we now have to devise a special means to let the CPU communicate to an I/O processor that there is work to be done. The only solution to this problem is to design a number of special I/O instructions that the CPU can execute. Such an instruction is then sent to a selected I/O processor, which in turn will do as it is instructed. For example, in the simplest form, the CPU may have a DOIO instruction which enables a selected I/O processor first to copy some data from main memory to its internal registers, after which it proceeds to send this copied data to the peripheral device to which it is connected.

As many modern processors do not employ this I/O scheme (a notable exception is the Intel 80x86 family), and because we will be using the conceptually much simpler memory-mapped I/O scheme throughout the remainder of this book, we shall discuss these matters no further.

3.4   Peripheral devices

Let's now take a closer look at peripheral devices. In particular, we shall pay attention to two subjects. First, we need to discuss how peripheral devices interact with processors and memories. Second, we will take a closer look at the kind of devices that are commonly used at present.

3.4.1   Interfacing devices and processors

As we have already mentioned briefly in the previous section, interaction with peripheral devices is generally taken care of by means of dedicated processors, called **I/O processors**. These are also frequently referred to as **I/O controllers**. I/O processors enable the transfer of data between a computer's main memory and a peripheral device: disks, terminals, printers, modems, etc. In general, each type of peripheral device requires a specific combination of a processing unit and additional circuitry which makes I/O processors special (where it should be noted that devices such as, for example, simple printers and keyboards are so similar with respect to their communication protocol that they can be controlled by the same I/O processor).

I/O processors are very similar to the general processor discussed in Section 3.1.4. The main difference is that they are capable of communicating directly with peripheral devices. They need to transform data as stored in their internal registers into a format that is acceptable for the device they control. For example, printers require special sequences of signals before they can be activated. A printer I/O processor allows an ordinary processor (i.e. the CPU) to write to its internal registers the data it wants to print, after which the I/O processor sends the correct signals to the printing components so that the data is actually hard-copied onto paper.

Now let's take a closer look at the interaction between a general processor and an I/O processor. In particular, we need to consider two aspects: (1) initiating data transfer, and (2) detecting that data transfer is completed.

Initiating I/O

We first consider how a general processor can actually initiate I/O. Assume we have a central processing unit (CPU) that wants to transfer N data items from a memory chip MEM to a peripheral storage device DEV. This device DEV has an associated I/O processor IOPROC. Transferring this data proceeds in two steps:

1. The data is transferred from MEM to some memory that is local to the I/O processor. This memory (which is often called a buffer) is denoted here as BUF.

2. From there on, the data is moved from BUF to the actual device for permanent storage, display on a screen, printing, etc.

There are several ways by which the first step can be executed, as illustrated in Figure 3.17. A simple scheme is to let the CPU start by issuing a bus request for reading a single data item from MEM into one of its internal registers. After that, it issues another bus request to write the contents of this register into a suitable location of BUF. This scheme is repeated until all data items have been stored in BUF. At that point, the buffer associated with the storage device DEV has been filled, so that its contents can now be

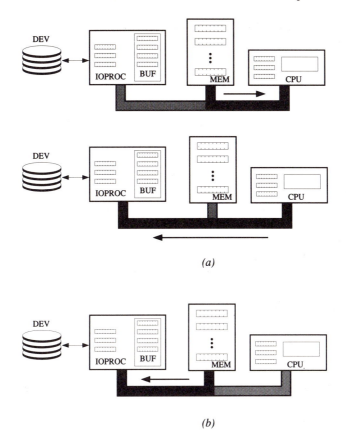

(a)

(b)

Figure 3.17 Transferring data for output via the CPU (a), or by means of direct memory access (b).

transferred to the device itself. This data transfer is the responsibility of the I/O processor associated with DEV. In order to accomplish this data transfer, the CPU will have to instruct the I/O processor to do so by sending a control signal to one of the I/O processor's internal registers.

▷ To illustrate, assume that we have a computer that uses memory-mapped I/O, and that the buffer BUF consists of a total of 100 words, mapped consecutively from memory location 11 and upwards. Also, we assume that DEV has an 8-bit register CTRLDEV mapped to address 10, used to indicate what kind of data transfer needs to take place. If the first two bits are set to ⟨01⟩, then this means that the data contained in BUF are to be stored on device DEV. Now, suppose that we need to transfer the data stored in the first 100 words of main memory, starting at address 1000. Omitting a number of details, the following sequence of instructions will accomplish just that:[7]

LOAD 1000, reg0	Load the 1st data item into register REG0
STORE reg0, 11	and store it as the 1st item in the buffer.
LOAD 1001, reg0	Load the 2nd data item into register REG0
STORE reg0, 12	and store it as the 2nd item in the buffer.
...	
LOAD 1099, reg0	Load the 100th data item into register REG0
STORE reg0, 110	and store it as the 100th item in the buffer.
LOAD #01000000, reg0	Set the appropriate values to transfer the data from the buffer to the device
STORE reg0, 10	and instruct IOPROC to do the actual transfer.

The sequence of LOAD and STORE instructions first copy the data into memory locations where they can be accessed by the I/O processor. Note that these transfers all take place over the bus. Each data item is thus physically moved from main memory to the memory associated with the device DEV. The last two instructions are used to instruct the I/O processor to store the data on DEV.

A more advanced scheme is to let IOPROC do all the work. In this case, the CPU starts by passing information to IOPROC on which data stored in MEM is to be permanently stored on DEV. It then lets IOPROC take care of the data transfer from MEM to BUF. The important distinction with the previous scheme is that the CPU no longer moves the data items from MEM to BUF. This is done entirely by IOPROC. Because IOPROC apparently has direct access to MEM, this second scheme is also referred to as **direct memory access** (DMA). Direct memory access is especially important in cases where large chunks of data are to be transported at high speed between main memory and a peripheral device. Obviously, it permits the processor that initiated the data transport to do other things during the time that the I/O processor is moving data.

▷ What the effect is of direct memory access can be illustrated by rewriting our program given above. Assuming that data transfers always take place in a fixed amount of bytes, the only thing we have to do now is tell the I/O processor where it can find the data. Assume IOPROC has another register, called STARTADDR, which should contain the address in main memory of the first datum that is to be stored on DEV. Assume STARTADDR has been mapped to address 9. Using a binary numbering convention (meaning that address 1000, where the first datum is located, is represented as the bit string ⟨1111101000⟩), we then need only execute the instructions

LOAD #1111101000, reg0	First get the start address (1000) into a register...
STORE reg0, 9	and store that address in register STARTADDR.
LOAD #01000000, reg0	And start the data transfer by setting the correct value
STORE reg0, 10	into the control register of the device.

(Suppose, by the way, that our control register is now used to instruct the I/O processor to do a DMA transfer, rather than transferring data between itself and the peripheral device.)

---

[7]We note that this solution is a rather foolish way of doing I/O. Better solutions will be presented in the next chapter.

From there on, IOPROC will independently fetch the data from main memory and transfer it to the buffer. As soon as this is finished, it will then store the data on DEV. Meanwhile, the CPU can be used for executing other instructions.

Detecting completion of I/O

But what about detecting that I/O has completed? In principle, we need to make a distinction between two cases: (1) the I/O controller has completed transfer of data between a peripheral device and itself, and (2) data transfer through DMA has completed. The two cases have in common that they both require the CPU to notice that *another* processor has finished a task.

When giving this matter some thought there is one scheme that immediately comes to mind, namely the one by which the CPU simply checks from time to time at the I/O processor if it has completed its work. This can easily be done, for example, by letting the CPU check the contents of a special control register at the I/O processor. This scheme is referred to as **polling**. The main drawback of polling is that it is not very efficient. If the CPU wants to initiate a second data transfer as soon as possible, it will have to frequently request the status of the first data transfer, prohibiting it to do other work in the meantime. On the other hand, if I/O completion is only tested after considerable time has elapsed, the overall rate at which I/O takes place may be too slow. The I/O processor would then simply not be working at its maximum speed.

But there is another simple solution to this problem. We let the I/O processor inform the CPU when it has completed its work by generating an **interrupt**. Generating an interrupt by an I/O processor causes the CPU to stop its current execution of instructions and devote itself to initiate a next I/O request, or otherwise indicate that no more I/O is currently needed. As we shall see in Chapter 5, this so-called **interrupt handling** is done completely by executing a series of special instructions. When this execution is finished, the CPU automatically resumes its interrupted work. But for now, let's take a closer look at what happens at the hardware level.

Whenever the I/O processor generates an interrupt, it sends a signal to a special digital circuit, called an **interrupt controller**. Normally, several I/O processors are attached in this way to a single interrupt controller. The interrupt controller in turn, sends the signal to the CPU. As soon as the latter sends a signal back to the interrupt controller that it is capable of handling the interrupt, the interrupt controller issues a bus request, and, after the request has been granted, propagates the identification of the device that initially caused the interrupt to the CPU's internal registers. From that moment on, the CPU "knows" that the device is ready to accept new data to transfer, and starts executing the instructions to initiate another data transfer or otherwise indicate that no further I/O is currently needed.

3.4.2   Examples of peripheral devices

Now that we have discussed the interaction between a CPU, memories, and I/O processors, let's look at some peripheral devices that are generally attached to computers. We briefly discuss storage devices, terminals, and printers.

Storage devices

Computers as we have discussed so far are magnificent devices indeed. Yet, when storing information they have one major drawback. As soon as the power supply is switched off, all the data that is contained in registers and main memory is lost. Consequently, this makes them unsuitable for *permanently* storing data. On the other hand, computers would be a lot less useful if we did not have the means to save our data as long as we wish regardless of the availability of power supplies. The means to these ends are so-called **storage devices**. Because the amount of data that we wish to keep intact is so large, we also find ourselves in the position that storage devices should not only preferably have a very large capacity, they should also be relatively cheap. In this subsection, we shall look at some popular storage devices.

Magnetic storage devices.   Traditionally, storage media have always appeared in the form of magnetic devices, particularly tapes, hard disks, and floppy disks. The principal working of these devices is always the same. There is a medium (plastic in the case of tapes and floppy disks, and metal or glass in the case of hard disks) that is **coated** with magnetic material. This means that uncountable microscopic parts (each forming a small magnet) are spread all over the medium. The quality of the coating in combination with the underlying medium determines how long this magnetic surface will remain intact. In practice, this will be for many years. The essence of having a magnetic surface is that its parts can be pointed in any direction under the influence of an external magnetic field. In other words, we can force the magnetic surface into a specific *pattern.* Moreover, once we have established a pattern, it will remain unaltered as long as it is not exposed to some external magnetic field again.[8] This also implies that if we expose the magnetic parts to an external magnetic field in a *controlled* manner we can actually store information.

Enforcing a specific magnetic pattern is done by means of a **read/write head**. The head is capable of inducing a magnetic field based on electrical signals. Consequently, the electrical signals that are passed to the head can said to be transformed into a unique magnetic pattern. More commonly, we say that we *write* data onto the device. The advantage about read/write heads, however, is that they also work the other way around. In other words, if we do not pass electrical signals to the head, but instead move the head across a magnetic surface, it will induce electrical signals in accordance with the pattern that is being scanned. In that case, we say that we are *reading* data.

As we have said, the principles underlying magnetic storage devices are all the same. The difference between the devices is to be sought in the way that they are physically organized. Let's look at three types of magnetic storage devices: *tapes*, *hard disks*, and *floppy disks*.

Magnetic tape.   Magnetic tapes are not the most attractive storage medium when it comes to flexibility. However, due to the fact that they can contain very large amounts of

---

[8]It is for this reason that you are often warned not to put your floppy disks on top of loudspeakers, which almost invariably produce a strong, permanent magnetic field.

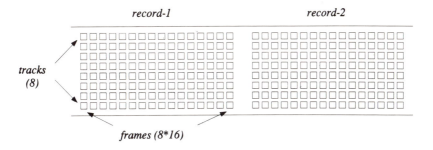

Figure 3.18 The organization of magnetic patterns on a tape.

data at an extremely low cost, they are still frequently used for archiving purposes. Typically, the storage capacity of tapes as used in many personal computer and workstation configurations is in the order of tens to hundreds of megabytes. In terms of money, this storage capacity is not going to cost much: it is comparable to the price of a video tape. Using advanced recording techniques, we can now store 5 gigabyte of data on a single video tape.

The magnetic pattern of a tape is organized into a number of **tracks** which in turn are divided into **frames** as shown in Figure 3.18. A number of frames together form a **record**. Data transfer to or from tape takes place in units of so-called **blocks**. A block typically contains a few thousand bytes. The problem with tapes is that they need to be wound or rewound in order to position the head above the block in which we are interested. This takes a lot of time as you can also experience with your own cassette or video recorder, making them unsuitable in cases where data needs to be stored permanently but still be easily, i.e. quickly, accessible.

Hard disks.   In order to increase access speed, hard disks were introduced. A hard disk consists of one or more metal (or glass) platters with a magnetizable coating, and for each disk surface, a movable read/write head, as shown in Figure 3.19. Each surface is divided into a number of **tracks**, which in turn are divided into **sectors**, as shown in Figure 3.20. Tracks that are at the same distance from the center jointly form what is called a **cylinder**. Data can be transferred to or from a hard disk in units that equal the size of a sector. The total storage capacity of a hard disk can vary considerably. Smaller personal computers, such as notebooks, are often equipped with a 120 or 340 megabyte hard disk. Larger hard disks may have a storage capacity of several gigabyte.

In order to transfer data to or from a hard disk, we have to specify exactly in which sector we are interested. In practice, this means that we have to specify (1) a cylinder, (2) a head, and (3) a sector number. The heads are then jointly positioned above the correct cylinder, and the disk itself is rotated so as to read or write the correct sector. Note that if information is to be transferred from or to the same cylinder, hardly any mechanical movement is involved, because the heads can remain positioned above the same cylinder. Because heads can be positioned above any cylinder, hard disks are so-called **random**

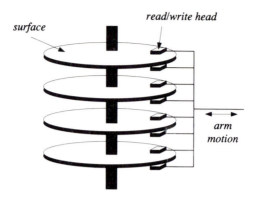

Figure 3.19 A typical organization of a hard disk.

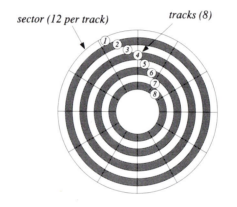

Figure 3.20 Layout of a surface of a hard disk.

access devices, as opposed to **sequential access devices** such as tape devices. Obviously, the average access time for hard disks is much shorter than that for tape drives.

One disadvantage of hard disks is that they are generally vulnerable to transportation. Although so-called removable disks are now commonly available, hard disks are not the most convenient means of physically transporting information from one computer to another.

Floppy disks.   With the advent of personal computers, floppy disks were introduced. They are conceptually the same as hard disks, although each floppy disk drive can handle only a single diskette rather than a stack of disks. Also, as their name suggests, a floppy disk is physically a lot more flexible with plastic being used as the underlying medium for the magnetic surface. The storage capacity of floppy disks is typically just over 1 megabyte. Another major difference is that the read/write head of a floppy disk drives actually touches the surface of the diskette, in contrast to hard disks (where the head floats just above the surface). Consequently, floppy disks are subject to more wear and tear. To overcome this problem, the heads are generally removed from the surface, and the motor of the disk drive is stopped when there is no need for data transportation. Floppy disk drives tend to have a much larger access and data transport time than hard disks, because time for rotation and head movement is much slower.

Optical storage devices.   An attractive alternative to magnetic tapes for storing data are optical stores, such as, for example, CD-ROM. The main advantage of an optical disk compared to a magnetic tape is the fact that it is far less vulnerable to external influences like heat, humidity, and, of course, electromagnetic fields. Consequently, optical disks are much better for storing information for a long period of time. The storage capacity of optical disks lies somewhere between that of high-capacity tapes and hard disks. In general, you can store in the order of 500–1000 megabytes of data on a single disk.

At the heart of an optical disk is a reflective layer which is used to store information. In most cases, this is done by burning holes at the surface, called **pits**, which are separated by unburned parts called **lands**. Due to their difference in reflectivity, it is possible to distinguish the two by making use of light (which is why these disks are referred to as optical disks). The difference in light can, as in the case of magnetic read/write heads, be transformed into electrical signals. The reflective layer itself is protected on both sides by an additional plastic or glass layer.

The problem with optical disks is that the data they contain are hard to modify. In practice, most disks to date can only be used for data retrieval: there is no way that the optical pattern burned into the disk can be changed. Special so-called **write-once read-many** disks allow data on a disk to be changed only once. It is expected that full erasable optical disks will become widely available in the near future. ⬭

In general, the data on an optical disk is organized in a single spiral, similar to the layout of vinyl records. This is perfectly in order for storing continuous data such as voice and video, but is less suitable when storing discrete data as found in most computers. The problem with the spiral organization is that the data, as in the case of magnetic tapes, is only sequentially accessible. This means that if no special measures are taken, the head will always have to be positioned at the start of the spiral, after which the scanning of the disk can start. In practice, this is circumvented by dividing the data into records, analogous to the organization of magnetic tapes. An alternative solution is to follow the layout of magnetic disks by organizing the data into tracks and sectors. This approach is still at the research stage, but would have the advantage that the data is then randomly accessible. Combining this with full erasure possibility of disks, optical storage devices may then form a strong alternative to hard disks.

Terminals

Terminals are the primary means for interactively communicating with a computer. They consist of a *keyboard*, sometimes a *mouse*, and a *monitor*.

Keyboards.   Keyboards are in principle nothing but a large collection of switches. With the introduction of personal computers by IBM, a so-called **geographic coding system** was used. Each key has an associated 7-bit binary code which is related not to what the key logically stands for but instead only its position on the keyboard. For example, on a PC compatible keyboard, the key "W" has the geographic code 46. The interesting aspect of this coding system is that a distinction is made between depressing a key and releasing it again. Whenever a key, say with geographic code *keycode*, is depressed, the keyboard sends its code to the keyboard controller. As soon as the key is depressed, the number *keycode* + 128 is sent. By associating two events with any keystroke, it is possible to distinguish complex key combinations.

To illustrate, many developers of word processors have found it useful to force their users to learn combinations of keys such as "CTRL-CEB" which means that the CTRL-key should be depressed while typing in the sequence "ceb". Using the notation "KEY↓" to denote that the key KEY is depressed, and likewise "KEY↑" denoting its release, our example key combination generates the following series of events:

event number:	1	2	3	4	5	6	7	8
event:	CTRL ↓	C ↓	C ↑	E ↓	E ↑	B ↓	B ↑	CTRL ↑

which is a total of eight events that are passed as keycodes to the keyboard controller. Each event generates an interrupt that is to be handled by the keyboard controller in combination with the CPU. Because the events can be separately distinguished, it is also possible to recognize which key combination has been typed in. In this way, appropriate action can be taken.

Mice.   A mouse is a small device that is capable of recording movements in two directions relative to an initial position. In it simplest form, whenever a mouse is moved it updates two internal counters: one for the X direction and one for the Y direction. For example, moving to the right increments the X-counter, whereas moving downwards decrements the Y-counter. The counters are updated by means of an electromechanical interface, where the mechanical part is formed by a simple tracking ball. Movement of the ball is then translated into electrical signals. The values in the counters are sent to the mouse controller every 100 milliseconds or so, where they are further processed by the CPU. In addition, each mouse generally has two or three buttons in order to generate additional events to the mouse controller, similar to the organization of keyboards as discussed above.

Monitors.   Monitors are comparable to normal TV screens. By using electrical signals as input they direct an electron beam to a phosphorescent screen that subsequently produces a light spot. The screen itself is divided into a number of **pixels** per square inch, also referred to as the **screen resolution**. The more pixels into which a screen is divided, the better the definition. In practice, ordinary screens have resolutions in the order of 640 pixels horizontally and 480 pixels vertically. High-definition screens may have a resolution of 1280×1024 pixels, or even 2048×2048.

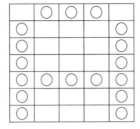

Figure 3.21 The representation of the character "A" by means of a 7-dot matrix printer.

In order to form a complete image on the screen, the electron beam scans each horizontal line separately, updating each pixel as the beam passes it. The information on a pixel (its color, luminosity, etc.) is generally encoded in one or several bytes, and which is stored in so-called video memory. This memory is generally mapped to the same address space as main memory, so that updating an image becomes relatively simple as far as interfacing is concerned. The information on a pixel is read each time the electron beam passes a pixel when scanning a line. Now, in order to generate an acceptable image, a screen has to be completely updated at least 25 times per second. This means that with a screen resolution of 640×480, at least 7,5 million updates have to be made per second. In practice, monitors often have an update rate that is two or three times as large. In order to realize these rates, a separate video processor is required.

Printers

There are various types of printers. Probably the three most common are *matrix printers*, *ink-jet printers*, and *laser printers*.

Matrix printers.   Matrix printers have a print head that consists of a number of needles that can be electrically activated and withdrawn. For example, a print head may contain seven vertically positioned needles. The letter "A" can then be put onto paper as a 5×7 matrix, as shown in Figure 3.21. Each character is then constructed in five subsequent steps of seven vertically placed dots.

There are roughly three techniques for matrix printing. The simplest one uses a ribbon as on a typewriter. The head moves along the ribbon ejecting needles when necessary. Another form which is used for many facsimile machines uses special thermosensitive paper. In that case, a head with pins is heated causing a local coloring when brought into contact with the paper. The third technique, which is also based on thermal principles, uses a special ribbon from which microscopic ink particles are removed when brought into contact with a heated needle. The ink particles are then transferred onto paper. In general, this form has a much higher quality than the other two types of matrix printing.

Ink-jet printers.   Ink-jet printers also encode characters and symbols in the form of matrices, but do not make use of a special head with needles to process the paper. Instead, a continuous, very fine stream of ink droplets is produced. Each drop can either be transferred to paper (producing a black spot), or diverted into a separate reservoir (leaving a blank on the paper). Drops that have been diverted into the reservoir can later be used again. An alternative technique is to only produce droplets on demand, making the need for a separate reservoir obsolete. Due to their excellent price/quality ratio, ink-jet printers have become popular for personal use.

Laser printers.   Laser printers are similar to photocopiers. The heart of a laser printer is formed by a rotating drum that is charged up to about a 1000 volts and coated with a photosensitive material. Using laser technology, the coated drum is hit with a light beam on those areas where the original input is "white". These spots then lose their electrical charge. As soon as a line of the input has been put on the drum in the form of electrically charged areas, the drum rotates and picks up black powder exactly on those parts that are still charged. The effect is that the drum contains a mirrored image of the input, that can now be transferred to a blank sheet of paper.

Laser printers are more expensive than ink-jet printers, but have a higher quality and speed. Compared to ink-jet printers, laser printers are capable of attaining a resolution that can be 10–20 times higher. And where ink-jets sometimes take tens of seconds to print on a sheet of paper, laser printers are often capable of processing tens of sheets per minute.

3.5   Discussion and further reading

It is worth taking a closer look at where we are now, before we move our discussion further away from hardware. In the following two sections we shall reconsider our approach towards the development of a processor by taking a look at microinstructions and instruction sets from the perspective of a design engineer. As we shall see, much of the difficulties involving processor design relate to performance demands that are to be met. Performance is put into context in Section 3.5.2.

3.5.1   Processor development

Microinstructions

We started our discussion with the introduction of microinstructions. We have shown how we we can control the transfer and manipulation of bit strings by storing the signals by which this control is done. A microinstruction was, in fact, a group of such control signals. Moreover, by adding a timer mechanism we are also capable of *executing* a series of microinstructions. A series of microinstructions is referred to as a microroutine. By storing several microroutines in a microstore, we subsequently showed that we can construct a processor having several useful instructions.

It should be clear that, to a certain extent, we can change this set of instructions by storing other microroutines. In other words, if we change the contents of the microstore we would effectively have a different processor. This perspective makes a processor less hardware than one would initially think. On the one hand, there are "hard" components such as registers, an ALU, etc. On the other, there is also a "soft" component in the form of the replaceable microprogram. Moreover, a microprogram is not something you can touch. It is merely an ordered collection of bit strings. However, microprograms are not very flexible – on the contrary. Because their primary goal is to control specific hardware, we will probably be forced to adapt a microprogram when making changes to the hardware. Moreover, microprograms hardly abstract from the hardware, they are truly meant as a convenient means to design and implement hardware control signals. This strong dependency on hardware makes microprograms a typical example of **firmware**.

Computers had been around for some time before microinstructions were invented. Until the 1950s when Maurice Wilkes introduced the concept of microprogramming, all instructions were hardwired, i.e. implemented directly into hardware. Microinstructions have had a serious impact on processor design, but their influence is gradually now declining in the face of performance demands (we shall return to this).

The advantage of microinstructions is that, to a certain extent, you can make your own instruction set without having to adapt the hardware. You only have to change the microprogram stored in the microstore. But this advantage does not always outweigh the disadvantage that constructing microprograms is an extremely hard and error-prone process. If you want to know more about firmware, the tutorial provided by Rauscher and Adams (1980) is a good point to start. A thorough treatment of the subject is given in Andrews (1980); for a more recent treatise, consult Mange (1992). The original work on firmware is presented in Wilkes (1956). Viewing microprogramming from the perspective of high-level languages makes it much easier to deal with than speaking in it in terms of bits. Patterson's (1976) paper was the first one to address this approach. It is instructive, as it provides a clear way of looking at microprogramming issues.

On complex and reduced instruction sets

The main goal of processor development, however, is, of course, not the development of advanced microprograms, but rather that of instruction sets. The instruction set determines the power and flexibility of a computer system from the programmer's point of view. The computer architect designs the instruction set as a compromise between what is thought of being useful to programmers and compiler writers and what is technologically possible. The advances in technology have been used to enhance instruction sets with more powerful and elaborate instructions and more complicated addressing schemes. For a long time there had been no validation whether or not the instructions are actually useful, in the sense that they are frequently executed by average programs.

When people started measuring and gathering statistics about instruction usage frequencies, they found out that some instructions were actually never used and others were used frequently. It even turned out that some instruction sequences appeared very often, while there was no appropriate instruction available to perform that operation in a single step. This happened, for instance, in the case of so-called subroutine calls. We will see in the next chapter that executing a subroutine involves saving a lot of context information (register contents, program counter, etc.). When the calling program is to resume execution, this context information has to be restored. Current programming practice tends to use subroutines much more frequently then three decades ago, among other things because of the popularity of the so-called modular programming paradigm. Another important aspect is that the translation of high-level programming languages into series of machine instructions only required rather simple and, above all, straightforward instructions to be available. Complex instructions, often only implementable by microprogramming techniques, were thus simply not needed.

Another consequence of more complex instruction sets is that the decoding of the instruction takes more time and leads to more complex decoding circuitry. This also slows down instruction execution, but this was thought to be compensated by more processing work done per instruction.

To overcome the above-mentioned problems, a number of computer architects started to design so-called **Reduced Instruction Set Computers** (RISC) as opposed to the **Complex Instruction Set Computer** (CISC). Their recipe is to reduce the number of instructions by deleting all instructions that are not frequently used, simplify the remaining instructions as much as possible to ease the instruction decoding process, and enlarge the number of registers to accommodate subroutine calls and high-level language translation optimizations. A faster computer system will then result. The first RISC processors had some 40–50 instructions as opposed to 200–300 instructions in earlier CISC designs. This approach has been adopted by some computer manufacturers, who now offer systems which are claimed to have been developed according to this concept. However, more recent RISC processors such as the PowerPC (May *et al.*, 1994) again have more than 200 instructions, deviating markedly from the original goal of reducing the number of instructions. Instead emphasis is put on fast decoding of instructions, leading to less well-structured instruction sets. It is nevertheless expected that both CISC and RISC designs will continue to co-exist, possibly merging both techniques into hybrid designs. A nice comparison of both approaches can be found in Smith and Weiss (1994).

The approach we have outlined in this chapter is clearly based on the development followed for CISC processors, and can also be found in general textbooks. For the design of RISC processors, Patterson and Hennessy (1994) is an excellent and thorough treatise starting from scratch.

Computer architecture and organization

The instruction set of a computer is one of the most important architectural features of a computer system. It is the link between hardware and software. Computer manufacturers have their proprietary instruction sets for their range of machines. In architectural features they can find a way to be different from the competition and to protect investments. In reality, however, instruction sets are not really that different, since many machines share equal or almost equal instruction types. Until recently, there was no trend or pressure to obtain uniformity. However, with the introduction of personal computers we can observe a change. Since only a few manufacturers of personal computers can afford to design and build their own processor, most of them adopt a processor from an independent manufacturer. Also, investment in designing and manufacturing a new processor is becoming so high, that only a few manufacturers will survive.

It is useful to make a distinction between computer *architecture* and computer *organization*, similar to the distinction given in Chapter 1. The architecture of a computer system comprises those attributes of the system that can be reached and used by a program (either application or system program). The organization of a computer system refers to the actual configuration of the system, e.g. the sort of ALUs, how many are built in, and their interconnection.

The main *architectural* specifications of a computer system are the instruction set, the built-in data type representations (integers and floating-point representation), the memory organization, and the I/O system organization. For example, a multiplication instruction in the instruction set is an architectural feature. However, *how* the multiplication is performed is an organizational issue. We can do multiplication by means of implementing an ALU capable of performing multiplication or by repetitive use of an ALU performing addition, for example.

The distinction between architecture and organization becomes important in view of introducing new processors. If we left the *architecture* of a processor unaltered, but instead, improved its *organization*, we would have obtained a situation in which all programs that could be in execution on one processor could also be executed by its successor without any adaptations. This concept of **processor families** was first introduced in the IBM 360-series of computers (Blaauw and Brooks, 1964) and caused a true revolution in the computer industry. The family concept protects the user investment in programs and provides a growth path for future needs. Most current manufacturers of large systems offer one or more families of computer systems. Typical examples of this upward compatibility feature in the case of processors are the Intel 80x86 and Motorola 680x0 processors.

There are many excellent textbooks on computer architecture and organization. Besides Tanenbaum's book (1990a), you might also find Shiva (1985) worthwhile as it provides a more gentle introduction to the material, although it is becoming rather out of date. A more in-depth presentation is given in van der Goor (1989) which also covers related subjects such a data representation. For advanced architectures, as in the case of so-called **parallel computers** that consist of several CPUs, an excellent treatise can be found in Hwang (1993).

3.5.2   Processing power

Clocks and speed

We have shown that the clock, or rather a timer as we have called it, plays an essential role in dictating the pace of operations in a digital computer system. However, we have not described clock rates in a quantitative sense. Nevertheless, it must be clear that a clock signal must be made as fast as possible, since the speed of the basic fetch execute cycle is directly dependent on the clock rate.

Now, how fast can a clock be? To obtain some insight into this issue, remember that the basic operation of a computer is retrieving a bit string from memory, providing an operation on it and storing it back into memory. An operation means in practice that a series of gates have to be passed. Physically, each gate causes a small time delay in propagating the signal from the input to the output lines. Therefore, the maximum number of gates to be passed from any position in the input bit string to any other position in the output bit string determines the maximum time delay for carrying out an operation. Hence the next clock pulse can only come *after* that maximum delay.

There are only two ways to influence the delay time of operations. The first is to minimize the number of gates to be passed from input to output. This is a design issue, often leading to intricate designs. The second way is changing the technology of manufacturing gates. This only concerns the physics of making transistors on silicon or another suitable substrate and can be done without changing the design of a computer system. Much of the speed improvement comes from the ongoing reduction in the size of transistors on a chip. Generally, smaller devices lead to increased switching speeds.

Pipelining

A technique frequently used to increase processor speed and minimize the number of gates to be passed per clock cycle is called **pipelining**. The idea behind pipelining is quite simple; one breaks down a complex operation into more simple suboperations, such that each suboperation executes in an equal amount of time. If we separate the suboperations by storage elements (pipeline-registers), a number of equal and mutually independent calculations can be executed in an overlapped manner.

Therefore, in principle, with a so-called *n*-stage pipeline, a total of *n* suboperations can be executed at the same time, yielding a potential *n*-fold increase in overall execution speed. In practice, the yield is a little less, among other things due to the time overhead caused by the pipeline registers. Several operations in computer systems can be pipelined. Examples are arithmetic operations, such as floating-point addition (with possible suboperations as exponent comparison and mantissa addition) and instructions (with possible suboperations as fetch, decode, and execute). As an example, reconsider the fetch and execute cycle of Figure 3.7. Here the cycle is done in a strict sequential order. Only after execution, can the next instruction fetch proceed. By putting an extra register between the microstore and the microinstruction register, both phases can be overlapped. During execution the next instruction is being fetched. By pipelining the fetch and execute cycle we effectively double the speed of operation.

Performance measures

Although clock speed and instruction execution have a close relation, they are not the same. Only when the internal design of the processors is the same, can clock speeds be directly used to assess performance differences. For instance, a 60 MHz version of processor of type X is twice as fast as a version of X with a clock speed of 30 MHz.

In general, when new and improved processors are being brought to the market, we would like to have an indication of their performance. What we want to know is how much faster a program can run on this new machine. In general, this question is difficult to answer for various reasons. Gathering statistics from production programs is almost impossible, since it requires the new computer to be completely installed in that production environment. Second, many computer systems run a mixture of programs, making judgment even more complicated.

However, measures of performance are still much wanted by users and vendors to have some means of comparing systems. The simplest performance indicators are the average instruction execution rate, denoted in **million instructions per second** (MIPS), and the average operation execution rate, denoted in **million floating-point operations per second** (MFLOPS). As a measure, the MIPS is not a very accurate one, since instruction sets can differ quite profoundly. Some computers can perform a certain operation with a single instruction, while others need several instructions to perform the same job. In order to compare average instruction execution times, we also have to give weight to the use of those instructions in typical programs. Still, the MIPS is a frequently (mis)used measure in comparisons between computer systems.

Within computer families comparisons between different models are a little easier, since they all share the same architecture. In this case, comparisons can be made relative to some model in the series. For estimating the CPU power this can be done quite well. However, different models may have a different computer organization. This can have serious effects on, for example, the I/O performance of the system. If a program is I/O bound, that is, if the transfer of data between the CPU and the disk dominates the total processing time of a program, putting more MIPS into the CPU has minor effects on the system's performance, while improving the I/O bandwidth would help a lot. A difficulty in this case is, that the I/O performance is dependent on many factors in the computer organization. Therefore, defining measures which can be used for comparison between the I/O performance of systems is not a simple task, not even within a family.

To obtain more accurate estimates of the real performance of a computer system, several measures have been developed, based on so-called **synthetic benchmark tests**. A benchmark suite is a relatively small collection of programs, of which the behavior approximates the behavior of a class of applications. The most well-known benchmark suites are the Whetstone and the Dhrystone (Serlin, 1986) benchmarks. The Whetstone is the older and is biased towards numerical types of programs, while the Dhrystone puts more emphasis on operations occurring in system programs. Currently, the so-called SPEC benchmarks are often used to indicate performance. These benchmarks consists of two programs: one for integer calculations and one for floating-point calculations. But even benchmark suites have serious flaws as indicators of performance. Because benchmark suites are programs written in a high-level programming language, the way that they are translated into machine instructions can have a large influence on the final result. Consequently, great care has to be taken in interpreting data obtained from executing benchmark suites.

Designing processors primarily from the perspective of performance is an approach that until recently has only been implicitly followed. With their textbook Hennessy and

Patterson (1990) introduced a new way of looking at matters. However, the reader should be warned: understanding performance issues is generally not easy, as it often requires a relatively strong background in mathematics. A general treatise on performance issues can be found in the classic textbook by Kobayashi (1979). A more recent presentation with a strong emphasis on designing performance analysis experiments, is discussed in Jain (1991).

Exercises

1. Derive a circuit implementation of the LOGUNIT8 function $f(\mathbf{a},\mathbf{b}) = \mathbf{a} + \mathbf{b}$ of Section 3.1.1.

2. Design a microprogram based on the components introduced in Section 3.1.1, for doing the calculation $\overline{((x \bullet y) + z)}$, where x is in W_1, y in W_2, z in W_3, and the result r is to be placed in W_4. What are the microroutines in this case?

3. Show how the simple dedicated calculator of Figure 3.3 can also be made to work by removing L_1 and connecting it to the output lines of LOGUNIT8.

4. Using the wiring scheme of the previous exercise, what would be the sequence of microinstructions for calculating $\mathbf{r} = \overline{(\mathbf{x} + \mathbf{y})} \bullet \mathbf{z}$?

5. *Can processors be constructed solely using memories? If so, why is this not done?

6. Explain the main reason for grouping microinstructions into a consecutive series of microroutines.

7. *Explain the principle of implementing microinstructions in the form of hardwired control and discuss the primary advantages and disadvantages of applying this technique.

8. By introducing instructions, we have obtained a separation between (1) telling a processor *what* it should do, and (2) letting designers of processors work out *how* things are to be done. Explain what is meant by this statement, and why such a separation is useful.

9. Provide arguments for combining data and instructions into a single memory.

10. Explain what the function of a program counter is, and why it is best to use a *counter* to implement that function.

11. Explain the basic components of the von Neumann computer, and what their function is.

12. What is meant by a *family* of processors?

13. If we would like to implement N instructions, what would be the size of the field for the operation code?

14. When data and instructions reside in the same main memory, how can a computer distinguish between data and instruction?

15. What type of addressing modes can be recognized when addressing operands? What are the advantages and disadvantages of each mode?

16. *Considering the transfers over the address and data lines in order to execute various instructions, explain what is meant by the "von Neumann bottleneck".

17. Explain the function of a bus and how we can logically subdivide its components. Also explain the role of a bus arbiter.

18. Explain the working of the daisy chain in the case of bus arbitration.

19. *At present, the time it needs to access main memory is lagging behind the improvements made with respect to the performance of processors. How would you imagine that this problem can be alleviated?

20. Explain the concept of an address space, and how this relates to memory-mapped I/O and non-memory-mapped I/O. What do you see as the main benefits of using memory-mapped I/O?

21. What is the distinction between a *double-density* and *high-density* floppy disk? Why isn't it such a good idea to try to use a double-density disk as a high-density one?

22. If you have an MS-DOS computer, typing in the command chkdsk returns information on the size of a so-called allocation unit, as well as the amount of allocation units available. Explain what is meant here.

23. *Many personal computers allow you to install a so-called RAM drive. This is a peripheral device similar to an ordinary disk drive, but which makes use only of main memory. Explain the principal working of this mechanism, as well as its main advantages and disadvantages.

Chapter 4

From hardware to software

In this chapter we will concentrate on the concept of programs. The objective is to show how you can actually program hardware, given an instruction set implemented by a processor. However, instruction sets are generally very low-level and make programming a rather tedious and error-prone process. This problem can be alleviated by making use of a high-level programming language. As we shall illustrate, such a programming language can be automatically translated to a low-level instruction set. What we have achieved then is something we refer to as a virtual processor. This concept will be further exploited in the succeeding chapters when discussing realization aspects of operating systems and communication systems.

4.1 Introduction

The material presented in the previous chapter has brought us a long way towards processing. At this point, we have the appropriate means for constructing programs in the form of a series of instructions that can be executed in an automated way.

4.1.1 Towards software solutions

In our discussion on microinstructions we argued that we are gradually diverting from hardware to things that can no longer be considered as being constructed solely of digital circuits. Microprograms, or **firmware** as we have referred to them, are constructed as series of bit strings that are (more or less permanently) stored, and that control the way that data (in the form of other bit strings) are manipulated in order to arrive at something that we feel is useful to us. On reflection, it should be clear that the approach of firmware construction offers us *flexibility*. Without having to change any digital circuits, or even change the wiring between these circuits, we are capable of implementing a different set of instructions by merely changing the processor's microprogram. From a somewhat different perspective, one might say that we can change the functionality of a processor by

133

replacing its microprogram. An important observation is that this change is *not* accomplished through hardware, but instead by changing the way that we *control* the hardware through bit strings.

But this approach can be taken several steps further. As we have said, a microprogram implements an instruction set that characterizes the behavior of a processor. It is through instructions that we again have the right means to control exactly what a computer does. This leads to the concept of a **program**: a series of instructions that can be executed in an automated way by a processor. Programs are also referred to as **software** as opposed to firmware and hardware.

But whereas microprograms are used to control the hardware that make up a single processor, we shall use programs to control the hardware that constitute a complete computer: processors, memories, and peripheral devices. In fact, we shall even use programs to control the way that computers communicate. Therefore, we need to say more about *how* computers can actually be programmed. In particular, we need to concentrate on two issues:

- How we express programs that can be executed by a processor.

- How we can have a processor that executes a program.

These two issues form the main theme of this chapter. Before we go into details, let's first briefly outline the approach that will be followed.

4.1.2   Expressing programs

Our first concern is to provide the right means to express programs. What we are thus seeking is a convenient **programming language**. A programming language is in many senses similar to ordinary languages, but with one important difference: programs expressed in a programming language describe something that can be executed by a processor. In particular, a program expresses precisely *what* a processor should do.

Machine languages

The most primitive programming languages are so-called **machine languages**. A machine language consists of the instructions that make up the instruction set as implemented by a processor. Moreover, each instruction is expressed as a bit string. Although it is primitive, we can indeed sensibly speak about a language in the sense that instructions adhere to a specific syntax and grammar. But expressing programs in a machine language is not something that many people favor, and for obvious reasons. Instead, rather than using bit strings, it is much more convenient to use a **symbolic** notation for each instruction. We have already encountered this form of expressing instructions in the previous chapter. Using a textual, symbolic representation for instructions instead of bit strings leads to the concept of a so-called **assembly language**. It should be clear that an assembly language and a machine language are tightly coupled. The former can be considered as an immediate representation of the instructions implemented by a processor. For this reason, we shall often hardly make a distinction between the two.

An example of an assembly language is discussed in Section 4.2. The purpose of presenting such a language is twofold. First, a concrete assembly language provides insight into what an instruction set looks like in practice, and thus about the basic functionality of a single processor. Our example language is derived from an existing one: we have merely left out specific details that are not important for the purposes of this book. Second, by using such a language to express some simple programs, it becomes apparent to what level of detail we need to go before we can get a processor to do something useful. And as we shall see, the level of detail is hopelessly inadequate to express solutions to complex problems. In fact, programs written in an assembly language are generally difficult to construct, and, except for the relatively simple ones that we shall discuss, are often even more difficult to comprehend.

High-level programming languages

Rather than expressing programs in an assembly language, we need something different. In particular, we need a so-called **high-level programming language** that allows us to concentrate on expressing solutions at an adequate level of abstraction. Such a programming language is presented in Section 4.3. Again, we have taken an example from real life by considering a subset of the programming language Ada which we have named BASAL. Our example programming language will be used throughout the remainder of this book to express software solutions to constructing computer systems and networks.

But what do we mean by an adequate level of abstraction? When we compare a high-level language such as BASAL to assembly languages, there are at least two striking differences. First, BASAL will allow us to express representations of common data in a way that is much more convenient than by using only bit strings. This is achieved through so-called **data abstraction**. To illustrate, suppose we want to represent an $N \times M$ matrix containing integer values. Assembly languages will provide us with little support to represent such a matrix easily. Using BASAL, however, we can write

```
type MATRIX is array (1..N,1..M) of INTEGER;
```

What we have done is express the matrix precisely as we imagine it: a data structure consisting of N rows and M columns where each element is an integer. We will see many more examples.

Second, high-level languages provide the facilities to **structure** our programs properly. In particular, where assembly languages only allow us to express a program as a single series of instructions, high-level languages provide the right means to hierarchically organize a program into logically coherent blocks of **program statements**, where a program statement is to be seen as an abstraction over a machine language instruction. Properly structuring programs is extremely important when expressing complex solutions. The clearer we are able to express a solution in the form of a program, the easier it becomes to comprehend that solution. And this is precisely what we wish to achieve when explaining the organization of computer systems and networks.

4.1.3   Executing programs

Having a convenient means to express programs is one thing; we also need to have a means to execute programs. Recall that the reason for using programs in the first place is that we wish to obtain solutions that can be constructed more easily than by using hardware alone. By subsequently executing programs, we control the way that the underlying computer operates. Expressing programs in a machine language is not going to lead to any fundamental problems of execution, because a machine language is always implemented by means of a processor. Using a symbolic notation as in the case of an assembly language requires that we at least transform our symbolic notation into instructions expressed as bit strings. Due to the tight coupling between an assembly language and a machine language, we need not expect many problems in such a transformation.

But problems will arise if we are going to express programs in a high-level programming language, for in that case, we may not assume that there is a processor available that can immediately do the execution. The point is, that a processor is capable only of executing a much more primitive machine language. It is here where we are faced with the problem of **program translation**. What we need to do in the end, is convert a program written in some high-level language into an *equivalent* program expressed in a machine language. If we were to do this manually, then not very much would have been gained by using a high-level language in the first place. Instead, the translation process itself should be automated. Programs that do this translation are called **compilers** and are briefly discussed in Section 4.4. This finally leads to the organization in Figure 4.1 in which three different layers with their interfaces are shown.

The lower and middle layers have been discussed in the previous two chapters. The lowest layer is that of digital circuits, which, as we said above, is pure hardware. As we have already indicated in Section 2.4.3, by adding (selection and) control pins to these circuits, and subsequently wiring them in different ways, we can select the functionality of the circuit. In this sense, these pins form an important part of the *programming interface* of digital circuits. The second layer consists of the microprogram that *implements* a machine language by *controlling* the setting of signals at the control pins of the digital circuits. The hardware and firmware form the real processor.

The third layer is the one that allows development of software solutions that are expressed at a convenient level of abstraction. In fact, as we shall see, our solutions are expressed at such a level that many details of the underlying hardware need not even be considered as part of the solution. Explaining a convenient high-level language and its relationship to hardware that can execute programs in that language is the main subject of this chapter. In order to execute programs written in a high-level language, these programs need to be translated into a machine language. If the translation process itself is automated, then, from a programmer's point of view, the machine language into which programs are translated is of little or no interest. In other words, the combination of an automated translator and a real processor provides a programmer with a **virtual processor** for the high-level language.

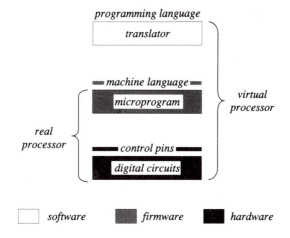

Figure 4.1 The relation between real and virtual processors.

In this chapter we are going to explore the concept of virtual processors. In order to do so, we need to discuss at least three subjects:

1. A machine language that we can use as interface to a real processor.

2. A high-level programming language that allows us to abstract from this machine language.

3. The translation of a high-level programming language into a machine language.

In the following three sections we shall discuss these subjects.

4.2   A primitive machine language

The first step we shall take towards software solutions is the introduction of a processor that implements a small set of instructions, which we refer to as **PRIMAL**: a **pri**mitive **ma**chine language.[1] PRIMAL is not an invention of our own. It is in fact (almost) a subset of a popular machine language implemented by the Motorola 680x0 family of processors. The 68000 machine language is generally considered a well-designed instruction set, inspired by another popular but now out-of-date machine language implemented by Digital's PDP-11 processors (Digital, 1975).

We have deliberately chosen to focus on a subset of the 68000 instruction set for reasons of illustration. By choosing an existing machine language as the basis for PRIMAL,

---

[1]It would have been more appropriate to say that PRIMAL is a **primitive assembly** language. As we have said, assembly languages are always directly based on a machine language, but represent instructions in a symbolic way. This makes it easier to construct programs. However, throughout this chapter we shall hardly make a distinction between the two.

you will nevertheless have the opportunity to experiment with writing your own programs if so desired. However, the 68000 instruction set does have some characteristics that we do not want to discuss here. Therefore, our PRIMAL language shall deviate somewhat from the original 68000 machine language. The examples we give in the succeeding sections can nevertheless be easily converted to executable programs (and in fact, they have first been constructed as such before writing them down in PRIMAL).

4.2.1   A basic PRIMAL instruction set

Let's first concentrate on a basic collection of instructions that will allow us to write simple PRIMAL programs. In order to do so, we need to say something about the registers of the PRIMAL processor.

Introduction

We assume that the PRIMAL language itself is implemented by a processor similar to the one discussed in the previous chapter. This so-called PRIMAL processor consists of the following registers.

- **Data registers.** There are eight so-called data registers available, denoted D0, ..., D7. These registers are truly *general-purpose* ones in the sense that they can be used to store all kinds of data, and that it does not matter which register you use for what purpose. These eight data registers are all 32 bits wide.

- **Address registers.** Apart from eight data registers, there are also eight address registers, denoted A0, ..., A7. As their name suggests, address registers can only be used to contain references to memory locations. In contrast to the data registers, not all address registers can be used for any purpose. In particular, register A7 is used as a so-called **stack pointer**. Its use will be explained in Section 4.2.2. Address registers are also 32 bits wide.

- **Program counter.** This register, denoted PC, is used to keep track of where we are during program execution. In particular, it always contains the address in main memory of the next instruction to be executed. As we have explained in Section 3.2, the program counter is always updated automatically. It will come as no surprise that the program counter is also 32 bits wide.

- **Status register.** A special register, also referred to as the **conditional code register**, and denoted CCR, contains additional information after an operation has been performed. For our purposes, we merely need to assume that CCR indicates whether the result of the last computational operation was zero or not. This register is used in combination with control flow instructions to be discussed below. The status register is assumed to contain only bit strings of length 8.

This is all you need to know about the registers of the PRIMAL processor when constructing programs.

Our next step consists of looking at some of the more important instructions. In the following discussion each instruction is only *symbolically* represented. We omit any details concerning its actual representation in the form of a bit string (these can be found in Motorola, 1986). The PRIMAL instruction set can be grouped into four different types of instructions: those for transferring data, for changing the order of execution, for doing computations, and finally, for handling subroutines. Here, we shall first concentrate only on the first three groups; subroutines are discussed in a separate section. In order to explain what exactly an instruction stands for, we will sometimes use the following notation that allows us to conveniently make a distinction between a register or memory location and its contents:

- If ADDR denotes a location in main memory, we use the notation M(ADDR) to denote the actual value stored at that location.

- If REG is one of PRIMAL's registers, then [REG] denotes its present contents. So, for example, to denote that register D4 contains the integer value 78, we write [D4] = 78. Combining this notation with the one above, M([REG]) denotes the value stored at the location of which the address is stored in REG.

- Replacing the contents of a register or memory location is denoted by means of a left-arrow "←". For example, the notation "[D4] ← 78" denotes that the contents of D4 is replaced by the integer value 78.

An instruction operates on one or more **operands**. In our notation, an instruction is written as a description of the operation, followed by the listing of the operand(s). The method used to specify the operands is the **addressing mode**, which we already encountered in Section 3.2.3. Now let's take a look at some of the basic instructions in PRIMAL.

Data transfer

Basically, there is just a single data transfer instruction, referred to as the **MOVE** instruction. Keeping the symbolic name used in the base language of PRIMAL, the 68000 assembly language, the MOVE instruction essentially comes in just one form:

      MOVE src, dst

which effectively copies the bit string stored as a 32-bit word at the location identified as the source src, to the destination identified as dst. Let's see how the source and destination can be identified. First, for our purposes, we require that when using the MOVE instruction at least one of the two operands should refer to one of the eight data registers, or otherwise to one of the eight address registers. Using this restriction, we can now take a closer look at LOAD and STORE instructions as mentioned in Chapter 3.

LOAD instructions.   LOAD instructions basically have five different forms. The following are supported, with their meaning explained after the vertical bar "|":

(L1)	MOVE #number, Rx	[Rx] ← number
(L2)	MOVE Rx, Ry	[Ry] ← [Rx]
(L3)	MOVE address, Rx	[Rx] ← M(address)
(L4)	MOVE (Ay), Rx	[Rx] ← M([Ay])
(L5)	MOVE offset(Ay), Rx	[Rx] ← M([Ay] + offset)

In these cases, Rx refers to either a data or an address register. Likewise, Ay always refers to one of the eight address registers. The meaning of each instruction is as follows.

- **(L1):** This is an example of an instruction employing **immediate addressing**. The effect is that an integer number as given in the instruction is copied into register Rx. Numbers can be represented in several ways. A number such as "#12" is considered as a decimal number, whereas "#%0110" is interpreted as the binary number $0110_2 = 6_{10}$. The term "immediate" refers to the fact that the operand is immediately available: it need not be transferred from another register or main memory.

- **(L2):** Execution of this instruction yields that the data contained in register Rx is copied to register Ry. The instruction is said to use **(register) direct addressing**. Anticipating our further discussion, we note that an instruction of this type can equally be qualified as a STORE instruction.

- **(L3):** Instruction (L3) is quite similar to (L2), except that the data that is to be copied to register Rx is now taken from the memory location address. It employs so-called **(memory) direct addressing**.

- **(L4):** This is an example of **(register) indirect addressing**. The address stored in register Ay identifies the location containing the actual data.

- **(L5):** This instruction *calculates* an address from where to copy data for register Rx. In this example, we have that Rx will be loaded with the data that is found at the location [Ay] + offset. The addressing mode exemplified by this instruction is referred to as **(register) indexed addressing**. Note, by the way, that we can use an address register only to denote the source.

STORE instructions.   The STORE instructions are used to copy data from registers to main memory and have three forms:

(S1)	MOVE Rx, address	M(address) ← [Rx]
(S2)	MOVE Rx, (Ay)	M([Ay]) ← [Rx]
(S2)	MOVE Rx, offset(Ay)	M([Ay] + offset) ← [Rx]

Instruction (S1) is comparable to (L3). Using direct addressing, it stores the data or address contained in register Rx at memory location address. Indirect addressing is used in (S2). The address or data contained in Rx is copied to the memory location found in register Ay. Finally, indexed addressing is employed in (S3), similar to the load instruction (L5).

There is one strange thing about PRIMAL when it comes to addressing and word length that deviates from the way we have been talking about instructions so far. Because all our

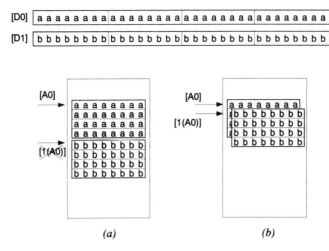

Figure 4.2 The effect of indexed addressing in PRIMAL.

registers have length 32, it would seem that main memory is organized into words having a size of 4 bytes. Well, this is not true: the PRIMAL processor assumes that memory can be addressed per byte. The only thing is that each instruction for transferring data copies 4 *consecutive* bytes into or from a register. This becomes particularly important to note when using indexed addressing. To illustrate, assume that we have the following code fragment

```
MOVE  D0, (A0)
MOVE  D1, 1(A0)
```

The idea is that we first copy the data contained in register D0 to the memory location identified by register A0, and store the contents of D1 in the *next* location, as illustrated in Figure 4.2(a). However, what actually happens is shown in Figure 4.2(b). The data stored in D1 is written partially over the data just stored. The correct code should have been

```
MOVE  D0, (A0)
MOVE  D1, 4(A0)
```

Control flow instructions.

This group of instructions is used to change the order of execution. First, we have a so-called **JUMP** instruction which takes the form

```
JMP     address          | JuMP unconditionally to address
```

After executing this instruction, the processor will continue with executing the instruction that is stored at the memory location address. However, this instruction is not used often in practice. Instead, so-called relative jump instructions, or **BRANCH** instructions as they are called, are actually used. One such BRANCH instruction that we shall encounter is

BRA   offset | BRAnch to the address at 'offset' units

The effect of executing this instruction is that the selected *next* instruction is chosen offset memory locations away from the current instruction. In other words, the effect is that

BRA offset $\equiv$ [PC] $\leftarrow$ [PC] + offset

Related to this instruction are the following two instructions:

BEQ   offset | Branch if EQual to zero
BNE   offset | Branch if Not Equal to zero

which are so-called *conditional* BRANCH instructions. In this case, the instruction located at memory location [PC] + offset will be selected as the next one to execute *only if* the register CCR indicates that the result of the last computation operation was zero or non-zero, respectively. Otherwise, the instruction following this BRANCH instruction will be selected as the next one to execute. There are many other conditional BRANCH instructions available in 68000 assembly languages, but as far as our PRIMAL subset is concerned, the above two will suffice for illustration purposes.

Computation instructions

These instructions actually set the ALU to work. Most of the instructions take two operands and are available in two forms:

(C1)   <oper>#number, Dx
(C2)   <oper>Dx, Dy

where "<oper>" stands for a binary operation such as addition, subtraction, etc. The first form (C1) operates directly on a given number, whereas the second (C2) operates on the value of a register. In both cases, the value in the second register is *updated* by the first operand. So, for example,

ADD   Dx, Dy

adds the contents of register Dx to the contents of Dy, i.e. [Dy] $\leftarrow$ [Dx] + [Dy]. Similarly,

SUB   #12, Dx

updates the value of register Dx by subtracting 12 from it. The computation instructions that require two operands are: ADD (addition), SUB (subtraction), DIVS (division), MULS (multiplication), AND (bitwise AND) and OR (bitwise OR).

▷ A comment on the relationship between PRIMAL and the 68000 instruction set, is in order. The computational operations we discuss here generally are in various forms. In particular, the 68000 instruction set makes a distinction between operands that have length 8, 16, or 32. And, as you may imagine, making this distinction indeed does make sense. Recall our discussion in Chapter 2 on the representation of negative numbers when having to deal with finite bit strings. In our case, we will assume that the operations work as they should, and we will be ignoring the length of their operands. For the programming examples we are about to see our notation is generally correct, and the programs will work well. In practice, subtle adaptations will generally be necessary. The interested reader is referred to Clements (1994) for further details.

Some simple examples

Before we continue, let's consider some example programs to illustrate what a PRIMAL program might look like.

Example 4.1. Suppose we have a number X stored at memory location 1000. Incrementing X with 12 can then be done by means of the following program (text that follows the vertical bar "|" is merely comment).

```
MOVE  1000,D0      | Load value of X into D0: [D0] ← M(1000)
ADD   #12,D0       | [D0] ← [D0] + 12
MOVE  D0,1000      | Store result back into X: M(1000) ← [D0]
```

The first MOVE instruction uses direct addressing. The data stored at location 1000 is copied into register D0. We then subsequently add 12 to the value contained in this register, and the result is then copied back again to location 1000.

□

In this example, we simply state that we have a variable X at memory location 1000. What we are stating is that X denotes a memory location (namely, 1000), or, in other words, is a *placeholder*, that we consider to be variable with respect to its contents. In what follows, we shall abstract from exact locations when we speak about variables. In particular, if X, Y, and Z denote distinct variables we simply assume that "X", "Y", and "Z" are just *synonyms* or *aliases* for distinct memory locations. In fact, this is completely consistent with the way that variables are dealt with in programming languages.

Example 4.2. Assume we need to perform the calculation $Y \leftarrow X^3$. This can be done as follows by using D1 for storing the intermediate and final result:

```
MOVE  X,D0      | Load X into D0: [D0] ← M(X)
MOVE  D0,D1     | Store X¹ into D1: [D1] ← [D0]
MULS  D0,D1     | Store X² into D1: [D1] ← [D0]*[D1]
MULS  D0,D1     | Store X³ into D1: [D1] ← [D0]*[D1]
MOVE  D1,Y      | Store the result into Y: M(Y) ← [D1]
```

This looks much like our previous example, except that we are using the symbolic name "X" to denote the place that we have associated with variable X. Note that register D1 is updated by first multiplying it with the contents of D0, and storing the result back into D1. In PRIMAL, these two steps are implemented by means of a single instruction.

□

```
        MOVE  X,D0          | Load X into D0
        MOVE  N,D1          | Load N into D1
        MOVE  D0,D2         | Store X¹ into D2
        SUB   #1,D1         | Calculate N ← N − 1: [D1] ← [D1] - 1
        BEQ   END           | If N = 0, we are finished, so continue with the instruc-
                            | tion labeled at 'END'

CALC:   MULS  D0,D2         | Calculate X^{K+1} ← X · X^K
        SUB   #1,D1         | Calculate N ← N − 1
        BNE   CALC          | Continue if N ≠ 0

END:    MOVE  D2,Y          | Store the result into Y
```

Listing 4.1 A PRIMAL program for calculating X^N.

If we followed the approach shown in the example above, it would become quite tedious to calculate, for example, $X \leftarrow X^{100}$. In that case we would have to repeat the instruction

MULS D0,D1

numerous times. Repeating instructions can be elegantly solved by using BRANCH instructions. Consider the following example.

Example 4.3. We want to calculate $Z \leftarrow X^N$ where $N > 0$. The idea, of course, is that we repeatedly calculate an intermediate result $X^{K+1} \leftarrow X \cdot X^K$, where X^K has been calculated in the previous step. Now look at the program shown in Listing 4.1.

This piece of PRIMAL code makes use of so-called **labels**. A label is a simple means of attaching a symbolic name to a location containing an instruction. In most assembly languages, a label is followed by a colon. For example, the label CALC identifies the location of the instruction

MULS D0,D2

We use labels in combination with control flow instructions. In particular, rather than specify the address of the next instruction to execute, we identify the instruction by means of a label. So, for example, the execution of the instruction

BEQ   END

yields that the status register CCR is first checked to see if the last performed operation had a zero result. If this is the case, then the first instruction of the next series of instructions that will be executed is identified by the label END, which, in our example, coincides with the instruction

MOVE D2,Y

Now, what is seen in this example is that we simply decrement the value of N each time we do an iteration. As soon as N becomes 0, we know that the work is completed.

□

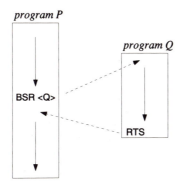

Figure 4.3 The principle of calling and executing a subroutine in PRIMAL.

It should be clear by now what simple PRIMAL programs look like. In the next section we shall see how more complex programs can be constructed by introducing the concept of subroutines.

4.2.2 Subroutines in PRIMAL

An important concept for any programming language is that of a **subroutine**, also referred to as a **procedure** or **function**. A subroutine is just another program, but whose instructions can be executed on behalf of some other program. The principle is shown in Figure 4.3. By executing the so-called **BRANCH-TO-SUBROUTINE** instruction:

      BSR   label | Branch to SubRoutine starting at "label"

execution continues with the series of instructions starting at the indicated label. The label itself is calculated as an address relative to the current value of the program counter, i.e. label = [PC] + offset. As soon as the **RETURN-FROM-SUBROUTINE** instruction

      RTS | ReTurn from Subroutine

is encountered, execution continues where it had previously left off.

Subroutines are extremely important when constructing large programs, no matter what language you are using. And although the concept may seem simple at first, it does take a special mechanism in order to realize it. In practice, many low-level machine languages incorporate a so-called **stack** to this end, and which is discussed next.

The concept of a stack

A stack is a collection of ordered elements, such that removing elements from a stack can only be done in the *reversed* order in which they were added to that stack. A stack can thus be seen as an abstract means for *storing* data. It has only two associated operations: *push* by which an item is said to be put on top of the stack, and the operation *pop* by

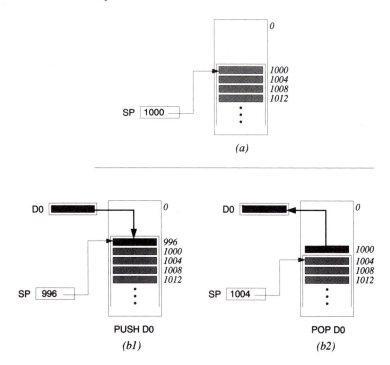

Figure 4.4 The organization of stacks in PRIMAL. (a) The initial situation; the effect of pushing an item onto the stack is shown in (b1); that of popping an item in (b2).

which the item on the top of the stack can be removed again. Before we explain how the concept of a stack plays an important role in subroutines, let's first see how stacks can be produced in PRIMAL.

Any stack in PRIMAL is associated with a series of consecutive memory locations. In order to identify a stack, we need a so-called **stack pointer**. A stack pointer is a reference to the **top** of a stack. It refers to the memory location of the element that can be popped from the stack, or on top of which a new element can be placed. To this end, PRIMAL uses one of the eight address registers, namely A7, as its general stack pointer. Due to its special role, A7 is also symbolically denoted as SP. Another issue that needs to be agreed is how stacks shrink and grow. In other words, if we *pop* an item from the stack, what happens to the contents of the stack pointer? If we decide to *increment* its value, then this means that a stack *shrinks* towards the higher locations in address space. This is the same as saying that a stack *grows* towards the lower memory locations. In PRIMAL, we assume that stacks are indeed organized according to this shrink and growth scenario. This is illustrated in Figure 4.4.

Now, in order to *push* an item onto the stack we need merely use the special **PUSH** instruction. To illustrate, the instruction

```
PUSH   D0
```

first adjusts the value of the stack pointer, and then copies the data stored in register D0 to the (new) top of the stack, as shown in Figure 4.4(b1). More formally, we have that

PUSH Rx   ≡   [SP] ← [SP] − 4;   M([SP]) ← [Rx]

where Rx can be any data or address register. The semicolon in this case denotes that we *first* adjust the stack pointer, and *then* store the value on the stack. Likewise, in order to pop an item from the stack, we use the **POP** instruction:

```
POP    Rx
```

which copies the data on top of the stack to register Rx, and adjusts the stack pointer accordingly. Again, we can express this more formally as

POP Rx   ≡   [Rx] ← M([SP]);   [SP] ← [SP] + 4

In this case, note that the semicolon indicates that we *first* copy the data from the top of the stack to the appropriate register, and *then* adjust the stack pointer. This is precisely the opposite order to the PUSH instruction.

▷   A comment is in order here. The 68000 machine language, and thus also PRIMAL, has, in fact, no special stack operations. In order to manipulate the stack, you should use a special form of indexed addressing instead. Without going into too many details, the correct way for pushing an item onto the stack would be to use the instruction

```
        MOVE   Rx, −(SP)
```

What effectively happens is that *before* the actual data transfer takes place, the stack pointer is decremented by 4 so that it refers to the right memory location to store the 4 bytes contained in Rx.

Similarly, popping an item from the stack can be done by the following instruction:

```
        MOVE   (SP)+, Rx
```

In this case, the data stored at the top of the stack is *first* copied into the specified register, after which the value of the stack pointer is incremented (implying that the top of the stack is lowered).

Stacks and subroutines

We can now explain how branching to a subroutine works in PRIMAL. The first point you have to realize is that with each program we associate precisely one stack. When executing the instruction

```
        BSR    label
```

```
POWER:  POP    A6          | Save the return address in A6
        POP    D1          | Save the value of P in D1
        POP    D0          | And save that of U in D0

        MOVE   D0,D2       | Store U¹ into D2
        SUB    #1,D1       | Calculate P ← P − 1
        BEQ    ENDPOW      | If P = 0, we are finished

CALC:   MULS   D0,D2       | Calculate U^{K+1}
        SUB    #1,D1       | Calculate P ← P − 1
        BNE    CALC        | Continue if P ≠ 0

ENDPOW:PUSH    D2          | Push the result onto the stack
       PUSH    A6          | As well as the return address
       RTS                 | And return
```

Listing 4.2 An alternative implementation for X^N.

where label indicates an address that can be found at, say, offset locations from the current location, the current value of the program counter is pushed onto the program's stack, after which the value of the program counter is incremented by the value offset. In other words, branching to a subroutine has (almost) the same effect as executing the two instructions

```
PUSH  PC
BRA   offset
```

with the difference that the execution of BSR performs the two instructions above as a single instruction.

As soon as the RETURN instruction RTS is executed, the value of the program counter is restored by popping the stack. This immediately leads to the selection of the instruction that initially followed the branch instruction. Thus, execution of RTS is similar to executing

```
POP   PC
```

Subroutine examples

To illustrate the semantics of combining the stack and subroutines, consider the following example.

Example 4.4. Our first consideration is to adapt the program of Example 4.3 so that it implements the function $power(U,P) = U^P$ by means of a subroutine. To that end, we assume that it is necessary to push the value of U onto the stack, followed by the value of P just before calling the subroutine. The result of the subroutine, i.e. U^P, will be pushed onto the stack just before a return is made to the calling program. Now look at the PRI-MAL code shown in Listing 4.2.

```
MAIN:   PUSH  X              Push value of X onto the stack
        PUSH  N              Push value of N onto the stack
        BSR   POWER          Branch to POWER
        POP   D0             Pop the result
        MOVE  D0,X           Store the result back into X

        PUSH  Y              Push value of Y onto the stack
        PUSH  M              Push value of M onto the stack
        BSR   POWER          Branch to POWER
        POP   D0             Pop the result
        MOVE  D0,Y           Store the result back into Y

        MOVE  X,D0           Store new value of X into D0
        MOVE  Y,D1           Store new value of Y into D1
        ADD   D0,D1          Store X + Y into D1
        MOVE  D1,Z           Store the result into Z
```

Listing 4.3 Calling the subroutine POWER twice in a row.

In order to understand what this program does, keep in mind that as soon as a BRANCH instruction

```
        BSR   POWER
```

has been executed, we assume that the stack has on its top the address of the next instruction to be executed when returning from the subroutine, followed by the value of the parameter P, and the value of U. By first popping these three values in the right order, we bring the stack into its original state. The major part of POWER looks the same as that of Example 4.3. The final series of instructions starting at label ENDPOW take care of the stack. First, we push the result of our calculation onto the stack, as well as the previously saved return address. Executing RTS will return us to our original position by popping the return address. The top of the stack now contains the calculated result.

□

Using the subroutine POWER we can now easily implement more intricate functions.

Example 4.5. We want to calculate $Z \leftarrow X^N + Y^M$ by using the program in Example 4.4. The idea is quite simple. We first calculate $X \leftarrow X^N$, and later $Y \leftarrow Y^M$. This leads to the PRIMAL program shown in Listing 4.3.

In the first section, we calculate $X \leftarrow X^N$. To that end, we can simply push the values for X and N onto the stack and execute subroutine POWER, and will find that the result is now on the top of the stack. Simply popping the stack, and copying the result back to X, accomplishes what we wanted in the first place. The rest of the program should now be clear.

□

4.2.3   Discussion

The examples discussed so far illustrate how programs can be constructed in PRIMAL. And although it is seen that even simple calculations require many instructions to be executed, it should be clear that our small PRIMAL instruction set is powerful enough to handle more intricate calculations. However, it seems that we are running into a number of problems. First, expressing calculations in PRIMAL is not very comprehensible. In other words, it is difficult to determine *what* a program does simply by looking at it. In this sense, PRIMAL, and any other machine language, is considered a *low-level* programming language. From a programming perspective this is a problem that should not be underestimated. The main issue is that constructing a program that does what it is expected to do has now become a serious engineering problem. Also, as these programs are difficult to comprehend at first, changing them is no longer a trivial task.

Another problem is that our programs will work only on PRIMAL processors. This is really a problem, because our solutions seem to be general enough for any reasonable processor. In other words, we have found general solutions, but have implemented them for only a single processor. Consequently, we will have to do our programming work all over again if we have a different processor at our disposal. As we have mentioned in Section 4.1 this implies that generally useful programs such as word processors will have to be rewritten entirely when adapting them for various real processors. This is not acceptable.

It is clear that the source of the problems we are encountering is the lack of abstraction that can be provided by our PRIMAL machine language. In other words, the *expressive power* of PRIMAL, or any machine language, is simply not enough to describe software solutions in a comprehensive and sufficiently abstract manner. There are too many details that we are forced to take into account that, in fact, have nothing to do with the solution we wish to describe. As we have argued in Section 4.1, the solution to this problem is to be found in high-level programming languages. Such languages (1) provide us with the right level of abstraction, and (2) can be translated in an automated way into machine languages, thus still allowing us to execute programs. In the next section we introduce such a high-level language.

4.3   A structured programming language

Our intention at this point is to introduce a high-level programming language which we have called BASAL. There are two main reasons for introducing BASAL. The first, and to us the most important reason is that we need a vehicle to express implementation issues of computer and communication systems at a more convenient level of abstraction than is possible with the material discussed so far. This implies that it is important that you attain a *reading knowledge* of our language. In other words, you need to know what BASAL programs do; it is not necessary to be able to write them yourself.

Second, constructing advanced computer and communication systems is not just a question of building the right hardware. As we have said, most of the effort is spent in getting the software to work. Software is seldom written in machine languages like PRIMAL. Instead, high-level languages are used for this purpose. By introducing a simple high-level language, we want to illustrate two things: (1) how we can construct machines merely by using software, and (2) how these abstract machines can be implemented by low-level machine languages such as PRIMAL. The first issue is, in fact, the topic of all the material yet to follow. The second issue will be further discussed in Section 4.4.

We have no intention of teaching you how to construct software. Instead, our focus in this section will be on providing you with a reading knowledge of a programming language that will serve our purposes. Here, we informally introduce BASAL, which stands for a **ba**sic **s**ubset of the **a**da **l**anguage. BASAL is derived from Ada (ANSI, 1983), an advanced programming language, and certainly not the most simple one to be learned by a novice. However, Ada is well established and, as we shall see below, suitable to be used as a vehicle for our purposes relating to system and communication software. Rather than use all its features, we shall restrict ourselves to a rather small but specific subset. Most of BASAL's language constructs will be explained in this section. In later chapters we shall extend our descriptions as appropriate. We shall have more to say about Ada in our discussion at the end of this chapter.

When discussing developing programs it should be clear by now that a distinction can be made between two different concepts: data and instructions that manipulate data. What we are seeking at this point is a convenient means of describing (1) what the data we wish to manipulate looks like, and (2) how this data is manipulated. We first concentrate on a notation for representing data. How data can be manipulated is discussed in Section 4.3.2. Then, we will describe complete programs in Sections 4.3.3 and 4.3.4.

4.3.1   Data types and variables

As we have said, in order to describe programs, we need a way to describe the data that is manipulated. An important concept fundamental to most high-level programming languages is that of a **data type**. We have already encountered a few data types such as integers, characters, etc. A data type is to be seen as a *definition* of a collection of abstract values, together with the operations by which these values can be manipulated. To illustrate, consider the character data type. This data type defines exactly what we mean by a character (namely the symbols, or values, "a", "b", "c", etc.), as well as the operations that can be used. An example of such an operation (and indeed, which only makes sense in the case of characters) is the operation *ascii*, defined as:

$$ascii(x) = the \text{ ASCII } code \ of \ character \ x$$

So, for example, using Table 2.3 on page 37, we have that $ascii(\text{"a"}) = 97$, and likewise, $ascii(\text{"8"}) = 56$.

In machine languages however, there is essentially only one data type: the bit string. In this sense, you might say that the only thing we have been discussing so far is how we can *represent* our common data types in the form of finite bit strings. This is a situation we want to change. In the following two subsections we are going to take a closer look at how we can define and represent, on the one hand, **simple data types**, and, on the other, **composed data types**.

Predefined, simple data types

An important simple data type that is available in most programming languages, is the integer. BASAL is no exception. In order to express that we are dealing with an integer variable k, we use the notation

    k : INTEGER;

Variables are also referred to as **data objects,** and we say that k has been **declared** as an INTEGER variable. The integer data type in BASAL is said to be **predefined**: it simply comes with the language. As we shall see, there are only a few predefined data types – most types will have to be explicitly defined. With integers, the arithmetic operators "+" (addition), "–" (subtraction), "*" (multiplication), and "/" (division) can be used in combination with integer variables. The result of using these operations is, again, always an integer value.

Example 4.6. Valid expressions in BASAL are, for example:

$$2 + 3, k - 6, (i / 2) * 2,$$

where we assume that k and i are INTEGER variables. Note that if i has the value 7 "i/2" yields the integer result 3. Integer division always rounds off to the nearest integer smaller than or equal to the exact result.

□

Another predefined data type in BASAL is the character. Expressing that some variable c can only take characters as its values is carried out by means of the notation

    c : CHARACTER;

Analogous to integers, we say that we have *declared* c to be of type CHARACTER. Character values (or literals, as they are more commonly called) are expressed by using single quotes. For example, the character "a" is expressed in BASAL as 'a'. Characters are assumed to be encoded according the ASCII code. Only a few operations are defined for characters. In order to get the ASCII value of, for example, the character "a" we can write

    CHARACTER'POS('a');

which yields the result 97. In other words, the expression above is the way we represent the function *ascii*(x) discussed before. Likewise, by writing

    CHARACTER'VAL(65);

we obtain the character "A" which has ASCII code 65. We will find these two character operations in some of the examples to follow.

The last predefined data type that we will discuss here, is the Boolean. Using our BASAL notation, a Boolean variable b can take on only two values TRUE and FALSE, and should be declared in the usual way:

    b : BOOLEAN;

The Boolean operators 'not', 'and', 'or', and 'xor' apply to Boolean values and yield Boolean results. Boolean values also result when using the relational operators '>', '≥', '≠', '<', '≤', '=' in conjunction with two integers.[2] These relations adhere to the conventional mathematical semantics.

Defining your own simple data types

Besides using predefined types, BASAL also provides notations for defining your own data types. Defining a data type D essentially means specifying the elements of D. There are various ways of doing this, but probably the most straightforward is simply naming all the elements (note that this may not be the most convenient way of defining a data type – and, in fact, it may not always be possible). Where a data type consists of a finite number of elements we can use a so-called **enumeration type declaration** for defining the data type. For example, a data type containing symbols for the days of the week can be defined in BASAL as follows:

    type DAY **is** (MON, TUE, WED, THU, FRI, SAT, SUN);

Using this notation, we have expressed that the data type DAY consists precisely of the seven elements MON . . . SUN. It is now easy to talk about variables of this data type, and which can be declared in the usual way.

But what if we want to specify a data type that consists of too many values to name explicitly? In that case, one possibility is to base your definition on an already specified data type. In terms of BASAL, you can declare a **subtype**. To illustrate, in order to define a restricted set of positive integers, we can declare a subtype CARDINAL as follows:

    subtype CARDINAL **is** INTEGER **range** 0..65535;

What we have expressed here is that any cardinal variable is just the same as an integer variable, except that it cannot take on negative values, nor values that are greater than 65535. We shall encounter more examples of enumeration types and subtypes in later sections.

---

[2]We note that our notation here deviates somewhat from that of Ada.

Composed data types

Besides simple data types such as integers, Booleans, and characters, BASAL also provides notations for defining so-called *composed data types*. A composed data type is (at first instance) constructed from simple data types, and is in two basic forms.

Array data types.   First, BASAL provides a notation to define *indexed sets* by means of an **array declaration**. To illustrate, suppose the data we wish to manipulate is in fact a finite bit string of length 8. Now *all* bit strings of length 8 can be considered as an indexed set of bits, each bit being a variable that can take on the value 0 or 1. This brings us to the two data types BIT and BITSTRING8 that can be declared in BASAL as follows:

> **subtype** BIT **is** INTEGER **range** 0..1;
> **type** BITSTRING8 **is array** (0..7) **of** BIT;

Now suppose we are using a variable bitstring, which we have declared as

> bitstring : BITSTRING8;

In this case, bitstring itself consists of eight simple variables, denoted as bitstring(0), bitstring(1), ..., bitstring(7), respectively. Each of these variables is of type BIT. The **index set** of type BITSTRING8 has been defined as $0\ldots7$.

As another example, suppose we wish to define a data type for representing the usual number of working hours per day of the week. In that case, it would be convenient if we could use our previous definition of the data type DAY as an index. In fact, this is possible, for we can write

> **type** WORKING_HOURS **is array** (DAY) **of** CARDINAL;

If we had a variable work of data type WORKING_HOURS we could then use the notation work(MON) to refer to the number of working hours on an ordinary Monday.

Record data types.   Similarly, we can also declare so-called **record data types**. Record data types are – in principle – composed of *different* data types. This is best explained by an example.

Example 4.7. Suppose we wish to have a representation of characters as displayed on an ordinary screen. In particular, we assume that characters can be displayed either in reverse video or not, but can also be displayed in a normal, bold, underlined, or italic typeface. We can then represent each position on the screen by means of the following record data type:

```
type CHARACTER_MODE is (NORMAL, BOLD, UNDERLINE, ITALIC);
type CHARACTER_DISPLAY is
   record
      char : CHARACTER;
      reverseVideo : BOOLEAN;
      format : CHARACTER_MODE;
   end record ;
```

yielding a data type CHARACTER_DISPLAY which is composed from a character, a Boolean, and an enumerated type CHARACTER_MODE.

□

The different components of a record are denoted as **fields**, and can be referred to by using a dot notation. For example, if we had the variable declaration

```
charDisplay : CHARACTER_DISPLAY;
```

then charDisplay.char denotes the actual character variable associated with charDisplay. Similarly, if charDisplay.reverseVideo has the value TRUE, then this would mean that charDisplay.char would be shown in reverse video on the screen.

Combining arrays and records. Of course, it is also possible to denote complex data types by combining the notations introduced so far.

Example 4.8. Assume that our screen consists of 72 rows and 120 columns, where the rows are counted down-wise, and the columns from left to right. This means, for example, that the upper-left corner of the screen can be represented by the coordinates $(1,1)$ and the lower-right corner by the coordinates $(72, 120)$. Representing an entire screen is then easily expressed in BASAL by the following declarations:

```
type DISPLAY_ROW is array (1..120) of CHARACTER_DISPLAY;
type DISPLAY is array (1..72) of DISPLAY_ROW;
```

Suppose, then, that we had the following variable declaration:

```
screen : DISPLAY;
```

In this case, screen(1)(120).char would denote the character that is displayed in the upper-right corner.

□

Using array declarations for defining the fields of a record is, of course, also possible. To illustrate, consider a completely different representation of a screen by considering complete rows, instead of only a single position.

Example 4.9. We assume that a screen is now represented by entire rows, each row consisting of 120 characters. We first introduce a separate data type for representing rows as follows:

```
type CHARACTER_MODE is (NORMAL, BOLD, UNDERLINE, ITALIC);
type DISPLAY_ROW is array (1..120) of CHARACTER;
type ROW_OF_CHARACTER is
  record
    column : DISPLAY_ROW;
    reverseVideo : BOOLEAN;
    format : CHARACTER_MODE;
  end record ;
```

It should be clear that we have lost some flexibility here. In this case, a row can only be displayed, for example, in reverse video or not; it is not possible to just select one or several characters in that row to be displayed otherwise.

Representing an entire screen can now be done by means of the following data type declaration, and accompanying variable:

```
type DISPLAY_BY_ROW is array (1..72) of ROW_OF_CHARACTER;
screen : DISPLAY_BY_ROW;
```

In this case, the character in the upper-right corner of the screen is represented by the variable screen(1).column(120).

□

We shall encounter several examples of (combinations of) record and array data types in subsequent sections.

4.3.2 Statements

So far, we have introduced only a notation for defining data types and variables. Nothing has been said about the way we can describe operations on variables. In this section we shall start by discussing the most elementary ones, referred to as **statements**. Statements are comparable to instructions in the sense that they are assumed to be *executed*. However, where program counters are used to indicate precisely which instruction is to be executed next, there is nothing comparable in high-level programming languages. The reason for this is that although statements are executed one by one, statements in high-level programming languages may be contained in other statements. This situation does not occur in machine languages. Rather than going into these matters here, we shall make this point clear in the following sections.

Again, we start with the simple notations for operations in BASAL: the statements for assignment and control flow.

Assignment statement

An **assignment statement** is used to express the assignment of a value to a variable. This is denoted in BASAL by means of a special symbol ":=" as in:

```
k := 2;
```

Assuming that k is an integer variable, this assignment expresses that the present value of the variable k is *replaced* by a new one, namely 2. The semicolon at the end of the assignment is important. It indicates the *termination of the execution* of the assignment. This is relevant when we have to specify a series of assignments, as in:

```
k := 2; b := TRUE; c := 'a';
```

In this case, the assignments are executed in sequence. First, k is assigned the value 2, then b becomes TRUE, and finally c is assigned the literal 'a'. Again, note how we are implicitly assuming some kind of execution mechanism by which these assignments take place, and in the order just mentioned.

Related to the assignment statement is the **initialization** of variables. In BASAL it is possible to assign an initial value to a variable which is specified as part of its declaration. For example, after declaring

```
k : INTEGER := 0;
```

we have not only declared a new integer variable k but have also provided it with the initial value 0.

Initialization is not only a convenient means for providing an initial value for a variable. The same mechanism must be used for declaring so-called **constants**. A constant is considered a variable that is initialized once, but whose value can never be replaced. For example, if we wanted to express the value "0" by means of a constant ZERO, the way to do this in BASAL would be:

```
ZERO : constant INTEGER := 0;
```

Let's illustrate this by means of another example.

Example 4.10. Suppose we wish to initialize our variable screen as declared in Example 4.8. In particular, we assume that the screen is initially to be entirely blank, for which we can use the character representation of a single space. Our aim is to use a constant BLANK for this purpose, which then leads to the following declarations in BASAL (see also Table 2.3 on page 37):

```
BLANK : constant CHARACTER := CHARACTER'VAL(32);

type CHARACTER_MODE is (NORMAL, BOLD, UNDERLINE, ITALIC);
type CHARACTER_DISPLAY is
   record
      char : CHARACTER := BLANK;
      reverseVideo : BOOLEAN := FALSE;
      format : CHARACTER_MODE := NORMAL;
   end record ;

type DISPLAY_ROW is array (1..120) OF CHARACTER_DISPLAY;
type DISPLAY is array (1..72) of DISPLAY_ROW;
```

Recall that CHARACTER'VAL(x) stands for the character associated with ASCII value x. In our case, BLANK will be correctly initialized as the character representing a space. Now in this case, a declaration such as

    screen : DISPLAY;

will automatically initialize the variable screen in such a way that it represents a completely blank screen.

$\square$

We shall encounter initializations and constant declarations a number of times in the example programs yet to follow.

Control flow statements

Our notation for describing operations assumes, as in the case of processors, that statements are executed in the order in which they appear in a description. In order to alter the order of execution we shall make use of a number of **control flow statements**. Control flow statements are basically in two forms, conditional statements and repetitive statements.

The conditional statement.   The conditional statement, also referred to as the **if statement**, is used to *guard* the execution of a series of statements, in the sense that execution will only take place if some condition is met. To illustrate, consider the following example, which is a rather strange way of calculating the difference between two integer variables m and n:

```
if m < n then d := n − m;
elsif m > n then d := m − n;
else d := 0;
end if ;
```

The semantics of a conditional statement are quite obvious. Starting with the evaluation of the first Boolean expression (in our case "m < n"), the statements associated with the Boolean expression that evaluates to TRUE the first time are executed. If neither of the first two conditions holds, the statements of the ELSE-part are executed. So, if m had the value 5 and n had the value 3 when the statement above was executed, then only the statement "d := m − n" would be executed.

Repetitive statement.   As its name suggests, a repetitive statement is used to express the repeated execution of a series of statements. In the case of BASAL there are two forms. The so-called **while statement** is the most general one and is used to execute a series of statements until some general condition is met. For example, consider the following program fragment:

```
row := 1;
while row ≤ 72 loop
  -- initialize a complete row first:
  col := 1;
  while col ≤ 120 loop
    screen(row)(col).char := BLANK;
    screen(row)(col).reverseVideo := FALSE;
    screen(row)(col).format := NORMAL;
    col := col + 1;
  end loop ;
  row := row + 1;
end loop ;
```

Listing 4.4 An implementation for initializing a screen with blanks.

```
i := 1; x := 1;
while i ≤ 12 loop
  x := 2 * x; i := i + 1;
end loop ;
```

In this case, the two assignment statements that are part of the **while** statement are repeatedly executed as long as the value of the integer variable i is less than 12. It is not hard to see that the statements above specify how 2^{12} can be calculated.

Example 4.11. It should now be clear that we can also use a **while** statement to *explicitly* initialize our variable screen from Example 4.8, rather than the initialization method as discussed in Example 4.10. Consider the piece of BASAL code in Listing 4.4 (where row and col are integer variables).

What happens is that we initialize the screen, *row by row*, by setting the right values for each column element. In other words, the screen is initialized by first considering the upper-left corner, then moving to the next position to the right until a complete row has been initialized. After that, we continue with the second row, and so forth. We leave it as an exercise for the reader to adapt the code so that a screen is initialized *column by column*.

□

Alternatively, we can also sometimes use a so-called **for statement**. In this case, an **index variable** is used to repeat the execution of a series of statements. To illustrate, we could also have expressed the simple **while** statement above in the following way:

```
for i in 1..12 loop
  x := 2 * x;
end loop ;
```

In this case, the index variable i is automatically initialized to 1, and incremented by 1 after each time the assignment "x := 2 * x" is executed. As soon as i reaches the value 13, i.e. its value would lie outside the specified *range* $1 \ldots 12$, execution continues with the

```
for row in 1..72 loop
   -- initialize a complete row first:
   for col in 1..120 loop
      screen(row)(col).char := BLANK;
      screen(row)(col).reverseVideo := FALSE;
      screen(row)(col).format := NORMAL;
   end loop ;
end loop ;
```

Listing 4.5 An alternative implementation for initializing a screen with blanks.

statement following the **for** statement. Incidentally, index variables are assumed to be *implicitly* declared as integer variables. In other words, they need not be declared explicitly in a program. Also, they may only be used within the **for** statement in which they occur.

Example 4.12. Our explicit initialization of a screen variable in Example 4.11 can now be written more conveniently by making use of a **for** statement as shown in Listing 4.5. Again, note that neither the index variable row or col, respectively, needs to be declared as previously.

□

4.3.3   Procedures

We have presented the most important notations for expressing data and operations on data in our BASAL programming language. It should now also be clear why we can talk about *programming* in BASAL. We are implicitly assuming that there is some kind of execution mechanism underlying BASAL; a mechanism that is quite similar to the fetch-decode-execute cycle discussed in Chapter 3. This will now enable us to consider **program units**: logical units that constitute a complete program, consisting of declarations for data types, variables, and statements. We first start by providing a notation for rather simple programs. Later, we shall see how we can combine several programs into a single so-called package.

Procedures declarations

The simplest form of a program description is by means of a so-called **procedure**. A procedure is a collection of declarations for data types and variables, combined with a collection of statements. As an example of a procedure declaration, consider the following description of a program that calculates 2^{12}:

```
procedure POWER is
   x : INTEGER := 1;
begin
   for i in 1..12 loop
      x := x * 2;
   end loop ;
end POWER;
```

Note that we need not declare the index variable i as explained above. The data types and variables declared within a procedure are said to be **local** to that procedure. This means that their declaration is valid only within the procedure and nowhere else. When we say that a procedure is executed, we mean that the statements specified after the word **begin** are executed in the order of their appearance.

Now, just as we have illustrated how convenient it can be to have subroutines during our discussion of PRIMAL, the same holds when dealing with high-level descriptions. But in that case, it is convenient also to be able to **parameterize** a procedure, i.e. we need a way to specify exactly what the input and output are of a procedure. Therefore, we need to make a distinction between three types of parameters:

- First, we will wish to make use of parameter values that serve merely as **input**. In that case, the value that is passed on to the procedure should only be read; under no circumstances must it be changed.

- Opposed to input parameters, there are also **output parameters**. An output parameter is a value that is computed by the procedure, and which is to be returned as a result.

- Finally, there is also something in the middle, namely values that are to be *changed* by a procedure. These so-called **in/out parameters** have the property that they act as input as well as output parameters.

This distinction between parameters is also made in BASAL. In general, parameters are declared as ordinary variables, as illustrated by the following parameterized version of our procedure POWER given above:

```
procedure POWER(p : in INTEGER; u : in INTEGER; v : out INTEGER) is
   x : INTEGER := 1;
begin
   for i in 1..p loop
      x := x * u;
   end loop ;
   v := x;
end POWER;
```

What does this notation mean? It is easily seen that this version of POWER is essentially the same as our previous one, except that we have added three parameter declarations:

- The input parameter p replaces the value 12 that we previously had. In particular, this parameter is used to calculate how often a multiplication should take place, i.e. it represents the exponent of our calculation.

- The input parameter u is used as the base of the calculation and replaces the value 2 of our previous version. Like p, it is required only to know the value of u; there is no need to change it.

- Finally, the output parameter v represents the result of POWER. In fact, it is not difficult to see now that we have described a procedure that calculates the value of v as u^p.

Let's first see how we can make use of (parameterized) procedures. The first point to make is that procedures are much like the subroutines in PRIMAL. In particular, as PRIMAL's BRANCH instruction, procedures in BASAL can be **called**. To illustrate, suppose we had the following declarations:

```
exponent : constant INTEGER := 12;
base : constant INTEGER := 2;
result : INTEGER;
```

In that case, we can assign the value 2^{12} to result by means of the **procedure call statement**

```
POWER(exponent, base, result);
```

Because the first two parameters are used as mere input to the procedure POWER, we could have also assigned the value 2^{12} to result by immediately providing the values 2 and 12 as in

```
POWER(12, 2, result);
```

Examples of using procedures

Let's illustrate the use of procedures by considering a number of examples.

Example 4.13. We first return to our explicit initialization of a variable screen from Example 4.11. In particular, we wish to provide a procedure that will allow us to initialize an arbitrary variable of type DISPLAY with a given initial character. Consider the BASAL code shown in Listing 4.6.

Now suppose again we had declared a variable screen of type DISPLAY. In order to initialize this variable with spaces, we would then need to call the procedure INIT_DISPLAY as in:

```
INIT_DISPLAY(screen, BLANK);
```

The point to note is that because the parameter someScreen of INIT_DISPLAY is specified as **out**, the variable screen will be *completely changed* when calling INIT_DISPLAY. In particular, none of the values it had previously can even be inspected. This is exactly what we needed, as the whole idea of initialization is to provide a value for each variable of which screen is composed. On the other hand, there is no reason to change the value of

```
procedure INIT_DISPLAY(someScreen : out DISPLAY; char : in CHARACTER) is
begin
   for row in 1..72 loop
      -- initialize a complete row first:
      for col in 1..120 loop
         someScreen(row)(col).char := char;
         someScreen(row)(col).reverseVideo := FALSE;
         someScreen(row)(col).format := NORMAL;
      end loop ;
   end loop ;
end INIT_DISPLAY;
```

Listing 4.6   The procedure INIT_DISPLAY for initializing any screen with a user-specified character.

the parameter char; instead, we need merely to know its value. For this reason, it has been declared by using **in**.

□

Many programming languages have a number of standard procedures which simply come with the language. Often, such procedures are used for I/O purposes. For example, the language Modula-2 (Wirth, 1983) has two standard procedures for handling terminal I/O. Using our BASAL notation, these procedures can be specified as follows:

```
procedure READ(c : out CHARACTER);
procedure WRITE(c : in CHARACTER);
```

The procedure READ is used for reading a character that has been typed in at the keyboard, whereas WRITE is used to display a character at the current position of a screen. Each time WRITE is called, a character will be displayed *next* to the previous one, possibly continuing on the next line.

Example 4.14.   Suppose we wish to construct a procedure that will automatically display on our screen the character that has just been typed in. This can then be described in BASAL as shown in Listing 4.7. Note that our procedure requires no parameters at all. Once called, the only thing it will do is echo the characters that have been typed in.

□

We can produce something more sophisticated by using the two procedures READ and WRITE. In particular, we can make a simple calculator. First, we assume that someone can type in a sequence consisting of a maximum of 10 digits, starting with a digit between "1" and "9" and terminating the sequence by a period ("."). For simplicity, we assume that only correct sequences are typed in.

Example 4.15.   Our first concern is to convert a sequence of digits into an integer value. This is really not that difficult (at least if we assume that the person at the keyboard follows the rules of the game). To this end, note that if someone types in the *character* "8"

```
procedure ECHO is
  key : CHARACTER;
begin
  while TRUE loop
    READ(key); –– Read the next character that is typed in,
    WRITE(key); –– and show it on the display.
  end loop ;
end ECHO;
```

Listing 4.7 A procedure for echoing typed-in characters on a screen.

```
procedure READ_NUMBER(number : out INTEGER) is
  key : CHARACTER;
  digit : INTEGER;
  result : INTEGER := 0;
  more : BOOLEAN := TRUE;
begin
  while more loop
    READ(key); –– read a character from the keyboard
    WRITE(key); –– and display it on the screen
    if key ≠ '.' then
      –– the sequence is not over yet: a digit has been typed in
      digit := CHARACTER'POS(key) – CHARACTER'POS('0');
      result := result * 10 + digit;
    else
      –– a period had just been typed in, so that we need to stop
      more := FALSE;
    end if ;
  end loop ;
  number := result;
end READ_NUMBER;
```

Listing 4.8 Reading an integer number from the keyboard.

we can easily convert this to an *integer value* and storing it in a variable, say digit as follows:

```
digit := CHARACTER'POS('8') – CHARACTER'POS('0');
```

This can easily be verified by considering Table 2.3: CHARACTER'POS('8') is equal to 56, and CHARACTER'POS('0') is equal to 48, yielding that the value of digit is equal to $56 - 48 = 8$. Now look at the procedure shown in Listing 4.8. What is seen here is that we gradually construct the final result by systematically multiplying the number constructed so far by 10. It is not difficult to verify that number will now correspond to the integer typed in at the keyboard.

□

Our next assumption is that, after having typed in the first sequence, either a "+" or a "−" can be typed in, to indicate what the actual result should be.

```
procedure CALCULATE(result : out INTEGER) is
   key : CHARACTER;
   firstNumber : INTEGER;
   secondNumber : INTEGER;
begin
   READ_NUMBER(firstNumber);
   READ(key);
   WRITE(key);
   READ_NUMBER(secondNumber);
   if key = '+' then
      result := firstNumber + secondNumber;
   else
      result := firstNumber − secondNumber;
   end if ;
end CALCULATE;
```

Listing 4.9 The actual calculator.

Example 4.16. Based on this assumption, we can now almost complete our trivial calculator. What we need to do is (1) read the first number, (2) check what operation is required, (3) read the second number, and (4) do the calculation. This can be described by the procedure CALCULATE (Listing 4.9). Note how this procedure makes use of the procedure READ_NUMBER but for different variables that are passed on as parameters (firstNumber and secondNumber, respectively). The final result is returned as a parameter of the procedure CALCULATE.

□

Finally, we now only need to write the result back onto the display. It will come as no surprise that this is precisely the reversed form of the procedure READ_NUMBER. Let's see what this looks like.

Example 4.17. The basic conversion from an integer number to a sequence of digits is rather straightforward. In principle, if we have an integer digit having a value in the range $0, \dots, 9$, we can simply convert this to a character char as follows:

```
char := CHARACTER'VAL(digit + CHARACTER'POS('0'));
```

But suppose we had an arbitrary integer number? In that case, the *last* digit can easily be converted as:

```
char := CHARACTER'VAL(number − (number / 10) * 10);
```

where it should be noted that, because we are dealing solely with *integers*, for example,

$$278 \quad - \quad (278/10) \cdot 10 \quad = \quad 278 - 27 \cdot 10 = 8$$

$$\uparrow \qquad\qquad \uparrow$$

number (number / 10) * 10

```
procedure WRITE_NUMBER(number : in INTEGER) is
   sequence : array (1..20) of CHARACTER;
   strippedNumber, newNumber, digit : INTEGER;
begin
   newNumber := number;
   for k in 1..20 loop
      strippedNumber := (newNumber / 10) * 10;
      digit := newNumber – strippedNumber;
      sequence(k) := CHARACTER'VAL(digit + CHARACTER'POS('0'));
      newNumber := strippedNumber / 10;
   end loop
   WRITE('=');
   for k in 1..20 loop
      WRITE( sequence(20 – k + 1) );
   end loop ;
end WRITE_NUMBER;
```

Listing 4.10 The procedure for writing calculations onto the screen.

The basic scheme for converting an integer can then be done by making use of a character array in the following way (note that the multiplication of two 10-digit numbers results in a number with a maximum of 20 digits):

```
sequence : array (1..20) of CHARACTER;
strippedNumber, digit : INTEGER;
...
for k in 1..20 loop
   strippedNumber := (number / 10) * 10;
   digit := number – strippedNumber;
   sequence(k) := CHARACTER'VAL(digit + CHARACTER'POS('0'));
   number := strippedNumber / 10;
end loop
```

The only thing we need to be aware of is that converting an integer in this way, starts at the least significant digit, i.e. the *right-most* one. In our example this means that sequence(1) denotes the right-most digit, and that sequence(20) the left-most one. We can now complete our example by adding the procedure shown in Listing 4.10. The only thing that remains to be done is to combine the procedure CALCULATE and WRITE_NUMBER in a procedure CALCULATOR. We leave this as an exercise for the reader.

□

4.3.4   Packages

Procedures and variables can be grouped into so-called **packages**. Packages are a convenient and practical means to denote that certain variables and procedures form a logical unit. In other words, they allow us to split a program description into different *modules*. In addition, they also provide a means for indicating which specifications of procedures, data types, and variables can be used within *other* packages and procedures. Therefore, a distinction is made between a **package specification** and a **package body**. A package specification specifies exactly those things that can be used within other packages; a package body describes how things are implemented.

Package specifications

A package specification in BASAL merely describes what is available to other packages and procedures. In this sense, it describes *what* can be used, rather than *how* things are actually implemented. A package specification is generally expressed in BASAL as:

```
package PACKAGE_NAME is
   ...
end PACKAGE_NAME;
```

where the ellipsis indicate the place where data types, variables, etc. are declared. To illustrate, the two procedures READ and WRITE we encountered in the previous section could well have been encapsulated into a package specification such as:

```
package TERMINAL is
   procedure READ(c : out CHARACTER);
   procedure WRITE(c : in CHARACTER);
end TERMINAL;
```

In this case, the package specification TERMINAL merely provides descriptions for reading and writing characters for a combination of a keyboard and monitor. In order to use these two procedures we have to reference them explicitly by making use of a dot notation, which we already encountered in the case of records. For example, a correct implementation of the procedure ECHO from Example 4.14 would have been:

```
procedure ECHO is
   key : CHARACTER;
begin
   while TRUE loop
      TERMINAL.READ(key);  -- Read the next character that is typed in,
      TERMINAL.WRITE(key);  -- and show it on the display.
   end loop ;
end ECHO;
```

To illustrate the way that package specifications are given in BASAL let's look at a more sophisticated example. Suppose we wish to specify a collection of procedures and the like that jointly describe what an **integer stack** is, including its associated operations. Informally, an integer stack is just like any other stack, but is restricted to merely storing integer values. Assume that our integer stack should be capable of storing a maximum of 1000 integer values. The description of such a package can be elegantly expressed in BASAL as illustrated in the following example.

Example 4.18. The whole idea when using BASAL to specify user-defined data types by means of packages is to start with a specification part. In the case of our example, we use the following specification outline (details will be filled in later):

```
package STACK_PACKAGE is
    MAXSTACKSIZE : constant INTEGER := 1000;

    subtype ELEMENT is INTEGER;
    type STACK is ...

    procedure INIT(s : out STACK; ...);
    procedure PUSH(s : in out STACK; value : in ELEMENT);
    procedure POP(s : in out STACK; value : out ELEMENT);
end STACK_PACKAGE;
```

Let's take a closer look at what we have outlined here. First, in order to emphasize that this is just another stack except for the fact that it can store only elements of the INTEGER data type we have deliberately declared a separate ELEMENT data type which, in our case is defined as a subtype of INTEGER. Second, we have declared a constant MAXSTACKSIZE which reflects the maximum amount of (integer) values that *any* stack can have. The package specification also contains a description of a data type STACK (which is further detailed below), and the operations that can be applied to variables of this type: INIT for initializing the stack, and PUSH and POP for manipulating it.

Consider the procedure specification PUSH first. By declaring the parameter s by using **in out**, we specify that this procedure will *change* the stack s. Indeed, this is what we would expect it to do. In particular, we would expect it to store the value given by the input parameter value. That this parameter should not be changed is also obvious. It should merely be pushed onto the stack. A similar reasoning explains why the procedure POP has an **in out** parameter s, and an **out**put parameter value. In this case, calling POP would change the stack s, and the value stored at the top would be returned in the form of value.

The procedure INIT, finally, is to be used for initializing a stack. We leave it to the reader to verify that specifying s as an **out**put parameter for the INIT is precisely what we would need for initialization.

□

Let's fill in some more details. In particular, we assume that when a stack is initialized it can be explicitly stated what the actual maximum size should be, provided that this is smaller than 1000. We can complete our specification as follows.

Example 4.19. We now need to provide a complete specification of a stack. First, we need to have a means of storing integer values. This can be solved by a simple array. Also, we have to stipulate exactly what the present top of the stack is, as well as the maximum size as specified at initialization. This then leads to the complete package specification shown in Listing 4.11.

When a stack is initialized, the actual maximum size will have to be provided, which is subsequently recorded in the field max of the data type STACK. Likewise, we use the field top to indicate the present top of the stack. Not surprisingly, top in all cases will be initialized to 0 as will be shown below.

□

```
package STACK_PACKAGE is
    MAXSTACKSIZE : constant INTEGER := 1000;

    subtype ELEMENT is INTEGER;
    type ELEMENT_SET is array (1..MAXSTACKSIZE) of ELEMENT;
    type STACK is
        record
            max : INTEGER range 0..MAXSTACKSIZE;
            top : INTEGER range 0..MAXSTACKSIZE;
            content : ELEMENT_SET;
        end record ;

    procedure INIT(s : out STACK; maxSize : in INTEGER);
    procedure PUSH(s : in out STACK; value : in ELEMENT);
    procedure POP(s : in out STACK; value : out ELEMENT);
end STACK_PACKAGE;
```

Listing 4.11 The specification of the package STACK_PACKAGE.

Package bodies

However, as we have said, this is only the specification part: it tells us precisely what a stack is, together with the procedures that can be applied to it. It says nothing about *how* the stack is manipulated. Therefore, we use a separate notation, namely that of a **package body**. A package body generally has the form

```
package body PACKAGE_NAME is
    ...
end PACKAGE_NAME;
```

where, at the ellipses, the implementation for the procedures in the package specification are given. Additional declarations for types, variables, etc. may also be included here. Let's see how this works for our stack example so far.

Example 4.20. We can continue by further describing *how* (integer) stacks work. Consider the package body shown in Listing 4.12. It can now be easily seen that, for example, our implementation of the procedure PUSH accomplishes precisely what we expect from it.

□

The example so far shows how we can construct a logically coherent group of data type declarations and operations by means of a package. The package specification describes what is *public*. These are the things that can be used within other packages as well. What's described by a package body, however, is considered to be *private*. No declarations given in a package body can be used in other packages. We shall explain other details of packages as we come across them.

We note that our package body as given in Example 4.20 is not complete. For example, we have not provided any adequate means to deal with the situation when a value is

```
package body STACK_PACKAGE is

  procedure INIT(s : out STACK; maxSize : in INTEGER) is
  begin
    if maxSize ≤ MAXSTACKSIZE then
      s.max := maxSize;
    else
      s.max := MAXSTACKSIZE;
    end if ;
    s.top := 0;
  end INIT;

  procedure PUSH (s : in out STACK; value : in ELEMENT) is
  begin
    if s.top < s.max then
      -- We adopt the same convention as used in PRIMAL, by first
      -- incrementing the value for top, and then storing a new value there.
      s.top := s.top + 1;
      s.content(s.top) := value;
    end if ;
  end PUSH;

  procedure POP (s : in out STACK; value : out ELEMENT) is
  begin
    if s.top ≥ 1 then
      -- Here, we should do exactly the opposite to PUSHing a value: we
      -- first remove the value stored at the top, and then lower the stack.
      value := s.content(s.top);
      s.top := s.top - 1;
    end if ;
  end POP;

end STACK_PACKAGE;
```

Listing 4.12 An implementation for (integer) stacks.

pushed onto a full stack or when an attempt is made to pop a value from an empty stack. We leave it as an exercise for the reader to correct this situation.

Parameterized packages

Before we divert our discussion from how programs can be expressed in BASAL, there is one aspect that we want to bring to your attention. Despite the fact that our package STACK_PACKAGE will only work for the INTEGER data type, it should be clear that the same solution can also be used for constructing stacks for other data types. For example, if we wanted to construct a package for CHARACTER stacks then only minor changes to our package would be needed. In particular, we need change only the declaration of the type ELEMENT to:

```
subtype ELEMENT is CHARACTER;
```

This is the *only* adaptation required. The rest of our package specification and implementation remains as shown above. Of course, if we want to have a separate package for integer stacks as well a package for character stacks, we would still need to copy our initial package and make the above-mentioned adaptation of the type ELEMENT. This, however, can be avoided by means of so-called **parameterized packages**. The original concept of a parameterized package comes from Ada, where it is referred to as a **generic package** and which is more sophisticated than is required for the purposes of this book. In BASAL we support parameterized packages in the following way.

In order to a construct a package for a specific kind of data we first construct a general stack package using the following notation:

package STACK_PACKAGE(**type** ELEMENT) **is**
   ...as before, but omitting the declaration of ELEMENT.
end STACK_PACKAGE;

Then, if we wish to construct a package INTEGER_STACK for integer stacks, we do this by writing:

package INTEGER_STACK **is new** STACK_PACKAGE(ELEMENT $\Rightarrow$ INTEGER);

Likewise, defining a package for handling character stacks is accomplished through the following declaration:

package CHARACTER_STACK **is new** STACK_PACKAGE(ELEMENT $\Rightarrow$ CHARACTER);

Here, we can conceive the *data type* ELEMENT as being a parameter of STACK_PACKAGE. The difference with parameters as used in procedures, lies in the fact that we are now using data types instead of actual data.

Example 4.21. As another example of a general package, and one that we shall encounter a few times in this book, consider the parameterized package specification for queuing elements shown in Listing 4.13. We have omitted the specific details with respect to the actual definition of the type QUEUE, but as you might expect, these will not differ radically from that of our STACK data type. In fact, if you realize that a queue is precisely the opposite of a stack, i.e. elements are added to the *end* of a queue and removed from the *front*, it is seen that the implementation of the procedures APPEND and REMOVE will also be quite similar to those of PUSH and POP, respectively. We leave it as an exercise for the reader to outline these implementations.

Using our general queue package, we can now easily construct other queuing packages for queuing specific elements. For example, a package for integer queues may be declared as:

package INTEGERQ **is new** GENERAL_QUEUE(ELEMENT $\Rightarrow$ INTEGER);

$\square$

```
package GENERAL_QUEUE (type ELEMENT) is
  type DEFINITION is ... definition is omitted for the sake of brevity

  procedure APPEND(q : in out DEFINITION; elem : in ELEMENT);
  -- Append the given element [elem] to the queue [q].

  procedure REMOVE(q : in out DEFINITION; elem : out ELEMENT);
  -- Remove the element at the head of the queue, and return it as [elem].

  procedure CHECK_EMPTY(q : in DEFINITION; status : out BOOLEAN);
  procedure CHECK_FULL(q : in DEFINITION; status : out BOOLEAN);
  -- Check if the indicated queue is empty or full, respectively.

end GENERAL_QUEUE;
```

Listing 4.13 The specification of general package for queuing elements.

4.4   A BASAL virtual processor

So what have we actually accomplished? Not very much, to be honest. We have described only two programming languages. The PRIMAL language may be assumed to be implemented by a processor, but is not really the kind of programming language that one would enjoy for constructing programs. On the other hand, BASAL at least allows us to perhaps enjoy program construction, but there's no such thing as a BASAL processor. So, we have a problem. One way or the other, BASAL can only be of use to us if we can provide a *language implementation*. What does this mean? When considering machine languages, their implementation is always provided by means of a real processor. In BASAL, we have no choice other than to find something analogous. But constructing a real processor that implements BASAL is simply impossible. The language is too intricate to seriously consider such an approach. Instead, we should try to construct a **virtual processor** which forms an implementation of BASAL. This virtual processor will be partly implemented in software.

In this section we shall concentrate on a number of issues. First, we shall explain the principal working of a virtual processor by taking a global view on the execution of a BASAL program in terms of a PRIMAL program. Then, in Section 4.4.2 we shall discuss how the execution of BASAL programs can be automated by making use of a compiler or interpreter.

4.4.1   The principle of a virtual processor

Our first concern at this point is to explain the principal working of a virtual processor. We start by taking a global view of what programs are actually all about. Starting in Chapter 2, we have consistently made a distinction between *data* and *operations* that manipulate data. This is particularly emphasized by our initial architecture of a processor, shown in Figure 3.10, in which we separated a memory module for instructions from a memory module containing only data. And again, in our presentation of PRIMAL the dis-

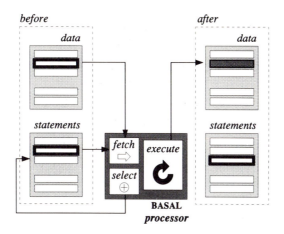

Figure 4.5 The effect of fetching and executing a BASAL statement.

tinction between the two was made explicit. Instructions were there to manipulate variables. In this sense, BASAL is no exception. Variables need to be declared explicitly, and by combining assignment statements with control flow statements, we discussed how we could describe the manipulation of variables. The major difference between the sophisticated notation provided by BASAL and the rather low-level notations available in PRIMAL is to be sought in the *structural organization* of operations and mechanisms for data abstraction. The principal distinction between data and operations, however, remains.

Using this distinction, we can now be more explicit about our concept of a virtual processor. First, consider Figure 4.5, which illustrates the principle of the execution of a BASAL program. What happens is the following. As we have mentioned, we assume the existence of some abstract execution mechanism underlying BASAL. This mechanism works just like the fetch-execute cycle of a processor. First, a statement is fetched from the set of statements that comprise a BASAL program. In addition, any values of variables that are needed to execute the statement are fetched from the data part of the program. During the execution of the statement two things are accomplished: (1) the *next* statement to be executed is determined, and (2) the value of variables are replaced by new ones when executing an assignment statement. Thereafter, the selected next statement is fetched and executed again.

Of course, we do not yet have a processor that repeats the fetch-execute cycle for BASAL programs. Nevertheless, we can *simulate* its effect by means of the PRIMAL processor. The principle is shown in Figure 4.6. What we need to do is construct a PRIMAL program that has the same effect as the execution of a BASAL program. To this end, we use a translator. Such a program does two things:

- First, it associates with each BASAL variable one or more memory locations, in which it subsequently stores bit strings that uniquely correspond to the value of that variable.

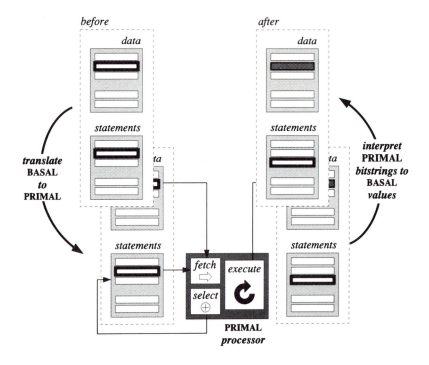

Figure 4.6 Simulating the BASAL fetch-execute cycle by the PRIMAL processor.

- Second, each BASAL statement is converted into one or several PRIMAL instructions, with appropriate references to the memory locations that correspond to the variables occurring in the BASAL statement.

The result of this translation is a PRIMAL program consisting of a data part representing all the BASAL variables and their initial values and a series of PRIMAL instructions corresponding to the converted BASAL statements. When this PRIMAL program is executed its data part will change in the sense that the bit strings representing the *initial* values of the BASAL variables will generally be replaced by other bit strings. These bit strings, in turn, are representations of the *final* values of the BASAL variables. Now suppose that we could execute our BASAL program directly, i.e. without having it translated first into a PRIMAL program. In that case, all the initial values of the BASAL program will also have been replaced by final values. If the final values resulting from this direct execution correspond to those resulting from the execution of the PRIMAL program, we say that the two executions have the same effect. We can now be more specific about virtual processors. Such a processor first translates a BASAL program into a PRIMAL program of which the execution has the same effect as the direct execution of the BASAL program. It then executes the PRIMAL program by means of the real PRIMAL processor.

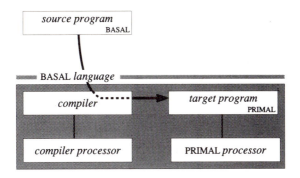

Figure 4.7 The general architecture of a virtual processor.

4.4.2 On automated translation

Suppose we have written a BASAL program. In order to execute this program, we will have to translate it into a PRIMAL program whose execution will have the same effect. Now, it would be rather frustrating if we had to do the translation manually, for in that case, we might as well have programmed directly in PRIMAL. The whole idea, of course, is that we should *automate* the translation process. And what would be a better means than to use a real processor for that purpose? In particular, if we can construct a program that takes a BASAL program as input, and produces a PRIMAL program as output that establishes the same as our original program, then we would no longer have to consider the PRIMAL instruction set, but instead could resort to constructing programs in BASAL. What we are talking about here is the construction of a so-called **compiler**.

More formally, a compiler is a program that establishes a translation from a **source language** to a **target language**. In our case, we are considering BASAL as our source language and PRIMAL as our target language. Because it is a program, a compiler is also to be written in a programming language. For now, assume it is written in a language implemented by a processor which we refer to as the **compiler processor**. The compiler, the compiler processor, and the target processor together form an implementation of what we have called a **virtual processor**. This approach is illustrated in Figure 4.7. Summarizing, the compiler is executed on the compiler processor and its execution results in the translation of a BASAL program into an equivalent PRIMAL program. The latter, in turn, is executed by the PRIMAL processor.

These abstractions may be fine, but you may justifiably ask yourself what this all means in practice. Let's get down to earth again and see what compilation is actually about. We note that the following subsections may be skipped on first reading.

▷ **The compiler**

So how do we start? The first point to make is that in order to compile a program we should at least make it *available* for translation by the compiler. This means that we have to get it into main memory, or perhaps store it somewhere on disk or tape, so that the program is at least accessible. Now the best we can do at this point is type it in. This means that by making use of a terminal we enter our BASAL program *character by character*. In the end, what we will have is a *textual* representation of our BASAL program, stored in the main memory of our host computer. From there on, we can leave it in main memory, but perhaps also store it safely on some storage device. The important point is that our program has now been made accessible for translation. We can then execute the compiler.

Now, compilers are not the simplest programs you can imagine. In fact, languages such as Ada are so intricate that it generally takes a few years before an acceptable compiler is developed. Acceptable in this sense means two things: (1) the compiler can translate every language construct correctly, and (2) the efficiency of the generated code is comparable to that of compilers for competitive languages. To illustrate, although the definition of the Ada language was established in 1983, it took approximately another four to five years before the first commercial compilers became available. To manage the complexity of translation, compilers are generally organized into a number of modules (or packages if we use BASAL terminology), each covering a specific phase of the translation process. Three phases can be distinguished: lexical analysis, parsing, and code generation.

Lexical analysis.   During lexical analysis the textual representation is read, character by character, and transformed into a series of so-called **tokens**. The concept of a token is rather simple, and we shall illustrate it by means of a brief example. Suppose we have the following initialization statement:

val : **constant** INTEGER := 3;

This may seem acceptable to us, but you have to realize that, initially, this statement appears only as a series of *characters*, namely the sequence

(where '◇' is used to denote a space). However, from a *logical* point of view, the statement consists of the following elements:

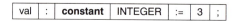

Each of these elements is called a token. In this example, we can distinguish four different types of tokens:

- There is a *keyword token* denoting the keyword "**constant**"
- There are two *identifier tokens*: one denoting the variable val and one denoting the type INTEGER
- There are two *delimiter tokens*: one for the colon separating val from the rest of the declaration, and one for the semicolon which refers to the end of the statement
- An *operator token* representing the assignment symbol ":=".

During lexical analysis, the character sequences are transformed into token sequences, implying that the compiler has to *recognize* that the first three characters of our example form a representation of a variable called "val". The space is then to be recognized as not being relevant. The colon and subsequent space implies that we are dealing with a declaration here, which is to be further recognized as being a constant declaration as soon as the character sequence that make up the word "**constant**" has been read. Continuing in this way, the compiler should recognize that "INTEGER" stands for the fact that we are dealing here with an integer declaration. And when reading the characters ":" and "=" the compiler must record that these two stand for an assignment token, implying in this case the analyzed statement is an initialization statement. Continuing in this way, the character "3" is to be recognized as a constant, and ";" as a so-called delimiter. This information (and more) is stored by the compiler for further analysis.

Parsing.   After the program has been scanned its actual organization is known. The next step consists of checking if the program obeys the syntactical rules of the programming language, and is known as the **parsing** phase. For example, suppose we had inadvertently typed in the following:

procdure proc (i : **in** INTEGER) **is** ...

The lexical analyzer, while scanning the sequence

p, r, o, c, d, u, r, e

can do no better than to record that it had just read a variable named "procdure" instead of what we actually intended, namely the keyword "**procedure**" for designating a procedure. It is the task of the parser to notify that something is wrong here. In particular, while reading the series of tokens produced by the lexical analyzer it is the job of the parser to recognize that a variable-token followed by a sequence of tokens that correspond to a procedure declaration does not make sense. The correct sequence, of course, should have started by a keyword-token for "**procedure**".

If no errors are found, the parser will construct an internal representation of the program which is more convenient for further processing. This internal representation is called a **parse tree**. To illustrate, consider the assignment statement

int := 3 + (2 * 5);

The interesting part about assignment statements in general is that they consist of two sides. A left-hand side corresponding to some *variable*, and a right-hand side that evaluates to some *value*. Essentially, what the parser does is organize the tokens of the above statement into a single group T, and records that this group stands for an assignment. It then divides T into two subgroups: T_{left} which is recorded as the left-hand side of the statement, and T_{right} which is recorded as its right-hand side. It is not difficult to see that T_{right} can be further divided into an addition and a multiplication. We can graphically represent the statement above as shown in Figure 4.8. The structure we see there is generally referred to as a tree.

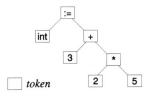

Figure 4.8 The representation of an assignment in the form of a parse tree.

In effect, we see that the complete program is broken down into elementary parts, which in turn are organized in a hierarchical way. This organization turns out to be particularly useful for the last phase: code generation.

Code generation.   The code generation part of a compiler is actually the hard part. In this case, the parse tree of the program as constructed by the parser and is traversed until a group is encountered (which may be organized into subgroups) for which a **translation rule** can be applied. For example, reconsider the assignment statement given above. The tokens for an assignment statement are first always grouped together by the parser, and subsequently partitioned into two subgroups. One group represents the left-hand side and the other represents the right-hand side. As far as the code generator is initially concerned, each assignment statement should in general be translated into the following two PRIMAL instructions:

MOVE <**RHS**>, D0	Move the value of the RHS into D0
MOVE D0, <**LHS**>	and assign this value to the variable in the LHS

The next step is to evaluate both sides of the assignment in order to complete the code generation. To this end, both subgroups T_{right} and T_{left} can be evaluated separately and independently of each other. By evaluating the tokens in T_{left}, the code generator will merely need to generate a reference to the variable int. In other words, it concludes that

$$<\textbf{LHS}> \quad \equiv \quad \text{int}$$

The right-hand side is rather more complicated. Assuming a rather naive approach towards code generation, the generator first generates the following code based on its evaluation of the addition:

MOVE #3, D0	[D0] := 3
MOVE <**2 * 5**>, D1	[D1] := 2 * 5
ADD D1, D0	[D0] := [D0] + [D1]

The multiplication needs to be evaluated as well, which leads to:

MOVE #2, D0	[D0] := 2
MOVE #5, D1	[D1] := 5
MULS D1, D0	[D0] := [D0] * [D1]

Its final task is to combine these pieces of code, leading to the following PRIMAL code:

```
MOVE   #2, D0          | [D0] := 2
MOVE   #5, D1          | [D1] := 5
MULS   D1, D0          | [D0] := [D0] * [D1]
PUSH   D0              | Store intermediate result on the stack

MOVE   #3, D0          | [D0] := 3
POP    D1              | Pop intermediate result from stack
ADD    D1, D0          | [D0] := [D0] + [D1]
PUSH   D0              | Store intermediate result on the stack

POP    D1              | Pop intermediate result from stack
MOVE   D1, int         | And finally do the assignment
```

The important point to note is the *systematic* approach that is being followed here. Admittedly, code generation is greatly simplified in the example above. For example, we have said nothing about the translation of data. However, the principles remain the same, although their realization is more intricate than we are prepared to demonstrate here.

Before we continue with our discussion on virtual processors, recall that in Section 3.2 we mentioned that an instruction memory and a data memory are always joined into a single main memory. By doing so, we argued that we were unifying data and instructions. Now you can see why this is such an important step. By unifying the two, we can treat instructions as data, and can thus sensibly speak about automated translation. To the compiler, the PRIMAL instructions it generates are just bit strings, i.e. data. To the PRIMAL processor, however, these bit strings are perfectly sensible instructions.

Choosing a language for the compiler

So far, we have been deliberately vague about the language in which the compiler is implemented and have implicitly suggested that this is a different language from either the source language (BASAL) or the target language (PRIMAL). In practice, this is not the case. Let's first pursue the thought that the compiler language is the same as the target language. In other words, in our case we construct a compiler written entirely in PRIMAL.

When giving the matter some thought, this would indeed be an attractive choice. What we would have then is a computer, based on a PRIMAL processor, that we could immediately use to enter, translate, and execute BASAL programs. In other words, when writing programs for that computer we can simply *pretend* it is a true BASAL computer. There is only one problem with this approach. We will have to write the compiler in PRIMAL, a language which we showed to be rather cumbersome for program development. An excellent candidate to alleviate this problem is, of course, BASAL itself. In other words, we could more conveniently write our compiler in BASAL rather than in PRIMAL. But, of course, this is not going to work because in order to let the compiler be able to do its work we need to execute it on a processor. But to do so requires that we first have to translate the compiler, which brings us back to our original problem, namely the translation of BASAL. Strangely enough, most compilers are written in a high-level language. In fact, many compilers are written in the same language that they are meant to translate.

How can this be? The answer is quite simple. We start with constructing a compiler *comp*₁ for a small subset of BASAL. We denote this subset by BASALSMALL. This compiler will

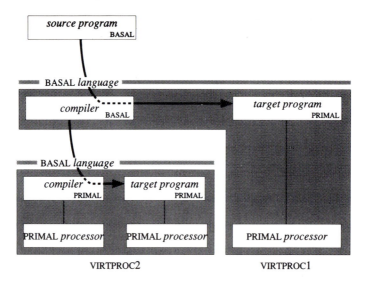

Figure 4.9   The adapted architecture of the BASAL virtual processor, using a BASAL virtual processor (VIRTPROC2).

have to be written in PRIMAL. We then write a second compiler *comp₂*, but now in BASAL-SMALL that implements the full language. In order to be usable, *comp₂* is then compiled by *comp₁*. Because the compiler written in BASALSMALL cannot make full use of all the BASAL features we may then decide to write a third and even better compiler *comp₃*, but now using the full capabilities of BASAL. Of course, *comp₃* is to be compiled using *comp₂*. In other words, our third compiler would be one written entirely in BASAL, and would form part of the implementation of BASAL. The above-mentioned compiler language and source language are now the same. (We note that in practice this situation hardly ever occurs: due to the fact that so many compilers for high-level languages are available, we can simply choose a suitable language for implementing the compiler and use one of its compilers.)

These observations lead to the architecture shown in Figure 4.9. Note that there are *two* implementations of a BASAL virtual processor. The first, denoted as VIRTPROC1, is to be considered as a general implementation which uses the PRIMAL processor as its real processor. The second, denoted as VIRTPROC2, is the one that executes the compiler of VIRTPROC1, and which also uses the PRIMAL processor. To complete the story, the two implementations may be exactly the same; they are merely used for different purposes.

Compilation versus execution

Now let's see how we can execute a BASAL program. Assume we have already entered the program into the computer, i.e. its textual representation is stored somewhere in main memory or on a storage device. This textual representation is then read by the compiler, analyzed, and translated. After this has been completed, we can execute the translated program. We can write these steps as the following algorithm:

Algorithm 4.1. The **compilation** algorithm:

1: Read program P_{BASAL} from storage or main memory.

2: Analyze program P_{BASAL} and translate it into an equivalent program P_{PRIMAL}.

3: Execute P_{PRIMAL} on the PRIMAL processor.

□

This should look familiar. It is another version of the fetch-execute cycles we have discussed in Chapter 3. The only difference is that the first two steps are executed once, whereas the last may be executed several times. In this sense, Algorithm 4.1 reflects the usual process of compilation and execution which is used in the case of many high-level programming languages. The algorithm can, however, often be refined. The approach outlined above is rather coarse-grained in the sense that a *complete* program is first read, then analyzed and translated, and subsequently executed. An alternative approach is repeatedly to read only the *minimal* amount of program text that can be sensibly analyzed, translated, and executed, and then continue with the next piece of minimal program text. Expressing this in an algorithm, we have the following:

Algorithm 4.2. The **interpretation** algorithm:

1: Read the next minimal piece of program text P_{BASAL} from storage or main memory that can be processed.

2: Analyze and translate P_{BASAL} into an equivalent piece of PRIMAL instructions P_{PRIMAL}.

3: Execute P_{PRIMAL} on the PRIMAL processor. Then continue with Step 1.

□

This algorithm reflects the usual behavior of so-called **interpreters** (although, in practice, there are a few subtleties that we have ignored here). Typically, so-called command languages that form the (textual) interface between a human being and a computer are executed by interpretation. There are also interpreted implementations for some high-level languages such as Pascal, and even Ada, although with some restrictions.

Algorithm 4.2 resembles our fetch-decode-execute cycles more than Algorithm 4.1 does. But as you can imagine, using compilers instead of interpreters will generally lead to more efficient target programs, as the *complete* source program can be analyzed, rather than just small parts of it. Nevertheless, it is important to realize that the effect of both algorithms is the same, namely that a program written in a high-level language is eventually executed in the form of a translated version at a lower level of abstraction.

4.5   Towards an extensible BASAL computer

We have come a long way. At this point we have demonstrated that we can sensibly speak about a virtual processor that implements the BASAL programming language. For one thing, this allows us to construct programs at a satisfactory level of abstraction. Unfortunately, BASAL as presented so far is not useful enough. It has no facilities for I/O – features that simply cannot be missed when talking about computers. In terms of virtual hardware, our BASAL processor lacks any means of controlling virtual peripheral devices. There are essentially two solutions to this problem.

First, we can add a number of language constructs to BASAL that will permit us to describe how I/O takes place. It would then be up to the developers of the virtual processor to ensure that such I/O constructs are properly implemented. What it means is that the BASAL compiler generates the right instructions by which disks, terminals, etc. are manipulated. The disadvantage of this approach is that the language determines to a certain extent what kind of peripheral devices are useful or not. This is not always such a good idea.

The second solution is to employ memory-mapped I/O facilities. What do we mean by this? Assuming that the real processor which is part of the virtual processor uses memory-mapped I/O, it would be convenient if we could manipulate the registers associated with peripheral devices, as if they formed part of our BASAL language. In particular, suppose we could explicitly associate variables with memory locations of the real processor, which in turn correspond to I/O registers. In that case, replacing a value of such a variable would mean that we would be changing that register. The only problem with this approach is that if we use a different real processor as part of our language implementation we might need to change the association of variables with memory locations.

In this section we shall see how, by employing memory-mapped I/O in BASAL, we can gradually build a true **virtual computer**, consisting of a virtual processor as well as several virtual peripheral devices.

4.5.1   Controlling the translation process

As we have mentioned above, each variable in BASAL is associated with one or more memory locations when the compiler starts doing its work. By associating variables to memory locations, we are capable of later executing a BASAL program by means of its PRIMAL counterpart. Exactly which memory locations are associated to a variable is not known in advance, and in fact, should be of no concern in general. However, if we are to make peripheral devices that are attached to our real processor also available to BASAL programs the association between variables and memory locations does become important.[3]

---

[3]We note at this point, however, that associating variables to specific memory locations is not something that should be left to a normal BASAL user. As we shall discuss further below and in the next chapter, it is the task of operating system developers to make various hardware-related facilities available through so-called service programs. An ordinary user can then subsequently make use of these programs. Hardware-related details should thus be hidden from normal users.

Being a subset of Ada, BASAL has inherited Ada's advanced features to express the relationship between, on the one hand, data types and variables, and on the other, the organization of memory. We start with looking at a simple example.

Organizing memory

The BASAL language has no predefined data type for representing bit strings. Suppose we wish to make such a data type available. In that case, we might begin with the following two type declarations:

```
subtype BIT is INTEGER range 0..1;
type BITSTRING32 is array (0..31) of BIT;
```

Now suppose we declare a variable bitstring as

```
bitstring : BITSTRING32;
```

When compiling our program, the compiler will probably reserve one or several memory locations so that a complete series of 32 integer variables (that, admittedly, can only take the value 0 or 1) can be stored. Which memory locations the compiler reserves, or how it represents the values that can be assigned to bitstring is, in principle, not important, as long as it is done in a unique way. Nevertheless, we can change this in two ways if so desired: (1) we can explicitly instruct the compiler to organize bit string variables in a way that we like, and (2) we can instruct the compiler to associate variables to specific memory locations.

With respect to the organization of memory, we can specify in BASAL how many bits each variable of the type BITSTRING32 should occupy by writing

```
for BIT'SIZE use 1;
for BITSTRING32'SIZE use 32;
```

What we have specified here is that each variable of the type BITSTRING32 should occupy precisely 32 *consecutive* bits in main memory. We say that its **size** is 32 bits. This means that each time we declare a variable of the type BITSTRING32 it will be associated with exactly 32 consecutive bits of main memory. *Which* bits can be specified by stating with which memory location a variable is to be associated. For example, by writing

```
for bitstring use at 40;
```

the variable bitstring will be associated with memory location 40: it is the compiler's job to ensure that this happens. Now, in all cases, variables in BASAL are also assumed to occupy a consecutive series of words, the first word referred to as #0. This means, for example, that if each word in main memory consists of 16 bits, that bitstring(0) ... bitstring(15) correspond to the word at memory location 40, whereas bitstring(16) ... bitstring(31) will correspond to memory location 41. Figure 4.10 shows this placement of bitstring into main memory. Of course, if the size of a word is 32, then bitstring will fit nicely into

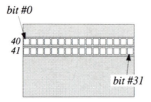

Figure 4.10   The placement of the variable bitstring in main memory by additional specifications.

one memory location.

Let's look at another example of defining the memory organization which, in fact, we shall come across a few times in succeeding chapters. Consider the following type declarations

```
subtype CARDINAL is INTEGER range 0..65535;
type SOME_RECORD is
   record
      field1 : CARDINAL;
      field2 : CARDINAL;
   end record ;
```

At this point we want to associate each variable of the type SOME_RECORD with precisely *two* consecutive memory locations, of which the first is reserved for element field1, and the second for field2. It is not difficult to see that each variable of the type CARDINAL requires only 16 bits of storage in order to represent all $65536 = 2^{16}$ different values. In order to ensure that indeed precisely 16 bits are used for this purpose, we write

```
for CARDINAL'SIZE use 16;
```

Now first assume that main memory is organized into 16-bit words, i.e. each memory location occupies 16 bits. In order to ensure that each variable of type SOME_RECORD occupies precisely two locations, we use the following **representation clause**:

```
for SOME_RECORD use
   record
      field1 at 0 range 0..15;
      field2 at 1 range 0..15;
   end record ;
```

What we have specified here is that element field1 of each variable of type SOME_RECORD is to be associated with the (first) 16 bits of word #0 of the memory locations that the variable uses. The second field is to be associated with word #1. To ensure that precisely two words are used to store variables of this type, we need to specify the required size. This can be done by means of the following representation clause:

```
for SOME_RECORD'SIZE use 2*16;
```

Now how can we actually associate a variable someObject with, say, memory locations 156 and 157? This is actually quite easy. We first declare the variable someObject:

someObject : SOME_RECORD;

and proceed by specifying precisely where it is to be stored by specifying the location of the first word in memory:

for someObject **use at** 156;

The effect of this is that someObject.field1 will be associated with memory location 156, occupying precisely 16 bits, and that someObject.field2 is associated with location 157.

▷ But suppose now that each word in main memory consists of 32 bits instead of 16. In that case, we need to change our representation clauses. First assume that we still want to associate each field of SOME_RECORD with a different memory location. The problem then is that we need to specify exactly which 16 bits of each memory location the respective fields are to occupy. Suppose we decide that this should always be the last 16 bits. In that case, we need to change the representation clauses for SOME_RECORD as follows:

```
for SOME_RECORD use
    record
        field1 at 0 range 16..31;
        field2 at 1 range 16..31;
    end record ;
for SOME_RECORD'SIZE use 2*32;
```

It should also be clear that each variable of SOME_RECORD will also nicely fit into one word. An alternative representation clause to achieve just that would be the following:

```
for SOME_RECORD use
    record
        field1 at 0 range 0..15;
        field2 at 0 range 16..31;
    end record ;
for SOME_RECORD'SIZE use 1*32;
```

In this case, the first field would always be mapped to the first 16 bits, whereas the second field would occupy the second series of 16 consecutive bits.

Exploiting memory-mapped I/O

By controlling the way that a compiler organizes main memory when translating variables, we can now easily make various peripheral devices available to BASAL programs, assuming that the real processor employs memory-mapped I/O. This is best illustrated by means of a simple example.

Assume that the I/O processor handling all communication to a (character-oriented) screen uses the registers shown in Table 4.1, which have been mapped to the indicated

Table 4.1 The memory-mapped registers of a display I/O controller

register	address	purpose
MONXPOS	20	requires an integer value for the *x*-position of the cursor
MONYPOS	21	requires an integer value for the *y*-position of the cursor
CHARREG	22	a register containing the ASCII representation of the character to be represented
SCRCTRL	23	a register for controlling what should happen with the screen as a whole

addresses. All registers are assumed to have length 8. An important register is SCRCTRL which is further specified as follows. The I/O processor continuously reads this register, and as soon as the last bit is "1" (i.e. SCRCTRL contains the bit string $\langle xxxxxxx1 \rangle$), it subsequently reads the values in the other registers and sends these to the display. Hereafter, we assume the I/O processor resets the last bit to "0".

For simplicity, also assume that each word in memory occupies precisely 8 bits. What we need at this point is a means to display a character on the screen by providing its position, as well as the character itself. This can be described in BASAL by means of the following package specification:

```
package DISPLAY is
   subtype SMALLCARD is INTEGER range 0..255;
   for SMALLCARD'SIZE use 8;
   procedure WRITE(char : in CHARACTER; xpos, ypos : in SMALLCARD);
end DISPLAY;
```

Note how we have deliberately forced each position to be specified by means of a positive integer smaller than 255, and that each *x* or *y* position will occupy precisely 8 bits of storage. In other words, it will fit nicely into one of the registers of our display controller. Now look at the package body of Listing 4.14 in which further implementation details are given.

A few remarks about package DISPLAY are in order. First, we have declared a type BITSTRING8 in order for us to manipulate the registers as ordinary bit strings. Again, a bit string is organized as a consecutive series of bits. In the declaration of the data type SCREEN_REGISTERS, each field corresponds to exactly one of the registers of the display controller. Its representation clause ensures that variables of type SCREEN_REGISTERS will be associated with precisely four consecutive memory locations. Consequently, the fragment

```
screenRegSet : SCREEN_REGISTERS;
for screenRegSet use at 20;
```

```
package body DISPLAY is
    subtype BIT is INTEGER range 0..1;
    type BITSTRING8 is array (0..7) of BIT;
    for BITSTRING8'SIZE use 8;

    type SCREEN_REGISTERS is
        record
            xScreenPos : SMALLCARD;
            yScreenPos : SMALLCARD;
            asciiChar : SMALLCARD;
            screenCtrl : BITSTRING8;
        end record ;

    for SCREEN_REGISTERS use
        record
            xScreenPos at 0 range 0..7;
            yScreenPos at 1 range 0..7;
            asciiChar at 2 range 0..7;
            screenCtrl at 3 range 0..7;
        end record ;
    for SCREEN_REGISTERS'SIZE use 4 * 8;

    screenRegSet : SCREEN_REGISTERS;
    for screenRegSet use at 20;

    procedure WRITE(char : in CHARACTER;xpos, ypos : in SMALLCARD) is
    begin
        screenRegSet.xScreenPos := xpos;
        screenRegSet.yScreenPos := ypos;
        screenRegSet.asciiChar := CHARACTER'POS(char);
        screenRegSet.screenCtrl(7) := 1;
    end WRITE;

end DISPLAY;
```

Listing 4.14 An implementation of the package DISPLAY.

ensures that the variable screenRegSet is not only associated with the memory locations of the display registers; its fields are appropriately organized with each register in the way we intended. The procedure WRITE should now be easy to understand. We first set the correct values in each register, after which the control bit is set to 1 in order to display the character on the screen.[4]

---

[4]It should be noted that our implementation is rather simple, and missing a number of details, for some characters may become lost because we are not **synchronizing** with the display. We leave these matters at the moment, but shall return to synchronization in the next chapter.

4.5.2   Virtual devices

Displays revisited

If we assume that package DISPLAY is always available (i.e. it is always placed in main memory when the PRIMAL computer is switched on), it is clear that we now at least have one albeit rather simple I/O function available. By simply writing, for example,

```
DISPLAY.WRITE('A',10,30);
```

we are now able at least to display a character (in this case 'A') on the screen at the specified position. Of course, our package DISPLAY is too simple to be of any practical use. For example, there is no easy way of clearing a screen, or perhaps scrolling it up or down. In fact, we have not even assumed that the display controller supports such operations. Nevertheless, such functions can be added with relative ease. To illustrate, suppose we wish to make a procedure available that would clear the entire screen. In that case, our package specification would become something like:

```
package DISPLAY is
    subtype SMALLCARD is INTEGER range 0..255;
    for SMALLCARD'SIZE use 8;
    procedure WRITE(char : in CHARACTER; xpos, ypos : in SMALLCARD);
    procedure CLEAR_SCREEN;
end DISPLAY;
```

All we need to do next is add an implementation of the procedure CLEAR_SCREEN to our package body. This is really not too difficult. Assume that our display is constructed from 72 lines, each line having a width of 120 characters. We could then extend the package body of DISPLAY with the following procedure CLEAR_SCREEN:

```
procedure CLEAR_SCREEN is
    BLANK : constant CHARACTER'VAL(32);
begin
    for yPos in 1..72 loop
        for xPos in 1..120 loop
            WRITE(BLANK, xPos, yPos);
        end loop ;
    end loop ;
end CLEAR_SCREEN;
```

Now the important point to note here is that we have *added* something to the working of a display that was not provided previously. In other words, we have extended the *functionality* of that what was provided by the hardware. The display now appears to support additional functions. We have thus created a **virtual display**, one that is partly implemented in hardware, and partly in software. Staying in this line of reasoning, we can say that we have extended our BASAL virtual processor with a component that may justifiably be referred to as a **virtual (peripheral) device**. The actual implementation of this device is shielded from other packages. Only what we can do has been made available by means of the procedures described in the package specification.

Service programs

Why are we making such a big fuss about this? Well, there is a good reason. Suppose that the BASAL virtual processor is to be implemented by means of a compiler that generates instructions for a PRIMAL processor. Also, assume that this real processor can be attached to various peripheral devices. Following the approach we have outlined above, it should be clear that these devices can be made available to BASAL programs by means of a number of packages. Each package corresponds to a partial implementation of a **virtual device**, and consists of two parts: (1) a specification part describing the *functionality* of the device by describing *what* you can do with it; and (2) a body describing *how* this functionality is actually realized. The point is that you never need to know what a package body looks like, and that's just fine because you will never be able to make use of this knowledge in any case.

But what does this mean when compiling a BASAL program? First, assume that all packages used to access peripheral devices have already been compiled, and that their PRIMAL counterparts have been placed somewhere in main memory. In that case, the BASAL compiler for our own program need merely to know exactly where these packages are placed, and subsequently generate code just for our BASAL program, adding references to the appropriate procedures and variables implemented by the packages. In this sense, the packages cannot only be seen as a convenient means for accessing the hardware, they can also be viewed as an extension of the BASAL programming language. Putting it differently, we say that we have made a collection of **services** available to BASAL programs.

Developing services, and implementing them in the form of what we refer to as **service programs**, is a major issue when developing general-purpose computers and communication systems. What it means, is that if we can standardize the services in the sense that we can come to a common agreement on

- Which services should be provided and
- How they should be made available

we can then develop programs for a wide range of different hardware. Because there is no need to know anything about how service programs are actually realized, it is clear that if we choose to use a different real processor, then this should have no effect on our BASAL programs: we should still be able to compile them in the usual way. Developing and implementing the type of services we have been discussing so far is the problem of developing **operating systems**. Operating systems form the topic of the next chapter.

4.5.3   Linking and loading

We need to discuss one more important issue: how do we make service programs (or any program for that matter) available? The point to note is that our BASAL programs, as well as all the service programs that we wish to make use of, are compiled separately. In the end, we will find ourselves with a collection of PRIMAL programs that need to be connected to each other in such a way that their instructions can be executed as if belonging to a single program. Making service programs available, and subsequently getting the final result to work as intended, is the job of a **linker** and a **loader**.

Linking programs

Linking programs together is really not difficult, at least if the compiler takes special measures. Let's start by considering a general problem. Suppose we were to compile a BASAL program. As we have mentioned, the compiler will associate variables to memory locations, although in most cases it is completely irrelevant which locations these are. The exception to this rule is, of course, formed by variables that need to be explicitly associated with memory-mapped I/O registers. Now suppose that the compiler, when translating a program $prog_1$, associates some variable var1 to memory location LOC1. Likewise, assume that when it subsequently compiles a second program $prog_2$, it associates a variable var2 belonging to $prog_2$ with location LOC2. This may all seem acceptable, but we are going to be in trouble if we want $prog_1$ and $prog_2$ to be placed in memory at the same time, and it turns out that LOC1 = LOC2.

The problem is easily solved if all addresses in a program are interpreted as being *relative* to the program's start address. So, for example, if $prog_1$ is placed in memory starting at address 1200, then LOC1 actually denotes memory address 1200 + LOC1. Now suppose that we wish to link several programs $prog_1, \ldots, prog_N$ together, to which end we start by first concatenating the programs into one large program *totalProg*. Clearly, all addresses occurring in $prog_1$ can be left unaltered. Addresses in $prog_2$, however, will have to be converted to addresses that are now relative to the start address of *totalProg*. If $size(prog_i)$ denotes the size of program $prog_i$, then the addresses occurring in $prog_2$ are to be incremented by $size(prog_1)$. Likewise, the addresses occurring in $prog_3$ are to be incremented by $size(prog_1) + size(prog_2)$, etc. Concatenating a collection of programs and converting the addresses in this way is precisely what a **linker** does.

Loading programs

The last step that needs to be done is placing, i.e. loading the linked program into main memory. This step is so easy that it is often directly done by the linker. What it implies is that the linked program generally needs to be transferred from disk into main memory. As soon as it has been placed, the loader must take care of the fact that the CPU starts executing the first instruction. This is really simple. The points to note are that:

1. The loader knows exactly where the first instruction has been placed, and

2. When loading the program into main memory, the *current* program that is being executed is the loader.

Consequently, the loader need essentially consist of the following instruction as its last one to be executed:

```
JMP    instr1
```

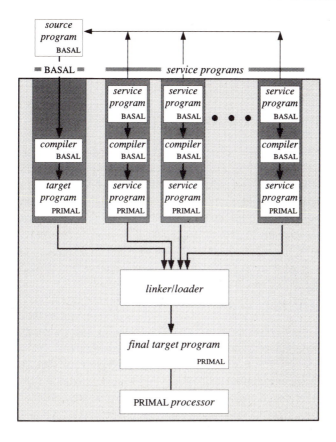

Figure 4.11 Extending the BASAL language with a number of service programs.

where instr1 is the address of the first instruction of the loaded program that needs to be executed.

The overall view

We can now summarize our approach to the development of a virtual computer as follows. First, in order to access the hardware in a convenient way we write so-called service programs in BASAL, and compile these programs into PRIMAL. The objective is that these service programs will be made available to ordinary BASAL programs. Therefore, we need merely write a BASAL program, compile it, and *link* it with the service programs we wish to use. After linking all the compiled programs together into one big program we simply load the latter into main memory, and start its execution. This is outlined in Figure 4.11.

And this is where we end for now: with a virtual computer that is now easy to program because it has a high-level programming language as its interface, combined with a number of services that hide hardware details of the underlying real processor. Indeed, we have gained this level of abstraction not by extending the hardware but by making use entirely of software solutions. The only topic we have not said much about is the type of service programs that we want to make available. This is the subject of the next chapter.

4.6   Discussion and further reading

The material presented in this chapter is essential for an understanding of computer and communication systems. It forms the bridge between systems that are implemented solely in hardware and those that are additionally implemented through software. In essence, we have discussed only two issues: (1) the principle of constructing executable programs in terms of machine instructions, and (2) the same principle, but now applied to programs written in a high-level programming language. The crux of the matter lies in the automated execution of the latter. A quick review of what we have been doing seems to be in order here.

4.6.1   Machine languages

By the end of the previous chapter, we had reached a point where it should be clear that we could program a computer by providing it with a series of instructions that it would subsequently execute. In this chapter we have introduced a simple yet effective instruction set, also referred to as a **machine language**. Our PRIMAL instruction set has been derived from an existing language, namely that of the Motorola 680x0 family of processors. The instructions it comprises have been represented in the form of symbols, i.e. rather than giving instructions in their pure form as bit strings, we have used a textual representation. Such a representation is called an **assembly language**. The development of instruction sets has already been discussed in the previous chapter, and we shall therefore leave that issue here. But in order to complete the picture, we do need to be more specific about the distinction between machine and assembly languages, and put the latter into context when using high-level languages such as BASAL.

Assemblers.   Using a textual representation for machine languages is the common way of developing programs at that level. But this does bring us to the same problem that we encountered with high-level languages such as BASAL, namely that we need to convert our symbols into the actual bit string representations of instructions in order to have our assembly language programs executed. To that end, a so-called **assembler** is used. An assembler is much like a compiler. It is a program that takes a textual representation of a program as input and produces an equivalent representation in the form of a series of bit strings representing the actual instructions. The point to realize when using assemblers (or machine languages for that purpose) is that programs are highly dependent on the hardware. In principle, an assembly program can only be executed by the processor that implements the underlying machine language.

Assembly languages in practice.   As we have stated, this hardware-dependent feature of assembly languages is not attractive when writing programs that are inherently independent of the processor that executes them. But there are more serious drawbacks in using assembly languages. Above all, assembly programming is difficult. The reason for this is that the languages are completely tailored to getting a processor to execute instructions – they are in no way supportive when expressing solutions to general, i.e. hardware-independent problems. In other words, they lack sufficient means for abstraction.

This feature is already demonstrated by the simple examples of PRIMAL programs: they are difficult to comprehend if you do not know in advance *what* they should be doing. And indeed, developing assembly programs is generally an extremely error-prone process. Many mistakes are introduced and more time is often spent in removing these mistakes (or "bugs" as they are called) than developing the initial program in the first place. Nevertheless, assembly programs are still being developed to date, and mostly just for two reasons: (1) when high-level languages lack sufficient support for capturing machine dependencies, or (2) when performance starts playing a crucial role. We return to the first issue below when putting BASAL into context.

Performance criteria are often used to justify the need for assembly programming instead of using some high-level language. These justifications were completely in order during the period when compilers for the first high-level languages became available. Then, it was simply a fact that the machine language programs generated by compilers were not as efficiently executable as their hand-coded counterparts. This is no longer true. In fact, when comparing some hand-coded solutions to those generated by a compiler when using a high-level language, the opposite can even be observed (Patterson and Hennessy, 1994). This should come as no surprise. The great amount of expertise which has been gathered by engineers in the last three decades has found its way into compilers. This expertise is such that it cannot be expected to be comprehended in its total by a single person hand-coding assembly solutions. Compilers are simply better in many cases.

Despite these discouraging words on the use of assembly languages, it is our opinion that they still form an excellent vehicle to comprehend what is going on at the level of processors. In this sense, an assembly language is the primary representative of many design decisions taken during the development of processors. If you want to experiment with writing PRIMAL programs or, more precisely, programs for the 680x0 processors, you will find Clements (1994) an excellent starting point. Not only does the author provide a comprehensive and well-structured approach to 680x0 program development, the book also contains a software package that will allow you to develop programs on Intel 80x86-based machines. In addition, a good introduction is also given by Bacon (1986). Full details on the 680x0 instruction set can be found in Motorola (1986). If you have difficulties understanding the various addressing modes of the 680x0, it is instructive to take a look at the PDP-11 instruction set, which inspired the developers of the Motorola processor. In that case, consult Meyer (1982) who not only explains the PDP-11, but also puts the machine into context by describing computer architecture and organization.

4.6.2   High-level languages

However, as we have said, machine (or assembly languages) are not the way to go in the case of program development. For that purpose we need to abstract from the hardware and be able to write solutions in the form of programs that are relatively easy to comprehend. For this reason, we have introduced the high-level programming language BASAL. This language is (almost) a subset of the language Ada, developed in the early 1980s. It is instructive to see why and how Ada has been developed, and to see what its present status is. After that, we shall briefly look at some other popular languages, motivating our choice to use Ada as our basis for the rest of this book.

The Ada programming language

The development of the Ada programming language is an initiative of the United States Department of Defense (DoD). The problem that the DoD was confronted with, was the very large amount of money spent on software development. Most administrative software was written in a language called COBOL, most scientific and engineering programs were written in FORTRAN, but the diversity of programming languages for so-called **embedded systems** was very large. Embedded systems consist of a mixture of components, of which a computer is just one (Cooling, 1991). For example, an aircraft control system typically consists of many components that measure all kinds of characteristics and that subsequently pass these data to a computer for analysis. The computer, in turn, passes control signals back to other components in order to keep the aircraft properly in flight. A problem with embedded systems is the intricate interaction between components and a computer. The construction of software for such systems is often a tremendous engineering task. The idea arose that if a single programming language were used in this area, that software development costs would drop considerably. The development of Ada in the late 1970s and early 1980s was the result.

Ada is typically the result of a committee. With some exaggeration one might say that it has every compromise that you can think of. Indeed, the language is a difficult one to learn, but if you take into account the goals that had to be fulfilled, then this will come as no surprise. The most important among these are:

- Ada should support the development of large programs. This implied that programs should be able to be developed by teams of engineers, each team working on its own and providing other teams with finalized parts of the complete software system. The concept of a package (of which we have discussed only the most salient features) was developed towards this aim.

- Software parts should be amenable to *re-use* i.e. teams should be able to develop solutions that could easily be adopted for other problems. The so-called **generic units** was one of the results. Generic units are not an easy concept to implement.

- It should be possible to define separately executable units within a single Ada software system. These units, called **tasks**, will be introduced in Chapter 6. In practice, they not only have intricate semantics but are even more difficult to implement efficiently.

- For our purposes perhaps the most important requirement was that of advanced means for **data abstraction**. In particular, this meant that the language should incorporate facilities that would allow developers to completely separate the logical organization of data from its actual representation at the level of processors. We have discussed many of these features in Section 4.5.1.

It is primarily for the third and fourth issues that we have chosen Ada as our base language. To date, no other popular language has integrated these two features into a single language the way that Ada has done. The facilities for data abstraction puts Ada in a remarkable position compared to other languages. From a practical point of view, however, Ada is not always the best high-level language to use when building computer and communication systems, as we shall discuss next. The main reason for this is that the language is so intricate that developing compilers that generate (1) correct code and (2) efficiently executable code is still a difficult task to accomplish. It is mostly for the latter reason that other, simpler programming languages are used. However, the expressiveness of the language makes it an excellent vehicle to demonstrate low-level programming at a sufficient level of abstraction.

If you want to learn more about Ada, Barnes (1980) provides an overview of the language and a complete description can be found in Barnes (1994). Using Ada for the development of software is described in Booch and Bryan (1994). But if you really want to know what the language is all about, you will have to consult the reference manual (ANSI, 1983). A recent update of the language is described in ISO/IEC (1995).

Alternative programming languages

It is completely beyond the scope of this book to go into any detail on programming languages. But we feel it would also be a serious omission if we did not say a few words on high-level languages in general. In particular, we shall pay some attention to three popular languages that in flavor are similar to BASAL, but for one or other reason were not used as a basis in this book. In the following we shall briefly discuss Pascal, Modula-2/3, and C/C++. A general overview on programming language concepts is presented in Ghezzi and Jazayeri (1987); a more recent presentation can be found in Bal and Grune (1994).

Pascal. A popular language that is generally used as a first programming language, is Pascal (Wirth, 1971). Pascal is a descendant of so-called structured programming languages developed in the 1960s, but was one of the first that could easily be implemented on small computer systems. This was due to its simplicity. As such, it has become not only widely used for educational purposes but also for programming personal computers. Approximately 25 years after its invention, Pascal has grown into a language with many variants, and often ill-engineered constructs in order to support access of all possible hardware features. Also, constructs have been added in order to support the construction of large programs. Nevertheless, the core language is still an excellent vehicle for learning programming in the first place. In that sense, Wirth (1973, 1976a) will show you how to do it the right way.

Modula-2/3.   Wirth recognized that Pascal was not suited for *systems programming*, i.e. developing programs at a sufficient level of abstraction, but still being able to access all hardware features. To this end, and also to provide the right means for developing large programs, he developed Modula (Wirth, 1976b). Modula was later followed by Modula-2 (Wirth, 1983) which to date is often used as an alternative to Pascal. The language is similar to BASAL in many ways, in that it allows programmers to modularize their software into so-called modules (comparable to packages), and to map variables onto specific memory address, thus allowing a convenient means of memory-mapped I/O programming. The language has been kept small, and is practically suitable for the development of what we have called service programs. Comparing it to Ada, however, Modula lacks the concept of a task. Instead, there is only a primitive way of specifying so-called co-routines. If you want to know more about Modula-2, especially for low-level programming, Christian (1986) will be of help.

Recently, Modula-2 has been upgraded to its third version, known as Modula-3. The main distinction with its predecessor is that more advanced data structuring techniques have been added, and that co-routines have been replaced with the more advanced concept of so-called threads. The language still needs to find its way to widespread use. A good introduction to Modula-3 is given by Harbison (1992), whereas Nelson (1991) provides more specific information on its advanced features.

C and C++.   The C programming language is perhaps one of the most disliked, and at the same time most used language for developing systems programs. The language was developed by Kernighan and Ritchie in the 1970s when they wanted to have the right means for developing an operating system. Their ideas had two remarkable results: the C language and UNIX (we will talk about UNIX later). The language proved that it was possible to develop almost entirely *portable* system software, in particular so-called operating systems, something that until then was considered hardly realistic. The crux of C lies in its simplicity. Comparing it to assembly languages, a programmer has just enough facilities to make the latter readable. Indeed, this meant that developing C programs is not always that simple. Data abstraction was hardly provided, and certainly, there were no advanced features such as tasks. Worse still, the data typing facilities that were incorporated into the language could easily be misused to do all the things that characterize ill-engineered software. Nevertheless, when in good hands, the language is extremely powerful and compilation of programs that can be efficiently executed on a wide range of platforms is yet to be seen supported by other languages. At present, the language has been standardized, and the interested reader is referred to Kernighan and Ritchie (1988) for a complete description of the language, augmented with many illustrative examples.

An extension that allows for better program construction is C++ developed by Stroustroup (1987). However, although C++ does provide for enhanced data structuring (in the form of so-called object-oriented constructs), it does not allow low-level programming in the way that Ada or Modula-2/3 supports. Also, you will find no concept of a task in C++. A good source on learning C++ is Lippman (1991).

4.6.3 Compiler technology

An important topic that we have hardly touched upon is the automated translation of BASAL into PRIMAL through a compiler. But if we are to use high-level programming languages, then compilers that can translate programs written in such languages into efficiently executable code are essential. And, of course, compilation should be correct, i.e. the (machine) program which is the result of compilation should do exactly the same as if the original program were immediately executed. Constructing correct compilers that generate efficiently executable code is difficult.

The correctness of the compiler is often affected in an unexpected way: the language that is to be translated is simply not well defined. This may seem strange but you have to realize that developing a language is no easy task. The consequence may be that some language semantics may simply not have been provided, or may not be precise enough to allow a compiler developer to achieve a correct set of translation rules. To this end, a large area of (theoretical and practical) research has been explored for developing means to express the semantics of programming languages in a complete and unambiguous way. We have skipped this subject entirely. A good starting point for the fundamentals of specifying what a programming language stands for is Watt (1991).

But assuming that in some way or other we have a good idea of the syntax and semantics of a programming language, we are still confronted with the considerable task of actually developing the compiler. Fortunately, a lot of work can be avoided by making use of so-called **compiler-compilers**. A compiler-compiler is a program that *generates* a compiler, or at least an important part of it. What it means in practice is that the less critical parts of a compiler, namely the lexical analyzer and the parser, can be generated almost entirely if a precise definition of the syntax of a language is given. Without going into any further details here, the reader is encouraged to experiment with the Lex and Yacc toolkit (Mason and Brown, 1990) which is standard available for UNIX systems, and for MS-DOS systems. In that respect, it is also worth taking a look at Kernighan and Pike (1984) in which the implementation of a simple desk calculator is given.

The really difficult part of compiler construction starts with the actual translation rules, i.e. taking a parse tree as input and generating code. The problem is that if we were to apply simple code generation rules such as the ones illustrated in Section 4.4.2 the result would be an unacceptable inefficiently executable program. Instead, we have to consider all kinds of *code optimizations*. In practice, this often means that the code generator should take into account that (1) hardware resources (such as memory and registers) are optimally used, and (2) code should not be generated on a per-statement basis, but rather for complete portions of a program. The second requirement simply states that a code generator can perform better if it first analyzes what a series of statements actually accomplishes, instead of just generating code for each statement separately. Intuitively, this is clear. How it can be realized in a compiler is something totally different. A brief but highly instructive and readable account on code generation is given in Aho and Sethi (1977).

A classic and excellent textbook on compilers is Aho *et al.* (1986). A practical, illustrative approach on how to construct compilers is presented in Fischer and LeBlanc (1991). Loaders and linkers are discussed in Graham (1975) and Presser and White (1972). But, as is the case with much intricate software, it is probably most illustrative to look at the actual implementations of compilers. Unfortunately, few references actually provide the source code of compilers. Nevertheless, the code presented in Welsh and McKeag (1980) describing a compiler for a subset of Pascal will be a good, and well-documented starting point. Many details can also be found in Barron (1981). One of the few books that provide many details of source code is Holub (1990), in which a complete compiler (written in C) is described for a subset of C.

Exercises

1. Writing down PRIMAL instructions is fine, but how do we get the computer to "understand" these instructions?

2. Explain the difference between a JUMP and BRANCH instruction. Take into account the role of the status register.

3. Why is it not should a good idea to also map the registers of the PRIMAL processor into the same address space as main memory? It would seem that we could do with far fewer instructions in that case.

4. Can you think of a good reason why PRIMAL does not have any instructions for dealing with floating-point numbers?

5. Explain in detail what happens when using subroutines in a PRIMAL program. Take into account the working of the stack and the role of the program counter.

6. Why is the instruction

       BSR   offset

   not *exactly* the same as executing the two instructions

       PUSH PC
       BRA   offset

7. Consider the following BASAL statements:

       for i in 1..12 loop
          x := x + 2;
       end loop ;

How would you express this in PRIMAL?

8. Consider the following declarations in BASAL:

```
type SOME_RECORD is
   record
      field1 : INTEGER;
      field2 : INTEGER;
   end record ;

someRecord : SOME_RECORD;
```

How would you represent the variable someRecord in PRIMAL?

9. Adapt the program shown in Listing 4.4 so that initialization is done column by column.

10. What kind of PRIMAL addressing mode would you use when representing BASAL array variables in PRIMAL?

11. Explain the difference between the three types of parameters supported by BASAL procedures.

12. Modify the package STACK_PACKAGE so that, for example, the situation that a value is pushed onto a full stack is properly handled. (Hint: provide additional parameters that indicate whether an operation succeeded or not.)

13. Outline the implementation of the package body for the parameterized package GENERAL_QUEUE as given on page 172.

14. Provide an outline for representing BASAL procedures in PRIMAL. Assume that a procedure has no parameters.

15. *How would you expect that an **in**put parameter as used in BASAL is represented in PRIMAL? And what about an **out**put parameter?

16. Explain in your own words what the underlying principles are of a virtual processor.

17. *What is the difference between compilation and interpretation?

18. Explain what is actually specified by a representation clause, and why you would want to have such clauses in the first place.

19. Do representation clauses make any sense if the underlying real processor does not support memory-mapped I/O?

20. Justify the term "virtual device" as introduced in Section 4.5.2.

21. Explain what is meant by a service program, and how such programs can be seen as an extension to a language such as BASAL.

Chapter 5

Operating systems

In this chapter we consider the problem of extending a computer with service programs that will allow us to execute several programs simultaneously. In essence, we shall discuss the core functionality of so-called operating systems. Therefore, we start with identifying a simple problem which can only be solved by a computer that supports multiple, independent programs. From there, various derived problems need to be solved. In particular, we consider memory management, scheduling issues, and program interference. We finish our discussion by taking a closer look at some architectural features of operating system kernels.

5.1 Support for multiple programs

In the previous chapter we demonstrated how we could implement a virtual processor, and how we could subsequently extend its programming language by constructing service programs. Most of these programs are directly or indirectly related to managing peripheral devices. In this section, we start with taking a closer look at one such service program, namely one that is used to transfer data between a disk and main memory. What we will see is that if no special measures are taken during the data transfer the CPU will simply have to wait until the transfer is completed. This is really something we do not want. Instead, it would make more sense to put the CPU to work by letting it execute the instructions of some other program. And just as simple as this strategy may seem, we will demonstrate that it raises many problems that need to be solved. These problems, and their solutions will be discussed in this chapter. But let's start by taking a look at the source of all the troubles we are yet to encounter.

5.1.1 An example: disk I/O

Imagine that our processor lies at the heart of a computer to which a number of peripheral devices is attached. In particular, assume we have a simple hard disk which is interfaced

Table 5.1 The registers, their mapping, and their meaning of the example disk controller

register	address	semantics
DISKSECTOR	10	specifies the sector number.
DISKTRACK	12	specifies the track number.
DISKSURFACE	14	specifies the required surface.
DISKMEMADDR	16	specifies the start address in main memory where the data is located that is to be either read from or written to the hard disk.
DISKCTRL	20	used to initiate the actual data transfer.

to the computer by an I/O controller which we refer to as the disk controller. We are assuming that the controller uses direct memory access (DMA) for data transfer. As we have explained in Chapter 3, this means that the controller can directly access main memory, from which it can either copy data into its internal buffer or, similarly, copy data from its buffer to main memory. In order to do so, it must know (1) exactly where data is (to be) located on the disks of the actual hard disk, (2) where it is (to be) located in main memory, and (3) how much data it needs to transfer. This means that on the one hand, the surface, the track, and the sector are to be specified, as well as on the other the start address of the data in main memory. With respect to the third point, we shall simplify matters and assume that our disk controller always transfers data in blocks of 512 bytes. Communication with the disk controller takes place through a number of 16-bit registers which are accessible via memory-mapped I/O. The registers and their addresses are specified in Table 5.1.

It is important to recall that our PRIMAL processor assumes that memory can be addressed per byte. This means that each (16-bit) register DISKSECTOR, DISKTRACK, and DISKSURFACE occupies 2 bytes. Register DISKMEMADDR is used to contain the start address in main memory of the data that is to be transferred. In the case of PRIMAL, we need 32 bits, i.e. 4 bytes, to store such an address. Register DISKCTRL is assumed to be 8 bits wide. The disk controller will only start transferring data if the first, i.e. left-most, bit is "1". As soon as data transfer has completed, we assume it then resets this bit to "0". The second bit is used to indicate if data should either be written to disk (in which case it should be set to "0") or read from disk (to which end it is set to "1").

Now first consider a software specification for our hard disk. This can be done by means of the BASAL package specification DISK, given as Listing 5.1. We assume the existence of a package MEMORY that provides a data type MEMORY.ADDRESS, which can be used for representing memory addresses. Our own data type DISK.ADDRESS is used for specifying the exact location of data on a disk. Note that the representation clauses ensure that a variable of type DISK.ADDRESS can be mapped to registers DISKSECTOR, DISK-TRACK, and DISKSURFACE respectively. The procedures READ and WRITE are used for transferring data. In both cases they take a disk address and a memory address as input,

```
package DISK is
    -- We assume that there is a package MEMORY available that will provide
    -- us with, at least, a data type ADDRESS representing locations in main
    -- memory. Recall that this data type is to be referenced using a dot
    -- notation, i.e. MEMORY.ADDRESS.

    subtype CARDINAL is INTEGER range 0..65535;
    for CARDINAL'SIZE use 16;

    -- Analogous to MEMORY.ADDRESS, we define a separate data type ADDRESS
    -- for representing where data blocks are located on a disk. Because we are
    -- using memory-mapped I/O, we also have to provide the representation
    -- of this data type in main memory.

    type ADDRESS is
       record
          sector, track, surface : CARDINAL;
       end record ;

    for ADDRESS use
       record
          sector at 0 range 0..15;
          track at 2 range 0..15;
          surface at 4 range 0..15;
       end record ;
    for ADDRESS'SIZE use 3*16;

    procedure READ(source : in ADDRESS; destination : in MEMORY.ADDRESS);
    procedure WRITE(source : in MEMORY.ADDRESS; destination : in ADDRESS);
end DISK;
```

Listing 5.1 The specification of the package DISK.

after which the disk controller handles the transfer. An implementation of our package DISK is given in Listing 5.2.

First, we have used three variables headPosition, memoryAddress, and diskControl which are mapped onto the respective registers of the disk controller. The implementations of the procedures READ and WRITE are rather straightforward. For example, in order to read a block of data, we first copy the right disk address and memory address into the appropriate registers, set the second bit of register DISKCTRL, and start the data transfer by setting the leftmost bit to "1" by the assignment

```
diskControl(0) := 1;
```

Then, we simply wait until the hardware resets this bit to "0" again, indicating that data transfer has completed. This is done by repeatedly checking the value of the leftmost bit through the **while** statement (execution of a **null** statement has no effect whatsoever)

```
package body DISK is

    subtype BIT is INTEGER range 0..1;
    type BITSTRING8 is array (0..7) of BIT;
    for BITSTRING8'SIZE use 8;

    headPosition : ADDRESS;
    memoryAddress : MEMORY.ADDRESS;
    diskControl : BITSTRING8;

    for headPosition use at 10;
    for memoryAddress use at 16;
    for diskControl use at 20;

    procedure READ(source : in ADDRESS; destination : in MEMORY.ADDRESS) is
    begin
        headPosition := source;
        memoryAddress := destination;
        diskControl(1) := 1; -- set to read data from disk to memory
        diskControl(0) := 1; -- start data transfer
        while diskControl(0) = 1 loop
            null ;
        end loop ;
    end READ;

    procedure WRITE(source : in MEMORY.ADDRESS; destination : in ADDRESS) is
    begin
        headPosition := destination;
        memoryAddress := source;
        diskControl(1) := 0; -- set to write data from memory to disk
        diskControl(0) := 1; -- start data transfer
        while diskControl(0) = 1 loop
            null ;
        end loop ;
    end WRITE;

end DISK;
```

Listing 5.2 An implementation of the package DISK.

```
    while diskControl(0) = 1 loop
        null ;
    end loop ;
```

This type of waiting is a form of **polling**. Within a program P, a procedure is called in which a check takes place on a regular basis to see whether some *external event* has taken place. In our example, the external event is the setting of the leftmost bit to "0" by the disk controller. Because this is the only event that is checked, and moreover because it is checked continuously, this form of polling is referred to as **busy waiting**.

Now the point is that data transfer may take some time, at least in the order of several to tens of milliseconds. This may not seem much, but if you realize that processors to

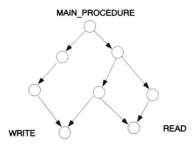

Figure 5.1 An example of related procedures, together forming a program.

date can execute in the order of (tens of) millions of instructions per second, it should be clear that we are indeed wasting valuable CPU time. There is one obvious solution to this problem: let the CPU devote its time to executing instructions of some *other* program P^*. And here's where the problems start.

5.1.2   The problems

We first have to identify the programs that are candidates for having their instructions executed. Now how did we execute the instructions of, for example, READ in the first place? In general, this procedure will have been called from within some other procedure P1 also forming part of our program P. In turn, we may expect that P1 has been called by yet another procedure, say P2, and so on. In the end, there will be a **main procedure** whose instructions were executed by the processor and which eventually resulted in calling the procedure READ. This is illustrated by the graph shown in Figure 5.1 in which a node represents a procedure, and an arc from node p to q the fact that procedure p will *sometime* during its execution call procedure q. A program is thus considered as consisting of a main procedure and all those procedures that are eventually executed due to the fact that they are directly or indirectly called from the main procedure.

Returning to our initial problem of not wanting to waste CPU time during data transfer on behalf of a program P, we wish to identify another program P^* whose instructions can be executed in the meantime. Denote by **P** the collection of procedures belonging to program P. Assume that data is to be transferred between main memory and a peripheral device on behalf of a procedure $p \in$ **P**. Now first suppose we select another procedure $q \in$ **P** whose instructions are to be executed in the meantime.[1] It is easily seen that selecting q is not only senseless, it is wrong. The whole idea of executing instructions of P is that this occurs in a purely sequential order. If we were to simply start executing some other instructions of P (now contained in our selected procedure q), we would violate this sequential execution order – something which is simply not permitted. The only solution, therefore, is to select procedures from some other program P^* which do not be-

---

[1] It should be noted that the assumption that we could even select such a procedure is not realistic. However, the assumption *is* made here for the sake of argument only.

long to **P**. In that case we would really let the CPU execute instructions from a completely different set of procedures. For now, assume that we have such a program P^* available. Introducing multiple programs then quickly leads to the following issues:

Problem 1: Placing several programs in main memory.   The first problem we will have to deal with is the placement of more than one program into main memory. This is not really a major problem until you realize that programs may have varying memory requirements in terms of size, and that these requirements may even change during the execution of a program (think of stacks, for example). Also, we have to ensure that the execution of instructions belonging to one program does not corrupt the data that belongs to another program.

Problem 2: Getting a suitable program.   Stating that we can simply let the CPU execute instructions from some other program is fine, but does impose two problems. First, we have to *find* a suitable program. Clearly, a program that is also waiting for the completion of I/O is not a candidate for the CPU. We are thus confronted with a *scheduling problem*. And even if we have found a suitable program, our problems are not over. In particular, we have to address the question how we can let the CPU continue with executing instructions for program P^*, but later continue where it had left off in program P. This is the problem of *context switching* and which we shall briefly discuss in Section 5.3.1.

Problem 3: Avoiding program interference.   This is a serious problem. Suppose that we have duplicated the package ᴸ'ˢᴷ so that program P^* can also issue data transfers for the hard disk. Duplicating the package, i.e. placing another copy of it into main memory, will not lead to duplication of the hard disk. In particular, all communication with the disk controller still proceeds through its single set of registers. And as long as the disk controller is doing its work on behalf of program P, P^* should be prohibited from manipulating these registers. This is the problem of *program synchronization*, a topic to which we will also need to pay attention.

Problem 4: Reacting to hardware signals.   Our problems started with the fact that we wanted the CPU to execute the instructions of another program. This is fine, but one way or another we will have to complete the execution of the program that we left off when the I/O is finished. This is a problem of *interrupt handling*. It is not a major problem, but it does require that the software for handling peripheral devices be properly organized. In general, we shall see that this problem can be generalized to that of properly handling hardware signals.

In the following four sections, each of these problems will be further explained and solutions presented. At the end, we will have discussed the basic functionality of an **operating system**. We conclude this chapter by taking a look at operating systems in general, and will show how we have been working towards the implementation of a rather sophisticated **virtual computer**.

5.2 Memory management

The first problem that we are going to tackle is that of placing several programs into main memory.

5.2.1 Program relocation

Suppose we have written a BASAL program, i.e. a collection of packages consisting of procedures, and that these packages are subsequently compiled to PRIMAL code. As we have discussed, the compiler will need to allocate memory locations to variables, and also keep track of the memory locations that contain the generated PRIMAL instructions. If we knew for certain that we would always have the main memory all to ourselves, we could instruct the compiler to allocate memory locations to data and instructions starting at, say, address 0. However, if several other programs are also to reside in main memory, we have to be careful about allocating memory locations for they might already have been taken for use in another program. When giving the matter some thought, this approach is seen to be unworkable. For one thing, it is unacceptable to let the process of compilation depend on the previous allocation of memory to programs that have nothing to do with the program that is currently being compiled.

But why not *pretend* that we have main memory all to ourselves? The only thing we need to do is adapt the hardware so that it can make a distinction between **relative** and **absolute** addresses. A relative address in this case is always considered to be relative with respect to the first address of memory that is occupied by a program, where it is assumed that a program always uses a contiguous piece of main memory. If we simply register this first address, we can easily convert relative addresses to absolute addresses which denote actual physical memory locations. What it means is that we implement (in hardware), a function ABS that converts a relative address a_{rel} to an absolute address a_{abs} according to

$$a_{abs} = ABS(a_{rel})$$
$$ABS(a_{rel}) = a_{rel} + a_{base} \tag{5.1}$$

where a_{base} denotes the so-called **base address**, the absolute start address of a program. This principle is shown in Figure 5.2.

The figure illustrates a program of which the translated procedures have been placed in a contiguous piece of memory starting at address 1400. This start address has been loaded into the so-called **base register**. Relative addresses are given to the left of the program, starting at relative address 0. At relative address 100, the value 2304 has been stored. Now assume the PRIMAL instruction

        MOVE 100, D0

is executed. In this case, addresses are taken relative with respect to the value stored in the base register. In other words, in order to obtain the right data, we first add the value

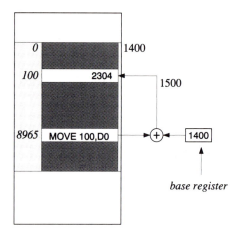

Figure 5.2 Using relative addressing and its conversion to absolute addresses.

contained in the base register to *each* address occurring in an instruction, in this case resulting in the absolute address 1500. In our example, the value 2304 is then loaded into register D0. The only exception to this rule is when variables have been allocated to specific memory locations, as is the case with memory-mapped I/O. Consequently, the PRIMAL instruction set will have to provide the means to indicate if addressing is relative or not. It should be clear, however, that calculating the absolute addresses can be entirely done in hardware.

5.2.2   Procedure protection

There is still another fundamental problem when several programs may reside in main memory: how we prevent a program from corrupting the data of another program. As an example, consider the following piece of PRIMAL code, a subroutine which is assumed to be a part of a program:

```
NASTY:
        MOVE  #END, A0      | Move the address of the last instruction into register A0
LOOP:   MOVE  #0,(A0)       | And store 0 at the location identified by A0
        ADD   #4, A0        | Increment the address stored in A0 by 4
        BRA   LOOP          | And repeat this forever
END:    RTS                 | This instruction will never be executed
```

The point is that as soon as NASTY is called, we first save the address of the last instruction of the subroutine. From that point on, we simply store the value 0 in this memory location, as well as in each location beyond NASTY. Although we may expect that the hardware will refuse to execute any more instructions at the point when memory is exhausted, clearly, if no special measures are taken we will presumably have corrupted a lot of data. In particular, all the data that is stored in those memory locations that are located at addresses higher than the last instruction of NASTY will have been changed. Now

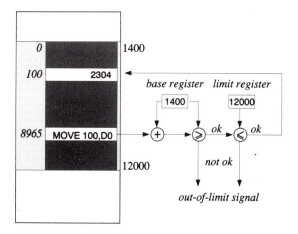

Figure 5.3 Using hardware to check if addresses are referenced within the proper limits.

if some of this data belonged to another program that was also placed in main memory, our subroutine is a problematic one indeed. A rather unacceptably problematic one to be sure.

To solve this problem, computers may have in addition to a base register, a **limit register** in which the absolute end address of a program is saved. Each time an instruction addresses some data or the address of a procedure or subroutine, this relative address is first converted to an absolute address, and then checked against the end address. If it is out of range, the execution of the instruction will simply not take place, but instead, an out-of-limit signal will be generated (we will return to this later). In terms of our above-mentioned function *ABS* that converts relative addresses, we have

$$a_{abs} = ABS(a_{rel}) = \begin{cases} a_{rel} + a_{base} & \text{if } 0 \le a_{rel} \le a_{limit} - a_{base} \\ out\text{-}of\text{-}limit & \text{otherwise} \end{cases} \tag{5.2}$$

The use of a limit register is shown in Figure 5.3. Note that for *each* program there will be a separate value for the (base register, limit register) pair.

5.2.3 Memory allocation

Now that we have seen that we can load a program anywhere in memory without having to affect its addressing, it is time to consider how we can manage the placement of several programs. Suppose we have five programs as shown in Table 5.2, where the completion time denotes the time to complete the program from the moment it is placed in memory. The size of each program is given in units of kilobytes (KB).[2]

---

[2]1 KB = 1024 bytes.

Table 5.2 Five programs to be placed into memory

program	P_1	P_2	P_3	P_4	P_5
size	1024	595	320	560	482
completion time	2	3	4	4	2

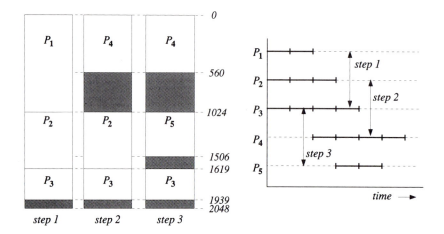

Figure 5.4 Placing programs into memory.

Now assume we have a total main memory of 2048 KB at our disposal. We then attempt to load as much programs in main memory as possible, starting with P_1. Initially, programs P_1, P_2, and P_3 can be loaded, as shown in step 1 of Figure 5.4. After 2 time units have elapsed, program P_1 is finished and can be replaced by P_4, so that we obtain the situation as shown in step 2. Finally, program P_2 will finish after another time unit has elapsed, so that P_5 can be loaded into memory.

Although everything seems to be in order, it is, in fact, not. Imagine what would happen if we had a very large number of programs. In the course of time, memory would be partitioned into contiguous chunks each allocated to a program, and a number of free chunks that can still be used. The problem is that the free chunks tend to scatter all over memory, and moreover, also tend to grow increasingly smaller. And as free chunks tend to become smaller, it should be clear that the maximum size a program can have in order to be loaded into memory decreases as well. The result is that we have what is called a completely **fragmented memory**. The solution to this problem is quite simple. If an allocated chunk of memory is no longer needed (so that it becomes free), we simply try to amalgamate it with a neighboring free chunk. This principle is shown in Figure 5.5.

The question that needs to be addressed is how we can keep track of allocated and free chunks of memory. The answer is quite simple. We do this by means of software. First, it is not hard to imagine how we can represent a contiguous chunk of memory. We merely need to record its start address and its size. This can be represented by means of

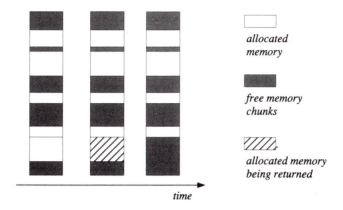

time

Figure 5.5 The process of returning a previously allocated chunk of memory.

the following BASAL data type:

```
type MEMCHUNK is
  record
    startAddress : MEMORY.ADDRESS;
    sizeOfChunk : INTEGER;
  end record ;
```

where, again, we assume that the data type ADDRESS is provided by a package MEMORY, used for representing memory addresses. In addition, we simply need to keep track of the free memory chunks, to which end we can use an array freeChunks declared as:

```
freeChunks : array (1..NCHNK) of MEMCHUNK;
```

In this case, we assume that a maximum of NCHNK free chunks can be administrated. Now, in order to load a program into main memory (which, as we have seen in Section 4.5.3, is done by means of a loader), the loader will have to request a contiguous piece of available memory. Later, when the program has finished, this memory chunk will have to be returned. Therefore, if we implement our memory administration by means of a package MEMORY (the same one that provides us with a definition of what a memory address is), we can expect that its specification will be quite similar to the following:

```
package MEMORY is
  type ADDRESS is ...;

  procedure REQUEST(
     size : in INTEGER; start : out ADDRESS; done : out BOOLEAN);
     −− Request a contiguous piece of free memory of [size] units. If allocation
     −− succeeded, [start] will indicate the start address of the allocated chunk and
     −− [done] is set to TRUE. If allocation was not possible, [done] is set to FALSE.

  procedure RELEASE(start : in ADDRESS; size : in INTEGER);
     −− Return a contiguous chunk of memory starting at address [start] and having a
     −− size of [size] units.
     ...
end MEMORY;
```

The actual BASAL implementations of these two procedures is not very interesting. It merely involves manipulating the array freeChunks, although, admittedly, the amount of code is more than you might expect at first. However, there is nothing really sophisticated about the implementation. The important point to note is that we have constructed a piece of *software* in the form of a service program MEMORY that allows us to keep track of available memory. Combined with the hardware solutions for program relocation and protection, we are now at least capable of placing multiple programs in a single main memory.

It is worth taking a closer look at two more advanced methods of memory management. (We note that the following two subsections can be skipped on first reading.)

▷ 5.2.4   Advanced memory management: paging

The main disadvantage with memory management as described above is that whenever a large program is to be placed into memory it may take a long time before there is a contiguous block of free memory available in which the program fits. This problem can be alleviated by making use of a **paging mechanism**. Paging is the subject of this section.

Principles of paged systems

In paged computer systems memory is partitioned into equally sized **pages**. Typically, the page size (which is generally fixed per computer system) ranges between 128 and 4096 memory locations. An address is broken into a *page number* and a *page offset*, as illustrated in the following example.

Example 5.1. Suppose that main memory consists of $2^{20} = 1\,048\,576$ locations, and that it is partitioned into pages each having a size of $2^8 = 256$ memory locations, so that there is a total of 2^{20} div $2^8 = 2^{12} = 4096$ pages. If an instruction in a program refers to address 26251, then this is converted into a page number p and page offset o, according to

$$
\begin{array}{rcllcl}
p & = & 26251 & \text{div} & 2^8 & = & 102 \\
o & = & 26251 & \text{mod} & 2^8 & = & 139
\end{array}
$$

where "div" denotes integer division and "mod" is the modulo operator, i.e.

$$26251 \bmod 2^8 = 26251 - (26251 \operatorname{div} 2^8) \times 2^8 = 139$$

Calculating the page number and page offset may seem a lot of work, but due to the fact that addresses are just bit strings, and page sizes are always chosen a multiple of 2, we can easily find the page number and offset by stripping off bits in the representation of the address. To illustrate, because our example computer has a total of 2^{20} memory locations, we can represent addresses as bit strings of length 20. In that case, address 26251 corresponds to the following bit string of length 20:

$$26251 \mapsto \underbrace{000001100110}_{12}\underbrace{10001011}_{8}$$

As can be readily verified, the last 8 bits correspond to the binary number $10001011_2 = 139_{10}$, whereas the first 12 bits correspond to $1100110_2 = (26251 \operatorname{div} 2^8) = 102_{10}$.

$\square$

Now suppose we have a program that cannot be loaded into memory because there is not a contiguous block of free memory available that is large enough for it. What we can do then is partition the program into *logical* pages and subsequently try to assign *physical* pages that are available in memory. Let's see how this works. Again, assume that we have a page size of 256 memory locations, and that our program requires a total of 9 logical pages, numbered $L_0, \ldots, L_8$. Now suppose that the first free page in memory is physical page P_6. What we then do is use this page for logical page L_0. In other words, we apply the mapping

$$L_0 \longleftrightarrow P_6$$

We then continue our search. If the next free page is page P_{29}, we then assign L_1 to P_{29}. This process continues until we have assigned all logical pages to free physical pages. While doing so, we keep track of these mappings in a so-called **page table**. In the end, we may find that for our example program we have constructed the following table:

logical page:	L_0	L_1	L_2	L_3	L_4	L_5	L_6	L_7	L_8
physical page:	P_6	P_{29}	P_{67}	P_{289}	P_{723}	P_{1879}	P_{2643}	P_{2644}	P_{3802}

What happens is that whenever an instruction is executed that refers to the **relative** address a_{rel}, this relative address is converted to an **absolute** address a_{abs} using the page table. In terms of our address-conversion function *ABS*, we can specify this as follows. Denote by $PAGE_{\text{PT}}[L]$ the physical page corresponding to the logical page L for a given a page table PT. Let K denote the page size. In that case, it should be clear that for any relative address a_{rel} we can find its logical page $LOG(a_{\text{rel}})$, and thus its corresponding physical page $PHYS(a_{\text{rel}})$ as

$$LOG(a_{rel}) \quad = \quad a_{rel} \text{ div } K$$
$$PHYS(a_{rel}) \quad = \quad PAGE_{PT}[LOG(a_{rel})]$$

We then have for the absolute address a_{abs}:

$$a_{abs} = ABS(a_{rel}) \quad = \quad (PHYS(a_{rel}) \times K) + (a_{rel} \text{ mod } K) \qquad (5.3)$$

For example, suppose our program contains the instruction

```
MOVE   1000, D0
```

Address 1000 is then converted to the logical page number $L_{1000/256} = L_3$, and the offset in that page 1000 mod 256 = 232. Because L_3 was mapped to physical page P_{289} which was recorded in the page table, we see that the instruction is effectively converted to

```
MOVE   74216, D0
```

where $74216 = 289 \times 256 + 232$. Note that, in the context of our discussion on program relocation, the address 1000 is indeed a *relative* address, whereas 74216 is an *absolute* address. However, the base register in paged computer system has been completely replaced by the concept of a page table.

A note on the page table

An interesting aspect of paged systems is the interaction between hardware and software. Obviously, if we want these systems to work efficiently, conversion of logical to physical page numbers should be done by the hardware. But in order to do so, we need a page table. What we can do is put this page table in main memory, and adapt the hardware such that it has an additional **page table register** that contains the address of the first entry of the page table. Each time a memory location is referenced, the hardware interprets the logical page number as an index in the page table. To that end, it adds this number to the value stored in the page table register in order to locate the physical page number.

Example 5.2. Returning to our example computer which had 2^{20} memory locations available, we can use the first 12 bits as an index into a page table that can contain $2^{12} = 4096$ entries. The relative address 1000 corresponds to the following bit string:

$$1000 \mapsto \underbrace{000000000011}_{12}\underbrace{11101000}_{8}$$

We then take the value of the entry #3 in the page table to find the physical page to which logical page L_3 has been mapped. This principle is illustrated in Figure 5.6.

□

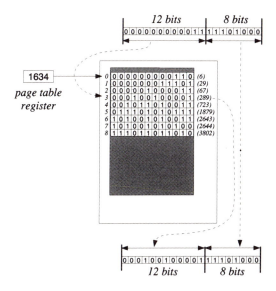

Figure 5.6 Address conversion in paged computer systems.

The important point to note here is that a memory manager which is entirely constructed in *software* fills a page table with appropriate physical page numbers. The *hardware* subsequently uses this table to do the actual conversion from logical to physical page number. To illustrate, suppose a loader wants to place a program into main memory. In that case, it will first request the memory manager for a page table, instead of just a contiguous chunk of memory as previously. A page table can be represented in BASAL by the following data type:

type PAGETABLE **is array** (0..MAXPAGES-1) **of** INTEGER **range** 0..MAXPAGES-1;

where MAXPAGES indicates the maximum amount of pages that can be allocated to a program. Now, for each program there will be a separate variable table of type PAGETABLE that contains the mapping of logical pages to physical pages. This page table will be filled by means of the service program implemented as the package MEMORY. As soon as this has been done, the loader need merely load the address of the variable table into the page table register in order for the program to be executed.

Sharing pages

An important advantage of paging is that certain pages can be **shared** by several programs. For example, the instructions of a program can be considered as non-modifiable data.[3] If

---

[3]Writing so-called self-modifying code was once considered to be a well-engineered solution to problems. A program could modify itself by treating its own instructions as data, and subsequently modify the bit strings that made up certain instructions. Today, you should not say to anyone that you like this.

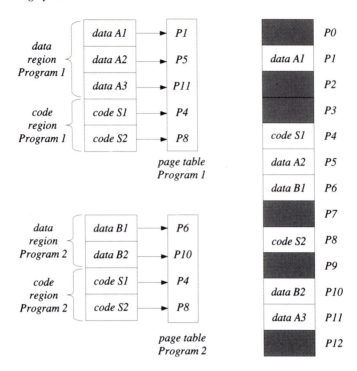

Figure 5.7 Sharing of pages in a paged computer system.

we were to duplicate instructions because several programs execute the same procedures, then it would seem that we are wasting memory. Instead, it would be more efficient if the instructions were placed in memory once, and used by several programs. Paging offers us a convenient means to implement this scheme.

When compiling a program, the compiler can separate the program into at least two different, non-overlapping regions. One, which we refer to as the **data region**, contains all the variables associated with the program. The data region is unique to each program. The second region, called the **code region**, contains only instructions. The code region may be shared with other programs. (Note that making a distinction between data and code regions is indeed feasible. What it means is that the program counter is always loaded with an address that refers to an instruction located in a code region, whereas almost every other address refers to data located in the data region.) In order to load a program into memory, we start with requesting a page table for the data region. Then, if the code region is already located in memory (on behalf of another program), we merely need to fill in the remaining entries of the page table so that they refer to the associated pages containing instructions. Otherwise, the page table will have to be handled by the memory manager because we would need additional memory to place the code region as well. This principle is shown in Figure 5.7.

An excellent candidate program for sharing its code region is a service program. Recall that in our description of the problem of avoiding program interference we assumed that we had duplicated the package DISK on behalf of a program P^*. We needed to duplicate the package in order to let this program also make use of the hard disk. Using shared pages, it is then necessary to assign only additional pages for the variables that occur in the package. All translated instructions need not be duplicated but can instead be located in a number of shared pages. Each time a new program is to be executed, pages are allocated for its own data and code regions, plus additional pages for containing the data related to the service programs.

There is, however, an important exception to this rule and which is the source of many problems related to program interference. Without going into too much detail at this point, reconsider our package MEMORY on page 211. Now clearly, the variable freeChunks which records the available chunks of memory should not be copied for each program, but instead, should be *shared* between all programs. This is caused by the fact that it is *global* information on the availability of main memory that should be maintained independently of the program currently being executed. What this means is that each reference to this data should not be considered as a relative reference, but rather as an absolute reference to a specific part in memory where this variable has been stored. How can we achieve this? Giving the matter some thought, it is not hard to see that we can actually store this, and similar global variables, in a separate physical page that is to be shared by all programs. Indeed, this solution is perfectly in order, except for the fact that we need to prevent two programs from modifying that page at the same time. How such program interference can be avoided is discussed below.

5.2.5   Advanced memory management: virtual memory

In the previous section we discussed how relative addresses can be converted to physical addresses by using a page table. So far, we have assumed that the length of a relative address is the same as that of a physical address. This means that the logical address space is exactly the same as the physical address space. Perhaps somewhat surprisingly, we can do better than that. In particular, we can make the logical address space considerably larger than the physical address space. In other words, to programs it will seem as if the size of main memory is much larger than it actually is. This technique, which we shall briefly describe here, is therefore known as **virtual memory**.[4]

In order to extend the logical address space beyond the size of main memory, a part of secondary storage (i.e. disks) is used to store logical pages that currently cannot be placed in main memory. This part of the secondary storage is also known as the **swap space**. What happens is the following. First, as in paged systems, a memory manager maintains a page table indicating the relation between the logical pages of a program and the actual physical pages with which they are associated. However, whereas in pure page systems each logical page was *always* associated with a physical page, this need hold no longer for virtual memory systems. Instead, a logical page may temporarily not be associated with a physical page implying that it has not been placed in main memory. This is illustrated in Figure 5.8. An additional bit is used to indicate the presence of a page in main memory. In the example,

---

[4]We note that this technique has until recently been used only in fairly large computers. However, now you can buy laptop computers that also support virtual memory.

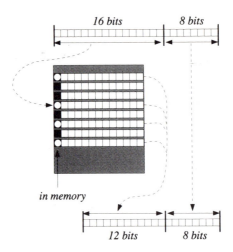

16 bits　*8 bits*

in memory

12 bits　*8 bits*

Figure 5.8 Address conversion in virtual memory systems.

we have expanded the width of an address from 20 to 24 bits, effectively leading to a virtual memory that is $2^4 = 16$ times larger than physical memory.

In terms of our address-conversion function *ABS*, we can then express the calculation of an absolute address as follows. We use the notation $PAGE_{PT}[L] = \perp$ to indicate that the logical page L is presently not associated with a physical page, i.e. L is not placed in main memory. Using our previous notations *LOG* and *PHYS* with

$$
\begin{aligned}
LOG(a_{\mathrm{rel}}) &= a_{\mathrm{rel}} \text{ div } K \\
PHYS(a_{\mathrm{rel}}) &= PAGE_{PT}[LOG(a_{\mathrm{rel}})]
\end{aligned}
$$

We then have for the absolute address a_{abs}:

$$
a_{\mathrm{abs}} = ABS(a_{\mathrm{rel}}) = \begin{cases} (PHYS(a_{\mathrm{rel}}) \times K) + (a_{\mathrm{rel}} \bmod K) & \text{if } PHYS(a_{\mathrm{rel}}) \neq \perp \\ \textit{out-of-memory} & \text{otherwise} \end{cases} \tag{5.4}
$$

This definition of *ABS* strongly resembles (5.3) except for the fact that calculation of an absolute address may fail because there is no associated page. Also, you should realize that in the case of pure paged systems we have

$$
\max\{a_{\mathrm{rel}}\} = \max\{a_{\mathrm{abs}}\}
$$

whereas in virtual memory systems,

$$
\max\{a_{\mathrm{rel}}\} \geq \max\{a_{\mathrm{abs}}\}
$$

Now suppose an instruction refers to an address in a logical page that is currently not placed in main memory. This means that the data or instructions contained in that page are still to be found in the swap space and that, one way or the other, this page will have to be transferred from swap space to main memory in order for the CPU to continue execution of the program. Of course, this can be done by yet another service program. The moment it is detected that a logical page should be transferred to main memory, this service program is automatically invoked (how this is actually done is described further below). The service program initiates a data transfer from swap space to main memory, thereby merely *copying* the logical page from swap space. As soon as the requested page is in main memory, the memory manager updates the page table to which the logical page belonged, and the execution of the program can proceed where it had left off.

Of course, there is a problem when we are running low on available physical pages. In that case, room will have to be made by removing one or several other logical pages from main memory. An important design decision is choosing the right **replacement strategy** that prescribes which logical page is to be removed. To illustrate, suppose we were to remove a logical page that will soon be needed again. In that case, another data transfer will soon have to be initiated again, a situation which we would preferably want to avoid. Page replacement strategies are targeted towards finding the *best* page to replace. But how do we know what the best page is? When giving the matter some thought, you will come to the conclusion that finding such a page requires knowledge of which pages will be referenced in the future. That's asking rather too much.

Therefore, to alleviate such problems, most strategies attempt to select the *least recently used* logical page, i.e. a logical page to which no reference has been made for a long time. The hypothesis is that such a logical page can be expected to remain unreferenced for some time in the future. In addition, logical pages that have not been modified while placed in main memory are preferred to modified ones. Because the memory manager always *copies* a logical page when placing it in memory, non-modified pages can simply be removed without having to update their counterpart as stored in the swap space. Modified pages thus require an additional data transfer from main memory to the swap space. As it turns out, maintaining an administration in order to find the least recently used page is so time-consuming that compromises have to be made. What happens in practice is that the hardware generally provides an additional two administration bits per physical page. The **reference bit** is automatically set whenever a reference to that page is made. The **modify bit** is set by the hardware whenever data contained in the page is changed. Furthermore, the reference bit is periodically reset to 0 so that referenced pages that have not been referenced for some time will appear as non-referenced ones. So, for example, a page with its reference bit equal to 0, and its modified bit equal to 1, indicates that this page has been modified, although some time ago. We shall not go into further detail here, but instead refer the interested reader to Silberschatz and Galvin (1994) or Tanenbaum (1992).

5.3 Process management

At this point it should be clear that we can indeed place several programs in main memory. This brings us to our next problem, namely finding a suitable program with which to continue when I/O is being done on behalf of another program. But before doing so, we first take a closer look at the more fundamental problem of switching over from one program to another.

5.3.1   Context switching

Suppose the CPU has been executing instructions of a program P and has come to a point where data transfer between main memory and a peripheral device is to take place. Rather than letting the CPU wait until data transfer is completed, we assume that it should continue with executing the instructions of another program, say P^*. In this section we shall only be concerned with the problem of how we can switch from executing instructions that belong to P to executing instructions that belong to P^* in such a way, that we can later switch back to P to the point where we had previously left off.

When giving the matter some thought, the solution is – in principle – quite simple. At the moment we initiate a data transfer on behalf of P we also know the *next* instruction of P that is to be executed: its address has been stored (by the hardware) in the program counter. So what we can do is simply save this address somewhere, and load the program counter with the address of the next instruction of P^* that we want to execute. Of course, we assume that we had previously saved this address as well. The moment we load the program counter with this new address, the CPU continues with the execution of instructions that belong to P^*.

But surely, this is not enough. For one thing, the stack that has been constructed on behalf of P has nothing to do with the one which was built on behalf of P^*. Consequently, we have to save the value of the stack pointer (i.e. register SP) which it had when executing P, and reload it with the value it previously had when executing P^*. And this method can be repeated for any other register of the CPU. What it means is that we have to save the complete **processor context** of P, and restore the processor context of P^*. The processor context of a program P at a time t is thus the collection of values stored in the registers of the CPU (and which are affected by P). An important observation is that the processor context changes during the execution of instructions. Now the whole idea is that the processor context also uniquely determines the **execution status** of a program. In other words, if we restore a previously saved processor context of a program P, we expect that execution continues at the point where we had last saved the processor context of P. The effect of saving and restoring a processor context is shown in Figure 5.9.

How can we realize such a mechanism? As may be expected, a solution can be found in software and in particular by means of another service program. We start with developing a data type for representing a processor context for the PRIMAL processor. To that end, we make a distinction between data and address registers, as well as the program counter and the status register (see also Section 4.2.1). These data types will form part of a package called CONTEXT, outlined in Listing 5.3.

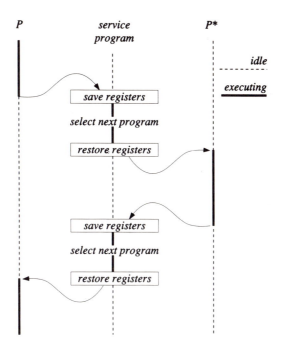

Figure 5.9   Context switching: relinquishing the CPU in favor of another program. Adapted from Silberschatz and Galvin (1994).

```
package CONTEXT is
   ...
   type DATA_REGISTER is (D0,D1,D2,D3,D4,D5,D6,D7);
   type DATA_REGISTER_SET is array (DATA_REGISTER) of BITSTRING32;

   type ADDRESS_REGISTER is (A0,A1,A2,A3,A4,A5,A6,A7);
   type ADDRESS_REGISTER_SET is array (ADDRESS_REGISTER) of BITSTRING32;

   type DEFINITION is
      record
         dataRegister : DATA_REGISTER_SET;
         addressRegister : ADDRESS_REGISTER_SET;
         programCounter : BITSTRING32;
         statusRegister : BITSTRING8;
      end record ;
   ...
end CONTEXT;
```

Listing 5.3 The data types for defining a processor context.

```
package CONTEXT is
  type DATA_REGISTER is (D0,D1,D2,D3,D4,D5,D6,D7);
  type DATA_REGISTER_SET is array (DATA_REGISTER) of BITSTRING32;

  type ADDRESS_REGISTER is (A0,A1,A2,A3,A4,A5,A6,A7);
  type ADDRESS_REGISTER_SET is array (ADDRESS_REGISTER) of BITSTRING32;

  type DEFINITION is
    record
      dataRegister : DATA_REGISTER_SET;
      addressRegister : ADDRESS_REGISTER_SET;
      programCounter : BITSTRING32;
      statusRegister : BITSTRING8;
    end record ;

  MAXPROG : constant INTEGER := ...;
  subtype PROGRAM_ID is INTEGER range 1..MAXPROG;
  type PROCESSOR_CONTEXTS is array (PROGRAM_ID) of DEFINITION;
  currentProgram : PROGRAM_ID;
  processorContext : PROCESSOR_CONTEXTS;

  procedure SWITCH(nextProgram : in PROGRAM_ID);
  -- Switch processor context from the calling program, registered as [currentProgram],
  -- to [nextProgram], so that execution proceeds with instructions belonging to the
  -- next program.
end CONTEXT;
```

Listing 5.4 The complete specification for describing processor contexts.

For each program, we have to be able to save and restore its processor context. Also, we have to keep track of the program that is currently executing. This can be achieved by means of the following declarations (exact declarations are given below):

```
currentProgram : INTEGER range 1..MAXPROG;
processorContext : array (1..MAXPROG) of CONTEXT.DEFINITION;
```

where MAXPROG is the maximum number of programs that can be supported. At this point we have all the necessary declarations for saving and restoring processor contexts. By putting these into a separate service program in the form of the package CONTEXT, we need merely supply a procedure for actually switching from one processor context to another. This leads to a more accurate specification for the package CONTEXT as shown in Listing 5.4.

Ignoring for now where and how the procedure SWITCH is actually called, saving and restoring the processor context roughly consists of executing the following three consecutive steps:

1. Save the value of each register into the appropriate field of processorContext.

2. Administrate that there is another program that is now current by assigning the value of nextProgram to currentProgram.

3. Restore the value of each register by assigning it the value as stored in the appropriate field of processorContext(nextProgram).

These steps coincide with what is shown in Figure 5.9.

▷ However, there is a subtle issue that we are ignoring here if these three steps were indeed to be executed as indicated: we are saving the *wrong* value for the program counter. To explain, note that the value of the program counter is saved during the first step above. In particular, assume it is the last thing we do as part of the first step. This means that the program counter refers to an instruction that forms part of the second step. What this implies is that when we *restore* the program counter during the third step we will immediately continue where we had previously left off. We thus continue with executing the first instruction of the second step. This eventually leads us to restoring the program counter *again* (in the third step), which thus brings us into an infinite loop of executing the second and third step.

What we should have done is the following. First, we should have saved the location of the first instruction that follows the call to the procedure SWITCH. As soon as we restore the value of the program counter, execution then immediately continues with this instruction. Second, this implies that restoring the program counter should also be the *last* thing we do as part of the third step, for any instruction of Step 3 that follows the restoring of the program counter will never be executed. How these matters are dealt with in practice is beyond the scope of this book, as they involve discussing some detailed and specific parts of PRIMAL code. We therefore refer the interested reader to Clements (1994) which includes a detailed discussion on context switching.

5.3.2   From processor contexts to processes

Before we discuss our original problem of selecting a *suitable* program, let's take a step back and see what we are doing at this point. With the concepts introduced so far, we are capable of placing several programs into main memory, and also of switching the CPU between those programs. The approach so far has been strictly bottom-up. We identified what a program was and how we could use the CPU more efficiently by switching between programs at appropriate moments. But from the perspective of a program, nothing really spectacular is happening. When we observe how its instructions are executed, it seems as if there is one CPU that is devoted entirely to executing the program. One way or the other, we have created yet another image of a virtual processor.

Let's see what this virtual processor looks like. First, it consists of a processor context: a true image of the registers that belong to the real processor executing the instructions of a program. But there is more. Whenever a program *P* is not being executed, it is as if its virtual processor is *waiting* for some event to happen. For example, when we choose to let the CPU start executing the instructions of a next program because it had just initiated I/O on behalf a previous program, it is as if the virtual processor that was executing *P* is indeed waiting for I/O to complete. Similarly, when a program has not been placed in main memory, its virtual processor is completely idle: it really has nothing to do. The idea of having a virtual processor exclusively dedicated to executing the instructions of a single program brings us to the concept of a **process**.

> Let P denote a program described in the programming language $LANG(P)$.
> A **process** $PROC(P)$ of P is a *description* of a series of actions or operations
> towards the completion of P, as if the program were executed by the (virtual)
> processor implementing $LANG(P)$.

Note that a process is a description of the *behavior* of a program. Consequently, if we
pretend that the procedures that make up a program are actually executed, we can indeed
view a program in execution as a process.

▷ Our definition deviates slightly from what is given in many textbooks on operating systems.
Most textbooks indeed define a process as a program in execution. However, this definition
is not a very accurate one. To see this, let's consider a program $P\{p,q\}$, where P is a program
consisting of the procedures p and q. So $PROC(P\{p,q\})$ denotes the process associated
with P.

Now nothing prevents us from bringing the program P in execution by two *different* processes $PROC_1(P)$ and $PROC_2(P)$. These processes execute the same program, but may in
the end do different things depending on the input data of a process. Examples are service
programs for identical devices (disks, terminals). On the other hand, we might have another
program $P^*\{p,r\}$ which has the procedure p in common with $P\{p,q\}$. P and P^* have different associated processes, because they are different programs. By association this also
holds for their contained procedure p, which is the same in both programs.

Now, what we need is a description that will allow us to talk about processes as *consumers of resources and services*. For example, a process requires the CPU in order to
have its associated program executed; similarly, it requires memory and peripheral devices, etc. This implies that in order to implement processes for our purposes we have
to administrate the use of hardware resources. In particular, this means that we have to
provide variables for administrating the processor context (which has already been discussed above), as well as variables for keeping track of the page table, data and code
regions (discussed in Section 5.2.4), CPU execution time, etc. Last, but not least, we will
also have to provide the right means for describing when the program of a process is
ready to be executed by a CPU. Therefore, we introduce the concept of a **process state**.
In particular, we make a distinction between the following situations, which are shown
in Figure 5.10. Let P denote the program associated with the process $PROC(P)$.

1. **New.** The process has just been created.

2. **Ready.** The instructions of P can be executed.

3. **Running.** The program is currently being executed by the CPU.

4. **In waiting.** The instructions of P that are to be executed next are placed in main
   memory, but execution must wait for the availability of one or other resource.

5. **Out waiting.** The instructions of P that are to be executed next are no longer placed
   in main memory. In addition, execution must wait for the availability of one or
   other resource.

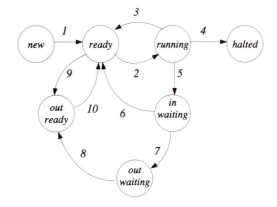

transition	reason
1	the process has been created.
2	the process has been selected for execution.
3	a time slice has expired.
4	the process has terminated.
5	the process requires a resource that is currently not available.
6,8	the required resource has become available.
7,9	the process has to make room for another process.
10	the process is placed back into main memory.

Figure 5.10 The general state-transition diagram of a process.

6. **Out ready.** The instructions of *P* can be executed, but are currently not placed in main memory.

7. **Halted.** The process has terminated.

Of course, it is not possible to make a transition from one state to an arbitrarily chosen next state; Figure 5.10 also shows the transitions that are possible.

Clearly, processes that are suitable for execution by the CPU are those that are residing in state **ready**. And these are precisely those processes that are not waiting for a resource to become available, and of which the associated program has been placed in main memory. Selecting one of these so-called ready processes can proceed according to different

```
package CPU_SCHEDULER is
   subtype PROCESS_ID is CONTEXT.PROGRAM_ID;

   type BASIC_STATE is (NON_EXISTENT, EXISTS, HALTED);
   type EXISTS_STATE is (READY, RUNNING, WAITING);
   type MEMORY_STATE is (IN_MEMORY, OUT_MEMORY);

   type PROCESS_STATE is
      record
         basic : BASIC_STATE;
         exists : EXISTS_STATE;
         memory : MEMORY_STATE;
      end record ;

   procedure SET_BASIC_STATE(
      proc : in PROCESS_ID; state : in BASIC_STATE);
   procedure SET_EXISTS_STATE(
      proc : in PROCESS_ID; state : in EXISTS_STATE);
   procedure SET_MEMORY_STATE(
      proc : in PROCESS_ID; state : in MEMORY_STATE);
   procedure GET_PROCESS_STATE(
      proc : in PROCESS_ID; state : out PROCESS_STATE);

   procedure SCHEDULE_NEXT(nextState : in EXISTS_STATE);
   -- To be called when the current process wants to relinquish the CPU, thereby setting
   -- itself in [nextState]. The process returns from this procedure call only after
   -- it has been scheduled again by some other process.

   currentProcess : PROCESS_ID; -- A globally accessible variable.
end CPU_SCHEDULER;
```

Listing 5.5 Initial data types for describing CPU scheduling.

strategies. For example, each process may have an associated priority, or the least recently selected ready process may be chosen. So, finding a suitable program is no longer a real problem. But who is going to do this? Again, the answer is to be found in software by means of a so-called **CPU scheduler**. Let's start by describing some data types that will allow us to administrate processes adequately. First, the state of a process can be represented by means of the data types and operations in Listing 5.5. For completeness, we have also added procedures for setting and retrieving the state of a process, as well as a procedure SCHEDULE_NEXT, and a global variable currentProcess which are used for scheduling purposes. Scheduling is discussed below.

But, of course, we need to keep track of more things. Using the declarations from the previous sections, we can represent a complete process by means of a so-called **process control block**, which can be represented in BASAL as shown in Listing 5.6.

Now suppose a process needs to give up the CPU for some reason. In that case, it need merely call the CPU scheduler in order to find a next program that can be executed. Therefore, we provide a procedure SCHEDULE_NEXT as part of a package CPU_SCHEDULER which also contains the declarations given so far, and some additional administration

```
type PROCESS_CONTROL_BLOCK is
   record
      state : PROCESS_STATE;
      dataTable : MEMORY.PAGETABLE;  -- See Section 5.2.4
      codeTable : MEMORY.PAGETABLE;
      ...
   end record ;
```

Listing 5.6 Definition of a process control block.

```
package body CPU_SCHEDULER is
   ...
   processTable : array (PROCESS_ID) of PROCESS_CONTROL_BLOCK;

   procedure SCHEDULE_NEXT(nextState : in EXISTS_STATE) is
      nextProcess : PROCESS_ID;
      nextIsFound : BOOLEAN;
   begin
      -- The process that is calling this procedure will be'currentProcess'.
      -- A good candidate to start searching for next is its successor as
      -- administrated in the process table. But before doing so, set the
      -- current process in its desired [nextState].
      processTable(currentProcess).state.exists := nextState;
      nextProcess := currentProcess mod CONTEXT.MAXPROG + 1;
      nextIsFound := FALSE;
      while not nextIsFound loop
         if processTable(nextProcess).state.basic = EXISTS and
            processTable(nextProcess).state.exists = READY and
            processTable(nextProcess).state.memory = IN_MEMORY
         then
            -- You found an appropriate candidate for executing next.
            nextIsFound := TRUE;
         else
            -- The presently inspected process is not eligible to be executed.
            -- Continue searching by inspecting its successor.
            nextProcess := (nextProcess mod CONTEXT.MAXPROG) + 1;
         end if ;
      end loop ;
      currentProcess := nextProcess;
      CONTEXT.SWITCH(nextProcess);
   end SCHEDULE_NEXT;
end CPU_SCHEDULER;
```

Listing 5.7 Outline of an implementation for a CPU scheduler.

variables. This procedure (shown in Listing 5.7) takes as parameter the EXISTS_STATE
to which the *calling process* should be set. We will see how this feature is used when we
reconsider our implementation of the package DISK.

The point is that a process which is going to give up the CPU keeps searching (now pre-
tending to be the CPU scheduler) for the next existing process that is ready and in memory.

Other selection criteria can be taken into account as well but have not been included in our outline. The first process that meets all criteria is then selected as the current process, and a context switch is made. (It should be noted that the code shown is rather simplified. In practice, much more checking needs to be done to find the *most* suitable program.)

At this point we are now able to adjust our DISK package as presented in Section 5.1. Instead of using the repetitive statement

```
while diskControl(0) = 1 loop
   null ;
end loop ;
```

we can now let the CPU continue with executing the most suitable program by means of the statement:

```
CPU_SCHEDULER.SCHEDULE_NEXT(CPU_SCHEDULER.WAITING);
```

where we indicate that the calling process should be put into the state WAITING. How we can eventually continue with the disk driver is discussed further below. For now, it should be clear that we have achieved the means to let a number of processes *share* a single CPU. But if we look again at what we have done from the perspective of a process, we have actually accomplished something quite spectacular. For example, suppose a process $PROC_1$ wants to read some data from disk. To that end, it calls the procedure READ from package DISK. This procedure call will eventually lead to the required data transfer, but will also suspend the process by letting the CPU continue with the execution of instructions that belong to an entirely different process, say $PROC_2$. That some other process will be executed, however, is completely hidden from $PROC_1$. To $PROC_1$ it still seems as if the CPU is executing instructions on its behalf. What we have thus accomplished is an image of a computer that consists of *several* processors or, in other words, we have a **virtual multiple processor** computer at our disposal. The spectacular thing about it is that we have realized this image entirely in software, and it turned out that it was not that difficult either. But we also introduced new problems as will be discussed in the next section.

5.4   Process interference

Probably one of the most intricate issues to deal with in cases where multiple processes co-exist, is unwanted interference. Generally, this can happen when the CPU is executing instructions on behalf of a process $PROC_1$ and which alter data that is stored on behalf of another process $PROC_2$. There are several solutions for avoiding interference, depending on the type of interference that can occur:

1. First, it may be necessary to let processes explicitly *synchronize*, meaning that a process $PROC_1$ is forced to wait until a process $PROC_2$ has reached a certain situation. Synchronization can generally be realized through software, although it is convenient to have some rudimentary hardware support.

2. Besides synchronization, we also have to deal with the fact that during execution, the hardware may interrupt the CPU. In that case, any execution of instructions by the CPU should not interfere with those it was executing just before the interrupt occurred.

3. Finally, providing service programs may seem in order, but they become useless if we cannot impose their use. What we need is a mechanism to force processes to make use of service programs so that we can *control* the avoidance of unwanted process interference.

Each of these subjects is discussed in the following three subsections.

5.4.1 Synchronization: semaphores

Imagine that a process $PROC_1$ has just issued a data transfer by calling the procedure READ as part of the service program DISK. This call will eventually result in a context switch to another process $PROC_2$ as explained in the previous section. Now assume that while data transfer is taking place on behalf of $PROC_1$, process $PROC_2$ calls the procedure WRITE from DISK, which, of course, should be perfectly in order. There is only one problem. The disk driver can handle only a single request at a time. This means that process $PROC_2$ will have to *wait* until the data transfer on behalf of $PROC_1$ is finished. It can then issue a new request by setting the disk driver's registers, and subsequently wait again until its own request has been processed. We first identify exactly *where* process $PROC_2$ should be suspended. Reconsidering our implementation of WRITE, it is not too difficult that this point can be identified as follows:

```
procedure WRITE(source : in ADDRESS; destination : in ADDRESS) is
begin
— WAIT HERE UNTIL A PREVIOUS REQUEST IS FINISHED —

    headPosition := destination;
    memoryAddress := source;
    diskControl(1) := 0;
    diskControl(0) := 1;

    CPU_SCHEDULER.SCHEDULE_NEXT(CPU_SCHEDULER.WAITING);
end WRITE;
```

It would seem that a solution to this problem should not be that difficult to find, but, it did take a few years before a generally accepted mechanism was introduced. In 1965 the Dutch mathematician Edsger Dijkstra devised the concept of a **semaphore**. A **binary semaphore** is a Boolean variable which, apart from its initialization, can be accessed by only two standard operations: *wait* and *signal*. The definition of these operations is given as follows:

wait(s)	::	**when** s **do** $s \leftarrow$ **false**
signal(s)	::	$s \leftarrow$ **true**

where

> **when** s **do** $s \leftarrow$ **false**

adheres to the semantics that the execution of a process is postponed until s is TRUE. Then the process will continue, but will also immediately set s back to FALSE again.

An important aspect of the *wait* and *signal* operations is that they are both **atomic**. An atomic operation is characterized by the fact that if N processes $PROC_1, \ldots, PROC_N$ simultaneously execute such an operation, then the result is the same as if the operation was executed N times in some arbitrary sequence, once by each process $PROC_i$. This is best explained by means of a simple example.

Example 5.3. Suppose that several people have access to the same bank account. There are only two operations that can be performed: *withdraw*(x) by which an x amount of money is removed, and *deposit*(x) which increases the savings at the account. Now, as you might imagine, drawing money from the account or depositing some money each requires a series of actions. For example, in order to draw money, we first have to check if enough money is available, and if so, decrease the savings by the amount that is required. Expressing this informally in BASAL could be done as follows:

```
procedure WITHDRAW(amount : in INTEGER; result : out INTEGER) is
    currentAmount : INTEGER;
begin
    currentAmount := the present savings;
    if currentAmount > amount then
        -- It is safe to withdraw some money. Adjust the savings.
        present savings := present savings - amount;
        result := amount;
    else
        -- Only give the amount that has been saved.
        result := present savings;
        present savings := 0;
    end if ;
end WITHDRAW;
```

Apart from the fact that this is not a very realistic way of getting money, it does illustrate that we need to perform several activities to achieve the final result. Moreover, in order to keep the savings account *consistent*, it is essential that no two persons draw money at the same time. Instead, one will have to wait for the other to finish. The order in which they draw money is irrelevant; what is relevant is that our administration is still correct. In that sense, WITHDRAW (and likewise its counterpart DEPOSIT) will have to be an atomic operation.

□

Let's take a closer look at the operations *wait* and *signal*. First, assume we have an implementation available as a BASAL package with the following specification part (we return to its implementation later):

```
package SEMAPHORE is
    subtype DEFINITION is BOOLEAN;

    procedure WAIT(sema : in out DEFINITION);
    procedure SIGNAL(sema : in out DEFINITION);
end SEMAPHORE;
```

Assume that the program of a process has included the procedure call

```
SEMAPHORE.WAIT(sema);
```

somewhere in one of its programs. Then, when sema is FALSE, the execution of the program is postponed until sema becomes TRUE. Moreover, if the program call succeeds (which can happen only if sema is TRUE), execution proceeds but the semaphore is also immediately set to FALSE again. Consequently, any other process that called the procedure WAIT will be postponed when it is executed. Postponement is maintained until the statement

```
SEMAPHORE.SIGNAL(sema);
```

is executed. It is thus seen that semaphores can be used to *serialize* the behavior of a collection of processes. In a sense, a semaphore acts as a lock through which only one process can pass at a time. Entering that lock can only take place by execution of WAIT; leaving the lock is accompanied by a call to SIGNAL.

It should be clear that our problem of the disk driver can indeed be solved by using semaphores. The point is that the code section of the procedure WRITE (and that of READ as well) should only be executed on behalf of, at most, one process at a time. In terms of the lock we mentioned above, the code section forms a lock for all processes that want to make use of the disk driver. We can then adapt our implementation as shown in Listing 5.8.

The important point to note here is that semaphores provide us with a means to let communication take place according to a simple *protocol*, namely that a process must *wait* until a semaphore has the right value. This is quite similar to the way processors synchronize by means of a bus. They first try to *claim exclusively* the bus for themselves by setting a high signal on the bus request line, and wait until the grant signal is passed on. This action corresponds to the execution of a WAIT(sema) operation for a semaphore sema. When the grant signal is set on the line, exactly one processor can pick it up and prevent any other processor from taking over the bus. As soon as the processor has finished its bus transfer, it puts a high signal on a bus release line, so that the grant signal can be propagated to the other processors (of which, again, only one will succeed in getting access to the bus). From a certain perspective, we see that we have made a *software equivalent* to something that was already available in the hardware.

```
package body DISK is
  lock : SEMAPHORE.DEFINITION := TRUE;
  ...
  procedure WRITE(source : in MEMORY.ADDRESS; destination : in ADDRESS) is
  begin
    SEMAPHORE.WAIT(lock);

    headPosition := destination;
    memoryAddress := source;
    diskControl(1) := 0;
    diskControl(0) := 1;

    CPU_SCHEDULER.SCHEDULE_NEXT(CPU_SCHEDULER.WAITING);

    SEMAPHORE.SIGNAL(lock);
  end WRITE;
  ...
end DISK;
```

Listing 5.8 An adaptation of the procedure WRITE for our example disk driver.

▷ **Implementing semaphores**

There is, however, a practical problem with semaphores: their implementation. For example, if we strictly followed the definition of the *wait* operation, the following implementation would seem to be in order:

```
procedure WAIT(sema : in DEFINITION) is
begin
  while not sema loop
    null ;
  end loop ;
  sema := FALSE;
end WAIT;
```

There are two problems with this solution. First, we see that valuable CPU time can still be wasted due to the **while** statement. As avoiding busy waiting was the main reason we started our discussions, the solution above does not seem to be a very good one. The second problem is perhaps more serious. As we have stated, the *wait* and *signal* operations need to be *atomic*. In other words, they should be executed without any interference. The solution above does not meet this demand. Let's take a closer look at these two issues.

Avoiding busy waiting.   A solution to the problem of busy waiting is to apply the same technique as we did previously. If a process notices that the *wait*-operation cannot immediately be successfully completed, it records itself as waiting for the semaphore in question, and schedules another process. Likewise, upon executing the *signal*-operation by a process $PROC_1$, this process activates exactly one other process $PROC_2$ that was waiting (by setting processTable($PROC_2$).state.exists to READY) if the latter was waiting for the semaphore to become TRUE again.

```
type DEFINITION is –– Definition of a semaphore type.
   record
      value : BOOLEAN;
      queue : QUEUE.DEFINITION;
   end record ;

procedure WAIT(sema : in out DEFINITION) is
begin
   if not sema.value then
      QUEUE.APPEND(sema.queue, CPU_SCHEDULER.currentProcess);
      CPU_SCHEDULER.SCHEDULE_NEXT(CPU_SCHEDULER.WAITING);
   else
      sema.value := FALSE;
   end if ;
end WAIT;
```

Listing 5.9 An initial implementation of the *wait* operation.

This scheme can be realized as follows. First, let's assume we have a package QUEUE at our disposal that will allow us to handle queues of processes. This package can be derived from our parameterized package GENERAL_QUEUE described in Listing 4.13 (page 172) as follows:

```
package QUEUE is new GENERAL_QUEUE(ELEMENT ⇒ CONTEXT.PROGRAM_ID);
```

Using this package allows us to implement the procedure WAIT as shown in Listing 5.9. To that end, we have adapted the definition of semaphores in such a way that each semaphore has not only an associated value but also an associated queue for administrating processes that are waiting for the value to become TRUE.

If a process finds that the semaphore is currently FALSE, it appends itself to the semaphore's queue, and schedules another process. Otherwise, it simply sets the value of the semaphore to FALSE and immediately continues. By setting the value to FALSE, no other process can pass beyond the procedure until it becomes TRUE again. We leave it as an exercise for the reader to outline a solution for the procedure SIGNAL.

Implementing atomicity.   The problem of atomicity is perhaps a more serious one. In order to understand, you have to realize that a process can be interrupted in its execution by a peripheral device. As we shall explain below, the effect of such an interrupt is that some *other* process may temporarily continue its execution. On this account we may assume that, conceptually, there may be two processes $PROC_1$ and $PROC_2$ *simultaneously* executing WAIT(sema). Assume that the value of the semaphore sema is initially TRUE. What can happen is that first, process $PROC_1$ starts with testing this value, and finds it to be TRUE. At that moment, and before it comes to setting the value to FALSE, an interrupt may occur, eventually leading to process $PROC_2$ executing the **if** statement as well, and *also* finding sema.value to be TRUE. However, this may never be allowed to happen. At any moment, at most one process may conclude that sema.value is TRUE, and thus that it may proceed.

The problem is that the statements of the procedures WAIT and SIGNAL, respectively, should again be protected as if they were locks, just as the statements of WRITE above. Obviously, we cannot immediately use semaphores to establish what we want (this is also left as an exercise for the reader). What it means in practice, is that we have to resort to hardware solutions. For example, the 680x0 family of processors supports a special **test-and-set** instruction that takes the form

```
TAS     address
```

To simplify matters, what this instruction does is first test if the value stored at memory location address is zero (i.e. TRUE), and then immediately sets it to a non-zero value (i.e. FALSE). This allows us to implement rather primitive binary semaphores by means of the following two subroutines (where sema is a symbolic name for a memory location):

PWAIT:	TAS	sema	Test if the value at address sema is zero, and
			set it to a non-zero value
	BNE	PWAIT	If the value was not zero, try testing it again
	RTS		Otherwise, return from this subroutine
PSIG:	MOVE	#0, sema	Simply set the value at address sema to zero
	RTS		And return from this subroutine

But, you might say, this solution is also not satisfactory because we are still making use of busy waiting. However, there is an important difference from our previous implementations. The solution above is to be applied only in those cases where we may expect that a *wait* operation will shortly be followed by a *signal* operation. In other words, if any process that calls PWAIT finds the semaphore's value to be FALSE, it can expect that it need only wait briefly before this value becomes TRUE again. Only in these cases is busy waiting justified. It is beyond the scope of this book to show in detail how procedures like WAIT and SIGNAL can be made atomic. The matters are simply too technical, and the interested reader is referred to references at the end of this chapter. It is important, however, to note that semaphores are nearly always supported by the collection of service programs that are provided as part of the software that goes with the computer you buy. In the end, their implementation is always supported by hardware.

5.4.2   Interrupt handling

It is time to look at another problem that we mentioned in Section 5.1: reacting to hardware signals. The point is that after data transfer has completed the hardware will signal this completion by interrupting the CPU. How this is done at the hardware level has been discussed in Section 3.4.1. But we have to ensure that the CPU eventually continues with executing the instructions of the program that it had left off. The problem is easily generalized to the following question: How can we ensure that certain instructions are executed on account of a hardware signal, and in such a way that this does not interfere with the current execution of instructions?

When giving the matter some thought, it is seen that we have to deal with a rather strange problem. We have to devise a *software* response to a *hardware* signal. The problem is less intricate than it seems. As explained in Section 3.4.1, any signal that interrupts

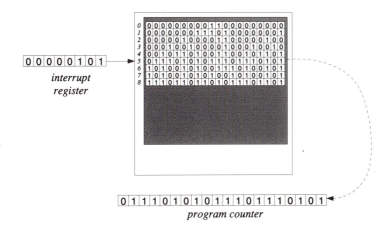

interrupt
register

program counter

Figure 5.11 The principle of an interrupt table.

the CPU is always accompanied by an *identification* of that signal, for example, by storing a unique number in some special-purpose register. This number can then be used to identify the first address of a series of instructions that the CPU should execute when it is interrupted. To that end, we can use an **interrupt table**, which works in the same way as the page table discussed in Section 5.2. The principle is illustrated in Figure 5.11.

Each time the hardware wants to interrupt the CPU, the identification of the interrupt signal is first loaded into a special register, which we refer to as the **interrupt register**. Then, as soon as the CPU can handle the interrupt, it starts with automatically pushing the current value of the program counter (and presumably also of other registers) onto the stack. In order to find exactly how it should handle the interrupt, it takes the value found in the interrupt register as an index to the interrupt table, which contains the address of the first instruction to execute. It continues to execute the series of instructions starting at the indicated address until it encounters a so-called **return from interrupt** instruction. At that point, the interrupt has been completely handled, and execution returns to the point where it had left off before the interrupt occurred. The instructions that are executed as a consequence of an interrupt form a special type of program, called an **interrupt handler**.

To illustrate, we construct a simple interrupt handler in BASAL. We add the following procedure INTERRUPT_HANDLER to our package specification of DISK:

```
package DISK is
   ...
   procedure INTERRUPT_HANDLER;
   for INTERRUPT_HANDLER'CALL use at 5;
end DISK;
```

What we have specified here is that the procedure INTERRUPT_HANDLER can only be CALLed via interrupt #5. (We note that we have purposefully deviated from the syntax and semantics of Ada for the sake of simplicity. Precise details on how interrupt handlers can be specified in Ada can be found in ANSI (1983).) Using this information, the compiler will then insert the start address of the first instruction of INTERRUPT_HANDLER into entry #5 of the interrupt table. The implementation of the interrupt handler can now be outlined as follows:

```
package body DISK is
    ...
    procedure INTERRUPT_HANDLER is
        waitingProcess : CPU_SCHEDULER.PROCESS_ID;
    begin
        waitingProcess := process that originally initiated the data transfer;
        CPU_SCHEDULER.SET_EXISTS_STATE(
            waitingProcess, CPU_SCHEDULER.READY);
    end INTERRUPT_HANDLER;
    ...
end DISK;
```

In this case, we assume that we can identify the process that had originally initiated the data transfer via the variable waitingProcess. The package CPU_SCHEDULER includes a procedure SET_EXISTS_STATE for altering the present state of a process. Furthermore, also assuming that the disk controller uses interrupt #5 to identify itself, the CPU will execute the procedure INTERRUPT_HANDLER by simply setting the state of the process waiting for completion of the data transfer to READY. In principle, this is enough to schedule the process later (i.e. restore its processor context) so that it can continue where it had left off. The complete implementation of our simple disk driver is summarized in Listings 5.10 and 5.11.

▷ It should now also be clear how we can handle other hardware signals. For example, in the case of virtual memory we have to initiate a data transfer when a logical page is not in memory. What happens is that the hardware inspects the first bit of an entry in the page table as shown in Figure 5.8. If the bit indicates that the logical page is not in memory, the identifier of a *page fault* is first stored in the interrupt register, after which the actual signal is generated that will interrupt the CPU. From there on, the story continues analogously to our disk driver interrupt handler. In this case, a procedure is executed that initiates the data transfer and which then schedules another process to be executed.

5.4.3   Forcing the use of service programs

We are gradually approaching our final topic on service programs. What we have been doing so far is introducing problems that are related to supporting multiple programs in a computer. We have shown that by introducing service programs most of the problems could be handled by software, occasionally with some additional help by the hardware. So far, so good. There is only one thing we have to ensure, namely that processes indeed make use of these service programs. Otherwise, we will still find ourselves in a lot of trouble. For example, suppose that someone writes a private version of the package DISK, including a procedure that sets the registers of the disk driver. Obviously, something like this should not happen, but can we prevent it with the solutions introduced so far? The answer is negative.

```
package DISK is
   subtype CARDINAL is INTEGER range 0..65535;
   for CARDINAL'SIZE use 16;

   type ADDRESS is
      record
         sector, track, surface : CARDINAL;
      end record ;

   for ADDRESS use
      record
         sector at 0 range 0..15;
         track at 2 range 0..15;
         surface at 4 range 0..15;
      end record ;
   for ADDRESS'SIZE use 3*16;

   procedure READ(source : in ADDRESS; destination : in MEMORY.ADDRESS);
   procedure WRITE(source : in MEMORY.ADDRESS; destination : in ADDRESS);

   procedure INTERRUPT_HANDLER;
   for INTERRUPT_HANDLER'CALL use at 5;
end DISK;
```

Listing 5.10 The specification part of the revised version of DISK.

What we need is an additional mechanism that prevents non-service programs making use of certain parts of memory. In particular, those memory locations that are used for the registers of I/O controllers, as well as those for page tables, interrupt tables, etc. should not be directly accessible by non-service programs. In order to establish this, we need support from the hardware. In general, the problem is solved by making a distinction between two operation modes for the CPU. When operating in **kernel mode** *all* special memory locations may be accessed. In **user mode** only the remaining memory locations can – in principle – be referenced. Of course, an individual program may be further restricted by means of a limit register. The use of the user and kernel mode varies from system to system, and generally differs between processors. Indeed, it is a highly hardware-dependent feature.

The next step is to organize the service programs into a separate part of memory, as shown in Figure 5.12. Now because we need to separate service programs from ordinary programs, we shall also have to find a safe way of passing parameters to service programs. This can be accomplished by means of a **system call** which is generally implemented by using a special hardware **TRAP instruction**. The mechanism is illustrated in Figure 5.12. What happens is that in order for a program to call a service program it first identifies the service program, and then copies the parameters to a commonly accessible location. Typically, the registers of the CPU can be used for this purpose. Then the TRAP instruction is executed by which the CPU switches to kernel mode.

At that point, the CPU continues with executing a so-called trap handler that identifies the required service. This corresponds to step 1 in Figure 5.12. The trap handler, which

```
package body DISK is
  subtype BIT is INTEGER range 0..1;
  type BITSTRING8 is array (0..7) of BIT;
  for BITSTRING8'SIZE use 8;

  headPosition : ADDRESS;
  memoryAddress : MEMORY.ADDRESS;
  diskControl : BITSTRING8;
  lock : SEMAPHORE.DEFINITION := TRUE;

  for headPosition use at 10;
  for memoryAddress use at 16;
  for diskControl use at 20;

  procedure READ(source : in ADDRESS; destination : in MEMORY.ADDRESS) is
  begin
    SEMAPHORE.WAIT(lock);

    headPosition := source;
    memoryAddress := destination;
    diskControl(1) := 1;
    diskControl(0) := 1;
    CPU_SCHEDULER.SCHEDULE_NEXT(CPU_SCHEDULER.WAITING);

    SEMAPHORE.SIGNAL(lock);
  end READ;

  procedure WRITE(source : in MEMORY.ADDRESS; destination : in ADDRESS) is
  begin
    SEMAPHORE.WAIT(lock);

    headPosition := destination;
    memoryAddress := source;
    diskControl(1) := 0;
    diskControl(0) := 1;
    CPU_SCHEDULER.SCHEDULE_NEXT(CPU_SCHEDULER.WAITING);

    SEMAPHORE.SIGNAL(lock);
  end WRITE;

  procedure INTERRUPT_HANDLER is
    waitingProcess : CPU_SCHEDULER.PROCESS_ID;
  begin
    waitingProcess := process that originally initiated the data transfer;
    CPU_SCHEDULER.SET_EXISTS_STATE(
      waitingProcess, CPU_SCHEDULER.READY);
  end INTERRUPT_HANDLER;

end DISK;
```

Listing 5.11 The implementation part of the revised version of DISK.

is similar to an ordinary interrupt handler, is followed by a jump to the requested service program (step 2). Again, the start address of the service program will have been stored in

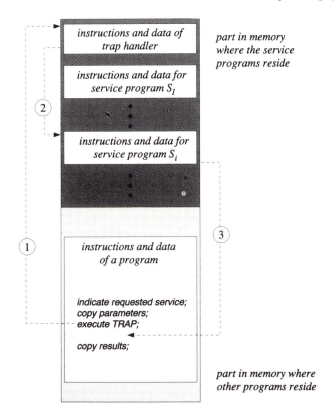

Figure 5.12 The interaction between service programs and a program requesting a service S_i to be performed.

a *service table*, which is comparable to the page table and interrupt table mentioned previously. After the service has finished, execution continues where it had left off (step 3), thereby switching the CPU back to user mode and leaving it to the program to copy the results into its own variables.

5.5 On operating systems

So where do we stand? So far we have illustrated how a number of service programs can be constructed that allow multiple programs to be placed in memory and which can jointly make efficient use of the available hardware. Moreover, when we consider these service programs, it is seen that they make the hardware much easier to use. For example, a program that wants to initiate a data transfer need not be concerned with other programs, because any interference is handled entirely by the service programs. What we have been doing is explaining the core functionality of a so-called **operating system**. An operating system can be defined as a collection of service programs that allow the hardware of a computer system to be used *easily*, and to be used *efficiently*. In this section we shall take a closer look at operating systems, in particular how they are organized and what type of functionality they generally offer.

5.5.1   The evolution of operating systems

If you read most textbooks on operating systems, you will find that many subjects are presented that will not be discussed in this chapter. In order to put things into perspective, and to understand why we are diverging from the more usual approach, let's take a brief look at the history of operating systems.

Conventional operating systems

Conventional operating systems originated from the same problem we described in Section 5.1: waste of valuable CPU time. In the 1950s computers were only capable of executing a single *job* (comparable to our concept of a program) that had to run to completion until the next job could be executed. Hardly any support for programming a computer was provided. For example, the first systems required that programmers explicitly programmed the hardware in machine language, including *all* routines to handle I/O. Later, service programs and high-level languages and their compilers were made available so that at least some convenient level of abstraction was supported. But although the problem of programming these systems was somewhat alleviated, it still required the intervention of a human operator to run a series of jobs. Also, while a job was doing I/O (mostly printing its results) the computer would remain idle. And each time a job was finished, the computer would then need to be activated again in order to process the next one.

The first solution to tackle the problem of wasted CPU time was found in **batch processing systems**. The idea was to first collect a number of jobs onto a single tape, or as a consecutive series of sets of punched cards, then execute these jobs in a row, and finally collect the output on a separate tape. While the next batch was being executed, the output tape was processed separately by printing the results *off line*. This approach at least had the advantage that computational work and printing was done simultaneously. And with a bit of luck, you could have your nice program calculating $z \leftarrow x^n + y^m$ for various values of x and y completely processed within several hours.

This approach had two severe problems. First, users had to wait too long for their jobs to be completely processed, and second, the manufacturer had to provide two separate computers. The solution was found in the 1960s by means of **timesharing** systems. Using a single computer, users could be connected to the system by means of terminals that would allow them interactively to edit, compile, and execute their programs. The only thing that was needed was support for having multiple programs in a single system. With the price of hardware still very high, it was felt that only large *general-purpose* computing systems would provide a sufficiently low price/utilization factor. Apart from whether this was true, it did bring a major problem, namely that the operating systems that had to accompany these large computing systems were extremely difficult to develop, and many projects have failed for precisely this reason.

Now while manufacturers were developing large *mainframe* computers to satisfy everyone's needs, there was also an approach to the development of so-called minicomputers. These much smaller systems could often deal with only a few different programs at a time, but were far cheaper than their mainframe counterparts, because the operating system was much easier to develop. Consequently, these systems became affordable for small groups who would then no longer need to rely on the large, centralized, and often bureaucratic computing centers where the mainframes were sited. The trend towards smaller systems continued rapidly, although buying a computer system still involved putting a lot of money on the table. Software, i.e. the operating system, had become more sophisticated in order to get the most out of the hardware. In fact, it was becoming a major task of manufacturers to provide not only the right hardware but also the right software to support program development and user interaction adequately.

Towards smaller systems

But things started to change. In the mid-1970s AT&T Bell Laboratories developed an operating system called UNIX.[5] UNIX was unique in two ways. First, more than 90% of the system's core functionality was written in a high-level language (C). The functionality included all the aspects we have discussed in the previous sections, plus one extra, namely that of a file system (we will return to this later). But above all, this functionality could be realized in no more than approximately 10 000 lines of code. Up to then, this approach was unheard of. In order to make the system really useful, numerous general-purpose *utility programs* were added for the user's convenience. However, where such programs were normally included as part of a complete operating system, in the case of UNIX they were just add-ons to the kernel (which comprised only 5–10% of a complete system). The developers of UNIX demonstrated that operating systems could be kept small, flexible, and hardware-independent.[6]

But the real impact came with the introduction of microprocessors in the early 1980s. Microprocessors made personal computing affordable and created a large demand for software that is flexible and user-friendly. Two operating systems have dominated the world of personal computing: MS-DOS for Intel-based microprocessors, and UNIX for the more powerful workstations (often based on RISC processors). Now at first, personal computers were stand-alone systems meaning that a single computer was supplied with a keyboard, monitor, mouse, and printer. The only way to exchange data with another computer was by carrying floppy disks from one system to another. During the mid-1980s it became custom to connect personal computers by means of a **network**, which put an additional burden on operating systems. They now also had to provide the right means for *communication* with other computers.

---

[5]This is the only statement we shall make concerning the story of UNIX – and it is far too little to appreciate what actually happened. The interested reader is referred to Salus (1994) for a historical overview.

[6]You should read Garfinkel *et al.* (1994) if you want to know why some people think UNIX is not so good.

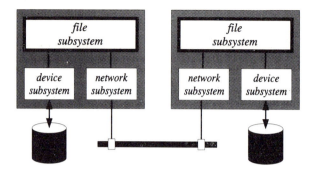

Figure 5.13   The global interaction between two different operating systems connected in a computer network.

Current technology: microkernels

This communication involved the exchange of data. Now one of the core functionalities of operating systems is providing a flexible means of storing data and programs through **files**. A file is a software abstraction of actual storage devices such as disks and tapes. This means that you can write data to a file, as well as read data from it. In addition, files that contain programs can be compiled and executed. By incorporating it as a *core* functionality it is easier to keep operating systems efficient. And this is what most (older) operating systems usually do in the sense that the complete organization of a file system is constructed as part of the **kernel** of the operating system. This has an important implication: if you want to change that part, you will (1) have to have the source code of the operating system at your disposal, and (2) know exactly what you are doing, for you may expect that any change in the kernel will affect other parts as well. In other words, any changes to the kernel of an operating system will generally have to be done by the manufacturer.

When hooking different computers into the same network, this is an unfortunate situation, for each kernel will presumably have to be adapted in order to accept data from another system. In order to transfer data from one file to another, where both files each resort under the regime of a different operating system, each kernel must be adapted in order to allow for the communication and conversion of files to take place. This approach is illustrated in Figure 5.13, where we see that the kernel itself needs to be adapted. So much for flexibility.

The solution to this problem is evident. Rather than incorporating the notion of a file into the core of an operating system, devise a file system as an additional *utility service*. And this is precisely the current trend in operating systems. The idea is to develop so-called **microkernels** that only have a bare functionality. Then, in the case of coupling several computers in a network, the microkernels need only provide for basic communication means which is generally restricted to transferring small packets consisting of a series of bytes. Figure 5.14 illustrates this approach. In this case, the file subsystem can

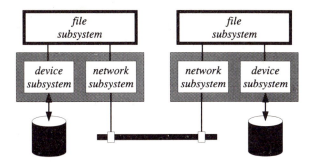

Figure 5.14 The global interaction between two microkernels.

be completely replaced by the user of the microkernel, as it has been placed outside that kernel. And although it can still be expected that only an expert can do this, it should be clear that no adaptations to the kernel are necessary. In fact, replacement of the file subsystem can actually be done during normal operation of the microkernels.

What we have been doing in this chapter is discussing what these microkernels look like and how they are realized. The only functionality we have not considered is that of communication. This subject will be treated extensively in succeeding chapters. File systems will be treated in the next section as an example of how the functionality of a microkernel can be extended. For now, in the following subsections we shall resort to paying attention to the *organization* of microkernels.

5.5.2   Architectural aspects of operating system kernels

Despite the fact that microkernels may be relatively small, they are still to be considered intricate pieces of software. Organizing a microkernel into a structured set of modules is essential in order to keep the system manageable and flexible. In general, microkernels are organized into four groups of modules, each providing a separate service:

1. Process management
2. Memory management
3. Device management
4. Interprocess communication.

Interprocess communication is discussed extensively in the following chapters. Here, we shall consider briefly the organization of each of the other services, and how they interact with each other. The overall architecture is shown in Figure 5.15.

Process management

Process management can be logically organized into three components: a *dispatcher*, a CPU *scheduler*, and some general *process administration*, as shown in Figure 5.16.

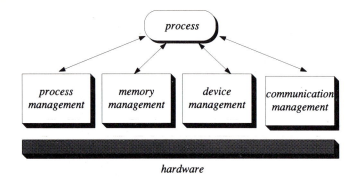

Figure 5.15 The overall architecture of a microkernel with four modules.

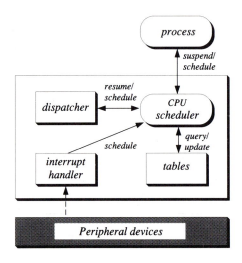

Figure 5.16 The logical organization of process management.

A dispatcher is a small procedure which establishes context switches between processes. In this sense, it is the program CONTEXT.SWITCH explained in Section 5.3.1.
From a logical point of view, a dispatcher always interacts with the CPU scheduler. It
either dispatches the CPU to the scheduler so that the latter can find a suitable process to
which to assign the CPU, or is activated by the scheduler again when such a process has
been found. There are two situations when the dispatcher is activated. First, a process
that needs to synchronize with another process (including synchronization on account of
I/O) will eventually have to relinquish the CPU. Second, whenever an interrupt has been
handled, it is generally the case that the interrupted process will no longer be the most
suitable one to which to assign the CPU. In that case too, the scheduler must be set to
work by activating the dispatcher.

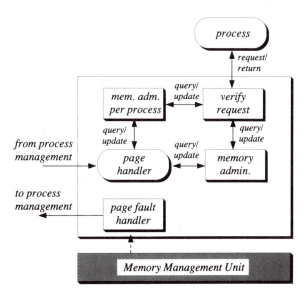

Figure 5.17 The logical organization of memory management.

As we have already discussed, in order to find the most suitable process for the CPU, we will need to have a scheduler that takes care of that. Conceptually, a CPU scheduler is just another process that inspects and updates the process administration in order to schedule the next process. For efficiency reasons, however, the scheduler is generally implemented as an ordinary procedure similar to our procedure SCHEDULE_NEXT shown in Listing 5.7. In that case, a process or interrupt handler directly calls the scheduler procedure in which a suitable next process is found, and in which the dispatcher is then activated.

Memory management

Memory management is generally organized into a few components as shown in Figure 5.17. A key role is played by the actual memory administration unit which keeps track of the occupied and available chunks of memory. Generally, it need not be much more sophisticated than our example administration discussed in Section 5.2.

Processes may request more memory, or otherwise return previously allocated memory chunks. In systems that do not support advanced memory management such as paging or virtual memory this is about all there is to it.

▷ However, when paged or virtual memory is supported, some additional checking will need to be done to see if requests are valid. To this end, there will be a separate memory administration per process in which all information concerning the page tables and current memory usage per process is stored. Some interaction with process management will be required, which primarily concentrates on properly activating the so-called *page handler*. Like the

CPU scheduler, a page handler can be conceptually considered as a separate process which is activated whenever a page needs to be transferred between main memory and the swap space. There are two occasions when this can happen:

1. In the case of virtual memory systems, as soon as a virtual address refers to data that is not located in main memory the hardware (by means of a so-called **memory management unit**, or **MMU**) will generate an interrupt which in turn causes a *page fault handler* to be invoked, as explained in Section 5.4.2. This interrupt handler, in turn, will require the process manager to schedule the page handler so that the required data can be brought into main memory.

2. When no virtual memory is supported, the page handler will occasionally be scheduled in order to allow a complete program to be placed in main memory. The page handler in that case may have to remove another program in order to make room. Obviously, the page fault handler shown in Figure 5.17 which is only responsible for passing interrupts to the dispatcher will then not be needed.

Again, in many systems the page handler is a procedure that is directly called rather than explicitly scheduled. However, it is important to note that this is only done in order to achieve efficiency. Conceptually, we can consider the page handler as a separate process.

Device management

Device management is generally organized in the form of so-called **device drivers**. There are all types of device drivers. Some can be almost as small as our example package DISK, others are so complex that it takes an expert to understand them. Nevertheless, device drivers are always more or less similarly structured. In general they consist of three parts:

- A *request handler* that deals with communication between the driver and processes requesting I/O

- A *device handler* that passes information from the request handler to the I/O controller

- An *interrupt handler* that deals with information that is passed by the I/O controller to the driver.

This general organization is shown in Figure 5.18. When the driver is rather simple (which is often so when dealing with simple keyboards, monitors, and storage devices), the request handler and device handler are rarely explicitly distinguished. The main difference between the two is that the request handler is *device independent* in the sense that it has no knowledge of the actual means of communication with the I/O controller. Details concerning the location and setting of registers are completely hidden in the device handler. However, in the case of extremely difficult drivers, like those used for laser printers, the device driver itself is organized as a layer of handlers, with only the lowest layer being programmed for a specific I/O controller. Also, the interrupt handler is sometimes not required, e.g. in the case of a monitor.

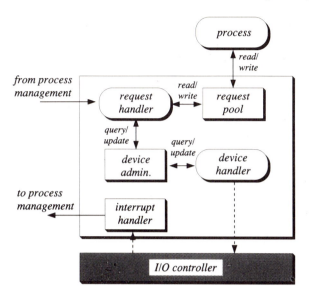

Figure 5.18 The general architecture of a device driver.

Whenever a process issues an I/O request, it passes this to the request handler, which again can be considered as a separate process. The request handler generally queues the request in such a way that several I/O requests can be handled simultaneously, and in the most efficient way. For example, in most disk drivers the request handler organizes the requests such that arm movement is minimized. In the end, it passes the best request to the device handler which sets the registers of the I/O controller.

As soon as I/O has completed, the I/O controller will generate an interrupt which is subsequently handled by the *interrupt handler*. This interrupt handler, in turn, will request process management to schedule the request handler as soon as possible so that the next I/O request can be processed. This explains the two arrows in Figure 5.18 between the device driver and process management. Again, in most systems this scheduling of the request handler is done directly without interference of the CPU scheduler. In other words, the request handler returns as an ordinary program that is immediately called as soon as an interrupt occurs.

5.5.3   A global architecture

Operating systems tend to be large programs, and, not surprisingly, they can be extremely complex. It is therefore mandatory to have a general organization of the operating system that makes it a manageable piece of software. In the preceding section, we discussed the organization of individual components. Here, we shall look at one possible global organization, namely that of a **client-server architecture**. Although many other architectures exist, this one is particularly interesting in light of the discussion on commu-

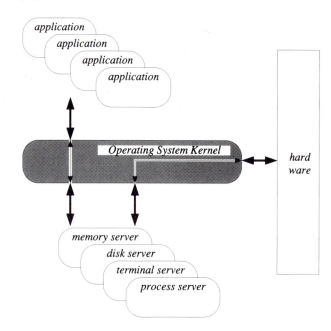

Figure 5.19 A client-server architecture applied to an operating system.

nication systems to be presented in the next chapters. The organization of an operating system following the client-server model not only provides a manageable organization for computers having a single processor, but is particularly attractive when extending an operating system in order to support multiple computers.

In a client-server architecture, the collection of programs is divided into two groups: those of **clients** that can issue **service requests** to, so-called **servers**. In practice, clients as well as servers are implemented as processes. In operating systems, a striking aspect is that in general only a small part of all its programs refer to I/O registers and shared variables. In other words, a major part of the programs constituting an operating system could be executed by the CPU while it is in user mode. This is what happens when adopting the client-server architecture for operating systems.

In particular, the system is split into two parts. The first part, which we have referred to as the **(micro)kernel**, consists of a minimal set of programs that make use of special memory locations and shared, global variables such as page and interrupt tables. In addition, the kernel is augmented by a small set of service programs that allow for **interprocess communication**. In other words, programs that allow processes to synchronize and exchange data. The rest of the operating system's programs are simply implemented *as if they were normal processes*. In particular, this means that they communicate with the kernel in the same way as other processes: by means of service programs that are called via system calls.

But, of course, there should be some kind of distinction between user processes (clients)

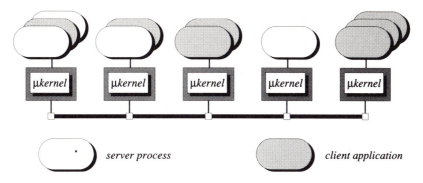

Figure 5.20 A distributed version of a client-server based operating system.

and operating system processes (servers). The general situation is shown in Figure 5.19. User processes communicate as clients with the kernel as described in Section 5.4.3. The kernel (being executed in kernel mode) checks the service request, and if it is found to be in order, passes it on to the appropriate server. The server, in turn, handles the request and, if necessary, passes a hardware-oriented request to the kernel. For example, a file server may request that a complete block of data is to be written to a specific hard disk. The actual data transfer is handled by the kernel, and the server is notified when the request has been processed. The latter then proceeds by finishing the request and notifying the client, again via communication through the kernel.

The advantage of this scheme should be clear. Because servers are executed in user mode, it is almost impossible to include hardware-dependent programs. Servers are only dependent on the operating system's kernel. Second, it is easy to modify a server. Because it is just another process running in user mode, we can replace it without affecting the other parts of the operating system, just as we can remove any user process and replace it with another. Anticipating our discussion on networks in later chapters, it is not hard to imagine that if the kernel is connected to a network, a client and a server need not be executed by the same CPU. In that case, we are **distributing** the operating system over several computers as shown in Figure 5.20.

5.6   An example extension: file systems

It is about time we said something about an important and probably the most visible part of many operating systems: file systems.[7] A file is an abstraction of a storage device. It is possible to store data in a file and retrieve data from it. Files are mapped (by the operating system) onto actual storage devices such as tapes, disks, etc. In our discussion here we shall not only focus on what file systems are, but also use them as an example of

---

[7]This is a rather crude remark. The most visible part is without doubt the so-called **command shell**. A command shell is a program that lets you interactively make use of important service programs. Command shells are not discussed in this book.

a component of an operating system which is, in fact, hardware-independent. As we shall see, in order to construct a file system we need only assume the existence of a microkernel which in its own right is a virtual computer. In other words, file systems can be seen as a pure software extension of the virtual machine we have been discussing so far. Therefore, we will first briefly see what files look like from the outside, after which we discuss their implementation on top of a microkernel. Files are organized into directories, which, in turn, basically need *only* the concept of a file in order to be implemented. In this sense, directory services form yet another extension of a virtual computer, but this time one which incorporates files.

5.6.1   The concept of a file

There are various types of files, but here we shall consider only a simple kind of file. Logically, we consider a file as an abstract storage device which is organized as a consecutive series of bytes. When talking about files in this way, it means that we can specify exactly which byte we wish to read from or write to a file. This can be easily expressed in BASAL by means of the following outlined package specification for a FILESYSTEM:

```
package FILESYSTEM is
    subtype FILESIZE is INTEGER range 0..MAXFILEPOS;
    subtype FILEPOS is INTEGER range 1..MAXFILEPOS;
    type FILE is ...;

    procedure READ(f : in FILE; pos : in FILEPOS; b : out MEMORY.BYTE);
    procedure WRITE(f : in FILE; pos : in FILEPOS; b : in MEMORY.BYTE);
end FILESYSTEM;
```

where we assume that the package MEMORY provides an appropriate definition of the data type BYTE. The actual definition of the data type FILE is left for now. Further details will be provided later. We further assume that the size of a file is limited to MAXFILEPOS bytes, which is also not further specified. We shall illustrate our package further below. But before doing so, we need to say more about files in general. The distinction between a file's size and a position in a file (represented by FILEPOS) is discussed now.

First consider the procedure READ which is to be called when a byte b is to be read from a file f and stored at position pos in that file. Now, typically, not all files will have the same amount of data stored. In other words, each file will have a *size*. The data stored as bytes in a file will then reside at positions $1 \ldots size$, and in order to read data, the value of pos will have to lie somewhere in this range. Of course, reading data from an empty file, i.e. a file have size 0, makes no sense.

When writing data, two situations can occur. Assume the size of a file f is presently $size(f)$. Writing a byte to position P with $1 \leq P \leq size(f)$ then implies that we are *updating* the contents of a file: the data that was stored at position P is replaced by some other data. On the other hand, we can also *expand* a file by writing data to position $P = size(f) + 1$. In that case, the size of the file increases by exactly one byte.

An important aspect of a file is that it acts as a **virtual storage device**. This means that as soon as we have written a byte to a file, we may assume that if the computer is

```
package FILESYSTEM is
  MAXFILEPOS : constant INTEGER := ...;

  subtype FILESIZE is INTEGER range 0..MAXFILEPOS;
  subtype FILEPOS is INTEGER range 1..MAXFILEPOS;
  subtype FILE_ID is INTEGER;

  procedure GETSIZE(id : in FILE_ID; size : out FILESIZE);

  procedure CREATE(id : out FILE_ID);
  procedure DELETE(id : in FILE_ID);
  procedure OPEN(id : in FILE_ID);
  procedure CLOSE(id : in FILE_ID);

  procedure READ(id : in FILE_ID; pos : in FILEPOS; b : out MEMORY.BYTE);
  procedure WRITE(id : in FILE_ID; pos : in FILEPOS; b : in MEMORY.BYTE);
end FILESYSTEM;
```

Listing 5.12 A package specification for a file system.

switched off, that byte will have been permanently stored somewhere. It is the task of the operating system to ensure this. In contrast to real storage devices, files can easily be added and removed. This means that an operating system allows you, in principle, to create as many files as you like, and if so required, is also prepared to remove them permanently. In practice, a file can only expand by writing a byte to its end. Removing a byte is generally not possible. In that case you will have to copy all the bytes you want into a new file, and subsequently delete the old file.

Using this information, we can refine our package specification at a number of points. First, whenever a file is created, operating systems generally provide a unique **file identifier** that is to be used to further identify the file when applying other operations. In most systems, before a file can be read from or written to it is mandatory to *open* it. Strictly, opening files before using them is not really necessary. However, it does allow the operating system to simplify its own administration as we shall see further below. Likewise, *closing* a file is done to inform the operating system that you (for now) will no longer be needing the file.

This then leads to the refined package specification shown in Listing 5.12. Note that we have omitted the data type FILE, whose specification need in fact be of no concern to users of files. Instead, we need merely to identify files, which is now done by means of a FILE_ID data type. The procedure GETSIZE has been added so that we can find out how large a file actually is. When a file is created by calling the procedure CREATE, a unique file identifier is returned to the calling process. The created file is assumed to be initially empty, i.e. its size will be 0.

Example 5.4. To illustrate how files can be used in practice, consider the situation where we want to store an array of characters in a file. For simplicity, we assume that a character corresponds precisely to a single byte (which it usually does), but above all that we can

```
package body MY_PROGRAM is
  type CHAR_ARRAY is array (1..NCHAR) of CHARACTER;

  procedure DO_SOMETHING is
    myData : CHAR_ARRAY;
  begin
    myData := fill the array with characters that make sense to you;
    FILESYSTEM.CREATE(newFile);
    FILESYSTEM.OPEN(newFile);
    for k in 1..NCHAR loop
      FILESYSTEM.WRITE(newFile, k, myData(k));
    end loop ;
    FILESYSTEM.CLOSE(newFile);
  end DO_SOMETHING;
end MY_PROGRAM;
```

Listing 5.13 An example of storing data in a newly created file.

use the procedures READ and WRITE directly, without having to *convert* a character to a byte or vice versa. Look at the program shown in Listing 5.13.

What we see here is that we (1) create a new file, then (2) open it, (3) subsequently append data to the file, and (4) finally close it again. By the end of the execution of DO_SOMETHING, the file newFile will have a size of NCHAR bytes.

□

Example 5.5. A useful procedure that is almost always available to users, is one by which you can copy one file to another. In particular, copying a file implies that we create a second version of the first. The BASAL procedure COPY shown in Listing 5.14 will do just that.

□

Although our treatment of files at this point may seem simplistic, you should realize that, in essence, there is not much more that needs to be said. Most real file systems will indeed provide a somewhat more elegant way of manipulating files, but from a user's perspective, they would not be much more advanced than those we have presented here. The real difference between file systems lies in the way that they are implemented and organized into directory structures. These two issues are discussed next.

5.6.2   File implementation

Our next concern is to see how our concept of a file can be realized. As we have said, we shall assume that we have a microkernel at our disposal that at least allows us to manipulate a hard disk. In fact, assume that we have access to our example disk driver discussed in the previous sections. That means we can read and write blocks of data from and to a hard disk, respectively, and which is controlled by the microkernel.[8] In that case, *im-*

---

[8]For simplicity, we assume that there is only a single hard disk available. Normally, a microkernel would allow access to at least several disks.

```
procedure COPY(
      oldFile : in FILESYSTEM.FILE_ID;
      newFile : in out FILESYSTEM.FILE_ID) is
    size : FILESYSTEM.FILESIZE;
    data : MEMORY.BYTE;
begin
  FILESYSTEM.CREATE(newFile);
  FILESYSTEM.OPEN(oldFile);
  FILESYSTEM.OPEN(newFile);
  size := FILESYSTEM.GETSIZE(oldFile);
  for k in 1..size loop
    FILESYSTEM.READ(oldFile, k, data);
    FILESYSTEM.WRITE(newFile, k, data);
  end loop ;
  FILESYSTEM.CLOSE(newFile);
  FILESYSTEM.CLOSE(oldFile);
end COPY;
```

Listing 5.14 An implementation of a procedure that copies one file to a new one.

plementing our file system now reduces to providing the right *mapping* of files onto the disk. And yes, there are some problems that need to be solved. First, we have to account for the fact that our files can handle *individual* bytes, whereas our disk driver can transfer only *blocks* of bytes. Second, we also have to consider how we are going to administrate where bytes are eventually stored on a disk. These two questions are dealt with next.

Bytes versus blocks

An important distinction between our notion of a file and that of a hard disk is that the former is capable of storing individual bytes. In other words, it is possible to transfer only a single byte between a file and main memory. Disks, on the other hand, support only the transfer of blocks of bytes. In particular, assume that a disk block always consists of 512 bytes. We have to devise a mechanism that allows us to manipulate individual bytes, but in such a way that we can still transfer data from and to disk in blocks of 512 bytes. The solution to this problem is really not that difficult: we can organize files *internally* in units of 512 bytes as well, which we refer to as **file blocks**. (We note that choosing a file block having a size other than 512 bytes is also possible. But in that case, the relation between a file block and a disk block becomes somewhat more difficult than we are willing to discuss here.) A file block can easily be represented in BASAL as follows:

type FILE_BLOCK **is array** (1..512) **of** MEMORY.BYTE;

Following this line of thought, we then consider a file as a consecutive series of file blocks, starting at block #1. The position *pos* of a byte in a file is then to be transformed into a pair consisting of a **file block number** *num* and a **file block offset** *offset*, with

$$pos = (num - 1) \times 512 + offset \quad \text{with } 1 \le offset \le 512$$

To illustrate, if a process wants to read the byte at position 3412 we need to first fetch file block number 7 from disk and subsequently pass byte number 340 to the requesting process.

Notice how we have silently modified our way of considering file blocks: they now are associated with a file, and are also numbered. This change can be reflected by adapting our previous definition of the FILE_BLOCK data type:

```
type BLOCK_CONTENTS is array (1..512) of MEMORY.BYTE;
type FILE_BLOCK is
    record
        fileId : FILE_ID;
        blockNumber : INTEGER;
        data : BLOCK_CONTENTS;
    end record ;
```

At this point, we first need to say something about how file blocks can be associated with disk blocks before we continue our discussion on file implementation.

Keeping track of disk blocks

In order to implement files, we need to associate each file block uniquely with a disk block. Conceptually, this is simple: as disk blocks are identified by a sector, track and surface, we need merely administrate for each file block precisely where it is located on disk. To this end, we can introduce, per file, a so-called **file index block**, which can be represented in BASAL as follows:

```
type INDEX_BLOCK is array (1..MAXINDEX) of DISK.ADDRESS;
```

where MAXINDEX now indicates the maximum number of blocks per file. So, for example, if indexBlock is the index block for file f, then indexBlock(k) will contain the exact location on disk of the kth file block of f. This approach also suggests a first representation of a file in BASAL:

```
type FILE is
    record
        fileId : FILE_ID;
        numOfBlocks : INTEGER range 0..MAXINDEX;
        indexBlock : INDEX_BLOCK;
        ...
    end record ;
```

where the field numOfBlocks indicates the actual size of the file, now expressed in the number of file blocks contained in the file. Note that our FILE data type contains information *about* a file, in particular, it tells us where we can find the actual data that is stored in the file.

It should be noted at this point that, in practice, index blocks are more sophisticated than we are presenting here. In particular, file systems may support index blocks that can vary in size in order to support small as well as large files without having the need to also use large index blocks for small files. However, it is beyond the scope of this book to go into these matters in detail, and we refer the interested reader to the references given at the end of this chapter. References to other methods of associating file blocks to disk blocks can be found there as well. The remainder of this subsection can be skipped on first reading.

▷ **Disk space management**

But associating file blocks to disk blocks is not the entire story. Before we can make such an association we have to find a disk block that is *available*, i.e. which is not already being used for storing data. What we need is a **disk storage manager**. This is a service program that keeps track of disk blocks that are in use and those that are available. In this sense, it is very comparable to our memory manager discussed in Section 5.2. There is only one point about keeping track of available disk blocks that needs some attention. To explain, we need to know something about the way a disk storage manager does its administration.

In many systems, a disk is administered as a consecutive series of disk blocks, with each disk block having a unique disk address. For each disk block, the storage manager simply records if the disk block has been allocated to a file, or not, by means of a **block allocation table**. In terms of BASAL, we can represent this as the following data type:

```
type BLOCK_ALLOCATION_TABLE is array (1..MAXDISKBLOCK) of BOOLEAN;
```

Then, if bat denotes a block allocation table, bat(k) = TRUE indicates that block number #k is free, whereas bat(k) = FALSE indicates that it has already been allocated to a file. Now the point to note is that for each disk its allocation table will need to be changed whenever files are created, deleted, or expanded. This can only be done when the allocation table is in main memory. Remember that the disk storage manager is just another service program and that all its administration must be in main memory in order to be manipulated. But when the computer is switched off, the allocation table may not be lost. Therefore, in contrast to our service program for managing main memory, the storage manager will have to ensure that the allocation table is stored on disk as well. Therefore, it will reserve enough disk blocks in advance to store its own administration.

Putting it together

We are now in a position to be more explicit on how a file system can be implemented on top of a microkernel. In particular, we want to outline some of the characteristic implementation aspects of our package FILESYSTEM given above. As we have said, in order to transfer data to and from a file we need first to copy the appropriate file block from disk and temporarily store it in main memory. Moreover, before we can transfer any file data, the file in question will have to be opened first. In practice, file system implementations allow only a maximum number of files to be open at any time. For each opened file, space in main memory will be reserved so that one or several of its file blocks can be temporarily stored for reading or writing purposes. We can represent this in BASAL by means of two variables: openFiles is an array for keeping track of opened files, and fileBlocks is an array for temporarily storing requested file blocks. Expressed in BASAL, this leads to the following declarations:

```
type OPEN_FILES is array (1..MAXOPENFILE) of FILE;
type OPEN_FILE_BLOCKS is array (1..MAXOPENBLOCKS) of FILE_BLOCK;

openFiles : OPEN_FILES;
fileBlocks : OPEN_FILE_BLOCKS;
```

Now let's see what happens when we open a file. Without going into too many implementation details, assume that openFiles(k) is presently not referring to an opened file. In that case, we can use that entry to store all relevant information on a file we wish to open. It is not hard to imagine where this information comes from: it is stored somewhere on disk (how it came there in the first place is discussed below). This so-called **file header** is then read from disk and stored in main memory as a FILE variable in openFiles(k). At that moment, all information on a specific file is now available to the file system.

Reading information from an opened file is then straightforward. First, the appropriate file block number is calculated as discussed above. By means of the index block stored as part of the file header, the associated disk block can be identified, and the disk driver will be instructed to read that block into main memory. The block itself will be stored as, say, file-Blocks(m).data; the file system will set the two fields fileBlocks(m).fileId and fileBlocks(m).block-Number as appropriate. As soon as the file block has been fetched from disk, the requested byte can be handed over to the process that originally initiated the data transfer. Now suppose the process wanted to read the *next* byte as well. Of course, unless the byte that was first requested was the last one of the file block, there will be no need to initiate another data transfer from disk, because the file block containing the next byte is already in main memory. Any file system will therefore always check if a referenced file block is already in memory or not.

Writing data to files proceeds in an analogous way. The interesting situation is when a process wants to append data to a file, such that it is necessary to allocate a free disk block. In that case, the file system will require the disk storage manager for an available disk block, assign one of its entries in fileBlocks for that block, and from there on allow the process to write data to the file. At a certain point in time, the file block which is still located in main memory will be transferred to disk as soon as the file system has instructed the disk driver to do so.

In order to create a file, we need to accomplish two things: make sure (1) that we have a file header, and (2) that we know where to find that header on disk. Now, for simplicity, assume that a file header will fit into a single disk block, i.e. in order to create a file we need only request the disk storage manager for an available disk block. Assuming such a block is available, the storage manager will pass back the disk address of that block to the file system. We have to be able to store that disk address permanently (why?). Therefore, many file system implementations, in particular those based on UNIX, maintain a so-called **index list**. This *fixed-sized* list can be represented in BASAL as:

```
type INDEX_LIST is array (1..MAXFILE) of DISK.ADDRESS;
```

The index list itself is stored on disk at a number of *pre-determined* disk blocks. In other words, these locations are always the same. It should now be clear what needs to be done in order to create a file. The file system has to (1) search in the index list for an entry that is not yet used for a file, and then (2) request the disk storage manager for an available disk block in order to store the header of the new file. The entry used for the file can actually be its unique identifier.

Storing file blocks in main memory

Above, we assumed that a file block could simply be read into main memory, and stored as an entry of fileBlocks. However, as soon as MAXOPENBLOCKS have been transferred from disk, there is no more reserved space available. In that case, the file system will have to make a decision to remove one or several file blocks from main memory. If it decides to remove a file block that has been changed, that block will have to be written back to disk; blocks that have not been changed (e.g. those from which a process only reads information) can simply be replaced by new file blocks. In this sense, the **replacement strategy** for file blocks in memory is quite analogous to that for replacing logical pages in the case of virtual memory.

Another interesting aspect about keeping file blocks in memory as illustrated here is that we can increase efficiency if carefully designed. To illustrate, suppose a process wants to modify a file block. The block is brought into memory after which it can be manipulated by the process. Now suppose we keep this block in memory for a reasonably long time. In that case, if the process wants to later modify the block again, we will have avoided a data transfer from disk if that block is still stored in main memory. In other words, it may be worth keeping file blocks relatively long in main memory before writing them back to disk. In practice, this is indeed an effective way to increase the performance of a file system. This organization of keeping file blocks in main memory before writing them to disk is referred to as **software caching**. The main problem, however, is that if a file block is not written to disk immediately after it has been modified we may find ourselves in an unfortunate situation if the computer crashes, for in that case the file as stored on disk will be inconsistent with the last modification. The problem is somewhat alleviated by periodically writing *all* modified blocks to disk. For example, in many UNIX systems this is done approximately every 30 seconds.

5.6.3   File organization: directories

File systems are seen to form an extension of physical storage devices. An important feature is that they need only rely on the availability of a (micro)kernel providing access to storage devices by means of, for example, one or several disk drivers. Once the concept of a file is readily available in the form of an implementation, we are able to *organize* them into so-called **directories**. Conceptually, a directory is a collection of files. More precisely, a directory contains *information* on files. The kind of information is discussed below. Important for now is that this information is so relevant that it is worth storing it somewhere permanently. And what would be a better place to do so than ... in a file? In other words, we can *hierarchically* organize files by means of directories, which consist of information on "ordinary" files, as well as information on other directories. This organization is illustrated in Figure 5.21.

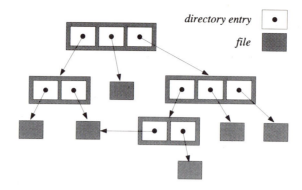

Figure 5.21 The logical organization of files by means of directories.

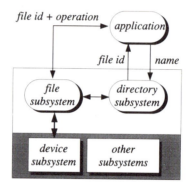

Figure 5.22 The organization of a file system and directory package on top of a microkernel.

Now what kind of information would we want to keep track of when organizing files? In fact, not much. The only disadvantage about files as discussed so far is that they can only be identified by means of the file identifier. Humans tend not to be good at remembering numbers. Instead, it is a lot more convenient for us to use names. And this is often the only information that is stored in directories. In particular, a directory can be considered as a *structured* file, consisting of records that pair a human-readable name to a file identifier. This also implies that a directory service program need have nothing to do with a (micro)kernel. Its only exchange of information takes place with the file system. In particular, many operations provided by a directory service program will be the same as those provided by a file system, but instead of using a file identifier the operations require a name given as a string of characters. The overall architecture of a file system combined with a directory service program is shown in Figure 5.22.

5.7   Discussion

5.7.1   Summary and further reading

Let's see what we have accomplished so far. In the previous chapter we had introduced a *virtual processor*, which implemented a high-level programming language, much in the same way that a real processor is an implementation of an instruction set. In Chapter 4 we showed how we could extend our virtual processor with *virtual peripheral devices*. Analogous to virtual processors, these devices were implemented as a combination of hardware and software, the latter in the form of so-called device drivers. In any case, virtual devices formed a convenient abstraction over peripheral devices such as hard disks. It is by means of device drivers that we can more easily control access to the peripherals that form part of real-world computer systems.

But having these abstractions of virtual processors and devices is not enough when using the available resources *efficiently*. In particular, we began by showing that during the transfer of data between main memory and a storage device on behalf of a program P it would make more sense to let the CPU continue with the execution of the instructions of some other program P^*. Being able to support the execution of several programs required a further consideration of three important problems:

- **Memory management.** In order to continue with another program that program will have to be in main memory as well. To be able to place programs in arbitrary contiguous pieces of memory the use of a base register and limit register was found to be convenient. The management of free memory chunks can be completely dealt with by means of software. Requiring a contiguous piece of memory before placing a program can be avoided by introducing a paging mechanism, and mapping a consecutive series of *logical* pages onto arbitrary available *physical* pages. To this end, we introduced the concept of a page table, which is filled by software but read through hardware. Paging was later extended to virtual memory by which the number of logical pages can exceed the number of physical pages.

- **Process management.** In order to switch from one program to another we need to apply a selection mechanism. In Section 5.3 we gradually introduced the concept of a process, informally referred to as a program in execution. We showed that by keeping track of a program's processor context, it was possible to switch from one program to another, and later continue where we had left off. Processes are an extremely important concept when discussing communication systems.

- **Process interference.** This is a subject that we shall return to extensively in the following chapters. Here, we discussed that if two processes $PROC_1$ and $PROC_2$ co-exist, and the CPU is switched between the two, we may find ourselves in the situation that while a peripheral device is acting on behalf of $PROC_1$, the same device should also start work on behalf of $PROC_2$. In other words, the processes need to *share* a single resource. Because devices can do only one thing at a time, we needed a mechanism to synchronize processes. Our solution was based on the use of semaphores, for many operating systems supporting multiple processes an essential mechanism. A semaphore is used to postpone the execution of a process by letting it wait until some condition has been met. The implementation of semaphores is not trivial. In the end, some hardware support is even required.

The interesting part of our solutions was that they were all presented as software extensions to the virtual processor introduced in the previous chapter. However, a close collaboration with hardware is sometimes still required, for example in the case of interrupt handling and forcing processes to use service programs.

Our discussion continued by showing how the essentials of an operating system, referred to as a **microkernel**, could be organized into a number of modules. In particular, we showed how the important modules for *memory management*, *process management*, and *device management* could more or less be isolated, together enabling further extensions. Structured organization of operating systems is essential to keep it manageable. One particular global organization was presented here, namely that of a client-server application in which client processes *communicate* with server processes, the latter capturing different functionalities of an operating system. The kernel in such an architecture plays a small but important role. It acts as an interface between clients, servers, and the hardware.

Our final subject was that of file systems: an extension to the material presented so far that allowed the use of abstract storage devices in the form of so-called files. We showed how the concept of a file could be readily implemented on top of a microkernel, and that their organization could even be completely dealt with without making use of that kernel. This approach is illustrative of the way that operating systems are often built today. A small kernel is extended by means of separate, more or less isolated components that completely encapsulate specific functionality. We shall return to this approach in succeeding chapters.

Operating systems are to be considered as intricate pieces of software, and much more can be said about them than what we have discussed in this chapter. Fortunately, the construction of operating systems is to date well understood, and a number of excellent textbooks exist that will help you find your way further. For those wishing to get some more overview material, Lister and Eager (1988) provide a good starting point. Another, more thorough treatment at a conceptual level can be found in Silberschatz and Galvin (1994) and Part I of Tanenbaum (1992). These two also provide many more references to specific subjects. If you still find the interaction between hardware and software a difficult subject to comprehend, Patterson and Hennessy (1994) provide a more thorough discussion than can be found in this book. File systems are discussed in Grosshans (1986), and many design and implementation details are also presented in Wiederhold (1983).

But general textbooks are not always the best way to become acquainted with the intricacies of operating systems. It is necessary to look at existing systems at a more detailed level. Tanenbaum (1987) discusses and presents the source code of the MINIX system, which has been designed (and is available) for IBM-compatible PCs. A relatively simple operating system, called XINU is presented in Comer (1984). Both MINIX and XINU are simplified versions of UNIX. An excellent treatment of UNIX itself can be found in Bach (1986). Without going into too many implementation details, the author manages to provide a clear understanding of the data structures and internal behavior of this well-known operating system. A similar approach is followed by Leffler *et al.* (1989) who deal with the Berkeley version of UNIX, and Goodheart and Cox (1994) who discuss another important version of UNIX. Finally, Joseph *et al.* (1984) discuss a major part of the source code of an operating system that can support multiple CPUs. In contrast to the other systems mentioned, which have been implemented in C, this multiprocessor system has been developed using a Pascal-like language.

5.7.2 Operating systems today

The material presented in this chapter belongs to the classical parts of research into operating systems. Once considered as being an extremely difficult subject, the basics of operating systems are well understood to date. In new developments, much research is motivated for adapting or inventing solutions so that performance demands can be met. In addition, modern operating systems are gradually adapting structures that seemed inconceivable in the past.

Performance issues: the I/O bottleneck

As we have mentioned, one of the main objectives of operating system design is to allow efficient use of the available hardware resources. When operating systems were first introduced, attention was drawn primarily towards efficient use of (1) the CPU, (2) main memory, and (3) peripheral storage media. If you realize that processing power is increasing much faster than I/O-related measures, and that memory chips are now so cheap that it is hardly realistic to consider memory as a *scarce* resource, it will be no surprise to learn that performance demands on operating systems are largely restricted by the I/O subsystem they support. Faster processors and larger memories allow us to construct sophisticated operating systems, but relatively slow peripheral devices force developers to think carefully about the design of software components for I/O.

The I/O problem is being attacked from different angles. One approach is the development of alternative storage devices, particularly so-called **disk arrays**. These devices appear logically as one very large disk, but are physically organized as a collection of hard disks that operate in parallel. Roughly speaking, an array of N disks increases the data transfer rate by a factor N. At the same time, the storage capacity is increased N-fold. Unfortunately, there is a problem. Having a number of disks work in parallel increases the probability that something will go wrong. And this is simply too much (instead of having a disk crash once every two years, imagine it occurring once a week). However, by applying special redundancy techniques and improving the quality of the disks, high-performance I/O subsystems have been realized and are already commercially available. If you want to know more about this technology, Chen *et al.* (1994) will provide you with enough details to make a good start.

While peripheral devices are being improved, so are the logical storage devices, i.e. file systems. One way of improving file systems is not to make any use of storage devices, at least for some time. This has led to main memory file and database systems, of which an overview is given in Garcia-Molina and Salem (1992). In practice, however, a compromise is made by applying advanced software caching techniques by which complete blocks of data are kept in main memory. The problems related to I/O caches in operating systems are similar to that of paged memory systems. An alternative approach is to concentrate on minimizing the frequency of (expensive) disk operations. For example, pure sequential disk access (which prevents the heads being moved all the time) is much better than random access patterns. Sequentializing disk access is done in so-called *log-structured file systems* which are discussed in Rosenblum and Oosterhout (1991). Disk access can also be greatly improved if only so-called *immutable files* are allowed, i.e. files that cannot be modified after being created. The advantage is that file sizes are known in advance so that (1) it is easier to optimize disk access, and (2) files can be placed in contiguous memory blocks. Their main benefit, however, is to be found in distributed systems (which we shall discuss in the next chapter). More details on immutable files can be found in Gifford *et al.* (1988) and Tanenbaum *et al.* (1990b).

Architecture and organization

Due to their size and mixture of functionality, it is important that operating systems are organized in an orderly way. The first systems tended to be completely unorganized in the sense that everything was more or less put into a single program. We briefly mentioned properly organizing operating systems. Here, we concentrate on some of the more recent trends.

Modern operating systems are almost invariably organized in the form of a microkernel, augmented with several server programs executing in user mode. In other words, the client-server architecture that we have discussed in Section 5.5.3 is generally adopted. This, however, does not imply that modern operating systems all look the same. The differences already appear when we consider the sizes of several kernels. For example, the microkernel of the Mach operating system has approximately four times as many service programs as one of the earlier versions of the UNIX system. The latter were definitely not considered to be microkernels. But apart from a discussion on when to call the core of an operating system a microkernel or not, the aim is to minimize the number of programs that should be executed only in kernel mode. This also means that many operating system services will be executed in user mode.

In order to organize these services, a trend that is increasingly finding its way into systems is the **object-based** approach. In systems that follow this approach, any resource in the system is treated as a single entity, called an object, that can be manipulated by (conceptually) sending it a message telling the resource what it is supposed to do. In this sense, the object-based approach bears a strong resemblance to the client-server model. In both cases, a process (client) issues an explicit request to an object (server) to provide a service. A good introduction to object-orientation is given in Meyer (1988). The object-based approach is presently successfully used in the area of distributed systems which we shall consider in later chapters.

Another structuring aspect besides that of using objects is the use of so-called **threads**. Conceptually, a thread is much the same as what we have termed a process. The main distinction with processes in practice is that threads have a simple implementation. What this means is that much protection, security, and authentication administration which is normally maintained in the case of processes is omitted for threads. This allows threads to be efficiently implementable. Having said this, structuring operating systems can then be done in a radically different way: we build them as a collection of threads that exchange information which each other. This approach was advocated some 20 years ago, but has found widespread support in practical system development only recently. Discussions on thread support by operating systems can be found in Silberschatz and Galvin (1994) and Tanenbaum (1992).

Exercises

1. Explain what polling is and why it is something you should generally avoid. An alternative to polling is reacting to hardware interrupts. How does this mechanism work?

2. Having support for multiple programs does lead to a number of fundamental problems. What are the main problems?

3. What is the purpose of having base and limit registers? Describe the memory mapping function and explain what happens if an *out-of-limit* signal is given. Would you classify such a signal as a hardware interrupt?

4. In placing programs into free memory areas we can adopt several strategies. For instance, we could select the largest or the smallest free block available in which the program still fits. Elaborate on the advantages and disadvantages of either approach.

5. *The Intel 8086 processor uses 20-bit addresses, meaning that addressable memory is restricted to 2^{20} words. Many 8086-based computers, however, have much more physical memory available. Would it be fair to say that such computers have a larger physical memory than virtual memory?

6. *Explain why page sizes on computer systems are invariably chosen equal to some power of 2.

7. *Explain in detail the function of a page table, and its role with respect to virtual memory. Also explain how the interaction between hardware and software proceeds when an *out-of-memory* signal is given.

8. Explain what context switching is, and why it is needed in order to support multiple programs.

9. Suppose that we have an operating system that provides support for multiple processes. What will happen when there is no more process available with the state READY?

10. *In this chapter we have implemented the CPU scheduler by means of a procedure. Explain how we could also achieve an implementation in which this scheduler is

just another process.

11. Is it possible that the CPU scheduler as implemented by SCHEDULE_NEXT shown on page 227, selects as the next process the one which invoked that procedure?

12. Suppose we have two processes $PROC_1$ and $PROC_2$ acting on a semaphore sema. Assume that at a certain time we have that sema is TRUE. Also assume that both processes will issue in turn a WAIT(sema) operation. Explain what will happen.

13. *Outline a solution for the implementation of the procedure SIGNAL based on that of WAIT as given in Listing 5.9.

14. *Explain why we need a different implementation from that used for semaphores to realize atomicity of the WAIT and SIGNAL operations.

15. *Can we implement the functionality of WAIT and SIGNAL by a normal BASAL program if we had a single instruction to switch interrupts generated by the hardware on or off?

16. When a computer is switched on the hardware automatically loads a set of instructions from, e.g. a hard disk into main memory. These instructions in turn will load the operating system into main memory. As soon as this is finished, would you expect that the computer is executing in kernel mode or in user mode?

17. In BASAL we can directly address memory locations. Assuming that our computer is running in user mode, how can we prevent users of BASAL addressing, for example, registers that belong to a hard disk? In other words, how can we prevent users from switching the computer to kernel mode?

18. Explain how an operating system can be organized as a collection of *server processes* that are executed in user mode. Say why such an organization may be preferable to one in which all service programs are executed in kernel mode.

19. Explain why we can view files as virtual storage devices, i.e. as an abstraction over actual storage devices such as hard disks.

20. *An administration on files (e.g., a directory) will have to stored somewhere. To that end, we generally use another file. However, there comes a moment when file administration has to be stored in another way than by means of files. Explain why, and outline a solution to this problem.

21. Directory servers need hardly ever be implemented as a basic service that needs to be executed in kernel mode. Explain what is meant by this statement, and why it is true.

Chapter 6

Basic communication models

Up to this point we have hardly described how communication between processes takes place. In this chapter we shall take a closer look at these matters by considering two basic models. The first, in which processes communicate through so-called shared data, is described in Section 6.2. The model can only be used in a restricted number of cases, but nevertheless illustrates fundamental problems that underlie communication in general. The main part of this chapter deals with so-called message-based communication models. In these models, communication takes place by having processes send messages to each other. As we shall show, message-based communication is much better suited for implementation in terms of computer networks, meaning that much larger systems consisting of multiple connected computers can be built than in the case of communication of shared data.

6.1 Describing communication models

6.1.1 Introduction

In the previous chapter we saw that a computer system supporting multiple programs was a good thing to have in view of utilizing the CPU. Therefore, we introduced the concept of a process by which we could describe a series of actions towards the completion of a program. Having multiple processes allowed us to let the CPU be *shared*: while one process was being postponed on account of I/O, the CPU could be used to execute the instructions of another process. This sharing of a hardware resource (i.e. the CPU) is effectively accomplished for almost every other resource as well. For example, main memory can said to be shared by multiple processes if we allow several to reside there at the same time. Similarly, a single disk can be shared by storing data from different processes. Having multiple processes thus allows us to devise allocation schemes that effectively increase resource utilization. This is useful from a hardware management point of view.

But although important, effective resource management is something we are not really interested in here. Instead, throughout this book we wish to explain the technical principles of communication systems. In this chapter, we will make a first attempt to show how we can achieve a better understanding of our own concept of communication with respect to computers. Processes will form the means to that end in the sense that all communication that we wish to describe will be in the form of communication that takes place between processes.

6.1.2   Processes in BASAL

But if we are going to follow this approach, we must have a means by which we can describe processes. Therefore, we extend our concept of BASAL with a so-called **process type**. (We note here that process types are *not* a part of the programming language Ada, from which BASAL has been derived. We will return to this below.) The general method of declaring a process type in BASAL is by writing

```
process PROCESS_NAME is
  ...declarations of data types used in this process
begin
  ...description of the general behavior of this process
end PROCESS_NAME;
```

For example, in order to describe a process that continuously displays characters on a screen as they are typed in at the keyboard we could declare the following process type ECHO_PROCESS:

```
process ECHO_PROCESS is
  key : CHARACTER;
begin
  while TRUE loop
    TERMINAL.READ(key);
    TERMINAL.WRITE(key);
  end loop ;
end ECHO_PROCESS;
```

where we are using the procedures READ and WRITE as declared in the package TERMINAL described in Section 4.3.4. But this is only a *description* of what a process type ECHO_PROCESS looks like. In order to have such a process available we also need to *create* a process that behaves according to this description. This is done in the same way that variables are declared:

```
echoProcess : ECHO_PROCESS;
```

This leaves us with one subtle point: when do processes such as echoProcess become active, i.e. when do they start doing their work? This simple question cannot be answered without going into a number of rather intricate details on the relation between BASAL and its compiled counterpart in PRIMAL. But to give you an idea, suppose we had declared the following procedure ACTIVATE:

```
procedure ACTIVATE is
    echoProcess : ECHO_PROCESS;
begin
    null ;
end ACTIVATE;
```

This procedure contains only a single **null** statement. Now when the procedure ACTIVATE is called, the following happens. Because we have declared echoProcess as part of ACTI-VATE, a procedure call will first result in creating a process of the type ECHO_PROCESS. When the **null** statement is executed, echoProcess will become active, and the procedure call will terminate as soon as echoProcess is finished. In our example, this means that we will *never* return from calling ACTIVATE.

Throughout the remainder of this book, *when* processes are activated will hardly be an issue. Instead, we shall use process types in a descriptive manner, i.e. as a means to express processes in general, and assume that processes are already active. For completeness, however, a more precise description of the subject now follows but it can be skipped on first reading.

▷ **Process activation**

The problem with our explanation of activating processes in BASAL is that we ignored how the procedure ACTIVATE is called. In other words, although we have described when processes are activated, we have done so by assuming that there is already some other process that calls ACTIVATE. When and how this calling process is activated has not been described. In order to do this, we need to take a closer look at the relation between BASAL programs and their compilation and execution on a computer.

As we have explained in Chapter 4, BASAL is a means of expressing programs at a convenient level of abstraction. In order for a BASAL program to be useful, we will have to compile it (for example, to an equivalent PRIMAL program), and execute it on a computer. We have also explained that a compiled program is first loaded into main memory by means of a special program called the loader. After the loader has loaded a program into main memory, we have explained that it continues with executing the first instruction of that program. In practice, what happens is that a new process is started, let's call it *PROC(main)*, that executes the program that has just been loaded into main memory.

When *PROC(main)* executes the (compiled version of the) procedure ACTIVATE, i.e. it calls the procedure, it creates another process *PROC(echo)*. This latter process is then responsible for executing the instructions as described by the BASAL process echoProcess. In other words, the description of echoProcess is treated as just another program that is to be executed by a process, in this case *PROC(echo)*. Then, just before *PROC(main)* continues with executing the single **null** statement of the procedure ACTIVATE, *PROC(echo)* is set into the state READY as explained in Section 5.3.2. It can thus be scheduled for execution by the CPU. The semantics of process creation and activation in BASAL further dictate that *PROC(main)* can only terminate, i.e. enter the state HALTED, if *PROC(echo)* has terminated.

The concept of a process in Ada

Processes as they are used in BASAL deviate from the way that the programming language Ada supports them. This has been done for simplicity and clarity. However, the concept of processes in BASAL do have a direct counterpart in Ada, where they are denoted as so-called **tasks**. Each process declaration in BASAL

```
process PROCESS_NAME is
    ...declarations of data types used in this process
begin
    ...description of the general behavior of this process
end PROCESS_NAME;
```

corresponds to the following task declaration in Ada, which consists of two parts:

```
task type TASK_NAME;

task body TASK_NAME is
    ...declarations of data types used in this process
begin
    ...description of the general behavior of this process
end TASK_NAME;
```

The first part consists of a task specification, which, when we restrict ourselves to the way that its process counterpart in BASAL is used, merely consists of declaring a name of the task. The second part shows the implementation of the specified task, and is almost the same as the way that BASAL processes are described. In contrast to BASAL, Ada not only allows tasks to be declared in numerous other ways but also more or less dictates how communication between tasks should be described. In particular, communication between Ada tasks is generally described by means of the so-called rendez-vous model, which we shall discuss in Section 6.4.2. Processes in BASAL are assumed to communicate only through special communication packages, the subject of this chapter. It is for these reasons that we deliberately deviated from Ada, and have adopted a simpler model for describing communication.

6.2   Making use of shared data

Our first concern is to take a look at some simple models that can be fairly easily implemented by making use of so-called **shared data**. In these cases, data that can be directly accessed by a number of processes. In the following two subsections we first give some examples that illustrate what it means to make use of shared data. Then we shall gradually come to a discussion of a communication model that is no longer based on the use of shared data, but for which we can, at this point, only describe an *implementation* in terms of shared data.

6.2.1   Handing over notes

We start with considering some simple communication schemes in which a single *source* process *PROC*(*source*) hands over notes to some other process *PROC*(*target*), designated as the *target* process. The actual content of each note is not important, and is assumed to take the form of a series of NCHAR characters. Therefore, we introduce the following data type:

```
type CONTENT is array (1..NCHAR) of CHARACTER;
```

The issue that we are initially interested in is how we can describe the communication between *PROC*(*source*) and *PROC*(*target*) in such a way that the target process will always read a note *after* the source process has written it.

Passing a single note

The simplest situation occurs when we are dealing with only one note. In that case, we merely need to ensure that if *PROC*(*target*) wants to read the content of the note it will somehow be delayed until *PROC*(*source*) has finished writing it. It is not hard to see how we can accomplish this by making use of semaphores – a means that we have used previously in order to delay a process while some data was being used by another process. In our case, using just a single semaphore (as defined in the package SEMAPHORE on page 231) will do the trick. Consider the following description of the type SHARED_NOTE:

```
type SHARED_NOTE is
   record
      data : CONTENT;
      isWritten : SEMAPHORE.DEFINITION := FALSE;
   end record ;
```

A SHARED_NOTE has a field data that contains the actual information that is to be passed on. In addition, the semaphore isWritten is used to indicate whether the note has already been written. A process that wants to read a SHARED_NOTE will first have to wait for this event to take place. In particular, we can describe reading and writing a note by means of the following two procedures:[1]

```
procedure READ(note : in out SHARED_NOTE; data : out CONTENT) is
begin
   SEMAPHORE.WAIT(note.isWritten);
   data := note.data;
end READ;
```

```
procedure WRITE(note : in out SHARED_NOTE; data : in CONTENT) is
begin
   note.data := data;
   SEMAPHORE.SIGNAL(note.isWritten);
end WRITE;
```

---

[1] Our implementation is based on the assumption that changes to the values of **in out** parameters are immediately visible outside the procedure. In Ada, this is not so. In most cases changes become visible *after* the procedure call is completed. This is also referred to as **copy-in/copy-out** semantics.

note : SHARED_NOTE;

```
process SOURCE_PROCESS is          process TARGET_PROCESS is
   data : CONTENT := ...;             data : CONTENT;
begin                              begin
   WRITE(note, data);                 READ(note, data);
end SOURCE_PROCESS;                end TARGET_PROCESS;

sourceProcess : SOURCE_PROCESS;    targetProcess : TARGET_PROCESS;
```

Listing 6.1 A simple example of one process handing a note over to another process.

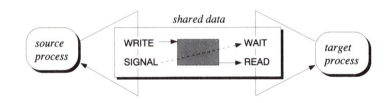

Figure 6.1 Outline of two processes communicating via a single, shared note.

We can then describe the communication between the two processes *PROC*(*source*) and *PROC*(*target*) as shown in Listing 6.1. In this case, the processes sourceProcess and targetProcess communicate by using just a single note, described by the variable note. The data field of this variable is modified by the source process, and subsequently read by the target process. That modification takes place before the note can be read has been accomplished through the use of a single semaphore.

Now, what's so special about this communication scheme? Not very much, except for the fact that you have to realize that both the source and target process have access to one and the same variable note. In other words, the two processes **share** the variable note. This variable is passed to the procedures WRITE and READ, respectively, where in *both* cases it is modified. The procedure WRITE modifies not only the data field but also the semaphore isWritten, whereas READ modifies only the note's semaphore. It is the fact that the processes share a single variable that makes this communication scheme special. As we shall see below, sharing variables is generally not possible in more elaborate communication schemes. This outline of communication between the two processes is illustrated in Figure 6.1.

Continuous communication by a single note

Let's take a look at a slightly more advanced communication scheme. We now wish to describe the situation where the source and target process may use the same note repeatedly in order to exchange information. In other words, the note itself should be rewritable. Of course, the note cannot be re-used for writing until after the target process has read its contents. What is seen now is that the source process may sometimes have to wait for the target process before it can continue writing the note. Therefore, we add a semaphore isRead which is initialized to TRUE to indicate that the source process may start with writing the note for the first time:

```
type SHARED_NOTE is
  record
    data : CONTENT;
    isRead : SEMAPHORE.DEFINITION := TRUE;
    isWritten : SEMAPHORE.DEFINITION := FALSE;
  end record ;
```

The procedures READ and WRITE are adapted accordingly:

```
procedure READ(note : in out SHARED_NOTE; data : out CONTENT) is
begin
  SEMAPHORE.WAIT(note.isWritten); –– wait until the note has been written to
  data := note.data;
  SEMAPHORE.SIGNAL(note.isRead); –– and indicate that it can be re-used
end READ;


procedure WRITE(note : in out SHARED_NOTE; data : in CONTENT) is
begin
  SEMAPHORE.WAIT(note.isRead); –– wait until the previous note has been read
  note.data := data;
  SEMAPHORE.SIGNAL(note.isWritten); –– signal that new note can now be read
end WRITE;
```

A useful aspect of our solution is that we need not restrict communication to just a single source and target process. It can be readily verified that several source and target processes may communicate by using just the single note. Whenever a source process wants to pass information to one of the target processes it merely needs to call the procedure WRITE. However, *which* target process will actually read the note cannot be specified. Instead, the note will be read by an arbitrary target process that calls the procedure READ.

But if there are many source and target processes, it may be worth having more than just one shared note available. How this situation can be handled is described next.

6.2.2   Shared streams for continuous communication

The examples we have been discussing show how processes can communicate by means of some shared data. Shared in this sense means that all processes can directly access a *common* variable. Communication takes place by modifying and reading the value of that variable. In effect, all we really need to be concerned about is the proper synchronization between the communicating processes. In other words, we have to devise schemes by which each source or target process accesses the shared data at the right time. This is done entirely by means of semaphores.

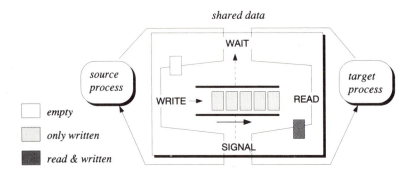

Figure 6.2 The principle of communicating by means of a shared stream.

However, all the communication described so far is based on the existence of only a single shared note. This means that no more than one piece of information can be exchanged at a time. In practice, this is much too restrictive. How we can correct this situation is discussed next. While doing so, we shall also gradually introduce terminology that is commonly used for a completely different type of communication model that we come to discuss in Section 6.3: message-passing. The concepts that we shall be using there can be illustrated by describing how we deal with shared data.

The concept of a stream

In the previous section we discussed how a source process can pass a series of notes to a target process. One way of describing how the source and target communicate is by stating that the two processes are connected by means of a **stream**. A source process writes data to a stream that subsequently flows to a target process where it is removed. So far, our stream was capable of handling only one note a time. Communication involving a stream that carries several notes can easily be described if we make use of a queuing mechanism. Writing a note at a stream then coincides with appending an element to a queue, whereas removing a note is the same as removing an element from the head of the queue. This communication scheme can be illustrated as shown in Figure 6.2.

Streams using non-blocking communication

What we are initially interested in here is describing communication between several processes that make use of one and the same stream. Therefore, assume we have a package QUEUE which we derive from the parameterized package GENERAL_QUEUE described on page 172 as follows:

> **package** QUEUE **is new** GENERAL_QUEUE(ELEMENT ⇒ NOTE);

where the NOTE data type is left unspecified. This declaration provides us with the right means to create and manipulate a queue which allows notes to be either appended to its end or removed from its front. Using such a queue, it is now simple to describe stream communication between source and target processes. Our first approach is to devise two simple procedures: READ and WRITE, that take into account that something may go wrong with the communication, i.e. there may be no notes in the stream to remove, or the stream may be too full for any more notes. If something went wrong, both procedures merely report that communication failed. This leads to the descriptions shown in Listing 6.2, where we have provided a complete (parameterized) package specification and implementation. (We point out that by providing the data type NOTE as a *parameter* of our package specification we can indeed omit any further details at present.)

Implementation of the procedures READ and WRITE is quite straightforward. In both cases we first ensure that the calling process gains exclusive access to the stream, after which it checks if the stream is either empty or full, respectively. As soon as a note has been read or written, exclusive access is given up, and the operation is completed after having set the appropriate value for the parameter done.

What we have accomplished now is a means of communication between several source processes and several target processes such that:

- Any source process can pass a note to one of the target processes, although it will not know exactly which target process has picked up its note

- Any target process can pick up a note from the stream, although likewise, it will not know which source process originally forwarded it

- There is no restriction with respect to the number of times the stream can be accessed, although it is possible that communication could not take place.

We still have to realize, that all communication takes place through shared data, in this case the queue of notes, which in turn is protected against simultaneous access by means of a semaphore.

But there is also something special about our implementation: we *never* delay a process if communication cannot proceed because the stream was either too full to write another note or because there was simply no note to read. In other words, we have introduced a form of **non-blocking** communication. An alternative implementation is that of blocking communication, which is discussed next.

Streams with blocking communication

Of course, when communication is not possible, we can also choose to delay a source or target process until notes can be written or read again, respectively. This is completely analogous to the situation where we re-used a single note to provide continuous communication between a source and target process. There, we delayed the source process until the note had been read by the target process, and likewise, the target process was delayed until the note had been written again by the source process. Using two semaphores to delay the source and target process was sufficient in that case. Unfortunately, a simple adaptation of that solution will not work where *several* notes may be exchanged at the same time. What we need now is a mechanism that delays a source process after a

```
package STREAM(type NOTE) is

  package QUEUE is new GENERAL_QUEUE(ELEMENT ⇒ NOTE);

  type DEFINITION is
    record
      noteQueue : QUEUE.DEFINITION;
      exclusiveAccess : SEMAPHORE.DEFINITION := TRUE;
    end record ;

  procedure READ(
    stream : in out DEFINITION; data : out NOTE; done : out BOOLEAN);
  procedure WRITE(
    stream : in out DEFINITION; data : in NOTE; done : out BOOLEAN);
end STREAM;

package body STREAM is

  procedure READ(
    stream : in out DEFINITION; data : out NOTE; done : out BOOLEAN) is
    empty : BOOLEAN;
  begin
    SEMAPHORE.WAIT(stream.exclusiveAccess);
    QUEUE.CHECK_EMPTY(stream.noteQueue, empty);
    if not empty then
      QUEUE.REMOVE(stream.noteQueue, data);
    end if ;
    SEMAPHORE.SIGNAL(stream.exclusiveAccess);
    done := not empty;
  end READ;

  procedure WRITE(
    stream : in out DEFINITION; data : in NOTE; done : out BOOLEAN) is
    full : BOOLEAN;
  begin
    SEMAPHORE.WAIT(stream.exclusiveAccess);
    QUEUE.CHECK_FULL(stream.noteQueue, full);
    if not full then
      QUEUE.APPEND(stream.noteQueue, data);
    end if ;
    SEMAPHORE.SIGNAL(stream.exclusiveAccess);
    done := not full;
  end WRITE;

end STREAM;
```

Listing 6.2 A complete description of simple stream communication.

certain maximum number of notes have been written but not yet read. Similarly, a target process is to be delayed only if there are no more written notes in the stream, and not just one unwritten note. What we are thus seeking is a means of constructing streams based on **blocking** communication.

The solution is found by adapting our concept of a semaphore. As we have mentioned in Section 5.4.1, a **binary semaphore** is a Boolean variable with two associated operations *wait* and *signal* formally defined as:

wait(s)	::	**when** s **do** $s \leftarrow$ **false**
signal(s)	::	$s \leftarrow$ **true**

So far, we have been making use only of binary semaphores. An extension to binary semaphores is given by so-called **counting semaphores**. A counting semaphore is an *integer* variable rather than a *Boolean* variable, with the operations *wait* and *signal* replaced by the two operations *down* and *up*:

down(s)	::	**when** $s > 0$ **do** $s \leftarrow s - 1$
up(s)	::	$s \leftarrow s + 1$

where

> **when** $s > 0$ **do** $s \leftarrow s - 1$

means that a process will decrement the value of s by one if $s > 0$, and that otherwise its execution will be delayed. A delayed process will continue as soon as s becomes larger than 0, after which it will then immediately decrement the value of s by one.

Returning to our initial problem, assume we have the following extended package available for semaphores:

```
package SEMAPHORE is
   subtype BINARY is BOOLEAN;
   subtype COUNTING is INTEGER;

   procedure WAIT(sema : in out BINARY);
   procedure SIGNAL(sema : in out BINARY);

   procedure DOWN(sema : in out COUNTING);
   procedure UP(sema : in out COUNTING);
end SEMAPHORE;
```

Devising a solution by which source and target processes are blocked until notes can be written and read again, respectively, is now fairly straightforward. First assume that the maximum number of notes that can be carried by the stream is NNOTE. In that case, we first need to adapt our definition of a stream as shown in the package specification in Listing 6.3.

Writing and reading notes can now be expressed by the procedures shown in Listing 6.4. A few points need to be kept in mind in order to understand the correctness of our implementation. First, note that the value of stream.isRead always corresponds to the number of notes that can be appended to the stream before it becomes full. Likewise, the value of stream.isWritten corresponds to the present number of notes that have been written. Second, we have to take into account that the queue associated with the stream is still shared by several processes. Moreover, it can happen that several processes want to

```
package STREAM(type NOTE) is
  package QUEUE is new GENERAL_QUEUE(ELEMENT ⇒ NOTE);

  NNOTE : constant INTEGER := ...;
  type DEFINITION is
    record
      noteQueue : QUEUE.DEFINITION;
      exclusiveAccess : SEMAPHORE.BINARY := TRUE;
      isWritten : SEMAPHORE.COUNTING := 0; -- no notes have yet been written
      isRead : SEMAPHORE.COUNTING := NNOTE; -- equals the stream capacity
    end record ;

  procedure READ(stream : in out DEFINITION; data : out NOTE);
  procedure WRITE(stream : in out DEFINITION; data : in NOTE);
end STREAM;
```

Listing 6.3 The package specification for a stream with blocking communication.

append or remove notes at the same time. Therefore, we still have to protect the stream against simultaneous access, to which end we use the semaphore stream.exclusiveAccess as before.

It is seen that by using counting semaphores we can devise solutions for blocking stream communication by which as many as NNOTE notes may be carried by the stream at the same time. Moreover, it is also seen that we need no longer check if the queue associated with the stream is either full or empty, as was the case with non-blocking communication. But suppose that we did not want to set a maximum on the number of notes in the stream, for example because we did not know in advance how many notes the stream can carry simultaneously. In that case, we *would* have to check if the associated queue was presently full or empty, and in addition, would possibly have to delay a source or target process. Here, binary semaphores can provide a solution to this problem. How exactly is left as an exercise for the reader.

▷ On the implementation of counting semaphores

A question that may come to mind is whether or not we actually *need* counting semaphores. The answer is no: counting semaphores can easily be implemented by assuming that we have only binary semaphores at our disposal. The point is that a process that wants to execute the *down* operation on a counting semaphore first checks whether the semaphore's value is 0 or not. If so, it registers itself as a process waiting for that value to become larger than 0, and delays itself by means of an additional binary semaphore upIsCalled. A process executing the *up* operation always checks whether there are any waiting processes, and if so, invokes one of these by SIGNALing the binary semaphore upIsCalled. This principle is shown in Listing 6.5.

When a process calls the procedure DOWN, it starts with checking the current value of the counting semaphore, given by the field value. If it is 0, it needs to delay itself until that value becomes positive. To that end, it first increments the value of the field waiters which indi-

```
package body STREAM is

  procedure WRITE(stream : in out DEFINITION; data : in NOTE) is
  begin
    -- Check if there is room in the stream to append a note. The current value of
    -- stream.isRead denotes exactly the number of notes that can still be appended.
    -- If it is 0, the calling process is delayed by definition of the operation DOWN.
    SEMAPHORE.DOWN(stream.isRead);

    -- The calling process must now get exclusive access to the stream, for there may
    -- be other processes that are also writing or reading notes at the same time.
    SEMAPHORE.WAIT(stream.exclusiveAccess);

    -- Simply append the note to the stream, give up exclusive access, and indicate to
    -- the target processes that there is a next note that can be read.
    QUEUE.APPEND(stream.noteQueue, data);
    SEMAPHORE.SIGNAL(stream.exclusiveAccess);
    SEMAPHORE.UP(stream.isWritten);
  end WRITE;

  procedure READ(stream : in out DEFINITION; data : out NOTE) is
  begin
    -- Check if there is a note that can be read, i.e. removed from the stream. The
    -- current value of stream.isWritten denotes exactly the number of notes presently
    -- in the stream. If it is 0, the calling process will be delayed by definition of DOWN.
    SEMAPHORE.DOWN(stream.isWritten);

    -- The calling process must now get exclusive access to the stream, for there may
    -- be other processes that are also reading or writing notes at the same time.
    SEMAPHORE.WAIT(stream.exclusiveAccess);

    -- Remove a note from the stream: it is certain that there is one. Then,
    -- exclusive access to the stream is to be given up, and the source processes are
    -- notified that there is room for the next note in the stream.
    QUEUE.REMOVE(stream.noteQueue, data);
    SEMAPHORE.SIGNAL(stream.exclusiveAccess);
    SEMAPHORE.UP(stream.isRead);
  end READ;

end STREAM;
```

Listing 6.4 The two procedures for passing notes via a stream with blocking communication.

cates the total number of waiting processes. The actual delay is achieved by WAITing on the binary semaphore upIsCalled. A process calling UP does exactly the converse: after incrementing the semaphore's value by 1, it checks whether there are any waiting processes. If so, it invokes one by decrementing that value of waiters by 1, and SIGNALs the binary semaphore upIsCalled. This will allow exactly one waiting process to continue where it had previously left off, after which the latter finally decrements value by 1 again in the procedure DOWN. Because the counting semaphore itself is shared among several processes, we need to protect it against simultaneous access through an additional binary semaphore exclusiveAccess.

```
type COUNTING is
  record
    value : INTEGER; −− value associated with the counting semaphore
    exclusiveAccess : SEMAPHORE.BINARY := TRUE; −− to guarantee exclusive access
    waiters : INTEGER := 0; −− number of processes waiting for value to become positive
    upIsCalled : SEMAPHORE.BINARY := FALSE; −− for delaying waiting processes
  end record ;

procedure DOWN(countSema : in out COUNTING) is
begin
    SEMAPHORE.WAIT(countSema.exclusiveAccess);
    if countSema.value = 0 then
      −− register the calling process as one that is waiting for value to become positive
      countSema.waiters := countSema.waiters + 1;
      SEMAPHORE.SIGNAL(countSema.exclusiveAccess);
      −− delay the calling process until further notice
      SEMAPHORE.WAIT(countSema.upIsCalled);
    end if ;
    countSema.value := countSema.value − 1;
    SEMAPHORE.SIGNAL(countSema.exclusiveAccess);
end DOWN;

procedure UP(countSema : in out COUNTING) is
begin
    SEMAPHORE.WAIT(countSema.exclusiveAccess);
    countSema.value := countSema.value + 1;
    if countSema.waiters > 0 then
      −− there are delayed processes waiting for this counting semaphore, so one of them
      −− can now be invoked
      countSema.waiters := countSema.waiters − 1;
      SEMAPHORE.SIGNAL(countSema.upIsCalled);
    else
      SEMAPHORE.SIGNAL(countSema.exclusiveAccess);
    end if ;
end UP;
```

Listing 6.5 An implementation of counting semaphores based on binary semaphores.

Stream communication and process synchronization

Having given a blocking and non-blocking form of stream communication, it is not hard
to imagine that we can also combine the two. In particular, we can make a distinction between, on the one hand, blocking versus non-blocking communication, and on the other,
whether this applies to writing or reading notes. So, for example, it is possible to have
a blocking WRITE operation as used by a source process combined with a non-blocking
READ operation at the target's end.

Whenever a process manages to write a note to a stream it is certain that eventually
the note will be read by one of the target processes (assuming that the target processes
regularly inspect the stream for incoming notes). In the case of blocking communication, we are certain that as soon as a WRITE operation completes, the note is on its way
to one of the target processes. However, we cannot know exactly *when* that note will
be read. In other words, the particular source process and the target process do not *synchronize*; the interaction between the two is therefore said to adhere to **asynchronous**

communication. A characteristic feature of asynchronous communication is that any data that is being communicated between a source and target process may be "in transit" without either of the two processes waiting until that transmission is completed. In the stream models we have discussed, a note is "in transit" as long as it remains in the queue associated with the stream.

Describing **synchronous communication**, i.e. communication in which a source process and a target process both continue only after the target process has read the note written by the source process, requires some additional exchange of information. In particular, in order for the source process to continue, it must be informed exactly when its note has been read. In a synchronous communication model, the source process will be delayed until that moment.

▷ Let's see how we can solve this problem of synchronous communication by assuming that source and target processes communicate *only* through streams. The basic idea is that whenever a target process has read a note from a stream it writes back an acknowledgment to the source process that wrote the note. To this end, we assume that there is an additional stream that flows in the opposite direction, namely from the target processes back to the source processes, and which carries such acknowledgments. We denote this stream as the *acknowledgment stream*, whereas the stream carrying the notes as written by the source processes is denoted as the *main stream*. We assume that a source process always attaches a unique identifier to a note when writing it to the main stream. The behavior of the source and target processes can now be roughly outlined as follows:

- A source process *PROC(source)* composes a note *note* consisting of the data that is to be communicated, as well as a unique identifier *id(source)* for itself. This note is then written to the main stream, and process *PROC(source)* is delayed until further notice.

- As soon as *note* has been read by some target process *PROC(target)*, the latter composes an acknowledgment *ack*, which is just another note, but now containing the unique identifier *id(source)* that came with *note*. The acknowledgment is written to the acknowledgment stream, and *PROC(target)* continues.

- After the acknowledgment *ack* has been removed from the acknowledgment stream, process *PROC(source)* is informed that it can continue. At this point we know that note *note* has been read.

Describing the third step in a BASAL program is rather tedious, and does not contribute much to the clarification of process synchronization in the case of stream communication. For this reason, we have resorted to providing only an outline of the solution.

Discussion

Before we continue, let's see what we have been doing so far. We started by discussing a simple communication model in which one process passes a note to another. We expressed this model in BASAL by making use of a variable that is **shared** between two processes. Having a shared variable means that the variable can be directly accessed by both processes. It is therefore also referred to as a common variable. Shared data, as we have already seen in Chapter 5, requires protection against simultaneous access by several processes. To that end, we can use semaphores.

Our next step consisted of extending the communication model so that several processes could exchange information by using only a single note that could be re-used repeatedly. The extension that followed was that of communication through a stream which allowed several processes to communicate with each other, but in such a way that several notes could be in transit at the same time. Streams are fairly flexible. A process can write a note to a stream, and another can read notes from a stream. From an abstract point of view, it would almost seem as if communication is no longer based on the use of shared data, except, of course, that the stream itself is shared between processes. But this is an *implementation* detail, although it is too important to ignore. What we are saying here is that although the stream model of communication is well suited to describe all kinds of communication, even the kind that takes place across computer networks, the implementation of the model as we have described so far is completely inadequate.

The problem is that we have described a solution in which shared data is stored at one particular place: main memory. This requires that all processes that make use of shared data should have direct access to the memory locations that contain that data. This direct access can only be realized if the processor that is executing a process is directly connected to the memory module in which the shared data is contained.[2] And it is for this reason that our approach will fail in the general case. When dealing with geographically distributed processes (and thus processors), we cannot simply assume that hardware is available that will allow these processes to access shared data directly. Instead, we will have to provide other solutions.

Returning to our concept of streams, the problem that we are now confronted with is that, on the one hand, it seems that we have a fairly good communication model, even for describing communication across a network, but on the other, that we will have to devise an implementation of that model which is supported by those networks as well. How we can implement this model, and similar ones, is the topic of Chapter 7 and beyond. It is indeed rather more intricate than you might imagine at first. In the next section we shall concentrate on so-called message-passing models, which are suited for network communication; as we will discuss, communication through streams is just one of the many models based on message-passing.

6.3   Basic message-passing

As we have said, communication through shared data requires that the communicating parties have direct access to the place where that shared data is stored. This is practically impossible when dealing with systems in which processes are geographically distributed. In that case, communication proceeds in an entirely different way. Instead of modifying commonly accessible data, processes communicate by passing messages to each other. In order to do so requires that there must be some underlying communication network

---

[2]This is not entirely true, see Section 6.5 for further information.

through which messages can be sent. Such communication networks form the topic of the following chapters. In the remainder of this chapter, we concentrate on message-passing as a model of communication. In other words, we will discuss what message-based communication looks like from the perspective of the communicating processes. To that end, we start in this section with presenting only relatively simple message-based communication models. In the following section more advanced models will be discussed.

6.3.1   The basic model

Fundamental to message-based communication is the distinction between two kinds of roles in which processes can be involved: that of a **sender**, and that of a **receiver**. In particular, a process may send a message to another process that is willing to receive that message. Moreover, as soon as a message has been sent, it can no longer be accessed by the sending process, i.e. it becomes impossible for the sender to read or modify that message. Likewise, a receiver cannot do anything with messages that are not yet received. From the moment that a message has been sent until the moment it is received the message is said to be **in transmission**.

This is indeed a simple communication model and also one with which we are fairly familiar. For example, it is completely analogous to the way that we communicate through regular mail. Unfortunately, the applicability of the message-passing model is rather restricted and certainly much more difficult to handle than communication through shared data. First, there is the problem of having to identify explicitly the sender and receiver. Let's start by taking a look at this particular issue.

Point-to-point communication

In order for a process to send a message it is necessary to identify uniquely to whom that message is to be delivered. In particular, many message-based communication schemes require that both the sender and the receiver can be explicitly identified through a unique **address**. An important assumption that we are making here is that each address has precisely one associated process. In other words, when we send a message to some specific address we assume that there is precisely one process that can receive that message at that address. In this way, providing an address is the same as stating exactly who is the other communicating party. The fact that both the sender and the receiver have to be explicitly identified is something with which we are generally familiar: when sending mail to someone we usually provide our own address on the envelope.

Of course, it may be possible that a process itself can be contacted at more than one address. Again, this is something we are also familiar with. It is common to make a distinction between someone's home address and the address of the company or institution where that person works. An alternative solution, and one that is normally adopted in communication across computer networks, is that each process has *precisely one* address where it can be contacted. If we adopt this scheme as well, we can then assume that a sending or receiving process provides its own address *implicitly*, which is expressed by

```
package MESSAGE_PASSING(type MESSAGE) is
  type ADDRESS is ...;

  procedure SEND(receiver : in ADDRESS; mess : in MESSAGE);
    -- Send a message [mess] from the calling process to the process identified at the
    -- address [receiver]. The address of the sender is automatically sent along with
    -- the message.

  procedure RECEIVE(sender : in ADDRESS; mess : out MESSAGE);
    -- Receive a message [mess] by the calling process which was sent by a process
    -- identified by the address [sender].

  procedure RECEIVE_ANY(sender : out ADDRESS; mess : out MESSAGE);
    -- Receive any incoming message [mess] by the calling process. The original sender
    -- of the message is identified by the address [sender].
end MESSAGE_PASSING;
```

Listing 6.6   The specification of a basic message-passing package where processes have exactly one associated address.

the package specification shown in Listing 6.6. The procedure RECEIVE_ANY is discussed below.

What we are discussing here is generally known as **point-to-point** message communication. The only way that communication can take place is to have a sender explicitly identify the receiver. Whether or not, for example, these two processes synchronize is not important, and indeed, we have omitted any further details with respect to such aspects, but will return to them below. However, for the sake of our further discussion, we assume at this point that *receiving* messages always adheres to blocking communication.

Point-to-point communication: an example

Let's take a closer look at our basic model by first considering how we can express the situation that a source process passes notes to another target process. First, we assume that we have created a package MPNOTE using our parameterized message-passing package:

```
type NOTE is array (1..NCHAR) of CHARACTER;
package MPNOTE is new MESSAGE_PASSING(MESSAGE ⇒ NOTE);
```

In order for a process to write a note note to a process at, say, address TARGET_ADDRESS, it simply needs to call the procedure SEND as in:

```
MPNOTE.SEND(TARGET_ADDRESS, note);
```

Likewise, in order for a process to read a note, it needs to specify the address of the source process and call the procedure RECEIVE:

```
MPNOTE.RECEIVE(SOURCE_ADDRESS, note);
```

The main distinction with our model based on shared data is that in order for two processes to communicate both have to provide *explicitly* the address where the other can be reached. In this sense, point-to-point communication is quite different from the communication models we have discussed so far.

Any-to-one communication

But, in fact, having to identify explicitly both communicating parties directly is found to be impractical, and sometimes even makes it impossible to express certain communication schemes. For example, although it is easy to describe the situation that precisely one source process passes notes to precisely one target process, it is impossible to describe the situation where a group of source processes passing notes to a group of target processes using only point-to-point message-passing. A more elaborate model of communication is needed.

The least we may expect is that a process should also be able to receive a message from *any* sender. In fact, this model coincides better with a regular mail model: many different senders may choose the same receiver, and the latter will still be able to pick up the incoming messages. We therefore extend our model by adding a procedure RECEIVE_ANY as shown in Listing 6.6, that allows a process to receive an arbitrary incoming message. The subtle difference between the procedures RECEIVE and RECEIVE_ANY lies in the fact that the first identifies the sender from which a message *is to be received*, while the second returns the sender of the message that *has been received*.

6.3.2 Passing notes revisited

Our extended model provides much more flexibility than when having just point-to-point communication available. To illustrate this, let's reconsider the situation of passing notes between processes.

Having a single target process

We first consider the situation where there is just one target process reachable at, say, address TARGET_ADDRESS. Describing communication in this case is quite simple. The only thing we need to do is adapt the way we read notes, which should now become:

    MPNOTE.RECEIVE_ANY(source, note);

where source is an **out**put parameter returning the address of the process from which the note was received. As far as the source processes are concerned, nothing changes for they can still send notes as before:

    MPNOTE.SEND(TARGET_ADDRESS, note);

This situation is illustrated in Figure 6.3.

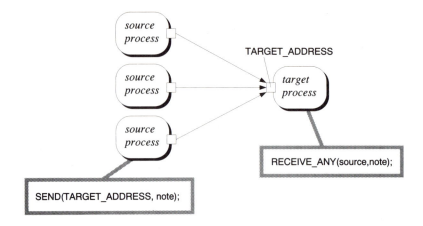

Figure 6.3 The situation of passing notes from several source processes to one target process.

Having only one source process

Now consider the opposite situation: a single source process wants to pass notes to any target process that is willing to read them. This situation is slightly more complicated because we do not have the means to *send* a message to any receiver. Indeed, having such a facility would not immediately make sense in the general case. Nevertheless, this situation can easily be captured if target processes first announce their willingness to read a note, and then wait until a note is passed on to them. This implies that we have at least two kind of messages: requests for notes, and notes. We can express our basic communication system as follows:

```
type CONTENT is array (1..NCHAR) of CHARACTER;
type INFO_KIND is (NOTE, REQUEST);
type INFORMATION is
   record
      infoKind : INFO_KIND;
      data : CONTENT;
   end record ;

package MPNOTE is new MESSAGE_PASSING(MESSAGE ⇒ INFORMATION);
```

The field infoKind in any message sent identifies whether we are either dealing with a REQUEST or with an actual NOTE. Assuming the source process can be reached at address SOURCE_ADDRESS, the behavior of a target process can then be expressed as follows:

```
procedure READ(data : out CONTENT) is
    message : INFORMATION;
begin
    message.infoKind := REQUEST;
    MPNOTE.SEND(SOURCE_ADDRESS, message);
    MPNOTE.RECEIVE(SOURCE_ADDRESS, message);
    data := message.data;
end READ;
```

First, a target process sends a request to the source process announcing its willingness to read a note. Then it simply waits until a note comes in, and copies its content. Again, we are assuming that receipt of messages adheres to blocking communication.

It is now quite straightforward to express the behavior of the source process. It first waits for any incoming request, and then passes its note to the target process that has just announced its willingness to communicate. This leads to the following description of WRITE:

```
procedure WRITE(data : in CONTENT) is
    request, message : INFORMATION;
    targetAddress : MPNOTE.ADDRESS;
begin
    MPNOTE.RECEIVE_ANY(targetAddress, request);
    message.infoKind := NOTE;
    message.data := data;
    MPNOTE.SEND(targetAddress, message);
end WRITE;
```

The overall behavior of this communication is illustrated in Figure 6.4.

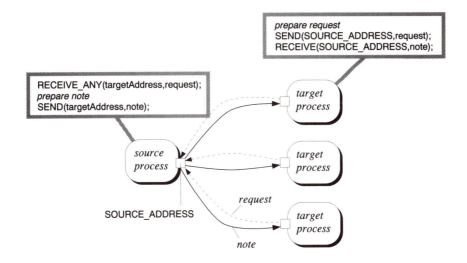

Figure 6.4 Passing notes from one source process to one of many target processes.

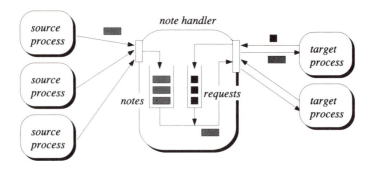

Figure 6.5 The global organization of the note-handling system.

Multiple source and target processes

As our last example, let's now consider the situation where multiple source and target processes want to exchange notes. In particular, we want to express the situation where *any* source process can write a note that will subsequently be received by one of *many* target processes. Simply combining the two solutions described above will not work because a target process would have to announce its willingness to read a note to *all* source processes, which may then each decide to write a note. Instead, what we do is introduce a separate process NOTE_HANDLER that handles all communication between the group of source processes and the group of target processes. The behavior of the note handler can be described as follows:

- The communication between a source process and the note handler proceeds as follows. A source process simply sends a note to the handler, which must then locate a target process to which it can forward the note. To that end, we adopt a solution in which the handler temporarily stores the incoming note by appending it to a queue. It then continues to search for a suitable target process.

- In order to know which target process is willing to read a note, a target process must first pass a request to the handler. The handler, in turn, will also temporarily store this request (again by appending it to a queue), after which it checks to see if there was also a pending note.

- If (1) a note is indeed pending, and (2) there is a target process that has issued a request for reading the note, the handler then removes the note at the head of the note queue, and removes the request at the head of the request queue, and sends that note to the requesting target process.

Again, there are two kinds of messages that can be communicated with the note handler: notes and requests, as shown in Figure 6.5. We can therefore use the MPNOTE package from our model with one source process and many target processes. Assuming that the note handler itself can be contacted at address HANDLER_ADDRESS, writing and reading notes can then be easily expressed by slightly modifying the procedures WRITE and READ from our previous example. In fact, the only two things we have to take into account is the address of the note handler and the fact that writing a note implies that a message can be sent from the source process to the handler without having to delay the source until a target has announced itself. We therefore leave these adaptations as an exercise for the reader.

▷ The behavior of the note handler can be expressed by further extending our package with the two procedures shown in Listing 6.7. In order to queue incoming requests and notes, we have also added two additional packages. For simplicity, we ignore the fact that queues have a maximum length, and leave an adaptation of our package that takes such maximum lengths into account as an exercise for the reader. The behavior of the note handler is described by the process HANDLER, also shown in Listing 6.7.

6.3.3 Semantics of message-based communication

So far, we have said hardly anything about the precise semantics of sending and receiving messages. Considering the vast number of variations in message-passing, it is important to know exactly what it means to send or receive a message. And this, in turn, generally implies that we have to know how message transmission is realized by an underlying communication system. Fortunately, describing the underlying communication system can be done by focusing on just a few issues: its capabilities for message buffering, blocking communication, and process synchronization.

Buffered communication

One aspect of message-based communication that is easily overlooked is whether communication is **buffered**. The principle of using buffers is shown in Figure 6.6. Each sending process has an associated **output queue** (also called an output buffer) to which messages are first appended before being transmitted to the receiver. After transmission, a message is appended to the receiving process' **input queue** (i.e. input buffer), from which it will later be removed. When a message is removed from the receiver's queue, the message is said to be **delivered** to the receiving process.

Let's look at some of the implications of buffered communication. First, it should be clear that whenever the sender's output queue has room left to append messages, a sending process need only append a message to its queue without having to be further delayed. A problem arises if the sender queue is already full. In that case we can either block the sender until a message has been removed from the head of the queue for transmission or simply report that there was no more room. This corresponds exactly to the blocking and non-blocking semantics we presented in our discussion on streams.

At the receiver's end we have a similar situation. In order to have a message delivered, a receiving process inspects its input queue and if it finds the queue is not empty, it simply removes the first message. If there are no messages pending, we have the choice either to block the receiver until a message comes in or have it continue immediately by reporting back that nothing has been sent.

```
package REQUESTQ is new GENERAL_QUEUE(ELEMENT ⇒ MPNOTE.ADDRESS);
package NOTEQ is new GENERAL_QUEUE(ELEMENT ⇒ CONTENT);

...
targets : REQUESTQ.DEFINITION;
notes : NOTEQ.DEFINITION;

procedure GET_INFORMATION is
   senderAddress : MPNOTE.ADDRESS;
   message : INFORMATION;
begin
   -- Simply let the note handler wait for any incoming message. If it is a request
   -- from a target process, then queue that request. Otherwise, the incoming message
   -- is a note that is also to be queued.
   MPNOTE.RECEIVE_ANY(senderAddress, message);
   if message.infoKind = REQUEST
      then REQUESTQ.APPEND(targets, senderAddress);
      else NOTEQ.APPEND(notes, message.data);
   end if ;
end GET_INFORMATION;

procedure PASS_NOTE is
   noTargets : BOOLEAN;
   noNotes : BOOLEAN;
   targetAddress : MPNOTE.ADDRESS;
   nextNote : INFORMATION;
begin
   -- In order to forward a note, there should at least be a pending request, as well
   -- as a pending note. If this is the case, remove both from their respective queues
   -- and pass the note to the selected target process.
   REQUESTQ.CHECK_EMPTY(targets, noTargets);
   NOTEQ.CHECK_EMPTY(notes, noNotes);
   if not (noTargets or noNotes) then
      REQUESTQ.REMOVE(targets, targetAddress);
      NOTEQ.REMOVE(notes, nextNote.data);
      nextNote.infoKind := NOTE;
      MPNOTE.SEND(targetAddress, nextNote);
   end if ;
end PASS_NOTE;

process HANDLER is
begin
   while TRUE loop
      GET_INFORMATION;
      PASS_NOTE;
   end loop ;
end HANDLER;

noteHandler : HANDLER;
```

Listing 6.7   The main behavior of the note handler expressed by two procedures, and combined in the process HANDLER.

▷ But from the viewpoint of the sender and receiver, what really counts is whether they need to block when they communicate. The situation is shown in Figure 6.7.

The simplest situation is that of buffered, non-blocking communication as shown in Figure 6.7(a). When the sender finds its output queue full (indicated at "send(1)") the sender continues immediately without any communication taking place. When a message can still

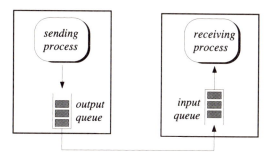

Figure 6.6 The organization of buffered message-passing.

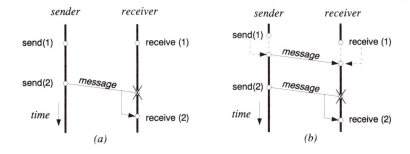

Figure 6.7   The basic message-passing protocols for buffered communication using (a) non-blocking and (b) blocking communication.

be appended to the output queue, communication will take place but the sender will not be delayed, as shown by the point marked "send(2)". From the receiver's point of view, we have a similar situation. At the point marked "receive(1)" the receiver finds its input queue empty so it will continue immediately without communication taking place. However, it may also find that a message has arrived (at "receive(2)"), which it subsequently removes from the input queue.

Buffered, blocking communication is illustrated in Figure 6.7(b). In that case, we see that a sender, when finding its output queue full at the point marked "send(1)", is delayed until there is room to append another message. At the point marked "send(2)" no delay takes place as a message could be immediately appended to the output queue. Likewise, the receiver is either delayed ("receive(1)") or can continue almost immediately ("receive(2)") depending on whether its input queue was empty.

But the real problems start when the receiver's input queue is full so that no transmitted message can be appended to it. The problem is that in most communication systems that use buffering mechanisms, whenever a message is transmitted it is *first* removed from the appropriate output queue and then transmitted. This implies that if the input queue at the receiver turns out to be full, there is nowhere the message can be temporarily stored. Consequently, all that can be done is *discard* the message: it is lost for ever. And this is

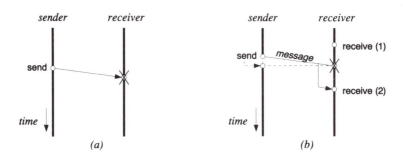

Figure 6.8   Buffered communication using message-discarding (a) without and (b) with information on success of transmission.

what often happens in practice. The result is that our communication is no longer **reliable**. One way or the other, a sending process has to take into account that there may be occasions when the message it sent never arrives at the destination.

▷ There are several solutions to this problem. The first is to do absolutely nothing, i.e. the sender is not even informed that transmission failed. This is a rather difficult situation which requires that the sender and receiver cooperate explicitly, because the underlying communication system provides no support whatsoever. How the two can come to an agreement on which messages have arrived, and which ones did not is discussed in the following chapters. A second solution is at least to inform the sender that transmission failed. The difference with providing no information is that the receiver is not bothered with transmission failures. All it sees are the messages as appended to its input queue. The sender, on the other hand, is put into a position in which it may decide to make another attempt to send the lost message to the receiver.

These two situations are shown in Figure 6.8. In Figure 6.8(a) it is seen that the sender will never know whether its message reached the other end. Figure 6.8(b) illustrates what happens when the sender is informed about the success of message transmission. An important observation here is that the sender will be delayed until it receives information on the status of the transmission. This implies that there is no need to maintain an output queue at the sender's end. The sender will never have more than one outstanding message, and this message will then be in transit.

Synchronized communication

When discussing streams in Section 6.2.2 we made a distinction between, on the one hand, blocking and non-blocking communication, and on the other, synchronous and asynchronous communication. We observed that if a source process used blocking communication, it was always certain that the note which it wrote to a stream would eventually be read by a target process. However, using blocking communication did not provide assurance as to *when* a note was read. To that end, the source and target processes needed to **synchronize** explicitly.

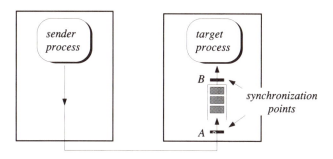

Figure 6.9 The two points of possible synchronization in message-based communication.

In the case of message-passing, the situation is certainly not better than our idealized implementation of streams. First, when communication uses buffering mechanisms, we have argued above that even blocking communication at the sender's end is not enough to ensure that a message will indeed be successfully transmitted to a receiver. All that a blocking send ensures is that the message to be transmitted is eventually appended to the sender's output queue. If we are going to use process synchronization in order to be able to say something sensible about message transmission and delivery, we will have to devise a rather specific mechanism.

First, we need to make a distinction between two kinds of synchronization which are also shown in Figure 6.9. If we are only concerned about successful transmission of a message, then it is sufficient to have a sending process block until the message passes what we have indicated as synchronization point "A". On the other hand, if we have to be certain that a message is actually delivered, i.e. read by the receiving process, then the sending process will have to be delayed until the message passes synchronization point "B" in Figure 6.9. Note that because we are delaying the sending process as soon as it submits a message for transmission, there is no need to maintain an output queue. The sender will never be in a position to have several pending messages waiting to be transmitted in any case.

In practice, communication systems at best support process synchronization for the case that messages pass synchronization point "A". In other words, they may provide the means for delaying a sending process until the message that is to be transmitted has been appended to the receiver's input queue. If a sender and receiver need to synchronize on the fact that a message passes synchronization point "B", only few systems will provide support. In general, it is left to the receiver to reply explicitly by sending an acknowledgment back to the sender. But independent of which synchronization point is actually chosen, both forms of communication are referred to as **synchronous message-passing**. The fact that this terminology refers to different situations is unfortunate, as it tends to lead to confusion. When a sender and a receiver do not synchronize, we speak of **asynchronous message-passing**.

Of course, there is one situation in which the distinction between the two vanishes completely: when there is also no input queue, i.e. when communication is completely

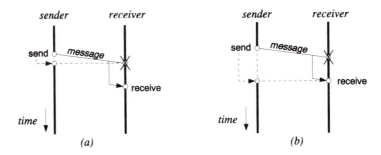

Figure 6.10   Synchronizing two processes at the point of message receipt (a), and message delivery (b).

unbuffered. In that case, synchronous communication implies that message transmission can only take place at the moment that *both* the sender and receiver are prepared to communicate. Also, it is not hard to imagine that if communication is unbuffered the only alternative for message transmission to take place is when sender and receiver synchronize. In other words, talking about unbuffered, asynchronous communication makes little or no sense.

▷ Let's take a closer look at process synchronization from the viewpoint of the communicating parties. We assume that messages can always be appended to a receiver's input queue. In that case, we need to take into account that the sender should be delayed until the message has arrived at the other end. This situation is illustrated in Figure 6.10 where we have made a distinction between the point where the message is appended to the receiver's input queue in Figure 6.10(a) and synchronization at the point of delivery in Figure 6.10(b). In both cases we are assuming that the receiver is not yet prepared to read an incoming message at the instant the sender's message arrives. Delivery takes place at the point marked "receive".

But the situation becomes much more difficult if we assume that input queues may become full. Synchronous communication more or less implies that messages should always arrive at the receiver. In any case, the sender is prepared to wait until that event takes place. Consequently, we have to devise a mechanism that allows us to cope with full input queues. The first point to note is that as long as a sender is waiting until its message has been successfully transmitted, it will, by definition, not send another message. This is an important difference with asynchronous communication where a sender has an output queue, for in that case, a sender can immediately issue another message transmission as soon as the previous message has been appended to its queue.

This observation suggests two solutions. First, suppose that we know in advance that for any receiver there will be a maximum *maxSend* of senders trying to pass a message to it. In that case, it is sufficient to ensure that the receiver's input queue can contain a total of *maxSend* messages. It can easily be verified that message transmission will always succeed. The weak point here, of course, is that we have assumed that we know what *maxSend* is. In practice, this is not possible (try to imagine why). Therefore, a second approach is not to maintain an input queue at the receiver's end at all. Instead, a message that is to be transmitted is kept

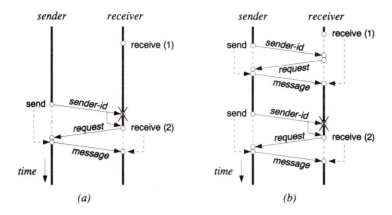

Figure 6.11   The refinement of synchronous communication with finite input queues using (a) non-blocking receive, and (b) blocking receive.

at the sender's end until the receiver indicates that it can accept it. Consequently, we only have to maintain, for each sender, an output queue having capacity 1.

But this second solution does create another problem: how will the receiver know that there is a message pending for it? A practical solution in this case is to let the communication system merely pass the *identification* of a sender to the receiver. This identification will have to be stored in an **identification buffer**. In contrast to message buffers, realizing an identification buffer need not lead to serious problems. The point to note is that messages, in general, can be quite large. An identification, however, need not take more than just a few bytes. In other words, the storage we need to reserve when implementing an identification buffer is much smaller than that required for the implementation of a message buffer. This implies that it is fairly easy to guarantee successful delivery of identifications.[3] Now, when a receiver detects that an identification has been stored in its buffer it sends a request to the identified sender that it can accept the sender's message. The sender, in turn, will then transmit the message via the communication system to the receiver. Assuming that message transmission will always succeed, the sender may continue the instant the message starts its way towards the receiver. This refinement of synchronous communication is shown in Figure 6.11.

6.4   Advanced message-based communication

There are many types of message-based communication models. So far, we have paid attention only to the most primitive forms of message communication. In practice, the simple send and receive operations discussed so far are not entirely adequate when building communication systems. In many cases, this concerns identifying where a message has to be sent, and possibly also knowing who has sent it. In this section, we shall take

---

[3]Assuming, at least, that message transmission itself is free of errors. In the next chapter we will see that this is not always an entirely realistic assumption.

Figure 6.12 The principle of a channel in message-based communication.

a closer look at communication models that make message-passing easier. In all cases, you should realize that these more advanced communication models are generally implemented by means of the basic models discussed in the previous section.

6.4.1   Channels

So far, we have assumed that whenever a process sends a message it knows exactly where it should send that message in the sense that it explicitly identifies the receiver. But, of course, this need not always be the case. For example, if you write a letter to an organization you will generally address the letter to a specific department and probably also use a post box. You are not interested in *who* actually handles your letter, nor in *where* the organization is sited. The same holds for a receiver. In many cases you may be interested in receiving *any* message, or, on the other hand, messages in which you have a particular interest. This type of anonymity is not only common in our daily lives; it is also something which is useful when dealing with communication systems.

Avoiding a sender and receiver having to identify each other explicitly is supported in communication systems through the concept of so-called **channels**. A channel is to be considered as a general communication medium between a set of senders and a set of receivers. The principle is shown in Figure 6.12. Channels are capable of transporting messages from one end to another.

Instead of sending a message to an explicitly identified receiver, a sending process simply puts a message on a channel. Likewise, receiving a message is now expressed by providing the channel from which a message should arrive. This can be expressed quite easily in BASAL by assuming the existence of a service program implemented as the following package CHANNEL:

```
package CHANNEL(type MESSAGE) is
   type ADDRESS is ...;

   procedure SEND(chan : in ADDRESS; mess : in MESSAGE);
   procedure RECEIVE(chan : in ADDRESS; mess : out MESSAGE);
end CHANNEL;
```

By using the data type ADDRESS, we reflect the fact that channels can be uniquely identified. And this is indeed what happens in practice. If you want to send data across a specific channel you need to provide an explicit reference to that channel. Such a reference is denoted by the more general term "address" in most communication systems. The important point about channels is that they allow a sender and receiver to be anonymous which provides us with at least more flexibility than using the addressing schemes discussed so far.

Channels as message queues

There are various types of channels. An important channel is the one that behaves as a **message queue**. Channels that appear to the communicating parties as message queues correspond to what we have previously referred to as a stream. The difference lies in the fact that channels have a (theoretically) infinite capacity. Upon sending a message to a channel, the message is immediately transmitted without further delaying the sender. If several messages have already been sent but not yet accepted by receivers, the newly sent message is simply buffered *as the last one*, and kept in the channel until it is removed. In other words, a channel delivers messages in the same order as they are delivered. In particular, if a sender executes the following two statements:

```
CHANNEL.SEND(chan, message_1);
CHANNEL.SEND(chan, message_2);
```

then the semantics of a channel as message queue ensures that message_1 will always be delivered *before* message_2. This preservation of message ordering is often extremely important in communication. To illustrate, suppose we were to send a complete document, page by page. If the order of receipt could not be guaranteed, we would have to (1) let the sender explicitly provide a number on each page that is sent, and (2) require that the receiver subsequently sorts the pages as they arrive.

Now assuming that message ordering is preserved may seem a perfectly reasonable thing to do, but the problem is that *realizing* such an ordering in practice often turns out to be not that easy. What it means is that the **route** a message follows from sender to receiver need not be unique in all cases. For example, if we had a channel between Amsterdam and San Francisco, message_1 may possibly be routed via New York, whereas message_2 may be sent to Tokyo first, giving it a chance to arrive before message_1. How this problem can be solved is discussed when we discuss implementation issues in the following chapters. Not being able to preserve message ordering is something that not only occurs with channel communication. It is inherent for most forms of message-passing, including the point-to-point and any-to-one communication schemes that were discussed in the previous section. Of course, message ordering is automatically preserved in the case of synchronous communication. Why this is so is left as an exercise for the reader.

At the receiver's end, a process will generally wait until a message arrives. In other words, message receipt adheres to blocking communication. But suppose that several receivers are waiting at the same time to receive a message from the same channel? In

```
package PORT is
  type ADDRESS is ...;
  type MESSAGE is ...;

  SERVER_PORT : constant ADDRESS := ...;

  procedure SEND(port : in ADDRESS; mess : in MESSAGE);
  procedure RECEIVE(port : in ADDRESS; mess : out message);
  −− Send and receive messages to and from a given port. Sending adheres to
  −− non-blocking communication, receipt adheres to blocking communication.

  procedure BIND(port : in ADDRESS; done : out BOOLEAN);
  procedure UNBIND(port : in ADDRESS);
  −− The calling process first requests the operating system to assign the indicated port
  −− so that it can act as a server for messages sent to that port. UNBINDing yields
  −− that the calling process will no longer handle incoming messages via that port.

  procedure ACQUIRE_PORT(port : out ADDRESS; done : out BOOLEAN);
  procedure RELEASE_PORT(port : in ADDRESS);
  −− The calling process requests (returns) a port that can be used to receive
  −− messages that are explicitly sent to that port.
end PORT;
```

Listing 6.8 The specification of a package for handling ports.

that case, nothing sensible can be said about message delivery. In other words, we cannot predict precisely which receiver will receive which message. In addition, there are also implementations that allow non-blocking receipt of messages via a channel. Channels that behave as message queues and that allow multiple senders and receivers are also referred to as **mailboxes**.

Ports

Channels in many communication systems have only one receiver, in which case they are also referred to as **ports**. As this concept of ports is heavily used in practice, let's pay some attention to it. The importance of ports becomes apparent when you realize that they can be used to *identify* processes. In particular, they can be used to identify processes that provide some kind of *service*. The use of ports is best illustrated by means of a simple example.

Suppose we have an operating system that provides us with the package specification shown in Listing 6.8. We assume that the procedure SEND adheres to non-blocking communication, but that RECEIVE employs blocking communication. Of special interest are the other procedures. First, we have provided a special port SERVER_PORT as part of our package specification. The intention is that this port represents a specific set of services that other processes may use. By declaring it in our package specification, this port becomes **known** to the outside world. Now suppose a process server calls the procedure BIND as in:

PORT.BIND(PORT.SERVER_PORT, okay);

In this case, the process server is requesting to use the port SERVER_PORT as the *only* process that is allowed to receive incoming messages via that port. If this permission is granted, then okay will be set to TRUE, otherwise, it will be set to FALSE. In general, there is only one reason why a process should not be allowed to use a known port: there is a process already using it.[4] The fact that a port is *known* simply means that other processes can send *specific* messages to that port. For example, in order to read and write files that are located on another computer, many UNIX operating systems have reserved port numbered 21 to let processes communicate with a special file server that can handle these file requests. All messages sent to port 21 must then adhere to a predefined format, i.e. the kind of information they contain is subject to strict, predefined rules. Now, if a process requires to be bound to port 21, it is effectively requesting to act as this special file server. Calling the procedure UNBIND establishes that the calling process can no longer act as the server for the indicated port.

The procedure ACQUIRE_PORT is used to request the operating system for a port that is not already being used. So, for example, if a process client calls

PORT.ACQUIRE_PORT(clientPort, okay);

then clientPort will contain the address of an unused port. In this case, that port is now bound to process client, and this process can receive messages via that port. If there are no more ports available (i.e. all ports have been used), the parameter okay will be set to FALSE. An important assumption that we are making here is that the collection of ports that can be managed by an operating system is finite. In practice, this is indeed the case, although hundreds or thousands of ports will generally be available. Ports are returned to the operating system as soon as a process finishes by calling the procedure RELEASE_PORT.

We are now in a position to let our processes communicate. To that end, we assume that the process client always provides a port by which server can send messages back, i.e. we assume that the data type MESSAGE looks something like:

```
type MESSAGE is
    record
        replyPort : PORT.ADDRESS;
        data : SOME_DATA;
    end record ;
```

In that case, our client process can easily communicate with the server process through the known port SERVER_PORT. The global behavior of the process server can be outlined as shown in Listing 6.9(a); that of a client process is given in Listing 6.9(b).

Observing what we are actually doing here should at least make one thing apparent: the communicating processes have barely any knowledge of each other. The only real

---

[4]In practice, there's another reason: the process is simply not *privileged* to use the port. This is typically something that is due to security reasons which we shall not take into account here.

```
process SERVER_PROCESS is
    okay : BOOLEAN;
    request, reply : PORT.MESSAGE;
    clientPort : PORT.ADDRESS;
begin
    PORT.BIND(PORT.SERVER_PORT, okay);
    if okay then
        while TRUE loop
            PORT.RECEIVE(PORT.SERVER_PORT, request);
            clientPort := request.replyPort;
            do something with the incoming message, and then reply
            reply.data := ...;
            PORT.SEND(clientPort, reply);
        end loop ;
    end if ;
end SERVER_PROCESS;
```

(a) The server process

```
process CLIENT_PROCESS is
    okay : BOOLEAN;
    request, reply : PORT.MESSAGE;
    clientPort : PORT.ADDRESS;
begin
    PORT.ACQUIRE_PORT(clientPort, okay);
    if okay then
        request.replyPort := clientPort;
        request.data := ...
        PORT.SEND(PORT.SERVER_PORT, request);
        PORT.RECEIVE(clientPort, reply);
        PORT.RELEASE_PORT(clientPort);
        do something with the reply.
    end if ;
end CLIENT_PROCESS;
```

(b) The client process

Listing 6.9 General outline of a server and a client process communicating through ports.

fact that has been determined in advance is how communication should proceed when referring to the known port SERVER_PORT. Reference to that port can be done in two ways. A **server process** can request to be the one that will *implement* the service related to this port, whereas a **client process** can request that service to be provided. There is no need for a client process to know exactly which process is handling its service requests. And by providing a port when requesting that service, the server need also not know to whom it is actually providing the service. As you can imagine, this admits for a large degree of flexibility: if we were to decide to implement the service related to port SERVER_PORT in a completely different way, then this is simply established by replacing the server process. No client processes are affected in any way.

Links and connections

A special type of channel is one with only a single sender and a single receiver, often referred to as a **link**. In practice, links mainly occur at two levels of abstraction. First, they are referred to as such when two geographically remote computers are directly connected to each other (i.e. through wires) that can only be used by those two. At a much higher level of abstraction, they appear in some programming languages, most notably those providing only unbuffered synchronous communication.

But there is also something between these two levels of abstraction, which, rather confusingly, is referred to as a **connection**. A connection is a (bidirectional) link between a pair of processes which preserves the order of message transmission. What this means is that if one of the processes sends a series of messages to the other, then these messages arrive in the same order they were sent. Bidirectional means that *both* processes can send and receive messages to and from the other, respectively. Although at first this may seem as a rather strange communication mechanism, connections as discussed here appear frequently in our daily lives, the most prominent form being perhaps the way we communicate by telephone.

The main distinction with all communication models we have been discussing so far is that connections need to be *set up*. Using communication by telephone as an example, this corresponds to having to dial a number first before it is possible to talk to the other party. Likewise, when communication is finished, a connection should be *closed* again. We can express this model of communication in BASAL by the package specification shown in Listing 6.10. Apart from the usual procedures for sending and receiving messages, as well as procedures for setting up and closing a connection, there is also a procedure LISTEN which blocks a calling process until another process has established a connection to it. LISTENing for a connection is similar to waiting at the telephone for someone to call you.

Rather than using the term connection, we shall generally speak of **connection-oriented communication** in order to avoid as much confusion with the more general term connection. Connection-oriented communication has some important properties:

- First, and as we have already mentioned, once a connection has been established, message ordering between two processes is maintained during the period of communication. This means that messages are received in the same order they were sent.

- Second, connection-oriented communication is generally also reliable, meaning that messages are guaranteed to be delivered at the other end. However, it may occur that the connection itself is abruptly broken caused by some external event.

These two properties form an important distinction from **connectionless communication**, which generally refers to the basic message-passing models discussed in Section 6.3. In practice, connectionless communication neither preserves message-ordering, nor does

```
package CONNECTION(type MESSAGE) is
    type ADDRESS is ...;
    type DEFINITION is ...;

    procedure OPEN(addr : in ADDRESS; conn : out DEFINITION; done : out BOOLEAN);
        –– Set up or open a connection to a process that can be reached at address
        –– [addr]. If a connection is established, [done] is set to TRUE, and [conn] is
        –– returned as an identifier of that connection. Otherwise, [done] is set to FALSE.

    procedure CLOSE(conn : in DEFINITION);
        –– Close the indicated connection [conn], thereby finishing the communication.

    procedure SEND(conn : in DEFINITION; mess : in MESSAGE);
        –– Send a message [mess] to the process at the other end of the connection.
        –– Communication is assumed to adhere to non-blocking semantics.

    procedure RECEIVE(conn : in DEFINITION; mess : out MESSAGE);
        –– Receive a message [mess] from the process at the other end of the connection.
        –– Communication is assumed to adhere to blocking semantics.

    procedure LISTEN(conn : out DEFINITION);
        –– Listen to discover whether someone is trying to establish a connection. When
        –– this procedure is called, the caller is blocked until a connection [conn] is established.

end CONNECTION;
```

Listing 6.10 A specification of a package for connection-based communication.

it guarantee message delivery, although this depends much on the capabilities of the underlying communication system. The distinction between connectionless and connection-oriented communication is an important one that we shall come across several times in succeeding chapters.

An example: connection-oriented communication.   To illustrate the difference between connectionless and connection-oriented communication, consider a situation where several source processes want to write notes to a single target process. In particular, we now assume that each note consists of several pages that are to be sent one after the other before a next note can be written. Each note can be represented by the following data type NOTE:

```
type PAGE is array (1..NCHAR) of CHARACTER;
type NOTE is array (1..NPAGE) of PAGE;
```

where NPAGE denotes the number of pages contained in each note. In order to set up communication based on connections for passing notes on a per-page basis, we first declare an appropriate package as follows:

```
package NOTE_CONNECTION is new CONNECTION(MESSAGE ⇒ PAGE);
```

Using this package, we can then express the behavior of a source process by means of the following procedure WRITE:

```
procedure WRITE(someNote : in NOTE; done : out BOOLEAN) is
   conn : NOTE_CONNECTION.DEFINITION;
   opened : BOOLEAN;
begin
   NOTE_CONNECTION.OPEN(TARGET_ADDRESS, conn, opened);
   if opened then
      for page in 1..NPAGE loop
         NOTE_CONNECTION.SEND(conn, someNote(page));
      end loop ;
      NOTE_CONNECTION.CLOSE(conn);
   end if ;
   done := opened;
end WRITE;
```

The basic idea is quite simple. The source process calling the procedure WRITE first establishes a connection to the target process, which is assumed to be reachable at address TARGET_ADDRESS. If a connection is established, the source process continues by sending each page separately to the target process through the established connection, after which it is closed again. The important point to note is that all pages arrive in the order they have been sent. Also, no other process can send notes across the same connection in the meantime because the source and target process are exclusively communicating with each other. The target process can now be described by means of the following procedure READ:

```
procedure READ(someNote : out NOTE) is
   conn : NOTE_CONNECTION.DEFINITION;
begin
   NOTE_CONNECTION.LISTEN(conn);
   for page in 1..NPAGE loop
      NOTE_CONNECTION.RECEIVE(conn, someNote(page));
   end loop ;
end READ;
```

What we see here is that the target process waits until *any* connection is established as initiated by one of the source processes. Then it simply reads all the incoming pages, and knowing that message-ordering is maintained, immediately puts them in the right place of someNote.

An example: connectionless communication.   But suppose now that we want to pass notes using our original package for message passing as described in Listing 6.6. The first point to realize is that we now have no guarantee that messages will arrive in the same order as they were sent. In other words, if we first send someNote(1), and then someNote(2), it may happen that the second page arrives before the first. What we need to do, therefore, is provide explicitly the number of the page that is being sent, leading to the following adaptation of our NOTE data type:

```
type CONTENT is ARRAY(1..NCHAR) of CHARACTER;
type PAGE is
  record
    pageNumber : INTEGER range 1..NPAGE;
    data : CONTENT;
  end record ;

type NOTE is array (1..NPAGE) of PAGE;
```

In order to use basic message-passing for our connectionless communication, we declare the following package:

```
package NOTE_CONNECTIONLESS is new MESSAGE_PASSING(MESSAGE ⇒ PAGE);
```

The fact that messages may not arrive in the same order they were sent is of particular concern to the receiving process. Therefore, we concentrate on the adaptation of the procedure READ and leave that of the procedure WRITE as an exercise for the reader. In order for a target process to receive an entire note, it can first receive a page from *any* source process. Then, the remaining pages should come only from that particular source process. In addition, the target process will also have to insert the incoming pages into the right position. This can be expressed by the following adaptation of the procedure READ:

```
procedure READ(someNote : out NOTE) is
  source : NOTE_CONNECTIONLESS.ADDRESS;
  somePage : PAGE;
  numOfReceivedPages : INTEGER := 0; -- the total number of pages received so far.
begin
  -- First wait for any incoming page. This will also identify the source process.
  NOTE_CONNECTIONLESS.RECEIVE_ANY(source, somePage);
  -- Insert the received page into the right position of the note that is being assembled.
  -- This is done by looking at the page number and doing the appropriate assignment.
  someNote(somePage.pageNumber) := somePage;
  numOfReceivedPages := 1;
  -- Now get the rest of the pages from the same source process.
  while numOfReceivedPages < NPAGE loop
    NOTE_CONNECTIONLESS.RECEIVE(source, somePage);
    someNote(somePage.pageNumber) := somePage;
    numOfReceivedPages := numOfReceivedPages + 1;
  end loop ;
end READ;
```

What is seen here is that the target process is now completely responsible for assembling the note by ordering the pages explicitly when they arrive.

Our solution is still relatively simple because we assume that a process can explicitly specify from which sending process it is prepared to accept incoming data. In practice, this is not always possible. Instead, many basic message-passing systems support only the RECEIVE_ANY procedure. In other words, a receiving process also has to account for the fact that messages from other processes may arrive, which have to be handled as well. We shall return to this situation in later chapters, but it should be clear that in such cases having connection-oriented communication available may indeed be convenient.

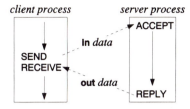

Figure 6.13 Synchronization between client and server in a rendez-vous.

▷ 6.4.2   The rendez-vous and remote procedure call

Using channels allows us to express message-based communication much more easily than using direct addressing schemes (i.e. schemes in which the sender and receiver have to explicitly know each other). But things can be made even more simpler if we take into account the communication *scenario* as well. One particular scenario that occurs frequently in practice, and which we also saw above, is the one in which a client process *first* sends a request to a server process, and then *immediately* delays itself until it receives a reply. In other words, the communication pattern expressed as the send-receive pair

```
SEND(server, request);
RECEIVE(server, answer);
```

is one that you will often see in practice. There are two points immediately worth noting about this scheme. First, the client process *fully synchronizes* with the server process, i.e. from the moment the client issues a service request,the process will have to wait until an answer has been sent back. Meanwhile, it cannot do anything else. During this waiting, the server handles the request. Second, when issuing a request, the client will generally have to provide some input data; similarly, the returned answer will generally contain output data that can be used by the client. This is illustrated in Figure 6.13.

When we compare this figure with Figure 4.3 (page 145), which describes the principle of a subroutine call in PRIMAL, these two aspects bear an immediate resemblance to ordinary procedure calls. The only real difference is that the instructions of the implementation of the service are executed by a separate process (the server), rather than the calling process, as is the case with procedure calls. And because we are dealing with *two* processes, we say that the client and server are engaged in a **rendez-vous**.

An example

To illustrate the use of this mechanism, assume our operating system provides a service program in the form of the package RENDEZVOUS shown in Listing 6.11. Furthermore, suppose that our system consists of a number of computers which are connected together, and of which exactly one operates as a so-called **file server**. The task of this file server is to maintain a file system like that discussed in Section 5.6. All operations on files are handled by the file server. In other words, if a process client wants to manipulate a file, this can only be done

```
package RENDEZVOUS is
   type ADDRESS is ...
   type IN_DATA is ...
   type OUT_DATA is ...

   procedure CALL(server : in ADDRESS; input : in IN_DATA; output : out OUT_DATA);
      -- Issue a request for a service at the indicated [server], passing on input data in
      -- in the form of [input]. The answer will be returned as [output]. The
      -- requesting process is postponed until an answer has been returned.

   procedure ACCEPT(caller : out ADDRESS; input : out IN_DATA);
      -- To be called by a server process, so that it can handle the service request
      -- issued by process [caller], with input data [input].

   procedure REPLY(caller : in ADDRESS; output : in OUT_DATA);
      -- To be called by a server process in order to answer a reply to process
      -- [caller] in the form of the output data [output].

end RENDEZVOUS;
```

Listing 6.11 The specification of a package for rendez-vous communication.

by requesting the file server to do so on behalf of the process client. The latter will therefore have to *request* the file server to perform a specific operation, and wait for the server's *reply*.

Let's start by considering what kind of messages a client process and the file server can exchange. We assume the file server provides the services as given by the package specification shown in Listing 5.12 on page 251. These services can be summarized by the following data type:

```
type SERVICE is (GETSIZE, CREATE, DELETE, OPEN, CLOSE, READ, WRITE);
```

In order to *request* a service, a client process will have to indicate exactly which service it wants to have the file server perform, as well as the necessary input data for that service. Input always consists of a FILE_ID except when a file is to be created. In addition, when reading or writing a file, the client will have to indicate the position in that file where the data is to be either read from or written to, and in the latter case, it will also have to provide the data. Therefore, we can represent the input data by a single data type IN_DATA:

```
type IN_DATA is
   record
      request : SERVICE;
      fileId : FILESYSTEM.FILE_ID; -- used always, except for the creating a file
      pos : FILESYSTEM.FILEPOS; -- needed to read or write data from and to a file
      data : MEMORY.BYTE; -- used when data is to be written to a file
   end record ;
```

Likewise, it can be verified that reply messages can be jointly represented by the following data type OUT_DATA:

```
type OUT_DATA is
  record
    fileId : FILESYSTEM.FILE_ID; –– returned after creating a file
    size : FILESYSTEM.FILESIZE; –– returned after asking for the size of a file
    data : MEMORY.BYTE; –– returned as the result of reading data from a file
  end record ;
```

The communication between a client process and the file server can now be represented by the following package specification, which is a specific version of the package RENDEZ-VOUS given in Listing 6.11.

```
package FILE_RENDEZVOUS is
  type ADDRESS is ...;
  type SERVICE is ... as given above
  type IN_DATA is ... as given above
  type OUT_DATA is ... as given above

  procedure CALL(server : in ADDRESS; input : in IN_DATA; output : out OUT_DATA);
  procedure ACCEPT(caller : out ADDRESS; input : out IN_DATA);
  procedure REPLY(caller : in ADDRESS; output : in OUT_DATA);
end FILE_RENDEZVOUS;
```

To illustrate, assuming that the file server can be reached at address SERVER_ADDRESS, the behavior of a client process that wants to know the size of a file can be expressed as the following procedure GETFILESIZE:

```
procedure GETFILESIZE(fileId : in FILESYSTEM.FILE_ID; size : out FILESYSTEM.FILESIZE) is
  input : FILE_RENDEZVOUS.IN_DATA;
  output : FILE_RENDEZVOUS.OUT_DATA;
begin
  input.request := FILE_RENDEZVOUS.GETSIZE;
  input.fileId := fileId;
  FILE_RENDEZVOUS.CALL(SERVER_ADDRESS, input, output);
  size := output.size;
end GETFILESIZE;
```

The file server, on the other hand, will need to get the requested file size. But not only that, it should also be capable of handling any other kind of service request. We can easily express the behavior of the server as shown in Listing 6.12.

Remote procedure calls

When taking a look at the way that we organize the communication between a client process and the file server, it is seen that our implementation is rather clumsy. In the approach so far, each procedure available in the package specification of FILESYSTEM needs to be separately implemented by a similar procedure for the client process. For example, the procedure GETFILESIZE as given above does exactly the same things as the procedure GETSIZE of FILESYSTEM. However, the latter is not available to the client process, but can only be called by the file server.

But this is a situation that can easily be corrected, and which will result in an elegant way of hiding communication altogether. What we can do is provide *two* package bodies for

```
process FILESERVER is
    input : FILE_RENDEZVOUS.IN_DATA;
    output : FILE_RENDEZVOUS.OUT_DATA;
    caller : FILE_RENDEZVOUS.ADDRESS;
begin
    while TRUE loop
        FILE_RENDEZVOUS.ACCEPT(caller, input);

        if input.request = GETSIZE then FILESYSTEM.GETSIZE(input.fileId, output.size);
        elsif input.request = CREATE then FILESYSTEM.CREATE(output.fileId);
        elsif input.request = DELETE then FILESYSTEM.DELETE(input.fileId);
        elsif input.request = OPEN then FILESYSTEM.OPEN(input.fileId);
        elsif input.request = CLOSE then FILESYSTEM.CLOSE(input.fileId);
        elsif input.request = READ then FILESYSTEM.READ(input.fileId, input.pos, output.data);
        elsif input.request = WRITE then FILESYSTEM.WRITE(input.fileId, input.pos, input.data);
        end if ;

        FILE_RENDEZVOUS.REPLY(caller, output);
    end loop ;
end FILESERVER;
```

Listing 6.12 The behavior of a simple file server.

the package specification FILESYSTEM. One package body implements all the procedures as necessary to handle a file system in the normal case, i.e. as we have discussed in Section 5.6. The other package body is to be made available to client processes, and implements the communication between the client and the file server. To illustrate, the procedure GETSIZE would be part of a special package body (also named FILESYSTEM) which is available only to client processes, as follows:

```
package body FILESYSTEM is
    ...
    procedure GETSIZE(fileId : in FILE_ID; size : out FILESIZE) is
        input : FILE_RENDEZVOUS.IN_DATA;
        output : FILE_RENDEZVOUS.OUT_DATA;
    begin
        input.request := FILE_RENDEZVOUS.GETSIZE;
        input.fileId := fileId;
        FILE_RENDEZVOUS.CALL(SERVER_ADDRESS, input, output);
        size := output.size;
    end GETSIZE;
    ...
end FILESYSTEM;
```

Now the special point about this is that a client process can call the procedure GETSIZE in the usual way, i.e.

```
    FILESYSTEM.GETSIZE(fileId, size);
```

What it does not see, however, is that calling this procedure establishes a rendez-vous communication with the file server, which also calls the procedure GETSIZE, but now the one that acts directly on the indicated file. In other words, what we have established is that the call to the procedure GETSIZE as done by the client process leads to a *remote* execution of the orig-

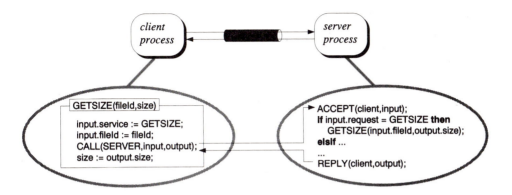

Figure 6.14 The principle of a remote procedure call mechanism.

inal implementation of GETSIZE by the file server. All communication aspects, however, have been made transparent to the client process. This mechanism is referred to as **remote procedure calling** and is illustrated in Figure 6.14.

The remote procedure call mechanism, often abbreviated simply to **RPC**, is a popular means of establishing communication and, in particular, hiding it. The main benefit is that to client processes the complete communication is hidden in the implementation of services as offered through some package. Consequently, the dependence of client processes on where or how services are implemented has more or less vanished. A desirable property indeed. To make it even more convenient, most implementations as used for client processes, like our alternative package body for FILESYSTEM, can be generated automatically. We shall leave this topic at this point, and refer the interested reader to the references provided at the end of this chapter.

▷ 6.4.3 Group communication

So far, we have discussed mostly communication between *two* parties. This may be rather restrictive in certain situations. For example, suppose we want to set up a communication system that supports (electronic) conferencing. In that case, several people have to communicate within a complete group. **Group communication** is an important topic when considering communication systems, and special measures have to be taken in order to support it the way involving parties would expect.

Group communication is characterized by the fact that a single sender wants to transfer a message to a group of receivers. This is also known as **multicasting** as opposed to **unicasting**, which merely involves communication from a sender to a single receiver. A related form of communication is **broadcasting** which involves sending a message to anyone capable of receiving it. That broadcasting is less efficient is illustrated in our daily lives by the fact that direct mailing has become so popular. Direct mailing (which is a form of multicasting) involves sending advertisements only to those people who are expected to be interested in the advertised product. Until recently, the alternative was to send the ads to all people (within a neighborhood or city) regardless whether they were expected to be interested. This last form is typical of broadcasting.

In the following, we shall briefly discuss some of the issues concerning group communication. A full description of the subject is simply not possible here. Therefore, we will mention only some of the problems without providing any solutions. In this sense, group communication reflects the current status of many communication systems: there are many problems for which no single solution has yet been found, or which can be classified as the best solution. References for further reading are provided at the end of this chapter.

Basic group communication

Like any other communication mechanism we have described so far, group communication should allow for sending and receiving messages to and from a group, respectively. As the basis for our discussion, suppose that we have the following package available:

```
package GROUP(type MESSAGE) is
   type ADDRESS is ...

   procedure SEND(group : in ADDRESS; mess : in MESSAGE);
   -- The calling process sends a message [mess] to all members in the indicated group.

   procedure RECEIVE(group : in ADDRESS; mess : out message);
   -- The calling process is blocked until it receives a message that is sent by one of
   -- members in the group.
end GROUP;
```

The first point to note is that these two procedures are less symmetric than you might initially think. Sending a message implies that *every* group member receives a copy. Receiving a message, however, implies that a receiver can accept a message from *any* member; it does not imply that it receives messages from *all* members simultaneously. Let's start by taking a look at sending messages.

When a message is sent to a group, it is clearly the intention that the message should be received by all members of that group. If one receipt fails (for whatever reason), we can conclude that our message has not been transferred properly. In other words, sending a message to a group can only be considered correct if and only if it is received by every member. This means that if only one member does not receive the message, the message transfer as a whole should be discarded in the end. This all-or-nothing property is called **atomic multicast**.

Suppose that in order to implement this scheme, we can make use of a communication system that supports reliable point-to-point communication. In other words, whenever a process sends a message to another process it is guaranteed that the message will find its way to the receiver's input queue. In that case, realizing atomic multicast is not so difficult. One particular simple (but not always efficient) implementation is sending the message separately to each group member. Because the underlying communication system guarantees message delivery, it is always certain that each group member eventually receives the message.

The problems start when reliable communication is not available. In that case, the sending process has to face the fact that if one message does not reach a group member, all copies of that message that were sent to the other members become invalid. For simplicity, assume that although point-to-point communication may fail, the sender will at least be notified that something went wrong. In that case, the sender may try to resend the message a couple of times, but if that does not lead to any result, it will have to inform the other group members that the previously sent message is invalid. And in that case, we will just have to hope that none of them have made important decisions based on the message, for all such decisions will have to be withdrawn. Considering the complexity of handling atomic multicasts in the presence of lost messages, it seems preferable first to build a scheme by which reliable point-to-point communication is supported, and then construct an atomic multicasting mechanism on top of that.

Message ordering

But even if atomic multicasting is realized, problems with group communication are not over. Probably one of the most prominent aspects that also needs to be taken into account is that of message ordering. As we have said, basic message-passing schemes generally do not preserve message ordering in the sense that all messages are delivered in the same order they were sent. In practice, many problems dealing with preserving message ordering between two processes can be handled in rather straightforward ways. For example, one particular simple solution is to number each message that is sent and delay the delivery of a message until all preceding ones have arrived.[5] This is, in fact, the basic implementation mechanism that underlies the way connection-oriented communication works.

In group communication, however, the problem is more serious. First, consider a process that sends two messages in a row as in

```
GROUP.SEND(someGroup, message_1);
GROUP.SEND(someGroup, message_2);
```

In this case, if we want to preserve message ordering, each group member belonging to someGroup must first have message message_1 delivered, before the delivery of message_2 can take place. Realizing this is not really that difficult if we number each message. If a group member receives message_2 first, its delivery to that member is simply delayed until message_1 arrives.

But now consider the following scheme:

```
GROUP.SEND(someGroup, message_1);
GROUP.RECEIVE(someGroup, message_2);
GROUP.SEND(someGroup, message_3);
```

In this case, message ordering should at least be preserved between message_3 and message_1, of which the latter should be delivered to all group members first. But when we consider the relationship between message_2 and message_3, we have that because (1) message_2 is delivered to all group members as well, and (2) message_3 is sent after the delivery

---

[5]Recall the distinction between the arrival and delivery of a message. When a message arrives at a process, it can be held for some time in the process's associated input queue before it is removed. Removing a message from the input queue corresponds to delivering it.

of message_2, message_2 should be delivered to all group members before message_3. The reason for this ordering is quite simple. Message_3 may contain information that is based on information contained in message_2. Achieving this so-called **causal ordering** is much more difficult, although solutions do exist. However, it is beyond the scope of this book to go into such details here, and we therefore resort to providing some references at the end of this chapter.

But in addition to causal ordering, it may be necessary to impose a more strict ordering. Again, consider a scheme in which two processes send a message to a group as in:

GROUP.SEND(someGroup, message_1);   GROUP.SEND(someGroup, message_2);

process #1   *process #2*

The problem is that we cannot say in which order these two messages will be delivered. In fact, some group members may receive message_1 before message_2, while for others the converse may hold. This is a situation that cannot always be accepted. For example, if the group members act on a common database, it is essential that they all have the same view on the state of that database. What we are thus demanding is that *all* group members either receive message_1 before message_2, or that all of them receive message_2 before message_1. With respect to implementation aspects, this so-called **total ordering** is generally even more difficult to realize. Again, we shall not go into any further details at this point but refer the interested reader to the references at the end of this chapter.

6.5   Discussion and further reading

In this chapter we have focused primarily on basic communication models for distributed systems. Basic, in this sense, means that we have taken a look at models by which *two* communicating parties can exchange information by either using shared data or passing messages. In distributed systems message-based communication is prevalent. In the following sections we shall summarize what we have been talking about in this chapter in order to allow you to understand the big picture. In doing so, we shall also make clear that we have indeed only touched upon the subject.

6.5.1   Communication models

Overview of basic models in this chapter

We started our presentation of communication models by assuming the existence of a number of processes that need access to some common data. This model can be viewed as a primitive way of exchanging information, and many examples exist in the real world by which this form of communication takes place. Most notably, perhaps, is where a number of people are using a blackboard such as in a classroom for presenting information, or in a meeting to write down ideas and solutions to a problem. The major disadvantage of this approach is that it is commonly required that processes have immediate access to the shared data. In terms of hardware, this often means that processors need to be connected to a single main memory module. If we are to implement geographically distributed systems, another approach will then have to be followed (we shall weaken this point further below when discussing a novel approach for supporting shared data in geographically distributed systems).

An alternative solution that has been widely accepted, and which has also its counterparts in real life, is that of sending and receiving messages. In this case, an important distinction that should be made is between the ways that the communicating parties synchronize. In particular, a distinction should be made between synchronous and asynchronous communication. Full asynchronous communication, i.e. by which both sender and receiver will never wait until the communication has taken place, is immediately comparable to the way that we handle regular mail. In fact, when taking a look at communication between people, you will find that in many cases it is based on asynchronous behavior. Synchronous communication occurs when a sender and receiver are both willing to wait idly from the moment communication is initiated until it has completed. An example of synchronous communication in real life is that of passing a box from one person to another.

Shared data: further reading

These two basic communication models – shared data versus message-passing – have received a large amount of attention. Initially, discussions focused on the use of shared variables by several processes. This is not too surprising if you realize that the whole idea of processes comes from the area of operating systems. As we have seen in the previous chapter, the main point that we had to take care of is prevention of unwanted process interference, which almost invariably meant avoiding simultaneous manipulation of shared variables and registers. A brief account on how this can be dealt with without using semaphores can be found in Silberschatz and Galvin (1994).

But since the introduction of semaphores by Dijkstra (1968), the problem of communicating by shared variables has been dealt with in a more elegant way. Initially, attention focused on the development of solutions to problems that were specific to operating systems, many of which are discussed in Ben-Ari (1982). An important impact on devising solutions in this area came with the introduction of so-called monitors by Hoare (1974). In terms of BASAL, monitors can be seen as packages consisting of procedures that can only be called by at most one process at a time. How monitors can be used to develop operating systems is discussed in Brinch Hansen (1976, 1977). Another treatise can be found in Welsh and McKeag (1980). A multiprocessor operating system based on monitors is discussed in Natarajan and Sinha (1979) and Joseph *et al.* (1984). A general overview of synchronization and communication operations in operating systems based on shared variables appears in Bacon (1993) and Maekawa *et al.* (1987).

The shared-variable model remains an important model for program development. Especially since the introduction of affordable multiprocessor systems in which several processors are connected to a single main memory module, interest in so-called **parallel programming** has substantially increased. Parallel programming primarily deals with exploiting parallelism in a solution in order to increase efficiency. The subject is discussed extensively in Quinn (1994) and Foster (1995) which both contain many references for further reading. Finally, a more thorough and systematic approach towards program development using shared variables in general can be found in an excellent textbook by Andrews (1991a).

The shared data model is so popular that researchers have sought solutions to also support the model for geographically distributed systems. This has resulted in so-called **distributed shared memory** systems. Different types of systems exist, although most of them are still in a research or experimental phase. What it means is that data can appear to be directly accessible by all processors. To explain, it is necessary to make a distinction between *referencing* shared data and *accessing* it. Only when shared data is accessed can it be read and updated. Referencing shared data merely means that you can *identify* the data you are interested in. What happens in distributed shared memory systems is that shared data can be referenced by all processors in the same way as would be the case with ordinary references to data. When shared data is referenced it may be necessary to explicitly fetch it from somewhere else in order to allow for inspection or modification. Automatically getting referenced data to processors in order for them to access it is precisely what happens in distributed shared memory systems. It is far beyond the scope of this book to go into any details here. A good starting point for further reading is Stumm and Zhou (1990) and Nitzberg and Lo (1991). Overviews can be found in Coulouris *et al.* (1994) and Tanenbaum (1995). The original work that started much of the research on distributed shared memory is found in Li and Hudak (1989).

Message-passing: further reading

But, as we have said, using shared variables is not the way to go when having to deal with remote communication. Analogous to shared variables, message-passing paradigms were originally conceived in the field of operating systems, although not because remote communication needed to take place. In Brinch Hansen (1970) the kernel of an operating system is discussed in which processes communicate merely by means of messages. The concept was later adopted by many other operating systems, as it allows a uniform way of dealing with interprocess communication. This is achieved by letting the kernel handle all message exchanges, so that, consequently, processes need no longer find out exactly where shared data is stored in main memory. This approach is also discussed in Bacon (1993).

Although message-passing may initially seem a useful way of communication, in practice it turns out to be relatively difficult to develop a program as a collection of processes that merely exchange messages. This is primarily caused by the fact that processes are much more dependent on each other: messages have to be sent and received at the right moment, and between the right processes. Nevertheless, message-passing is important for the simple reason that remote communication would otherwise not be possible. A friendly introduction to distributed programming can be found in Ben-Ari (1980). A good survey on interprocess communication based on basic message-passing (as well as shared variables) is Andrews and Schneider (1983). A clear overview of different ways of message-based communication is Andrews (1991b) and a more extensive treatise can, again, be found in Andrews (1991a).

6.5.2   Advanced communication models

Although the basic communication models discussed in this chapter will suffice our purposes for describing the principles of communication across large distances, we feel it would have been unwise not to mention the models that are currently used in many existing systems. These advanced models have been primarily developed from an *engineering* point of view. As message-passing is (1) almost inevitable, but (2) hard to use in practice, much research has been devoted to developing advanced models that would ease the development of communication-based systems, but which at the same time could be efficiently implemented on top of primitive message-passing operations. Without question, new models have primarily found their way into programming languages for distributed systems, of which an extensive overview is given in Bal *et al.* (1989).

But besides programming languages, advanced models of communication are generally also supported by operating systems in the form of service programs. For those of you who wish to become acquainted with programming details, Stevens has written two excellent books for UNIX based systems, although both of them do require programming experience. Stevens (1992) concentrates, among other things, on interprocess communication for single-processor versions of UNIX. Implementation of processes communicating across a network is discussed in depth in Stevens (1990). A popular communication library that employs message-passing as the basis for application development is the Parallel Virtual Machine, described in Sunderam (1990). Its successor, the so-called Message-Passing Interface, is described in MPI Forum (1993) and which will certainly become popular in the field of parallel and distributed programming.

Rendez-vous and remote procedure calls

The term "rendez-vous" originated in the programming language Ada (ANSI, 1983), the basis for our programming notation in this book. The principle underlying the rendez-vous mechanism, however, had already been investigated before the language was defined. We have not discussed how Ada supports distributed programming. For that purpose, the reader is referred to Barnes (1994) and Booch and Bryan (1994).

As we have illustrated, the principle of rendez-vous and remote procedure call (RPC) are conceptually the same. The essence of both mechanisms is that they allow communication to be dealt with in much the same way as ordinary procedure calls. In particular, processes that require some service to be provided need merely initiate that service by means of a procedure call. The effect of that call may result in communication with another computer, namely the one where the service *provider* resides. This communication, however, is transparent to the requesting process.

Remote procedure calls are an important subject when discussing so-called distributed systems. But to be honest, we have hardly addressed the practical implications of this mechanism. It is far beyond the scope of this book to go into any details on how the RPC mechanism is implemented, and what the problems are when true transparency is to be achieved. A brief account of these matters can be found in Tanenbaum (1992). Implementation issues can be found in Spector (1982), and in the (now considered classical) article written by Birrell and Nelson (1984). A general discussion on interprocess communication, with emphasis on remote operations, is presented in Mullender (1993). How RPC is supported in the UNIX environment can be found in Stevens (1990). For detailed information, the interested reader is referred to Bloomer (1992).

Group communication

As we have said, we have barely touched upon an important issue in distributed systems, namely that of group communication. In essence, group communication is concerned with sending messages to an entire group of processes, and likewise, receiving messages from members that belong to a specific group. A major problem with this model is how to deal with the ordering of messages.

Our approach towards treating the subject was one by which we stated the requirements and subsequently indicated that meeting those requirements could be a hard thing to do. Admittedly, this may be rather unsatisfying. In order to get a better feeling for what is going on, Liang *et al.* (1990) will be a good start, as well as Birman (1993). Also, in Tanenbaum (1992) you will find sufficient material to help you on your way. A discussion on message ordering and taking failure of message delivery into account appears in Hadzilacos and Toueg (1993). Finally, Birman and van Renesse (1994) contains a collection of papers on Isis, a system which is probably the most widely used one when building applications based on group communication. Many details concerning concepts, design, and implementation of the system can be found there.

Exercises

1. What is the difference between a BASAL process and the concept of a process as explained in Chapter 5?

2. Why does a process never return from the procedure ACTIVATE as discussed in Section 6.1.2?

3. We sometimes say that processes *communicate* through shared data, and *synchronize* through semaphores. Explain what is meant by this statement.

4. Suppose that we have two distinct shared data objects that we want to protect by also using two semaphores, sema1 and sema2, respectively. Explain what might happen if the following two BASAL processes are simultaneously executed:

```
process PROCESS1 is                process PROCESS2 is
begin                              begin
    WAIT(sema1);                       WAIT(sema2);
    WAIT(sema2);                       WAIT(sema1);
    ...                                ...
end PROCESS1;                      end PROCESS2;
```

5. Explain why semaphores are generally only applicable to situations where communication can take place through shared data.

6. *Outline a solution for blocking stream communication where an unknown maximum of notes can be carried by the stream, requiring that its associated queue needs to be inspected to see whether it is empty or full.

7. Explain what is meant by blocking communication, taking into account that messages may be buffered.

8. Explain the difference between asynchronous and synchronous message-passing, thereby taking into account the roles of a sender and a receiver.

9. Analogous to Exercise 4, we may find ourselves in trouble if the following two processes (which are only informally expressed in BASAL) were executed simultaneously:

```
process PROCESS1 is                process PROCESS2 is
begin                              begin
    SEND(PROCESS2, mess1to2);          SEND(PROCESS1, mess2to1);
    RECEIVE(PROCESS2, mess2to1);       RECEIVE(PROCESS1, mess1to2);
    ...                                ...
end PROCESS1;                      end PROCESS2;
```

However, we have to be more accurate in this case. Explain whether or not things might go wrong, thereby making a distinction between synchronous and asynchronous communication in the case of sending messages. Receipt is assumed to be always blocking.

10. *Many communication-based systems such as electronic mail only support asynchronous message-passing where messages may become lost. Why do you think this model has been adopted? Would a more sophisticated model be more appropriate?

11. *We have stated that full synchronous communication, illustrated in Figure 6.11(b) on page 293, has the disadvantage that a sender cannot do any useful work as long as the receiver has not picked up the message. How can this problem be alleviated? (Hint: think of solutions that were adapted to avoid polling.)

12. Why is message ordering automatically preserved in full synchronous communication?

13. Explain the difference between channels, ports, and links. In particular, outline a solution for developing a client-server architecture using ports.

14. There are several advantages when using connection-oriented communication instead of connectionless communication. Name the most important ones. Also mention some of the disadvantages.

15. *Explain in your own words what a remote procedure call is, and outline how it can be implemented.

16. *Can the remote procedure call mechanism be used for implementing group communication? If not, in what sense would we need to change the *semantics* of the mechanism?

17. *Passing messages to a group does impose some problems. Describe a few of them.

Chapter 7

Connecting computers

In the previous chapter we have discussed some basic communication models, but have neglected the issue of actually connecting several computers. In this chapter the fundamentals of connecting several communicating devices are discussed. The material we present here is somewhat technical and anticipates some basic understanding of electrical and physical issues. Also, many topics that have to do with physically connecting computers are often only touched upon, omitting details that appear not to be immediately relevant for the remaining chapters. For these reasons, a relatively large part of the material presented here may be skipped entirely, or skimmed on first reading. An exception, however, is Section 7.5 in which we outline the lower layers of the OSI reference model, an important topic when discussing computer networks in general.

7.1 Introduction

If we look at what we have accomplished so far, it becomes obvious that our discussion should start focusing on a subject that we have been more or less neglecting: connecting computers to each other. First, we have explained how computers are basically assembled and how we could extend the concept of a real processor into a virtual processor. A virtual processor supports a programming language that can be far more sophisticated than the primitive set of instructions of real processors. So, at least our programming efforts can be done more easily. In Chapter 5 we went even further by introducing operating systems that allowed several programs to share the hardware resources of a computer. In particular, these programs shared the central processing unit, and each program need not be aware of the existence of other programs. In this sense, it is as if a number of processes are executed simultaneously on a single computer.

Of course, there are situations in which processes do need to communicate. So here we are capable of modeling complex systems in terms of communicating processes, and even modeling systems which are inherently distributed. Meanwhile, we have silently neglected the fact that we are still talking about computers with a single CPU. So much for reality. Of course, we have given some hints about how communication can take place.

317

We have mentioned that you should be able to imagine that we can connect a number of computers together, and let processes residing at different computers communicate by passing messages. However, although you may understand by now the principles of message-based communication, the actual connections between computers is still left entirely open to your imagination. It is time we returned to earth and said what we mean by connecting computers.

Unfortunately, connecting computers is easier said than done. It is quite difficult for two reasons: (1) hardware (and software) failures, and (2) getting people to agree. The first issue is something we can handle and which will form the major topic of this chapter. The second issue is much tougher. What we are referring to is agreement by people on communication protocols. As long as no agreement is reached, communication is virtually impossible, although protocol converters do alleviate some of the major problems. The following chapters deal more extensively with communication protocols.

After reading this chapter you will have a basic understanding of how one computer can send a large chunk of data to another computer to which it is directly connected. The most important aspect of this communication is that it apparently is free of transmission errors: the data is received as it is sent. In the following sections we shall show that this may not be easy to accomplish. In particular, all kinds of errors may occur which effectively are all caused by the fact that our means of transmission (i.e. the wires) are simply never good enough – and can never be made good enough.

7.2   On wiring

It may be rather frustrating at this point, but if we are going to talk about connecting computers and how the hardware is going to let us down, we might as well start where the first problems arise: wiring. So far, we have stated that we can build all kinds of electrical devices by simply wiring them together. And if you open up your personal computer, you will see a number of boards containing integrated circuits where wires have been etched into the board.[1] You will also see some wires that look the same as those used for connecting the components of stereo and video sets. In this section we shall take a closer look at two problems: (1) why the simple wiring scheme in personal computers cannot be used for connecting computers, and (2) why picking up a signal can be rather frustrating. Most of the material that follows can be skipped on first reading.

▷ 7.2.1   Transmitting signals

When connecting two computers we have to consider the type of wires, or better, **transmission medium** we are going to use. This is something we also see in our daily lives. For example, if you want to connect a TV set to an external antenna or perhaps the local cable net, you will need to use a special coax cable. Otherwise, the chance that you will be able to really enjoy watching TV will be small as reception will be poor. Moreover, it can be observed that if you relay the wires, reception may become better or worse – a rather strange

---

[1] These boards are commonly referred as printed circuit boards, on which the wires have been "printed."

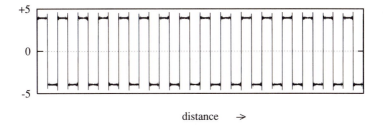

+5

0

-5

distance   →

Figure 7.1 A periodic digital signal.

situation if you thought that signals could only be transmitted through the wire between the TV set and the antenna or cable socket. When connecting computers, we have a similar situation: signals sent through a wire, or any transmission medium for that matter, may be completely different at the other end. In order to appreciate why people bother looking into these matters, let's take a closer look at the kind of problems that we can have with using transmission media.

Fundamental problems

In Chapter 2 we explained that every computer works with two types of signal values: a high and a low one. For example, a high signal value can be used to represent the binary digit 1, whereas a low signal value can be used to represent a 0. In order to send a bit string over a wire, we merely need to send a series of high and low signals. This is called **digital signal transmission**. As an example, Figure 7.1 shows the transmission of a series of alternating bits (i.e. the sequence ⟨10101010...⟩), generated by a *source*. A positive signal value (5 volts) is interpreted as a 1, whereas a negative signal value (−5 volts) is used to represent a 0. The *x*-axis represents the distance from the source, and the signal value that will be received there.

Now there are several problems. First, we may not expect that our signal will have the same strength at the other end of the line. In other words, if we send a 5 volt signal across a line, it may be received as a 4 volt signal.[2] This phenomenon is called **signal attenuation**. So, in the extreme case, it may be impossible to detect any signal at all at the other end of the line.

But worse is to follow. The problem is that the *form* of our input signal is going to be different from the one we observe at the other end. In particular, the attenuation that will occur is dependent on the **frequency** of our signal. How can this be? To understand what is going on here, you have to realize that every periodic digital signal can be regarded as an infinite sum of **analog signals**. An analog signal differs from a digital signal in that its amplitude (strength) *continuously* varies in the course of time. In particular, digital signals can be thought of as composed of an infinite summation of sines, which, by themselves, are analog

---

[2]Where did the 1 volt go? Imagine (and only that) using a thin double wire to connect your washing machine to a wall socket and you will find out. You will smell some plastic melting, and probably also see some smoke before a fuse blows.

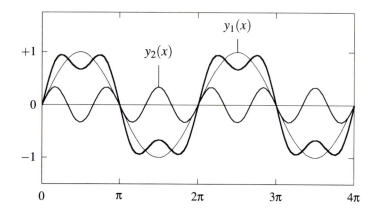

Figure 7.2 An example of two sines $y_1(x)$ and $y_2(x)$ and their summation $y_1(x) + y_2(x)$.

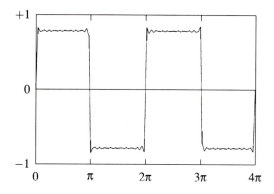

Figure 7.3 The summation $y_1(x) + \cdots + y_{35}(x)$.

signals. To illustrate, Figure 7.2 shows the two sines $y_1(x) = \sin(x)$ and $y_2(x) = \frac{1}{3}\sin(3x)$. Note the contrast between these two analog functions and the digital signal shown in Figure 7.1.

Figure 7.2 also shows the resulting function if we add $y_1(x)$ and $y_2(x)$ for each value of x. Note that the *form* of this function starts to resemble a digital signal. This is even more emphasized if we add, say, 35 such signals, as illustrated in Figure 7.3. In this case, we have constructed the function $Y(x)$ with

$$Y(x) = y_1(x) + \cdots + y_{35}(x) = \sum_{k=1}^{35} \frac{1}{2k-1} \sin((2k-1)x)$$

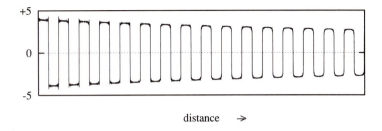

distance   →

Figure 7.4 The effect of frequency-dependent attenuation on a digital signal.

Now recall that sines are *periodic* functions, i.e. their form is repeated after a certain time, called the period T. For example, the period of $\sin(x)$ is 2π. The **frequency** of a function is the number of times it can be repeated within a given unit, and is thus equal to $1/T$. In terms of signals, the frequency is generally expressed as the number of repetitions per second, referred to as **Hertz** (abbreviated to Hz). So, for an analog signal with a period of 2π seconds, its frequency will be equal to $1/(2\pi)$ Hz. Returning to our original problem, we have the unfortunate situation that attenuation is *frequency-dependent*. In other words, the extent to which a signal is reduced is dependent on its frequency. Consequently, as digital signals are composed of analog signals with varying frequency, and attenuation is frequency-dependent, our digital signal shown in Figure 7.1 may be received at the other side as the signal shown in Figure 7.4. This problem of frequency-dependent attenuation is caused by the **limited bandwidth** of the transmission medium. Depending on the transmission media, signals with a high frequency will simply not reach the end. (The bandwidth of a medium is often expressed as a range of frequencies that can still be transmitted without too much loss of strength. Alternatively, the bandwidth is often also expressed as the number of bits per second that can be transmitted without too many errors.)

But even if we had a line with a large bandwidth, our problems are not over. There is yet another factor we have to account for, namely **delay distortion**. Any signal takes some time to reach the other end of a line. Now realizing that digital signals are constructed as a number of sines, and that the time to transmit a signal is *also* frequency-dependent, you can guess what the problem is. The various sines out of which the digital signal is made up each have a different transmission speed. Consequently, they simply will not reach the end all at the same time. Consequently, we will receive a distorted signal. Returning to our original digital signal, the combined effect of attenuation and delay distortion may result in the signal illustrated in Figure 7.5.

A final and important source of distorted transmission is due to **noise**. You should take the word "noise" literally here. Noise is a group of signals that disturb the communication. For example, so-called impulse noises are often caused by electro-mechanical switches that make part of the physical connection (as used in conventional telephone systems), but can also be caused by environmental sources such as lightning, traffic, etc. And although various methods can be applied to reduce these noises, establishing a completely noise-free connection through physical means is simply impossible. Taking all these factors into account, our original digital signal may finally look like the signal shown in Figure 7.6

So, connecting computers seems simple to do, but, due to all kinds of physical phenomena,

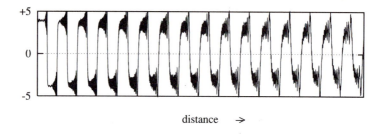

distance   →

Figure 7.5 The effect of delay distortion when transmitting a digital signal.

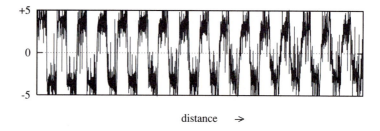

distance   →

Figure 7.6 The possible final result of sending a digital signal across a line.

sending a digital signal across a line may end in rubbish at the other end if no special measures are taken. We will not pursue this any further. By now, you should be able to appreciate why some people bother to think about the actual physical composition of transmission media. Typically, these problems are handled by experts in the field of telecommunication.

Types of transmission media

So far, we have spoken about wires and lines by which we implicitly meant the ordinary copper-like wires we see daily. Of course, there's more to it. In particular, a distinction can be made between the following transmission media:

- **Copper-based media**, such as those in which a copper wire is coated with an insulating material (the ones you can find at home), coaxial cables as used for TV sets, or so-called twisted pair connections. Most *local area computer networks* use these type of transmission media.

- **Fiber-optic media** by which information is transported in the form of light. These media have the advantage that they allow for high propagation speeds and bandwidths, but above all, their signals cannot be influenced by electro-magnetic fields, thus making them highly reliable.

- **Satellite media** which use radio waves to transmit data. These type of media are important in the case of geographically remote sites. Connection is established by means of sending information to a satellite typically located at some 30 000 kilometers above

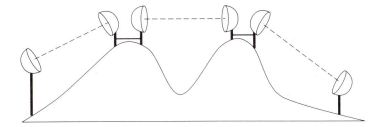

Figure 7.7 Terrestrial microwave connection

the earth's surface. The satellite then retransmits the information to a ground station from which it is transported by conventional media to the target.

- **Terrestrial microwave media**, by which radio waves are sent from one dish to another. The important point here is that dishes are located in each other's sight, as shown in Figure 7.7. The signals sent through this medium can come as far as approximately 40–50 kilometers.

So it is seen that there is more to wiring than one might suspect at first. Nevertheless, we shall continue to speak of wires and lines throughout this book when we mean the physical connection between two or more components. Wires in this sense should be taken to be one of the transmission means mentioned above.

7.2.2 Receiving signals

Assume we have connected two digital devices with an appropriate transmission medium that suits our purposes. Then all we have to do is let the sending device start putting bit strings on the line in the form of high and low signals and let the receiving device pick these up. For simplicity, assume we have an ideal transmission medium. In other words, the signals we send at one end can be recognized without any distortion at the other. There is only one problem: how can the receiver pick up a signal? When giving the matter some thought, it is seen that we really do have a problem.

For example, when no signal is sent, our line will be at rest. The first time a bit is transmitted, the receiver will have to notice that a signal has indeed been put on the line. This should not be too difficult. If a 0 is represented by −5 volts, and a 1 by +5 volts, then any change from 0 volts (the line at rest) to either −5 volts or +5 volts indicates that something is being sent. Unfortunately, this does imply that the line has *three* possible states: at rest (0 volt), carrying a low signal value (−5 volt), and carrying a high signal value (5 volt). And although this approach is followed in practice, schemes that fit better into the binary world which can handle just *two* types of signal values are perhaps more commonly used.

First, assume that when a line is at rest it will permanently carry a high signal value. Now, before we send a bit string, we first send a low signal value indicating to the receiver that some bits are on the way. In other words, *changing* the signal value on the line is an indication that data is going to be sent. Using this first bit as a **start bit** will allow the receiver

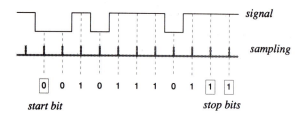

Figure 7.8 Bit synchronization by using start and stop bits.

to prepare itself for receipt. But what if the first bit to be sent is a 0? Certainly, the receiver cannot distinguish the start bit from the first bit of the bit string. To solve this problem, the sender and receiver should have agreement on the **transmission rate**, which is generally expressed as the number of bits sent per second (**bps**). The transmission rate is thus the pace at which the *sender and receiver* decide to exchange bits. This pace is primarily determined by the communicating parties. If one of them is simply a "slow" computer, then the transmission rate will necessarily be low. Once the transmission rate has been agreed, the receiver knows how long a single bit is put on the line by the sender, and can thus deduce when the next bit has been transmitted without having to observe a signal transition. In practice, the receiver inspects the line at regular intervals (namely each time when it expects that a new bit has arrived), and stores the bit in a 1-bit memory.

In addition, the sender and receiver also agree on the number of bits that can be transmitted in a row, as well as one or more **stop bits** that indicate that the line is at rest again. This principle is illustrated in Figure 7.8, where it is assumed that two 1's in a row after having transmitted eight bits denote the end of the transmission. Note that by sending two 1-valued stop bits it is possible for the receiver to detect the next start bit.

The scheme we have just described is referred to as **bit synchronization**. It is generally employed in so-called **asynchronous transmission** where the sender sends only characters at (more or less) irregular intervals. The characteristic feature of asynchronous transmission is that the receiver entirely determines when it should inspect the line. Once a transmission rate of, say, k bps has been agreed, it will inspect the line every $1/k^{\text{th}}$ second (we will return to this below). Each character (consisting of 8 bits) is always preceded by a start bit, and terminated by one or two stop bits. Alternatively, some schemes allow several characters in a row to be transmitted, followed by the stop bits. The term asynchronous is used to indicate that the receiver always needs to synchronize explicitly with the sender each time a character is sent. In addition to bit synchronization, a receiver may also employ **character synchronization** in which case streams of characters can be received. Normally, such character streams start and end with a special character. For example, using ASCII coding, the start character can be STX to designate the start of a text data stream, which is subsequently ended with an ETX character (see also Table 2.3). Using this information, the receiver can store the complete stream into main memory, knowing that it can stop as soon as the ETX character has been received.

An alternative form of transmission is so-called **synchronous transmission**. Synchronous transmission differs from asynchronous transmission in that the receiver stays at the same

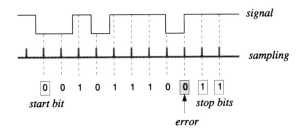

Figure 7.9 The effect of a receiver sampling too quickly for an incoming signal.

rate as the sender for a long time. To understand this, note that in order for a receiver to pick up a series of bits at a rate of k bps, it should have a clock that allows the receiver to inspect the line every $1/k^{th}$ second. But this is ideal. Due to the finite accuracy of any clock, the receiver will inspect the line at intervals of, say, $1/k + \varepsilon$ seconds (where ε is small, and either negative or positive). This is acceptable if only a few bits are sent (as in the case of asynchronous transmission); it is going to lead to problems when the series is long. In that case, the receiver is sooner or later going to miss a bit (when $\varepsilon > 0$), or read the same bit twice (when $\varepsilon < 0$). The latter is illustrated in Figure 7.9, where we have taken the same signal as in Figure 7.8, but have increased the sampling frequency. In synchronous transmission, mere *changes* in the received signal are additionally used by the receiver to adapt (i.e. synchronize) its own clock. The effect is that the sender's and receiver's clock stay more or less in step, allowing for extremely high transmission rates compared to asynchronous transmission. For example, where asynchronous transmission is generally limited to approximately 20 000 bps (i.e. 20 Kbps), it is not unusual for synchronous transmission to operate at 10 000 000 bps (10 Mbps).

We shall leave these matters at this point. A thorough description lies completely beyond this book, and is something more suited for electrical engineers. The point you have to realize, though, is that conceptually it may be simple to pick up bits from a line; in practice, however, there are a few problems to be solved.

7.2.3   In the event of errors

In Section 7.2.1 we discussed how a digital signal could be completely distorted by simply sending it across a transmission medium. And signal distortion is a fact of life that we will have to live with. In particular, this means that no matter what the quality of our transmission medium is, or how long the bit strings that we send, there is always the possibility that the receiver will inadvertently interpret a signal incorrectly. In other words, we need to deal with the situation that a transmitted bit string **b** is interpreted by the receiver as a different bit string **b̂**. In this section we shall look at how a receiver can detect that something went wrong, and possibly even derive the correct string without having to request a retransmission.

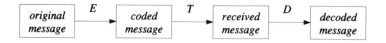

Figure 7.10 The process of encoding, transmitting, and decoding messages.

Encoding and decoding

Our starting point is the transmission of a so-called **frame**, which is a series of bits that is to be sent across a line. The question that we need to address is the following:

> Can we devise a method such that any errors resulting from the transmission of a frame can be detected, or possibly even corrected by the receiver?

The answer is simply no. However, it is possible to devise methods that at least allow a receiver to detect and correct errors with a relatively high probability. What we need to do is to **encode** a bit string **a** to a bit string **b** containing additional information on **a**. Bit string **b** is then transmitted, and on arrival may have been received as a possibly different bit string $\hat{\mathbf{b}}$. The point is then that we **decode** $\hat{\mathbf{b}}$ either back to the original bit string **a** or at least detect that something went wrong. In the latter case, a receiver can simply request the sender to retransmit **a** after having encoded it again.

This scheme of encoding, transmitting, and decoding is shown in Figure 7.10. Formally, we can describe this scheme by means of three functions:

$$E : 2^m \to 2^n, T : 2^n \to 2^n, D : 2^n \to 2^m \quad \text{with } m \leq n$$

where 2^k represents the set of all bit strings of length k. E is the encoding function, T the transmission function, and D the decoding function. The pair (D, E) is called a **code**. In order to transmit a bit string **a** we first need to encode it, then transmit it, and then decode it again, implying that at the receiver's side, we get the bit string $D(T(E(\mathbf{a})))$. Now, if we denote the set of bit strings that we would ever want to transmit as the set $A \subseteq 2^m$, then ideally we would want that

$$\text{for all } \mathbf{a} \in A :: \mathbf{a} = D(T(E(\mathbf{a})))$$

In order to obtain a code that, at least to a certain extent, allows us to detect and possibly even correct transmission errors, we need to introduce a few important concepts.

One, which is a key concept of coding theory, is the **distance** between two bit strings. Let $\mathbf{a} = \langle a_0 \dots a_{m-1} \rangle$ and $\mathbf{b} = \langle b_0 \dots b_{m-1} \rangle$ be two bit strings of length m. The distance between **a** and **b** is defined as the number of indices i with $a_i \neq b_i$. For example, the distance between the bit strings $\langle 0110 \rangle$ and $\langle 1100 \rangle$ is 2. If $A \subseteq 2^m$ is a set of bit strings of length m, then the **Hamming distance** of A is the smallest distance between any two bit strings in A. The Hamming distance is important when coding. If (D, E) is a given code, then it can be shown that the following two properties hold:

1. For the code (D, E) to *detect* all sets of k or fewer errors, it is necessary and sufficient that the Hamming distance of $E(A)$ be $k + 1$ or more.

2. For the code (D, E) to *correct* all sets of k or fewer errors, it is necessary that the Hamming distance of $E(A)$ be $2k + 1$ or more.

These properties seem fine, especially the first. What it says is that by *adding* a sufficient number of bits to each bit string from a set A, it is possible to detect whenever transmission in the encoded bit string fails for one (or more) bits. Unfortunately, neither of the two statements reveals *how* we should add bits in order to detect or correct errors. And this turns out to be the really difficult part. But before we look at solutions that are applied in practice, we first consider some simple coding schemes to illustrate what coding is about.

Simple coding schemes

Parity-check code. Let's first look at the simple yet effective **parity-check code** that allows a receiver to detect that a transmitted bit string contains exactly one error. For this code, we take $A \subseteq 2^m$. If $\mathbf{a} = \langle a_0 \ldots a_{m-1} \rangle \in A$, then the parity-check code encodes $\mathbf{a}$ according to the following scheme:

$$E(\langle a_0 \ldots a_{m-1} \rangle) = \langle b_0 \ldots b_{m-1} b_m \rangle$$

where $a_i = b_i$ for $0 \leq i \leq m - 1$, and b_m is defined as

$$b_m = \begin{cases} 0 & \text{if } \sum_{i=0}^{m-1} a_i \text{ is even} \\ 1 & \text{if } \sum_{i=0}^{m-1} a_i \text{ is odd} \end{cases}$$

Thus, for example, if $m = 2$, we then have the following encoding scheme:

$$\langle 00 \rangle \mapsto \langle 000 \rangle, \langle 01 \rangle \mapsto \langle 011 \rangle, \langle 10 \rangle \mapsto \langle 101 \rangle, \langle 11 \rangle \mapsto \langle 110 \rangle$$

It is not difficult to see that if $\mathbf{a}$ is encoded into $\langle b_0 \ldots b_{m-1} b_m \rangle$ that $\sum_{i=0}^m b_i$ is always even, and consequently, the minimum distance between any two bit strings in $E(A)$ is 2. The decoding scheme is simple as well:

$$D(\langle b_0 \ldots b_{m-1} b_m \rangle) = \langle c_0 \ldots c_{m-1} \rangle$$

where $c_i = b_i$ for $0 \leq i \leq m - 1$. Now, of course, the receiver only sees encoded bit strings. If it is found that for such a bit string $\sum_{i=0}^m b_i$ is *odd*, then the decoder knows something went wrong.

But this, of course, is just a lot of mathematics. In order for a code to work in practice, it should also be *efficient*, in other words it should also be possible to implement the scheme without causing too much overhead. To illustrate that this is indeed possible, consider our encoding scheme as an ordinary Boolean function. So, for example, if we assume that $m = 3$, we can construct the following function table for a function with three input variables (a_0, a_1, and a_2) and that produces a bit string $\mathbf{b} = \langle b_0 b_1 b_2 b_3 \rangle$ as output:

a_0	a_1	a_2	b_0	b_1	b_2	b_3
0	0	0	0	0	0	0
0	0	1	0	0	1	1
0	1	0	0	1	0	1
0	1	1	0	1	1	0
1	0	0	1	0	0	1
1	0	1	1	0	1	0
1	1	0	1	1	0	0
1	1	1	1	1	1	1

For the first three bits of **b** we, of course, have that

$$b_0 = a_0, b_1 = a_1, b_2 = a_2$$

Deriving an expression for the fourth bit is really not difficult. It can be readily verified that we have

$$b_3 = (a_0 \oplus a_1) \oplus a_2$$

where "$\oplus$" denotes the exclusive-or operator discussed in Section 2.3. In other words, the parity-check code can easily be implemented with elementary combinatorial logic. In general, we have that for a bit string $\mathbf{a} = \langle a_0 \dots a_{m-1} \rangle$ of length m the additional bit b_m that is to be added is equal to

$$b_m = a_0 \oplus a_1 \oplus a_2 \oplus \cdots \oplus a_{m-1}$$

Consequently, implementing the parity-check code is not the most serious problem.

Triple-repetition code. The parity-check code is a 1-error *detecting* code. As an illustration of a 1-error *correcting* code, we now consider a version of the so-called **triple-repetition code**. This is an extremely simple although not very efficient code. The encoding scheme is as follows. For any bit string $\mathbf{a} = \langle a_0 \dots a_{m-1} \rangle$, we transmit the bit string **b**:

$$E(\langle a_0 \dots a_{m-1} \rangle) = \langle b_0 \dots b_{m-1} b_m \dots b_{3m-1} \rangle$$

where $b_i = a_{i/3}$ with $0 \leq i \leq 3m - 1$. In other words, each bit from the bit string **a** is simply sent three times in a row. The decoding function is now as follows:

$$D(\langle b_0 \dots b_{3m-1} \rangle) = \langle c_0 \dots c_{m-1} \rangle$$

where $c_i = 1$ if and only if $b_{3i} + b_{3i+1} + b_{3i+2} \geq 2$. Consequently, if we consider a block of 3 transmitted bits of which one has been incorrectly interpreted by the receiver, then it should be clear that despite this error the receiver will decode the 3 bits into the correct one. It should also be clear that this is indeed not an efficient code as all bit strings need effectively be sent three times. In other words, the transmission rate over any medium is brought back to a third of what could be possible if no errors occurred. Incidentally, note that we can easily implement this code through the majority function discussed in Chapter 2. Details of such an implementation are left to the reader.

The triple-repetition code is, in fact, not a bad one when considering error-correcting code. However, devising error-correcting codes generally implies that so many bits have to be added during encoding that it simply is not worth the trouble because the effective transmission rate decreases too fast. For this reason, dealing with transmission errors in practice is restricted to merely *detecting* that something went wrong, and subsequently requesting the sender to retransmit the bit string.

Error detection: polynomial code

In this section we take a closer look at an error-detection code which is in widespread use. The code serves two purposes. First, it illustrates some of mathematical intricacies related to coding in practice. Second, we shall see that despite the complexity that is encountered at first, the implementation of the code is so simple that it can be implemented in hardware similar to the parity-check code discussed above.

The scheme we present here is called **polynomial code** or **cyclic redundancy code** (CRC) and is based on interpreting bit strings as the coefficients of a polynomial. Consider a bit string $\mathbf{a} = \langle a_0 \ldots a_{m-1} \rangle$. Polynomial code associates a unique polynomial $a(x)$ with $\mathbf{a}$ as follows:

$$\mathbf{a} \mapsto a(x) = a_0 x^0 + a_1 x^1 + \ldots + a_{m-1} x^{m-1}$$

Note how each coefficient a_i is associated with the term x^i. So, for example, the bit string $\langle 01101 \rangle$ would be uniquely associated with a polynomial as follows:

$$\langle 01101 \rangle \mapsto 0 \cdot x^0 + 1 \cdot x + 1 \cdot x^2 + 0 \cdot x^3 + 1 \cdot x^4 = x + x^2 + x^4$$

Now, the objective in polynomial code is to encode a bit string by extending it with bits from a **generator polynomial**. This works as follows. Let $g(x)$ be the polynomial

$$g(x) = g_0 + g_1 x + \cdots + g_k x^k, \text{ with } g_0 \neq 0 \text{ and } g_k \neq 0$$

Each bit string $\mathbf{a} = \langle a_0 \ldots a_{m-1} \rangle$ is encoded into a bit string $\mathbf{b} = \langle b_0 \ldots b_{n-1} \rangle$ with $n = m + k$ such that

$$b(x) = b_0 + b_1 x + \cdots + b_{n-1} x^{n-1} = a(x) \cdot g(x)$$

where all coefficients are calculated using modulo 2 arithmetic. This is best explained by an example.

Example 7.1. Suppose we have the bit string $\mathbf{a} = \langle 01011 \rangle$ and the generator polynomial $g(x) = 1 + x^2 + x^3$. The polynomial $a(x)$ associated with $\mathbf{a}$ is equal to

$$a(x) = 0 \cdot x^0 + 1 \cdot x^1 + 0 \cdot x^2 + 1 \cdot x^3 + 1 \cdot x^4 = x + x^3 + x^4$$

Consequently, we have that $a(x) \cdot g(x)$ is equal to

$$
\begin{aligned}
a(x) \cdot g(x) &= (x + x^3 + x^4)(1 + x^2 + x^3) \\
&= x + 2x^3 + 2x^4 + x^5 + 2x^6 + x^7
\end{aligned}
$$

In modulo 2 arithmetic, we are capable of dealing only with 0 and 1. In particular, in addition, the following rules apply:

$$0 + 0 = 0, 0 + 1 = 1, 1 + 1 = 0$$

This means that when multiplying two polynomials using modulo 2 arithmetic, we simply ignore those terms that have coefficient 2. This means that our multiplication $a(x) \cdot g(x)$ becomes:

$$a(x) \cdot g(x) = x + 2x^3 + 2x^4 + x^5 + 2x^6 + x^7 \Rightarrow x + x^5 + x^7$$

which results in the bit string $\langle 01000101 \rangle$.

$\square$

Now, once we have calculated the result $b(x) = a(x) \cdot g(x)$, we simply transmit the bit string $\mathbf{b}$ associated with $b(x)$, and decode the transmitted vector $\hat{\mathbf{b}}$, which may possibly differ from the original encoded bit string $\mathbf{b}$. Decoding proceeds by **factoring** the polynomial $\hat{b}(x)$, i.e. we write it as the following multiplication and addition of polynomials:

$$\hat{b}(x) = \hat{a}(x) \cdot g(x) + \hat{e}(x)$$

where we have that

$$
\begin{aligned}
\hat{a}(x) &= \hat{a}_0 + \hat{a}_1 x + \cdots + \hat{a}_{m-1} x^{m-1} \\
\hat{e}(x) &= \hat{e}_0 + \hat{e}_1 x + \cdots + \hat{e}_{k-1} x^{k-1}
\end{aligned}
$$

The point is that only if $\hat{e}(x) \equiv 0$, i.e. all coefficients $\hat{e}_i = 0$, transmission succeeded. In fact, if we choose an appropriate generator polynomial $g(x)$, we can devise a polynomial code in which the number of coefficients of $\hat{e}(x)$ with $\hat{e}_i \neq 0$ correspond with the number of bits that are in error in the bit string $\hat{\mathbf{b}}$. It is beyond the scope of this book to go into any further details. The interested reader is referred to the end of this chapter where pointers to the literature are provided.

But why have we been discussing all this? First, you should note that polynomial codes are extremely efficient. By systematically adding k bits to a Boolean bit string it is possible to detect k errors. Not many encoding schemes are known to have this property.

But there is more. Although our coding scheme seems rather intricate, it is not difficult to see that operations on polynomials such as multiplication and factorization effectively reduce to simple manipulations with bit strings. For example, multiplication by 2 means shifting all the bits one position to the left. Such operations can easily be implemented in hardware. And indeed, polynomial coding is almost invariably implemented by means of a digital circuit, or otherwise by a straightforward software solution. So what we see here is that a mathematically rather intricate computation eventually resorts to something that can be built rather easily into an automated solution.

7.2.4 Making networks

Assume we can wire two computers together by a suitable transmission medium that allows them to exchange data. Having mastered this technology, we should now also be able to extend our collection of communicators by adding more computers. The question is, how to proceed? Wiring two computers A and B does not give us much choice, but what do we do with the next one? Should we connect it to A? Or perhaps to B? Or better still, perhaps this third computer should be connected to both A and B. Numerous alternatives will come to mind when giving the matter some thought, and thinking about it is not such a bad idea when you realize that our ultimate goal is to allow thousands of computers to exchange information. The problem that we are faced with is that of designing a **topology**: a network in which each node consists of a computer. This network must be designed so that communication is not only possible between pairs of computers, but also that several pairs of computers can communicate at the same time (just imagine that the worldwide telephone system could, at any time, support a conversation between only two people).

Network topologies fall more or less naturally into two categories based on which communication strategy is followed when transferring messages between parties:

- **Broadcast:** The first strategy is that of broadcasting by which a message is sent to every other computer in the network. If a message arrives at a computer for which it was not intended, then it will simply be discarded. This strategy is not so bad as it may seem. Compare it to the way radio programs are transmitted. In principle, anyone who has a radio can tune into stations but it is up to the receiver to decide whether to do so.

- **Unicast:** In this case, messages are sent specifically to a single receiver, and the goal is to make transmission as efficient as possible. This means that preferably only the computer for which the message is intended should receive it.

Broadcasting is generally applied in so-called **local area networks** (LAN), where the mechanism has proven to be highly efficient and reliable. Unicasting is typically adopted in **wide area networks** (WAN), where geographical distances prohibit the use of efficient

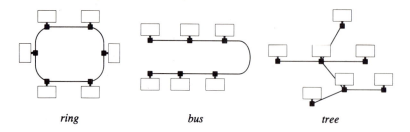

ring   *bus*   *tree*

Figure 7.11 Commonly applied LAN topologies.

transmission media that are needed to exploit broadcast mechanisms effectively.[3] Let's take a closer look at these two types of networks. We will return to both types at length in the next chapters; here, we just concentrate on our original problem, namely that of designing a topology.

Local area network topologies

As we have said, local area networks are based on the principle of message broadcasting. Two dominant topologies for supporting this principle are the **ring** and **bus networks**. The latter also have a variant in the form of a **tree network**, as shown in Figure 7.11. The connections generally consist of copper or fiber-based wires (i.e. you can actually *see* how parts are hooked up to each other).

In a ring topology, the computers are connected to each other by means of unidirectional links. This means that messages are forwarded in a single direction from one computer to its neighbor until it reaches its destination. In a bus topology, all computers are directly connected to the same wire (compare this to connecting several telephones to the same wall socket). This means that if any computer puts a message on the line, all other computers will be capable of picking it up almost immediately. In a tree topology, finally, whenever a message reaches a node with several branches, the message is simply forwarded onto every branch.

The fact that messages are broadcast across the network has a serious consequence. Whenever a message is being transmitted it means that all connections that make up the network will need to be free of other message transmissions. In other words, from a conceptual point of view, the computers in a local area network make use of a *shared* transmission medium, to which we have to guarantee exclusive access. Indeed, in terms of channels as introduced in Section 6.4.1, we can say that the computers in a LAN make use of a single **shared broadcast channel**. The problem that we have to deal with is how we can allocate this shared medium to a single computer so that it can transmit its message. This will be discussed at length in Chapter 8.

---

[3]An exception in this case is to be made for long-range communication by satellites. In this book, however, we consider mostly wide area networks that are constructed through point-to-point links between computers.

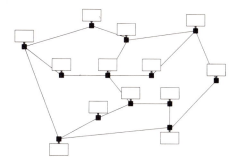

Figure 7.12 A WAN topology.

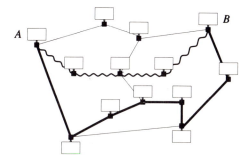

Figure 7.13 Two different routes in a WAN.

Wide area network topologies

Wide area networks are organized completely differently from local area networks, and for a good reason. Imagine that we wanted to construct a network consisting of thousands of computers using, for example, a ring topology and employing the principle of a broadcast channel. We would indeed have problems. Instead, WANs are typically organized into a graph in which point-to-point connections are now taken as they are: messages are forwarded according to some **routing scheme**. The principle is shown in Figure 7.12.

The main distinction with LANs is that each node in a WAN has to determine to which *single* other node it should forward an incoming message. In LANs a message is simply forwarded to *every* neighboring node. To illustrate, Figure 7.13 shows two alternative routes for getting a message from node *A* to node *B* in a WAN. Determining the route is something we shall discuss in Chapter 9. Here, we focus on the elementary aspects, generally referred to as **switching technology**, as each node in a WAN acts as a switch selecting alternative outgoing lines for incoming messages. WANs are generally classified as either **circuit-switched** or **packet-switched** networks.

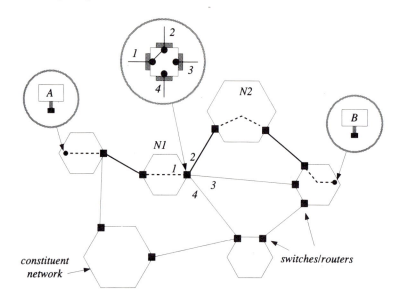

Figure 7.14 The principal working of a circuit-switched network.

Circuit-switched networks.   Whenever a message is to be sent in a circuit-switched network it is first necessary to set up a complete physical connection from the sender to the receiver. In other words, switches are set up all over the WAN in such a way that the sender and receiver are directly connected. This principle is shown in Figure 7.14. There, we show a WAN that has been constructed by connecting several smaller networks (called constituent networks). An essential part of the WAN are the so-called **routers**, which act as true switches in the case of circuit-switched networks. One such switch is shown, having four connectors. In our example, connectors 1 and 2 have been circuit-switched, effectively establishing a direct connection between constituent networks $N1$ and $N2$. A typical example of a circuit-switched network is our telephone system. As you dial a number, a connection is gradually established by appropriately setting switches until a complete connection is made. When the conversation is finished, the connection is broken and each intermediate switch can be used for the next call.

This behavior is characteristic of circuit-switched networks, and always contains the following three steps:

1. A sender requests a connection to be made with a receiver. This implies that a series of nodes in the WAN will have to set up a route.

2. The message exchange takes place, possibly for some time as the receiver may have some information to send back as well. Meanwhile, the nodes in the WAN maintain the connection.

3. The sender (or receiver) indicates that the connection may be broken. From that

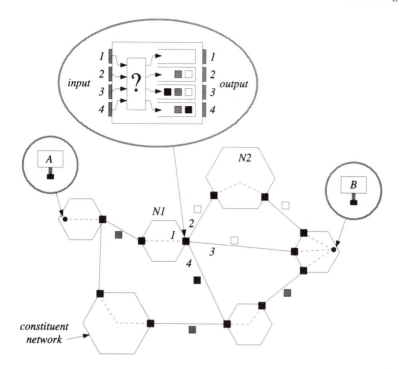

Figure 7.15 The principal working of a packet-switched network.

moment, each node in the WAN can divert its attention to other requests for connection.

Note the resemblance between circuit-switching and connection-oriented communication as discussed in the previous chapter. We shall see more examples of this method of communication in later chapters.

Packet-switched networks.   A disadvantage of circuit-switched networks is that as long as neither the sender nor the receiver has indicated that communication has ended, the connection should be maintained. This also implies that no other connection can be made across any link in the route, even if the sender and receiver are not communicating. As you may imagine, this approach may result in a poor utilization of the network. Alternatively, **packet-switching technology** can be employed. In this case, a message is disassembled into a number of **packets** which are then subsequently sent across the network. No full connection between sender and receiver is required. Instead, each packet carries the address of the destination and nodes in the WAN will forward a packet in the right direction. This principle is shown in Figure 7.15.

In the figure, there are three messages being routed through the network, each consisting of a number of packets (indicated by white, grey, and black boxes, respectively). The indicated router has four input ports, and likewise, four output ports, one pair of ports for each link it has with another router. Now as soon as a packet arrives, the router takes a decision to which link it should forward the packet (indicated by the box marked "?"), based on the destination address found in the packet. It then queues the packet for the selected output port, after which it can be forwarded to the next router.

We will return to packet-switched networks in Chapter 9, but already it can be seen that there are a number of important differences from circuit-switched networks. The most important is that the route a packet should follow is not reserved in advance. Instead, packets are gradually forwarded through the network on a strict node-to-node basis. Consequently, in order to send a packet, we need to reserve only a single connection between two nodes, which can be immediately released when the packet has reached its intermediate destination.

Another important difference is that packets comprising a message need not follow the same route, as illustrated in Figure 7.15. There, all packets having the same color (white, grey or black) are assumed to belong to the same message. Changing a route may be a good thing to do in order to avoid congestion in the network. It does have a serious consequence, though: packets may not arrive in the order they were sent. This means, in the end, that the destination node will have to assemble the message by putting the packets in the right order before passing the message to the receiver. Assembling messages seems a straightforward operation, but may be difficult in practice as we shall see later.

7.3   Frame transmission

So far, we have been discussing a few of the issues that are related to simply wiring computers together:

- Transmission of digital signals, and observing that signals can be significantly distorted

- Reception of signals, which requires some form of synchronization between the sending and receiving device

- The detection by a receiving device that something went wrong during transmission

- Alternatives for wiring several computers together.

It is time that we concentrated on sending data and left the wiring. So, let's focus on a situation where we have two computers A and B that have been wired together and in which A wants to transmit data to B. Simply putting the data on the line by continuously sending bits is not going to work. In order to manage all kinds of transmission errors, and to allow the two computers to keep pace with each other, we will have to resort to sending relatively small portions of data. These portions of data are referred to as **frames**. The total amount of data is thus partitioned into frames, and each frame is subsequently sent to the receiver. For example, a sender may decide to split a large piece of text into frames by sending the text character by character. Each frame then consists of a single character (with some additional information as we shall see). By splitting the data into frames, data transmission then reduces to sending a *series* of frames. Splitting data into frames and sending these frames one by one is perfectly in order if at least one rule is obeyed: the frames should be pasted together by the receiver in the order they are sent. We will see later that this rule imposes some serious difficulties.

Now, returning to our two computers A and B, two problems need to be addressed:

1. How do A and B cooperate so that we are certain that B has received all frames, and it is possible to paste them together into the original data that A wanted to transmit in the first place?

2. What should B do when it finds that a received frame is not the right one, or that a frame has been damaged on account of a transmission error?

The first question addresses the issue of **flow control**; the second that of **error control**. Both issues are discussed in the following two subsections.

7.3.1 Flow control

Imagine the following situation. A has split its large amount of data into N frames, and starts transmitting each frame to B without paying attention as to whether or not B can handle them. This can easily lead to problems, because, typically, in order to handle incoming frames, B will temporarily store each of them in an **input buffer** before processing its contents. For example, the data contained in each frame will generally have to be copied into B's main memory. Consequently, if frames arrive too fast for B to remove them from its internal buffers in order to make some space again, things will indeed go wrong. The principle of communicating frames is shown in Figure 7.16. We require that A and B will have to run at the same speed. Let's see how this can be accomplished.

Stop-and-wait protocol

The simplest scenario for synchronizing a sender and receiver, is for the sender to transmit a single frame, and subsequently let it wait until the receiver has received and processed the frame. To that end, the receiver will always send an *acknowledgment* back to the sender as soon as the frame has been processed. This is illustrated in Figure 7.17.

In this case, the line is used for bidirectional traffic: it is said to operate in **half duplex mode** because although transmission can occur in either direction, only one direction can be used at a time.[4] This is an extremely simple, so-called **stop-and-wait** protocol. And although it appears satisfactory, in many cases, it is in fact very inefficient. To see this, we need to consider the so-called propagation and frame transmission time.

---

[4]Compare this to traffic over a one-lane bridge in which vehicles can go in either direction.

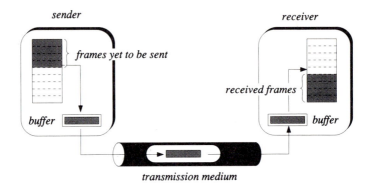

Figure 7.16 The principle of frame transmission.

Propagation time.   The propagation time is the time it takes for a single signal to reach the receiver. To illustrate, imagine we are using a satellite as our transmission medium, circulating in an orbit at, say, 35 000 kilometers above the earth. Transmitting a signal at the speed of light (3×10^8 meters per second) means sending it over a total distance of 70 000 kilometers, which takes about 230 milliseconds. This is a factor that cannot be ignored. On the other hand, coax cables are often used to connect computers up to approximately 10 kilometers. With a propagation speed of approximately 2×10^8 mps (meters per second), it will take only 50 microseconds for a signal to reach the receiver.

Frame transmission time.   The frame transmission time is the time it takes for a complete frame to reach the receiver. In this case, we need to also consider the **transmission rate**. The transmission rate is the speed by which a sender and receiver can put bits on a line, and pick them up, respectively. For example, using satellites, computers can generally transmit and accept approximately 64 000 bits per second (i.e. 64 Kbps). In this case, it takes a frame of 4000 bits approximately 60 milliseconds to reach the receiver. In contrast, if we have a transmission rate of 10 Mbps, it will take only 400 microseconds to transmit the complete frame, at least as far as the sender and receiver are concerned.

Now the propagation time is completely determined by the transmission medium and its length, whereas the transmission rate is determined by the speed with which the sender and receiver are capable of putting a signal on the line, and picking it up, respectively. In cases where the propagation time is much larger than the frame transmission time, we will have a problem with our stop-and-wait protocol. To see this, consider how much time it takes to send and acknowledge the receipt of a frame. We assume that the acknowledgment is a bit string having a length that can be ignored compared to the length of the transmitted frame. Then, sending a frame will take a total of

$$\textit{sending time} \;\; = \;\; T_{\text{prop}} + T_{\text{frame}}$$

sender *receiver*

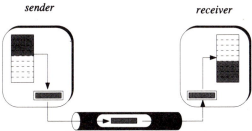

transmit frame #k from sender to receiver

transmit an acknowledgement from receiver to sender

transmit frame # k+1 from sender to receiver

Figure 7.17 Frame transmission following a stop-and wait protocol.

time units, where T_{prop} is the propagation time and T_{frame} denotes the transmission time of the frame. Likewise, returning an acknowledgment will take an additional

$$acknowledgment\ time\ =\ T_{prop}$$

time units. The total transmission time, also called the **transmission cycle time** T_{cycle}, then adds up to

$$transmission\ cycle\ time\ =\ 2T_{prop} + T_{frame}$$

Consequently, the *efficiency* of our transmission is then equal to:

$$\frac{ideal\ transmission\ time}{transmission\ cycle\ time} = \frac{T_{\text{frame}}}{2T_{\text{prop}} + T_{\text{frame}}} \qquad (7.1)$$

which is poor when $T_{\text{prop}} > T_{\text{frame}}$, as is the case when we are using satellites. What it means is that the propagation time is so long that it dominates the transmission cycle time. In other words, the transmission medium itself is simply too slow (or too long) for the sender and receiver.

This can easily be compared with real-life examples. One way of looking at this is the use of a conveyer belt, where boxes are loaded on one end and removed from the other. No matter how fast we put boxes on the belt, if the belt itself is slow, or long, it will take a long time for a box to reach the other end. In any case, the transmission medium (i.e. the belt) actually determines the speed at which communication can take place. To see the effect of this protocol, imagine you could measure the traffic intensity of the transmission medium by counting the number of frames that pass a certain point. What you will see is that only occasionally a frame will pass in one direction, followed by an acknowledgment in the other direction. The **utilization** of the medium will thus be extremely low.

▷ The ratio expressed in equation (7.1) is an interesting one that we will return to later. In particular, if we consider its reciprocal:

$$\theta = \frac{2T_{\text{prop}} + T_{\text{frame}}}{T_{\text{frame}}}$$

then θ denotes the *multitude* of frames that could have been sent in ideal circumstances, i.e. without any propagation delay, and without any errors. We shall refer to θ as the **ideal transmission factor**. Another way of viewing θ is that it denotes the number of frames that can be transmitted in sequence before the first acknowledgment arrives. In the next chapter we shall replace this factor by one that it is more commonly used for performance analysis.

Sliding-window protocol

Returning to our problem of having a low efficiency, there is an obvious solution to this problem. Assume that we can use the medium for simultaneously transmitting messages in *both* directions, i.e. we use the medium in **full duplex mode**.[5] What we can do then is send a number of frames in a row without having the sender wait for each frame to be acknowledged before sending the next one. The receiver will return an acknowledgment for each frame upon receipt, and continue to wait for the arrival of the next frame which may already be on its way. This situation is illustrated in Figure 7.18.

Of course, we have to ensure that the sender will not be sending too many frames for the receiver to handle. Assume that the receiver can store up to a maximum of N_{win} frames (called a **window**) before having processed each of them. Each time a frame arrives,

---

[5]Relating this to half-duplex mode, this situation is comparable to having a two-lane bridge.

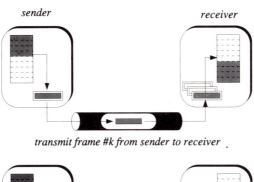

transmit frame #k from sender to receiver .

transmit frame # k+1 from sender to receiver,
and return an acknowledgment for frame #k

Figure 7.18 Allowing multiple frames to be in transit before acknowledgment.

the receiver temporarily stores it in one of its (free) buffers, and subsequently sends an acknowledgment. Now suppose the sender wants to send the kth frame, where $k > N_{\text{win}}$, denoted as F_k. If it has not yet received an acknowledgment for frame $F_{k-N_{\text{win}}}$, the sender will know that N_{win} frames are apparently still in transit. Consequently, it should wait because this is the maximum number of frames that the receiver can handle in sequence.

The protocol we have just described is referred to as a **sliding-window** protocol. What it means is that the sender maintains a list (a *window*) of frames that have been sent, but not yet acknowledged. If the maximum number of frames on this list is N_{win}, the sender will have to wait until the first frame on the list is acknowledged before sending a new one. Acknowledged frames are removed from the list, whereas recently sent ones are appended to it. Note that if $N_{\text{win}} = 1$, this protocol is exactly the stop-and-wait protocol described above.

▷ **Comparison of the two protocols**

Let's see how the sliding window protocol compares to the stop-and-wait protocol which exploits only half-duplex transmission. Again, we assume that the transmission time for an acknowledgment is negligible, so that we only have to take the propagation time into account. Suppose A sends a first frame F_1 which then arrives at B after $T_{\text{prop}} + T_{\text{frame}}$ time units. B acknowledges the receipt of the frame, which will reach A after an additional T_{prop} time units. In other words, each time A sends a frame, the acknowledgment for that frame will arrive after $2T_{\text{prop}} + T_{\text{frame}}$ time units. This is referred to as the **transmission cycle time**

T_{cycle}:

$$\text{transmission cycle time } T_{\text{cycle}} \quad = \quad 2T_{\text{prop}} + T_{\text{frame}} \qquad (7.2)$$

(Note that the transmission cycle time is measured from the instant that A starts to transmit a frame, not from the moment the frame has been sent, in which case it would be equal to $2T_{\text{prop}}$.) Denote by N_{win} the window size, i.e. the number of frames that B can store before processing them. After sending F_1, A can continue to send frames $F_2, F_3, \ldots, F_{N_{\text{win}}}$, which will take an additional $(N_{\text{win}} - 1) \cdot T_{\text{frame}}$ time units. We now need to consider two cases:

1. The acknowledgment for frame F_1 reaches A before it had the chance to transmit the remaining $N_{\text{win}} - 1$ frames. In other words, $T_{\text{cycle}} < N_{\text{win}} \cdot T_{\text{frame}}$, which is the same as stating that $N_{\text{win}} > \theta$.
2. The acknowledgment for frame F_1 reaches A after all remaining $N_{\text{win}} - 1$ frames have been sent. In this case, $T_{\text{cycle}} > N_{\text{win}} \cdot T_{\text{frame}}$, or, in other words, $N_{\text{win}} < \theta$.

In the first case, A can continue to transmit frames without any delay: B will always be capable of receiving and subsequently processing them. In this case, the efficiency of the transmission will be equal to 1 because A will never have to wait for B. In other words, the ideal transmission time is the same as the transmission cycle time.

In the second case, A will have to wait until it receives the acknowledgment. Now the point to note is that if we assume that nothing went wrong during the transmission (i.e. if we assume a completely error-free line), A can immediately send another N_{win} frames as soon as it receives the acknowledgment for frame F_1. To see this, note that $T_{\text{cycle}} > N_{\text{win}} \cdot T_{\text{frame}}$ implies that we necessarily have that *all* frames will have been received by B by the time A receives the acknowledgment of the receipt of F_1 (assuming a constant acceptance rate). Taking the first case into account as well, we can now state that the overall efficiency in the case of a sliding-window protocol is equal to:

$$\frac{\textit{ideal transmission time}}{\textit{transmission cycle time}} \quad = \quad \begin{cases} 1 & \text{if } N_{\text{win}} \geq \theta \\ N_{\text{win}}/\theta & \text{if } N_{\text{win}} < \theta \end{cases} \qquad (7.3)$$

Figure 7.19 shows how the efficiency relates to the size of the window (N_{win}) as the transmission factor θ increases. For example, it can be concluded that in the case of satellite transmission (where θ can be very large), a large window will be needed to keep efficiency high. In practice, a window size of 7 for most transmission media and 127 for satellite media are sufficient.

7.3.2   Error control

What have we accomplished so far? At this point, we are able to send frames from one computer to another such that:

-   The receiver has the chance to process frames, i.e. remove a frame from its internal buffers before a next one arrives

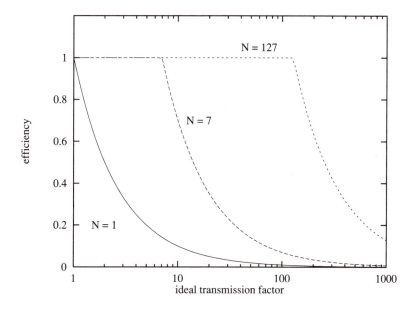

Figure 7.19 The efficiency of a transmission medium when using a sliding-window protocol.

- The transmission medium is used efficiently in the sense that we can transmit as many frames as the medium can hold, while keeping the sender and receiver in synchronization.

But, of course, things may still go wrong. Due to the fact that no line can ever guarantee error-free transmission of data, we may not expect that all frames will reach the receiver without being damaged. In particular, we need to distinguish two types of errors:

1. A frame that has been picked up by the receiver is found to contain errors. This is a so-called *damaged frame*. That a frame has been damaged can be determined with a certain high probability by using, for example, polynomial coding as described in Section 7.2.3.

2. A frame never arrives, or better, the receiver fails to detect that a new frame arrives. This is generally referred to as a *lost frame*. This type of error may occur when the frame is so damaged that the receiver simply cannot recognize it.

Error control refers to the techniques that can be applied in the case of damaged and lost frames. Roughly, there are four general techniques (Stallings, 1993b):

- **Error detection**, by which it can be determined whether a frame is damaged. As we have said, a widely applied technique for error detection is polynomial coding.

- **Positive acknowledgment**, by which the receiver sends an acknowledgment back to the sender upon the successful receipt of a frame.

- **Negative acknowledgment and retransmission**, by which the receiver sends a negative acknowledgment for each damaged or lost frame so that the sender can retransmit it.

- **Retransmission after timeout**, implying that if the sender does not receive a positive acknowledgment after a certain time has elapsed, it simply retransmits the frame.

These techniques are collectively referred to as **automatic repeat request** mechanisms, or simply **ARQ**. The first technique has already been discussed and is fundamental to any error control technique as it provides the means to *detect* that something went wrong. The second and third technique seem to be in order as well. One way or the other, the sender is informed about the error status of a frame transmission so that it can handle the problem. The fourth technique is illustrative of the fundamental problem that we have to deal with: acknowledgments (being either positive or negative) can themselves be damaged or lost.

To illustrate, suppose the receiver acknowledges each successful receipt of a frame. If the sender does not receive an acknowledgment for, say, frame F_k there are two possibilities: (1) the frame was lost or damaged, or (2) its acknowledgment simply did not reach the sender. In the first case, retransmission is in order; in the second case, it is not, because transmission was successful. In any case, frame F_k is retransmitted and it is up to the receiver to conclude if retransmission was necessary (i.e. the frame was originally damaged or lost) or not (because the frame originally reached the receiver). One way or the other, we have to set up a protocol and corresponding administration to handle this form of error control.

Stop-and-wait ARQ

To see what this means in practice, we first consider an error control protocol which is based on the stop-and-wait protocol in the previous section. This so-called **stop-and-wait ARQ** error control scheme works as follows. Suppose a sender has just transmitted a frame F_k. After transmission, the sender will wait until it either receives a positive acknowledgment (ACK) indicating that transmission was successful, or a negative acknowledgment (NACK), indicating that the frame arrived but was damaged. If no acknowledgment is received after a certain time has elapsed, the sender concludes that either the frame or the acknowledgment was lost. When an ACK arrives, the next frame F_{k+1} is transmitted. When either a NACK is received or a timeout occurs, frame F_k is retransmitted to the receiver.

As we have explained, it may be that the frame F_k was unnecessarily retransmitted because its acknowledgment was lost. Consequently, the receiver may pick up the same frame twice in a row. By explicitly providing the frame number as part of the frame, retransmission of a successfully received frame can be detected by the receiver.[6]

---

[6]In fact, it is sufficient merely to indicate that a frame is being retransmitted. We shall not go into details

▷ How efficient is this simple protocol? To simplify matters, assume that ACKs and NACKs are never lost. Then, denote by p the probability that a frame is transmitted with an error. Let $\underline{r}$ be the stochastic variable denoting the number of times a frame has to be transmitted in sequence. Then the probability $\mathcal{P}[\underline{r} = i]$ that we need to retransmit a frame i times in sequence is equal to:

$$\mathcal{P}[\underline{r} = i] \;=\; p^{i-1}(1-p)$$

So the *expected* number of successive retransmissions is equal to

$$\mathcal{E}[\underline{r}] \;=\; \sum_{i=1}^{\infty} i \cdot \mathcal{P}[\underline{r} = i]$$

$$= \sum_{i=1}^{\infty} i p^{i-1}(1-p) = 1/(1-p)$$

Consequently, the efficiency of the overall transmission will be equal to

$$\frac{ideal\ transmission\ time}{transmission\ cycle\ time} \;=\; \frac{T_{\text{frame}}}{\mathcal{E}[\underline{r}]T_{\text{cycle}}} = \frac{1-p}{\theta}$$

which, as we have argued in the previous section, is generally not very good.

Continuous ARQ

An alternative error control technique is the so-called **continuous ARQ** which is based on a sliding-window protocol. The basic idea is that a sender can continuously send frames without waiting for each frame to be acknowledged by the receiver. When a negative acknowledgment arrives, or when the sender notices that an acknowledgment has been lost, two different procedures can be followed. Assume the sender notices that something has gone wrong with frame F_k while it had just finished the transmission of frame F_{k+N-1} (i.e. after sending a series of N frames the sender is notified that the first one has not reached the receiver). In that case, it can either (1) retransmit *all* frames $F_k, F_{k+1}, \ldots, F_{k+N-1}$ or (2) retransmit only frame F_k. The first procedure is characteristic of the so-called **go-back-N ARQ**; the second is referred to as **selective repeat ARQ**.

At first it would seem wasteful to retransmit all frames succeeding F_k. On the other hand, you have to realize that this scheme does make reception of frames extremely simple when comparing it to the selective-repeat mechanism. To see this, we first consider this last protocol. Assume that one way or the other the receiver detects that frame F_k has been damaged or lost so that it subsequently returns a NACK(k) to the sender. Now, the problem we have to deal with is that frames can only be processed in the order in which

here.

they are transmitted. For example, the receiver can only copy a frame F_i from its internal buffer to main memory if the previous frame F_{i-1} has been copied to main memory as well. This is exactly the rule we mentioned at the beginning of this section. And it is exactly this rule that is going to lead to serious difficulties when applying the selective-repeat protocol.

So, while the receiver is now waiting for retransmission of frame F_k, it should be able temporarily to store all succeeding frames $F_{k+1}, \ldots, F_{k+N-1}$. As long as frame F_k has not been received, the succeeding frames cannot be processed. Consequently, it may turn out that the number of buffers at the receiver's side may have to be quite large. And things can get worse. If it is found that one of the succeeding frames F_{k+p} $(k+1 \leq p \leq N-1)$ is damaged or lost, the receiver will have to account for that as well. In effect, the selective-repeat protocol puts a fairly heavy burden on the receiver's capability of administrating the reception of frames. As we shall discuss later, because the protocols we are discussing here are generally implemented in *hardware*, we do have a serious problem. Consequently, for implementation reasons the selective-repeat protocol is not often applied as an error control mechanism.

The go-back-N protocol does not have these buffering problems. Whenever a damaged or lost frame is detected by the receiver, it simply waits until the frame has been successfully retransmitted, thereby ignoring all succeeding frames. Consequently, there is no need for an intricate buffering scheme and administration.

▷ Now let's see how good the go-back-N protocol is.[7] Our first concern is to work out the number of expected transmissions. Assume the sender had transmitted N frames $F_k, \ldots, F_{k+N-1}$ and that it finds out that frame F_k has been damaged or lost. Again, assume that ACKs and NACKs are never lost, and that the probability of a transmission error for a complete frame is p. Let $\mathbf{r}_N$ denote the total number of frame transmissions required to get frame F_k successfully to the receiver. Note that $\mathbf{r}_N$ can only take on values $1, N+1, 2N+1, 3N+1$, etc. We then have

$$\mathcal{P}[\mathbf{r}_N - i] = \begin{cases} p^k(1-p) & \text{with } i = kN + 1, k = 0, 1, 2, \ldots \\ 0 & \text{otherwise} \end{cases}$$

With respect to the number of *expected* frame transmissions, it can be shown that we then have

$$\mathcal{E}[\mathbf{r}_N] \;\; = \;\; \sum_{i=1}^{\infty} i \cdot \mathcal{P}[\mathbf{r}_N = i] = \frac{1-p+pN}{1-p} \tag{7.4}$$

The question is, of course, how large N is. Again, we need to consider two situations taking into account the transmission factor θ and the receiver's window size N_{win}.

1. If $N_{\text{win}} < \theta$, NACK(k) will reach the sender *after* all frames that fit into a window have been transmitted. Consequently, all these frames will need to be retransmitted, so that $N = N_{\text{win}}$.

---

[7]The analysis presented here is an approximation of the actual one, and is based on the analysis presented in Stallings (1993b).

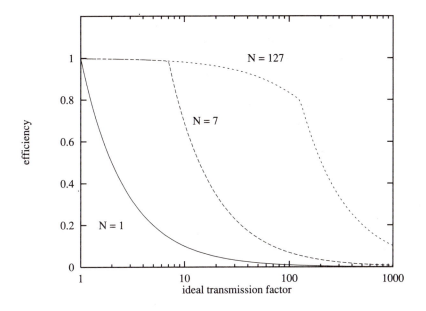

Figure 7.20 The efficiency of a transmission medium when using a sliding-window ARQ.

2. When $N_{win} > \theta$, NACK(k) will reach the sender before a complete window of frames has been transmitted. In particular, we may expect that approximately θ frames will have been sent while the NACK was making its way to the sender. In other words, $N = \theta$.

Using these values for N, we can now derive an approximation for the overall efficiency of the sliding-window ARQ analogous to formula (7.3):

$$\frac{ideal\ transmission\ time}{transmission\ cycle\ time} = \begin{cases} (1-p)/(1-p+\theta p) & \text{if } N_{win} \geq \theta \\ (1-p)N_{win}/((1-p+N_{win}p)\theta) & \text{if } N_{win} < \theta \end{cases} \quad (7.5)$$

Figure 7.20 illustrates these efficiencies for a error probability of $p = 0.002$. Again, it is seen that if the window size is chosen large enough when dealing with a high transmission factor, overall efficiency remains relatively close to 1.

Summarizing, we see that retransmitting frames may indeed be an adequate way to respond to transmission errors, but, as in the case of flow control, propagation times should be taken into account.

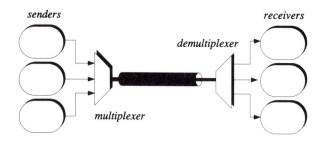

Figure 7.21 The principle of multiplexing a transmission medium

7.4   Multiplexing

In the previous section we have shown how we can effectively raise the utilization of a transmission medium by using sliding-window protocols. In this case, the sender simply puts a number of frames on the line without waiting for an acknowledgment by the receiver. This scheme is perfectly in order, and it does increase efficiency, as long as there is data to transfer. As soon as the sender and receiver are finished, the transmission medium is simply no longer used. As transmission media are generally not cheap, it would seem a good idea to use the same medium to connect two other computers while the initial sender and receiver have no need to communicate. Of course, removing connectors and physically relaying a wire is impractical. Nevertheless, the idea can be put into practice by applying a technique referred to as **multiplexing**. In this section we shall briefly consider some of the issues related to multiplexing.

The principle of multiplexing a transmission medium is illustrated in Figure 7.21. A number of senders and a number of receivers can share a single transmission medium without interfering with each other. Here, we shall present two different methods of doing so (of which the first, called frequency-division multiplexing, is of less importance for understanding the material that is to follow, so it may be skipped on first reading).

▷ **Frequency-division multiplexing**

Frequency-division multiplexing, or simply FDM, is a method of sending multiple signals simultaneously over a single transmission medium. How can this be done without signals destroying or interfering with each other? The solution is found by the observation that a digital signal can be practically represented by a limited number of sine waves of different frequencies, as was shown in Section 7.2.1. The range between the lowest and highest frequencies is called the **baseband frequency range** of that signal. This is analogous to saying that the frequency range of human hearing is usually from 40 to 16 000 Hz.

The bandwidth of a transmission medium (or, equivalently in this case, the allowable frequency range) is often much larger than the frequency range required to represent a signal. This would mean that a large part of the bandwidth of the transmission medium is effectively not used. If we could temporarily *shift* a baseband frequency range of 0 to B Hz to

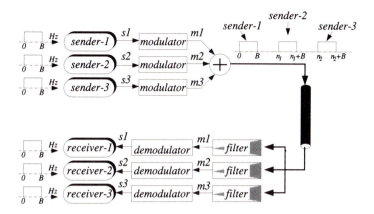

Figure 7.22 The principle of frequency-division multiplexing.

n to $n + B$ Hz, we could elegantly "fill" the available capacity of the transmission medium by choosing a different value of n for each baseband signal. By de-shifting at the receiving end, we would be able to retrieve the original signals.

The technique by which this shifting is done is called **modulation**. The way modulation is accomplished is beyond the scope of this book. That different forms of modulation exist can already be seen in the way that radio signals are modulated. There we have **AM** (Amplitude Modulation) or **FM** (Frequency Modulation). De-shifting back to the baseband is done by an operation called **demodulation**. The principle is shown in Figure 7.22.

The modulator changes each input signal to a modulated signal with a unique frequency range. In particular, each of baseband signals are associated with a different frequency range, which is generally referred to as a channel. These channels are conceptually the same as those discussed in Section 6.4.1. They allow a sender and a receiver to communicate without explicit reference to each other. Transmission systems which have multiple simultaneous channels are generally referred to as **broadband** transmission systems, as opposed to **baseband** transmission systems which allow only a single channel for communication.

As a practical example of FDM, consider hand-held telephones. Whenever a call is to be made, the telephone *searches* for an available frequency range that it can use for transmission. The cheapest hand-held telephones often support only two different frequency ranges, or channels. If your two neighbors happen to be using those channels, that is unfortunate for you. On the other hand, the more expensive systems support many more channels, and it is almost always possible to find a free channel that can be used for transmission.

Time-division multiplexing

Frequency-division multiplexing can only be used when analog signals are to be transmitted. Consequently, this means that when a digital signal is to be transmitted, it will first have to be encoded into an analog one. An alternative multiplexing scheme that is also suited for digital signal transmission, is **(synchronous) time-division multiplexing**,

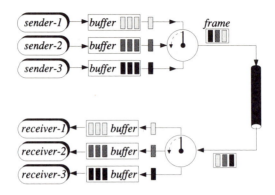

Figure 7.23 The principle of time-division multiplexing.

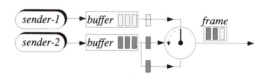

Figure 7.24 An example of using TDM for different transmission rates.

or **TDM** for short. The principle of TDM is illustrated in Figure 7.23 and is really quite simple.

What happens is the following. Suppose we have three senders as shown in Figure 7.23. Each sender stores a part of the data it wants to transmit (e.g. a single bit or byte) into a local buffer, which is *periodically* scanned. If data is available, it is removed from the buffer and appended to the data that has been removed from other buffers. After scanning each buffer once, a frame will have been composed which is then subsequently transmitted to the other side. There, the process is repeated inversely, and the data is stored in the appropriate buffers.

A few remarks are in order. First, note that each buffer is scanned for a *fixed* time slot. This is comparable to our concept of a clock signal that we introduced in Section 2.5. If no data is available during the time a buffer is scanned, then that part of the frame will remain empty. Second, note that we can indeed increase the efficiency of the transmission medium. If, say, one sender is temporarily not willing to transmit any data, the medium is still used for data transmission by the other two senders. Third, we can use TDM to use the transmission medium to support several transmission rates. This is illustrated in Figure 7.24.

What we see here is that the buffer of the second sender is scanned *twice* during a single period, whereas the first sender's buffer is scanned only once in that time. Consequently, the second buffer can be emptied at twice the rate of the first buffer. This implies that *sender-2* and its receiver can communicate twice as much data in the same time that *sender-1* and its receiver can. In other words, the transmission rate between *sender-2* and its receiver is twice as much as the rate between *sender-1* and its receiver. Being able to support different transmission rates over the same transmission medium is important. For one thing, different services can be offered, for example the same medium can be effectively used to (digitally) transmit voice (requiring a relatively low transmission rate) and video data (which requires a high transmission rate).

We shall return to the issue of supporting several transmission rates in our discussion on wide area networks in Chapter 9.

7.5   Towards a layered approach

We have now come to a point at which you should have an idea about some of the basic properties concerning communication between computers. In particular, we have presented issues on physically connecting computers and on transmitting data in the form of a series of bits, called frames. At first, the order in which we have presented the material may seem rather arbitrary. Therefore, we first concentrate explicitly on the structure of the material presented so far.

7.5.1   Review of basic communication properties

We started with some basic issues in Section 7.2: physically wiring computers to each other. In particular, we discussed fundamental problems related to actual transmission media, and also paid attention to different types of media. Furthermore, we focused on the problem on how a receiver can pick up a series of bits by briefly discussing transmission modes, and also how possible transmission errors can be detected. An important observation with respect to error detection was that its implementation could be done by means of relatively simple integrated circuits. At that point, we had shown that two computers could be physically connected, and that a series of bits could be put on a line on one end and picked up at the other with detection of possible transmission errors.

We then made a small digression by taking a closer look at physically connecting more than two computers to each other. New problems were introduced. In particular, we showed that there is no single means for connecting several computers and that it may be necessary to distinguish different switching technologies as is the case with wide area networks. Still, our attention was focused on basic (i.e. physical) connection schemes.

A first diversion from physical connections was introduced in Section 7.3. There, we discussed how it is possible to send large chunks of data by splitting the data into so-called frames. In particular, communication protocols were presented that dealt with the issue of getting a series of frames from one side to the other, taking into account that the transmission of a single frame may be subject to errors. Applying these flow and error control protocols establishes a situation in which large amounts of data can be transmitted between two computers in such a way as if no transmission errors had appeared. In other words, we have realized an error-free transmission means for data between two computers.

Flow and error control are greatly influenced by efficiency issues concerning the usage of a transmission media. The question of establishing efficiency, finally, brought us to the subject of multiplexing in the previous section. Multiplexing allows multiple senders and receivers to make simultaneous use of the same transmission medium. However, where we concentrated on transmitting *series* of frames in Section 7.3, multiplexing merely deals with sending a single frame over a transmission medium. In that sense, our discussion on multiplexing can indeed be considered as taking a step back.

Let's put these topics into a somewhat different perspective by considering different levels of abstraction. The following levels (starting at the lowest) can be distinguished:[8]

L1: Physical connections between two computers, particularly transmission media.

L2: Transmission modes, i.e. how a receiver can pick up the bits that have been put on a line by a sender.

L3: Multiplexing, which is concerned with sending several signals at the same time over a single medium in such a way that each signal can be recognized separately by various receivers.

L4: Switching technology, in which we can make a distinction between absence of switches (LANs) and circuit and packet-switched networks (WANs).

L5: Frame transmission, particularly the means to send and receive a *series* of bits, and the means to detect that something went wrong during transmission.

L6: Data transmission, involving error-free transmission of large amounts of data from one computer to another by splitting the data into a series of frames.

An important observation is that in order to realize each level, agreement must be reached between a sender and a receiver concerning how communication is going to take place *at that level*. But there is more. For example, in order to realize data transmission, it is essential that agreement with respect to frame transmission exists. Likewise, frame transmission can only be successfully accomplished if we know which switching technology is applied, which in turn requires agreement on whether or not multiplexing is used, and if so, according to which protocol. Again, multiplexing requires knowledge concerning transmission modes. And finally, of course, there can be no transmission at all if we do not have a medium at our disposal.

What we see here is the presence of two entirely different types of agreements. First, *intra-level* agreements, also referred to as *horizontal* agreements, deal with agreements between senders and receivers with respect to a single level. They describe how a sender can transmit information to a receiver in terms of the available communication means at just one level lower. For example, data transmission agreements assume that transmission of individual frames is possible. Second, there are *inter-level* agreements, also referred to as *vertical* agreements, that describe how a function at, say, level L_k can be

---

[8]We note that the hierarchy of levels presented is, in fact, rather too strict, and in some cases not completely realistic. In this sense, the levels are to be seen as an illustration of the type of structure that is commonly applied in communication systems.

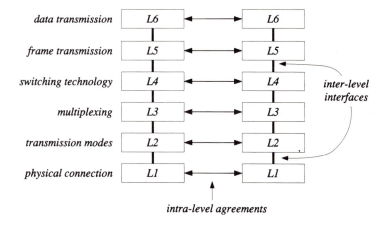

Figure 7.25 The principle of layered agreements.

realized by means of the functions available at one level lower, i.e. level L_{k-1}. These inter-level agreements form the **interface** between two adjacent levels. This principle of *layered agreements* is shown in Figure 7.25.

Communication systems can be extremely complicated and it is hardly possible to produce them without adapting some kind of structure. In the next section we shall introduce a widely adopted layered structure to which we will return throughout the remainder of this book.

7.5.2 The ISO/OSI reference model

As we have said, successfully constructing a communication system can be an extremely difficult task. In order to assist the development of such systems by different parties, the International Standards Organization (ISO) developed a seven-layered **reference model**, in which each layer is described in terms of *which* communication support it should provide. The reference model is generally referred to as the **Open Systems Interconnection** (OSI) model . At this point we shall only briefly describe its most commonly applied layers which deal with computer networks in general, i.e. independent of the actual use of a network in terms of applications.

The three lower layers of the OSI model are shown in Figure 7.26. A distinction is made between the physical layer, the data link layer, and the network layer.

The physical layer

The lowest layer, referred to as the physical layer, deals with protocols concerning the physical connection between computers. All issues mentioned in levels L_2, L_3 and L_4 of the previous subsection are dealt with in this layer, except for the actual transmission medium (which lies below this layer). In essence, it concerns agreements on the trans-

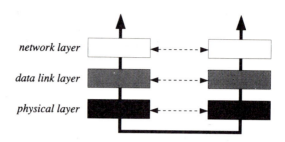

Figure 7.26 The three lower layers of the OSI reference model.

mission of a single signal: how we can transmit a single bit from a sender to a receiver. For example, agreement has to exist concerning the plugs and sockets that are used to connect a medium to a computer, which pins are used for which signals, the strength of signals in terms of volts, etc.

The data link layer

Typically, the issues mentioned on our levels L_5 and L_6 are dealt with at the data link layer. Essentially, protocols at the data link layer establish an error-free communication of data in terms of sending a series of frames. Consequently, agreement has to be reached with respect to flow and error control of frames. An important topic that we have not yet discussed is the issue of selecting a single sender to put a frame on a broadcast transmission medium when several computers are organized into a LAN, as discussed in Section 7.2.4. How this is accomplished will be a major topic of Chapter 8. Many of the protocols at the data link layer are implemented in hardware, but the more intricate ones which are to be found at the "top" of this layer are generally implemented in software.

The network layer

The network layer will be discussed at length when we describe the presentation of wide area networks in Chapter 9. The main functionality of network layer communication protocols is establishing a connection between several networks. In particular, protocols at this level deal with *routing issues*, i.e. determining the route of a message from a sender to its receiver(s) through a wide area network. We touched upon this subject in Section 7.2.4.

The OSI model also defines four other, higher, layers. The **transport layer**, which lies just above the network layer, is probably the most widely and consistently applied *general* layer in the world of communication systems. In effect, this layer provides users and applications with a consistent view of a true, worldwide expanding network in which it becomes irrelevant whether a communicating party is sited on the same floor or at the other side of the world. The transport layer as well as issues of the other higher layers will be discussed in later chapters. For now, the above-mentioned three lowest layers are of primary concern for understanding the more technical principles related to communication systems. These issues are discussed in the following two chapters.

7.6   Further reading

In this chapter we have briefly discussed some important issues that deal with physically connecting two or more computers. As a summary of our approach has already been given in Section 7.5.1, we shall give only some references for further reading.

Most of the material discussed in this chapter is generally contained in standard textbooks on data communication and computer networks, especially those that view it from the perspective of an electrical engineer. In this sense, both Halsall (1992) and Stallings (1994) provide adequate background material. Also, Beyda (1989) and Goupille (1993) may be of use. The material is also discussed in Tanenbaum (1988), which is more suited for those oriented to computer science and mathematics. Error correction and detection is discussed at length in Peterson (1968) and Clark and Cain (1981).

Exercises

1. *Explain the difference between digital and analog signals. Is this a fundamental difference or not?

2. *What can go wrong during the transmission of a digital signal through a medium?

3. *Explain the difference between synchronous and asynchronous transmission.

4. Suppose that we always transmit data in the form of bit strings of length 8, and that any bit string of length 8 has a sensible interpretation. Can a receiver then ever detect a transmission error? What does this imply for an error detection scheme?

5. *In devising error detection schemes, developers strive to minimize the number of additional bits that have to be sent in order to allow for error detection. Why do they do this?

6. *Outline a way of implementing the triple-repetition code in hardware. (Hint: think how you can use the implementation of the majority function as presented in Chapter 2 to do the decoding.)

7. What is the fundamental difference between LAN and WAN technology? Also explain the difference between circuit-switched and packet-switched networks.

8. There is one kind of circuit-switched local area network that we have not mentioned in this chapter. Which one do we mean? (Hint: think of how telephones are used in a building.)

9. The propagation time is determined by the transmission medium that is used; the frame transmission time is determined by the sender and receiver. Explain precisely what is meant by this statement.

10. Suppose that a sender transmits at a much lower speed than the receiver is willing to accept incoming messages. Do we need some kind of flow control scheme in this case?

11. Why is using a simple stop-and-wait protocol in the case of satellite communication not such a good idea?

12. Increasing the utilization of a channel implies that we would want to have several frames simultaneously in transmission. Does this always imply that the buffering capacity at the receiver should be increased as well?

13. *Show the correctness of equation (7.4) on page 346.

14. Can we still apply the *go-back-N* protocol if frames can be received out of order?

15. Explain how time-division multiplexing works, and in particular how it can be used to increase channel utilization.

16. Suppose we were to use some form of time-division multiplexing, but instead of skipping a slot in the case of detecting an empty buffer, we continued to search until data from another buffer was found. In that case, what kind of information must we add to each slot before sending the entire frame?

17. Explain what is meant by "layered communication protocols".

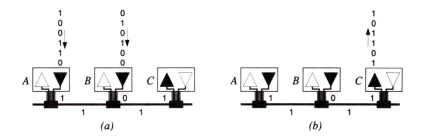

Figure 8.1 The effect of colliding messages, at the start (a) and end (b) of transmission.

8.2.1 General problems with broadcast channels

As we have already mentioned, broadcast channels impose a fundamental problem. Assuming that we do not use multiplexing techniques, we must prevent two stations simultaneously attempting to put information on the channel for garbled data will be the result. As an introduction to the following sections, we first concentrate on how these problems can be handled in general.

Message collision and detection

Let's start by considering what the result of simultaneous transmission over a broadcast channel might be. Suppose we have three stations A, B, and C, respectively, which share the same broadcast channel as shown in Figure 8.1. Station A wants to transmit the bit string $\langle 1011001 \rangle$, whereas B simultaneously wants to transmit $\langle 0001010 \rangle$. For simplicity, we assume that when both a 1 and a 0 are transmitted across the channel by different stations, the result signal will be 1 as well. This means that if A and B simultaneously transmit their bit strings, the first bit that will be received by station C will be 1, as shown in Figure 8.1(a). The final result, of course, will be the bit string $\langle 1011001 \rangle + \langle 0001010 \rangle = \langle 1011011 \rangle$ as shown in Figure 8.1(b). Indeed, this bit string is to be considered as rubbish as there was no station that sent it. We say that the messages that have been sent by A and B have **collided**.

Now clearly, collided messages is something we do not want and they should be discarded completely. But in order to do so, we must have a means of *detecting* a collision. Different techniques can be applied for detecting that things went wrong; one particular scheme is discussed here. The point is that while a station is transmitting a bit string across a channel, it is also in a position to *listen* at what is being transmitted on that channel at the same time. This is illustrated in Figure 8.2(a) where station B notices that although it is transmitting a 0, it is receiving only a 1. Consequently, it has to conclude that something went wrong. A similar situation occurs for station A, although much later as illustrated in Figure 8.2(b).

But what about station C? From its perspective it seems to be receiving just another bit string. One way or the other, C will also have to know that this bit string is indeed rubbish. The solution is quite simple. When a station transmits a message, it adds information to

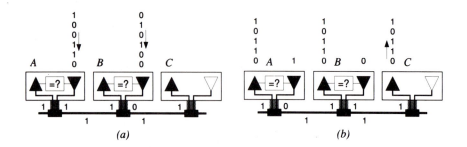

Figure 8.2 Detecting collisions by station *B* (a) and *A* (b).

that message that will allow for error detection by the receiver. This is in principle no different from the techniques that were discussed in Section 7.2.3. Note that we are here explicitly permitting errors through message collision, and are relying on error detection as a means of detecting collisions.

Getting exclusive access

Now that we have seen what can happen when two stations simultaneously transmit a message, we should start addressing the question of how exclusive access to a channel can be obtained. Here we are confronted with a fundamental problem. In order to agree on which station may access the channel, the stations will have to communicate. The only medium that they have at their disposal to do this is the same channel to which they need exclusive access. Therefore, special measures will have to be taken. Roughly, three types of techniques can be distinguished for controlling access to the channel:

- Exercise **no control** at all, i.e. simply let a station try to use the channel, and take appropriate measures when it finds that its message has collided with another message. This rather anarchic approach, applied to so-called **contention systems**, will work well when channels are not used intensively. The converse is the case when network traffic is heavy.

- Employ a **round-robin** technique, in which each station in turn is given an opportunity to use the channel. In practice, networks based on this technique make use of a so-called **token** that is circulated between stations. A token is a message acting as a marker. The station that has the token may use the channel. These systems work well when network traffic is high, but they are not very efficient when only a few stations wish to transmit.

- Let a station place a **reservation** for the channel. In practice, this happens by reserving so-called **slots**, which is an amount of time that a station can reserve for transmission. The problem here, however, is how to make a reservation. As we shall see, this need not really be difficult.

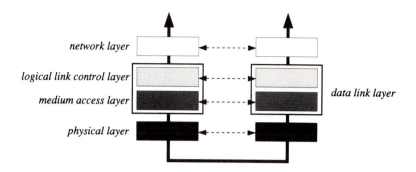

Figure 8.3 The position of the medium access and the logical link control layer in the OSI model.

In the remainder of this section we shall take a closer look at the way that broadcast channels can be shared between a number of stations. The protocols we describe here form an important part of OSI's data link layer. In fact, they are so important that they have been recognized as a separate sublayer, generally referred to as the **medium access layer**, positioned in the lower layers of the OSI model as shown in Figure 8.3. The sublayer that forms the upper part of the data link layer is referred to as the **logical link control layer**. We shall concentrate primarily on protocols that have been widely accepted, and have gone through a process of *standardization*. In what follows two types of systems each using a different access strategy are discussed: contention systems, and collision-free systems, the latter containing round-robin and reservation techniques.

8.2.2 Contention systems

Probably the simplest way of sharing a broadcast channel is allowing its stations to use it simultaneously. The point of these contention systems is that stations try to transmit something via the channel, and withdraw if they notice that something is wrong. After withdrawal, they make a new attempt, mostly after having waited a certain time. In order to appreciate the standardized version of contention systems, let's look at some protocols based on this principle, starting with a rather crude one for the sake of illustration.

▷ **ALOHA protocol**

As a first example, consider the so-called **pure ALOHA protocol** implemented at the University of Hawaii in the 1970s. In pure ALOHA systems stations simply transmit a frame whenever they need to. If the frame is destroyed, i.e. if it collides with another frame, the transmitter waits a random amount of time and makes a new attempt to transmit it. There are two characteristic features of this protocol: (1) a frame is always transmitted in its entirety, and (2) the channel is sensed *after* transmission has started. The sender will continue to retransmit the frame until no collision has been detected. Indeed, this is a rather crude method for getting access to a channel. Nevertheless, if we analyze the performance of this protocol, things are not as bad as they may seem. It can be readily shown that the **utilization** of a channel using the ALOHA protocol can be as high as 18%. This means that if we measure the frame traffic across the channel during 100 time units, and measure how much time is used for the *successful* transmission of frames, then this will be as much as 18 time units. The rest of the time is just wasted. The channel is either not used at all or is used for transmitting frames that will have to be retransmitted later.

Of course, much better protocols exist. For example, by letting stations attempt to transmit a frame during predefined time slots it can be shown that maximum utilization can be doubled. We will leave these matters at this point and continue with presenting protocols that are now in far more widespread use than those employed in ALOHA systems. We shall return to performance issues in Section 8.2.4.

▷ **CSMA protocols**

The problem with ALOHA protocols is that stations do not make use of the fact that the propagation time in a LAN for a frame is relatively short. Because the distance between any two stations in a LAN is short, a transmitted signal arrives at all stations almost immediately. Consequently, it makes sense for a station first to check if any other station is currently transmitting a frame. If this is the case, it is useless to start a frame transmission, and instead, the station should wait until the channel is free. Protocols that obey this rule are generally known as **carrier sense multiple access** (CSMA) protocols. Two types of CSMA protocols are briefly discussed here: non-persistent and persistent.

Non-persistent CSMA.   With a simple CSMA protocol a station starts with sensing the channel before trying to send a frame. Then, if the channel is free, the frame is sent, otherwise some *random* amount of time is allowed to pass before making another attempt. That this will indeed work is illustrated by considering what you often do when phoning someone and find that the line is busy. In that case, you will make a second attempt after having waited a few minutes. The underlying idea is that you *expect* that phone calls will generally take only a few minutes, and that phones are not continuously being used.

But the analogy with making phone calls also illustrates a problem that is inherent in non-persistent CSMA, for we may have a situation where a station is voluntarily waiting before making its next retransmission attempt, while in fact, the channel may be free. In other words, we are wasting transmission capacity. The solution is found in simply allowing a station to be more selfish.

p-Persistent CSMA.   A more greedy approach is followed by the **p-persistent CSMA** protocol. In this case, stations are allowed to make an attempt for transmitting a frame only at specific moments. What happens is the following. If a station finds that the channel is not being used, it will start transmission with probability p. If it decides not to start transmission (with probability $1 - p$), it waits a full **time slot** before making the next decision whether to start transmission. A time slot, in this case, is a predetermined fixed amount of time. On the other hand, if the channel is occupied, the station will simply wait until it becomes free, and then make the decision to start its transmission or not.

An important question is how large p should be. One extreme is to take $p = 1$, i.e. a station will never be prepared to wait voluntarily another time slot, but instead immediately starts frame transmission as soon as it detects that the channel is no longer occupied. This **1-persistent CSMA** protocol is not very efficient in heavily loaded systems as it can be expected that collisions may occur frequently because no station is prepared to delay starting its transmission. In practice, efficiency is improved by allowing stations that have noticed that a collision occurred to wait a random amount of time before making another attempt. Another extreme is to take $p = 0$. In this case the number of collisions will be zero as well, as each station is now prepared to wait indefinitely before starting transmission. In other words, there will be no frame transmissions at all. Indeed, a 0-persistent CSMA protocol makes no sense.

Finding the right value for p is not simple. For example, if it is expected that network traffic is low, i.e. that there will be relatively few frame transmissions, it is wise to choose $p \approx 1$. But if network traffic is heavy, having p close to 1 will lead to a catastrophe. Many collisions will occur and stations are repeatedly forced to make a new attempt to retransmit their frame. Meanwhile, new senders will appear on the scene making matters even worse. In the end, we may find ourselves in a situation in which the efficiency rapidly decreases to zero. In these cases, p should have been chosen close to zero, but, as can be seen, this does mean that stations will often unnecessarily wait before transmission in the case of light network traffic. For these reasons, more flexible protocols needed to be devised.

CSMA with collision detection

A widely used family of protocols in local area networks are the so-called **CSMA/CD** protocols, which stands for **carrier sense multiple access with collision detection**. This family of protocols is so widely applied that it has led to a standardization by the IEEE, referred to as IEEE 802.3. In contrast to the protocols described above, CSMA/CD prescribes that stations immediately abort transmission of a frame as soon as they detect a collision. As in the case of CSMA protocols, a distinction is made between persistent and non-persistent CSMA/CD protocols.

Probably the most famous CSMA/CD protocol is its 1-persistent version, generally referred to as **Ethernet**. The Ethernet standard is widely applied to local area networks. The standard stands for a family of implementations, in which distinctions are made between the diameter of the cable and whether or not a tree topology is supported. The standard transmission rate is 10 Mbps. Being 1-persistent CSMA/CD means in this case that stations will follow three steps in order to access the channel:

1. The station first listens to see whether the channel is free. Transmission is delayed until the instant the channel is no longer used.

2. During transmission, the station keeps listening in order to detect a possible collision. If a collision occurs, transmission immediately stops.

3. If a collision occurs, the station waits a random amount of time, and proceeds with the first step again.

Waiting some time after detection of a collision is essential in order to allow the protocol to work. In practice, the time to wait is chosen at random, with a mean value that doubles with every unsuccessful transmission attempt. If a collision still occurs after 16 attempts, the station will simply stop trying and report an error.

▷ Now let's take a closer look at the impact of a collision in CSMA/CD networks. The important point is the time it takes for a station to detect that something is wrong. We have argued that due to the fact that the propagation time of signals through a LAN is extremely short, we may assume that signals have been received *immediately*. However, this statement does not hold if we want to say something sensible about collision detection. Therefore, following our notation as introduced in Chapter 7, we denote the propagation time for a signal to travel from a sender to a receiver by T_{prop}. Again, the frame transmission time is denoted by T_{frame}.

Now, considering Figure 8.4, suppose we have two stations, A and B, connected to the same channel, and that A starts to transmit a frame F_A at time t. Of course, B cannot detect that A is transmitting F_A before the head of frame F_A has reached B, which will take T_{prop} time units. If B starts to transmit a frame F_B at time $t + T_{prop} - \delta$, where $0 \leq \delta < T_{prop}$, we have a problem. First, B is going to detect that its own frame collides with frame F_A at time $t + T_{prop}$, and so it will stop transmitting F_B. But we are already too late, because frame F_A will have been corrupted by the first signals that were sent by B. Consequently, A will have to stop transmitting as well. However, the first time that A can detect that a collision occurred is at time $t + 2T_{prop} - \delta$, because by then the first signals of frame F_B will have reached station A. Consequently, a station can never be sure that the head of its frame has reached its destination for at least $2T_{prop}$ time units after it started transmission.

What does this mean? First, it implies that if we want to use the CSMA/CD protocol, we have to take into account that whenever two frames are to be transmitted, at least $2T_{prop}$ time units will have to elapse before transmission of the second frame. This period of time is referred to as the **contention period** T_{cont}. It is during the contention period that collisions can occur. Note that the contention period is in fact "wasted time": we are not allowed to use the channel. This is no problem when T_{prop} is small and frames are relatively long (i.e. the frame transmission time $T_{frame} \gg T_{prop}$), but matters deteriorate when either T_{prop} increases or frames become shorter and transmission rates higher. (Note that these timing analyses are completely analogous to those presented in Section 7.3. The difference lies in the fact that we are now concerned with detecting when two frames collide, rather than synchronizing the transmission rate between a sender and a receiver.)

8.2.3 Collision-free systems

Contention systems are based on the principle that stations are allowed to start transmitting a message simultaneously. Special measures will have to be taken when a collision occurs. By detecting collisions and subsequently retransmitting frames, we can ensure

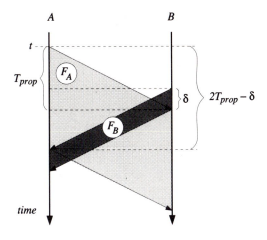

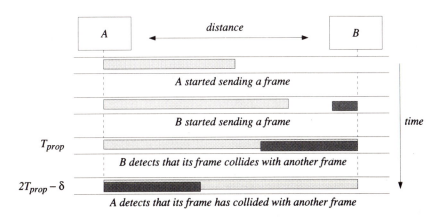

Figure 8.4 The detection of collisions in CSMA/CD protocols requiring a contention period of $2T_{\text{prop}}$.

that frames, in the end, will travel through the channel to their receiver(s). But obviously, each frame that has collided is a wasted frame, and it would seem worth looking at protocols in which collision would simply never occur. In this section, we shall briefly consider three collision-free protocols.

Token ring protocol

One particular example of a collision-free protocol is the so-called **token ring** protocol. This protocol (which has been standardized as IEEE 802.5) is used for LANs that are *physically* organized as a ring. A small frame, called a **token**, is continuously circulated from one station to another. If a station wants to transmit a frame, the first thing it should do

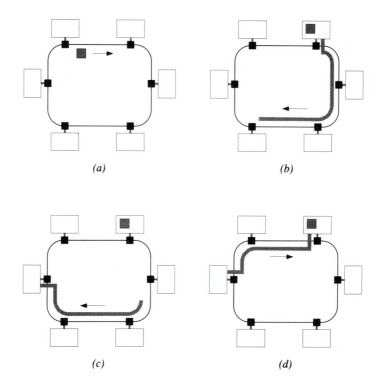

Figure 8.5 The token ring mechanism: a token circulates (a), which is then claimed by a station that subsequently starts transmission (b). The frame arrives at its destination (c), and is later removed from the ring by its sender (d).

is to claim the token. As soon as the token arrives, the station removes it from the ring and starts transmitting its frame. Because the frame is broadcast to every other station in the LAN, it will not only be received at the intended destination but will eventually also reach the station that sent it. In this way, the station will know when the frame has been completely transmitted so that it can then put the token back on the ring again. This principle is illustrated in Figure 8.5.

The principle of a token ring mechanism is quite simple. It is essential that stations each have an opportunity to transmit their data. Because a token is passed from station to station in accordance to their circular ordering, no station will be excluded from transmission. This is an important distinction from the CSMA/CD strategy where randomness is used as the basis for selection among competing stations.

▷ It is also not difficult to incorporate some priority scheme as well. Let's see how this principle works.

Using priorities. To simplify matters, assume we wish to make a distinction between two priorities, and that stations operating at a low priority should be excluded from transmitting their frame as long as there are stations which have a high-priority frame to send. (In reality, the IEEE 802.5 standard for token ring networks makes a distinction between eight priorities.) In this case, we can devise a simple scheme in which a low priority is indicated by 0, and a high priority by 1. If F is a frame, denote by $prior(F)$ the **reserved priority** at F. Likewise, denote by $prior(T)$ the current priority of the token, and by $prior(S)$ the priority of a station S. Adding a two-level priority is then expressed by the following algorithm.

Algorithm 8.1. Two-level priority scheme for token ring networks. The algorithm expresses what a station S should do in order to send a frame.

1. Wait until either a frame F or the token T arrives.

2. If a frame F arrives, then set $prior(F) \leftarrow \max\{prior(F), prior(S)\}$ and forward F (with its adjusted reserved priority) to the neighboring station. Note that the priority that is now reserved at F is the highest requested by any station that has received F. Continue with Step 1.

3. If the token T arrives, and $prior(T) > prior(S)$, then simply forward the token to the neighboring station, and continue with Step 1.

4. If the token T arrives, and $prior(T) = prior(S)$, then simply send your own frame F through the ring after having set $prior(F)$ to 0. Eventually, F will be returned with a possibly adjusted value for $prior(F)$. As soon as F returns, forward the token with its priority set to $prior(F)$, i.e. $prior(T) \leftarrow prior(F)$. Stop.

□

It is not difficult to see that this scheme will work. The essence lies in the priority reservation at a frame F that is currently in transmission. Any high-priority station that wants to transmit a frame instructs the currently transmitting station to insert a high-priority token as soon as its transmission has been completed. From that moment, only high-priority stations can transmit frames, and again, in a round-robin way. As soon as there is no more high-priority data to send (indicated by the fact that $prior(F) = 0$ for the frame presently in transmission), a low-priority token is inserted in the ring so that the other stations will have an opportunity to transmit data.

In practice, token ring systems admit more than just two priorities, and eight priority levels are generally supported. In that case, the algorithm becomes slightly more complicated, although the principle remains the same. The interested reader is referred to Stallings (1993b) for further details.

However, when comparing the token ring mechanism to CSMA/CD systems, there are also some potential flaws that have to be taken into account. First, tokens, like frames, can become lost due to transmission errors. Another source of error is a malfunctioning station. For example, assume a station has just transmitted a frame and, after transmission, crashes. In that case, the frame will continuously circulate through the ring as nothing has the authority to remove it. To solve these problems, token ring networks always have a special station which is elected as the **network monitor**.

The network monitor.   To illustrate, suppose that, for one reason or another, the token is lost. In order to detect this event, the network monitor uses a simple timeout mechanism. Each time the token or a frame passes, a timer is set to the maximum time that is needed to circulate it. If this timer expires, the network monitor will simply insert a new token into the ring. Detecting circulating frames is also easy. As soon as a frame passes the network monitor, it simply *marks* that frame. Clearly, if a marked frame passes the monitor, it should be removed as it has already circulated through the entire ring. In that case, the original sender of the frame has failed to remove it. The monitor removes the marked frame and inserts the token into the ring.

An interesting question is what happens when the monitor itself fails to work properly. First, we must have a means of knowing that there *is* a monitor present. This is not too difficult. The monitor simply inserts a control frame from time to time to indicate that it is still present. This control frame is received by every other station, so there's nothing to worry about. But suppose now that the monitor fails. In that case, the other stations will notice that there is no longer a monitor available, and a new monitor will have to be **elected**. Without going into too much detail, stations can start issuing election frames, stating that they are candidates to act as network monitor. As soon as each election frame has passed all other stations, enough information is known to select the next monitor.

But the real problems start when the ring breaks down, for example because a station is no longer capable of forwarding the token or frames. In many cases, such a situation cannot be resolved by automatic recovery means, implying that a human operator will have to intervene. This is not a disadvantage as long as the usage of the network is not critical. For example, in many offices it is acceptable that the network shuts down completely in order to upgrade the system or undertake repairs. In factories where networks need to be exceptionally reliable, this procedure is not acceptable and another solution is needed.

Token bus protocol

In contrast to token ring systems, the **token bus** protocol is used in those situations in which the LAN is organized in a bus or tree topology. The main difference from the token ring protocol is that each station in a token bus system has equal rights when keeping the network active. In particular, management of faults is not performed by a single monitor, but instead is distributed between the various stations. In a token bus system there is, as in token ring networks, a token that circulates between the various stations. In particular, the stations are *logically* organized as a ring but *physically* organized in a bus or tree topology, as shown in Figure 8.6. The token bus protocol has also been standardized by the IEEE (802.4).

The working of a token bus network is in principle the same as that of a token ring system. Whenever a station wants to transmit a frame, it waits until it receives the token from its (logical) neighbor, removes the token from the ring and broadcasts the frame on the network. When frame transmission is completed, the token is forwarded to its other neighbor. The main difference between the two systems lies in the management of the logical ring. We first briefly consider some issues to illustrate the increased complexity compared to the token ring systems described above.

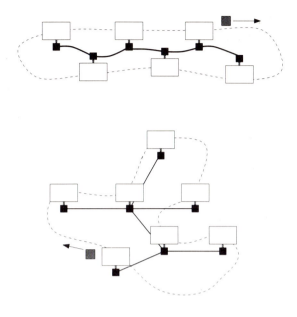

Figure 8.6 The organization of a token bus network.

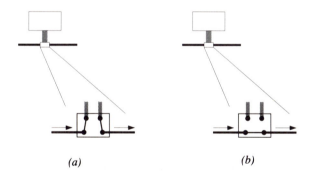

(a)   *(b)*

Figure 8.7 Setting a switch for participation (a), or no participation (b) of a station in a token ring network.

Removing a station from the bus. Let's start with the simplest issue, namely shutting down a station. In a token ring system each station is physically connected to the ring by means of a switch as shown in Figure 8.7. When this switch is open, frames are simply passed to the station. When this switch is closed, as shown in Figure 8.7, frames will simply pass by the station to its neighbor. Shutting down in that case can be done simply by closing the switch. In the case of a token bus network, however, we have to do a lot more work instead.

If station S_i wants to shut down in a token bus network it will first have to wait until it receives the token. It then transmits a frame to its logical *predecessor* S_{i-1} stating that it will no longer participate in the ring, and that the logical successor of S_{i-1} will now be S_{i+1}, the former successor of station S_i. As soon as S_{i-1} receives the frame, it will simply forward a new token to S_{i+1}. In this way, we have reconfigured the logical ring.

Adding a station to the bus.   But what if a station wants to enter the token bus network? With token ring systems we (in principle) simply have to open the switch in Figure 8.7. For token bus systems, this simple scheme cannot be used. Instead, each time a station S_i is holding the token it will broadcast over the bus a small *solicit-successor* frame to all stations, including those that are not yet participating in the logical ring. This frame contains the identification of S_i and its present successor S_{i+1}. It is important to note that this frame can indeed be received by all stations that are connected to the bus. Three possible responses can then be transmitted:

- **No response** can be returned, implying that there is no station that wants to enter the logical ring. In that case, S_i can forward the token as before.

- There is precisely **one response**, say from station S_{new}. In this case, there is also no real problem. Station S_i simply forwards the token to S_{new}, who then knows that it may now participate in the ring with S_{i+1} as its successor.

- There are **several responses**. No problem you might say: if S_{new} and S_{new}^* responded, simply let S_i decide how to reconfigure the ring by sending the appropriate configuration information to S_{new} and S_{new}^*. But there *is* a problem. Because both new stations are announcing their respective arrivals at the same time, the only information that will reach S_i is that two messages have collided. In other words, it detects rubbish on the bus, and the only thing it can conclude is that several stations want to join.

  In this case, it transmits a *resolve-contention* frame and waits for a number of time slots, say four. These time slots are important. The point is that each station has a unique (hard-wired) identification, represented as a binary number. Now, during the first time slot, only those stations with a number starting with "00" are allowed to respond; during the second slot, stations with their number starting with "01" may respond, etc. In this way, station S_i imposes an *ordering* on the responses of the stations that want to join the ring, so that message collision may be avoided, allowing proper reconfiguration of the ring. Of course, two stations whose identification number starts with the same two bits will still cause message collision. In this case they will have to try later (after having waited a random amount of time).

It should be clear that letting a new station join the ring is much more complex than is the case with token ring networks.

Token problems.   Problems with tokens can be particularly difficult. Let's focus on the situation where the token is lost. Detecting this is not too difficult. If there is no activity on the ring for some time (again, we have to detect this by means of a timeout mechanism), *all* stations can come to the conclusion that there is no token. So they try to transmit a new token. Obviously, in the end, only one station should succeed in doing so. The solution is like adding new stations. First, stations broadcast a *claim-token* frame. If message collisions occurs, each station can conclude that there are more claimants on the ring. Consequently, each station will decide for itself to wait for a specific number of time slots before sending the next claim-token frame. If, at any moment, message collision does *not* occur, then this means that a station has succeeded in transmitting its claim-token frame. It is that station that may then insert a new token, and the logical ring is active again. The other stations simply join in exactly the same way as described above.

We leave these matters at this point. The issue that should be clear by now is that token bus systems are far more intricate than token ring systems in terms of management. The intricacies are a result of the distributed nature of token bus management. Because all stations share equal responsibility for managing the network, they have to follow a distributed decision-making policy in order to reach a common agreement. The advantage of this scheme is that token bus systems are extremely reliable. For example, if one station malfunctions, its tasks with respect to network management are taken over completely by the remaining stations. Only in exceptional cases is it necessary for a human operator to intervene. For this reason alone, token bus systems have been widely applied in factory automation and process control.

▷ **Using time slots**

Both token-based protocols are typical implementations of access strategies that employ round-robin control. As a last example, let's consider a simple reservation system that is based on the use of time slots in bus-based systems.

Suppose we have a network with N stations. We introduce a contention period $T_{cont} \geq 2T_{prop}$ consisting of N time slots. Again, no two frames are ever transmitted in sequence by the same sender before T_{cont} time units have elapsed. Within these T_{cont} time units we distinguish N time slots each lasting T_{cont}/N time units. Now if station S_i wants to transmit a frame, it starts with transmitting a 1 during the ith slot of the contention period. No other station is allowed to transmit during this slot. Because each station indicates whether it wants to transmit a frame, it should be clear that after the contention period has elapsed it is known to all stations who are the competitors for the channel. This knowledge can then be used *jointly* to allocate the channel to one of the stations.

For example, we can agree to allow the station with the highest number to use the channel for transmitting its frame. A fairer strategy is to allocate the channel in turn. For example, suppose during the first contention period we detect that stations $S_1, \ldots, S_k$ want to transmit a frame. We then let S_1 transmit its frame, so we are left with contenders $S_2, \ldots, S_k$. Now assume that during the second contention period, $S_1^*, \ldots, S_n^*$ also indicate that they want to use the channel. It can then be jointly decided that S_2 can use the channel, and that S_1^* will have to wait until S_k has finished its transmission. What we are effectively doing is maintaining a queue of competitors at each station, following a first-come first-serve strategy.

The important point to note here is that by *globally* indicating that a station wants to use the channel it can be decided *locally* by each station when it is permitted to use the channel, using an allocation policy known by each station. In other words, we have found a way to arrive at a commonly agreed final decision whereas the making of that decision is completely distributed. This is an important decision-making policy to which we shall return a number of times throughout this book. Several improvements in using time slots can be made. Most attempt to avoid the situation where a station can start transmission only after the contention period has elapsed. We shall not go into any details here, but instead refer the interested reader to Tanenbaum (1988).

▷ ## 8.2.4 On the performance of broadcast channels

At this point, let's concentrate on seeing which network protocol is the best by focusing on the issue of performance.

Preliminaries

Basically, the performance of a network protocol is dependent on the number of active stations on the channel, the length and frequency of the messages, and the supported transmission rate, or **bandwidth** of the medium. Performance itself can be roughly expressed in three different ways:

- In terms of **throughput**, performance is expressed as the number of bits that are sent per time unit. Overhead bits, i.e. those which are also transmitted merely to make a protocol work, are not taken into account.

- In the case of **channel utilization**, we concentrate on the ratio of the number of bits that we wish to send, and the ones that we have to send in order for a frame transmission to succeed. We encountered this measure in our discussion of ALOHA protocols.

- Finally, it is also possible to measure various forms of **delays**. For example, the performance can be expressed as the mean transfer time between the moment a sender first attempts to transmit a frame and the moment it arrives successfully at the receiver.

In the following, we shall describe performance mainly in terms of throughput and utilization.

Now let's see what we can say about performance by merely looking at the two types of systems we have discussed so far. First, it can be expected that contention protocols work pretty well in systems where channel traffic is not heavy. The opposite will be the case with collision-free systems. This distinction is not too surprising when giving the matter some thought:

1. When taking a closer look at collision-free systems it is seen that a more or less fixed amount of overhead in the form of a circulating token is introduced to avoid collisions. This is acceptable when collisions can be expected to occur frequently, but not when it is known that the channel is seldom used. In the latter case, we will be forcing a station to do a lot of work to avoid a collision that will probably not happen in any case.

2. In contention systems there is nothing related to avoiding collisions; instead, collisions are simply corrected when they happen. When only a few corrections can be expected (i.e. retransmissions in the case of frame collision), it is worth doing this to avoid administrative overhead. But if many collisions are going to occur and stations are permitted to transmit frames on an *ad hoc* basis, we may find the stations in the network continuously correcting collisions rather than successfully transmitting information.

This is analogous to having traffic lights on a road crossing. When there is little traffic, traffic lights slow down access to the crossing. On the other hand, with heavy traffic and no traffic lights there is very low throughput; having traffic lights in that case at least guarantees a certain throughput. This qualitative reasoning reveals that protocols such as Ethernet may be in a difficult position when network traffic increases. And, in fact, they are.

Of course, more can be said if a more detailed analysis is made. To make matters not too complicated, we would like to have a single parameter that can be used for the analysis of the performance of a local network. In practice, the so-called **normalized propagation delay** is used. This parameter, denoted as **a**, is defined as:

$$\mathbf{a} \;=\; \frac{T_{\text{prop}}}{T_{\text{frame}}} \tag{8.1}$$

where T_{prop} denotes the propagation time, and T_{frame} the frame transmission time. Another way of looking at the value of **a** is interpreting it as *the maximum number of frames that can be in transmission* at a given time.

For example, suppose that $\mathbf{a} = 1$. In that case, we have $T_{\text{prop}} = T_{\text{frame}}$. Now, what does this mean? If the propagation time is the same as the frame transmission time, then by the time the *first* bit of a frame reaches the receiver (which is after T_{prop} time units), the *last* bit of that frame will just have been forwarded to the channel (which takes place after T_{frame} time units). Clearly, this implies that when $\mathbf{a} = 1$, at most one frame can be in transmission. A similar reasoning will show that if $\mathbf{a} = 2$, implying that $T_{\text{prop}} = 2T_{\text{frame}}$, at most *two* frames can be in transmission at the same time. It should now be clear that if $\mathbf{a} \gg 1$, we are dealing with the situation where many frames *can* be in transmission. This was the case with satellite communication in the previous chapter.

But suppose now that $\mathbf{a} \ll 1$. This can happen on several occasions:

- We have managed to keep the propagation time low, which is generally the case with LANs in which frames have to travel over at most a few kilometers.

- Our frames are relatively large, say at least a few hundred bytes. This can also be the case in LANs.

- The transmission rate is relatively low, so that, in combination with the frame size, the frame transmission time is large compared to the propagation time.

And indeed, when observing LANs, it will generally be the case that $\mathbf{a} < 1$. But this situation will not hold for very long. The need for extremely high transmission rates and smaller frame sizes is going to put some protocols in a difficult position, as we shall see in the next two sections.

Contention systems

We first look at contention systems. Based on an analysis found in Metcalfe and Boggs (1976), Stallings (1993b) derives the following formula for expressing the channel utilization S of CSMA/CD networks:

$$S \;=\; \frac{1}{1 + 2 \cdot \mathbf{a} \cdot (1 - A)/A} \tag{8.2}$$

where A denotes the maximum probability that precisely one station attempts to transmit and the others do not. Assuming that *any* station will make an attempt to transmit a frame during a single contention period with probability $1/N$, it can be shown that

$$A \;=\; (1 - 1/N)^{N-1}$$

in which N denotes the number of (active) stations in the network. Now what does this formula say? First, note that the number of stations N hardly has an impact on S. For example, when $N = 5$ we have $A \approx 0.41$ which is almost the minimum value for A (which is approximately 0.37). Assuming that there are generally more than five active stations, it is therefore in order to take the minimum value for A for our calculation of S, so that we can roughly state that for average to large CSMA/CD networks, we have

$$S \;\approx\; \frac{1}{1 + 3.44 \cdot \mathbf{a}} \tag{8.3}$$

Consequently, the predominant factor that determines the utilization is $\mathbf{a}$. If $\mathbf{a} \ll 1$, as is the case in many CSMA/CD networks, channel utilization will be good. In practice, $\mathbf{a}$ will lie somewhere between 0.05 and 0.1 for most of these types of networks.

But the real problems start if we want to employ CSMA/CD protocols, but with higher transmission rates than currently practiced. For example, suppose we increase the transmission rate by a factor 10 (and keeping the same frame length), effectively meaning that $\mathbf{a}$ increases by a factor 10 as well. If our original value for $\mathbf{a}$ was 0.05, we will see the utilization drop from 85% to a mere 37%. For this reason CSMA/CD protocols will probably have to be replaced by more efficient ones in the near future.

Token-based systems

In token-based systems, the situation is much better. First, it can be shown that channel utilization in the case of token ring networks is equal to:

$$
S = \begin{cases} \dfrac{1}{1 + \mathbf{a}/N} & \text{if } \mathbf{a} \le 1 \\[2ex] \dfrac{1}{\mathbf{a}(1 + 1/N)} & \text{if } \mathbf{a} > 1 \end{cases}
\tag{8.4}
$$

Token bus systems are logically equivalent to token ring systems, and if we assume that the token in a token bus system is always sent to the physically nearest active station, the same formula for S can be derived (see Stallings, 1993b, for further details).

It can be seen from equation (8.4) that token-based systems will outperform CSMA/CD based systems, especially in systems for which **a** remains smaller than 1. In those cases, almost regardless of the number of active stations, channel utilization will be approximately 1, which, of course, is the best one can hope for. Problems will arise, however, as soon **a** increases beyond 1. In those cases, a practical solution is simply to keep the physical length of the ring in accordance with the frame size, i.e. make the ring shorter, effectively returning **a** to 1.

8.3   Interconnecting LANs

Local area networks have proved to be extremely successful, and the result is that their application increases at a steady pace. This also means that there is an increasing demand on them with respect to the amount of stations that they can support, as well as the rates with which they support the transmission of data. In fact, we have gradually reached a situation in which it is impossible to scale networks simply using the technology described in the previous section. Instead, large-scale LANs supporting hundreds of stations and high transmission rates are presently built by connecting a collection of smaller LANs. In this section we shall explore how such large-scale LANs are actually constructed.

8.3.1   Constructing large, high-speed networks

Simply scaling existing LANs by adding an increasing number of stations is a means towards a dead end. The problems are caused by the fact that we wish to increase the transmission rate (which reduces the frame transmission time), and at the same time also physically expand the LAN in order to cover a geographically wider area (which increases the propagation time). In order to attain higher efficiencies, we should allow the network to be used for the simultaneous transmission of several frames instead of one. This can be achieved by dividing the network into smaller units each primarily accounting for *local* traffic. Alternatively, if we connect existing LANs without adopting the full-blown broadcast mechanism, we can achieve the same goal. And this is what is done in practice.

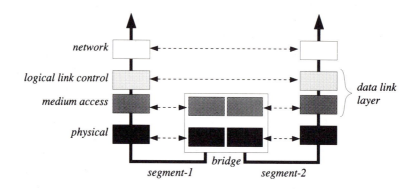

Figure 8.8 Connecting two LANs by means of a bridge.

▷ As we have argued previously, scaling a LAN in size and time effectively means that the normalized propagation delay **a** increases. In other words, the maximum amount of frames that *can* be in transmission increases. In order to attain that maximum, we will simply need to allow several frames to be in transmission at the same time.

The concept of a bridge

In practice, scalability of LANs is realized by connecting several so-called **LAN segments** together. A LAN segment is just another LAN, but having only relatively few stations attached to it. For example, a LAN segment may be constructed as an Ethernet network with, say, 25 stations all sited on the same floor of a department. In general, each LAN segment also forms a *logical* group in the sense that stations within the same segment generally require services from only those stations that are connected to the same segment. Occasionally, services may be needed from stations connected to other segments. LAN segments are connected to each other by so-called bridges.

A **bridge** is a device that picks up a frame from one LAN and subsequently forwards the frame to another LAN. Logically, bridges span the physical and medium access layer of the OSI model, as shown in Figure 8.8. Spanning the physical layer means that bridges are like any other station in the network with respect to their physical layer. They are connected to other stations in a LAN segment using the same connectors, transmission media, etc. In particular, they can pick up and transmit frames like any other station, the only difference being the fact that they are connected to at least two physically distinct LANs.

But the real difference from ordinary stations lies in the implementation of the medium access layer. For example, a bridge can be constructed to connect two CSMA/CD segments which use the same medium access protocol but which operate at different transmission rates. The bridge is then responsible for forwarding frames from one segment to another taking different transmission rates into account. For example, suppose a bridge connects segment L_1 operating at 10 Mbps with a segment L_2 operating at 4 Mbps. If a frame is sent from L_1 to L_2, the bridge will first have to receive and store the frame at a rate of 10 Mbps, and subsequently transmit it on L_2 at the much slower rate of 4 Mbps. You can imagine that although this scheme seems perfectly in order, we may find ourselves in difficulties if the rate at which frames are sent from L_1 to L_2 is high. The bridge will have to store these frames while it is still forwarding previous ones onto L_2. Consequently, we may encounter storage problems if the amount of available memory at the bridge gradually declines.

Bridges are also responsible for adapting frame sizes, a parameter which is defined by the protocol used in the medium access layer. For example, if frame transmission in segment L_1 is based on frames of length n, each frame F on L_1 and which is intended for segment L_2 will have to be converted to a frame F^* of length n^* that corresponds to the medium access protocol used in segment L_2. If $n \leq n^*$ conversion is no problem: the bridge simply adds a number of bits. When $n > n^*$ we will find ourselves in difficulties. Splitting F into smaller subframes is out of the question as no medium access protocol can handle fragmented frames as a frame is always assumed to be the only logically coherent unit of transmission data. In these cases, a bridge will have to discard conversion completely, i.e. the frame F cannot be forwarded to L_2.

Other problems with respect to converting frames from one segment to another exist, but will not be further discussed here as these highly technical problems more or less fall outside the scope of this book. Instead, we shall focus on two important general issues. In the remainder of this subsection we shall take a closer look at interconnection topologies, particularly so-called backbone networks. In the next section, the problem of routing frames through a network is discussed – an issue which is also important when dealing with wide area networks.

Interconnection topologies

Probably the most simple scheme for connecting a series of LANs is by cascading the segments as illustrated in Figure 8.9(a). What we have then is a very large, linear ordered LAN. Although this is an extremely simple way to scale a LAN it is not a very good one. The problem is that inter-segment traffic may have to cross segments for which it is not intended. For example, if station A wants to send a frame to station B as shown in Figure 8.9(a), the frame will have to be forwarded through all intermediate segments, unnecessarily burdening the traffic for each of those segments. For this reason, it is generally not acceptable to cascade more than two or three segments. An alternative solution is to use **multiport bridges** which enable more than two segments to be directly connected as shown in Figure 8.9(b). In general, multiport bridges allow up to a maximum of five to ten segments to be connected. A typical use of multiport bridges is to connect a number of segments in one building.

An interesting interconnection topology is the one based on a so-called **backbone**. A backbone is a LAN in its own right, although no user generally ever sees it. The point is that the bridges themselves are organized into a LAN as shown in Figure 8.10. A backbone serves only one purpose: connecting networks together. In principle, it can be built using exactly the same technology as used for each of the LAN segments that it connects.

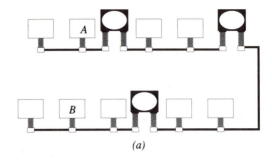

(a)

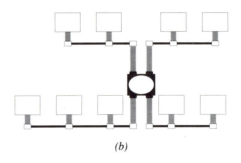

(b)

Figure 8.9   The construction of a LAN by cascading a number of segments (a) or using multiport bridges (b).

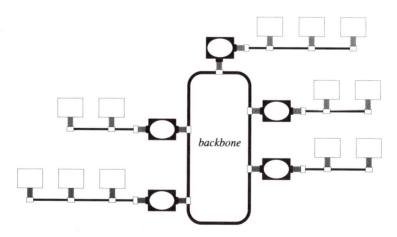

Figure 8.10 Using a backbone to connect multiple LAN segments.

However, if no special measures are taken, it can be easily seen that a backbone may become a bottleneck when intersegment traffic steadily increases. First, a backbone is often used to connect segments which are geographically distributed over a wider area than each of the LAN segments. Consequently, the physical length of a backbone may become so large that propagation times may start to be a problem. Second, backbones need to serve *all* the stations in each of the LAN segments. Consequently, if intersegment traffic increases (for whatever reason) we must ensure that transmission rates are extremely high or otherwise we will soon have the same problems encountered when a single segment is expanded by simply adding more stations.

To account for high transmission rates, two different techniques are generally employed which we shall briefly discuss here. The first employs an optical fiber-based ring technology which can support transmission rates of 100 Mbps. The second is a bus-based technology which supports transmission rates of 35–150 Mbps, and which can employ either fiber or electric transmission media.

FDDI. The **fiber distributed data interface** (**FDDI**) standard is used to connect a series of bridges into a token ring network. However, there are a number of important differences from the IEEE 802.5 standard for token ring networks. First, an FDDI-network consists of *two* (logical) rings, the second being available either as a backup facility or as an additional means of transmission. Furthermore, an FDDI-based backbone operates at a transmission rate of 100 Mbps. An important difference from the IEEE 802.5 token ring network described previously is the following. In the latter configuration, a token was retransmitted over the ring as soon as the transmitted frame reached its sending station again. In contrast, a station connected to an FDDI network transmits the token immediately after it has transmitted a frame. In other words, a sending station does not wait until the frame it has sent has been circulated entirely around the ring.

Another important distinction from the IEEE 802.5 token ring networks is that FDDI networks support a mixture of *asynchronous* and *synchronous* data. Asynchronous data consists of frames that can be sent at random time intervals. For example, when a large amount of text is to be transmitted from one station to another in, say, N_{text} successive frames, it is unimportant when exactly each frame arrives at its destination. The only issue is that all frames are successively transmitted. On the other hand, suppose we wish to transmit (digital) signals that constitute speech or video. In that case, it is essential that the data arrives at regular intervals due to the fact that speech or video is inherently "continuous". This is a typical example of synchronous data.

The point is to allow a station S to transmit synchronous data during a fixed time slot T_{sync} as soon as it has received the token. The time slot is assigned on a per-station basis. Consequently, some stations may be allowed to transmit synchronous data during a longer period than other stations. In addition, a common agreement is made between the stations concerning the time that it should take them to circulate the token around the ring once. This circulation time will be much longer than the minimum amount of time needed to circulate the token. If we denote this circulation time as T_{token}, then a station S that has transmitted the token at time t may *expect* that the token is received again at time $t + T_{token}$. Assume station S receives the token at time t^*. Then, two situations need to be distinguished:

1. $t^* < t + T_{\text{token}} - T_{\text{sync}}$. In this case, station S first transmits synchronous data during its time slot of T_{sync} time units. It then may have time to transmit asynchronous data, and may do so until time $t + T_{\text{token}}$. If there is no asynchronous data to be sent, the token is immediately transmitted to the next station.

2. $t^* \geq t + T_{\text{token}} - T_{\text{sync}}$. In this case, station S is allowed to transmit synchronous data only during its time slot of T_{sync} time units after which it must immediately forward the token to the next station. Note that if $T_{\text{sync}} = 0$ for station S, then in this case S is not allowed to transmit any data, despite the fact that it has received the token.

An important observation of this scheme is that synchronous data is not only sent during a fixed time slot (which is essential when transmitting "continuous" data such as speech and video), it is also given a higher transmission priority than asynchronous data. And indeed, such an assignment of priorities is perfectly justified.

DQDB.   An alternative to FDDI networks are backbones adhering to the **distributed-queue dual-bus (DQDB)** protocol. The DQDB standard has been developed to interconnect LANs over a relatively large geographical area. A standard has been adopted by the IEEE for its definition of metropolitan area networks (MANs).

The principal architecture of a DQDB network is shown in Figure 8.11(a). The network is organized into two bus-based subnets A and B. In contrast to ordinary bus networks, however, frames are now transmitted in only one direction. In particular, on bus A frames are transmitted *upstream* from station S_0 to station S_{N-1}, whereas on bus B they are transmitted *downstream* from S_{N-1} to S_0. Moreover, both endstations S_0 and S_{N-1} transmit frames at a regular time interval. Frames on bus A or B can be either empty or full.

The principal operation of a DQDB network is shown in Figure 8.11(b) and can be explained as follows. Suppose a station S_i wants to transmit a frame to another station S_j. If $i < j$, it will need to do so by means of bus A, otherwise the frame will have to be transmitted via bus B. Without loss of generality, assume that $i < j$, i.e. S_i wants to transmit a frame to an *upstream* neighbor S_j.

Frames in a DQDB network contain two additional bits: a **busy bit** indicating that the frame already contains data, and a **request bit** indicating that a frame has been requested by a station. In our case, station S_i will need to claim an empty frame which is going upstream towards S_j. Claiming the first empty frame will not do, for the simple reason that it is not fair to other stations located upstream that want to send a message upstream as well. Instead, stations will first have to issue a request for an empty frame. This is done through the frames going downstream, i.e. those transmitted across bus B. The crux of the matter lies in the fact that the request bit of frames going downstream can be set only by stations that want to send a message to an upstream station. Also, we are assuming that each station can have at most one outstanding request for an empty frame.

In our case, station S_i will continuously sense bus B for frames, thereby counting the number N_{req}^A of frames of which the request bit has been set to 1. At the same time, it will keep track of the frames transmitted upstream (i.e. on bus A) of which the busy bit is set to 0, indicating that the frame is empty. Each time an empty frame is detected on bus A,

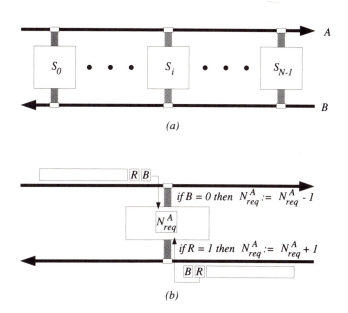

Figure 8.11 The architecture of a DQDB network (a) and its principal operation (b).

N_{req}^A is decremented. Consequently, N_{req}^A denotes the number of *outstanding* requests for empty frames on bus A as recorded by station S_i.

The moment that S_i wants to transmit a frame to S_j it will wait until the first downstream frame (i.e. on bus B) arrives of which the request bit is still set to 0. S_i subsequently sets the request bit of this frame to 1. In addition, it records the current value of N_{req}^A which denotes the number of outstanding or preceding requests for empty frames on bus A. As soon as N_{req}^A empty frames on bus A have passed S_i, it can use the next empty frame to transmit its data to station S_j.

An important observation of the DQDB protocol is that the channel is used efficiently regardless of the traffic load. When there are very few frames to transmit by any station, a station will always record a small number of outstanding requests for empty frames. Consequently, it will be able to access the network with only a small delay. On the other hand, when many frames are to be transmitted, a station need only wait until a frame is transmitted with its request bit set to 0. As can easily be seen, the worst situation that can happen is when there are $N-1$ outstanding requests for frames. But after that, the station will be able to access the network. What this means is that with a minimum of overhead, stations in a DQDB network maintain a distributed queue of requests for empty frames.

Finally, we note that like FDDI networks, the DQDB protocol supports transmission of synchronous and asynchronous data. To that end, a number of prioritized request bits are put into a frame, instead of only one. We shall not go into detail here, but instead refer the interested reader to Stallings (1993b).

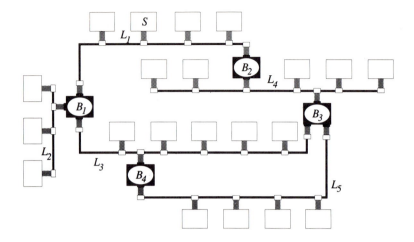

Figure 8.12 A network containing a cycle.

8.3.2 Routing between LANs

We have now come to a point at which we can construct fairly large local and metropolitan networks by interconnecting LAN segments by means of bridges. In essence, these larger networks use the same technology as the smaller LAN segments. A frame transmitted by a station S will in principle be broadcast to all other stations on the network. The role of a bridge is in principle rather modest. If it connects several LANs $L_1, \ldots, L_N$, then a frame transmitted on one of these LANs, say L_i, will be forwarded to LANs $L_1, \ldots, L_{i-1}$, $L_{i+1}, \ldots, L_N$. However, if we rigorously adhered to this simple forwarding scheme, we might find ourselves in difficulties. To illustrate, suppose we construct the network shown in Figure 8.12.

Now assume that station S transmits a frame F on L_1. Based on the forwarding scheme just mentioned, bridge B_1 will then forward F to L_2 and L_3. Denote these copies of F as F_{12} and F_{13}, respectively, where the subscript reflects the LANs through which the frame is transmitted. Similarly, bridge B_2 will pass the frame on to LAN L_4, resulting in a copy F_{14}. Now observe what happens with respect to bridge B_3. First, because it detects that frame F is on L_4 (in the form of its copy F_{14}), it will forward F to L_3, leading to a copy F_{143}. At that point, L_3 will have received *two* copies of F: F_{13} via bridge B_1 and F_{143} via B_3. This implies that all stations that are part of L_3 will receive F twice. Clearly, this was not our intention. But matters become worse. Because F was also forwarded via B_1 onto L_3, bridge B_3 will pick up copy F_{13} as well and pass it on to L_4, leading to another copy F_{134}. In other words, L_4 also receives two copies of F: F_{14} and F_{134}.

Now let's concentrate on F_{134}. It should be clear by now that this copy will be forwarded to L_1 (leading to frame F_{1341}), which is subsequently forwarded to L_2 (F_{13412}) and L_3 (F_{13413}). At that point, we have generated *three* copies of the original frame F for LAN L_3. The end of the story can easily be imagined: we are completely flooding the network with an endless stream of copies of the frame F. We are not only broadcasting the

Table 8.1 An example of a routing table for the network shown in Figure 8.12.

	L_1	L_2	L_3	L_4	L_5
L_1	—	B_1	B_1	B_2	B_2
L_2	B_1	—	B_1	B_1	B_1
L_3	B_1	B_1	—	B_3	B_4
L_4	B_2	B_2	B_3	—	B_3
L_5	B_3	B_4	B_4	B_3	—

frame to each station, we are also generating an infinite number of copies to all stations. Our broadcast is being performed rather too well.

What we need to do is deliberately **route** the frame through the network in such a way that each station will receive it exactly once. In fact, an even better policy would be to route the frame only to that LAN segment where its destination is sited. Decisions concerning a route will at least partially have to be made by bridges. In the following two subsections we will take a closer look at three commonly applied routing strategies.

Static routing

Probably the simplest way to avoid trouble is to provide a fixed **routing table**. For example, reconsider the network shown in Figure 8.12. Table 8.1 shows a possible routing table **R** for this network. Each LAN segment is represented by a row and a column, whereas each entry $\mathbf{R}(i, j)$ indicates the *first* bridge that should forward a frame that is to be transmitted from LAN L_i to L_j. So, for example, if a station on L_4 wants to send a frame to a station on LAN L_2, bridge B_2 will forward the frame from L_4 to L_1, after which it will reach L_2 via bridge B_1.

Static routing is extremely simple and is widely applied to relatively small local area networks. For reasons of maintenance, the routing table is often stored at a central location. If the topology of the network changes it will be necessary to adapt the table at only one place. However, we will encounter problems as the network grows, as each bridge will have to obtain its routing information from this central location. And as networks grow, the rate at which the network changes increases as well. In large networks, stations and bridges may occasionally fail to work properly, giving rise to the need to change routes dynamically.

Spanning tree

Our need for routing came from the fact that we could easily flood the network when transmitting only one frame. In essence, our problems were a result of the fact that there could be more than one way to get a frame from LAN L to L^*. It is not difficult to see that if there were always precisely one route for a frame to be in transmission, delivering several copies to the same LAN would not occur. And if the mere existence of alternative

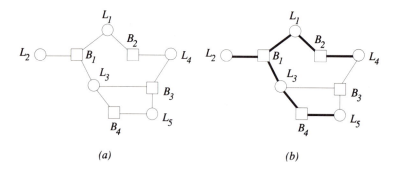

Figure 8.13 The representation of a network as a graph (a), and a tree spanning all its LANs (b).

routes is the problem, why not eliminate them in the first place? Of course, in view of possible failing connections, it is not such a bad idea to have some alternatives routes. If one bridge crashes, its task can be taken over by another. However, from a routing point of view, we have seen that alternative routes cause problems.

A solution to this problem can be found by first considering the network as a graph where the nodes are formed by the LAN segments and the bridges. For example, the network from Figure 8.12 can be represented by the graph shown in Figure 8.13(a). In Figure 8.13(b) we see a possible connection scheme through which all LANs are still connected, but now there is only one route between each two LANs. This connection scheme is an example of a **spanning tree**. The point is that when we are dealing with a network in which two LANs are connected by alternative routes (meaning that its corresponding graph will contain at least one cycle), we search for a subgraph that connects all LANs but in which alternative routes are no longer present. Frame transmission is then only allowed across the connection scheme corresponding to this spanning tree. For example, if we adopt the spanning tree shown in Figure 8.13, then a frame originating at L_4 will be forwarded to L_1 via bridge B_2, and subsequently forwarded to L_2 and L_3 via bridge B_1, and finally to L_5 via B_4. Note that bridge B_3 has effectively been disabled.

There are two important issues related to adopting routing by means of a spanning tree which we shall briefly discuss here. First, bridges can determine a spanning tree for the complete network without having to make use of centralized information. This means that each bridge can gradually update its own local administration in such a way that eventually all bridges in the network will have reached agreement on the same spanning tree. Second, bridges can also gradually construct an administration that provides them with information on how LAN segments are organized, i.e. which station is on which segment. This information will allow a bridge to forward frames *selectively*. Let's consider these two issues in more detail.

▷ **Finding a spanning tree.** In order to find a spanning tree in a distributed way, we assume that each bridge has a unique identification number. If bridge B is connected to LAN segment L, it will transmit its identification number to each other bridge that is connected to L as well. Consequently, per LAN segment it can be determined which bridge has the lowest identification number. Initially, the one with the lowest number is selected as the *root bridge*. So, per segment, there will initially be one root bridge. This can be illustrated by the network shown in Figure 8.13(a). Assume that bridge B_1 has identification number 3, whereas B_2, B_3 and B_4 have numbers 11, 10, and 8, respectively. Then, per LAN we have initially the following selection of root bridges:

bridge	id	L_1	L_2	L_3	L_4	L_5
B_1	3	√	√	√	–	–
B_2	11	–	–	–	–	–
B_3	10	–	–	–	√	–
B_4	8	–	–	–	–	√

Now the point is that eventually, there should only be one root bridge, and that all other bridges know how they are connected to this bridge. First, see what happens with bridge B_4. It initially detected that it is the root bridge for segment L_5, but not for L_3 which had bridge B_1 as its root. Instead, it will record that it is now directly connected through L_3 from B_1, which it expects to become the final root bridge.

The fact that B_4 is located at distance 1 from the expected root is forwarded by B_4 on LAN L_5, where it will be picked up by bridge B_3. At that point, bridge B_3 can record that it is located at distance 2 from B_1, and transmits the information to LAN segment L_4.

Meanwhile, bridge B_2 discovered that it could never be the root bridge for either L_1 or L_4. However, it will also find that its distance to B_1 (again, the expected root bridge for the entire network) is only one LAN segment away, and passes this information via segment L_4 to bridge B_3. So what happens at B_3? Although it found that it was located at distance 2 from B_1, it now concludes that messages for segment L_4 can be forwarded via a shorter route (namely via B_2). Similarly, it also knows that messages for L_5 are already forwarded via bridge B_4. It therefore draws the conclusion that it can play no role at all with respect to forwarding messages, and effectively disables itself by discarding any future messages passed to it via any LAN to which it is connected. The result is the spanning tree shown in Figure 8.13(b).

Locating stations. Now, a spanning tree gives information on how frames between the various LANs are to be routed. Its says nothing about frame transmission between stations. In this sense, a spanning tree is merely used to facilitate efficient broadcasts of frames over the entire network. But, of course, broadcasting frames may not be a wise thing to do. Instead, if frames could be routed directly from source to destination, we would be using the network more efficiently. And indeed, this can also be achieved once we have arrived at a point where a spanning tree has been agreed upon by all bridges. The idea is quite simple. Consider the five LANs shown in Figure 8.14. (Note that we may now assume that the network topology corresponds to that of a tree.) Now suppose bridge B_3 receives (for the first time) a frame *sent* by station S. At that point B_3 can store the fact that frames which are to be *received* by station S should always be sent via LAN L_3. This also means that if bridge B_3 notices that a frame destined for station S is being transmitted on LAN L_4, it need not forward this frame to LAN L_5, but can resort to just forwarding the frame onto L_3.

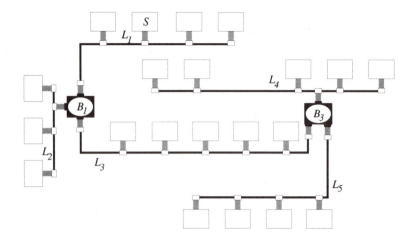

Figure 8.14 An example of five LANs connected by two bridges.

So what have we accomplished? First, we have illustrated that bridges can jointly determine a spanning tree over an interconnected network that will allow them to broadcast frames efficiently. Second, bridges can also locally determine that it may be senseless to forward frames to every segment they connect. Putting these two facts together, we conclude that in an interconnected network it is possible to determine efficient routing schemes (i.e. schemes that generate a minimum amount of network traffic) between stations without making use of centralized information, and, moreover, that these schemes can be determined dynamically. The implication of this observation is significant. Suppose that we repeat the construction of a spanning tree from time to time, and also reconstruct all local information concerning the exact location of stations on a periodic basis. In that case, it should be clear that we can add and remove stations and LAN segments without having to update any *global* information on the network manually. In other words, changing the network now reduces to simply connecting a station, or updating a bridge without having to be concerned with other stations or segments. The network will simply find out "by itself" what it looks like. A powerful property indeed. Bridges that cooperatively build a spanning tree, and which discover where stations are located, are called **transparent bridges**

Source routing

Although the spanning tree approach has the benefit of flexibility, there is also a price to be paid. The main drawback lies in the fact that bridges such as B_3 in our example become redundant. The primary role is that of a standby bridge in case any of the other bridges fails to work. Another drawback is that network traffic now only takes place according to the spanning tree, which may not be a well-balanced strategy if we are concerned about dividing the work between the various bridges and segments. As an alternative to the spanning tree approach, routing frames through an interconnected network can also take place according to the so-called **source routing** strategy. The basic idea underlying this strategy is that a sending station explicitly provides the route that a frame is to follow. Note that this does imply that the frame now contains not only data that is to be transmitted but additional information on the route as well. This is an important distinction with the spanning tree approach. In that case, stations merely transmitted frames on their LAN segment; the bridges would ensure that they arrived at their proper destination.

Now, it should be clear that in order to transmit a frame, the topology of the interconnected network should be available to the sending station. How does this information get there? To explain how a station can find a route, we first need to discuss the various types of frames that can be transmitted. In the extension of the IEEE 802.5 standard, dealing with source routing bridges, the following four types of **route directives** are distinguished:

- A **null directive** indicates that a frame should be delivered to all stations only on the same segment to which the sending station is connected.

- A **non-broadcast directive** specifies a unique route that is to be followed. The route is given as an alternating sequence of LAN and bridge numbers respectively.

- An **all-routes broadcast** indicates that the frame is to be forwarded over all possible routes in the network. As we have illustrated, this may imply that several copies of the frame will arrive at the receiver. It is there that the responsibility lies to discard any copies. The protocol avoids cyclic transmission of frames.

- A **single-route broadcast** implies that the frame is to be sent to each station, but only once. In effect, this means sending the frame according to a spanning tree.

In order to select a route from source to destination, the sending station first transmits a single-route request frame. This frame will eventually arrive at all stations, but only the destination will respond by transmitting an all-routes frame. Consequently, the sending frame will eventually receive multiple copies of this response, where each copy corresponds to a unique route between the source and the destination. After storing this information, the sending station can subsequently choose which route frames are to follow when transmitting data to the selected destination station. The criterion for choosing a route may be based on the length of the route or the expected amount of traffic.

The real problem with source routing is that discovering the collection of alternative routes between each (source, destination) pair is quite costly. Once this is done, however, spreading the load over the network can be much better than in the case of the spanning tree approach. However, the additional amount of work for discovering routes is generally a reason for not using source routing but for adhering to the spanning tree approach.

8.4   Basic network interfacing

At this point it should be clear that we can in principle construct large networks connecting tens to hundreds of stations. The principles of the underlying technology that we have discussed so far allows one station to send a frame to another station without having to be bothered about the fact whether the frame will arrive (it will), whether any other stations are transmitting as well (they are, but who cares?), and how a frame will get to its destination (the routing is being taken care of). As long as a station has an identification of the destination(s) of a frame, the network technology discussed so far ensures that the frame will get there.

This may all seem fine, but it is not really getting us much further in light of the discussion we had in Chapter 6 on communicating processes. There, we described how we could build *software solutions* that reflected the way we would want communication to take place. So far, we have essentially only described the solutions that provide us with the *means to connect computers* and getting a bit string, i.e. a frame, from one computer to another. It is time that we paid some attention to how these means can be applied to implement our communication models. And it is perhaps also here where normally the real intricacies of computer networks surface. The problems lie not so much in the concepts that are applied but much more in the level of abstraction that is pursued to explain them, reflected by a completely new language and terminology which often hides the underlying principles. This is not the approach that we wish to follow in this book. Instead, we feel that it is much better to introduce concepts at a relatively low level of abstraction by almost immediately giving some idea on how they can be implemented. It is our belief that this will allow you to understand more easily the concepts and terminology that are usually employed.

In the remainder of the book we *are* going to raise the level of abstraction. But before doing so we are first going to explain a number of important concepts following the approach outlined above. In this section we shall concentrate entirely on two issues: (1) how we can *access* a network by means of software, and (2) how we can *exchange information* in terms of software. The first issue has everything to do with network interfacing; the second with formatting frames such that they can be exchanged between software components.

This section is going to form a basis for the main topic of Section 8.5: the principle of devising computer networks in terms of **protocol suites**. In essence, we wish to construct a complete computer network only in terms of layers of communication protocols. Moreover, it should be possible to have several of these networks exist simultaneously, i.e. make use of the same hardware.

8.4.1   Networks as peripheral devices

Let's start with a relatively simple problem: how does a network manifest itself to a computer? At first, this may seem a rather puzzling question in view of the discussions we had so far. But, in fact, when you think about it, we have not described in any way how we can actually construct a frame and ensure that it gets transmitted on a network. In other words, we have not been very specific about the **network interface**. On the other hand, finding an answer to the question is really not that difficult from the perspective of a computer. In that case, a network can be considered as merely a peripheral device to which data can be transferred and from which data can be received. This also suggests how a network manifests itself: by means of a special I/O controller, referred to as the **network controller**. Transferring data to and from a network is then as usual, namely through registers associated with the network controller. This is best illustrated by means of an example of a hypothetical (and somewhat simplified) network interface for our PRI-MAL processor. In order to understand the essentials of network interfacing, the reader is encouraged to study the following example, although some parts may be skipped on first reading; these are indicated in the usual way.

The hardware interface

Imagine that our network controller allows us to transmit and receive frames adhering to some simple medium access control protocol. In particular, we assume that we have hardware support for sending and receiving a single frame containing a fixed amount of 1024 bytes of data. Frames are always buffered by the network controller, to which end it has *two* buffers: an **input buffer** for storing frames that come from the network and an **output buffer** for storing frames that are to be transmitted. If the input buffer is full, receipt of new frames is not possible. The controller's input buffer is assumed to be memory-mapped to locations $0, 1, \ldots, 1023$ (recall that each memory location of the PRIMAL processor contains one byte); the output buffer is mapped to locations $1024, \ldots, 2047$. The single 8-bit register NETCTRL is mapped to address 2048, and operates as follows. The 8 bits are grouped into three logical units as shown in Table 8.2.

Normally, the controller will either be ready to receive any incoming data, or in the case that it also has to transmit a frame, will at the same time make an attempt to send the frame stored in the output buffer. Being able to receive a frame while at the same time an attempt is being made to send one is very important. Suppose that station S_1 tries to send a frame to station S_2, and *at the same time* S_2 is making an attempt to send something to S_1. If we had only one buffer at each station, then clearly communication between the two would immediately come to a halt (generally referred to as a **deadlock**). Compare this to synchronous communication as discussed in Chapter 6 and you will find a strong similarity.

Clearly, the network controller distinguishes four kinds of actions, determined by the first two bits of NETCTRL. If the controller was prepared to receive a frame, indicated by the fact that the second bit is set to 1, this bit will automatically be reset by the hardware to 0 as soon as a frame is received. On that occasion, the controller will generate an interrupt (say interrupt number 7). Similarly, an interrupt is also generated as soon as a frame has been transmitted, causing the first bit to switch from 1 to 0. The remaining bits can always be inspected to see what caused the interrupt. If everything proceeds as planned, the last 4 bits will be set to $\langle 0000 \rangle$, otherwise they will indicate the kind of error that occurred (of which the specification is not important here).

To illustrate how transmission might work, suppose we wish to send the contents of

Table 8.2 The specification of the register NETCTRL for our example network controller

bit string	meaning
	CONTROL INFORMATION
00 xx xxxx	Idle: the controller will not do anything.
01 xx xxxx	Ready to receive: any incoming frame will be stored in the input buffer.
10 xx xxxx	Sending: the data stored in the output buffer is to be transmitted across the network.
11 xx xxxx	Ready to receive, and making an attempt to send as well.
	INTERRUPT INFORMATION
xx 00 xxxx	Nothing has happened so far.
xx 01 xxxx	Data has just been received.
xx 10 xxxx	Data has just been sent.
xx 11 xxxx	Data has been sent and received.
	ERROR INFORMATION
xx xx eeee	A 4-bit error code, with ⟨0000⟩ indicating that everything is correct.

the output buffer across the network. In that case, we simply need to set the first bit of NETCTRL to 1, and the controller will do its work. Completion of transmission is indicated by setting the first bit back to 0 and generating an interrupt, which is then there for us to handle. Two situations may occur when an interrupt is generated. The transmission of the frame was either completed (indicated by setting the third bit to 1) or a new frame had arrived in the meantime (indicated by the setting of the fourth bit). How these interrupts can be handled is discussed further below.

A question that comes to mind is how we are going to identify stations. Without going into too much detail, you can imagine that each station has a unique **address**. The hardware has, one way or the other, access to that address. Now, in order to send a frame to a specific station, we need to incorporate its address into the transmitted data. Because we are making use of broadcast channels, the data will be sent to each station. Upon arrival at a station, that station will first check if the address is the same as its own. If so, the frame is stored in the controller's buffer (if possible). Otherwise, it is simply discarded. (What is exactly meant by the latter is left as an exercise for the reader.)

It should now be clear that frame reception may fail for two reasons: (1) there was simply no station willing to pick up the frame, i.e. the destination address was not recognized by any network controller, or (2) the destination station did not have its receipt bit enabled. It is important to note that frame transmission itself was successful as far as the

```
type ERROR_CODE is (NO_ERROR, ... );
for ERROR_CODE'SIZE use 4;

type CONTROL_REGISTER is
   record
      sendFrame : BOOLEAN; −− for instructing the controller to send data.
      receiveFrame : BOOLEAN; −− for instructing to receive data.
      frameSent : BOOLEAN; −− set by the controller when a frame has been sent.
      frameReceived : BOOLEAN; −− set by the controller upon arrival of a frame.
      error : ERROR_CODE; −− indicates a possible error.
   end record ;

for CONTROL_REGISTER use
   record
      sendFrame at 0 range 0..0;
      receiveFrame at 0 range 1..1;
      frameSent at 0 range 2..2;
      frameReceived at 0 range 3..3;
      error at 0 range 4..7;
   end record ;

for CONTROL_REGISTER'SIZE use 8;
```

Listing 8.1 The definition of NETCTRL expressed in BASAL.

medium access control layer is concerned. In other words, the hardware ensures that a frame is sent over the network correctly. However, if the destination did not exist, or was simply not willing or able to pick up any frames, it is impossible for the medium access control layer to correct this situation. The only thing that can be done at that point is to indicate the status of the transmission through the error code bits of register NETCTRL.

▷ **The software interface: data types**

At this point, we can construct a piece of software that will allow us to send and receive frames. Let's start by taking a look at how we can describe the register NETCTRL in terms of BASAL. To that end, we choose to distinguish the first four bits of NETCTRL by means of Boolean variables and the last four by means of a separate date type ERROR_CODE to see what could have gone wrong when communication failed. This leads to the data types, and their mapping in terms of bit strings, as shown in Listing 8.1.

The data type CONTROL_REGISTER is the description of the register NETCTRL. It is important to note that the mapping of this data type onto main memory corresponds precisely to the organization of the bits in the register, where we assume that a BOOLEAN can indeed be represented by only one bit. In our case, FALSE will correspond to a 0 and TRUE to 1. Consequently, the only thing we need to do is declare the following variable:

```
networkController : CONTROL_REGISTER;
for networkController use at 2048;
```

and the compiler will arrange things in such a way that we can instruct the network controller what to do.

```
subtype ADDRESS is INTEGER range 0..16777215;
for ADDRESS'SIZE use 3*8;

type USERDATA is array (1..1021) of MEMORY.BYTE;
for USERDATA'SIZE use 1021*8;

type FRAME_FORMAT is
   record
      destination : ADDRESS;
      data : USERDATA;
   end RECORD;

for FRAME_FORMAT use
   record
      destination at 0 range 0..23;
      data at 3 range 0..8167;
   end record ;

for FRAME_FORMAT'SIZE use 1024*8;

inputBuffer : FRAME_FORMAT;
outputBuffer : FRAME_FORMAT;
for inputBuffer use at 0;
for outputBuffer use at 1024;
```

Listing 8.2 The (data) declarations for sending and receiving frames.

Our next step is defining the buffer. Anticipating our discussion on addressing in the next section, assume that each station can be uniquely identified by means of a 24-bit binary number (meaning that addresses lie between 0 and $2^{24} - 1 = 16\,777\,215$). Also, when sending a frame, this address should be the first data that is to be transmitted. This leaves a total of 1021 bytes for the rest of the data to be sent. Expressing this in BASAL leads to the declarations shown in Listing 8.2. We assume that the basic data type MEMORY.BYTE is already available, and that its size is precisely 8 bits.

▷ **The software interface: services**

By now, it should not be too difficult to imagine how we can actually send and receive frames, although there are some things that are rather difficult. First, we assume that any process can send or receive frames. This implies that we have to protect the network controller's register and buffers against simultaneous access by several processes. (Anticipating our further discussion, we shall see that in practice there will be only one process handling all incoming and outgoing data, making the need for protection against simultaneous access obsolete.) But there is more. Suppose that a transmitting process has just sent a frame across the network. While it is waiting for transmission to complete, no other process should be allowed to submit a frame for transmission. However, it should still be possible to *receive* frames. A similar situation holds for receiving processes. Although no other process should be allowed to wait for the receipt of a frame, sending a frame should still be possible. The solution to this problem can be found in using two different semaphores:

```
procedure REQUEST(frame : in FRAME_FORMAT) is
begin
    SEMAPHORE.WAIT(senderLock);
    outputBuffer := frame;
    confirmation := FALSE;
    networkController.sendFrame := TRUE;
end REQUEST;
```

Listing 8.3 An implementation for sending at the MAC layer.

- senderLock that is used to prevent more than one process to send a frame, i.e. manipulate the output buffer, and

- receiverLock used to prevent several processes manipulating the input buffer at the same time.

We note that a sender and receiver will *never* manipulate the same bits of register NETCTRL. Therefore, we need not use a semaphore for protection against simultaneous access of the bits of NETCTRL.[1]

Instead of constructing the "usual" procedures that will allow us to send and receive frames, we are going to stay close to what is defined by the OSI reference model when it comes to the MAC layer. OSI defines three basic **services** that should be provided by the MAC layer:

- A service REQUEST that will allow a process to issue a request for the transmission of a frame. What this means is that a frame is merely stored in the output buffer, and the controller is instructed to start sending that frame. The requesting process need not wait until transmission has taken place.

- The service CONFIRMATION is a signal that is to be returned to the sending process to indicate that the frame has been successfully transmitted. In our case, we assume this implies that the frame reached the receiver, although it could possibly not be stored.

- Finally, the service INDICATION can be seen as a signal generated at the receiver's end to indicate that a frame has just arrived and is stored in the input buffer.

Sending a frame. Let's concentrate on sending frames. First, we need a means for requesting the transmission of a frame, which, in our case, means filling the output buffer with the frame to be sent. Second, we should also allow a process to wait until the transmission can be confirmed. In any case, as long as there is no confirmation, other processes should be prohibited from submitting a frame for transmission. Filling the output buffer is rather straightforward, and can be expressed by the procedure REQUEST shown in Listing 8.3. The Boolean variable confirmation is used as a semaphore, and needs to be initialized to FALSE. This will be explained below.

---

[1] There is a much better reason for us to avoid this additional semaphore: we may safely assume that any BASAL statement involving register NETCTRL is atomic. In that case, we need only ensure that during the translation of BASAL to PRIMAL, the compiler will generate code that makes use of this atomicity property. How this can be achieved is not further discussed here.

Note that the only thing that can be done is to fill the output buffer and instruct the controller to start transmission. By using the semaphore senderLock we prohibit any other process from submitting a transmission request as well. Of course, when transmission is completed, other senders should be allowed to enter the scene. Because the controller will generate an interrupt as soon as transmission completes, we can deal with these matters by means of a BASAL interrupt procedure. In our case, the controller is associated with interrupt number 7, so that we can specify the following interrupt procedure:

```
procedure NETWORK_INTERRUPT;
for NETWORK_INTERRUPT'CALL use at 7;
```

Let's first concentrate on what needs to be done when the controller generates an interrupt because it has just emptied its output buffer. In that case, (1) new senders should be allowed to submit requests, and (2) a process waiting for this confirmation should be informed. The first issue simply implies that the semaphore senderLock should be SIGNALed. In order to let a process wait for confirmation, we introduce a semaphore confirmation, that will now need to be SIGNALed by the interrupt procedure as well.[2] This semaphore has already been introduced as a Boolean variable. This leads to our first version of NETWORK_INTERRUPT:

```
procedure NETWORK_INTERRUPT is
begin
   if networkController.frameSent then
      networkController.frameSent := FALSE;
      SEMAPHORE.SIGNAL(confirmation); -- acknowledge that sending took place
      SEMAPHORE.SIGNAL(senderLock); -- allow other senders to proceed
   end if ;
end NETWORK_INTERRUPT;
```

Finally, in order to allow for a process to wait for confirmation, we introduce an additional procedure WAIT_FOR_CONFIRMATION with the obvious straightforward implementation:

```
procedure WAIT_FOR_CONFIRMATION is
begin
   SEMAPHORE.WAIT(confirmation);
end WAIT_FOR_CONFIRMATION;
```

An interesting aspect of our implementation is that it allows for blocking as well as non-blocking transmission of frames. This depends entirely on whether the sending process calls the procedure WAIT_FOR_CONFIRMATION. However, in order to ensure that a process indeed blocks whenever it wants to wait for a confirmation, we have to be sure that the value of the semaphore is initially set to FALSE when requesting the transmission of a frame. This explains the initialization of confirmation in the procedure REQUEST above.

Receiving a frame. Now consider the receipt of a frame. The additional problem we are confronted with here is that although no one is waiting for an incoming frame, a frame

---

[2]We note at this point that although this mechanism works in principle, realizing it in the case of device drivers can be difficult. We will not go into details here, as they are not important for the principal working of device drivers in general.

```
procedure ACCEPT(frame : out FRAME_FORMAT; done : out BOOLEAN) is
begin
    SEMAPHORE.WAIT(receiverLock);
    if networkController.frameReceived then
        frame := inputBuffer;
        networkController.frameReceived := FALSE; -- the buffer has been emptied
        networkController.receiveFrame := TRUE; -- another frame can be received
        done := TRUE;
    else
        indication := FALSE; -- explained below
        done := FALSE;
    end if ;
    SEMAPHORE.SIGNAL(receiverLock);
end ACCEPT;
```

Listing 8.4 The procedure ACCEPT for receiving an incoming frame.

may still arrive. Consequently, if a process wants to receive a frame, it will first have to inspect whether a frame has already arrived (by inspecting networkController.frameReceived). From there on, there are two options. The process should continue immediately, regardless whether a frame has arrived, or it should be allowed to wait until a frame has arrived.

Checking to see if something had arrived is straightforward and can be expressed by means of the procedure ACCEPT shown in Listing 8.4. First, the receiving process gains exclusive access to the input buffer by WAITing for the semaphore receiverLock to become TRUE. It then inspects whether a frame has already arrived by inspecting the value of frameReceived which is always set to TRUE by the interrupt controller upon the receipt of a frame in the input buffer. If a frame has already arrived, it simply copies the contents of the input buffer, and stops. By setting frameReceived back to FALSE it indicates that the input buffer has been emptied. Also, it explicitly instructs the controller to receive frames when they arrive (recall that the controller sets receiveFrame to FALSE when the input buffer is full). The Boolean variable indication is analogous to the use of confirmation, and is explained below.

If no frame has arrived, a process should be able to wait for one. Analogous to sending frames, we use a semaphore indication embedded in the following procedure:

```
procedure WAIT_FOR_INDICATION is
begin
    SEMAPHORE.WAIT(indication);
end WAIT_FOR_INDICATION;
```

Again, we must ensure that if a process finds that no frame has arrived, it should block until one does if it wants to wait for an indication. To that end, we initialize the semaphore indication to FALSE as shown in the procedure ACCEPT.

By now, it should be clear what our interrupt procedure should look like. As soon as the controller generates an interrupt and finds that it has just filled the input buffer, it simply SIGNALs the semaphore indication. However, we also have to take into account that the interrupt was generated because a frame had just been transmitted. This leads to the adaptation of our interrupt procedure shown in Listing 8.5.

```
procedure NETWORK_INTERRUPT is
begin
    if networkController.frameSent then
        networkController.frameSent := FALSE;
        SEMAPHORE.SIGNAL(confirmation); -- acknowledge that transmission took place
        SEMAPHORE.SIGNAL(senderLock); -- allow other senders to proceed
    end if ;
    if networkController.frameReceived then
        SEMAPHORE.SIGNAL(indication); -- warn the process waiting for an incoming frame
    end if ;
end NETWORK_INTERRUPT;
```

Listing 8.5 The adapted interrupt network interrupt handler.

The complete picture

We have now reached an important point: access to the network, as far as its hardware counterpart is concerned, can be completely hidden. Indeed, we may expect that a microkernel implementation provides a simple package specification that allows frames to be communicated across the network by means of at most four procedure calls. Ignoring the way that data types are to be mapped onto main memory, we assume that the package MAC_LAYER as shown in Listing 8.6 is at our disposal. Most implementation details have been given above. Note that we are still assuming that errors will never occur. We leave it as an exercise for the reader to adapt the implementation so that it will include this as well.

8.4.2 Frame information

We are now in a good position to be more specific on the information that is to be contained in frames. In the next two subsections we concentrate on addressing in the case of medium access control layers and consider frame layouts.

Addressing

Suppose we want to construct a computer network consisting of a number of personal workstations. Also assume that none of these workstations contains any hardware that allows them to be connected to each other. How do we proceed? Taking a rather simplistic point of view, it is not really difficult. The first thing that has to be done is buy a large amount of hardware. In particular, we have to purchase cables, plugs and sockets, etc. But perhaps the most important hardware that we have to buy is an *implementation* of the physical and medium access control layer. Generally, such an implementation is purchased in the form of a **printed board** consisting of memory (the registers and buffers mentioned in the previous section), a network controller, and some additional circuitry as explained in Chapter 3. Each personal workstation will have to be equipped with such a **network interface**.

```
package MAC_LAYER is
   subtype ADDRESS is INTEGER range 0..16777215;
   type USERDATA is array (1..1021) of MEMORY.BYTE;
   type FRAME_FORMAT is
      record
         destination : ADDRESS;
         data : USERDATA;
      end RECORD;

   procedure REQUEST(frame : in FRAME_FORMAT);
   -- Submit a frame for transmission across the network. The calling process will be
   -- allowed to continue as soon as the frame has been stored in the controller's
   -- output buffer.

   procedure WAIT_FOR_CONFIRMATION;
   -- To be called by a process that had just submitted a frame transmission. The process
   -- will be delayed until the frame has actually been sent.

   procedure ACCEPT(frame : out FRAME_FORMAT; done : out BOOLEAN);
   -- Check if a new frame has arrived. If so, it is removed from the controller's input
   -- buffer and returned as [frame]; [done] is set to TRUE. If there was no frame in the
   -- input buffer, [done] is set to FALSE and the calling process continues immediately.

   procedure WAIT_FOR_INDICATION;
   -- To be called by a process that wants to be delayed until the arrival of a new frame
   -- in the controller's input buffer.
end MAC_LAYER;
```

Listing 8.6 The specification for the software interface to the MAC layer.

There are two important points here. First, most computers can be extended by simply plugging interface boards into standardized sockets. In particular, this immediately allows for memory-mapped I/O of the important registers and buffers of such a board. The locations have already been reserved. Second, in the case of most network interfaces each interface will have a unique, hardwired identification. Such an identification can either be already supplied by the manufacturer (as is often the case with Ethernet interfaces) or it can be set manually afterwards (either by setting switches or under software control). This identification is generally referred to as the **medium access control address**, or **MAC address** for short.

Depending on the protocol supported at the MAC layer, there are different forms of addresses. For example, Ethernet addresses are always 48 bits wide, and so are addresses for the standardized token ring and token bus networks. The important aspect of these unique addressing schemes is that we can identify the computers that constitute the network. And if we send a frame with the right destination address the computer whose interface board has that address will pick up the frame and store it in its internal buffer, where it can be removed for further processing. And that is about all there is to it. Of course, we have to *know* what these addresses are, but we will discuss that later.

Frame layout

Now suppose we want to send a frame from one computer to another. In addition to the data that needs to be sent, we must also include additional information. In general, the following needs to be provided:

- A **start delimiter**, which is usually a unique byte by which the start of a frame can be recognized. It is comparable to the start and stop bits of frames as discussed in Chapter 7.

- A **destination address** which is the unique address at the level of the MAC layer we mentioned above.

- A **source address**, by which the sender can be identified.

- Most frames reserve one to several bytes for error control also referred to as a **checksum**.

- Finally, an **end delimiter** to identify the last byte of which the frame consists.

The use of an end delimiter indicates that frame sizes may vary and indeed, this is often the case. For example, an Ethernet frame may consist of up to 1500 bytes of data, and a token ring may have up to 8192 bytes. Token bus systems impose no limit on the frame size.

▷ In our simple example, we assume that the maximum frame size is 1024 bytes. However, we will now additionally assume that apart from the destination address, the sending process will also have to provide the source address. This implies that at most $1024 - 2 \cdot 3 = 1018$ bytes can be used for sending data. We assume that the amount of data to be sent is always fixed, and that no checksum is provided.

8.5   Computer networks in software

Now that we have seen how we can interface to the network through software, we are also in a position to *extend* our system by means of software. As we mentioned at the beginning of Section 8.4, our goal at this point is to provide some insight into how we can construct computer networks in terms of software. Two concepts are vital to understanding this approach: (1) the layering of communication protocols, and (2) the co-existence of several protocols at the same layer. Again, we shall introduce these two concepts entirely through (albeit rather simplified) examples. First, we shall present in Section 8.5.1 an extension of our package MAC_LAYER in which we make use of the data types and procedures *only* available in that package. Moreover, our example will illustrate that it is possible to *hide* MAC_LAYER completely: we have thus provided a layer "on top" of the MAC layer.

The second problem that we will face is that of having two communication protocols that co-exist within the same layer. Therefore, we shall take a closer look in Section 8.5.2 at how we can implement the basic communication models discussed in Chapter 6. Our example will illustrate how we can have two independent communication systems, one based entirely on synchronous communication and one based entirely on asynchronous communication. The point is that these two communication systems can exist simultaneously but making use of only a single basic computer network.

8.5.1 Layering the network software

As an illustration of how we can continue in implementing our network interface in software let's consider the development of a module that implements part of the functionality of the **logical link control layer**, i.e. the upper half of OSI's data link layer with the lower half being formed by the MAC layer discussed so far. In particular, our LLC layer provides a means for submitting only one frame for transmission, without knowing whether it arrived (a so-called unacknowledged connectionless service). The extension we are interested in here is twofold, as we shall discuss next.

Preliminaries

First, we wish to allow *several* frames to be in transmission at the same time. Our implementation of the MAC layer was such that if a process *PROC* had submitted a transmission request, then any other process *PROC** that subsequently submitted such a request as well had to be delayed until the request by *PROC* was confirmed. For our LLC implementation, we want to avoid this. In particular, it should be possible to have at least NREQUEST outstanding requests at the same time. If any request is submitted after that, an error will be reported.

A similar situation should exist when accepting frames. Again, in our implementation of the MAC layer, no more frames could be received as long as the controller's input buffer had not been emptied. For our LLC implementation, we demand that at least NACCEPT frames should be accepted for receipt before new incoming frames are rejected.

We can achieve this by creating separate queues as illustrated in Figure 8.15. In particular, we make a distinction between an **output queue** for temporarily storing transmission requests and an **input queue** for storing incoming frames. Each queue is handled by a separate process as will be discussed below.

Addressing at the level of the LLC layer

In Section 6.4.1 we introduced the concept of a **port** as a means for letting two processes communicate without having to know each other's identity explicitly. A similar concept is used in the OSI reference model, where it is referred to as a **service access point**, or simply SAP. An SAP is used as an extension to the normal addressing at the data link layer in order to identify a particular process that can handle incoming requests. In other words, communicating processes at the LLC level identify each other by a combination of a number (i.e. SAP) and an address (i.e. a MAC address).

When sending frames at the level of the LLC layer it is common that not only the addresses of the source and destination station are provided but also a source and destination

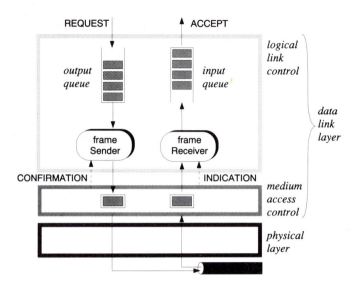

Figure 8.15 The outline of a software solution for queuing incoming and outgoing data.

```
package LLC_LAYER is
   subtype ADDRESS is INTEGER range 0..16777215;
   subtype SAP is INTEGER range 0..255;
   type USERDATA is array (1..1016) of MEMORY.BYTE;

   type FRAME_FORMAT is
      record
         dstStation : ADDRESS;
         srcStation : ADDRESS;
         dstSAP : SAP;
         srcSAP : SAP;
         data : USERDATA;
      end record ;
   ...
end LLC_LAYER;
```

Listing 8.7 Data definitions at the LLC layer.

SAP. An SAP is generally expressed as an 8-bit binary number. Taking into account that frames in our example are limited to 1024 bytes, and that addresses are each 24 bits wide, it should be clear that this leaves us with a total of 1016 bytes that can be used for the data. Expressing an LLC frame in BASAL can then be done as in Listing 8.7 (where, for clarity, we omit details with respect to the way the types are to be mapped to memory).

In our example, we have simply copied the definition of ADDRESS as was used within the package MAC_LAYER to reflect that this addressing scheme is exactly the same at the LLC layer. The point is that an LLC frame is converted into a MAC frame, and vice versa,

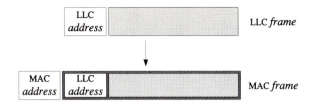

Figure 8.16 The construction of a MAC frame based on an LLC frame.

```
package LLC_LAYER is
   ...
   procedure REQUEST(frame : in FRAME_FORMAT; done : out BOOLEAN);
   -- Submit a frame for transmission. If [frame] could be submitted, [done]
   -- is set to TRUE, otherwise to FALSE.

   procedure ACCEPT(frame : out FRAME_FORMAT; done : out BOOLEAN);
   -- Accept any incoming frame. If there was one, [done] is set to TRUE,
   -- otherwise to FALSE.

   procedure WAIT_FOR_INDICATION;
   -- Delay the calling process until a frame has arrived.
end LLC_LAYER;
```

Listing 8.8 The specification of the LLC interface.

as shown in Figure 8.16. In effect, the data part of a MAC frame will consist entirely of an LLC frame, which only has the two SAP identifications as additional information.

Our package specification can now be completed by simply adding the procedures for requesting a frame transmission, and checking to see if anything arrived. Recall that, with respect to sending frames, we are not going to provide any means for confirming that the receiver has accepted a frame. The result is shown in Listing 8.8. Our next step is to see how these procedures are to be implemented. We note that the following subsections may be skipped on first reading.

▷ **Implementation of the services**

When implementing our services we have to realize that there are always two sides of any layer that require attention: (1) the lower half of a layer in which the interface with the layer underneath is to be taken care of, and (2) the upper half which forms the implementation of the layer's own interface to the outside world. Let's start by taking a look at the two halves that implement the submission of frames for transmission. To simplify matters, we assume that we have a package MACQUEUE at our disposal that will allow us to handle queues of frames. This package can be specified using our generic package GENERAL_QUEUE given in Listing 4.13 on page 172:

```
package MACQUEUE is new GENERAL_QUEUE(ELEMENT ⇒ MAC_LAYER.FRAME_FORMAT);
```

```
process FRAME_SENDER is
    newMacFrame : MAC_LAYER.FRAME_FORMAT;
    empty : BOOLEAN;
begin
    while TRUE loop
        SEMAPHORE.WAIT(outputQueueLock);
        MACQUEUE.CHECK_EMPTY(outputQueue, empty);
        if empty then
            -- There are no pending frames to send. Suspend the calling process, but make sure
            -- that it can be activated as soon as another process submits a frame to send.
            senderWaiting := TRUE;
            SEMAPHORE.SIGNAL(outputQueueLock);
            SEMAPHORE.WAIT(outputQueueNotEmpty);
            senderWaiting := FALSE;
        end if ;
        MACQUEUE.REMOVE(outputQueue, newMacFrame);
        SEMAPHORE.SIGNAL(outputQueueLock);
        MAC_LAYER.REQUEST(newMacFrame);
        MAC_LAYER.WAIT_FOR_CONFIRMATION;
    end loop ;
end FRAME_SENDER;
```

Listing 8.9 The implementation of a process that handles frames to be sent.

Frame submission: lower half.   As we have shown in Figure 8.15, we will construct
an independent process that is responsible for submitting frames for transmission to the MAC
layer. The behavior this process frameSender exposes is very straightforward: (1) it should
remove any outstanding frame in the output queue, and (2) it should pass this frame to the
MAC layer. To keep matters simple, we assume that queued frames are already suited for
being handled by the MAC layer, i.e. they already contain the source and destination address
that will allow them to be transmitted across the network. Now look at the process shown
in Listing 8.9.

The first point we have to realize is that the output queue (which we have expressed by the
variable outputQueue) is to be *shared* between frameSender and processes that submit a frame
to the LLC layer. This explains why we have used a semaphore outputQueueLock to ensure exclusive access to this queue. The process frameSender first checks whether the output queue
is empty. When the queue is not empty, it simply REMOVEs the first frame, gives up its exclusive access, and passes the frame to the MAC layer using synchronous communication.

The difficult part is when the queue is found to be empty, in which case frameSender will have
to postpone any further actions. Again, we can use a semaphore for that purpose as shown
in our example as outputQueueNotEmpty. The point is that this semaphore will be SIGNALed
by a requesting process as soon as it has (1) appended a frame to the output queue and (2)
finds that frameSender was waiting for the queue to be filled. In order to see that frameSender
is indeed waiting, the latter uses a Boolean variable senderWaiting, which is to be inspected
by the requesting process. This mechanism is further explained next.

Frame submission: upper half.   The behavior of a requesting process is also fairly
straightforward. First, a new frame will have to be created that fits the frame layout at the
level of the MAC layer. Data is then copied into that frame after which it is appended to

```
procedure REQUEST(frame : in FRAME_FORMAT; done : out BOOLEAN) is
   newMacFrame : MAC_LAYER.FRAME_FORMAT;
   full : BOOLEAN;
begin
   newMacFrame.destination := frame.dstStation;
   newMacFrame.source := frame.srcStation;
   newMacFrame.data(1) := frame.dstSAP;
   newMacFrame.data(2) := frame.srcSAP;
   for k in 3..1018 loop
      newMacFrame.data(k) := frame.data(k-2);
   end loop ;

   SEMAPHORE.WAIT(outputQueueLock);
   MACQUEUE.CHECK_FULL(outputQueue, full);
   if full then
      SEMAPHORE.SIGNAL(outputQueueLock);
      done := FALSE;
   else
      MACQUEUE.APPEND(outputQueue, newMacFrame);
      if senderWaiting then
         SEMAPHORE.SIGNAL(outputQueueNotEmpty);
      else
         SEMAPHORE.SIGNAL(outputQueueLock);
      end if ;
      done := TRUE;
   end if ;
end REQUEST;
```

Listing 8.10 The procedure that will be called by a process submitting a frame for sending.

the output queue. For an explanation, look at the implementation of LLC_LAYER.REQUEST (Listing 8.10).

The procedure implementation consists of two parts. In the first part we copy the data of the LLC frame into one that is suited for the MAC layer. Note how we copy the destination and source SAP into the first two entries of newMacFrame.data. The remaining elements are then used for the data that should be transmitted.[3]

The second part, in which the new frame is appended to the output queue, is again, somewhat difficult. First, exclusive access to the output queue is gained by WAITing for semaphore outputQueueLock. If the queue is full, we have finished: the request cannot be handled. Otherwise, the process appends the frame to the queue and then checks to see if it should SIGNAL frameSender that the queue is not empty. If frameSender is indeed waiting, the requesting process simply SIGNALs semaphore outputQueueNotEmpty, and immediately returns from the procedure call *without* SIGNAL*ing the semaphore* outputQueueLock. But this will not lead to any problems, for it can be readily verified that it is now frameSender that has exclusive access to the output queue. We leave this as an exercise for the reader.

Frame acceptance: lower half.   We can now construct the lower half of the LLC layer for accepting incoming frames. The behavior of the process frameReceiver that is responsi-

---

[3]We note that our implementation is not complete. Our solution requires that the type LLC_LAYER.SAP and MEMORY.BYTE are *compatible*, which we may not, in general, assume to be the case. We ignore these details as they are not considered entirely relevant here.

```
process FRAME_RECEIVER is
  newMacFrame : MAC_LAYER.FRAME_FORMAT;
  done, full : BOOLEAN;
begin
  while TRUE loop
    MAC_LAYER.ACCEPT(newMacFrame, done);
    if done then
      SEMAPHORE.WAIT(inputQueueLock);
      MACQUEUE.CHECK_FULL(inputQueue, full);
      if not full then
        MACQUEUE.APPEND(inputQueue, newMacFrame);
        SEMAPHORE.SIGNAL(inputQueueNotEmpty);
      end if ;
      SEMAPHORE.SIGNAL(inputQueueLock);
    else
      MAC_LAYER.WAIT_FOR_INDICATION;
    end if ;
  end loop ;
end FRAME_RECEIVER;
```

Listing 8.11   The process FRAME_RECEIVER for handling frames coming in from the MAC layer.

ble for handling such frames is fairly simple. First, it waits for an indication that a frame has arrived, and copies the new frame from the MAC layer. The frame is then subsequently appended to the input queue (if possible), and any process waiting at the LLC level for incoming data is signaled. To that end, we have used yet another semaphore inputQueueNotEmpty. This leads to the process FRAME_RECEIVER shown in Listing 8.11.

Again, we have protected the input queue (modeled as inputQueue) by means of a semaphore inputQueueLock. If a frame has arrived, it is appended to the queue, unless the queue is full, in which case the frame is simply discarded. If there is no frame, the process frameReceiver simply waits until one arrives.

Frame acceptance: the upper half.   Accepting LLC frames is similarly straightforward and like REQUEST, it consists of two parts. The first part concerns the removal of a frame from the input queue, which is possible unless the queue is empty. The second part again consists of converting the MAC frame to the appropriate LLC format. This leads to the code shown in Listing 8.12. We leave it to the reader to provide the (almost trivial) implementation of the LLC procedure WAIT_FOR_INDICATION, which is quite analogous to its MAC counterpart discussed earlier.

Initialization of the LLC layer.   Our final implementation detail is that of declaring and initializing the various variables used in our package LLC_LAYER. The package body can be described as Listing 8.13, where all upper- and lower-half procedures and process specifications are to be included as well. We assume that both queues have been properly initialized. Further initialization details have been omitted, as they require detailed attention that is not relevant at this point.

```
procedure ACCEPT(frame : out FRAME_FORMAT; done : out BOOLEAN) is
    newMacFrame : MAC_LAYER.FRAME_FORMAT;
    empty : BOOLEAN;
begin
    SEMAPHORE.WAIT(inputQueueLock);
    MACQUEUE.CHECK_EMPTY(inputQueue, empty);
    if empty then
        SEMAPHORE.SIGNAL(inputQueueLock);
        done := FALSE;
    else
        MACQUEUE.REMOVE(inputQueue, newMacFrame);
        SEMAPHORE.SIGNAL(inputQueueLock);

        frame.dstStation := newMacFrame.destination;
        frame.srcStation := newMacFrame.source;
        frame.dstSAP := newMacFrame.data(1);
        frame.srcSAP := newMacFrame.data(2);
        for k in 1..1016 loop
            frame.data(k) := newMacFrame.data(k+2);
        end loop ;
        done := TRUE;
    end if ;
end ACCEPT;
```

Listing 8.12 The procedure for accepting frames coming in at the level of the LLC layer.

```
package body LLC_LAYER is
    ...
    inputQueue : MACQUEUE.DEFINITION;
    outputQueue : MACQUEUE.DEFINITION;

    inputQueueLock : SEMAPHORE.DEFINITION := TRUE;
    inputQueueNotEmpty : SEMAPHORE.DEFINITION := FALSE;

    outputQueueLock : SEMAPHORE.DEFINITION := TRUE;
    outputQueueNotEmpty : SEMAPHORE.DEFINITION := FALSE;

    frameSender : FRAME_SENDER;
    senderWaiting : BOOLEAN;

    frameReceiver : FRAME_RECEIVER;
end LLC_LAYER;
```

Listing 8.13 Declaration and initialization of the LLC variables.

8.5.2   Supporting multiple protocols

Probably the main importance of adding the LLC layer to our basic hardware interface (the MAC layer) is that we have introduced the concept of a **service access point**. As we have explained, an SAP is a means to identify *services* at a particular site, or, in other words, to identify a process that is capable of handling the data that is being sent in a frame. In this sense, an SAP is not much different than the concept of a port. In this section we are going to use SAPs to construct two independent communication systems that co-exist on the same basic computer network.

Two basic communication systems

The two communication systems, or computer networks as they can also be called, are based on the communication models we have discussed in Chapter 6. Abstracting from the specifics of using these models, we shall assume that we need to implement one communication system that is based entirely on asynchronous communication. Its specification is expressed in BASAL as follows:

```
package ASYNCHRONOUS is
    type ADDRESS is ...;
    type MESSAGE is ...

    procedure SEND(dest : in ADDRESS; mess : in MESSAGE);
    -- The indicated message [mess] is sent to the destination [dest], without
    -- suspending the calling process while the message is being sent.

    procedure RECEIVE(mess : out MESSAGE; delivered : out BOOLEAN);
    -- Checks if a message has arrived. If so, it will be passed onto the calling
    -- process as [mess], and [delivered] is set to TRUE. If no message has
    -- arrived [delivered] is set to FALSE.
end ASYNCHRONOUS;
```

The second communication system is based entirely on synchronous communication, and, again using BASAL, is described by the package specification SYNCHRONOUS:

```
package SYNCHRONOUS is
    type ADDRESS is ...;
    type MESSAGE is ...

    procedure SEND(dest : in ADDRESS; mess : in MESSAGE);
    -- The indicated message [mess] is sent to the destination [dest], and the
    -- calling process is suspended until the message has been delivered, and
    -- its receipt acknowledged by the destination.

    procedure RECEIVE(mess : out MESSAGE);
    -- The calling process is suspended until a message [mess] has been received.
    -- The sending process will be acknowledged that [mess] has arrived.
end SYNCHRONOUS;
```

Assuming that we only have the implementation of the LLC layer at our disposal, you should have a rough idea of how either package can be implemented by using only the data types and procedures of that layer. Admittedly, there are many intricacies that need special attention, but these will essentially not differ much from the way we implemented the package LLC_LAYER by making use of package MAC_LAYER. Instead, the problem that we wish to address here is how we can implement *both* packages, but by making use of only *one* implementation of the LLC layer for each computer.

To fully comprehend our problem, consider Figure 8.17. There, we show the organization of the implementation of both packages on top of a single LLC layer per station A or B. The problem we are dealing with is the following. Suppose a process $PROC^A_{sync}$ sends a message M_{sync} by making use of synchronous communication. The point is that M_{sync} may be received only by a process $PROC^B_{sync}$ that, like the sending process $PROC^A_{sync}$, em-

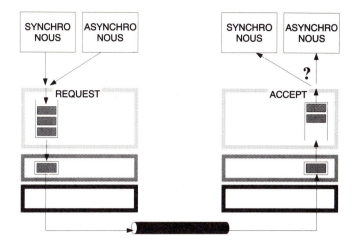

Figure 8.17 The organization of the two communication modules with respect to the OSI layers.

ploys synchronous communication. Something else would simply make no sense, just as it makes no sense to assume that a letter can be received through the phone, or vice versa. A similar reasoning can be applied to asynchronous communication. If a process $PROC^A_{async}$ sends a message M_{async} to station B using the package ASYNCHRONOUS, then we will have to ensure that the message is received only by a process $PROC^B_{async}$ at B that also employs asynchronous communication.

But there is more. If the two processes $PROC^A_{sync}$ and $PROC^A_{async}$ send their respective messages M_{sync} and M_{async} at the same time, then *both* messages should be sent across the network to B, and properly delivered *independently* of each other. That is, message M_{sync} should be delivered to the process $PROC^B_{sync}$ without having interfered with the delivery of message M_{async} to process $PROC^B_{async}$. The converse should, of course, also hold: delivery of M_{async} should in no way influence the delivery of M_{sync}.

What we are thus confronted with is the implementation of two mutually independent communication systems that have to share the same basic network, but in such a way that communication within one system does not affect communication within the other. In other words, we have to devise a means to let two unrelated communication protocols co-exist without mutual interference. The solution to this problem, which is that of **multiplexing** an underlying network, is surprisingly simple.

Architecture of a concurrent communication layer

In order to explain a general solution to our problem you first have to realize that the only thing we may assume is the existence of a computer network which can be interfaced through the data link layer, in the form of the package LLC_LAYER. This means that neither the implementation of this package nor that of the package MAC_LAYER may be changed. A second, important, issue has to do with addressing. We shall consider this further below.

Taking the LLC layer as our starting point gives us at least one powerful concept that we are going to use here: the service access point. By using an SAP we will be able to distinguish one message type from another, and in fact, this is in principle all that we need to construct our so-called **concurrent communication layers**, consisting of the implementations of the packages SYNCHRONOUS and ASYNCHRONOUS. The idea is simple. We associate a unique SAP with either package. For example, *all* implementations of the package SYNCHRONOUS will have SAP #1, whereas *all* implementations of ASYNCHRONOUS will have SAP #2.

Our next step is to add a simple process frameSplitter to each station, which is the *only* process allowed to receive frames from the LLC layer. Its behavior can be outlined in BASAL as follows:

```
process FRAME_SPLITTER is
begin
   while TRUE loop
      Wait for a new LLC frame [frame] to arrive
      if frame.dstSAP = 1 then
         append [frame] to input queue of SYNCHRONOUS
      elsif frame.dstSAP = 2 then
         append [frame] to input queue of ASYNCHRONOUS
      end if ;
   end loop ;
end FRAME_SPLITTER;
```

What is seen here is that the only thing frameSplitter does is accept new incoming frames, checks the value of the destination SAP field, and subsequently forwards the frame to the appropriate process by appending it to the (assumed) input queue of the package implementing that process. At that moment, the frame is to be further dealt with by processes adhering to the communication protocol as specified by the package SYNCHRONOUS or ASYNCHRONOUS, respectively. This solution is shown in Figure 8.18.

Sending messages is even simpler. The only thing we need to do is set the right value for the destination and source SAP fields of the corresponding LLC frames.

Address resolution

The final topic we need to discuss is that of addressing. So far, we have consistently used the concept of an address as a means to identify communicating parties. We have hardly touched upon **address resolution**. The problem can be stated quite easily. In order for two parties to communicate, they will make use of a unique addressing convention. For example, when mailing a letter, you will generally at least need to provide things like a street, a number, a city, and also a ZIP code to ensure delivery. On the other hand, when phoning someone, the addressing convention consists of dialing the right sequence of digits.

In communication systems, addressing is no different: each system will use its own scheme. But when a communication system has to make use of an existing perhaps more primitive system, addresses will need to be converted. For example, suppose that for our two packages SYNCHRONOUS and ASYNCHRONOUS we had the following addressing

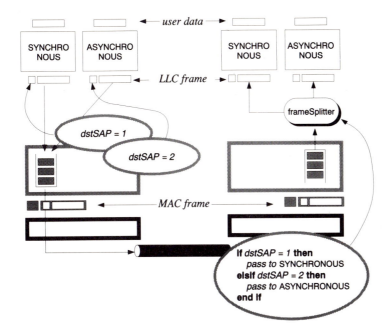

Figure 8.18 Handling incoming frames for different communication protocols.

conventions:

```
type SYNCHRONOUS.ADDRESS is ARRAY(1..10) of CHARACTER;
subtype ASYNCHRONOUS.ADDRESS is INTEGER range 0..4095;
```

These two addressing schemes have nothing in common, but that need not be a problem, for they belong to two completely independent communication protocols. The problem, however, is that both addresses will have to be uniquely converted to addresses that make sense at the level of the data link layer. Otherwise, sending frames across that network will be impossible.

A general solution to this problem is manually to maintain a **mapping** of addresses between two layers. For example, suppose the implementation of package SYNCHRONOUS on station *A* from our example, has address "MODULE_ONE_", which consists of precisely 10 characters. If station *A* has MAC address 519, then address "MODULE_ONE_" should be **resolved** into the LLC address 519 with SAP #1. Similar conversions hold for addressing in the case of ASYNCHRONOUS.

But how does this work in practice? As we have said, mappings are often maintained manually. This is done by storing address conversions into a file (that can be kept either local to each station or otherwise centralized at a dedicated station), and which needs to be read each time address resolution takes place. And this is a scheme that should look familiar to you. It is, in fact, not very different from the way that file names were converted into file identifiers as explained in Section 5.6.3, by means of directories.

8.6   Discussion

8.6.1   Summary and further reading

This chapter has been devoted entirely to the principles of operation of local area networks (LANs). These networks have been *technologically* characterized by the fact that they are based entirely on an interconnection scheme at the level of the data link layer, which employs broadcasting. This means that any station that has a message merely sends it to all other stations. Only the destination station (or destinations for that matter), picks up the message, while the others ignore it. As we shall see in the next chapter, this technological aspect makes LANs different from so-called wide area networks. At this point, let's briefly summarize the material presented so far.

Probably the main rationale for using a broadcast mechanism is its simplicity with respect to implementations. Either we use a single wire with various taps, as in the case of Ethernet of token-bus networks, or we physically organize the stations into a ring. In both cases the basic communication is simple: just put your message on the wire, and have it picked up by the appropriate listener. For one thing, there is no need to be concerned about *routing* messages.

But, as we have also discussed, LANs do have their drawbacks. In particular, although the number of stations within a single LAN segment can be quite large, eventually we are going to run into all kinds of problems if we continue to attach stations to the same segment. The solution, in that case, is to start connecting LAN segments into an interconnected network. In that case, routing does become an issue. Also, we have to invent constructions that allow us to maintain the high transmission rates that we were used to. It is probably here that network technology shows its more interesting sides. Nowadays, it is hard to imagine that a local area network is not constructed by interconnecting individual segments. The concept of a bridge is important in this respect. In principle, a bridge is responsible for forwarding frames from one segment to others, such that (1) the broadcasting principle is obeyed, but also that (2) broadcasting is done in a controlled way.

It should be apparent by now that developing networks is generally not an easy thing to do. An important structuring mechanism to at least make such developments more or less manageable is to make use of layers. The OSI model introduced in the previous chapter is seen to be of value in this case. How this layering approach can be used to guide implementations has been demonstrated in Section 8.4. In particular, we have seen there how, from an operating system's point of view, a network can be considered as merely another peripheral device. It is also there that we made the jump from hardware to software. And, as we have seen sometimes so far, making such a jump often leads to important improvements. We have also demonstrated that it is relatively easy to build several high-level protocols using the same underlying technology. The real improvement comes from the fact that several protocols can be used *simultaneously*, or, putting it differently, can be *multiplexed* on a single, lower-level protocol.

The literature on local area networks is large, and many books have overlapping subjects. A good general reference is Stallings (1993b) which concentrates solely on local area networking techniques. You will also find many references there to specific topics on LAN technology. A good survey of medium access layer protocols can be found in Kurose *et al.* (1984). On interconnecting networks, consult Perlman (1992) which contains many details on bridges and LAN routing technology. Local area network technology is also discussed in Halsall (1992) and Tanenbaum (1988). But, as with operating systems and compilers, it is highly instructive to look at actual network software when you really want to understand what's going on. In that case, Comer (1987), which augments its predecessor Comer (1984), will also be of help.

8.6.2   Improving local area networks

LAN technology is certainly not at the end of its development. As of this writing, new technologies are still being introduced and a large body of research is devoted entirely to improving network capabilities. Before we continue with expanding our view on networks in the next chapter, let's first consider where things are heading.

Performance issues

Probably the most significant improvements that have been made in the case of local area networks is related to overall performance. In particular, LANs to date not only allow for high transmission rates but are also capable of handling intensive communication by far more stations than when they were first introduced.

Looking back, a popular type of LAN has always been one based on the CSMA/CD protocol, generally referred to as Ethernet. As we have shown, the CSMA/CD protocol works well for small values of the normalized propagation delay **a**. Also, this generally occurs in networks consisting of a few stations that occasionally exchange relatively large portions of data, such as files. Indeed, it is under these circumstances that the protocol works well and for which it was intended in the first place (Metcalfe and Boggs, 1976). However, modern networked computers systems tend to interact more frequently with smaller frame sizes. For example, it is not uncommon these days to build a network as a cluster of disk-less workstations, implying that *all* I/O is to occur across the network. And if you realize that this statement also implies that virtual memory implementations are to make use of the network, it is indeed not hard to imagine that network traffic can be considerable. It will be no surprise that the original Ethernet implementations will not survive in the long run, and that they will be replaced by more efficient protocols. However, when this will exactly be the case is something that remains an open question. It is Metcalfe (1993) himself who poses this question in a highly readable and instructive article reflecting his experience with Ethernet.

When talking about the performance of local area networks, two factors need to be considered: the propagation time and the frame transmission time, which were both introduced in Chapter 7. What it means in the case of LANs is that the (required) frame transmission time is gradually coming too close to the propagation time in order for the network to be termed "efficient". A major research topic in the case of high-speed networks is to introduce efficient medium access protocols. Ethernet is certainly not such a protocol for networks allowing high transmission rates. Efficient MAC protocols are almost invariably based on the so-called **attempt and defer** principle. In these cases, a station (1) always waits until the channel is free before starting transmission, and (2) defers to transmissions from other stations that are logically placed "upstream" (compare this to the DQDB protocol). The introduction of an implicit ordering of stations seems important in order to attain efficiency. By doing it correctly, it can also be guaranteed that a station need not wait indefinitely before it can start transmission. A more recent comparison based on simulation studies, and which confirms previous results, is reported in Marsan *et al.* (1994).

Local area networks will continue to evolve in the near future. If you are interested in performance issues, Abeysundara and Kamal (1991) provide a good overview of high-speed networks, focusing on recent proposals for efficient MAC protocols. Understanding performance issues in the case of computer networks is discussed in Stuck and Arthurs (1985). A good starting point is also Bertsekas and Gallagher (1992), which presents network communication in connection with performance analysis.

Separating specification and implementation

Completely different technology can also be expected as well. An important development that we shall discuss in the next chapter is the so-called **asynchronous transfer mode** (ATM). In contrast to the broadcast mechanisms employed in LANs through the use of bus and ring topologies, ATM networks are based on a true switching technology as used in wide area networks. Broadcast mechanisms are then constructed *on top* of the underlying network. As discussed in Kung (1992), switching technology will form a prominent component of future high-speed local area networks. We shall have more to say about this mechanism later. The important point to note here, however, is that a distinction is being made between *specification* and *implementation* of network protocols.

This separation between specifying *what* a protocol does, and *how* it is subsequently implemented, is important. It is only by means of this explicit separation that investments in software can be protected. For example, at present, implementations of Ethernet exist (or, more precisely, of the IEEE 802.3 standard) in which the transmission medium is twisted pair instead of coax cable, and the topology of the network is based on one or several switches, with each switch having several stations attached to it. This topology, also referred to as a **star network**, is similar to that of local telephone branch exchanges. What happens is that when a frame is received at a switch it is subsequently forwarded to the appropriate station, or, if so required, forwarded to *all* stations connected to the switch. But how frames are actually transmitted from sender to receiver is of no interest to the users. As far as they can see, they are simply dealing with an ordinary Ethernet network (although the performance is considerably higher).

The number of LAN standards adopted by the IEEE is large and can be obtained from the IEEE Computer Society Press. If you are in search of an overview on future LAN technology, Stallings (1993a) provides a collection of articles that is worth consulting. Reprints of some of the references mentioned above can also be found there.

Exercises

1. What would be the political or legal implications of networks outside a building?

2. What happens in a contention system, when stations A and B are simultaneously transmitting the strings $\langle 110110 \rangle$ and $\langle 100010 \rangle$, respectively, to station C, when a 1 put by any station connected to the channel results in a 1 on the channel?

3. *Explain why a station connected to a contention-based channel must wait a contention period of $2 \times T_{\text{prop}}$ before it can send the next frame.

4. What happens if through an error there are two tokens in a token-based network?

5. Explain in your own words the essential difference between a token ring network and a token bus network, and why the latter is more difficult to implement.

6. Is the propagation time T_{prop} a constant between every pair of stations? What about the frame transmission time?

7. *When a file is transferred between two stations connected through a contention-based channel, is the normalized propagation delay $\mathbf{a} \ll 1$, $\mathbf{a} \approx 1$, or $\mathbf{a} \gg 1$? Explain.

8. *Suppose, in a token ring system, the normalized propagation delay $\mathbf{a}$ is larger than 1. Do we have to shorten or lengthen the ring to return it to $\mathbf{a} = 1$? What would be an alternative?

9. Why may it not be such a good idea to use a contention-based network as a backbone for connecting several LAN segments?

10. Explain why in a DQDB backbone protocol a station cannot monopolize the channel.

11. If we know in advance that the bridges in an interconnected LAN are going to route according to a spanning tree, why would we then still leave "redundant" bridges in the network after making the interconnections?

12. *The DQDB protocol is relatively insensitive to the normalized propagation delay $\mathbf{a}$. Explain why.

13. *Show that the efficiency of a token ring is $S = 1/(1 + \mathbf{a}/N)$, if $\mathbf{a} \le 1$. (Hint: normalize T_{frame}, i.e. set it to 1.)

14. *Show that the efficiency of a token ring is $S = 1/(\mathbf{a} \cdot (1 + 1/N))$, if $\mathbf{a} > 1$.

15. What would be the spanning tree of a network consisting of L_i segments, $0 \le i \le k$, each segment L_i connected only to segment L_{i+1} through a bridge B_i, where bridge B_k closes the circle and connects segments L_k and L_0?

16. How can a station report an error to a process that submitted a frame for transmission?

17. Describe precisely what is meant by discarding frames upon arrival at a station.

18. Explain why it is generally necessary to have the software that controls access to the network be part of the operating system. Is it also necessary to have this software run in kernel mode, or would it be sufficient to run (parts of) it in user mode, as adopted in a client-server architecture?

19. Service access points cannot be qualified as true addresses in the sense that they can be used to identify processes. Why not?

20. *Explain in your own words what the essential difference is between what we have called the upper and lower layer of the software for handling frame transmission. Did we find a similar distinction in our discussion on device drivers for hard disks in Chapter 5?

21. Verify the synchronization between the upper and lower halves of the frame transmission protocol.

22. Explain the principle of multiplexing a physical network between different higher-level network protocols.

Chapter 9

Wide area networks

Our next step towards computer networks is in fact a jump. In this chapter we shall concentrate on the construction of networks that literally span the world. The main problem that we shall encounter is that of finding a route from a source to a destination across a network. Routing in worldwide networks is of a completely different order of complexity than in local area networks. The problems arise from the fact that the broadcast mechanism inherent in the latter type of networks cannot be employed when communication has to span thousands and even millions of computers all over the world. In addition, we are confronted with the actual construction of worldwide networks. In particular, we shall also look at so-called internetworks which are built by connecting together wide area networks. In Section 9.4 we shall briefly look at an evolving type of network, the so-called integrated services digital networks. We conclude this chapter by paying some attention in Section 9.5 to the functions that are provided in OSI's transport layer.

9.1 Expanding communication systems

9.1.1 Introduction

The approach we have been taking with respect to the construction of computer networks so far is that of stepwise expansion. In Chapter 7 we have shown how we can start by simply connecting pairs of computers through various transmission media. Our attention initially focused on getting a single frame of data from one computer to another. The best we could do with respect to connecting several computers at that point was letting a single transmission medium be shared by means of multiplexing techniques. But multiplexing is only one way of sharing a communication channel. In Chapter 8 we introduced the concept of a LAN segment: a network in which several computers are connected employing broadcast communication through a common channel. However, rather than allowing several frames to be sent simultaneously as in the case of multiplexing, we showed how the channel could be temporarily allocated to a single computer by introducing several completely distributed allocation policies. In this way, dozens of computers were capable of communicating with each other all using the same communication medium.

Unfortunately, the strategy followed in these LAN segments cannot be easily expanded to support hundreds of computers. The main problem is that as more computers are connected to the channel, the probability of colliding frames increases rapidly. Alternative approaches of devising collision-free systems such as the token ring and token bus networks permit many more computers to be connected, but efficiency from the perspective of a single station does become difficult as there are simply too many competitors. In view of this scalability problem, we came to the point that LAN segments need to be interconnected into a larger network by using so-called bridges. In essence, a bridge is just an intermediate computer that operates at the level of the medium access control layer. In other words, it simply picks up frames from one LAN segment and forwards it onto another.

But as simple as this may seem, in order to guarantee that frames are indeed broadcast to every LAN segment (and thus to every station), we need explicitly to exploit routing strategies. In other words, where broadcast communication was initially an inherent feature of our means of communication, this is no longer the case with interconnected LANs and measures have to be taken to maintain it. Routing is a price to be paid in scalable solutions. Fortunately, there are also benefits. When devising routing strategies we can take into account the fact that a frame need not always be broadcast. Instead, when there is only a single destination we can reduce network traffic by avoiding frame transmission on those LANs where the frame has no business whatsoever. And it is precisely this strategy that we *need* to follow if we are to expand our networks even further.

In this chapter we shall concentrate on so-called **wide area networks**, or **WANs**. Wide area networks, as we mentioned earlier, cover nations, countries, and literally, the entire world. Routing data efficiently through the often intricate maze of interconnected networks that comprise a WAN is one of the major topics of this chapter. In order to simplify our discussion, we shall initially assume that all WANs are more or less the same, i.e. they all use the same protocols, so that it is relatively easy to connect them. This will allow us to start by discussing some general issues related to WANs in the next two subsections thereby omitting all kinds of technical details. Also, treating WANs as essentially uniform networks permits us to put the subject of routing data into a broader perspective. In particular, in Section 9.2 we shall discuss the necessity of data fragmentation, and consider the need for routing by describing network congestion. This provides us with a basis for discussing adaptive routing strategies, which are generally applied to WANs. As an example of an emerging WAN technology, we shall pay separate attention to ISDN and B-ISDN in Section 9.4 which can be considered as the ultimate global digital network of the future. Of course, that WANs are the same is not a realistic assumption and we shall discard this in order to discuss some of the additional problems we face when constructing so-called **internets**. Internetworking as it is also called, is discussed in Section 9.3.

9.1.2   Architectural features of WANs: routers

As we have mentioned in Section 7.2.4, WANs distinguish themselves from LANs and MANs in that they are constructed as a collection of computers connected by means of *point-to-point* communication channels. This means that each station in a WAN should explicitly decide to which other adjacent station(s) it should send or forward a message. For reasons we shall elaborate further below, we denote these stations as **routers**.

Routers are much comparable to bridges as used to interconnect LAN segments. It is illustrative to take a closer look at the two in order to get a basic idea of the technical distinctions between, on the one hand, local and metropolitan area networks, and wide area networks, on the other. First, consider their functionality with respect to routing. The main reason we needed to consider routing in LANs and MANs was due to the fact that we needed to (1) broadcast frames across the entire network, but (2) prevent the network from being flooded with an infinite number of copies of the same frame. In other words, routing in bridges essentially follows an *offensive* policy: forward frames but do not be too generous in the sense that the data should reach all stations precisely once. Effectively, this was established by cutting off alternative routes. Routing in WANs is fundamentally different. In this case, data should only be forwarded in precisely one direction in such a way that it will reach *only* its destination. Hence, instead of wondering which alternative routes to cut off, a router makes a well-founded choice for exactly one route.

Another distinction between routers and bridges related to their routing functionality is that routers assume that the lifetime of a packet is finite. In particular, each time a packet passes a router its age increases. If this age reaches a certain value while the data still has not reached its destination, it will be discarded. As we shall see, this prevents data circulating through a WAN indefinitely. Conversely, bridges in general do not take any aging criteria into account.

But there is more. Bridges assume that routes proceed through LAN segments. This means that they expect routes to be established at the level of the medium access control layer. Consequently, their own interface within an interconnected LAN is completely realized at the MAC layer. This means that whenever a frame is indeed forwarded, a bridge may have to convert the frame from, say, an Ethernet protocol to a token ring protocol. This is perhaps the only conversion that will take place. In any case, a frame is forwarded in its entirety to another segment only by taking the MAC protocols into account. A router does more. In particular, a router can accept data that may not fit into a single frame. For example, a router may need to forward a contiguous piece of data comprising 8192 bytes onto an Ethernet LAN which can only accept frames with a maximum size of 1500 bytes. In this case, it is the router's responsibility to fragment the 8192 bytes of data into several smaller frames, and subsequently forward each fragment onto the Ethernet network. Likewise, a router may also need to reassemble several fragments into the original piece of data. We shall return to this problem in more detail later. The important point to note is that fragmentation and reassembly of data is an *additional* functionality of routers.

Explicit routing and data fragmentation give routers a different status from bridges. In particular, where bridges are used to connect LAN segments, routers are generally used to interconnect (bridged) LANs into a wide area network. In terms of the OSI reference model, routers typically operate at the network layer as shown in Figure 9.1. Now, this network layer not only adds functionality by means of its routing and fragmentation algorithms, it also deals with flow and error control issues at a more advanced level than

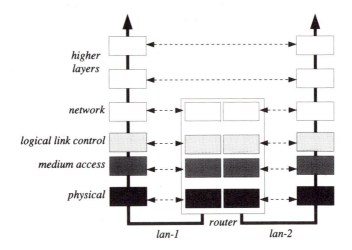

Figure 9.1 The position of a router in terms of the OSI reference model.

is done at the data link layer. And there is a good reason for this. In many cases the *only* connection between two routers is not a LAN but merely a simple transmission medium such as a satellite or a cable. Consequently, routers will have to take into account that data transmission may be subject to more errors than can be expected when connected by LANs. As we shall see, these additional flow and error control mechanisms prohibit fast communication, and can make the network layer relatively sophisticated. The specific functionality of routers, and thus also the communication protocols that form part of the network layer, will be discussed extensively in the following sections of this chapter.

9.1.3   Building a worldwide network

Viewing a WAN as a collection of interconnected routers puts us in a position to take a closer look at how these wide area networks can be organized. Again, as we have mentioned previously, we shall for now make the simplified assumption that all our WANs more or less behave according to one set of communication protocols. In that case, there are two issues that we need to consider: how we can organize routers, and how we can connect LANs to wide area networks.[1] Let's start by looking at these issues from the perspective of a LAN.

Addressing

The first question that we need to address is what is meant by connecting a LAN to a WAN. One way of answering this question is by using the perspective of *reachability*. When

---

[1] From now on we shall make no further distinction between LAN segments, LANs, MANs and bridged LANs or MANs. Instead, we shall collectively refer to them simply as LANs.

we say that a LAN L is to be connected to a WAN, we are stating that we need to *address* stations that are located at some site external to L. The term "address" is the keyword in this context.

Let's first take a naive approach. In the case of LANs, we mentioned in the previous chapter that each station in a network could generally be *uniquely* identified by means of an LLC address (which, in turn, was based on a MAC address). For now, suppose that this is indeed the case. Then, in view of our present discussion, addressing stations outside the current LAN effectively means that we use an LLC address that does not correspond to any LLC address known at the present LAN. So, the solution seems simple. Assuming that every station in the world has a unique LLC address, we can simply use that address to identify the destination of our messages.

But if we were to maintain to this addressing policy, we enter a danger zone. What this policy implies is that each LAN should now need to administrate not merely the stations that it constitutes, but, in fact, also the stations that lie outside it. This is not acceptable as it violates the main principle of local area networks, namely that they are *local*. In that case, you should be able to construct a LAN without having to know what is happening outside that LAN. In particular, this also means that, although addresses of stations within a LAN should be unique, it is unacceptable to insist that two stations in different LANs also have different addresses. The principle of locality would then indeed be violated.

Therefore, we have to suggest something different, and in particular an addressing policy which is completely independent of the addressing policies as invented and used for the construction of LANs. And it is here where OSI's network layer falls into place. Instead of addressing at the level of the data link layer, we invent a completely new *worldwide* addressing policy and place it "on top" of the addressing policy used at the data link layer. In other words, if one station wants to address another station, it does so by using a worldwide known addressing convention. It is then the responsibility of the software comprising the network layer to *resolve* each network address to an LLC address, i.e. find the LLC address in a specific network that corresponds to the given network address. We shall return to this topic in the next chapter.

This address resolution may either succeed or fail. If it succeeds, this implies that the destination station is on the same LAN as the sending station. In other words, if we can find an LLC address that corresponds to the given network address, then this implies that the message that is to be sent can simply be forwarded across the local network. On the other hand, if address resolution fails, then apparently the destination station is not part of the local network from where the message is being sent. In that case, we can forward the message to a dedicated station in our local network to further handle message delivery. Indeed, this dedicated station is a router that has a connection to other routers outside the current LAN. It is the responsibility of this router to forward the message to other routers. How this is done is explained later.

▷ **Some implementation issues**

We can be rather more specific by outlining a possible implementation of this scheme. Assume that in order to connect a LAN to a wide area network, a package NETWORK_LAYER is

```
package NETWORK_LAYER is
   type ADDRESS is ... -- the description of a worldwide addressing scheme
   type DATA_FORMAT is
      record
         destination : ADDRESS;
         source : ADDRESS;
         data : USERDATA; -- the actual data (not further specified)
      end record ;

   procedure REQUEST(message : in DATA_FORMAT; done : out BOOLEAN);
   -- Submit the indicated message for transmission across the network. If the
   -- message can be submitted, [done] is set to TRUE, otherwise to FALSE.
   ...
end NETWORK_LAYER;
```

Listing 9.1 The specification of the procedure REQUEST.

available that provides us with a data type ADDRESS for addressing stations worldwide:

```
package NETWORK_LAYER is
   type ADDRESS is ... -- the description of a worldwide addressing scheme.
   ...
end NETWORK_LAYER;
```

This package will, of course, be implemented as a layer on top of an implementation for the LLC layer of our network, similar to the way that we implemented the packages SYN-CHRONOUS and ASYNCHRONOUS in the previous chapter. Resolving network addresses will be done by means of a separate procedure RESOLVE, which we assume is specified as follows:

```
procedure RESOLVE(
   netAddr : in NETWORK_LAYER.ADDRESS;
   llcAddr : out LLC_LAYER.ADDRESS;
   isThere : out BOOLEAN);
   -- Check at the current local area network, whether there is a station having network
   -- address [netAddr]. If this is the case, [llcAddr] will contain that station's LLC
   -- address and [isThere] is set to TRUE. If there is no such station [isThere] is set
   -- to FALSE.
```

Now suppose we wish to send some data to another station. The first point to realize is that we will no longer directly use an LLC address to identify the destination. Instead, if we assume that our own station is part of a wide area network, we shall use the addressing policy as defined by the package NETWORK_LAYER, i.e. we adhere to addressing at the level of the network layer. Therefore, we may safely assume that our package will also have a procedure REQUEST for sending data in this WAN, as shown in Listing 9.1.

Now let's see how requesting the transmission of data can take place. The first thing that we have to do is to see if our destination station is part of the same LAN from where the request is being issued. In that case, sending the message is easy as we need merely use the communication primitives as provided by our local implementation of the package LLC_LAYER. However, if it turns out that we are addressing a station outside the current LAN, we have to forward the data to the world outside our local network. In particular, we may decide to

```
procedure REQUEST(message : in DATA_FORMAT; done : out BOOLEAN) is
    newLLCFrame : LLC_LAYER.FRAME_FORMAT;
    llcDestination : LLC_LAYER.ADDRESS;
    isThere : BOOLEAN;
begin
    RESOLVE(message.destination, llcDestination, isThere);
    if isThere
        then newLLCFrame.dstStation := llcDestination;
        else newLLCFrame.dstStation := ROUTER_LLC_ADDRESS;
    end if ;
    newLLCFrame.srcStation := LLC address of sender;
    newLLCFrame.dstService := SAP at destination station;
    newLLCFrame.srcService := SAP at sending station;
    newLLCFrame.data := message.data;
    LLC_LAYER.REQUEST(newLLCFrame, done);
end REQUEST;
```

Listing 9.2 An implementation outline for sending data at the level of the network layer.

forward the data to a dedicated station that has a connection to the outside world. Indeed, such a station will form a router in the sense of the WAN terminology we discussed above. However, this router is also part of our LAN, and thus, it has its own LLC address. Denoting this address as ROUTER_LLC_ADDRESS, we can then outline an implementation of the procedure REQUEST as shown in Listing 9.2.

We have omitted many details for the sake of clarity, but the outline above does reveal the essence of address resolution and message handling when discussing the role of a LAN participating in a wide area network. A few remarks are in order.

First, it is important to note that the *implementation* of message handling at the level of the network layer requires the existence of a network of computers at the level of the data link layer. In particular, messages that only make sense at the level of the network layer need to be converted into frames, which in turn, are the only things that make sense at the level of the data link layer. In other words, we are constructing a completely new network on top of an existing one. This is no different from our implementation of a communication layer as illustrated in Section 8.5.2.

Second, the main distinction with the approach followed in the case of LANs is that our local network has a dedicated station, i.e. a router, which has a separate connection to the outside world, in particular to one or more routers that may be part of other local area networks. It is by means of these routers that we are capable of passing information across local network boundaries, and which thus makes our higher-level network a wide area one.

The use of a service access point in our implementation of REQUEST is important. Using SAPs we are able to identify the package at the destination station which should handle the incoming frame. Again, this is completely analogous to our implementation of the packages SYNCHRONOUS and ASYNCHRONOUS in Section 8.5.2. And just as we had two concurrent communication layers in that case, we have the same situation when constructing wide area networks. This means that we may even support *several* wide area network implementations at the same time, where all implementations are based on just a single implementation of the data link layer at a particular local area network.

A general hierarchical WAN topology

So here we have it. First, we need to raise the level of abstraction by considering addressing conventions at a logically higher layer than the data link layer. This so-called network layer resolves addresses in the sense that it finds out if the addressed station is part of the current LAN. If we are addressing a station outside this LAN, it may be forwarded to one of the possibly several available routers. Each of these routers is just another station in the LAN. From here on, organizing a WAN is really not difficult. The first point to realize is that if we were to connect all routers into one very large worldwide network, we would probably find ourselves with a network comprising thousands of routers – indeed a situation we would like to avoid in view of maintenance. A generally accepted approach is to adopt a hierarchical scheme consisting of three levels.

- At the lowest level we have what is generally referred to as a **subnetwork**. A subnetwork is actually what we called a LAN. It is generally a bridged LAN or MAN with one or several routers that allow access to the outside world.

- Subnetworks, in turn, are organized into **areas**. An area thus consists of a collection of routers of which each is attached to a subnetwork. Two subnetworks may be connected to each other by one or several routers. In addition, each area will have special routers that allow communication with stations lying outside the area.

- Finally, areas are organized into so-called **domains**. Again, two areas within a domain can be connected by means of routers. Also, special routers are distinguished to allow communication to take place with stations lying outside a specific domain.

This general architecture is shown in Figure 9.2.

We will have more to say about this hierarchical layering when we discuss internetworking in Section 9.3. The important point to note here is that this hierarchical organization also implies a hierarchical routing scheme. For example, in order for data to transfer from subnetwork S_{111} in Figure 9.2 to subnetwork S_{232}, it will have to traverse to a router contained in area A_{11}, and from there to one of the routers comprising domain D_1. Once the data has reached that level, it can be forwarded to a router of domain D_2 which will need to forward it to (in this case) an area router of area A_{23}. It is then the responsibility of this latter router to get the data to subnetwork S_{232}, in this case implying that it will need to cross subnetwork S_{231} which is also contained in area A_{23}.

9.1.4   Communication models revisited

In Section 7.2.4 we mentioned that WANs can generally be classified by their switching technology which could be based on either **packet-switching** or **circuit-switching**. Let's briefly review these concepts here.

Packet-switching versus circuit-switching

In a packet-switched network a message is generally first divided into a number of smaller **packets** before sending it to its destination. A packet in a wide area network is the same

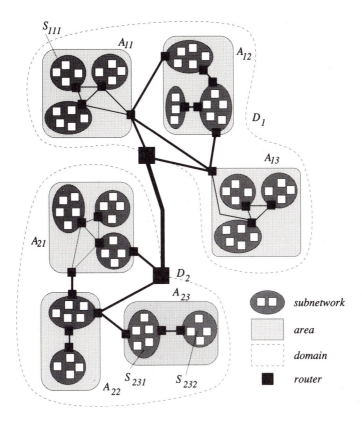

Figure 9.2 The general architecture of a WAN in terms of subnetworks, areas, and domains.

as a **frame** in a local area network: a single, and indivisible unit of data. More precisely, frame transmission takes place at the level of the data link layer, whereas packet transmission occurs at the level of the network layer. Each packet is augmented with the address of the destination and sent across the network. Each time a packet arrives at a router, the latter first stores it and inspects the destination address, and subsequently forwards it to another router according to a routing strategy. The point to note is that each packet that is part of the original message is stored and forwarded completely independently of any other packet of that message. This may imply that each packet follows a completely different route before it reaches the destination. Finally, when all packets have reached the last router, they are reassembled into the original message which is then passed on to the actual destination. Packet switching is thus comparable to national postal systems where envelopes are forwarded from one sorting office to another. It is mandatory to provide the complete destination address so that each office can decide where to forward the envelope.

In a circuit-switched network, on the other hand, communication starts by first setting up a complete physical connection between the sending and receiving station. To this end, each router makes a permanent connection between a preceding and a successive router which eventually results in a direct communication path from the source to the destination. This path is maintained as long as required by both communicating parties, and, moreover, it can *only* be used by these two. As long as the connection is maintained, each message from the source to the destination is sent across the same path. As soon as one of the communicating parties issues a disconnect request, the path will be broken and message exchange is further prohibited until a new connection is set up. In this sense, circuit-switched networks are comparable to the way we make phone calls.

The distinction between packet-switching and circuit-switching in networks is an important one and each switching method has its advantages and disadvantages. As an illustration, let's mention some more important examples of both:

- Although setting up a complete physical communication path between a source and destination station may indeed take some time, it should be clear that once a connection has been established, message exchange can be extremely efficient. For one thing, it is no longer necessary to provide any information on where messages are destined as this is completely determined by the physical connection itself. In this sense, communication in a circuit-switched network can be extremely efficient from a user's point of view.

- The main disadvantage of circuit-switched networks, however, is that a communication path is entirely dedicated to one source and one destination station. This means that if two other stations need to communicate, they should establish a completely distinct connection. Consequently, *overall* utilization of the network may be rather poor.

- Packet-switched networks, on the other hand, avoid this situation. Because each packet is stored and subsequently forwarded from router to router, connections between two routers immediately become available for other packets as soon as a transmission has been completed. Consequently, packet-switched networks tend to show a much higher overall utilization than circuit-switched networks.

- The primary disadvantage of packet-switched networks, however, is that each message must be partitioned into a number of packets, which are later to be reassembled. This may put a rather heavy burden on the routers when considering the fact that packets may follow entirely different routes, implying that they need not arrive at the destination in the order they were sent.

Both types of networks are important and the choice for either (or indeed, a mixture of the two) depends on many factors. In general, whenever communication has to be reliable and subject to timing constraints (e.g., constant transmission rate), a circuit-switched approach will be used. On the other hand, data communication is generally easier to realize and more efficient with regard to network utilization when using packet-switched networks.

Datagrams versus virtual circuits

Packet-switching and circuit-switching have their counterparts at a logical level as well. In particular, a distinction is made between networks supporting so-called datagrams and those supporting what is known as virtual circuits.

Datagrams are comparable to what we have termed packets above. At the logical level, a datagram is a self-contained message that can be sent across a network independently of any other datagram. This implies that it will include the address of the destination, which is subsequently used to forward it from station to station. In addition to containing the destination address, a datagram generally also contains the address of the source station, as well as information that will allow the destination station to see if the datagram has been corrupted on its way through the network. The major difference with packets is that datagrams exist only at the logical level. In contrast to packets, for example, a datagram may be fragmented into smaller parts which are sent independently of each other. It is the responsibility of the destination to ensure that the original message is reassembled as fragments arrive.

The logical equivalent of circuit-switching is the use of so-called **virtual circuits**. A virtual circuit is a logical connection between two stations across a network. Logical in this sense means that the underlying physical network need not employ circuit-switching technology, but may instead be based on packet-switching. In that case, it is the software which maintains the view of a circuit between two stations. Once a virtual circuit has been set up, messages can be sent across it, which are then guaranteed to arrive in the same order as they were sent. In contrast to datagrams, sending messages across a virtual circuit need not carry the destination address with them because the destination is identified as the endpoint of the virtual circuit.

Using datagrams or virtual circuits corresponds with the two basic communication models we discussed in Chapter 6. Datagrams are used in connectionless communication, where virtual circuits need to be set up in connection-oriented communication. When discussing wide area networks, these two models are important topics. In practice, WANs virtually always support a connectionless mode of communication. In other words, the means to communicate across such a network is by sending datagrams. But having only connectionless communication is really something we do not always want. Instead, it turns out that the connection-oriented model is far more appropriate in most cases. To that end, WANs provide additional connection-oriented services which are often built *on top* of their connectionless services. We shall have more to say about the implementation of these communication models in the following sections.

9.2   Routing in wide area networks

We are now able to concentrate on one of the major distinctions between LANs and WANs: routing. Selecting an appropriate route is an important task for a router, and differs from the way in which bridges select routes. In particular, routers are generally concerned with the selection of a route that will avoid **network congestion**. Network congestion may be

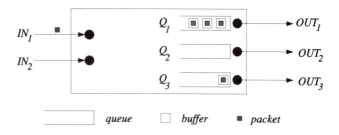

Figure 9.3 Accepting and storing incoming packets at a router.

observed when a number of routers are (temporarily) not adequately capable of processing incoming data. How congestion may occur and how it is dealt with is discussed in Section 9.2.1. In order to avoid congestion, routers need to generally adopt an adaptive routing strategy. In other words, selecting a route may be dependent on the overall state of the network. Routing strategies are discussed in Section 9.2.2.

9.2.1   Network congestion

In order to explain the phenomenon of network congestion, we first need to take a closer look at the organization of routers. We assume that all network traffic takes place in the form of transportation of so-called **packets**. We see that routers should be capable of accepting incoming packets, and forwarding these packets to other routers. The crucial point here is that routers need temporarily to *store* incoming packets before forwarding them. This can be illustrated by considering the logical organization of a router as shown in Figure 9.3.

In the figure we have depicted a router with two incoming links: IN_1 and IN_2. Packets destined for the router will thus arrive via either one of these links. Conversely, there are three output links: OUT_1, OUT_2, and OUT_3, respectively. We assume that a link is simply the direct connection from one router to precisely one other router. Now whenever a packet arrives via one of the input links the router will need to decide via which output link it is to be forwarded. As soon as the output link has been selected, the router then stores the packet in an output queue Q_j ($j = 1, 2, 3$) associated with that link. Queuing a packet is necessary when the link is already being used to send another packet, or when the receiving side is not ready to receive the next packet because it has too many packets arriving at that moment.

Here we come to the source of our problem. Queues associated with an outgoing link are generally limited to a maximum length. In other words, we may find ourselves in the situation where a router cannot store an incoming packet because a queue has become full. Network congestion is the result of the limited capacity of routers to temporarily store incoming packets while waiting for outgoing links to become available for packet forwarding. In essence, there are only two solutions to this problem: (1) simply discard a packet when it cannot be stored, or (2) refuse any incoming packets until they can be stored again. As we shall see, the second solution is in fact not a real alternative, and practice shows that discarding packets in packet-switched networks is almost unavoidable. In the next two sections we shall start with taking a look at the general policy of discarding packets. The effects of refusing incoming packets is discussed thereafter. How packet discarding can be avoided is our third topic with respect to network congestion.

Packet discarding

Probably the simplest way to control network congestion is to discard an incoming packet when there is nowhere to queue it. In other words, an incoming packet may still be accepted by a router, but is then simply thrown away. This may seem as a rather crude solution, but, in fact, it turns out to work well in practice. What it means is that the network simply does not guarantee **reliability**: it may happen that packets are simply lost. Clearly, packets are not actually lost; they are merely deliberately discarded somewhere on their route from source to destination.

A packet discarding policy requires that we have criteria to decide whether an accepted packet is to be forwarded. To this end, several strategies have been developed of which we outline one here. The point is that each router has a fixed number of buffers available that can be used temporarily to store incoming packets. In addition, each outgoing queue always has a minimum number of buffers at its disposal, but, on the other hand, it can never have all buffers in use. To illustrate, reconsider our router R shown in Figure 9.3, and assume it has a total of N_{buf} buffers available, implying that it can store at most N_{buf} incoming packets. Now suppose that a packet P arrives that should be forwarded to link OUT_3, which is connected to, say, router R^*. Assuming R^* cannot accept a packet at the time of P's arrival, the router R allocates one of its buffers to store P, and subsequently puts the buffer in queue Q_3 as shown in Figure 9.4.

Now suppose that *all* buffers have eventually been queued for link OUT_3. The problem that arises then is that new incoming packets have to be discarded, even if they could be forwarded to routers other than R^*. This is caused by the fact that router R has no more buffers available to store an incoming packet temporarily. The objective to prevent this situation is to allocate a *maximum* number of buffers to each queue Q_j. In that case, there will always be buffers available for the other outgoing links. For example, suppose the maximum queue length has been set at six, and that there are 12 buffers available. As soon as queue Q_3 has six buffers pending, any incoming packet for link OUT_3 will then be discarded, while packets for any other outgoing link can still be accepted and queued (assuming that the length of the respective outgoing queues is smaller than six).

Similarly, each outgoing link may always have a minimum number of buffers at its disposal. In this way, it can be guaranteed to a certain extent that packets for a specific route can always be forwarded. To illustrate, assume that in our example router we reserve two buffers in advance for each outgoing link. Now suppose that both links OUT_1 and OUT_2 each already have five pending packets, whereas link OUT_1 has no packets waiting to be forwarded. As we assumed that there were a total of 12 buffers, we thus still have two buffers available for incoming packets. Now, despite the fact that the maximum queue length has been set at six, the router will discard any packet for either link

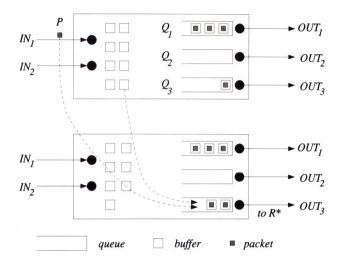

Figure 9.4 Allocating a buffer for an incoming packet destined for link OUT_3.

OUT_1 or OUT_2, for the simple reason that this would imply that there was only one buffer left for link OUT_3.

Using this combined strategy of allocating a maximum, and reserving a minimum number of buffers for outgoing links, turns out to work well in practice. It should be realized, however, that although packet loss may be reduced to an acceptable minimum, we have not achieved reliable communication. In other words, losing packets along the route is still possible.

Refusing incoming packets

Now look at the second alternative, refusing incoming packets. Refusing to process incoming packets can at best be a temporary solution. The problem is that as long as one router, say R, refuses to accept any packets, routers that wish to forward packets to R may gradually also come to a halt as their respective outgoing queues will also eventually become full. The result is what is called a **deadlock**, and is illustrated in Figure 9.5. What we see there is that each outgoing queue has reached its maximum length. Consequently, no one can forward a packet to a next station (because it cannot be queued there), and the system comes to a halt.

Deadlocks are a major problem. First, it may take a considerable amount of work just to detect them. But even if a deadlock has been detected, then it still is not easy to untie the routers that take part in the deadlock. The best alternative, therefore, is simply to avoid situations in which deadlocks can occur. This does mean, however, that routers may never refuse an incoming packet. Instead, they need to adopt a policy in which packets can always be accepted. Now, of course, if we adopted the general packet discarding policy as outlined above, deadlock would never occur. As soon as there are no more

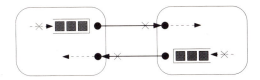

Figure 9.5 The presence of deadlock in a network due to incoming packets being refused.

buffers, the total amount of packets in the network is simply brought back by throwing packets away. In effect, the network traffic is not jammed, but rather, it is simply discarded until destination stations start accepting incoming messages again. Clearly, a less crude method would be preferable. Ideally, we would want to avoid the situation where packets need to be discarded altogether. And this is a difficult objective to meet in practice. A compromise is always to accept packets but to give preference to those that have already made considerable progress through the network.

▷ Let's take a closer look at one such solution. We assume that each packet is bound to a maximum lifetime, implying that each packet has an **age** attached to it. Initially, a packet starts with age 0. Each time it passes a router its age is incremented by 1. Consequently, the current age of a packet denotes the number of routers it has passed since it was initially sent by its source station. Now suppose that the maximum age for all packets is A_{max}. Furthermore, denote by $age(P)$ the present age of a packet P. What we can do then is organize the buffers at each router in a hierarchical way as follows.

For each age k, there will be a fixed number of buffers available, denoted as the set **class**(k). A buffer can be either *free* or *in use*. Now the point is that a buffer $buf(k)$ from **class**(k) can only be used for a packet P with $age(P) \geq k$. In other words, a packet must be "old" enough before it can be allotted a (free) buffer from **class**(k). Each time a packet P arrives, the router will proceed according to the following five steps:

1. **Initial.** Let i denote the currently inspected class of buffer. Set $i \leftarrow 0$.
2. **Inspect.** If there is a free buffer from **class**(i), allocate a buffer $buf(i)$ for storing packet P: go to Step 4. Otherwise go to Step 3.
3. **Increment.** No buffer from **class**(i) was free, so set $i \leftarrow i+1$. If $i \leq age(P)$, continue with Step 2, otherwise go to Step 5.
4. **Allocate.** Use the buffer $buf(i)$ found in Step 2 for storing P. Register it as being in use, and stop: allocation succeeded.
5. **Discard.** There is no buffer available for P, so discard the packet and stop searching.

To see that the network does not deadlock, assume the converse. In that case, we have a situation where, for a certain router R, all buffers are presently allocated to a packet. In particular, consider a buffer buf from **class**(A_{max}) allocated to a packet P. Clearly, we will have $age(P) = A_{max}$, otherwise buffer buf could never have been allocated to P in the first place. Two situations can occur. First, if P is queued for an outgoing link to which its destination station is connected, then there is no problem: P can be safely delivered and buf becomes available again. On the other hand, if the outgoing link for which P is queued is *not* connected to its destination, but instead to another router R^*, P can still be delivered to R^*, although $age(P)$ will be incremented by one. Consequently, upon arrival at R^*, P will be discarded because (1) there are no more buffers available at R^*, and (2) P has simply become too old. We conclude that our initial assumption, namely that the network was deadlocked cannot hold. What we effectively have, is that as soon as the buffers at each router are gradually all allocated to incoming packets, only those that have already traveled a relatively long way will continue to their destination. Clearly, the choice of A_{max} is crucial and will depend on the size of the network.

Avoiding network congestion

Discarding packets is a problem. The main disadvantage is that there is no way of guaranteeing reliable communication as long as there is the possibility that packets are lost during transmission. How reliable communications can be built on top of unreliable networks will be discussed in Section 9.5. At this point, however, it is illustrative to look into a situation in which packet discarding need never occur. In other words, there is an elegant way of preventing network congestion altogether.

The problem of network congestion was caused by the lack of available buffers at routers to store incoming packets temporarily. But in that case, there is an obvious way to ensure that there is always a buffer available: claim it in advance. And this is precisely what can be done when we are dealing with **connection-oriented communication**. In that case, before a source station starts transmitting packets to a destination, it first sends a request packet across the network. Now assume that this packet travels to the destination station according to a route consisting of routers $R_1, \ldots, R_N$. Such a route is called a **virtual circuit**. Then, each router R_i can preallocate a buffer for the packets that are yet to be sent from the source to the destination. Clearly, *all* future packets will follow the same virtual circuit, but it is also clear that none of these packets needs to be discarded as there will always be a buffer available to them. In this sense, as soon as a route has been successively established, no network congestion will be observed by either the source or the destination station.

And what if a request packet does not reach the destination? In that case, there was good reason not to preallocate a virtual circuit as the network was already congested. Instead, the source station will receive a packet indicating that the setup of a connection failed due to congestion. This situation is comparable to trying to phone someone during a peak period. Although the person you want to talk to may be sitting at home waiting for your call, you will still get the busy tone because the telephone lines are occupied by other calls. It is important to note that due to the practicalities of network congestion, many wide area networks do not support connection-oriented communication at the level of the OSI network layer. Instead, the best provided service is that of unreliable communication in the form of packet transmission as we have discussed so far.

9.2.2 Selecting routes

Until now, we have deliberately avoided any details concerning the routing strategies as applied in wide area networks. But by now, it should be clear that routing is not only an extremely important topic, it is also a difficult one when discussing WANs. The difficulties primarily arise from the fact that routers should adopt a policy in which network congestion can be circumvented. Again, notice that this is entirely different from routing in LANs. As we have mentioned, routing in that case is primarily concerned with getting a frame across the entire network, but also only once to each station. In the case of WANs we are dealing with a means to use the network as efficiently as possible, and to avoid the situation where somewhere along the line packets will have to be discarded due to limited buffering capabilities of the individual routers.

In general, most wide area networks have adopted routing strategies that vary with the state of network congestion. In other words, the fixed routing strategies for LANs as discussed in Section 8.3.2 generally have no counterparts in WANs. Instead, we need to explore **adaptive routing strategies**. In order to apply adaptive routing, we need to have criteria on which a decision can be based. Also, as its name suggests, these criteria will vary over time. Virtually all wide area networks we consider here base their decision making on some kind of *least-cost criterion*. In particular, when we consider a WAN as a graph in which the nodes are formed by the routers, and the links between these routers as the edges, then least-cost algorithms assume that each link l has an associated cost $cost(l)$. Whenever a packet P needs to traverse N links $l_1, \ldots, l_N$ the total cost $cost_{tot}(P)$ of sending P across these links is then simply computed as the sum of the individual costs:

$$cost_{tot}(P) \;=\; \sum_{i=1}^{N} cost(l_i)$$

This leaves us with two issues to address: (1) how we determine the cost of a link, and (2) how we can find a route for a packet P such that $cost_{tot}(P)$ is minimal.

Determining the cost of a link

There are numerous ways to associate a cost to a link. The simplest relation is to set the cost to 1. In that case, determining the minimum overall cost for sending a packet reduces to finding the shortest route from its source to its destination. Although this may seem a rather naive way of looking at things, in view of the fact that links may occasionally fail, and thus that the network topology may change over time, it is seen that we may indeed speak of an adaptive routing scheme.

A better criterion is to relate the cost to the transmission rate that is supported by the link. For example, if a link is merely an ordinary telephone line capable of supporting packet transmission at a rate of 20 000 bps, it would be reasonable to associate a relatively high cost to the link. On the other hand, high-speed links that support, say, a transmission rate of 10 Mbps would have a relatively low cost associated.

Another criterion may be related to the actual costs in terms of money. For example, satellite connections are generally not very cheap implying that packet transfer may indeed considerably increase the monthly bill of an institute that makes use of this transmission medium. This can already be seen with ordinary telephone lines. If you make many calls abroad you will undoubtedly be charged at the end of the month with an amount that is, in most cases, rather high. You may decide to resort to ordinary mail which is generally much cheaper, although also much slower.

Yet another means to measure the cost of a link is to take a look at the number of packets pending in its associated outgoing queue. If the length of the queue is high, it may be a wise decision to seek an alternative link as the network is apparently subject to local congestion.

In general, most adaptive routing strategies combine these criteria in order to arrive at a cost per link. The problem, however, is that most costs vary over time, implying that in order to find the best route we will have to calculate the costs at regular intervals. Doing this too fast may imply that we can never make a decision, for as soon as a best route has been found, it may turn out that the network may have changed in such a way that another route may be better. On the other hand, if costs are recalculated only after a long period of time has elapsed, they may not reflect the actual state of the network. Finding a compromise between these two is not always easy.

Link state routing

There are a number of ways of finding the cheapest route in a network, but two of the most popular ones are based on so-called link states and distance vectors, respectively. We start with considering link state routing.

In the case of link state routing, each router has to know the topology of the entire network. In particular, it has to know which routers are connected to each other and the cost of each link. Using this information, a router can easily calculate the cheapest route to each other router.

To find the cheapest route starting at a router R_0 we divide routers into two classes: a class $\mathbf{S}$ consisting of routers to which the cheapest route has been found, and a class $\overline{\mathbf{S}}$ for which this is not the case. A next cheapest route can then be constructed by finding a link $[R, \hat{R}]$, where $R \in \mathbf{S}$ and $\hat{R} \in \overline{\mathbf{S}}$, such that the route to $\hat{R}$ via R is the cheapest route that can be constructed in this way. The router $\hat{R}$ that is found according to this procedure is then added to the set $\mathbf{S}$. It is important to note that in order to find routes in this way, we must know exactly the topology of the network.

▷ We can formulate link state routing more accurately in terms of the following algorithm, which is due to Dijkstra (1959). As we have stated, adaptive routing strategies view the network as a graph in which the nodes are formed by routers, and links constitute the edges. Each link l is labeled with a cost $cost_{\text{link}}(l)$, representing the cost of sending a packet across that link. Dijkstra's algorithm proceeds as follows. Suppose we want to find the cheapest route from a router R_0 to any other router in the network. Denote by $cost_{\text{route}}^{\text{sofar}}(R_0, R)$ the cost of the cheapest route from R_0 to R found so far, and by $last(R_0, R)$ the last link of that cheapest route. Furthermore, denote by $\mathbf{S}$ the set of routers for which the cheapest route has been found and by $\overline{\mathbf{S}}$ those for which this is not the case (this will be further explained in the algorithm). The cost of link $[R,\hat{R}]$ between two adjacent routers is denoted as $cost_{\text{link}}(R,\hat{R})$. If there is no link between these two routers, we write $cost_{\text{link}}(R,\hat{R}) = \infty$, i.e. we set the cost to infinity.

1. **Initial.** Initialize the set $\mathbf{S}$ and the various values for $cost_{\text{route}}^{\text{sofar}}(R)$ and $last(R_0,R)$ as follows:

$$\mathbf{S} = \{R_0\}$$

$$cost_{\text{route}}^{\text{sofar}}(R_0,R) = \begin{cases} 0 & \text{if } R = R_0 \\ cost_{\text{link}}(R_0,R) & \text{otherwise} \end{cases}$$

$$last(R_0,R) = \begin{cases} [R_0,R] & \text{if } cost_{\text{link}}(R_0,R) < \infty \\ \emptyset & \text{otherwise} \end{cases}$$

Note that $\overline{\mathbf{S}}$ now consists of all routers except R_0.

2. **Expand.** During each expansion step, select a router $R_{\text{new}} \in \overline{\mathbf{S}}$ for which we have that $cost_{\text{route}}^{\text{sofar}}(R_0,R_{\text{new}})$ is minimal. Add this router to the set $\mathbf{S}$ of inspected routers, and finalize its costs, i.e.

$$\mathbf{S} \leftarrow \mathbf{S} + R_{\text{new}}$$

$$\overline{\mathbf{S}} \leftarrow \overline{\mathbf{S}} - R_{\text{new}}$$

$$cost_{\text{route}}(R_0,R_{\text{new}}) \leftarrow cost_{\text{route}}^{\text{sofar}}(R_0,R_{\text{new}})$$

In this step, $\mathbf{S}$ consists of all routers for which a cheapest path has been found. The router R_{new} is the next one that is nearest to these routers (nearest in the sense that it can be reached at minimal cost from one of the routers in $\mathbf{S}$). Therefore, we add it to $\mathbf{S}$, and remove it from the set of routers that need to be further inspected.

3. **Update.** If $\overline{\mathbf{S}} = \emptyset$, then stop. Otherwise, for each router $R_{\text{rest}} \in \overline{\mathbf{S}}$, calculate a new cost $cost_{\text{route}}^{\text{new}}(R_0,R_{\text{rest}})$ of a route from R_0 to R_{rest} taking the router R_{new} identified in the previous step into account, and where

$$cost_{\text{route}}^{\text{new}}(R_0,R_{\text{rest}}) =$$
$$\min\{cost_{\text{route}}^{\text{sofar}}(R_0,R_{\text{rest}}), cost_{\text{route}}(R_0,R_{\text{new}}) + cost_{\text{link}}(R_{\text{new}},R_{\text{rest}})\}$$

If $cost_{\text{route}}^{\text{new}}(R_0,R_{\text{rest}}) < cost_{\text{route}}^{\text{sofar}}(R_0,R_{\text{rest}})$, i.e. the newly calculated cost is smaller than the one found previously, then make the following replacements:

$$cost_{\text{route}}^{\text{sofar}}(R_0,R_{\text{rest}}) \leftarrow cost_{\text{route}}^{\text{new}}(R_0,R_{\text{rest}})$$

$$last(R_0,R_{\text{rest}}) \leftarrow [R_{\text{new}},R_{\text{rest}}]$$

After having done this update for each router in $\overline{S}$, continue with the following expansion, i.e. go to step 2.

This implies that if we find a cheaper route from R_0 to R_{rest}, now via the router R_{new} which had just been added to S, then this route is recorded by updating $last(R_0, R_{rest})$, and also updating the total cost for reaching router R_{rest} found so far. Clearly, R_{rest} may then be eligible for selection during the next expansion of S.

The cheapest route from R_0 to a destination router R is found by backtracking, i.e., starting at R, $last(R_0, R)$ will be the last link of the cheapest route to R. If $last(R_0, R) = [R_{pred}, R]$, then the next-to-last link will be $last(R_0, R_{pred})$, etc.

The algorithm is illustrated in Figure 9.6. The starting node is 1, from which the shortest path to each other node needs to be found. Initially, we have $S = \{1\}$, and $\overline{S} = \{2, 3, 4, 5, 6\}$, and $cost_{route}^{sofar}(1, R)$ for each node R is equal to:

node:	1	2	3	4	5	6
$cost_{route}^{sofar}$:	0	50	∞	40	25	10
inspect?	N	Y	Y	Y	Y	Y

We have also indicated whether a node needs to be further inspected. For the ones that require no further inspection, the cheapest path has already been found. Initially, this is only the case for node 1. During the first expansion step, node 6 will be selected, because $cost_{route}^{sofar}(1, 6)$ is the lowest for all nodes in $\overline{S}$. By selecting this node, we can update the cost to other nodes by taking a look at paths from node 1 via node 6. This leads to the following adjustments as part of the first update step.

node:	1	2	3	4	5	6
$cost_{route}^{sofar}$:	0	35	∞	35	25	10
inspect?	N	Y	Y	Y	Y	N

Note how we have discovered cheaper routes to nodes 2 and 4, respectively. Both routes go from node 1 via node 6.

The second expansion step will select node 5 from $\overline{S}$, thereby making a route available to node 3 at cost of 45. From there on, no further cost improvements can be made, and the selection of nodes from $\overline{S}$ proceeds as shown in Figure 9.6.

Distance vector routing

Distance vector routing employs a different strategy. In this case, a router maintains information on the costs of the cheapest route (referred to as the distance) to each destination in the network. The cost of this route is calculated by taking into account only the distance of each of its neighbors from all other routers. In this way, a router can easily determine what its own distance is from every other router.

To illustrate, suppose that a router R_0 has recorded for itself that the cost of reaching a destination router R_{dest} is 93 units, and that this is achieved by forwarding packets for R_{dest} to its adjacent router R_{succ}. If the cost of the link between R_0 and R_{succ} is 12, then clearly

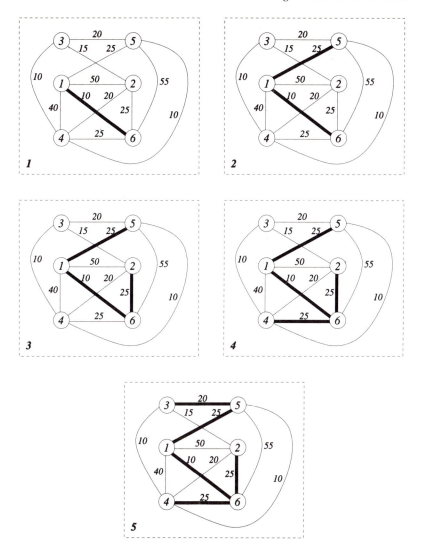

Figure 9.6 An example of finding all least-cost paths originating at node 1, using Dijkstra's algorithm.

it should cost R_{succ} precisely 81 units to get packets to R_{dest}. Now suppose things change in the network. In particular, assume that another router R_{succ}^* which is also adjacent to R_0 finds that it can get packets to R_{dest} at a cost of 85 units. If we let R_0 regularly request its neighbors to state at what price they can forward packets to R_{dest}, then R_0 will change its route to R_{dest} if the cost of the link between R_0 and R_{succ}^* is smaller than 8. In that case, the cost of sending a packet from R_0 to R_{dest} drops below the initial value of 93.

▷ Let's see how this works. Suppose we wish to determine the cheapest route starting at some router R_0. Denote by $cost_{\text{route}}^{(k)}(R_0, R)$ the cost of the cheapest route from R_0 to R, under the constraint that the **length** of that route be not longer than k. In other words, there should be no more than $k - 1$ intermediate routers from R_0 to R. For any router R, denote by $\textbf{adj}(R)$ the set of its adjacent routers. The cost of a link between two routers R and $\hat{R}$ is again denoted as $cost_{\text{link}}(R, \hat{R})$. Finally, denote by $first(R_0, R)$ the *first* router adjacent to R_0 to which a message for router R should be forwarded. The algorithm, generally referred to as the Bellman–Ford algorithm, works as follows:

1. **Initial.** Initialize the values for $cost_{\text{route}}^{(1)}(R_0, R)$ and $first(R_0, R)$ as follows:

$$
cost_{\text{route}}^{(1)}(R_0, R) = \begin{cases} 0 & \text{if } R = R_0 \\ cost_{\text{link}}(R_0, R) & \text{if } R \in \textbf{adj}(R_0) \\ \infty & \text{otherwise} \end{cases}
$$

$$
first(R_0, R) = \begin{cases} [R_0, R] & \text{if } R \in \textbf{adj}(R_0) \\ \emptyset & \text{otherwise} \end{cases}
$$

The initialization step effectively establishes that the cost of getting from R_0 to any other router by means of just one link is either finite by crossing the link to an adjacent router or infinite in the case of non-adjacent routers. By setting $first(R_0, R) = \infty$ for non-adjacent routers, we express that those routers cannot be directly reached.

2. **Update.** Starting at $k = 1$, during the kth update step, calculate first for *each* router R the alternative cost $cost_{\text{new}}^{(k+1)}(R_0, R)$ with

$$
cost_{\text{new}}^{(k+1)}(R_0, R) = \min_{R^* \in \textbf{adj}(R)} \{ cost_{\text{route}}^{(k)}(R_0, R^*) + cost_{\text{link}}(R^*, R) \}
$$

This alternative cost expresses the cost of reaching a router R by passing at most k routers by first considering routes of length k to any router R^* that is adjacent to R, and then crossing the link between R^* and R. Now suppose that the minimum value for $cost_{\text{new}}^{(k+1)}(R_0, R)$ is obtained if we traverse a route via router $R_{\text{min}} \in \textbf{adj}(R)$. Two situations may occur:

(1) $cost_{\text{new}}^{(k+1)}(R_0, R) \geq cost^{(k)}(R_0, R)$. In this case, an alternative, *longer* route from R_0 to R was not any cheaper than any route we had found so far. In that case, we leave things as they are, i.e.

$$
cost_{\text{route}}^{(k+1)}(R_0, R) \leftarrow cost_{\text{route}}^{(k)}(R_0, R)
$$
$$
first(R_0, R) \leftarrow \textit{unaltered}
$$

(2) $cost_{\text{new}}^{(k+1)}(R_0, R) < cost^{(k)}(R_0, R)$. In this case, we have found a longer route (via R_{min}) that is cheaper than any shorter route to R found so far. The following adjustments are then made:

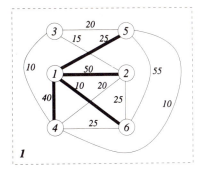 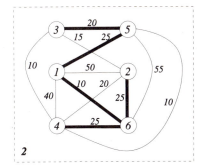

Figure 9.7 An example of finding the least-cost paths originating at node 1, using the Bellman–Ford algorithm.

$$cost_{route}^{(k+1)}(R_0,R) \quad \leftarrow \quad cost_{new}^{(k+1)}(R_0,R)$$
$$first(R_0,R) \quad \leftarrow \quad first(R_0,R_{min})$$

It is important to note that we already know the cheapest route to R_{min}, because $cost_{route}^{(k)}(R_0,R_{min})$ had already been calculated during the previous update step.

3. **Finalize.** If new cost values were found in the previous step, do another update step, thereby incrementing the value for k by 1. Otherwise, stop.

The algorithm is illustrated in Figure 9.7. The first step shows how all cheapest routes with a maximum length of one are found; the second, and also final step shows the cheapest routes of maximum length two. It can be verified that there are no *longer* cheaper routes originating at node 1.

Link state versus distance vector routing

If we compare routing based on either link states or distance vectors, an important distinction between the two is easily identified. In order for a router to find the cheapest routes to all routers when using link states it needs to know the entire topology of the network. But in the case of distance vector routing, a router can find the cheapest route to any other router by merely taking *local* information into account. In particular, it need only know the cost of the link to any adjacent router, as well as the distance from each of these adjacent routers to other routers.

Distance vector routing therefore seems more attractive than link state routing as decisions can be made using only local information, which, in turn, tends to make the work of a router simpler. However, there is one problem with distance vector routing. Although the algorithm is simpler, it generally does take more time eventually to discover the cheapest route. (This may seem to contradict our example where distance vector routing required only two steps, whereas link state routing required five steps. This difference arises entirely from the fact that we have considered only a small network. As networks grow, it can be shown that distance vector routing is indeed much more expensive in terms of network traffic and necessary computations.) In other words, the algorithm converges more slowly to a final solution than link state routing. This is particularly important in view of changes in the network as we shall see below.

9.2.3   Routing organization

Merely finding a good route is just one part of the story. It is also important to know *where* routes are actually calculated. In this section we shall concentrate on this organizational aspect of routing, following the classification discussed in Stallings (1994). In particular, we make a distinction based on where routing decisions are made, and where information on the network topology and congestion is maintained. This leads to three different classes of routing organization:

- **Isolated routing** which is characterized by the fact that *all* routing decisions are made locally; there is no central information available nor do nodes gather information on the global status of the network.

- In **centralized routing** schemes, each router takes its own decision with respect to routing packets, but information on network topology and congestion is obtained from a centralized location.

- **Distributed routing** is comparable to isolated routing, but routers additionally try to build up a view of the actual network traffic which they take into account when forwarding packets.

Let's take a closer look at these three classes of routing organization.

Isolated routing

An extremely simple example of an isolated routing organization is the **hot potato** algorithm. In this case, whenever a router accepts an incoming packet, it simply appends the packet to the shortest outgoing queue. The important point to note is that the router does not take into account whether the link associated with an outgoing queue is geared in the right direction. Consequently, a packet may be forwarded into a completely wrong direction, diverting it further from its destination. The hot potato algorithm can be considered as the bottom line for any routing algorithm. If an algorithm does routing worse, it can be better replaced by the simple and naive hot potato scheme.

▷ Of course, this algorithm can be easily improved if we place some information on the network topology at each router. In that case, the router can *bias* its decision with respect to selecting an outgoing link. To illustrate, assume there are N outgoing links $OUT_1, \ldots, OUT_N$. Denote by $len(Q_i)$ the current length of queue Q_i associated with link OUT_i. Then, for each destination station S in the network, we associate a (positive-valued) weight $weight_i(S)$ with link OUT_i. A low weight indicates that selection of the link will probably divert an incoming packet from its destination. A high weight, on the other hand, indicates that selection of the link will move the packet in the right direction. Using these notations, we can calculate the relative weight $weight_i^{rel}(S)$ of each outgoing link as:

$$weight_i^{rel}(S) \quad = \quad \frac{weight_i(S) \cdot len(Q_i)}{\sum_{i=1}^{N} weight_i(S) \cdot len(Q_i)}$$

and select the link for which $weight_i^{rel}(S)$ is the largest. Clearly, this scheme will only work if we provide each router with some information on the network topology. Due to the variance of the network topology, this information will need to be adapted at regular intervals. And in that case, much better routing strategies exist.

Centralized routing

Isolated routing organizations are rarely used by routers in practice for the simple reason that their decisions with respect to selecting appropriate routes are not very good. Much better decisions can be made when general information on network topology and traffic is available. To this end, some wide area networks employ a strategy in which a centralized **routing control center** maintains such information.

Each router in the network periodically sends information to the routing control center. This information may include average lengths of outgoing queues, how much traffic each outgoing link had during the last report period, malfunctioning links, etc. The routing control center gathers all this information and subsequently calculates for each router in the network the optimal routes along which it should forward packets. These routing tables, one for each router, are then passed back to the respective routers.

One of the major problems with this centralized approach is the fact that in order to respond quickly to changing overall network traffic, routing tables will have to be frequently updated. However, updating tables is a time-consuming task, especially if we take the additional communication between the routers and the control center into account. Consequently, the centralized approach may simply be too slow to respond adequately to changing traffic loads.

Another, and serious problem arises when the control center fails to work properly. In particular, imagine what happens when the center goes down completely. In that case, changes in network traffic cannot be responded to at all. This is an extremely vulnerable point, for example, in the TYMNET wide area network (Tymes, 1981) where each new user first has to communicate with the control center before even getting access to the network. If the center has broken down, then clearly new users cannot participate in communication across the network.

Distributed routing

A generally better but also more complex method of maintaining network information at each station is employed in distributed routing organizations. In these cases, each router attempts to maintain its own routing table for the entire network without having to consult a routing control center. The problem, of course, is how network information can be obtained. As an illustration of how distributed routing can work in practice, we will look at two strategies followed in the Internet (this example network is discussed further below.)

Distance vector routing.   A widely used distributed routing protocol in the Internet is the **routing information protocol**, or simply **RIP** (Hedrick, 1988). Under normal circumstances, a router that uses RIP generally sends its routing table to its adjacent routers once every 30 seconds. Each entry in a routing table essentially consists of the following information:[2]

- The address of a destination router R
- The address of an adjacent router to which packets for R should be forwarded
- The length of the route to R.

The cost of a link between two routers is then simply taken as 1. This means that routing is based on finding the *shortest* route. Whenever a router R_0 receives the routing table of an adjacent router R_{adj}, it can easily update its own routing table. For example, suppose R_0 finds that it has a route to, say, router R of length 9. If R_{adj} states that it can route packets to R through a route of length 6, then R_0 will adjust its entry for R by subsequently forwarding packets to R_{adj}. The shorter route between R_0 and R will then have length 7.

If a router R_0 has not received a routing table from its adjacent router R_{adj} for more than 3 minutes, it concludes that the link to R_{adj} has gone down. It then sets the cost of that link to infinity, and after another minute has passed (implying that the other adjacent routers will have been informed of the failure of that link), all routes via R_{adj} are removed from the routing table.

The main problem with RIP is that it takes a long time to stabilize after a link or router failure. By this we mean that other routers may still think that a route exists across a failed link, leading to additional traffic to correct this. Another problem is that the maximum length of a route that can be administrated is 15. Consequently, the size of the network expressed as the length of the shortest path between any two routers is limited as well.

Link state routing.   In the case of link state routing, a router determines who its neighbors are and the cost of the link to each neighbor. This information is gathered in a so-called **link state packet** (**LSP**), and subsequently *broadcast* to all other routers. Broadcasting an LSP is an essential difference with distance vector routing: it enables each router to build a complete picture of the topology of the network. We shall briefly discuss link state routing and the interested reader is referred to Perlman (1993) for further details.

---

[2]Note that for clarity, we have combined the information of a routing table and that which is actually sent by adjacent routers to allow updates.

The cheapest path to each other router is determined as soon as a complete picture of the network has been obtained through the incoming LSPs. To that end, Dijkstra's algorithm (or a variant thereof) as explained above is generally applied. The real problem with link state routing is the distribution of the LSPs throughout the network. Therefore, each LSP contains at least the following information:

- An address identifying the router that generated the LSP

- A sequence number in order to indicate newer LSPs generated by the same router

- A field containing an expiration time until the LSP is to be considered out of date, and thus that it should be discarded.

Now suppose a router R_0 broadcasts an updated LSP. If another router receives this LSP, it removes the previous one received from R_0. The fact that the LSP just received is indeed more recent can be seen by inspecting its sequence number. A router is forced to generate a new LSP approximately once every hour, which corresponds to the maximum time any LSP is considered to be valid. It is precisely because of this relatively long life of LSPs that broadcasting the network topology across the network is feasible. Of course, if links fail, then a router connected to a failing link can generate an LSP as well.

9.3 Internetworking

So far, we have tacitly assumed that all WANs look alike so that it is easy to send messages from one network to another. However, such an assumption is not realistic. In practice, wide area networks are constructed by interconnecting several different kinds of networks together, giving rise to a so-called **internetwork**, or **internet**.[3] The problem with internetworks is that their constituents networks need not be the same. And this causes a lot of trouble. In this section we shall take a closer look at the problems that need to be solved when dealing with constructing a wide area network from different networks.

9.3.1 What makes internetworks different

When constructing an internetwork from different networks, we should keep in mind that its users should not be aware of the fact that there *are* different underlying networks at all. In other words, the fact that the internetwork is built from different networks should be *transparent* to its users. No matter where the internetwork is accessed, it should always appear in the same way. This transparency is to be achieved at the level of the OSI network layer. In particular, we may assume that this layer is divided into two sublayers as shown in Figure 9.8. The lower part of the layer, which we refer to as the **subnet layer**, consists of the network protocols as supported by a specific constituent network.

---

[3]We shall use the term "internetwork" rather than the more popular "internet" in order to avoid confusion with an internetwork called "Internet".

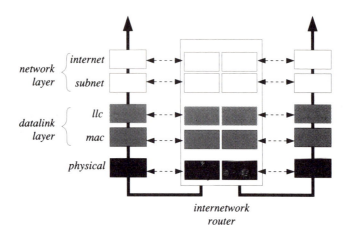

Figure 9.8 The subdivision of the network layer into two sublayers to support internetworking.

The upper part, called the **internet layer**, consists of the protocols that are specific to an internetwork. Note, by the way, that a constituent network may be *any* network that provides support at the level of the network layer. Such networks include WANs not only, but also LANs and MANs that have been extended with communication protocols for the network layer.

An internetwork will thus add an internet sublayer to the existing network layer which supports the transmission of packets across the internetwork. Let's refer to these packets as **internet packets**, in order to distinguish them from what we shall call **subnet packets** which are specific to the networks that constitute an internetwork. Now, in order to send an internet packet across an internetwork, we will have to make use of the facilities provided by each of of the constituent networks. In particular, this means that each internet packet will have to be converted into subnet packets that can be accepted by the constituent networks. Clearly, the responsibility for such a conversion lies with the routers. In order to see the kind of work that a router needs to do, reconsider Figure 9.2 and imagine how data exchange between a station in network S_{111} and one in network S_{232} would need to be supported. In particular, we may expect that a message must cross a number of different constituent networks as shown in Figure 9.9.

The problems start as soon as network boundaries need to be crossed. For example, the router in Figure 9.9 connecting S_{111} to network A_{11} will need to support two communication protocols: the one by which all stations in S_{111} communicate, and the one by which all routers in A_{11} communicate. But there is more. Not only should the router establish that messages can be transferred between the two networks, it should also ensure that the services as provided by the internetwork are kept intact.

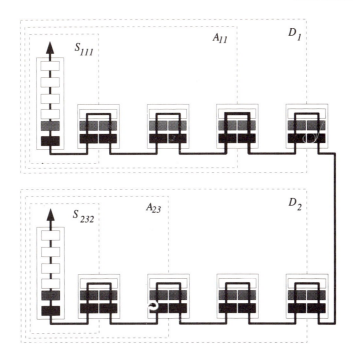

Figure 9.9 Passing a message across different networks through routers.

Additional problems

Let's be more specific, and look at some of the more apparent differences between networks that should be made invisible to a user when constructing an internetwork (see also Stallings, 1994).

- **Addressing schemes.** First, the internetwork should provide a uniform addressing scheme. Now this may seem an obvious thing to do, but when you realize that different networks generally have different addressing conventions, we may indeed have a problem to solve. In essence, the problem lies in the fact that a router should be capable of translating a source address at the level of the data link layer into a target data link address of a next router that may have a completely different format. In particular, how data link addresses are found may differ substantially from network to network.

- **Reliability.** Suppose that at the level of the entire internetwork we have agreed to support reliable communication. In other words, the internetwork must provide a mechanism by which it can guarantee delivery of packets. Now, of course, achieving reliability based on a constituent network that already guarantees reliable communication is not really a problem. Instead, we run into difficulties whenever one of the constituent networks does not support reliable communication. In that case, the routers connected to that network will need to adopt a communication protocol by which delivery of packets is guaranteed. And as we shall see later, this is not always easy to accomplish.

- **Packet size.** Of course, it should be clear what the maximum length of a packet for an internetwork may be. Unfortunately, we may run into problems if one of the networks that constitute the internetwork can support packets or frames only of a smaller length than the size of a packet as supported by the internetwork. In that case, a packet will have to be fragmented. This may be a serious problem to which we shall return below.

- **Modes of operation.** Like any network, an internetwork will generally provide connectionless communication and possibly also connection-oriented communication. However, it cannot be expected that each constituent network will support both modes of communication as well. And even if they do, their implementation may differ substantially from what is required from the point of view of the overall internetwork. This important issue is also discussed further below.

We shall leave addressing and reliability problems at this point. Addressing will be illustrated by means of an example in Section 9.3. Reliability is discussed in Section 9.5. How to handle different packet and frame sizes is discussed in Section 9.3.2, and the way to support different modes of operation is discussed in Section 9.3.3. But before doing so, we mention one other practical problem which arises primarily from organizational issues.

Internetwork routers

Figure 9.9 also illustrates another problem. Because the constituent networks of an internetwork will generally belong to different organizations, it may become difficult to have a single router connect two networks. For example, the two networks may be located at two distant locations making it almost impossible to connect them by a single router. Another problem is that whenever two networks run by different organizations need to be connected by a single router, this router will need to fall under the regime of either one or both organizations. And indeed, this may be virtually impossible in practice. The solution is quite simple: we can split the functionality of the router into two parts, leading to what we refer to as an **internetwork router**, but is usually called a **half-gateway**. As shown in Figure 9.10, we simply take two internetwork routers and directly connect them by a transmission medium. In that case, the two networks need to share merely the line that connects them, instead of a full-blown computer.

9.3.2   Internet packet fragmentation

An important problem that we have to face when dealing with internetworking is that sizes of internet packets and subnet packets may not match. In particular, we may have the situation where an internetwork supports packet sizes that are simply too large to be

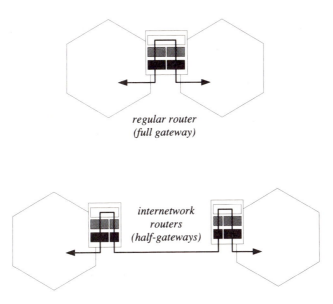

regular router
(full gateway)

internetwork
routers
(half-gateways)

Figure 9.10 Using internetwork routers to construct an internetwork.

handled by one or several of its constituent networks. Imagine the following situation. Suppose that we need to transmit an internet packet consisting of N_{inet} bytes, but that the constituent network through which it should be transmitted supports only subnet packets having a maximum size of N_{snet} bytes, with $N_{\text{snet}} < N_{\text{inet}}$. In that case, we are left with no other choice than to partition our internet packet into a number of subnet packets and send each of these subnet packets across the network, in order to reassemble them later.

Principal operation

Now fragmenting an internet packet into a number of subnet packets is not really difficult. The problems start at the other end, i.e. the destination, where these subnet packets have to be pasted together again in order to retain the original packet. To illustrate, we first assume that the constituent networks provide a completely reliable transportation of subnet packets. In other words, when a router transmits a subnet packet across a constituent network it is certain to arrive eventually at its destination. In that case, the major problem we are confronted with is that subnet packets may not arrive in the same order as they were sent. This may happen when routers follow an adaptive routing strategy and in which a route is strictly selected on a per-packet basis. In other words, each time a subnet packet arrives at a router the latter selects at that point only the best route for that the packet to follow. Consequently, subnet packets belonging to the same fragmented internet packet may follow completely different routes, and may thus arrive out of order.

So how do we paste subnet packets together again? First, we must bear in mind that a number of subnet packets comprise a specific internet packet. To that end, each subnet

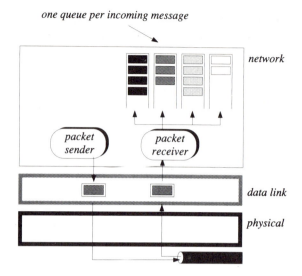

Figure 9.11 The principle of reassembling subnet packets to their original internet packet.

packet must carry an identification that uniquely determines the original internet packet. In addition, each subnet packet must also be augmented with a sequence number, and likewise, it should also carry information on whether it is the last packet in the series associated with the original packet. Given this information, the destination can now start building a list of incoming subnet packets. In particular, it will need to maintain a list for each unique internet packet it recognizes. This is illustrated in Figure 9.11.

As soon as all subnet packets have been received, the destination can be pursued by pasting them together in the right order, and subsequently handing the reassembled internet packet over to the higher layers. Although this principle is rather simple, it should be clear that as long as not all subnet packets have been received, a relatively large amount of buffer space will be required to hold all the subnet packets that have already reached the destination. In addition, the internet sublayer, in turn, will have to maintain a list of reassembled internet packets.

Responsibility of reassembling

But matters can get worse. The issue that we ignored above is that an internetwork consists of *several* constituent networks, and that each of these networks may have its own restrictions on maximum packet sizes. To explain, assume that an internet packet IP is partitioned into K subnet packets $SP^1, \ldots, SP_K^1$ for the first constituent network CN_1 that needs to be crossed. At that point, the internetwork router can follow two policies:

- First, in its role as router, it may decide to select a subsequent internetwork router (which is also attached to CN_1) to which the *entire* internet packet IP should be forwarded. This means that the constituent network CN_1 will have no choice but to route *all* subnet packets $SP_1^1, \ldots, SP_K^1$ to the next internetwork router.

- Alternatively, the internetwork router may decide to leave the routing entirely to the constituent network CN_1. This implies that each subnet packet SP_i^1 will be treated as an independent packet, and is thus simply routed to one of possibly several internetwork routers attached to CN_1.

Let's take a closer look at each of these two alternatives.

Intermediate reassembly.   Using the first option, reassembly becomes rather easy. Because all subnet packets are forwarded to the same (intermediate) internetwork router, the latter can reassemble the original internet packet *IP*. After this has occurred the internetwork router can decide to which router it should then forward *IP*, possibly after having fragmented it again into, say, N subnet packets $SP_1^2, \ldots, SP_N^2$ for the next constituent network. An important observation is that fragmentation of internet packets has become completely transparent at the level of the internetwork. Each internet packet simply travels in its entirety from one internetwork router to the next, although perhaps as a series of fragments.

Although this may seem an elegant scheme, there are two disadvantages with this approach. First, it can be expected that fragmentation and reassembly will have to be done several times, namely in those cases when a constituent network cannot handle the size of the internet packet. Second, we are losing flexibility in adaptive routing: the internetwork routers can take network congestion into account only at the level of the internetwork. Local traffic within a constituent network is simply ignored. Indeed, these two issues may degrade performance aspects.

Immediate forwarding.   The second alternative, also referred to as immediate forwarding, is often more attractive from a performance point of view, but it does have its own problems. In this case, reassembly is assumed to be done at the actual destination station; in other words, intermediate routers simply handle incoming packets on a purely individual basis. This may seem a good idea, but we do have a problem here. The point is that a subnet packet SP_i^1 may itself be too large for the next constituent network. In other words, it may happen that SP_i^1 needs to be fragmented into a number of subpackets $SP_{i,1}^2, \ldots, SP_{i,M}^2$. Consequently, the final destination will now have to deal with reassembling an internet packet from different-sized fragments.

This is really not a major problem, but we will encounter difficulties when a subnet packet becomes lost. Requesting the retransmission of merely a lost subpacket is out of the question as it means that we have to request the original sender to retransmit a part of the internet packet. But internet packets are considered by the internetwork to be indivisible (meaning that no one keeps a record of how packets are fragmented into subnet packets) so this will not do. Consequently, the sender will eventually have to retransmit the entire original packet, thereby discarding all subnet packets received so far.

Probably the simplest solution is to restrict internet packet sizes to the smallest packet size of any of the constituent networks comprising the internetwork. This at least alleviates the problem of receiving differently sized portions of an internet packet. In addition, if packets are lost, the subnet packets received so far are discarded and no retransmission request is issued. This last policy is completely in order when reliable communication is not supported by the network, as is often the case.

In conclusion, there is no single best solution to the problem of where to fragment and reassemble internet packets, and different internetworks indeed adopt different solutions. When required, a combination of immediate forwarding and intermediate reassembly may also be a viable way to solve the problem of fragmentation.

9.3.3   Modes of operation

In Section 9.1.4 we mentioned that wide area networks generally support connection-less communication, meaning that packets can be sent across the network, where each packet is treated as a separate and independent unit of data. At a logical level, connectionless communication is supported in the form of so-called **datagrams**. Although a datagram may appear to its users as an indivisible unit of data, a wide area network may choose to fragment a datagram into several packets, and send each of these packets separately. The destination station is then responsible for reassembling these packets. The alternative mode of communication is referred to as connection-oriented, which is generally supported through **virtual circuits**. After having set up a virtual circuit, it is then subsequently used to transfer packets across the network, which will now arrive in the same order as they were sent.

When connecting networks into a large internetwork we have to face the fact that some constituent networks may differ in the way that they support these two modes of communication. In particular, four combinations need to be examined:

1. Setting up a connection-oriented communication when all constituent networks support virtual circuits.

2. Setting up a connection-oriented communication but lacking the support of virtual circuits by one or several constituent networks.

3. Providing connectionless communication based on datagrams.

4. Providing connectionless communication based on virtual circuits.

The distinction between the mode of operation as offered by the internetwork (namely connection-oriented versus connectionless) and the way that each mode is *implemented* by either virtual circuits or datagrams is an important one. And although we are presenting this distinction in view of internetworking, it should be clear that it may be equally applicable within any layer. This issue is further addressed in the exercise section at the end of this chapter. For now, let's see what we need to deal with in any of these four cases.

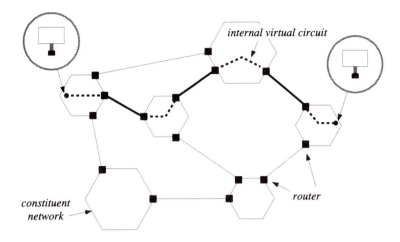

internal virtual circuit

router

constituent
network

Figure 9.12 The construction of a virtual circuit in an internetwork.

Connection-oriented communication using virtual circuits

The problem we now face is that our network no longer consists of a collection of intimately cooperating routers. Instead, we have to deal with networks having their own view on how to support communication, and generally also owned by different organizations. For one thing, we cannot set up a single virtual circuit, but instead, the best we can hope for is that a connection can be established by means of a series of virtual circuits. This is illustrated in Figure 9.12.

Each router shown in Figure 9.12 must adhere to two protocol suites: one of the internetwork and one of the constituent network for which it acts as a connector to the other routers. In order to establish an internetwork-wide virtual circuit, each internetwork router will have to establish an internal virtual circuit, and combine this with a connection to an internetwork router of a following constituent network. The principle is quite simple in this case. An internetwork-wide virtual circuit is simply constructed as the concatenation of several internal virtual circuits. It is the job of internetwork routers to maintain information on which two internal virtual circuits are connected to each other. An important observation is that packets can be sent through the virtual circuit on an individual basis. That is, whenever an internetwork router receives a packet traversing through an internetwork-wide virtual circuit *IVC*, it can immediately forward that packet across the next internal virtual circuit that forms part of *IVC* to the next internetwork router.

Connection-oriented communication using datagrams

What happens if the internetwork offers connection-oriented communication, but one of its constituent networks does not provide the means to set up an internal virtual circuit, but instead supports communication only through datagrams? In that case, it is the router's job to maintain the *view* of a virtual circuit. This is best explained by an example.

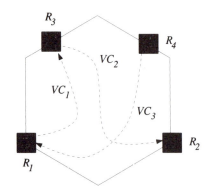

Figure 9.13 Realizing a virtual circuit between two routers in a network.

Consider Figure 9.13. Suppose router R_1 receives a request to establish an internal virtual circuit on behalf of, say sender S, to router R_3, but that the constituent network (CN) does not support connection-oriented communication. One way or the other, R_1 and R_3 will have to provide a solution that at least *imitates* the presence of an internal virtual circuit between them. This need not be a major problem if the two routers are directly connected to each other. It may, however, impose a rather large burden if this is not the case.

In order to imitate the presence of an internal virtual circuit (which is shown as VC_1), R_1 first sends a *call request* to R_3 stating that all succeeding packets from S will logically follow the same route. This generally implies two things:

- Packets sent from R_1 to R_3 may not be lost, i.e. the two routers will have to achieve reliable communication
- Router R_3 has to process packets in the same order as they are sent by R_1.

Realizing a reliable connection is discussed later, but need not be a problem if constituent network CN already supports it. This leaves us with the second problem. The point here is that because network CN does not support virtual circuits, packets sent from R_1 to R_3 may follow different routes *within CN*, and may thus arrive out of order at R_3. When maintaining the internetwork-wide virtual circuit, R_3 is forced temporarily to store a packet from R_1 until all its predecessors have been received (and forwarded onto the next internal circuit). Indeed, this does put an extra burden on the capabilities of an internetwork router. The effect, however, is that R_1 and R_3 jointly establish a view of a true internal virtual circuit through constituent network CN.

Connectionless communication using virtual circuits

When providing connectionless communication, things are a lot easier. However, where connectionless communication is generally more efficient when just a single piece of data needs to be transmitted, we may find ourselves in a difficult position when a constituent network provides communication only through virtual circuits. In that case, we will be forced to set up a complete virtual circuit for the transmission of only a single internet packet. And as soon as the packet has been transmitted, the circuit should be canceled.

Of course, this situation should be avoided as much as possible, and in practice, it is indeed rather hypothetical. Nevertheless, explicit attention must be paid to this phenomenon. To illustrate, the wide area network type ISDN, which we shall discuss in Section 9.4, is inherently based on the use of virtual circuits. In the case of ISDN, special measures have been taken to allow for efficient packet switching capabilities, i.e. means for providing connectionless communication through datagrams. And as we shall see, it is sometimes still necessary at least to set up a partial virtual circuit before the actual transportation by means of datagrams can take place.

Connectionless communication using datagrams

Undoubtedly, the simplest implementation scheme, apart from problems related to fragmentation and assembly, is that of a connectionless communication service through direct use of datagrams. And in practice, this is indeed the easiest mode of operation to provide in internetworks.

▷ 9.3.4   An example: the Internet

At this point it is illustrative to take a look at one of the world's largest internetworks, the **Internet**. We shall concentrate on some of the basic protocols on which this worldwide network is based, in particular the so-called **IP protocol**.

Background

The history of the Internet has its roots in the ARPANET project which concentrated on the development of a computer network in the late 1960s, financed by the US Department of Defense. Since its first introduction, ARPANET has rapidly expanded by adding more and more computers all around the world. In the beginning, ARPANET was a true wide area network, in the sense that all computers that were part of it made use of the same *protocol suite*. In other words, if a computer was part of the network, it ran exactly the same protocols as any other computer in the network.

The first step towards the construction of an internetwork was made by connecting a few (military) networks to ARPANET. These networks were adapted in such a way that a computer in the ARPANET could also communicate with a computer located in one of these added networks. In particular, this meant that internetwork routers were added (or existing routers enhanced to internetwork routers), and that stations in the added networks were supplied with packages containing implementations of ARPANET protocols. This growth of the network continued as many universities wanted their own local area networks to be connected to ARPANET as well. At this point, the network was becoming a true, worldwide internetwork consisting of a variety of smaller networks, and with tens of thousands of users. By then, it became generally known as the ARPA Internet.

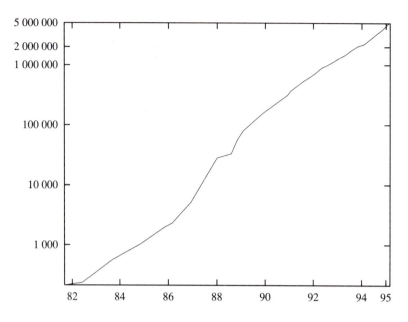

Figure 9.14   The growth of the Internet during the period 1982–1995. Source: Matrix Information and Directory Services, Inc. (MIDS).

The popularity of the Internet, as it is known today, is very large and continues to grow at an increasing pace. Figure 9.14 shows how the number of Internet computers has grown in a decade. Notice that the *y*-axis is scaled logarithmically implying that the growth is exponential. This popularity is not entirely surprising. First, as we shall see, the Internet protocol suite is a relatively simple one. But simplicity with respect to technology is not all. In particular, it is also kept simple from an organizational point of view. To illustrate, the Berkeley version of the UNIX operating system included the Internet protocols as part of its system – and this version of UNIX was (almost) freely distributed throughout the world. And because universities (1) like to experiment, (2) can easily make students acquainted with operating systems, and (3) love systems that can be purchased for little or no money, it should be no surprise why so many people initially used the Internet. To date, it is also the availability of good implementations of the Internet protocol for other systems, combined with the strong reduction of hardware costs, that make the system so attractive.

An important organizational aspect of the Internet is that its protocol specifications are publicly available. This is also true for many protocol implementations, as demonstrated by the Berkeley version of UNIX discussed above. The standards for the various protocols are published as so-called **Requests for Comment**s, or **RFC**s. An RFC is a document that describes a particular protocol adopted by the Internet. RFCs are published regularly and can be obtained by means of electronic mail (yes, via the Internet that implements them). Combined with the fact that many implementations are readily available at little or no cost, the Internet may truly be regarded as an *open system*: there are no hidden details that preclude participation of an organization in the network.

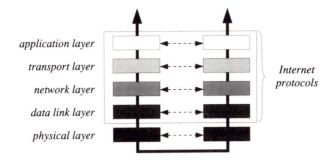

Figure 9.15 The layering of the Internet protocol suite.

The Internet protocol suite is structured according to the layering principles we have been discussing so far. However, its structure does not fit the OSI reference model very well, particularly the higher-level layers. Nevertheless, when speaking in terms of the OSI model, the Internet protocols can be organized into four main layers, as shown in Figure 9.15. Here, we shall concentrate mainly on the data link and network layer; the transport and application layers are discussed later.

Addressing

Let's start with one of the fundamental issues of any network: addressing. In the case of the Internet, each station has a unique address which is expressed as a 32-bit number. This implies that, in principle, a total of $2^{32} \approx 4 \cdot 10^9$ different addresses can be used, and thus that the same number of stations could be connected to the network. However, simply assigning addresses in this way is not practical as we shall see. Instead, addresses in the Internet are organized into five classes, numbered A to E. Each address belonging to class A, B, or C consists of a **network identification (*netid*)** and a **host identification (*hostid*)**. Hosts are considered to be stations located in a network which in turn is part of the Internet. This means that each address is constructed as a (*netid,hostid*) pair. Each class has a maximum number of networks, as well as a maximum number of hosts per network, as shown in Table 9.1. (We note that some (*netid,hostid*) combinations are special so that the actual number of networks and hosts per network is slightly less than mentioned.) The layout of the addressing schemes is shown in Figure 9.16. Class D networks are reserved for so-called **broadcast groups**. Class E addresses are reserved for future use. The latter two addressing schemes are not further considered here.

Internet addresses are usually represented in so-called **dotted-decimal notation** which corresponds to converting it to a number using radix 256. For example, the 32-bit number 2 188 611 653 can be written as:

$$2\,188\,611\,653 = 130 \cdot 256^3 + 115 \cdot 256^2 + 144 \cdot 256^1 + 69 \mapsto 130.115.144.69$$

Table 9.1 The networks and hosts per Internet class *A*, *B*, and *C*

class	max. networks	max. hosts per network
A	128	16 777 216
B	16 384	65 536
C	2 097 152	256

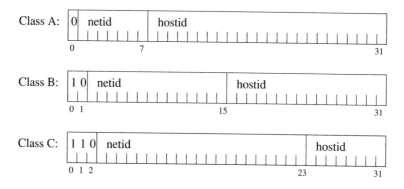

Figure 9.16 The address layout for the first three classes of the Internet addressing convention.

which happens to be the Internet address of one of the workstations on which this book has been written. The first number of the Internet address determines its class. In particular, we have the following:

class	range		
A	0.0.0.0	–	127.255.255.255
B	128.0.0.0	–	191.255.255.255
C	192.0.0.0	–	223.255.255.255
D	224.0.0.0	–	239.255.255.255
E	240.0.0.0	–	247.255.255.255

implying that the above-mentioned address falls into class *B*.

But how are addresses actually assigned? For example, suppose that an organization has a local area network that they want to connect to the Internet. In that case, at least one station in this LAN will need to be transformed into an Internet router, and subsequently connected to another, already existing, Internet router. This means enhancing the LAN software with packages that implement the IP protocols. Second, the organization will need to get its unique network identification. To that end, they need to contact the **Internet Network Information Center**, or InterNIC, who is responsible for assigning network identifications. The host identifications for the network are subsequently assigned by the organization – this is not the responsibility of the InterNIC. We shall return to these issues in the next chapter.

Table 9.2 Information contained in an IP header

field	length (bits)	purpose
source	32	The IP address of the sending station.
destination	32	The IP address of the receiving station.
identification	16	A number that identifies the datagram being sent.
amount-of-data	16	The size of the data part (in bytes).
protocol	8	Identifies the transport layer protocol by which this datagram was sent.
type-of-service	8	A parameter used to determine the way routing should take place: minimize delay, maximize throughput, maximize reliability, and minimize monetary cost.
time-to-live	8	The maximum number of routers through which the datagram pass.
flags	3	Used when fragmentation of the datagram is required.
fragment-offset	13	Used to identify the *next* fragment when fragmentation occurred.

The IP datagram

The network layer of the Internet is rather simple. The only thing it supports is the unreliable transmission of **IP datagrams**. Indeed, this is not very much. Reliable communication is supported at the transport layer by means of separate protocols which we shall examine in Section 9.5. An IP datagram consists of two parts: a header and a data part. The header consists of information that allows the data to travel from its source to its destination. To that end, the following information is contained in a number of fields,[4] as shown in Table 9.2.

The *source* and *destination* fields are obvious. The *identification* field uniquely determines which datagram is being sent by a host and plays an important role when a datagram needs to be fragmented (we shall return to fragmentation below). The *amount-of-data* field indicates the size of the data part. Being a 16-bit number, the data part has a theoretical maximum of $2^{16} - 1 = 65\,535$ bytes. In practice, however, the size of the data part is restricted to approximately 8192 bytes, and often even 512 bytes in order to avoid fragmentation.

The *protocol* field is used to identify the original higher-layer protocol that led to the construction of the datagram, and as such is comparable to what we have called a service access point (SAP) in Section 8.5.1. To explain this, recall that in Section 8.5.2 we discussed that it is often necessary to use several protocols simultaneously. For example, we showed that we

---

[4]We note that we have omitted a number of additional fields for the sake of clarity.

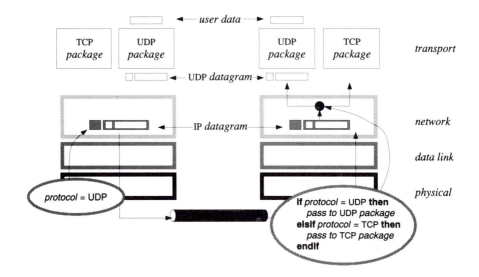

Figure 9.17 The transmission of a UDP datagram.

would want to have a package implementing synchronous communication at our disposal, as well as a package for asynchronous communication. The problem that we encountered, however, was that we needed a way to identify that messages which were sent using synchronous communication, were also processed at the receiver's end by the right package. Here, we have the same situation. For example, two widely used higher-level protocols in the Internet are UDP and TCP. In order to send a UDP datagram, this datagram is encapsulated into an IP datagram as shown in Figure 9.17, with its protocol field set to "UDP". Upon arrival, the datagram can be sent to the appropriate package.

The remaining fields are related to routing and fragmentation which we discuss next.

Routing

We have already paid some attention to the general routing scheme of the Internet in Section 9.2.2. As noted there, routing in the Internet has undergone a number of important changes in order to arrive at a strategy that is able to handle network congestion, malfunctioning of routers and links, etc. We shall not go into the details concerning the actual algorithms used today as these lie beyond the scope of this book. Instead, we shall briefly discuss the parameters that influence dynamic routing occurring as the *type-of-service* field in an IP header (see also Table 9.2).

Four different routing parameters are distinguished at the network layer of the Internet. Each parameter corresponds to a Boolean variable. If set to TRUE, the parameter should be satisfied, otherwise ignored. The four parameters are the following:[5]

---

[5]Only 4 of the 8 bits of the *type-of-service* field are actually used.

- minimize_delay: when this parameter is set, the routing strategy to be followed for the IP datagram in question should attempt to get the datagram to the destination as soon as possible. It is typically set in those cases that a datagram is sent to *control* a situation. For example, when a high degree of interactiveness is to be expected, it is essential that a destination can react quickly.

- maximize_throughput: this is typically a parameter that is set when large amounts of data are to be transferred. The parameter specifies that a route should be selected that allows many datagrams to be in transit at the same time. In other words, it indicates that maximum effort should be taken to avoid network congestion. It is less important when the data actually reaches the destination – it will presumably take some time, in any case.

- maximize_reliability: in this case, the routing strategy is geared towards getting the datagram to its destination in a single attempt. In other words, routing is chosen such that retransmissions are not or hardly ever necessary. Typically, this parameter is set for datagram transfer that takes entirely place *within* one of the constituent networks, or when the network itself needs to be examined, as is the case with discovering routes.

- minimize_monetary_cost: this parameter is typically set for news bulletins. These are applications that allow a large group of users to communicate with one another by "posting" messages in a way similar to the use of normal bulletin boards. The only requirement of these users when using the network is that it should be cheap.

The algorithms that make use of these parameters can be extremely intricate, and as we have already stated, are not further discussed here. An important observation, however, is that a user of the Internet has actual control over the way that a route is established. This is important as it allows totally different users and applications to make use of a single network for different purposes. Again, this type of flexibility is necessary if a network is to become popular.

Another parameter that is important when routing is the *time-to-live* field in the IP header. This 8-bit integer indicates the maximum number of routers that an IP datagram may pass when it is sent across the network. Typically, its value is set to 32 or 64. The *time-to-live* parameter prevents datagrams from circulating throughout the network forever. As soon as the maximum number of routers have been passed, the datagram will simply be discarded and the sender is subsequently notified (how this is done is discussed below).

Fragmentation

Fragmentation forms an important part of the IP protocol. A datagram may need to be split into two or more fragments when a constituent network can only support packets that have a maximum size smaller than the present size of the datagram. Fragmentation in the Internet is dealt with in a simple and pragmatic way. For one thing, whenever fragmentation occurs, it is up to the destination station to reassemble the original datagram. In other words, an **immediate forwarding** policy is followed as discussed in Section 9.3.2.

To explain how fragmentation works in the Internet, suppose we have a datagram D that needs to be fragmented into two parts. Denote these two fragments as D_1 and D_2, respectively. Now each of these fragments will need to be sent across the network, or, in other words, need to be IP datagrams in their own right. To that end, they will both have (almost) identical headers – in particular the original header from D is inherited by the two new datagrams. The data part of D is split into two pieces, each consisting of a multiple of 8 bytes. The first part is appended to D_1, with its *fragment-offset* field set to 0. The second part is appended to D_2, but its *fragment-offset* field will now be set equal to the length of the data part of D_1 expressed as multiples of 8 bytes. So, for example, if the data part of D_1 has a total size of 8192 bytes, then the *fragment-offset* field of D_2 will be set equal to 8192 div 8 = 1024. We shall return to this when we explain reassembly.

The *flags* field of each IP header is important in fragmentation. As shown in Table 9.2, this field has a length of three bits of which only two are used. The associated Boolean parameters are as follows:

- more_data: setting this parameter to TRUE implies that the current datagram is a fragment of a larger datagram, and moreover, that it is not the last fragment.

- do_not_fragment: when this parameter is set to TRUE, the datagram may on no account be fragmented. Consequently, if it is too large to transmit across one of the constituent networks, it will simply be discarded.

Returning to our example, it should be clear that for datagram D_1, more_data must be set to TRUE, whereas in the case of D_2, it must be set to FALSE.

But suppose now that both datagrams need to be fragmented again. In particular, assume that D_1 needs to be fragmented into M smaller datagrams $D_{1,1}, \ldots, D_{1,M}$, whereas D_2 is fragmented into N datagrams $D_{2,1}, \ldots D_{2,N}$. Because more_data of D_1 was set to TRUE, it is known that more data is to be received before reassembly can take place. Consequently, when fragmenting D_1, we will need to set the more_data parameters to TRUE not only for the first $M-1$ datagrams but also for the last one, $D_{1,M}$. In the case of fragmentation of D_2, it should be clear that for all but the last datagram $D_{2,k}$ we will have to set more_data to TRUE as well.

Reassembling a datagram is now rather straightforward. Denote by $len(F_k)$ the length (in bytes) of the data part of a fragment F_k, and by $offset(F_k)$ the value of its *fragment-offset* field. Finally, we use the notation $more(F_k)$ to denote the value of the more_data parameter of fragment F_k. Now, first the destination station needs to identify the first fragment F_1. Clearly, we have

$$offset(F_k) = 0, \ \textit{if and only if } F_k \equiv F_1$$

In other words, the *only* fragment with a zero-valued *fragment-offset* field is the first one. Also, it should be clear that the last fragment F_{last} is uniquely determined by its value for the more_data parameter:

$$more(F) = \text{FALSE}, \text{ if and only if } F \equiv F_{\text{last}}$$

But what about the second fragment F_2? It is not too difficult to see that for F_2 we uniquely have

$$offset(F_2) = len(F_1) \text{ div } 8$$

IP *datagram*

ICMP *control message*

Figure 9.18 An IP datagram containing a control message.

and that, in general, the kth fragment can be found for which the following equation holds:

$$offset(F_k) = len(F_{k-1}) \text{ div } 8 + offset(F_{k-1})$$

By using offsets, Internet datagrams can be repeatedly fragmented without having to be concerned about the order in which they arrive at the destination. No sophisticated numbering system is necessary to see where a fragment actually fits when it comes to reassembly. The only problem that can occur with fragmented datagrams is that one or several fragments may be lost. In order to detect this, the destination station uses a timeout mechanism. As soon as a next fragment arrives, the timer is set, depending on its current value and the value of *time-to-live* field of the fragment most recently received. If the timer expires *all* fragments received so far are discarded. Consequently, the original datagram will have to be retransmitted entirely.

Control messages

In order to communicate exceptional situations, for example when one of the fragments of a fragmented datagram failed to reach the receiver on time, a **control message** is sent across the network. Control messages, or **ICMP messages** as they are called, are sent as ordinary IP datagrams. The message itself is contained in the data part of the datagram, as shown in Figure 9.18.

Each ICMP message contains at least the following information:

- The *type* of the message, identified as an integer between 0 and 18. For example, when the type is equal to 11, this indicates that the message contains information on an expired timer.
- For each message type, there is a further specification by means of a *code*, also expressed as an integer. There can be at most 256 codes associated with a single type. To illustrate, when a timer expires due to the fact that a fragment did not reach the receiver in time the latter sends an ICMP message of type 11 with code 1.
- The complete header of the original IP datagram that caused the ICMP message to be sent. This allows the sender to identify precisely for which datagram the ICMP message is being sent and to take appropriate measures.

But not all ICMP messages indicate that something went wrong. In particular, a distinction is made between ICMP **query messages** and ICMP **error messages**. A typical example of a query message is the one used by routers for discovering routes throughout the network. To that end, a router sends its routing table to each of its neighbors by means of an ICMP query message (in this case having its type set to 9 with code 0), as discussed in Section 9.2.2. We shall omit further details here.

An interesting question is what happens when something goes wrong with an ICMP message. For example, we may find ourselves in the situation where a message is fragmented and one of its fragments is lost during its transmission. As a general rule, whenever an error occurs with an ICMP error message, no message is sent as response.[6] In this way, we avoid the network being flooded with error control messages. The problem we are faced with then, however, is that the source station is now not aware of the fact that something went wrong. There is no general solution to this. At best, we may expect that the source continues to behave as if nothing went wrong, resulting in unexpected situations at the receiver's end. The receiver, in turn, will then return a new ICMP error message, and if this one gets through, will probably be difficult to interpret by the source. But in any case, one conclusion can be drawn: communication failed and it is up to the source station to decide what to do.

9.4   Integrated services digital networks

The computer networks we have been discussing so far, from small LANs to the worldwide internetworks, are currently primarily used by professionals. Until recently, the applied technology was not available to domestic uses or small businesses. Not for technological reasons, but simply because the costs were too high to be affordable by these types of consumers. This situation, however, is rapidly changing. For example, the Internet is now made available by commercial Internet service providers, and anyone with a simple modem can connect to it. Further progress is being made with the introduction of so-called **integrated services digital networks**, or **ISDN** for short. An ISDN is a true, worldwide digital network that meets the demands of many small businesses. In this section, we shall concentrate on the technology of ISDNs.

9.4.1   Introduction

At present, carriers are rapidly changing their current telephone network into one that can support the transmission of digital information. In particular, the existing telephone lines are upgraded to a network that will allow the transmission of digitized *voice* and digital *data*. The resulting network is said to *integrate* these two forms of information and provides several advanced *services* to the public. For this reason, they are referred to as **integrated services digital networks** (ISDN). An ISDN will thus allow computers and telephones to be connected to a single worldwide network, quite similar to the way in which we currently use the telephone network to communicate either directly (by telephones) or indirectly (by means of modems that connect a computer to the present network).

An important issue is that ISDNs will gradually evolve from the presently available (public) digital networks. The starting point of this evolution is formed by the current

---

[6]There are also several other rules related to broadcasting that we shall not mention here.

digital telephone networks. This has an important implication, for the initial services provided by an ISDN will bear a strong resemblance to what we already use. In particular, emphasis will lie on initially providing various telephone services. This means that, besides being able to make calls in the usual way, additional features such as automatic redialing when a line is busy, displaying the phone number of a caller on the receiver's set, redirecting phone calls to another number if necessary, etc. will be made available (and, in fact, are often already provided nowadays). Other telephone-oriented services can easily be imagined. For example, the first generation of ISDNs allow several people to communicate as a group, or, in other words, support a simple form of *teleconferencing*.

The choice for using the existing telephone network is an important one. First, telephone networks employ circuit-switching technology rather than packet-switching. This means that initially ISDN components will be based on just a single type of switching technology, putting the very large number of existing packet-switched networks into second place. However, packet-switched networks are predominant in computer networks as we generally know them today. This is due to the fact that packet-switching is generally much better when asynchronous data is to be communicated instead of the synchronous type of data such as digitized voice. For this reason alone, existing computer networks cannot be ignored when integration of voice and data is to be taken seriously. Therefore, the evolutionary approach followed by the introduction of ISDN does dictate that existing networks should be used. In particular, those packet-switched networks that already adhere to the standards adopted by the telecom companies will soon form part of ISDNs. But adopting computer networks as an afterthought is not really viable.

This is already illustrated by the fact that ISDNs will never be the final word in worldwide networks as they will support a maximum transmission rate of only 64 Kbps. This rate is acceptable when transmitting digitized voice – it is completely inadequate for transmission of, for example, motion pictures (video). To that end, transmission rates in the order of (hundreds of) millions of bits per second are required. To meet such requirements, efforts are already underway to construct **broadband ISDNs** by applying completely new technologies. The main difference between ISDN and broadband ISDN lies in their implementation of the physical and data link layers. The functionality and principal working of both types of networks, however, is roughly the same. Therefore, we shall make no distinction here between ISDN and broadband ISDN, and concentrate mainly on the original concept of ISDN.

9.4.2   ISDN architecture

At this point, let's concentrate more on what an ISDN looks like. In order to understand the architecture of an ISDN, it is important to make a distinction between customers and carriers. The latter are the organizations that provide the means to connect remote sites to each other. For example, the telecom companies can provide a digital network to which customers can subscribe. In order for a customer to hook on to an ISDN, a carrier can place a so-called **network terminating device**, abbreviated to **NT1**, at the subscriber's premises. From the outside, this is a small box with a number of outlets, comparable to the wall socket used to connect a telephone. In terms of the OSI reference model, an NT1

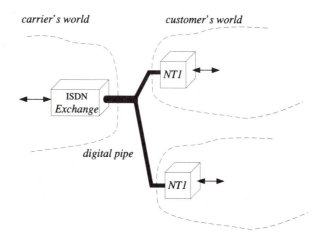

Figure 9.19 The basic architecture for an ISDN connection.

is found at the lowest, i.e. physical, layer. It is, in principle, the only way to connect to the carrier's part of an ISDN. This scheme is shown in Figure 9.19.

An NT1 is connected by means of a so-called **digital pipe** to an ISDN exchange owned by the carrier. This exchange forms the interface to the carrier's internal network. The digital pipe is a physical connection from the ISDN exchange to one or several NT1s. Now the reason for this digital pipe is to support the simultaneous transmission of several series of signals. To that end, a distinction is made between different types of **channels**, which are carried across the pipe using a form a time-division multiplexing as discussed in Section 7.4. Three different types of channels are distinguished:

- A **B channel** allows a transmission rate of 64 Kbps, and forms the basic channel for subscribers. This type of channel is, in principle, used for all types of communication supported by an ISDN: digitized voice and digital data.

- A **D channel** is used for *controlling* purposes, meaning that it will generally carry only small series of signals. Accordingly, its transmission rate has been set to 16 Kbps.

- An **H channel** is additionally provided when higher transmission rates are needed, for example in the case of offices requiring a connection to the outside world. Three different transmission rates are supported: 384 Kbps (a so-called H0 channel), 1536 Kbps (an H11 channel), and 1920 Kbps (an H12 channel).

A normal subscriber can get a **basic service connection** to an ISDN consisting of two B channels and a single D channel. This means that a total transmission rate is provided of $2 \times 64 + 16 = 144$ Kbps. This will generally be enough for most customers, but certainly not for organizations. The latter can acquire a so-called **primary service connection** which supports a maximum transmission rate of either approximately 1.5 Mbps (for

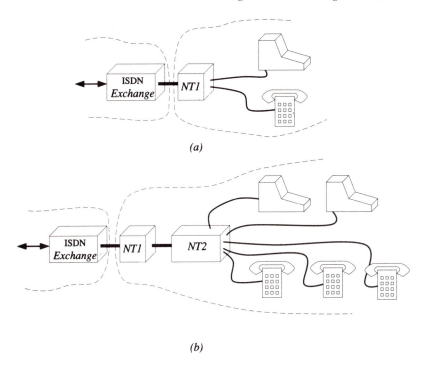

(a)

(b)

Figure 9.20 The use of network terminating devices at a customer's premises for (a) basic services and (b) primary services.

Canada, the USA, and Japan), or 2 Mbps (in Europe). This means, for example, that an organization (located in Europe) can simultaneously use 3 H0 channels, 5 B channels, and 1 D channel across the same NT1 to an ISDN.

Now, particularly when only a basic service connection is needed, a single NT1 at the customer's site will be sufficient. Simple devices that adhere to the ISDN protocols (such as telephones and adapted computers) can be directly connected to the NT1 as illustrated in Figure 9.20(a). For organizations having a primary service connection, an additional network terminating device, known as **NT2**, will generally be required, as shown in Figure 9.20(b).

An NT2 is more than just a small box. In terms of the OSI reference model it can provide functionality up through the network layer. For example, an NT2 may provide additional switching functions as required by local telephone exchanges. In that case, the device can make a distinction between phone calls that are internal to the organization (meaning that it does not need to access the ISDN but that, instead, a direct internal connection can be established) or external. Another example is using a special router as an NT2, connecting a LAN to the ISDN. It may even happen that the functionality of a telephone exchange is combined with that of a router.

A point to note is that the network terminating devices NT1 and NT2 are both true ISDN

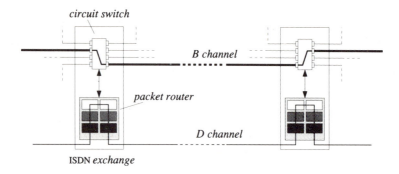

circuit switch

B channel

packet router

D channel

ISDN *exchange*

Figure 9.21 Establishing a circuit-switched based connection in an ISDN.

constituents. In other words, both devices adhere to the protocols adopted by ISDNs. This implies that all other devices such as telephones and computers that are connected to NT1s and NT2s should also adhere to the ISDN protocols. This puts existing equipment in a difficult position. In order to allow these non-ISDN devices to communicate over an ISDN, they will need to make use of specially constructed **terminal adaptors** (TAs), which are actually *protocol converters*.

9.4.3　ISDN communication support

As with all computer networks, communication over an ISDN can only be realized if source, intermediate, and destination stations adhere to a specific set of communication protocols. The general aspects of wide area networks discussed in the previous sections are equally applicable to an ISDN. The unique feature of an ISDN, however, is that it integrates voice and data by providing the full functionality of a true circuit-switched network, as well as that of a packet-switched network.

In this section we shall not go into details of the ISDN protocol suite, other than by taking a look at the more exceptional situations. In particular, we shall concentrate on the way a circuit-switched connection is set up, and consider the support for packet-switched communication.

Circuit-switched connections

Establishing circuit-switched connections will remain one of the most important features of an ISDN as it is the primary means for achieving standard telephone services. Telephone calls and related communications such as facsimile take place over a B channel. This implies that a complete physical connection should be made between two subscribers of the ISDN that supports a transmission rate of 64 Kbps. In practice, such a physical connection is made by setting switches at a number of ISDN exchanges as shown in Figure 9.21. The difference from the usual approach is that the switches are set by making use of D channels. This approach is generally referred to as **common channel signaling**.

Suppose a subscriber wants to establish a circuit-switched connection, to which end we shall have to make use of a B channel. In the situations we have discussed so far, establishing a complete connection would take place via the same medium that would be later used for the actual data transportation. In the case of ISDN, however, a different approach is used. Instead, a request packet is sent through a D channel towards the first ISDN exchange. The packet will contain information on the used B channel on the subscriber's side, as well as an identification of the required destination. From there on, the ISDN exchange will try to set up a route via one of its adjacent exchanges. To that end, it will use a separate **signaling network** which is part of the actual ISDN. This signaling network is an ordinary packet-switched network that uses the D channel. The information exchanged between ISDN exchanges is again encapsulated in packets sent across the D channel. Establishing a route implies that a direct connection is set up between ISDN exchanges. But the physical connection between two exchanges (i.e. a B channel) will be different from the connection via which the information packets are being sent.

The main advantage of this approach is that the time to set up a complete connection is relatively short compared to the traditional approaches by which information is sent through the same channel that will later be used for exchanging the actual information. Also, during the time the connection is maintained, the B channel can be used only for its initial purpose, which is presumably in this case transmitting digitized voice. Any other additional information (e.g. status of the connection, existence of additional requests to communicate with either sender or receiver, etc.) can be sent as a packet through the signaling network or directly via the D channel.[7]

Packet-switched connections

A packet-switched connection is established in much the same way as a circuit-switched connection when it concerns setting up a *virtual circuit* between two subscribers. Recall that a virtual circuit is a preallocated route between a sender and a receiver through which all packets are sent. The main advantage of setting up a virtual circuit is that the two communicating parties are hardly bothered by possible network congestion, and that all packets arrive in the order they were sent.

Virtual circuits for exchanging packets in ISDN are set up as follows. First, a circuit-switched connection is set up between the sender and an ISDN exchange, called a **packet handler**, that is directly connected to a true packet-switched network. In other words, a direct, *physical* connection exists between the sender and the ISDN exchange. This exchange then sets up a virtual circuit to a similar exchange located near the destination via the packet-switched network as usual. From there on, a circuit-switched connection is established to the destination, and packet exchange can commence. Again, the D channels are used to set up the two circuit-switched parts of the connection, and to transfer any control messages to and from the two subscribers. Control messages between the two

---

[7]It is illustrative to see how standardizations may not always turn out to be as applicable as one might initially hope. The approach of common channel signaling, for example, is something that is simply not considered in the OSI reference model. And indeed, although attempts have been made to fit the ISDN protocol suite into this model, such attempts can be considered only as partially successful.

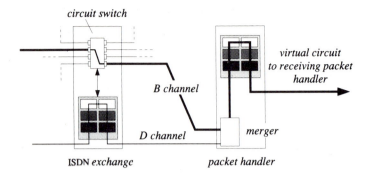

Figure 9.22 The principle of a packet-switched virtual circuit in ISDN.

exchanges are transmitted via the packet-switched network. This principle is illustrated in Figure 9.22.

Alternatively, an ISDN may also provide a complete packet-switched network by means of either B or D channels. In that case, no virtual circuit needs to be set up (for it would then have been better to establish a circuit-switched connection). The ISDN exchanges now operate as true routers comparable to the routers found in more traditional wide area networks.

9.4.4   Broadband ISDN

As we have stated, ISDN standards are not suited to meet the requirements for future data transmissions: the 64 Kbps transmission rate which is fundamental to ISDNs is hopelessly inadequate when supporting, for example, video services. And that these services will be required is just something that we must simply await. To that end, efforts have already been undertaken to produce so-called **broadband** ISDNs, generally abbreviated to **B-ISDN**.

A B-ISDN is a true extension of an ISDN in the sense that all the functionality that is provided by an ISDN will also be supported by a B-ISDN. The important extension of B-ISDNs is that they will provide the means to support very high transmission rates. In particular, it is anticipated that such networks will support channels that can transmit data at a speed of approximately 155 Mbps and 622 Mbps. From the user's point of view, there is this added functionality when comparing B-ISDNs to the original ISDNs. However, in order to establish such transmission rates, a completely different type of implementation technique needs to be applied. Let's just briefly consider the basic principle of this underlying technology.

▷ **ATM networks**

In order to achieve extremely high transmission rates, two, related basic requirements must be met:

1. The overhead introduced by communication protocols must be reduced to a minimum.
2. A large part of these protocols should be implemented in hardware.

In digital networks, it is not difficult to meet the first requirement. The point is that most overhead in communication protocols arises from the fact that transmission media need to be shared, and in addition introduce errors. Sharing requires that control information needs to be added to messages in order for stations to decide what to do with the incoming data. Errors require that error detection bits are to be added to messages, in addition to error control information such as sequence and acknowledgment numbers. Erroneous transmission is caused primarily by the transmission medium itself, which is generally metallic. Transferring electrical signals through metallic media makes these signals highly susceptible to (always present) external electro-magnetic fields, and consequently, erroneous transmission may result. This is no longer the case when using, for example, optical fiber. When combining transmission of digital signals with these type of media, we may expect the occurrence of erroneous frame transmission to fall to a minimum. In that case, it is no longer justified to introduce rather intricate schemes for error control, but instead, we should devise protocols that are targeted towards an occasional correction of errors. In practice, it turns out that error control can be completely removed from the data link layer, substantially reducing the overhead of communication protocols. Erroneous transmission is instead entirely dealt with at the higher-level layers.

Removing error control from the data link layer protocols makes these protocols much simpler. Simplicity at this level has two consequences. First, due to the reduction of overhead, processing of data, i.e. sending, transmission, and receipt of frames, can be done at a much higher rate compared to more complex protocols. In other words, less work needs to be done. Second, simplicity also allows for efficient implementation of protocols into hardware. The combined effect is the realization of high transmission rates.

This approach is followed by a technique known as **asynchronous transfer mode**. In so-called **ATM networks**, data is transferred in small units referred to as **cells**. A cell has a fixed size and consists of just 48 bytes of data, with a 5-byte header. When you realize that, for example, Ethernet frames carry at least 16 bytes of overhead information (and in most cases, this is actually 26 bytes), and allow for as much as 1500 bytes of user data, it is seen that cells are indeed small.

Now, in order to improve the utilization of the transmission media, a technique quite similar to time-division multiplexing as discussed in Chapter 7 is employed. However, there is one important difference. Recall that TDM simply scans the output buffers of a sending station in a round-robin fashion, each time reserving a slot S_i to store some data from output buffer B_i. If buffer B_i is empty, then so will be slot S_i when the frame is finally sent. In the case of ATM networks, this will never happen. Instead, if a buffer B_i is empty, then the slot will be filled with a cell from another buffer. Also, cells are transmitted immediately. In this way, we ensure a *continuous* stream of cells across the medium, at least as long there are cells to be sent.

Another important point about ATM networks is that routing is done entirely in hardware. To that end, a virtual circuit, known as a **virtual channel**, is set up between a sender and a destination. The administration needed to set up and maintain such a channel is implemented in hardware implying that the delay at each switch when a cell arrives is minimized. The

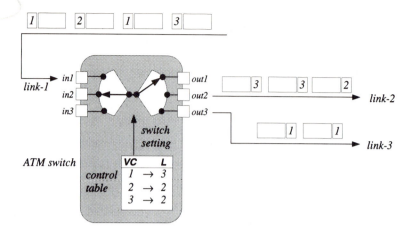

Figure 9.23 The principle of an ATM switch.

header of a cell contains an identification of the channel through which it is to be transported. This principle is shown in Figure 9.23. What is shown there are three virtual channels, each identified in the header of each cell. The switch is connected to one incoming link, and two outgoing links. Virtual channel 1 is always routed via *link-1* to *link-3*, whereas the other two are routed via *link-2*. The routing table itself is implemented in hardware, so that routing decisions can be made quickly.

Virtual circuits form an important aspect of ATM networks. First, by using virtual channels as discussed above, extremely fast cell switching can take place at each switch. But there is more. Virtual channels are grouped into so-called **virtual paths**. A virtual path is thus a virtual circuit between two stations, but which contains a number of channels. By allowing several virtual channels to be contained in a single virtual path, an ATM network can accommodate several transmission rates for different but logically related information. For example, when transmitting video information (which requires an extremely high transmission rate), it is now also possible to send its associated audio via the same path but through a different channel. In addition, data such as subtitles which requires even lower transmission rates can be sent through a third channel, but again, also along the same path. The main benefit of this approach is its simplicity. For example, instead of setting up a virtual circuit for each channel, it is now sufficient to establish a virtual circuit for the path only.

We have only briefly touched upon some of the issues of ATM networks, and indeed, this new technology deserves more attention than we have paid to it here. However, the technology is still emerging and no definite answers can be given concerning its impact. Rather than elaborating any further on this subject, we refer the interested reader to Section 9.6 where we provide references for further reading.

9.5 Making networks work

Let's see what we have accomplished so far. In the preceding sections our main concern has been the construction of computer networks that allow for transmission of data across geographically large distances. The distinctive feature of these so-called wide area networks when comparing them to local area networks is that routing should take place. Data is thus explicitly forwarded from computer to computer until it reaches its destination. We have also seen that extremely large networks can be constructed through internetworking technologies.

An important distinction that we have introduced is that between so-called connectionless communication (by means of datagrams) and connection-oriented communication (by means of virtual circuits). There is, however, one aspect that we have been deliberately ignoring: how we can make these wide area networks accessible to users. Some hints have already been given. For example, we have illustrated how we can produce several kinds of networks by providing software packages that are built directly on top of implementations of the data link layer. In general, these packages will form part of an operating system, and make the network accessible through what we have called service programs.

But this is simply not enough. In wide area networks it is essential that we provide the right means to enable completely different application programs, running on completely different computers, to communicate with each other. In other words, we should provide the right means to allow for the construction of **open systems**. An open system in our case can be defined as a communication system that will allow anyone to construct a program that can communicate with other existing programs (presumably built by someone else) as long as communication adheres to a collection of standardized protocols. There are two issues involved here: (1) what exactly these protocols look like, and (2) how they should be implemented. So far, we have concentrated mainly on the second issue. The first has hardly been touched upon. At this point, we are now in a position to correct this situation. In this section we shall concentrate on the so-called **transport layer**, which forms the bridge between what we may expect from *any* network and that which is available by means of an implementation of the network layer. Other issues of open systems are discussed in Chapter 10.

9.5.1 The transport layer

From a certain perspective, the transport layer can perhaps be considered as the most important layer of the OSI reference model. What this means is that any implementation of this layer should provide the right interface to users and application programs that need to communicate via some underlying network. The point is that this underlying network is completely shielded from the user.

But why is it needed? In particular, you may wonder why the network layer cannot provide enough functionality that will allow us to access networks. From a certain point of view, this is true. However, the network layer has been introduced primarily to cope with the problem of routing packets across wide area networks, and to allow for the construction of very large networks through internetworking technology. In this sense, the network layer merely provides the basic support that is needed for the construction of large networks. Separating this concern from the question of how such networks can then be subsequently made available to application programs is just a matter of good design. For one thing, you have to realize that the question of *how* data gets from a sender to a receiver no longer needs to be addressed. But in that case, what *are* the issues we need to consider? The most important, perhaps, is that the underlying communication network should be completely shielded from application programs. We now take a closer look at this issue.

Network types and protocol classes

When we describe computer networks at the level of the network layer, i.e. when we consider a network by what kind of services it has to offer by means of its implementations of the network and lower layers, we can make a distinction between three network types:

- **Type A:** This is an almost perfect network type. In this case, the network guarantees error-free delivery of packets. Also, if a packet is submitted for transmission, the network takes full responsibility for making sure that it reaches its destination.

- **Type B:** This is almost as good, except for the fact that the network cannot guarantee that delivery will actually take place. In other words, if packets can be delivered, then this will be done without error, but if transmission is not successful, the sender will be notified.

- **Type C:** This is the worst one can expect. In this case, packets may be damaged or become lost during transmission, and what is worse, the network will not notify the sender at all. Consequently, if the sender and receiver want to ensure reliable communication they cannot count on any support from the underlying network and will thus have to agree on a separate protocol.

Fortunately, LANs can generally be classified as type A networks. Many WANs fall into type B, which means that in general they take care of proper transmission, but from time to time fail to recover when things really go wrong. In that case, they will at least inform the sender that transmission failed. Type C networks are indeed a problem, and as it turns out, many internetworks fall into this category. This is not surprising when you realize that the best we can generally achieve in internetworking is aiming at the greatest common denominator, which is unreliable datagram delivery.

Protocol classes

With respect to providing communication services to application programs, there is more or less general agreement that the transport layer should allow for (1) unreliable connectionless communication, and (2) reliable connection-oriented communication. The first is generally fairly easy to provide. The second may impose severe problems if it is to be provided on top of a type C network. In any case, it should be clear that the complexity

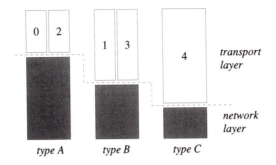

Figure 9.24 The relationship between transport protocols and different network types.

of the protocols contained in the transport layer will vary from case to case. In particular, five different classes of protocols are distinguished, each with increasing complexity:

(0) **Simple class**: protocols in this class are used for type A networks. They rely almost entirely on the reliable connection-oriented services offered by the underlying network.

(1) **Basic recovery class**: these kind of protocols, which are constructed for type B networks, assume that the underlying network is not capable of restoring a connection after a fault has occurred, but will otherwise handle transmission in case of lost and damaged packets.

(2) **Multiplexing class**: protocols in this class assume that the underlying network provides reliable connection-oriented communication, i.e. they assume a type A network. In addition to the functionality provided by this network, these protocols implement several logical connections through a single network channel. Consequently, a sender will now be allowed to set up several virtual circuits at the same time to the same destination.

(3) **Error recovery and multiplexing class**: a combination of class 1 and class 2 protocols. These protocols assume that the underlying network is of type B.

(4) **Error detection and recovery class**: the ultimate collection of protocols which assume that if anything can go wrong, it will. Clearly, these kind of protocols can be extremely intricate, and assume that the underlying network is of type C.

The relationship between these five classes and the network types mentioned above is shown in Figure 9.24. In this case, the height of the various layers suggests the complexity of its implementation. An important observation, however, is that in the end, the transport layer which is built on top of the network layer will provide the same functionality, regardless of the services offered at the level of the network layer.

In our discussion of WANs so far, it should be clear by now that we have discussed mainly the facilities which classify them as type C network. With respect to LANs which also provide flow and error control, we are justified in saying that the mechanisms discussed so far, place them more or less as type B networks. It is therefore time that we corrected this situation and described protocols for ensuring completely reliable communication. An important observation is that although we discuss these protocols as if they were part of the transport layer, you should realize that the same kind of mechanisms can be used at lower layers, having the effect that reliability is provided simply at a lower level.

▷ Although our discussion will be of a rather general nature, we have more or less based it on the structure of the transport protocols supported in the Internet. The Internet transport protocols are based on the IP protocol which forms part of the network layer. Two transport protocols are available: the so-called **unreliable datagram protocol** (**UDP**) which is just a minor extension of IP, and the important **transmission control protocol** (**TCP**), which implements much of the functionality that is to be discussed in this section. Detailed presentations of TCP and UDP can be found in the references provided at the end of this chapter.

9.5.2   Error control

When dealing with the transmission of packets across an unreliable network that supports merely connectionless communication, we have to account for two situations: (1) packets may be lost or damaged in which case a retransmission is required, and (2) acknowledgments may not reach the other end, in which case the transmission of duplicate packets may result. In the following we assume that a receiver should accept a series of packets, $P_1, \ldots, P_N$. A fundamental problem is that these packets may arrive out of order. In essence, this makes the (efficient) error control mechanisms discussed in Chapter 7 no longer applicable.

Transmission failure of packets

We first assume that packets will always arrive, but that a packet may be damaged. The first thing we have to ensure is that the receiving station is capable of detecting that a packet has been damaged. Consequently, we have to add information to each packet that will allow for the mere *detection* of an erroneous packet. In practice, one of the error detection schemes as discussed in Section 7.2.3 is used for this purpose. The strategy that is usually followed by the receiver when an error is detected is simply to discard the packet.

Consequently, a damaged packet is then considered as a packet which has never arrived. But how are we to handle the complete loss of a packet? For example, suppose that packets $P_1, \ldots, P_i$ have been successfully transmitted and that packet P_j, where $j > i + 1$, arrives at the receiver. The point to realize is that the receiver may *not* conclude that all intermediate packets $P_{i+1}, \ldots, P_{j-1}$ have been lost, for indeed, the network does not guarantee delivery of packets in the order they are sent. The solution generally adopted is to let the receiver acknowledge the successful receipt of packets. It is then up to the sender to conclude whether packets have been lost by inspecting the returned acknowledgments.

This immediately leads to another question: *when* should acknowledgments be sent? A rather naive solution is to acknowledge each packet separately. However, this may lead to considerable network traffic, requiring at least two communications per packet (one for the actual transmission, and one for the acknowledgment). A preferred scheme, therefore, is only to send an acknowledgment of, say, packet P_i if all preceding packets have been received as well. Further improvement can be accomplished if the receiver expects to send data back to the original sender. In that case, it waits some time before actually transmitting an acknowledgment, and instead, returns the acknowledgment along with other data. This approach, referred to as **piggybacking** has at least two benefits. First, we allow the receiver to accept more packets in the meantime, which can all be acknowledged by just one acknowledgment. Second, if the receiver indeed has a packet to transmit to the original sender in the form of a reply, it just adds the acknowledgment to that packet. In other words, we are avoiding separate transmission of an acknowledgment.

Transmission failure of acknowledgments

But matters become more intricate if acknowledgments are lost. The first point to note is that the sender will be waiting for acknowledgments. Because there will be some delay between the transmission of a packet and the receipt of its acknowledgment, the sender will have to wait some time before it concludes that a packet did not arrive. Two situations may occur:

- A packet may indeed have been damaged or lost, so that retransmission is perfectly in order

- The acknowledgment was lost, so that retransmission results in a duplicate packet.

If the sender does not wait long enough before initiating a retransmission, many duplicate packets will cross the network, unnecessarily burdening the network's capacity. Of course, duplicate packets must be discarded by the receiver. On the other hand, if the sender waits too long, the effective transmission rate may drop to an unacceptable level, and with it, the utilization of the network. Clearly, finding the right value for the time before a retransmission is incurred is an important design decision, and is often not easy to determine.

9.5.3   Flow control

But our problems are not over yet. Protocols at the level of the transport layer will also have to ensure that a sender and receiver more or less remain synchronized. This means that a sender should at least transmit packets at a rate that can be dealt with by the receiver. If this is not taken into account, the receiver will have no choice other than to discard incoming packets as soon as its input buffers become full. The sender, in turn, will repeatedly issue retransmissions for each discarded packet, for the simple reason that it has not received an acknowledgment. It is not hard to imagine that this situation is highly undesirable.

The solution to this problem is to adopt a sliding window protocol, similar to the one discussed in Chapter 7. In particular, a so-called **credit allocation scheme** is often used. What happens is the following. The receiver maintains a buffer of some length for storing incoming packets before passing them on to the application program for which the packets are intended. Each time the receiver acknowledges the receipt of one or several packets it accompanies the acknowledgment with a **credit grant** by which it specifies for the sender how many packets it may actually send next. The sender, in turn, will never exceed this grant. In other words, if it has a credit of N packets, it will stop transmitting new packets after N have been transmitted if the receiver has not adjusted the sender's credit in the meantime.

This scheme is quite robust. Suppose, for example, that a credit grant (traveling along with an acknowledgment) is lost. In that case, there is really nothing to worry about, as the next acknowledgment returned by the receiver can carry a new, updated credit grant. However, this scheme does rely on the return of a *following* acknowledgment, which is too optimistic. To illustrate, assume that the sender has passed its credit so that it is now waiting for a new grant from the receiver. Furthermore, assume that the latter has acknowledged the last packet sent, together with an update of the sender's credit, but that this acknowledgment is lost during transmission. Indeed, packet transmission may then come to a halt. The sender assumes it has no credit left, while the receiver assumes it has properly updated the sender's credit. The solution, of course, is straightforward. When the receiver returns a credit update, it should expect delivery of new packets after some time has elapsed. If this is not the case, it should assume that the last acknowledgment that has been returned has been lost, together with the updated credit grant. Consequently, the receiver will have to *retransmit* this acknowledgment and credit grant.

By now, note that the sender as well as the receiver should each have at least one timer mechanism. First, the sender will be waiting for acknowledgments to arrive, and will retransmit a packet if after some time the previous transmission had not been acknowledged. The associated timer is generally referred to as a **retransmission timer**. Second, the receiver will have to take into account that a credit grant had been lost, but that the sender is assuming it has no credit left. If the receiver has not had any incoming packets after some time has elapsed, it will have to retransmit the credit grant. In this case, we have to construct a so-called **window timer**.

9.5.4   Connection management

Managing a connection is perhaps hardest to accomplish when you have only an unreliable connectionless network at your disposal. Let's consider two situations: establishing and terminating a connection, respectively.

Establishing a connection

In order to establish a connection, a request packet must be sent across the network, by which a virtual circuit is set up from the sender to the receiver. In any case, the receiving side will have to reply by sending an acknowledgment back to the sender, confirming that the connection has been made. Now, many things can go wrong. First, assume that either the request packet or its acknowledgment is lost, damaged, or delayed. In any case, the originator of the connection will just be waiting some time for the acknowledgment to arrive, and if it has waited long enough, an attempt will be made to re-establish the connection. Let's examine some of the situations that might occur.

- First, assume that the request packet was lost or damaged. In that case, little harm is done because no connection had been established in any case.

- But suppose that the acknowledgment did not reach the originator. In that case, a connection had already been established, and an attempt is now to be considered to make an *additional* connection. This is not acceptable. Therefore, the receiver will simply ignore the request, but should conclude that the acknowledgment did not reach the originator. It therefore acknowledges the connection again.

- Similarly, suppose that the request packet is delayed too long, and that the originator assumes something went wrong. This is when we can get into real trouble. Assume the second attempt succeeds, some communication takes place, and the connection is terminated. After termination, the original request arrives, and the receiver can assume that it should set up a connection again. Unfortunately, this was not what we wanted at all. The acknowledgment returned to the originator will merely be ignored, but clearly, the receiver will still think it has a connection set up with the originator.

Depending on the way that the sender and receiver react, it is not hard to imagine that if no special measures are taken, we might find ourselves in trouble. A generally adopted solution to this problem is a so-called **three-way handshake** devised by Tomlinson (1975). The protocol consists of the following three steps:

1. The originator starts with sending a request packet, having a unique *initial sequence number*, say ISN1.

2. The receiver responds with an acknowledgment, confirming that it had just received a request packet with sequence number ISN1, but also passing its own initial sequence number, say ISN2.

3. The originator, finally, acknowledges that the connection has been established by sending back a packet acknowledging the receipt of the receiver's sequence number ISN2.

It is the combination of the sender's and receiver's unique initial sequence numbers for *each* connection that allows either side to detect that duplicate request packets exist. For example, suppose the receiver has a duplicate request packet. By acknowledging the receipt of this specific packet with a (again unique) sequence number, the originator can easily determine as soon as it receives this packet that something went wrong.

And again, we will have to introduce yet another timeout mechanism in order to guarantee that this scheme works. In this case, the originator of the connection will have to decide through a **retransmit-request** timer when to issue a next request for setting up a connection, because it has not received an acknowledgment from the other end.

Releasing a connection

So what about releasing a connection? Well, we have some problems here as well. Suppose we have a bidirectional connection between two sites. In other words, both sites can request a connection to be released if they think communication is completed. And here's where the problem starts. For imagine that site *A* requests a connection to be released, just after site *B* has sent some data, but which has not yet arrived at *A*. Clearly, this data will be lost if *A* immediately closes down the connection.

So what happens in practice is that if *A* wants to close down the connection, it sends a termination request to *B*. This request will first have to be acknowledged by *B*. There are in principle three options:

- *B* sends an acknowledgment, indicating that it will close the connection as well. This is the best that can happen: both sites have agreed to end the communication. In this case, *A* will acknowledge that the connection is now indeed closed, so *B* can also safely assume that communication is over. Why is this additional acknowledgment by *A* necessary? The reason is quite simple. *B* has no way of knowing that its termination acknowledgment reached *A*. So what it will do is wait for *A* to acknowledge that communication is now finished, and organize its administration. If, in turn, *A*'s acknowledgment did not reach *B*, the latter will decide to consider the connection closed in any case, but report an **abnormal close**.

- *B* does not send an acknowledgment, but instead transmits a separate termination request. In this case, *A* can assume that its own termination request had not yet reached *B*. Therefore, it will acknowledge *B*'s request, and subsequently wait until its own request is acknowledged by *B*.

- *B* sends nothing at all, in which case *A* can assume that either its termination request did not arrive or that *B*'s acknowledgment was lost. In this case, *A* will simply close the connection at the risk of data being lost. And, as in the first case, it will report an abnormal closing of the connection.

Figure 9.25 shows a state transition diagram for a site that is involved in the termination of a connection. The squares represent a global state of a site, whereas the transitions are written as "*event* ⇒ *action*" pairs. For example, if a site is residing in state *active*, and it receives a termination request, it will make a transition to state *received a request to close*, thereby sending an acknowledgment to the site that requested the termination.

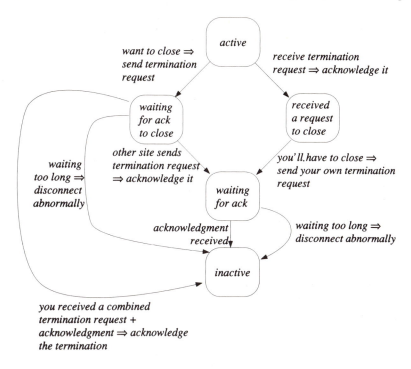

Figure 9.25 A state transition diagram for closing a connection. Adapted from Stallings (1994).

In addition to the three timers mentioned so far, it is seen that we again need a time-out mechanism in order ensure termination of a connection. In this case, a general **persistence timer** is used for dealing with the situation where no acknowledgments are received. This timer is also used for abnormally closing a connection. In fact, if a sender has not received any acknowledgments for some time, the persistence timer will be used as an indication that something is seriously wrong. In that case, the connection will always be closed.

Similarly, the connection will also be terminated abnormally by a receiver if it has not received any packets for some time. The point of having a connection is that communication can be done efficiently, and at a certain rate. Therefore, if no packets are transmitted through a connection, or at least are not perceived as such by a receiver, it may be assumed that something is wrong indeed. Indicating that a connection should be closed for this reason is performed through a so-called **inactivity timer**.

9.6 Summary and further reading

Where local area networks are often used for efficient sharing of local resources such as printers and the like, wide area networks are indeed tailored to support the exchange of information between users (or the applications they use). Let's see what we have accomplished so far.

9.6.1   Wide area networks

Routing

Our main concern in wide area networks is to find the correct way of exchanging information over relatively large distances. The broadcast channels that were used in the case of LANs have now been replaced by point-to-point links between routers, and a major concern is then how to *route* data through a network. Due to the size of the network, we have argued that adaptive routing strategies are the best. They are also considerably more complex than the static routing applied in LANs. Part of the problems arise from the fact that most wide area networks are indeed *large*, as they are constructed through internetworking technology. Consequently, we have to face the fact that several routing protocols are to coincide within one very large, but presumably hierarchically organized network. The principles of routing through networks has only been touched upon in this chapter. What routing is in practice has hardly been discussed. If you want to know more about routing, consult Perlman (1992) for an in-depth discussion. An overview of various routing protocols is given in Bell and Jabour (1986), as well as in Perlman (1993) which focuses more on the Internet.

One topic that we have neglected entirely is that of **multicasting** data. In that case, data is to be sent to several receivers, and as such, the problem strongly resembles that of group communication as discussed in Chapter 6. In the case of LANs the problems can, in general, be solved more easily due to the inherent nature of broadcasting that characterizes local area networking. In that case, data is sent to *all* stations, and those for which it is not intended simply ignore it. This makes implementation of multicasting relatively easy. But in multicasting in wide area networks, many problems arise. In particular, it is definitely not feasible to first broadcast data through the entire network, to be later ignored by those stations that are not supposed to receive it. Instead, multicasting has to be done explicitly in the sense that data has to be forwarded deliberately to all required recipients. A good starting point for further information on multicasting is to first look at broadcast algorithms as described in Chang and Maxemchunk (1984). Multicasting is further described in Frank *et al.* (1985), and a readable article by Deering and Cheriton (1990). Approaches towards wide area multicasting are described by Ballardie (1993, 1995), and Deering *et al.* (1994).

Internetworking

But there is more to wide area networks than routing. As we have already mentioned, WANs often exist only as an internetwork. The real problem with internetworking is generally the conversion from one protocol suite to another. This means not only that we have to adapt to different formats but also that several network routing strategies have to be supported at the same time. The definitive study on the construction of internetworks can be found in Perlman (1992) where you will find many problems, and their solutions, for the simultaneous support of several networks in large internetworks.

But without doubt, the best way to learn more about internetworking is to look at existing systems. In this sense, the extremely well-documented Internet forms a source of many unanswered questions and the reader is encouraged not only to explore the use of the Internet, but also to take a closer look at how things have came to be as they are today. A brief introduction to the Internet is given in Kehoe (1992) and Comer (1995b), whereas numerous other books will guide you through the Internet resources (Krol, 1992). An overview of the technical aspects is given in Lynch and Rose (1993). A first step towards understanding the network and transport protocols (TCP, UDP and IP) should be accommodated by Stevens (1994) and Wright and Stevens (1995), which is an excellent way of getting to know more about the internals of networks in general. A good reference to internetworking with TCP/IP is the two-volume set by Comer (1995a) and Comer and Stevens (1994), which is a good introduction to the many intricate details of the Internet's protocol suite. Nevertheless, the final word on the Internet is always in the so-called requests for comments (RFCs), which can be retrieved via electronic mail. Where these RFCs can be acquired is described in Crockner (1993).

9.6.2 Wide area digital networks

Without doubt, the future of wide area networks is heading towards advanced digital networks that operate at extremely high transmission rates. An intermediate stage will be formed by the present generation of ISDNs that still need to be matured, but it can be expected that the so-called **gigabit networks** will soon outgrow the experimental phase in which they are today.

ISDN

Although there has been considerable scepticism about ISDNs, it can nevertheless be expected that these networks will gradually enter the homes of many, despite the fact that at this moment, they are not capable of fully supporting advanced services such as digital video. For that type of services, we need broadband ISDN. But it is clear that in order to realize B-ISDN we have to make use of advanced transmission media such as optical fiber. And that's precisely where the main problems occur when introducing B-ISDN. Although many countries already have a complete digital telephone network based on optical fiber, this network has not been expanded to each home. At present, almost every home is attached to the telephone network by means of a simple metallic wiring scheme. Replacing these so-called **local subscriber loops** by optical fiber is probably necessary to support the high transmission rates for the kind of services that are to be provided by B-ISDN. Technically, this is not really a problem. From a financial point of view, it is. These costs imply that subscription to a B-ISDN is going to cost a lot of money, and it remains to be seen if customers are willing to pay the price for having, for example, instant video services brought to their homes.

But despite their drawbacks, "normal" ISDNs will probably be adequate in many cases and the additional services that can be offered will undoubtedly be found to be useful. If you want to know more about ISDN, Stallings (1992) will show to be a good reference to many of the details we have omitted from our presentation.

Gigabit networks

The real challenge for the future is the development of systems that are constructed on top of gigabit networks. A gigabit network is "simply" a network that supports transmission rates in the range of 10^9 bits per second. This is indeed extremely high. Roughly, there are two broad problems to be addressed: (1) how we can construct such networks, and (2) how we are to implement adequate systems on top of this technology.

Most attention is presently paid to the development of gigabit networks. An important role in their implementation will be reserved for the use of ATM switches as explained in Section 9.4.4. And it is here that much research is yet to be done. Although ATM switches are commercially available, they do not generally meet several important commercial requirements. For example, in order to allow for a gradual transition from existing network technology to full-blown ATM networks, switches should be able to support several low-level protocols for the coming years. These, and other problems are discussed in Rooholamini *et al.* (1994) which also presents different implementation technologies for switches. Introductions to ATM are given by Lane (1994), Le Boudec (1992), and Miller (1994), the latter putting ATM into the context of existing technology. Detailed information on ATM networks, containing also many references for further reading can be found in Händel *et al.* (1994).

The gradual transition from current technology to gigabit networks is something that plays a role not only at the lowest layers. Of course, we want our present distributed systems and applications to execute on top of these networks as well. For some time, this was thought of being the wrong way to go, for the simple reason that the existing protocol suites were far too tailored towards the underlying network technology. As a result, research has concentrated on the development of so-called **light-weight protocols** which attempted to reduce the administrative overhead as much as possible. Much of this overhead came from the assumption that the underlying network supported only unreliable connectionless communication, which indeed is not realistic in the case of many high-speed networks based on fiber optical media. An overview of the work on these light-weight protocols can be found in Doeringer *et al.* (1990). However, it remains to be seen how useful these alternative protocols are. Many existing protocol suites, such as for example TCP/IP have shown to be adaptable for faster networks as well (Jacobson *et al.*, 1992). As was already pointed out by Watson and Mamrak (1987), developers often fail to make the distinction between *what* a protocol is supposed to do and *how* they actually accomplish things, i.e. how they are implemented. Consequently, as of today, it seems that changing the network technology need not seriously affect the existing bulk of distributed systems and applications, and that to a certain extent, scalability of these systems and applications is even supported.

But implementing systems on top of gigabit networks is going to pose many more problems. Although these networks offer very high performance, the performance increase is only to be sought in the increase of *transmission rate*. That means that we can transfer more data per second than is presently possible. This does not mean, however, that data will be transferred *faster*. To illustrate, even when traveling at the speed of light, it is still going to take 70 milliseconds to get a bit to cross a distance of 20 000 kilometers. For interactive programs which generally require several communications between a client and a server per keystroke, this adds up to a few hundred milliseconds delay – and that is something that will not go unnoticed. This long delay in the case of wide area distributed systems (that will be built on top of gigabit networks) is going to be a major problem to be solved. At present, some important research in this area has been conducted, but more is required for these networks to be commercially attractive. It is also here that the existing protocols will probably fail to support gigabit networks adequately.

We shall leave gigabit networks here. If you want to know more about them, Partridge (1994) is the book to consult. Not only does the author provide details on the implementation of gigabit networks, he also supplies a lot of information on the problems when making a transition towards gigabit networks.

Exercises

1. Ethernet boards have a (worldwide) unique MAC address. Why is it still not such a good idea to use this address on a global basis when constructing a wide area network?

2. What is the real gain of having a hierarchical addressing scheme such as the one in which domains, areas, and subnetworks are distinguished?

3. Make the distinction clear between circuit-switching and packet-switching, and also between virtual circuits and datagrams. Is it possible to construct virtual circuits on a packet-switched network? And what about sending datagrams through a circuit-switched network?

4. Explain in detail how network congestion can occur. Take into account the functional organization of routers as well as the sources of congestion.

5. Packet discarding is in principle a rather crude way of getting rid of too much traffic. Name several policies that make the technique less crude to apply in the first place.

6. If we can avoid network congestion through virtual circuits, why not apply that technique to all communications across wide area networks?

7. Explain the difference between link state routing and distance vector routing. Identify advantages and disadvantages of both approaches, and explain why, despite some disadvantages, link state routing is often preferred.

8. *If we compare Figure 9.6 (page 435) with Figure 9.7 (page 437), it would seem that Dijkstra's algorithm requires more steps than Bellman's approach. What's your opinion? (Hint: think what happens in large networks.)

9. *Making a distinction between, on the one hand, routing algorithms and, on the other, routing organizations, is considered good design practice. But, in this respect, is distance vector routing actually not a distributed routing algorithm?

10. Name the main additional problems that need to be dealt with when constructing an internetwork.

11. Fragmenting packets can be avoided if the sender ensures that its packets are always small. Following this strategy is not always such a good idea. Why?

12. We have presented fragmentation as a problem inherent to internetworks. Why need it not be a major issue in homogeneous wide area networks (i.e. a WAN built on top of a single type of LAN)?

13. *Can you think of a reason why the Internet is growing *exponentially*? Wouldn't you expect the growth to be linear instead?

14. *If ICMP messages are sent as ordinary IP datagrams, how can we distinguish them from other IP datagrams?

15. An ISDN will offer a basic service connection to your home consisting of two B channels and one D channel, adding up to 144 Kbps. However, ISDN will actually reserve a total of 192 Kbps. Can you imagine why?

16. *Suppose I have an IP datagram of 2048 bytes that I want to send across a broadband ISDN implemented by means of an ATM network. How many cells will need to be sent?

17. *Taking the previous exercise into account, provide arguments for the fact that ATM networks, although intended to support computer communication which is strongly biased towards packet exchanges, employ circuit-switching technology.

18. *ATM networks are so reliable that cells will generally not contain any additional error detection bits, except for the header. Why? (Hint: work out where error detection takes place for the data contained in cells.)

19. Explain the main reason for introducing the transport layer, and also its main functionality.

20. Why would we want multiplexing capabilities in the transport layer?

21. Transport layer protocols often have extensive error detection capabilities, even if they are implemented directly on top of reliable networks such as those based on ATM. Does this make sense?

22. Is it possible to devise a completely safe protocol for closing down a connection taking into account that requests and acknowledgments may be lost?

Chapter 10

Towards communication architectures

In this chapter we shall discuss communication architectures. These define the functionality of communication services, which enable us to build distributed applications using various computers interconnected through a communication network. In fact, we will explore how the basic services provided by the operating system, such as file access and inter-process communication, can be lifted to the network level. In other words, we will discuss some of the problems encountered in trying to let computers collectively work across a network infrastructure and what kind of solutions can be provided.

10.1   From local to global systems

In the preceding chapters we have given the basic ingredients of computer systems, their structure, way of operation, and methods to interconnect them. After having dealt with all problems associated with hardware, system software, and networks, we might ask ourselves if we now have enough to allow us to construct programs using multiple computers in a relatively straightforward and easy manner. In other words, we ask ourselves if we have all the ingredients to build **distributed applications**. To that end, let's first be more specific about what a distributed application actually is.

10.1.1   The concept of distributed applications

We use the term distributed system to characterize properties of certain computer systems with *multiple active entities*. However, we are usually rather vague about the behavioral and physical nature of these entities. Not surprisingly, several definitions appear in the literature that deviate from each other quite substantially. The word "distributed" suggests that something is distributed, we can safely agree on that. However, it is much more difficult to agree on *what* is actually distributed, and *where* it is distributed. Concerning what to distribute, it seems obvious that the prime entities that can be subject to distribution are computations and data. Where to distribute these entities also does not seem to lead to any problems: entities should be distributed over available resources such as processors, memories, and other devices.

But is this enough to describe the nature of a distributed application? Let's take a degenerated example. Suppose we have written a BASAL program consisting of several processes. First, assume that we have a computer system with just a single CPU and one main memory module that is capable of compiling and executing BASAL programs. In that case, the computations and data of our program can be distributed only over these two main resources; the underlying operating system will have to ensure that the various processes each get an equal share of CPU time when executing instructions.[1] Intuitively, we would not be inclined to refer to our program implementation as being a distributed application. So let's add some more CPUs that are all connected to the same memory module, so that several processes forming part of our program can now be executed at the same time. Again, speaking of a distributed program seems to be wrong here. From the outside we see hardly any differences with our first implementation, except, perhaps that our implementation could be executed much faster. Similarly, if we assume that there are even several memory modules in our computer, and the data of our program is located in different memory modules, it would still feel strange to speak of a distributed application. From the outside we still see nothing special happening. Our BASAL compiler merely compiles our program for this (admittedly rather advanced computer), but there is nothing really to distinguish the program from our first one.

But then what? Some people would say: the active entities in a distributed system must be independent or autonomous to be able to speak of being truly distributed. For instance, if we take multiple independent computers, each running their own operating system and having their own memories, interconnect them through a communication system (e.g. a computer network) and agree on a message format, we would have a system that can be used for distributed programming. A couple of personal computers interconnected through such a network, each running an electronic mail program, is an example of a distributed system; the mail program is then an example of such a distributed application. Not a bad definition. However, this definition is rather biased by hardware terminology, leaving other sensible interpretations of the concept of a distributed program uncovered.

It is better to rely on the definition of an active entity we have already encountered, namely a **process**. Multiple active entities can then be interpreted as multiple processes, each executing a program that forms part of a larger, distributed application. However, more must be said to make an application distributed. We impose the following requirements on processes constituting a distributed application:

(R1): Several processes must provide a *service* to other processes.

(R2): Processes must have an agreed upon way of *communication*.

(R3): Processes must know how they can *request* a service, and provided services must be *used*.

(R4): The order of providing services to requesting processes must be immaterial and subject only to a fairness rule.

---

[1]Indeed, we might say that the processes are to be distributed in time, which is just another resource.

Let's go into more detail on these requirements.

(R1): Providing services.   This requirement indicates that a process providing a service must have a properly defined functional interface to enable other processes to use that service. In terms of BASAL, this means that there should be a *specification* of a service, for example in the form of a package specification containing definitions of relevant data types and procedures. It is extremely important to note that *how* the service is implemented is of no concern to a process requesting that service. This implies that a process providing a service has a certain **autonomy** in realizing that service.

(R2): Agreed way of communication.   To use a service, processes must be able to communicate with each other. This implies that they have to agree on the way that communication should proceed. In other words, they have to agree on a **communication protocol**. Again, such a protocol says nothing about the way it is realized.

(R3): Requesting and using services.   This requirement may seem strange, but it is, in fact, an important one. What we are saying here is that processes that have no knowledge of or means to use a service provided by another process simply are not considered as being part of the distributed application. Similarly, if a process merely provides services that are never used, it does not make sense to consider it as part of the application as well. What we are talking about here are (1) the identification and naming disciplines of the processes constituting a distributed application, and (2) identifying services that play a role in a distributed application. In other words, we are requiring that a distributed application consists of a **logically coherent** collection of communicating processes.

(R4): Fairness of service provision.   The last requirement implies that there is no imposed order on providing a service to requesting processes, i.e. service can be given in any order. The only thing we require is a certain fairness in handling service requests from processes. Otherwise, a chosen service discipline could prevent certain processes from making use of a service, effectively inhibiting them in taking part in the distributed application.

In using the above description of a distributed application, nothing was said about the hardware requirements. In fact this is not necessary. We can implement distributed applications obeying the requirements put forward on systems varying from a single processor to a worldwide web of connected computers. A good example of this is electronic mail which we shall discuss below. In practice users that are connected to the same computer still send each other messages in exactly the same way as when they are connected to computers that are located at geographically different sites.

10.1.2   Implicit assumptions made so far

A central role when building distributed applications is played by operating systems. As we have explained, an operating system provides users and programs with a **virtual computer**: a machine consisting of resources such as processes, files, and peripheral devices, constructed as a combination of hardware and software. Important in this respect is that the machine manifests itself in a *coherent* fashion. In other words, there is a more or less standardized interface that allows users and programs to access and use these resources. The interface, of course, consists of the numerous service programs that can be called by applications.

In Chapter 6 we took the approach followed then one step further. There we introduced several package specifications that allowed us to describe communication between computer systems. The implementations of these packages, which are merely other service programs, had been omitted. However, we returned to that issue in the two preceding chapters. By and large, using the presented implementation outlines and general descriptions of how implementations could be derived would seem to be enough to obtain a system that supports the development of distributed programs.

In fact, this is true, but we are ignoring one extremely important issue. The bottom-up approach described here is one we cannot follow in practice. What we have to accept is that the assumptions we are implicitly making by following a bottom-up approach will no longer hold when building applications on top of existing wide area networks. What are these assumptions? We mention some of the more important ones:

- **A single language environment.** All working principles of communication systems have been explained in this book by means of programs written in a single language, BASAL. This implies that the BASAL compiler will take all programs making up the complete application and translate them to executable entities as explained in Chapter 4. Because of this, we can be sure that identical declarations for data types in different program units have the same meaning. For example, if we declare a data type INTEGER, we may safely assume that it includes both positive and negative numbers in both programs. But what happens when other programming languages are used? Indeed, exactly *what* a data type stands for is no longer uniquely defined. And because many distributed applications are developed by using several programming languages, we have a problem to solve.

- **Identical processor architectures.** The same meaning of data types does not necessarily imply the same representation in memory. Different processor architectures may have different representations for integers and floating-point numbers. However, if the processor architecture of the processors in a system is identical, also their representation in memory can be assumed to be identical. So far, we have ignored any differences between the way that processors represent data in main memory.

- **A single file system.** We have also assumed that we have a single file system such that all processes in the system can name and access files in a uniform way. But, as you may know from experience, file systems may be considerably different in this sense. And when several distinct file systems are used within a single worldwide application, we will have to take those differences into account.

- **A local naming system.** In a computer system all kinds of resources need to be given a name or number for their identification. Examples of such resources are processes, users, files, and peripheral devices. The point to note is that when using a single operating system, it is the operating system which maintains the mapping between those names and the resources that they identify. One example is that of a directory service as explained in Section 5.6.3: it maintains the mapping between the name of a file and the file identifier. File naming, file identifiers, and the directory service itself fall under the regime of a *single* operating system. This local naming system is acceptable for small systems; it will not, however, suffice if we need to support wide area distributed applications.

It is thus seen that we do indeed have some problems to solve. In truly distributed applications, the assumptions listed above no longer hold. What we want is to let completely different applications (possibly written in different languages), running on computers with different architectures and operating systems, communicate with each other. In other words, we should provide the right means to allow for the construction of **open systems**. An open system was defined in Section 9.5 as a system that will allow anyone to construct a program that can communicate with other existing programs. Clearly, we can only do this if we have a collection of standardized services.

In this chapter we are going to look at several such services. To that end, we start by completing the OSI reference model in Section 10.2, and subsequently introducing a simplified model to structure our further discussion. In Section 10.3 we discuss four important commonly adopted communication services: terminal handling, file transfer, message handling, and global naming schemes. How these services can be used by a worldwide distributed application is illustrated in Section 10.4 where we briefly discuss the popular World Wide Web.

10.2 On open systems

10.2.1 The OSI model completed

The problems mentioned so far are not new and have also been addressed by the OSI reference model. At this point, it is worth considering the framework that OSI provides to handle solutions to problems dealing with open systems. We shall also see, however, that this framework is no longer considered entirely adequate and that another approach needs to be followed.

Our discussion so far on the OSI reference model has ended with the description of the transport layer in Section 9.5. With the transport layer in place, we can be certain of making a reliable connection between any two points in a network. However complicated these connections might be in terms of implementation (error control, fragmentation, connection management), from a user's perspective a *pipe* has been established

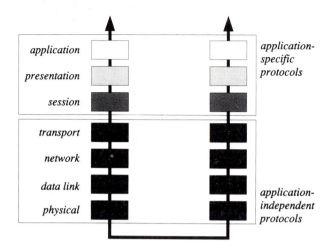

Figure 10.1 The complete OSI reference model.

over which bits can be pumped from one side to the other. More functionality needs to be added to be able to construct communicating systems.

The OSI reference model adds three more layers to the transport layer: the **session layer**, the **presentation layer**, and the **application layer**. These three layers work together to perform a specific user function. If we add them on top of the transport layer we get the picture as shown in Figure 10.1. We shall briefly describe the functionality of these three layers.

The session layer

The session layer is responsible for dialogue management between two application protocols. A dialogue is the set-up, synchronization, and clearance of a complete network transaction. When taking the connection management facilities of the transport layer into account, you might think that dialogue management at this level may not even be necessary. And, in fact, this is often true. There are, however, a few points that need clarification.

First, dialogue management may be skipped entirely, even at the level of the transport layer. For instance, if we have a simple connectionless mail service, there is no dialogue at all. The session layer can in that case safely be omitted or made transparent. And indeed, connectionless communication at the level of the transport layer is taken care of in the form of datagrams, so that dialogues are also non-existent at that level.

On the other hand, if we have a timely network transaction, we want to be able to correct things when something goes wrong in the middle of the transaction. For example, suppose we were to transfer the complete catalog of the Library of Congress overnight

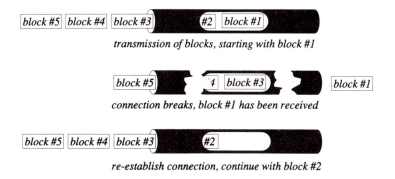

transmission of blocks, starting with block #1

connection breaks, block #1 has been received

re-establish connection, continue with block #2

Figure 10.2 The principle of maintaining a connection by the session layer.

to the other side of the world. If during this indeed lengthly transaction an error occurs (e.g. a connection was somehow broken), we would like to resend only the data affected by the error and not start all over again. To do so we have to split the data to be sent into blocks and insert synchronization points between the blocks. The session protocol uses these synchronization points to have reference points from where a transfer can be resumed after failure correction. The principle of operation is shown in Figure 10.2.

The presentation layer

The presentation layer is responsible for the *representation* of the data being transferred between two processes forming part of a wide area application. When we transfer data between two processes of such an application the data has a specific meaning, or in other words, has specific *semantics*. Now a transfer makes sense only when this meaning is the same for both parties in the communication, i.e. when both sender and receiver have *shared semantics*. What this means is best explained by an example.

Suppose two processes want to exchange a message consisting of several data fields, one of these fields being an integer. The point to note is that in the end the only thing the sender can transmit with the concepts introduced so far is a *bit string*. It is up to the receiver to *interpret* this bit string as the intended message. This leaves us with two problems. First, both the sender and receiver have to agree upon what the message looks like. In other words, they have to agree on the data fields and the types associated with those fields. This is called agreement on the **abstract syntax**.

But that's not all. As the sender will eventually transmit the message in the form of a bit string, both the sender and the receiver will have to agree on the way that the message is represented as a bit string. This is called agreement on the **concrete syntax**. For example, if the sender is executed on a computer in which integers are represented in one's complement notation, while the receiver's computer uses two's complement notation, somewhere a conversion needs to take place so that the receiver can still interpret the received bit string as containing the correct value of the integer data field.

It is the responsibility of the presentation layer to take care of these matters. In par-

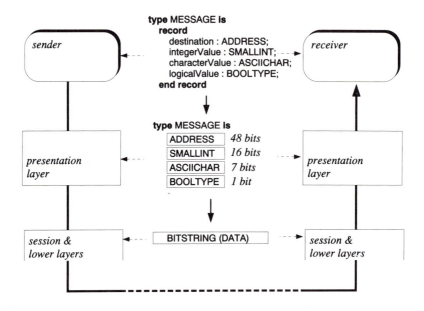

Figure 10.3 The principal working of the presentation layer.

ticular, the presentation layer provides the right means for a sender and receiver to reach an agreement on a common abstract and concrete syntax. This principle is illustrated in Figure 10.3.

▷ You might wonder how we can implement this functionality in the presentation layer. To illustrate, assume that within an application a sender wishes to pass messages of some kind to a receiver. Say that these messages are to consist of a field by which the receiver can be identified, as well as a field containing an integer value. In addition, messages will also contain a character corresponding to one of the 128 possible ASCII characters, as well as a Boolean variable. In order to reach an agreement on the abstract syntax of messages, both the sender and the receiver will use the same *notation*. For example, we could use BASAL for this. This implies that both the sender and the receiver will have BASAL at their disposal. For example, some of the basic data types can be represented as follows:

```
subtype ADDRESS is INTEGER range 0..16777215;
subtype SMALLINT is INTEGER range 0..65535;
subtype ASCIICHAR is CHARACTER range CHARACTER'VAL(0)..CHARACTER'VAL(127);
subtype BOOLTYPE is BOOLEAN;
```

so that a message can be specified as:

```
type MESSAGE is
  record
      destination : ADDRESS;
      integerValue : SMALLINT;
      characterValue : ASCIICHAR;
      logicalValue : BOOLTYPE;
  end record ;
```

The MESSAGE data type is specified to be composed of two integer data fields, a character data field and a Boolean data field. Both the sender and the receiver will use this specification of a message. They are said to agree on the abstract syntax of the messages they are to exchange. Note that by explicitly specifying the subtypes ADDRESS, SMALLINT, ASCII-CHAR, and BOOLTYPE both parties have also agreed on the values that any variable of these data types can have.

Our specification, however, says nothing about the way that the various data types are represented as bit strings, let alone how we are to convert a MESSAGE variable into a bit string and vice versa. To that end, we need to provide more information. In particular, we need to specify how the basic data types are to be represented as bit strings, and using these representations, how MESSAGE data types are represented in the form of a bit string. It will come as no surprise that we can use BASAL's representation clauses to this end, as explained in Section 4.5.1. We start by specifying precisely how the basic data types are to be represented:

```
for ADDRESS'SIZE use 3*8;
for SMALLINT'SIZE use 2*8;
for ASCIICHAR'SIZE use 7;
for BOOLTYPE'SIZE use 1;
```

The definition of the subtype ADDRESS is similar to the definition in Listing 8.2 and defines a 24-bit non-negative integer, occupying three consecutive bytes in memory. The subtype SMALLINT occupies two bytes of memory. Because there are only 128 ASCII characters, it suffices to use just seven bits to represent them all. Likewise, Boolean data types can be represented by only one bit. Specifying the complete representation for a MESSAGE is now not too difficult:

```
for MESSAGE use
  record
      destination at 0 range 0..23; -- occupies precisely 24 bits
      integerValue at 0 range 24..39; -- occupies the following 16 bits
      characterValue at 0 range 40..46; -- occupies precisely 7 bits
      logicalValue at 0 range 47..47; -- occupies exactly the last bit
  end record ;

for MESSAGE use 6*8;
```

Note how we have specified exactly which substrings of a 48-bit message correspond to the respective data fields of the MESSAGE data type. It is now up to the BASAL compiler running at both locations to ensure that this layout of MESSAGE data types is maintained.

But is this enough? The answer is easily seen to be no: the only thing we have done is specify by *how many* bits each data type is to be represented. We have said nothing about *what* these bits stand for. For example, should the value TRUE be represented by "1" or by "0"? Likewise, we have also not specified whether integers should be represented in one's or two's complement. How this additional information can be added is left as an exercise for the reader.

Having solved the problem of abstract and concrete syntax in BASAL, only one problem remains: not all programs will be written in BASAL (in fact, no program will be ever written in BASAL). Actual programs might be written in several different languages, such as C and Fortran. All those languages usually have a different syntax for data types, different capabilities to define data types, and different concrete syntax definitions (if any). To solve this problem, the language ASN.1 has been developed, which allows abstract and concrete syntaxes to be precisely defined. Only those data types that are to be used in communication need to be specified in ASN.1; a compiler subsequently translates these definitions into corresponding ones for the language in which the application is being written. Therefore, for example, there are ASN.1 to C compilers as well as ones to translate ASN.1 to Fortran.

The application layer

Having dealt with dialogues and data representation, we are left with one general problem: the mechanisms provided so far are simply *too* general to be used efficiently. For example, it is not hard to imagine that electronic mailing systems require a different way of communication from order handling systems in a manufacturing environment. Where the first type of systems mostly need to agree on the way that sender and receiver are specified in a message, as well as the allowable characters in a message, the latter will require information on the product that is ordered, the quantity, etc. In fact, many of these details can be more or less identified *per application domain*. And it is here where the application layer falls into place. The point is that if an application adheres to the general protocol laid down for its domain at the level of the application layer, it need not be further concerned about the way that information exchange takes place.

Clearly, if such communication protocols, or application protocols as they are also called, can be agreed upon, developing wide area applications would indeed become relatively simple. For one thing, the application developers need not be concerned about the way communication itself is handled as this is completely being taken care of. It will come as no surprise that this approach is only meaningful if the application protocols are highly standardized. This is an area where much work is still in progress, although standardization for certain domains has been reasonably successful.

But in the OSI reference model, the application layer is really not the final solution. This can be seen by imagining that, for example, an order handling system may be entirely based on an electronic mail handling system. In other words, orders are translated into messages that can be treated as electronic mail. At the other end, such messages can be converted back again to actual orders. This approach is already often used for electronically ordering books, or for even searching through remote data bases. What we then have in fact are two application protocols placed "on top" of each other. In other words, we have introduced yet another communication layer.

Unfortunately, the OSI reference model does not cover this approach towards applica-

tion development as it defines only a single application layer. Adding yet another layer
to the model is really not a solution, especially if you realize that other layers, such as the
session layer, have not always proven to be very useful. To simply matters we will define
in the next section a simplified reference model, which from an application developer's
point of view is more convenient than the standard model.

▷ A remark should be made at this point. The OSI reference model defines seven layers, where
the Nth layer for the realization of its communication functions relies on the services provided by the $(N-1)^{\text{th}}$ layer. However, the Nth layer needs to know nothing about *how* the
$(N-1)^{\text{th}}$ layer implements these services. This strict separation enables layers to be replaced and makes it possible to realize an application (say, an electronic mail application)
using different assemblies of layers. Such an assembly is also called a **protocol suite**.

Apart from protocols defined according to the OSI model, protocols are in use which do not
strictly adhere to this reference model. This is the case with, for example, the TCP/IP protocols, which have been outlined in Section 9.5. Although the TCP protocol can be regarded as
a protocol of the transport layer and the IP protocol as a protocol of the network layer, both
protocols do not separate functionality and implementation as strictly as required by the OSI
model. Another important difference is that the TCP/IP protocol suite does not have layers
defined on top of the TCP layer. This means that each application must implement presentation and session functions itself and no sharing of this functionality can be obtained.

10.2.2 A simplified model for open systems

To reduce complexity, we will now define a simplified reference model. This model has
four layers as opposed to the seven layers of the OSI model. The model is depicted in
Figure 10.4. The four layers describe the following functions:

- **layer 1:** transmission
- **layer 2:** transfer
- **layer 3:** communication
- **layer 4:** application.

We will describe the function of each layer of the simplified model in more detail in the
following subsections and relate each layer of the simplified model to the OSI layers.

Layer 1: Transmission

Layer 1 of the simplified model is equal to the physical layer of the OSI model. Since this
is the least spectacular layer of the OSI model, you might ask why we define a separate
layer for it. The main reason is one of economics. For example, cabling of buildings
carries large investments and the turnover frequency of these investments is in general
much higher than for other network equipment. Hence standardization of the electrical
and mechanical characteristics of transmission media will enable these investments to be
protected.

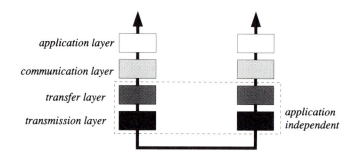

Figure 10.4 The four-layered alternative model.

Layer 2: Transfer functionality

For the second layer of the simplified model we make use of the fact that up to the transport layer of the OSI model all layers define application-independent protocols. These layers are to provide reliable data paths between two communication points. As long as this is secured, the more application-oriented layers above our transfer layer are not concerned how this is accomplished. Hence we can take the data link, network, and transport layer together and mold them into a single layer providing *transfer functions*. So, for example, the TCP and IP protocols as used within the Internet and which are implemented on top of a local area network protocol such as IEEE 802.3 (CSMA/CD) would give a complete definition of this layer.

Layer 3: Communication

The third layer in our model defines common communication services as needed by many applications. With common communication services we mean services that are needed by most network-based applications. The communication services generally adopted in this layer include:

- Terminal handling services
- File handling services
- Message handling services
- Name handling services
- Remote operation services
- Time handling services
- Security services.

The first four of these services will be explained in more detail in Section 10.3. Anticipating our further discussion, it can be noted that the functions provided by this layer are similar to those of traditional operating systems. For example, both name and file handling services are typically services that a local operating system should also provide. Likewise, having a facility to communicate as a user through a terminal is something that no operating system can ignore. Naming facilities is yet another service that each operating system will offer. Indeed, it is thus seen that the communication layer extends the concept of an operating system to that of a network-based environment.

The other three services (remote operation, time handling, and security) have been omitted from our discussion here for various reasons. Rather than elaborating on these reasons now, we defer a further discussion to the end of this chapter.

Layer 4: Application domain functions

The fourth layer defines additional standards for various application domains. Many of such application domain-specific standards deal with the definition of document formats. Examples of such document formats are purchase orders, shipping documents, and invoices. Standards for the format of these documents enable trade functions to be automated, such as automated ordering of parts at various suppliers. This book is not the right place to discuss these matters for the simple reason that they are application-specific.

10.3 Communication services

From the above, it can be concluded that our presentation so far has mainly lacked discussion of the communication layer when discussing general communication systems. It is time that we corrected this. In this section we shall pay some more attention on the various communication services as offered by our communication layer. As we have said, we shall concentrate on how this layer provides wide area support for dealing with communication through terminals, file transfer, message handling, and the important issue of providing naming facilities for resources. The reason for concentrating on exactly these four services has everything to do with their illustrative nature. As of today, they are probably not only the most widely used services, but they also reveal more clearly than any other service the present state of wide area distributed systems. Moreover, we shall see that these services can be relatively elegantly combined into a single user-oriented global information system: the World Wide Web which we will discuss in Section 10.4. Other important services, but which are more hidden from users, are briefly discussed in Section 10.5.

10.3.1 Terminal handling services

We normally communicate with a computer through a terminal. Most terminals consist of a keyboard and a screen (and sometimes other devices such as a mouse). If we are to expand the functionality of an operating system so that it can still work in a network-based environment, we will have to devise a way to connect terminals to remote sites of the system.

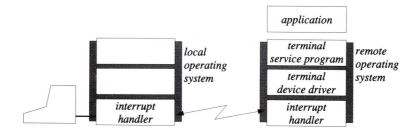

Figure 10.5 Having a remote device driver control a local terminal.

A straightforward expansion

Terminals are usually connected to the computer via an interface to the local bus as described in Chapter 3. In essence, a device driver, forming part of the operating system, takes care of the basic communication between a process requiring terminal input or output. Additional software, usually also forming part of the operating system, is capable of handling more sophisticated operations. To illustrate, recall that echoing characters on the screen was actually something that we needed explicitly to take into account as discussed in Chapter 4. Sometimes echoing is suppressed on purpose, as can be seen when the operating system requires you to type in a password after login. The point to note is that even for apparently simple operations such as echoing characters, we need to devise special software that implements such operations. In other words, terminals by themselves have very limited capabilities.

This is really not such a disadvantage as most basic operations can be handled at the level of the operating system. But matters do become more complicated when a terminal should also be attached to a non-local computer. Imagine that in this case we followed the same approach as attaching a terminal to the local computer. This would require that a *remote* device driver has access to the terminal. What does this mean? Take a look at Figure 10.5 which illustrates the minimal approach to follow in this case.

Each time a key is (de)pressed, the subsequent interrupt generated by the local hardware should initially be handled locally as well. Then, the interrupt handler associated with the terminal should pass, in the form of a message, the interrupt to the remote device driver. The driver, in turn, processes that message and sends a reply, which is subsequently handled by a minimal amount of software or hardware at the local site. In principle, this scheme would indeed work. There is, however, a problem with this approach which is related to the fact that there are so many different types of terminals. The simplest terminals are able to support character-oriented screens that scroll as information is displayed. The most sophisticated ones are graphical terminals. In general, different terminal types, and in general also terminals from different vendors, require their own, specific device driver. In the case of a network-based system, this means that a remote station will need the device drivers for any terminal that could possibly request a remote connection. Realizing that device drivers are also specific to operating systems, it is then not difficult to see that we are losing a lot of flexibility with respect to changes in the network.

Virtual terminals

A better solution is to define a **virtual terminal**. In order to explain what a virtual terminal is, first reconsider how an ordinary terminal may appear to a user or an application program. Using BASAL for this purpose, a simple scroll-based terminal can be specified by the following package:

```
package TERMINAL is
   procedure READ(char : out CHARACTER);
   procedure WRITE(char : in CHARACTER);
end TERMINAL;
```

When invoking the procedure READ, the calling process is suspended until a character has been typed, which is subsequently returned via the parameter char. Likewise, calling the procedure WRITE results in displaying the given character on the screen.

A virtual scroll-based terminal is not much different, except for one thing: characters are now read from a *remote* keyboard, and likewise, are written to a *remote* display. In addition, if we standardize the interface for virtual scroll-based terminals, *and* base their implementation on standard protocols available at the level of the communication layer (such as TCP/IP), we have accomplished three important things:

- Implementations are independent of operating systems, but instead rely on standardized implementations of interfaces to the transfer layer.

- There is no dependency between virtual terminals and vendor-specific products.

- The number of implementations is limited as there is only a single concept of (in our case) a virtual scroll-based terminal.

Now what does a virtual terminal look like? To produce a virtual terminal we make use of two components: a client terminal running at the local computer to which the real terminal is connected, and a server terminal running on the remote computer. This organization is shown in Figure 10.6(b). The original situation in which a program PROGRAM depends on a local terminal is shown in Figure 10.6(a). Note that in the case of a virtual terminal, PROGRAM will now be running on the remote computer. Also note how the two components of a virtual terminal are placed on top of the transfer layer, and indeed form part of the communication layer. All commands between the client and server terminal are to be translated into messages that can be handled by the transfer layer. It is important to note that neither component makes any assumptions concerning the actual hardware or the operating systems that are being used. Instead, it relies entirely on (1) the definition as provided by, in our case, the TERMINAL package specification, and (2) the functions provided by the transfer layer. We have thus established a clean separation between both systems and a decoupling of machine-specific information for both sides.

▷ **An example: TELNET**

A popular virtual terminal protocol based on TCP/IP is TELNET. The core of the protocol is formed by a set of commands that are sufficiently general to be found in one form or an-

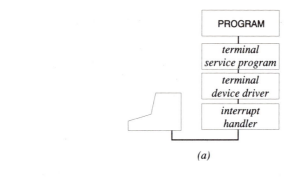

(a)

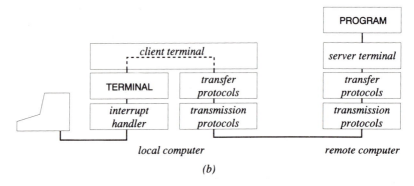

(b)

Figure 10.6   The principal working of a virtual terminal (b). The original situation is shown in (a).

other on most scroll-based terminals. These commands are used to let the client and server TELNET terminal communicate with each other. Of course, each command must be communicated between the client and server terminal in the form of a message. There is simply no other way of doing so. This does, however, impose a problem that we will encounter with other protocols as well: how can we distinguish commands from data? The solution is simple and straightforward. Like many other protocols, TELNET sends messages as a string of 8-bit bytes. However, data is restricted to the 7-bit ASCII coding as presented in Table 2.3. Commands can thus be recognized by the fact that the leftmost bit of a byte has been set to 1.

Before the information exchange between the client and server terminal takes place, the two are first involved in a *negotiation phase*. To that end, the following four TELNET commands can be used:

- DO: This command, which is sent as "DO option", is a request to *the receiver* to support the indicated option. For example, a client may request the server to support message encryption by sending the command "DO encrypt".

- WILL: This is a command sent to the other party to express that *the sender* is willing to support an option. For example, the server may indicate that message encryption will

Table 10.1   The six different scenarios for TELNET option negotiation (adapted from Stevens, 1994).

Sender	Receiver	Semantics
WILL option	DO option	The sender wants to enable option; the receiver agrees.
WILL option	DONT option	The sender wants to enable option; the receiver disallows it.
DO option	WILL option	The sender wants the receiver to enable option; the receiver agrees.
DO option	WONT option	The sender wants the receiver to enable option; the receiver won't do that.
WONT option	DONT option	The sender wants to disable option; the receiver acknowledges its cooperation.
DONT option	WONT option	The sender wants the receiver to disable option; the receiver acknowledges its cooperation.

be supported by sending the command "WILL encrypt" to the client terminal.

- DONT: This is the opposite of the DO command: the sender is requesting the receiver to disable an option.
- WONT: Likewise, this is the opposite of the WILL command: sending "WONT option" tells the receiver that the sender wants to disable the option.

These four commands can be used in six different scenarios as shown in Table 10.1. For example, the client terminal may want to encrypt all messages during the TELNET session to which end it sends the command "WILL encrypt" to the server terminal. Assuming the latter agrees to accept encrypted messages, it replies by sending the command "DO encrypt" to the client. After several of such options have been agreed upon, initiated either by the client or server terminal, communication between the two can commence.

Now how does TELNET appear to a user? In practice, the protocol is most often used when a user wants to login into a remote computer. For example, suppose that you want to login into a remote computer named hydra.cp.tn.tudelft.nl (where we assume that you have an account for that computer). To that end, you can invoke on your own computer system the program TELNET which forms an implementation of the TELNET protocol. What you might see on your own screen is shown in Figure 10.7.[2] Commands typed in by the user are shown in bold.

Let's see what is actually happening. After starting the TELNET program, we first instruct it to show the options that are negotiated on the screen. Then we instruct to open a connection to hydra.cp.tn.tudelft.nl, which happens to have the Internet address 192.31.126.72. As

---

[2]We note that this is, in fact, an edited version of an actual transcript from a TELNET session. In this case, we are requesting a connection from a computer in Amsterdam to one in Delft.

```
% telnet                                 start TELNET program
telnet> toggle options                   instruct to show info on options
Will show option processing.             response by program
telnet> open hydra.cp.tn.tudelft.nl      open connection to other site
Trying 192.31.126.72...                  TELNET seeks connection to other site
Connected to hydra.cp.tn.tudelft.nl.     connection has been made
Escape character is '^]'.                 more info by TELNET
SENT do SUPPRESS GO AHEAD                client requests to send character at a time
SENT will TERMINAL TYPE (don't reply)    client requests to negotiate terminal type
RCVD do TERMINAL TYPE (don't reply)      server acks terminal type negotiation
RCVD will SUPPRESS GO AHEAD (don't reply) server acks character transmission
RCVD will ECHO (reply)                   server requests that it handles echoing
SENT do ECHO (don't reply)               client acknowledges


SunOS UNIX (hydra)                       we are at the other site

login:                                   the login prompt at the other site
```

Figure 10.7   An example of how TELNET appears to a user on its own computer while opening a connection to another computer hydra.cp.tn.tudelft.nl.

soon as the connection has been made, negotiation starts. In our case, the client requests that all communication with the server terminal occurs on a per-character basis. Also, the client and server need to negotiate over the type of terminal that is being used. After these two steps, the client requests the server to handle echoing. This means that each time a character is sent to the server, the latter responds by sending that character back so that it will be displayed on the screen. At that point, we are ready to login at the remote site, and have connected our own terminal to the remote computer system. The fact that it is indeed remote will more or less be hidden from us. The remoteness of the other computer has thus been made *transparent* to us.

10.3.2   File handling services

A communication service for which there is clearly a need is remote access to a file. By this we mean that it is possible to access files that are normally only accessible from a remote computer system. In distributed applications based on a single operating system running on a local area network, file access is generally *transparent*. No matter where you are located within the network, you will be able to access files as if they had been stored on a storage medium directly connected to the computer you are using at that moment. In the case of wide area distributed applications, this is still an ambitious goal, although some steps in the right direction of making file access transparent have been taken. An alternative approach is to support **file transfer**. In that case, the only thing we can do is copy a file from a remote system to our own system.

A virtual file structure

Copying files is a lot easier said than done. What we wish to do is copy the contents of some remote file F_{remote} into a local file F_{local}. Unfortunately, how data is stored in files varies considerably between file systems. In turn, how files are organized into directories is also very different. Supporting file transfer can only be done if we are able to divert from these organizational details. In other words, we need some concept of a **virtual file system** which forms a common denominator of currently existing file systems.

The problem that we have to deal with is that a virtual file system should be able to support files from different real file systems. To get an insight into what we are dealing with, consider what file systems may provide on a per-file basis:

- A *file name*, which is a symbolic name to identify a file. In practice, the restrictions imposed on file names can be different with respect to length and allowable symbols.

- A set of *attributes*, containing information on a file. Typically, access permissions, the size of the file, its owner, and time and date of creation are recorded. But again, differences exist between file systems.

- A *file structure* which may vary between providing no structure at all, but merely considering a file as a series of bits, to organizing files in terms of, for example, indexed records.

In addition, many operating systems allow files to be arranged in different ways by organizing them into directories, as discussed in Section 5.6.3. Again, striking differences may exist. For example, whereas in MS-DOS files can only be organized in a strict hierarchical fashion in the form of a tree, UNIX systems allow files to be organized into a more or less arbitrary directed graph.

By now, it should be clear that defining a virtual file structure is no easy task. In practice, what happens is that directory structures are simply not taken into account, and that attention is focused merely on supporting individual files. This approach makes sense, for in the end, what we are really interested in is fetching a particular file from a file system, and copying it into a "new" file in our current system. Directory organizations become less important then. To a certain extent, this approach has also been followed within the OSI model, which includes the so-called **file transfer and management** standard (**FTAM**). The standard is intricate and reflects OSI's strive for completeness. We will not discuss FTAM here and refer the interested reader to the literature mentioned in Section 10.5. Instead, to illustrate how matters can also be kept relatively simple, we discuss a popular file transfer protocol as adopted by the Internet.

▷ **Internet's FTP**

A commonly used application in the Internet is the FTP program, an implementation of the Internet's file transfer protocol, also known as FTP. The virtual file structure that FTP sup-

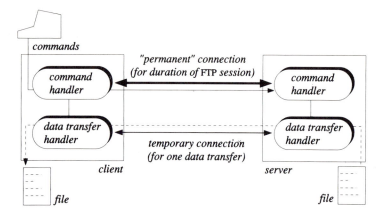

Figure 10.8 The architecture of Internet's FTP.

ports is certainly not general, but does cover a wide range of possible files. Different aspects need to be considered in the case of FTP:[3]

- The **file type** where a distinction is made roughly between (1) character files, which contain only (transmissible and printable) characters and (2) binary files, which are considered as a stream of bits.
- The **file structure**, by which a choice can be made between (1) unstructured files, which are considered as a stream of bytes, and (2) record structured files in the case of character files.
- The **transmission mode**, for which a choice can be made for *transmitting* the file as (1) a stream of bytes or (2) as a series of blocks of bytes.

In practice, most file transfers leave only the option of choosing between either character or binary files. The file structure is often assumed to be that of a stream of bytes which conforms to both MS-DOS and UNIX, which is naturally transmitted as a stream of bytes as well. Indeed, our concept of a virtual file structure can be reduced to something simple in many practical situations.

So how does FTP work? An important difference with the TELNET protocol is that FTP makes use of two separate components at each site as illustrated in Figure 10.8. Both the client and server process have a separate component that takes care of all *commands* that are exchanged. In addition, each has a component that is responsible for transferring data. When starting an FTP session, a *permanent* connection is set up between the two command handlers. Each time a file is transferred during that session, a separate connection between the data handlers is set up, and subsequently closed after file transfer has taken place. Only after the session is over will the connection between the two command handlers be closed as well.

Again, to illustrate how file transfer appears to the user, look at Figure 10.9 which shows an FTP session, again with our remote computer in Delft. As in the TELNET protocol, FTP is

---

[3]For clarity, we have omitted several options which are rarely used in practice.

`% ftp -d`	*invoke the* FTP *program*
`ftp> open hydra.cp.tn.tudelft.nl`	*request a permanent connection*
`Connected to hydra.cp.tn.tudelft.nl.`	
`220 hydra FTP server (SunOS 4.1) ready.`	
`Name (hydra.cp.tn.tudelft.nl:steen): henk`	FTP *requests for a user name and*
`---> USER henk`	*sends command* USER *to other site*
`331 Password required for henk.`	FTP *requests a password*
`Password:`	*and the user types it in (not echoed)*
`---> PASS XXXX`	*the password is sent to the other side*
`230 User henk logged in.`	*and we have got our connection*
`ftp> get Xloadimage`	*request transfer of a file*
`---> PORT 192,31,231,170,128,75`	FTP *tells where the client is reached*
`200 PORT command successful.`	
`---> RETR Xloadimage`	*and instructs server to transfer the file*
`150 ASCII data connection for Xloadimage`	*server starts the data transfer*
`     (192.31.231.170,32843) (111 bytes).`	*across new data connection*
`226 ASCII Transfer complete.`	*and indicates its completeness*
`local: Xloadimage remote:  Xloadimage`	
`113 bytes received in 0.22 seconds`	
`ftp> close`	*we close the permanent connection*
`---> QUIT`	*the* QUIT *command is sent*
`221 Goodbye.`	
`ftp> quit`	*and we can leave the* FTP *program*

Figure 10.9 An example of an FTP session with the remote host named hydra.cp.tn.tudelft.nl.

supported by means of a program FTP which, in our case, we have invoked with an additional debugging option in order to display additional information on what's really happening.

As in the case of using TELNET, we first set up a permanent connection between the client (our side) and the server (at the remote site). This happens as the first command, after which we get a reply (in the form of a 3-digit number) and some additional text. As FTP requires that we login at the remote site, we first have to pass a user name and valid password. The interesting part starts when we want to transfer the file Xloadimage from the remote computer to our own computer. After having instructed FTP to get the file, it first tries to set up a data connection between the server and the client. To that end, it requests a *port* at our local operating system, and passes this port as well as the IP address of the local system to the other side. As the transcript shows, our own IP address is 192.31.231.170, and the connection is to be made to port #32843 (note that the number of the port is passed to the server using decimal-dotted notation, i.e. as number $128.75 = 128 \times 256 + 75 = 32843$). The transfer takes place, the data connection is closed, and we are then ready to close the permanent command connection.

10.3.3   Message handling services

The next type of communication service, and probably the one that is used more often than any other service in user-oriented distributed applications, is that of handling messages. In this section we shall concentrate on one particular form, namely that of handling **electronic mail**, also known as **e-mail**.

Electronic mail

We have shown how in BASAL messages between processes could be exchanged by using the SEND and RECEIVE service calls. Such services are also generally available as communication services. But matters become more complicated then we have suggested in all our solutions so far. First, note that in almost every situation in which we used the SEND and RECEIVE operations we had identified the party with which communication takes place by making explicit use of some kind of ADDRESS variable. Now where does the value of this variable come from? You will notice that we have not said anything about that, and indeed we have a *naming* problem here. We defer a presentation to solve that problem to the next section.

A second problem that we have hardly touched upon is the distinction between several kinds of messages. Distinctions manifest themselves at different places. For example, contents and layout of messages may differ substantially. Likewise, we should also make a distinction between messages exchanged between human beings and those exchanged between applications. Yet another completely different kind of distinction can be made with respect to message handling itself. For example, some messages may require acknowledgment of receipt, or must be *encrypted* for security reasons.

These distinctions need to be taken into account when devising a message handling service. When providing solutions at the level of a general-purpose message handling facility, it is more common to speak about **electronic mail**. And as its name suggests, solutions largely mimic the way hand-delivered mail is organized. First, mail is delivered in the form of an **envelope** having a **header** and **contents**. The envelope header is the same for all sorts of mail, while the envelope contents, of course, depend on the type of message being sent. In Figure 10.10 an example of a message is shown for interpersonal e-mail exchange. The envelope contains publicly known originator and recipient addresses. These addresses are normally the addresses where the mail servers of a certain site are located. We note that in this case, most of the information shown in the envelope header has been generated for the convenience of the recipient.

The envelope contents, in turn, are again divided into two parts: the **contents header** and the **contents body**. The contents header contains additional information for the receiving party for which the mail was intended in the first place. In the case of interpersonal e-mail, the header may contain information on the person who sent it and on the main subject. When e-mail is sent directly to an application, such as the case with our library example, the header may contain items such as keywords that allow automatic further processing. Finally, the contents body contains the information to be exchanged.

It is important that both contents header and contents body can together be *encrypted*.

Figure 10.10 An example of the structure of an envelope sent via electronic mail.

This is relevant, because often we do not want other people to know the nature and contents of an information exchange. In normal hand-delivered mail systems this is usually covered by law, stating that the postal service is to keep this secret (privacy of letters).

Organization of a message handling system

Message handling systems are generally organized as follows. The core of such a distributed application is formed by a collection of **message transfer agents**, of which there is at least one per site participating in message handling. A message transfer agent is responsible for handling all incoming and outgoing messages, and as such, acts as both a client and a server.

When a message is to be sent, the transfer agent, in its role as client, sets up a connection across the transfer layer with the transfer agent located at the remote site where the message is to be delivered. After establishing this, it places the message in an envelope as described above. This scheme is shown in Figure 10.11. Likewise, whenever a message arrives across a previously established connection, the transfer agent, in its role as server, unwraps the envelope and delivers the message to the appropriate receiver. The connection between the two transfer agents is closed after mail transfer has taken place.

This scheme implies that some work has to be done in order to get a message from a sender to its local message transfer agent, and vice versa, delivering the message from the transfer agent to the actual receiver. To this end, each user has its own **user agent**. At the sender's end, a user agent is responsible for providing support to let the sender compose a message, after which it stores the message so that it can be picked up by the local transfer agent. At the receiver's end, we see a similar scheme. What the transfer agent actually does is store an incoming message into a **mailbox**, of which there is one per user. Physically, a mailbox is a special file in which messages are appended when they arrive. The receiver's user agent occasionally inspects the mailbox, and if a new message has arrived, notifies the user who can then read its contents.

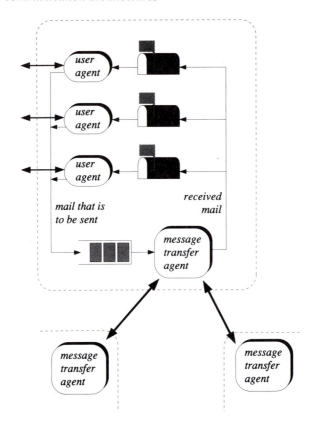

Figure 10.11 The general organization of a message handling system.

▷ **A simple mail transfer protocol**

The above description of how a mail handling system works is, of course, rather crude. In reality, mail systems can be complex. There are currently two major standards. The first is the *X*.400 standard, which comes from the OSI world. It is currently used in a large number of commercial applications. The second standard is SMTP (Simple Mail Transfer Protocol), which is heavily used in the TCP/IP world and is the *de-facto* standard on the Internet. As this latter protocol is by far the simplest of the two, we consider it here as an illustration of how electronic mail may work in practice.

Almost all message information in SMTP is simply provided as ASCII text. In addition, there are only a few commands available that message transfer agents use to exchange mail. However, in order to distinguish the actual message contents from e.g. envelope headers and message headers, SMTP uses the concept of reserved words, as in an ordinary programming language. Reserved words are followed by a text string, with a semicolon separating the two.

For example, in order to identify both the sender and receiver of a message, SMTP uses the reserved words **From** and **To**. Likewise, it also uses the reserved words **Date** and **Subject**

```
Date:  Fri, 9 Dec 94 11:32:22 MET


From:  Maarten van Steen <steen@cs.vu.nl>
To:  henk@cp.tn.tudelft.nl
Subject:  illustration
Message-Id:  <9412091132.aa01428@barkas.cs.vu.nl>
Status:  R


This is a message from Amsterdam to Delft
```

Figure 10.12 An example of the message from Figure 10.10 in SMTP format.

with obvious meaning. This is illustrated by the example message from Figure 10.10, whose contents are shown again in Figure 10.12 where keywords appear in bold.

The first text string after the reserved word **Date** gives the date and time the message was sent. Note the time reference "MET" indicating that the time is measured according to Mid European Time. The second and third text strings provide the addresses of sender and receiver of the message, respectively. Besides the **Subject** identifier, also other optional identifiers and associated text strings can be added to a message. For example, it is possible to attach a list of persons to which the message should be copied.

Now, as you might have concluded from our discussion above, there are many types of user agents. And in fact, their functionality is highly independent of whatever mail protocol that is used. The only restriction is that they pass mail to the transfer agent in such a way that it adheres to, in our case, SMTP, and likewise, can pick up messages in SMTP format as appended to the mailbox by a transfer agent. For this reason, it makes little sense to illustrate SMTP by means of a transcript showing how a user agent works.

Let's concentrate on what the message transfer agent does when it has to send mail to, for example, henk@cp.tn.tudelft.nl. Look at Figure 10.13(a) which shows part of a transcript providing information on the actions taken by a transfer agent at our site in Amsterdam. First, it expects that the receiver named henk has a mailbox at site cp.tn.tudelft.nl. Now it needs to find a connection with a computer at that site that can handle incoming mail. There are apparently two options:

- A host named orion.cp.tn.tudelft.nl with IP address 192.31.126.53
- A host named ph.tn.tudelft.nl with IP address 130.161.189.1

The transfer agent chooses to contact the transfer agent at the first computer via address 192.31.126.53, succeeds in doing so, and delivers the message. At that point, the connection is closed again and it is up to the transfer agent at the receiver's side to deliver the message.

What happens at the receiver's side is shown in Figure 10.13(b) which shows the complete message, including the envelope as received by user henk in Delft. The easiest way to trace the delivery of the message is starting from the bottom up. Apparently the message that was sent was

```
Trying cp.tn.tudelft.nl
henk@cp.tn.tudelft.nl: cp.tn.tudelft.nl matched by inet_hosts:
    routed henk@cp.tn.tudelft.nl --> henk@cp.tn.tudelft.nl at cp.tn.tudelft.nl
      transport hint mx 10 orion.cp.tn.tudelft.nl
        address hint orion.cp.tn.tudelft.nl 192.31.126.53
      transport hint mx 20 ph.tn.tudelft.nl
        address hint ph.tn.tudelft.nl 130.161.189.1
transport smtp uses driver tcpsmtp
lock retry/smtp/orion.cp.tn.tudelft.nl
lock succeeded (will defer failure) retry/smtp/orion.cp.tn.tudelft.nl
transport smtp: connect to host orion.cp.tn.tudelft.nl [192.31.126.53]/smtp
      ...connected
unlock (success) retry/smtp/orion.cp.tn.tudelft.nl
```

(a)

```
From steen@cs.vu.nl Fri Dec  9 11:32:51 1994
Return-Path: <steen@cs.vu.nl>
Received: from zephyr.cs.vu.nl by cp.tn.tudelft (5.67a/HB-1.18)
        id AA29642; Fri, 9 Dec 94 11:32:50 +0100
Received: from barkas.cs.vu.nl by zephyr.cs.vu.nl id aa21249; 9 Dec 94 11:32 MET
Date:     Fri, 9 Dec 94 11:32:22 MET
From: Maarten van Steen <steen@cs.vu.nl>
To: henk@cp.tn.tudelft.nl
Subject:  illustration
Message-Id:  <9412091132.aa01428@barkas.cs.vu.nl>
Status: R

This is a message from Amsterdam to Delft
```

(b)

Figure 10.13   The communication two message transfer agents delivering a message from steen@cs.vu.nl to henk@cp.tn.tudelft.nl.

"This is a message from Amsterdam to Delft"

having subject "*illustration*". The message came from a user named "*Maarten van Steen*" known to the sending site as steen@cs.vu.nl. The message was submitted to the transfer agent on a host named barkas.cs.vu.nl, and subsequently forwarded by that agent to the central message transfer agent at host zephyr.cs.vu.nl. Both these transfer agents are located in Amsterdam. About 30 seconds later, the latter transfer agent established a connection with the transfer agent in Delft on the host named cp.tn.tudelft.nl, but which we now know was actually on host orion.cp.tn.tudelft.nl. The message is deposited in the mailbox of henk@cp.tn.tudelft.nl about one second later.

A final note before we finish our discussion on mail handling systems. It would be rather unfortunate if SMTP and $X.400$ users could not communicate with each other. Hence, to be able to exchange mail between SMTP-based mail systems and $X.400$ mail systems, so-called **mail gateways** are used. We shall not go into any details here on how these gateways work, but you can imagine that their main task is converting messages between both systems and ensuring delivery of mail despite different systems being used.

10.3.4   Name handling services

At this point, it is time we started saying something about **naming** in distributed systems. At first, this may seem as a rather strange topic in the light of our discussion on communication services. For indeed, what does naming have to do with communication? Without going into too many details, picture the way we would use telephones without having any telephone directories. It would indeed become much more difficult to find out how we could reach other users.

In computers, normally, the operating system we are working with provides all kinds of naming services for resources. For instance, each process has a name or number which can be used to identify that process when needed. Likewise, other resources such as printers and users of the system also have identifiers. If we step outside the local operating system environment, we are suddenly confronted with a *resource identification* problem. This is caused by the simple fact that identifiers for local resources are never made available to the outside world. Therefore, in order to be able to communicate among different systems, we need a *global* naming convention for resources. Let's look in more detail at the problems encountered.

Global process identification

On our local system we would use a local process name (or number) to communicate with that process. If that process is running on another machine, a first thought could be to add a machine identifier to the process name. This machine identifier is then used to locate where the process is actually running.

Let's illustrate this by means of an example. Suppose that we wish to construct a file system similar to the one discussed in Chapter 5, where a single **file server** is responsible for carrying out file operations on behalf of a client process. We assume that the file server itself can be identified as a process called FILE_SERVER, whereas the machine (or site as we shall call it) where it is located is called SERVER_SITE. A complete identification that would allow us to *address* the file server could then take the following form:[4]

```
FILE_SERVER_ADDRESS :
   record
      site : INTEGER := SERVER_SITE;
      server : INTEGER := FILE_SERVER;
   end record ;
```

and a client would generally communicate with the file server as follows:

```
DFS.SEND(FILE_SERVER_ADDRESS, requested file operation);
DFS.RECEIVE(FILE_SERVER_ADDRESS, reply from file server);
```

where DFS stands for a message-based communication package supporting a Distributed File System, derived from the general package for message passing outlined in Listing 6.6 on page 282:

---

[4]Note that such a declaration is not permitted in BASAL or Ada.

package DFS **is new** MESSAGE_PASSING(MESSAGE ⇒ *some message type*);

In general, this looks like a sensible solution to the global identification problem. However, we have made a "hard" connection between the system sending the message and the system receiving it. To illustrate, suppose that the system on which we have implemented our distributed file system changes, thereby making it necessary to place the file server on a different machine, and thus having to change the part of its address identifying the actual site. In that case, we would be forced to change all our client programs, because they would now each refer to the wrong address for the file server.

If we had anticipated such changes, we could have followed a more defensive way of programming the clients. One solution would be to have the client programs first find out where the file server is located by checking all possible sites. This solution can be outlined as follows:

```
found := FALSE;
site := some initial machine, or site;
while not found loop
   DFS.SEND(site, request to see if FILE_SERVER is there);
   DFS.RECEIVE(site, answer from site);
   if file server is on the questioned site then
      FILE_SERVER_ADDRESS.site := site;
      FILE_SERVER_ADDRESS.server := FILE_SERVER;
      found := TRUE;
   else
      site := next site to check;
   end if ;
end loop ;
DFS.SEND(FILE_SERVER_ADDRESS, requested file operation);
DFS.RECEIVE(FILE_SERVER_ADDRESS, reply from file server);
```

Of course, finding the location of the file server need not be done separately for every file operation request, but only from time to time, based on how often we expect the file server's address to change. Note that the above solution employs a form of broadcasting called **multicasting.** Now if the number of sites that is broadcast to is limited, this would provide an elegant solution. The file server can be freely migrated to any machine and the clients will still be capable of contacting it.

However, distributed systems might not be so restricted as in our example. For example, if we are to address all companies in the country for an inquiry, it is immediately apparent that broadcasting is not always a viable solution. An alternative solution is the use of a separate **name server**. This is a server containing a name-to-address resolution mechanism. It means that a client first asks the name server where a certain service can be found in the network. The name server replies by sending back the appropriate **location** of that service. All that is now required is that the name server (hardly) ever changes its address. To illustrate, suppose that the name server is located at a fixed address NAME_SERVER_ADDRESS. In that case, client programs could issue a file operation request as follows:

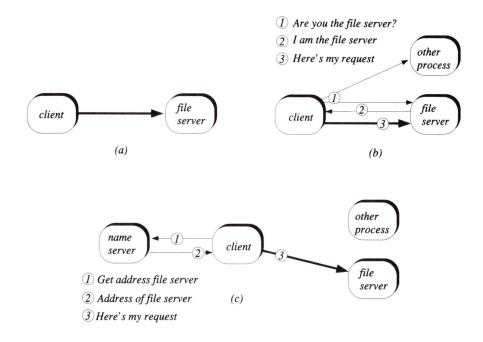

Figure 10.14   Three ways of identifying processes: (a) using direct naming, (b) broadcasting a request for identification, and (c) using a name server.

```
DFS.SEND(NAME_SERVER_ADDRESS, FILE_SERVER);
DFS.RECEIVE(NAME_SERVER_ADDRESS, FILE_SERVER_ADDRESS);
DFS.SEND(FILE_SERVER_ADDRESS, requested file operation);
DFS.RECEIVE(FILE_SERVER_ADDRESS, reply from file server);
```

When servers are migrated, only the information in the table as maintained by the name server has to be updated. We will return to this issue when we discuss more accurately the distinction between names and addresses. These three forms of identifying processes are illustrated in Figure 10.14.

Global naming systems

In an open system we also need a common way of locating resources. Most naming schemes for locating resources are based on a tree-like hierarchy, where, upon descending the tree, the set of possible destinations decreases rapidly. Such a scheme is often adopted when assigning global names to resources. The problem that is encountered, however, is that we have to decide on the actual subdivision of the naming tree.

To illustrate, assume that for our electronic communication services we follow the traditional ordering as used in the postal system. In that case, in order to locate a service it seems reasonable first to locate the country, followed by identifying the kind of organization, and then the actual organization which provides the service. This can be further subdivided by also considering perhaps the department, and perhaps even a group. This approach leads to the following **pathname**:

$$country \rightarrow org. \, domain \rightarrow organization \rightarrow department \rightarrow \ldots etc.$$

But there are some problems with this scheme, especially when describing resources within a wide area distributed application. To illustrate, suppose we had a worldwide operating company called trader with its main office in The Netherlands. It would then seem reasonable to assign its sales department a pathname such as nl.com.trader.sales. But in that case, we are ignoring the fact that this company operates worldwide. And in electronic services, the fact that the main office is located in The Netherlands is hardly interesting, except when it is necessary to reach exactly the sales department of the main office. And indeed, advocates of viewing the world as a global village with worldwide organizations would like to have a different structure: first comes the organization, then the country, organizational unit, etc. A typical pathname structure would then be

$$org. \, domain \rightarrow organization \rightarrow country \rightarrow department \rightarrow \ldots etc.$$

so that the actual pathname for our example sales department becomes com.trader.nl.sales.

Another problem is the **naming authority**. In order to avoid confusion, an authority should be established which issues names. In the postal system these authorities are organized nationwide. They establish things like ZIP codes, etc. The consequence, however, is a non-uniform naming structure between countries. In the modern age of electronics, this is clearly not what we want. Here a uniform structure of names is needed for electronic handling of messages. The syntax of a name is established by a worldwide authority. Such an authority is, for instance, the ISO. Also the top-level names are determined by such an authority. However, it would not be very efficient if more local names are also to be established by a central authority. The usual approach therefore is to follow the naming hierarchy in supplying names. So within a country, a local authority issues the organization names, the organization hands out the organizational unit names, etc. In this way, a flexible and decentralized naming authority is established, while keeping a worldwide uniform naming syntax.

▷ **Two examples**

There are two main naming schemes currently in use: one is based on the international $X.500$ standard and one for the Internet. The Internet uses the so-called **Domain Name System** (**DNS**) which we shall briefly discuss here. OSI's $X.500$ is discussed hereafter.

The Domain Naming System. Internet's DNS employs a hierarchical naming scheme. The top-level domains are fixed and include domains for commercial organizations (the so-called com domain), educational organizations (the edu domain), and country domains (us domain, nl domain, etc.). Hence it mixes the above-mentioned different ways of organizing the tree hierarchy.

Each domain has a domain authority, which issues the names in the next level of subdomains. Names are specified by separating domains and subdomains by points. An example of such a name is cs.vu.nl, which denotes the Department of Computer Science (cs) of the Vrije Universiteit (vu) in the Netherlands (nl). The naming structure also indicates where naming authorities are located. For example, the system administrators at the computer science department of the Vrije Universiteit have the responsibility of naming the department's machines. One such machine is named barkas, which we have encountered several times. Indeed, its full name is barkas.cs.vu.nl. Similarly, the system administrators in the Computational Physics group (cp) in the Department of Applied Physics[5] (tn) at the Technical University in Delft (tudelft) have called one of their machines hydra, which we have used by its full name hydra.cp.tn.tudelft.nl in our examples as well.

OSI's X.500 directory service. The X.500 naming system is slightly different. It is *object-based*, meaning that all names at a node in the tree belong to the same *class*. Each object class has a set of *attributes*, each attribute having a *type* and one or more *values*. The type of the attribute defines the type of the object, and the value its name. The idea behind this is rather practical. Let's give some examples to clarify matters.

Suppose we wish to denote our machine barkas located at the computer science department of the Vrije Universiteit in The Netherlands. What we have to realize is that we are dealing with several different kinds of objects: we have a *country* (The Netherlands), there is apparently a specific *group of organizations* (the universities), as well as *organizational units* within that group (the computer science department at the Vrije Universiteit), and *host computers* (the one denoted as barkas). This leads to a number of classes with the following possible attributes, types, and values:[6]

country	attribute	type	value
country	code (C)	2-char. string	nl
org. group	org. (O)	4-char. string	univ
org. unit	unit (OU)	arbitrary char. string	vu
	dept (DEPT)	arbitrary char. string	cs
host comp.	host (HOST)	arbitrary char. string	barkas

Using the convention to separate classes by a slash, and attributes by a comma, the full name for our host computer would then become /C = nl /O = univ /OU = vu, DEPT = cs /HOST = barkas.

From names to addresses

So far, we have been concerned only with naming conventions. But, of course, names make little sense if they are not associated with addresses. An address identifies the *location* where a resource can be found. The distinction between a name and an address

---

[5]Applied physics is a translation of the Dutch "Technische Natuurkunde".

[6]It should be noted that we have simplified matter for the sake of illustration.

is important. A name is something that can always be assigned to a resource, no matter where it is located (well, at least to a certain extent). An address is used by the network protocols to set up a complete path between a source and destination so that a connection between the two can be made.

▷ To give an example, in our discussion on the use of the TELNET facility we showed how we opened a connection to the host named hydra.cp.tn.tudelft.nl. A fragment from that session, shown in Figure 10.7 was:

```
telnet> open hydra.cp.tn.tudelft.nl   open connection to other site
Trying 192.31.126.72...               TELNET seeks connection to other site
```

What we see here is that our host can be found at IP address 192.31.126.72. And this is precisely the information we need to set up a connection. In other words, the Internet routers are not at all concerned about how resources are named. The only thing they can do is transfer packets from one location to another. Apparently, what happened was that our host *name* had been resolved to a host *address*.

Names are used by human beings only because it is convenient. Names are easy to remember as they generally reflect the way we think about how our system is organized. Computer networks, however, cannot use names. What they need in the end are addresses, as this is the only way by which they route packets from one location to another. Consequently, what we need is a mechanism for **resolving** names to addresses. And it is here where **name servers** fall into place.

A name server is a process that (1) maintains a table which associates names with addresses, and (2) can be queried by other processes to find the address of a named resource. There is only one problem. As we are dealing with a *global* naming scheme, it would seem that we would have to maintain a single name server which contains the complete mapping between all names and addresses. Clearly, this is impossible. The generally adopted solution is to construct a hierarchy of name servers. For example, accessing the host named hydra.cp.tn.tudelft.nl requires that we contact the name server at site cp.tn.tudelft.nl. If we do not know the address of that server, we could also try to see if there is a name server named tn.tudelft.nl, etc. For the sake of illustration, assume that such a name server exists and that we know its address. The best we can expect is that this name server knows only the locations for the name servers having names *ending* with tn.tudelft.nl, such as cp.tn.tudelft.nl. Using the returned location enables us to contact the name server we wanted (cp.tn.tudelft.nl), which, in turn, can return the address of the host computer hydra.cp.tn.tudelft.nl.

10.4   The World Wide Web

At this point you should have a fairly good idea of the way that wide area distributed applications can be built using the facilities provided by our communication layer. At this point, it is worth considering a popular application which employs many of the services we have discussed in this and the preceding chapters. In this section we shall pay some attention to the so-called **World Wide Web**, also known as **The Web**, **WWW** or **W3**.

10.4.1 The Web's basic functionality

The Web is becoming an extremely popular information system that, as its name suggests, is distributed across the entire world. Its main functionality is that of providing documents to users through a technique called **hypertext**. Let's first explain what a hypertext document is.

Most documents, like this book, are structured in such a way that you start reading at the beginning and continue until the end, perhaps occasionally skipping a few pages, paragraphs, or perhaps an entire chapter. In other words, most documents are structured in a strict *linear* fashion. It is precisely with respect to this strict linear ordering that hypertext documents distinguish themselves from ordinary documents.

A hypertext document is a collection of relatively small documents which have been made electronically available. Each document contains a number of **keywords**. For example, a chapter heading in a table of contents is an excellent candidate for being a keyword. Other examples of typical keywords are citations, references within the document to tables or figures, or to other chapters. The point is that each keyword is uniquely linked to another document through what is known as a **hyperlink**. By *selecting* a keyword the underlying hypertext system automatically fetches the document to which the keyword is linked, and displays it to the user.

Anticipating our further discussion, let's look at a simple example. Figure 10.15(a) shows an electronically available one-page document providing some information on one of the authors. That document contains six keywords, designated by means of underlining. If we select the keyword "Address info" our hypertext system automatically fetches another one-page document containing information on how the author can be reached, shown in Figure 10.15(b). Again, this document contains a number of keywords. By selecting the keyword "User's Home Page" the hypertext system will retrieve the page of Figure 10.15(a).

The World Wide Web is full of these documents. In fact, the reason it is called a web is that large collections of documents, spread all over the world, are directly, but of course most often indirectly, linked together in the way we have just illustrated. Moreover, it is sometimes hard to work out the precise structure of how these documents are linked together. Fortunately, there is also no reason to know about this structure.

10.4.2 The underlying technology

Now, let's see what's actually under the hood. In the following, we concentrate on two issues: what hyperlinks in the Web look like, and what happens when a link is activated.

Uniform Resource Locators

A key component in the Web is formed by its hyperlinks. By activating a hyperlink a document is retrieved and displayed on the screen. The term document is to be taken here in its broadest sense, including menus, images, but also the kind of pages we have shown above. In terms of the Web, anything that can be displayed on the screen is referred to

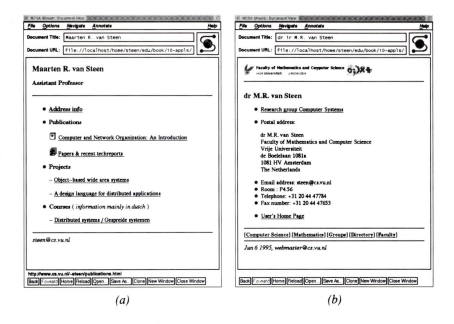

(a)   *(b)*

Figure 10.15 An example of part of a hypertext document.

as a **resource**, and a hyperlink is to contain information on *how* that resource can be retrieved, and *where* it can be retrieved. Indeed, hyperlinks contain all the information on the *type of communication service* that is required for retrieval of a resource. As such, the Web itself can be viewed as an application that is built "on top" of the communication layer introduced in this chapter.

In order to select precisely how and where a resource is to be retrieved, the Web makes use of so-called **uniform resource locators**, also known as URLs. A URL takes the following form:

communication service: // *host name* / *path name* / *resource name*

Each URL is divided into three parts: the first part identifies the required communication service by specifying its protocol. For example, the two most often used services are FTP and HTTP. The latter stands for HyperText Transfer Protocol, which, as its name suggests, is a protocol much like FTP but which has been tailored to transfer hypertext documents across the network. Hypertext documents in this case, are assumed to have been written making use of the HyperText Markup Language (HTML). In principle, almost any communication service can be specified, although most require some adaptation in order to fit into the framework of the Web. The second part of a URL specification deals with naming the host at which the required resource resides. Being based on the Internet, host names are given in the usual way, for example as barkas.cs.vu.nl. The third and last part consists of a pathname within the file system at the indicated host, plus the actual file name where the resource is assumed to be stored. Two examples of complete URL specifications are:

- ftp://ftp.cs.vu.nl/pub/steen/cno/answers.ps.gz

- http://www.cs.vu.nl/˜steen/cno.html

The first URL specifies a hyperlink to a resource (file) named answers.ps.gz, which can be found via FTP on the host ftp.cs.vu.nl, in the directory pub/steen/cno. If you access this file via the Web, you will get a document containing the answers to˙the book's exercises. The second URL specifies a hyperlink via HTTP to a one-page hypertext document containing general information on this book. The document itself is named cno.html; it is stored in the directory ˜steen/, and is accessible via host www.cs.vu.nl.

Organization of the Web

You will by now presumably have a fairly good idea how the Web is organized. It is easiest to think about its organization in terms of clients requesting resources from servers. A client program is executed at each host that wants to retrieve a hypertext document. Using a URL specification for links, the client will then seek contact with a server at the indicated host through the selected communication protocol. For example, activating the hyperlink with URL

ftp://ftp.cs.vu.nl/pub/steen/cno/answers.ps.gz

means that the Web client sets up an FTP session with the host ftp.cs.vu.nl; transfers the indicated file, then closes the session again. The server side in this case consists of only an FTP server. And that's about all there is to it.

The Web client plays a similar role as that of the message transfer agent in the case of message handling services: it acts as a central point where all communication on behalf of a single user goes through. In addition, in order to access the Web, you will also need an information browser which acts as an interface between the Web client and the user. Such a browser is comparable to the user agent in message handling systems.

10.5   Discussion and further reading

In this last chapter we have made the step from a local and relatively closed environment of computer systems using a single language and operating system to heterogeneous systems communicating with each other through networks, possibly on a worldwide scale. We have introduced the concept of open systems to make this possible. By simplifying the seven-layer OSI model to a four-layer model, a natural division between application-independent and application-oriented communication layers could be derived.

10.5.1   On distributed applications

In order to say anything sensible about communication architectures as used by applications, we started with giving a characterization of distributed applications. We identified four requirements that are to be met in order to call an application distributed: (1) processes should provide services to each other, which in turn are (2) accessible and which are used. In order to make use of services, (3) a communication protocol should have been agreed upon. Finally, (4) service providers should account for the fact that each request for service will eventually be honored, in order to prevent processes being inadvertently prohibited in taking part in the system.

This description of distributed applications takes hardly any hardware into account. In particular, our view of distributed applications can be seen entirely independent of whether the application is implemented on top of a computer network. In practice, of course, distributed applications will refer to *geographical* distribution of data and computations. And in that case, it makes sense only when we take a computer network into account. However, such a network is to be seen as an *implementation aspect*, and ideally, it should be hidden entirely from a user. In other words, to a user it should be completely transparent whether the system he or she is working on is built on top of a computer network or is just a single computer.

There are very few general textbooks on distributed systems and applications, and those cover the subject in the context of distributed operating systems. A good starting point is Tanenbaum's (1995) treatment of the subject. An excellent treatise of all the relevant issues is provided by Coulouris *et al.* (1994). Although discussing the material at a more conceptual level, Goscinski (1991) and Silberschatz and Galvin (1994) may also be of interest. Brief overviews of what can be expected from a distributed application are given in Schroeder (1993) and Stankovic (1994). The first steps that were undertaken in order to make the transition from operating systems to distributed applications, generally focused on file systems. Overviews on distributed file systems can be found in Levy and Silberschatz (1990) and Satyanarayanan (1993). Scaling file systems for very large distributed systems is discussed in Neuman (1994).

10.5.2   The communication layer

Communication services

Up to the OSI transport layer, network functions are application-independent and merely provide reliable connections between two end points in a network. In other words, the best you can get from transfer functions is a point-to-point connection that allows you reliably to send messages from one end to the other (we are not taking multicasting into account here). This is indeed the functionality as provided by the four lower layers of the OSI reference model. We have simplified this model by introducing only two layers: one dealing with physical connections, and one (admittedly large) layer dealing with producing reliable connections. Which approach is taken is really not that important; what counts is that you should realize that there are numerous ways of implementing transfer functionalities. And, as we have seen in the preceding chapters, numerous implementations indeed co-exist.

It makes sense to distinguish a separate layer on top of the transfer layer which we have denoted as the communication layer. This layer roughly covers OSI's three higher layers (i.e. the session, presentation, and application layers) by providing several communication services that cannot be classified as universal (which they are indeed not), but also not as application-specific. The services we have distinguished are, in fact, nothing more than services which are normally provided by a local operating system. From a certain perspective, we have made an attempt to raise the concept of an operating system to that of a system that spans the world. That we have only partially succeeded in doing this is already illustrated by the level of transparency offered by the communication services. For example, FTP has little to do with file management. It allows you only to transfer files from one site to another, an operation which is normally done through a copy operator that hides any details of actual locations.

Additional communication services

We have deliberately omitted the presentation of three important services that are generally provided at the level of the communication layer:

- Remote operations
- Time handling services
- Security.

Let's look briefly at each of these topics.

Remote operations.   This service has, to a certain extent, already been discussed in Section 6.4.2 where we described the principal working of the remote procedure calling (RPC) mechanism. As a communication service, RPC is a convenient way to build a distributed application in terms of clients and servers. Indeed, its implementation is directly dependent on the services provided by the transfer layer. As we have already explained the principle underlying the RPC mechanism, and because its actual implementation details go beyond the scope of this book, we have not treated the subject any further in this chapter. For more information, the interested reader should consult the literature mentioned at the end of Chapter 6.

Time handling services.   As it name suggests, a time handling service must give us the ability to determine the right time. Why do we need this? Well, as with many things, it is sometimes important to know exactly *when* something happened. For example, when communicating via electronic mail, it may be important for a receiver to know when an incoming message was actually sent. And if the original sender is someone on the other side of the world, an indication of the local time is not always going to be helpful. In that case, it may be possible to receive a message at 11:00 a.m. that was sent at 5:00 p.m. that same day.

A worldwide distributed system should take these differences into account. Unfortunately, solutions are not always found that easily, especially if it is necessary to let all components in the system have the same idea of what the time actually is. The problems stem from the fact that we cannot build a global view of time by using merely local information. In particular, any mechanism that makes use only of local clocks will sooner or later be inadequate, as these local clocks will start running out of sync in due course. Global synchronization is what is needed here, and how this can be obtained in a distributed manner lies outside the scope of this book. A good starting point for a further treatise on these matters is Tanenbaum (1995). Also, you will find Lamport's (1978) seminal paper definitely worth reading if you are interested in what is referred to as logical time. Keeping time on the Internet is described in Mills (1992). Without doubt this is an informative document on how global time in a wide area distributed system can be handled.

Security.   An extremely important topic that we have not discussed in this book is that of security. What do we mean by this? Security has everything to do with protecting your documents against malicious persons. It covers topics such as encrypting documents so that outsiders cannot make any sense of their contents, authentication of communicating parties ("are you really who you say you are?"), and things such as digital signatures. The subject is very large and can fill an entire book. We have made the decision to not say anything about security, mainly because its technicalities are of a different nature from any subject we have treated so far.

There is a wealth of books on security. The material is treated in a balanced and structured manner in Davies and Price (1989) and Kaufman *et al.* (1995). Also, Stallings (1995) may be of interest. On authentication, Lampson *et al.* (1992) will show to be good reading material.

The ideal of a common working environment across computer platforms and networks is far from being realized. Nevertheless, some environments are presently in development which appear to be quite promising. One is DCE (Distributed Computing Environment), which defines a number of communication services, similar to the ones outlined in this chapter, on which distributed applications can be built. More on DCE can be found in Rosenberry *et al.* (1992).

10.5.3   Wide area distributed applications

Having wide area computer networks is one thing; but having applications that actually exploit this technology in a manner that makes sense to users is a completely different story. Obviously, there is one domain in which these networks are useful: simple communication between people. But what does the term "simple" actually mean here? It is not hard to imagine the kind of systems that lie ahead of us. Apart from the use of electronic mail which has seen very large growth in the last decade, it can be expected that promises are going to be met on issues such as teleconferencing. In particular, it can be anticipated that within the next decade video-conferencing which requires the development of all kinds of *multimedia* techniques, will come into widespread use. Integrating voice, data, and graphics still has a long way to go, but with the advent of high-speed gigabit networks, applications requiring such an integration will indeed come into practical use.

Another area where much research is currently being conducted is that of wide area *information services*. We have briefly touched upon this subject by illustrating the already very popular World Wide Web. But the Web is just a means to access information. The real problem in this area lies in *finding* the information you want. This problem domain is generally referred to as **resource discovery**. If you want to know more about that subject, Bowman *et al.* (1994) is a good starting point. More on particular information browsers can be found in Obraczka *et al.* (1993), whereas Berners-Lee *et al.* (1994) and Vetter *et al.* (1994) provide good general introductions to the Web.

Exercises

1. Explain how a connection may be broken, as mentioned in our discussion of the session layer.

2. Why do programming languages not require the same representation for integers and reals?

3. Suppose we have two processes exchanging floating point numbers in an internationally agreed format. Do we have to worry about specifying a concrete syntax?

4. *Devise an extension to BASAL that allows for the specification of representing *values* of integers to either one's or two's complement notation.

5. Some public FTP sites contain large amounts of files that can be freely retrieved for personal use. In order to find the files you need, these sites often have an *automatic inquiry service* that accepts inquiries sent as electronic mail. When sending a message, you will automatically receive an answer, also by electronic mail, without any human intervention. Explain the principal working of such inquiry services.

6. The FTP file transfer protocol requires both a "permanent" and a temporary connection (see Figure 10.8). Does this imply that we need a (virtual) circuit type of connection between both systems to realize the above logical connections?

7. Virtual terminal protocols are shown to be relatively straightforward for ASCI-based scroll terminals. How would a modern window-based virtual terminal protocol be realized?

8. What would be the effect of requesting a virtual terminal on the same terminal you are presently logged into? And what about requesting a file transfer from your present machine?

9. Explain what happens when you send a copy of an electronic message to yourself.

10. Mistakes when identifying the destination of an electronic message can easily be made. Explain what happens when (1) the destination is an unknown user at the other site, and (2) the destination site is not known to the mailing system. In both cases, explain exactly where message delivery fails.

11. *Suppose an organization wants its network to be part of the Internet. To that end, they request a name that can be subsequently used to contact them. How can your computer succeed in locating that organization's network, without having previously heard of them?

12. Explain the difference between a name and a (network) address, and why maintaining such a distinction makes sense. To what extent are the names used for identifying machines, such as barkas.cs.vu.nl *location independent*?

13. The Uniform Resource Locators (URLs) are not pure resource identifiers. Why not?

References

Abeysundara, B. and Kamal, A. "High-Speed Local Area Networks and Their Performance: A Survey." *ACM Computing Surveys*, 23(2):221–264, June 1991.

Aho, A. and Sethi, R. "How Hard is Compiler Code Generation?" In Goos, G. and Hartmanis, J. (eds.), *Compiler Construction: An Advanced Course*, volume 52 of *Lecture Notes in Computer Science*, pp. 1–15. Springer-Verlag, Berlin, 1977.

Aho, A., Sethi, R., and Ullman, J. *Compilers: Principles, Techniques and Tools*. Addison-Wesley, Reading, Mass., 1986.

Andrews, G. *Concurrent Programming: Principles and Practice*. Benjamin/Cummings, Menlo Park, Calif., 1991a.

Andrews, G. "Paradigms for Process Interaction in Distributed Programs." *ACM Computing Surveys*, 23(1):49–90, March 1991b.

Andrews, G. and Schneider, F. "Concepts and Notations for Concurrent Programming." *ACM Computing Surveys*, 15(1):3–43, March 1983.

Andrews, M. *Principles of Firmware Engineering in Microprogram Control*. Pitman, London, 1980.

ANSI. *The Programming Language Ada Reference Manual*, volume 155 of *Lecture Notes in Computer Science*. Springer-Verlag, Berlin, 1983.

Bach, M. *The Design of the UNIX Operating System*. Prentice-Hall, Englewood Cliffs, N.J., 1986.

Bacon, J. *The Motorola MC68000: An Introduction to Processor, Memory, and Interfacing*. Prentice-Hall, Englewood Cliffs, N.J., 1986.

Bacon, J. *Concurrent Systems, An Integrated Approach to Operating Systems, Database, and Distributed Systems*. Addison-Wesley, Reading, Mass., 1993.

Bal, H. and Grune, D. *Programming Language Essentials*. Addison-Wesley, Reading, Mass., 1994.

Bal, H., Steiner, J., and Tanenbaum, A. "Programming Languages for Distributed Computing Systems." *ACM Computing Surveys*, 21(3):261–322, September 1989.

Ballardie, A., Francis, P., and Cowcroft, J. "Core Based Trees: An Architecture for Scalable Inter-Domain Multicast Routing." In *Proceedings ACM SIGCOMM '93*, pp. 85–95, San Francisco, September 1993.

Ballardie, A. *A New Approach to Multicast Communication in a Datagram Internetwork*. Ph.D. thesis, Department of Computer Science, University College London, May 1995.

Barnes, J. "An Overview of Ada." *Software – Practice and Experience*, 10(11):851–887, November 1980.

Barnes, J. *Programming in Ada, Plus an Overview of Ada 9X*. Addison-Wesley, Reading, Mass., 4th edition, 1994.

Barron, D. *Pascal – The Language and its Implementation*. John Wiley, New York, 1981.

Bell, P. and Jabour, K. "Review of Point-to-Point Routing Algorithms." *IEEE Communications Magazine*, 24(1):34–38, January 1986.

Ben-Ari, M. *Principles of Concurrent and Distributed Programming*. Prentice-Hall, Englewood Cliffs, N.J., 1980.

Ben-Ari, M. *Principles of Concurrent Programming*. Prentice-Hall, Englewood Cliffs, N.J., 1982.

Berners-Lee, T., Cailliau, R., Nielson, H. F., and Secret, A. "The World-Wide Web." *Communications of the ACM*, 37(8):76–82, August 1994.

Bertsekas, D. and Gallagher, R. *Data Networks*. Prentice-Hall, Englewood Cliffs, N.J., 2nd edition, 1992.

Beyda, W. *Basic Data Communications, A Comprehensive Overview*. Prentice-Hall, Englewood Cliffs, N.J., 1989.

Birkhoff, G. and Bartee, T. *Modern Applied Algebra*. McGraw-Hill, New York, 1970.

Birman, K. "The Process Group Approach to Reliable Distributed Computing." *Communications of the ACM*, 36(12):36–53, December 1993.

Birman, K. and van Renesse, R. (eds.). *Reliable Distributed Computing with the Isis Toolkit*. IEEE Computer Society Press, Los Alamitos, Calif., 1994.

Birrell, A. and Nelson, B. "Implementing Remote Procedure Calls." *ACM Transactions on Computer Systems*, 2(1):39–59, February 1984.

Blaauw, G. and Brooks, F. "The Structure of the System/360, part I – Outline of the Logical Structure." *IBM Systems Journal*, 3(2), 1964.

Bloomer, J. *Power Programming with RPC*. O'Reilly & Associates, Sebastopol, Calif., 1992.

Booch, G. and Bryan, D. *Software Engineering with Ada*. Addison-Wesley, Reading, Mass., 3rd edition, 1994.

Bowman, M., Danzig, P., Manber, U., and Schwartz, M. "Scalable Internet Resource Discovery: Research Problems and Approaches." *Communications of the ACM*, 37(8):98–107, August 1994.

Brinch Hansen, P. "The Nucleus of a Multiprogramming System." *Communications of the ACM*, 13(4):238–241, April 1970.

Brinch Hansen, P. "The SOLO Operating System: A Concurrent Pascal Program." *Software – Practice and Experience*, 6(2):141–149, February 1976.

Brinch Hansen, P. *The Architecture of Concurrent Programs.* Prentice-Hall, Englewood Cliffs, N.J., 1977.

Chang, J. and Maxemchunk, N. "Reliable Broadcast Protocols." *ACM Transactions on Computer Systems*, 2(3):251–273, August 1984.

Chen, P., Lee, E., Gibson, G., Katz, R., and Patterson, D. "RAID: High-Performance, Reliable Secondary Storage." *ACM Computing Surveys*, 26(2):145–186, June 1994.

Christian, K. *A Guide to Modula-2.* Springer-Verlag, Berlin, 1986.

Clark, G. and Cain, J. *Error-Correction Coding for Digital Communications.* Plenum Press, New York, 1981.

Clements, A. *68000 Family Assembly Language.* PWS Publishing Company, Boston, Mass., 1994.

Comer, D. *Operating Systems Design: The XINU Approach.* Prentice-Hall, Englewood Cliffs, N.J., 1984.

Comer, D. *Operating Systems Design: Internetworking with XINU.* Prentice-Hall, Englewood Cliffs, N.J., 1987.

Comer, D. *Internetworking with TCP/IP, Volume I: Principles, Protocols, and Architecture.* Prentice Hall, Englewood Cliffs, N.J., 3rd edition, 1995.

Comer, D. *The Internet Book.* Prentice-Hall, Englewood Cliffs, N.J., 1995.

Comer, D. and Stevens, D. *Internetworking with TCP/IP, Volume II: Design, Implementation and Internals.* Prentice Hall, Englewood Cliffs, N.J., 2nd edition, 1994.

Cooling, J. *Software Design for Real-time Systems.* Chapman & Hall, London, 1991.

Coulouris, G., Dollimore, J., and Kindberg, T. *Distributed Systems, Concepts and Design.* Addison-Wesley, Wokingham, 2nd edition, 1994.

Crockner, D. "Evolving the System." In Lynch, D. and Rose, M. (eds.), *Internet System Handbook*, pp. 41–76. Addison-Wesley, Reading, Mass., 1993.

Davies, D. and Price, W. *Security for Computer Networks.* John Wiley, Chichester, 2nd edition, 1989.

Deering, S. and Cheriton, D. "Multicast Routing in Datagram Internetworks and Extended LANs." *ACM Transactions on Computer Systems*, 8(2):85–110, May 1990.

Deering, S., Estrin, D., Farinacci, D., Jacobson, V., Liu, C.-G., and Wei, L. "An Architecture for Wide-Area Multicast Routing." In *Proceedings SIGCOMM '94*, pp. 126–135, London, August 1994. ACM.

Digital Equipment Corporation, Maynard, Mass. *PDP-11 Processor Handbook*, 1975.

Dijkstra, E. "A Note on Two Problems in Connection with Graphs." *Numerical Mathematics*, 1:269–271, October 1959.

Dijkstra, E. "Cooperating Sequential Processes." In F. Genuys (ed.), *Programming Languages*. Academic Press, London, 1968.

Doeringer, W., Dykeman, D., Kaiserswerth, M., Meister, B., Rudin, H., and Williamson, R. "A Survey of Light-Weight Transport Protocols for High-Speed Networks." *IEEE Transactions on Communications*, 38(11):2025–2039, November 1990.

Fischer, C. and LeBlanc, R. *Crafting a Compiler with C*. Addison-Wesley, Reading, Mass., 1991.

Foster, I. *Designing and Building Parallel Programs*. Addison-Wesley, Reading, Mass., 1995.

Frank, A., Wittie, L., and Bernstein, A. "Multicast Communication on Network Computers." *IEEE Software*, 2(3):49–61, May 1985.

Garcia-Molina, H. and Salem, K. "Main Memory Database Systems: An Overview." *IEEE Transactions on Knowledge and Data Engineering*, 4(6):509–516, December 1992.

Garfinkel, S., Weise, D., and Strassmann, S. *The UNIX-Haters Handbook*. IDG Books, San Mateo, Calif., 1994.

Garrod, S. and Borns, R. *Digital Logic: Analysis, Application & Design*. Saunders College Publishing, Philadelphia, 1991.

Ghezzi, C. and Jazayeri, M. *Programming Language Concepts*. John Wiley, New York, 2nd edition, 1987.

Gifford, D., Needham, R., and Schroeder, M. "The Cedar File System." *Communications of the ACM*, 31(3):288–298, March 1988.

Givone, D. *Introduction to Switching Circuit Theory*. McGraw-Hill, New York, 1970.

Goldberg, D. "What Every Computer Scientist Should Know About Floating-Point Arithmetic." *ACM Computing Surveys*, 23(1):5–48, March 1991.

Goodheart, B. and Cox, J. *The Magic Garden Explained: The Internals of UNIX SVR4, An Open Systems Design*. Prentice-Hall, Englewood Cliffs, N.J., 1994.

Goscinski, A. *Distributed Operating Systems, The Logical Design*. Addison-Wesley, Sydney, 1991.

Goupille, P.-A. *Introduction to Computer Hardware and Data Communications*. Prentice-Hall, Englewood Cliffs, N.J., 1993.

Graham, R. *Principles of Systems Programming*. John Wiley, New York, 1975.

Grosshans, D. *File Systems: Design and Implementation*. Prentice-Hall, Englewood Cliffs, N.J., 1986.

Hadzilacos, V. and Toueg, S. "Fault-Tolerant Broadcasts and Related Problems." In Mullender, S. (ed.), *Distributed Systems*, pp. 97–145. Addison-Wesley, Wokingham, 2nd edition, 1993.

Halsall, F. *Data Communications, Computer Networks, and Open Systems*. Addison-Wesley, Reading, Mass., 3rd edition, 1992.

Händel, R., Huber, M., and Schröder, S. *ATM Networks*. Addison-Wesley, Wokingham, 2nd edition, 1994.

Harbison, S. *Modula-3*. Prentice Hall, Englewood Cliffs, N.J., 1992.

Hedrick, C. "Routing Information Protocol." RFC 1058, June 1988.

Hennessy, J. and Patterson, D. *Computer Architecture: A Quantative Approach*. Morgan Kaufmann, San Mateo, Calif., 1990.

Hoare, C. "Monitors: An Operating System Structuring Concept." *Communications of the ACM*, 17(10):549–557, October 1974.

Holub, A. *Compiler Design in C*. Prentice-Hall, Englewood Cliffs, N.J., 1990.

Hwang, K. *Computer Arithmetic: Principles, Architecture, and Design.* John Wiley, New York, 1979.

Hwang, K. *Advanced Computer Architecture: Parallelism, Scalability, Programmability.* McGraw-Hill, New York, 1993.

ISO/IEC. "Ada Reference Manual: Language and Standard Libraries." International Standard ISO/IEC 8652:1995(E), 1995.

Jacobson, V., Braden, R., and Borman, D. "TCP Extensions for High Performance." RFC 1323, May 1992.

Jain, R. *The Art of Computer Systems Performance Analysis: Techniques for Experimental Design, Measurement, Simulation, and Modeling.* John Wiley, New York, 1991.

Joseph, M., Prasad, V., and Natarajan, N. *A Multiprocessor Operating System.* Prentice-Hall, Englewood Cliffs, N.J., 1984.

Kaufman, C., Perlman, R., and Speciner, M. *Network Security: Private Communication in a Public World.* Prentice-Hall, Englewood Cliffs, N.J., 1995.

Kehoe, B. *Zen and the Art of the Internet: A Beginner's Guide.* Prentice-Hall, Englewood Cliffs, N.J., 2nd edition, 1992.

Kernighan, B. and Pike, R. *The UNIX Programming Environment.* Prentice-Hall, Englewood Cliffs, N.J., 1984.

Kernighan, B. and Ritchie, D. *The C Programming Language.* Prentice-Hall, Englewood Cliffs, N.J., 2nd edition, 1988.

Knuth, D. *The Art of Computer Programming: Seminumerical Algorithms.* Addison-Wesley, Reading, Mass., 2nd edition, 1981.

Kobayashi, H. *Modeling and Analysis: an Introduction to System Performance Evaluation Methodology.* Addison-Wesley, Reading, Mass., 2nd edition, 1979.

Krol, E. *The Whole Internet User's Guide & Catalog.* O'Reilly & Associates, Sebastopol, Calif., 1992.

Kung, H. "Gigabit Local Area Networks: A Systems Perspective." *IEEE Communications Magazine*, pp. 79–89, April 1992.

Kurose, J., Schwartz, M., and Yemini, Y. "Multiple-Access Protocols and Time-Constrained Communication." *ACM Computing Surveys*, 16(1), March 1984.

Lamport, L. "Time, Clocks, and the Ordering of Events in a Distributed System." *Communications of the ACM*, 21(7):558–565, July 1978.

Lampson, B., Abadi, M., Burrows, M., and Wobber, E. "Authentication in Distributed Systems: Theory and Practice." *ACM Transactions on Computer Systems*, 10(4):265–310, November 1992.

Lane, J. "ATM Knits Voice, Data, on any Net." *IEEE Spectrum*, pp. 42–45, February 1994.

Le Boudec, J.-Y. "The Asynchronous Transfer Mode: A Tutorial." *Computer Networks and ISDN Systems*, 24:279–309, April 1992.

Leffler, S., McKusick, M., Karels, M., and Quarterman, J. *The Design and Implementation of the 4.3BSD UNIX Operating System.* Addison-Wesley, Reading, Mass., 1989.

Levy, E. and Silberschatz, A. "Distributed File Systems: Concepts and Examples." *ACM Computing Surveys*, 22(4):321–375, December 1990.

Li, K. and Hudak, P. "Memory Cache Coherence in Shared Virtual Memory Systems." *ACM Transactions on Computer Systems*, 7(3):321–359, November 1989.

Liang, L., Chanson, S., and Neufeld, G. "Process Groups and Group Communication: Classification and Requirements." *Computer*, 23(2):56–68, February 1990.

Lippman, S. *C++ Primer*. Addison-Wesley, Reading, Mass., 1991.

Lister, A. and Eager, R. *Fundamentals of Operating Systems*. Macmillan, New York, 4th edition, 1988.

Lynch, D. and Rose, M. *Internet System Handbook*. Addison-Wesley, Reading, Mass., 1993.

Maekawa, M., Oldehoeft, A., and Oldehoeft, R. *Operating Systems: Advanced Concepts*. Benjamin/Cummings, Menlo Park, Calif., 1987.

Mange, D. *Microprogrammed Systems, An Introduction to Firmware Theory*. Chapman & Hall, London, 1992.

Mano, M. *Digital Design*. Prentice Hall, Englewood Cliffs, N.J., 1984.

Marsan, M., Albertengo, G., Casetti, C., Neri, F., and Panizzardi, G. "On the Performance of Topologies and Access Protocols for High-Speed LANs and MANs." *Computer Networks and ISDN Systems*, 26:873–893, March 1994.

Mason, T. and Brown, D. *Lex & Yacc*. O'Reilly & Associates, Sebastopol, Calif., 1990.

May, C., Silha, E., Simpson, R., and Warren, H. *The PowerPC Architecture*. Morgan Kaufmann, San Mateo, Calif., 2nd edition, 1994.

Metcalfe, R. "Computer/Network Interface Design: Lessons from Arpanet and Ethernet." *IEEE Journal on Selected Areas in Communications*, 11(2):173–180, February 1993.

Metcalfe, R. and Boggs, D. "Ethernet: Distributed Packet Switching for Local Computer Networks." *Communications of the ACM*, 19(7):395–404, July 1976.

Meyer, B. *Object-oriented Software Construction*. Prentice Hall, Englewood Cliffs, N.J., 1988.

Meyer, T. *Computer Architecture and Organization*. Dilithium Press, Beaverton, Ohio, 1982.

Miller, A. "From Here to ATM." *IEEE Spectrum*, pp. 20–24, June 1994.

Mills, D. "Network Time Protocol (version 3): Specification, Implementation, and Analysis." RFC 1305, July 1992.

Motorola. *M68000: 8-/16-/32-bit Microprocessors Programmer's Reference Manual*, 5th edition, 1986.

MPI Forum. "Document for a Standard Message-Passing Interface." Draft Technical Report, University of Tennessee, Knoxville, Tennessee, December 1993.

Mullender, S. "Interprocess Communcation." In Mullender, S. (ed.), *Distributed Systems*, pp. 217–250. Addison-Wesley, Wokingham, 2nd edition, 1993.

Natarajan, N. and Sinha, M. "Language Issues in the Implementation of a Kernel." *Software – Practice and Experience*, 9:771–778, 1979.

Nelson, G. (ed.). *Systems Programming with Modula-3*. Prentice Hall, Englewood Cliffs, N.J., 1991.

Neuman, B. "Scale in Distributed Systems." In Casavant, T. and Singhal, M. (eds.), *Readings in Distributed Computing Systems*, pp. 463–489. IEEE Computer Society Press, Los Alamitos, Calif., 1994.

Nitzberg, B. and Lo, V. "Distributed Shared Memory: A Survey of Issues and Algorithms." *Computer*, 24(8):52–60, August 1991.

Obraczka, K., Danzig, P., and Li, S.-H. "Internet Resource Discovery Services." *Computer*, 26(9):8–22, September 1993.

Partridge, C. *Gigabit Networking*. Addison-Wesley, Reading, Mass., 1994.

Patterson, D. and Hennessy, J. *Computer Organization and Design, The Hardware/Software Interface*. Morgan Kaufmann, San Mateo, Calif., 1994.

Patterson, D. "STRUM: Structured Microprogram Development System for Correct Firmware." *IEEE Transactions on Computers*, C-25(10):50–59, October 1976.

Perlman, R. *Interconnections: Bridges and Routers*. Addison-Wesley, Reading, Mass., 1992.

Perlman, R. "Routing Protocols." In Lynch, D. and Rose, M. (eds.), *Internet System Handbook*, pp. 157–182. Addison-Wesley, Reading, Mass., 1993.

Peterson, W. *Error Correcting Codes*. MIT Press, Cambridge, Mass., 1968.

Presser, L. and White, J. "Linkers and Loaders." *ACM Computing Surveys*, 4(3):150–167, September 1972.

Quinn, M. *Parallel Computing, Theory and Practice*. McGraw-Hill, New York, 1994.

Rauscher, T. and Adams, P. "Microprogramming: A Tutorial and Survey of Recent Developments." *IEEE Transactions on Computers*, C-29(1):2–20, January 1980.

Rooholamini, R., Cherkassy, V., and Garver, M. "Finding the Right ATM Switch for the Market." *Computer*, 27(4):16–28, April 1994.

Rosenberry, W., Kenney, D., and Fisher, G. *Understanding DCE*. O'Reilly, Sebastopol, Calif., 1992.

Rosenblum, M. and Oosterhout, J. "The Design and Implementation of a Log-Structured File System." In *Proceedings 13th ACM Symposium on Operating Systems Principles*, pp. 1–15, October 1991.

Salus, P. *A Quarter Century of UNIX*. Addison-Wesley, Engelwood Cliffs, N.J., 1994.

Satyanarayanan, M. "Distributed File Systems." In Mullender, S. (ed.), *Distributed Systems*, pp. 353–383. Addison-Wesley, Wokingham, 2nd edition, 1993.

Schroeder, M. "A State-of-the-Art Distributed System: Computing with BOB." In Mullender, S. (ed.), *Distributed Systems*, pp. 1–16. Addison-Wesley, Wokingham, 2nd edition, 1993.

Serlin, O. "MIPS, Drystones and Other Tales." *Datamation*, June 1986.

Shay, W. *Understanding Data Communications and Networks*. PWS Publishing Company, Boston, Mass., 1995.

Shiva, S. *Computer Design and Architecture*. Little, Brown and Company, Boston, Mass., 1985.

Silberschatz, A. and Galvin, P. *Operating System Concepts*. Addison-Wesley, Reading, Mass., 4th edition, 1994.

Smith, J. and Weiss, S. "PowerPC 601 and Alpha21064: A Tale of Two RISCs." *Computer*, 27(6):46–58, June 1994.

Spector, A. "Performing Remote Operations Efficiently on a Local Computer Network." *Communications of the ACM*, 25(4):246–260, April 1982.

Stallings, W. *Computer Organization and Architecture*. Macmillan, New York, 1990.

Stallings, W. *ISDN and Broadband ISDN*. Macmillan, New York, 2nd edition, 1992.

Stallings, W. (ed.). *Advances in Local and Metropolitan Area Networks*. IEEE Computer Society Press, Los Alamitos, Calif., 1993a.

Stallings, W. *Local and Metropolitan Area Networks*. Macmillan, New York, 4th edition, 1993b.

Stallings, W. *Data and Computer Communications*. Macmillan, New York, 4th edition, 1994.

Stallings, W. *Network and Internetwork Security, Principles and Practice*. Prentice-Hall, Englewood Cliffs, N.J., 1995.

Stankovic, J. "Distributed Computing." In Casavant, T. and Singhal, M. (eds.), *Readings in Distributed Computing Systems*, pp. 6–30. IEEE Computer Society Press, Los Alamitos, Calif., 1994.

Stevens, W. *UNIX Network Programming*. Prentice-Hall, Englewood Cliffs, N.J., 1990.

Stevens, W. *Advanced Programming in the UNIX Environment*. Addison-Wesley, Reading, Mass., 1992.

Stevens, W. *TCP/IP Illustrated, Volume 1: The Protocols*. Addison-Wesley, Reading, Mass., 1994.

Stroustroup, B. *The C++ Programming Language*. Addison-Wesley, Reading, Mass., 1987.

Stuck, B. and Arthurs, E. *A Computer Communications Network Performance Analysis Primer*. Prentice-Hall, Englewood Cliffs, N.J., 1985.

Stumm, M. and Zhou, S. "Algorithms Implementing Distributed Shared Memory." *Computer*, 23(5):54–64, 1990.

Sunderam, V. "PVM: A Framework for Parallel Distributed Computing." *Concurrency: Practice and Experience*, 24(4):315–339, December 1990.

Tanenbaum, A. *Operating Systems Design and Implementation*. Prentice-Hall, Englewood Cliffs, N.J., 1987.

Tanenbaum, A. *Computer Networks*. Prentice-Hall, Englewood Cliffs, N.J., 2nd edition, 1988.

Tanenbaum, A. *Structured Computer Organization*. Prentice-Hall, Englewood Cliffs, N.J., 3rd edition, 1990a.

Tanenbaum, A. *Modern Operating Systems*. Prentice Hall, Englewood Cliffs, N.J., 1992.

Tanenbaum, A. *Distributed Operating Systems*. Prentice-Hall, Englewood Cliffs, N.J., 1995.

Tanenbaum, A. *Computer Networks*. Prentice-Hall, Englewood Cliffs, N.J., 3rd edition, 1996.

Tanenbaum, A., van Renesse, R., van Staveren, H., Sharp, G., Mullender, S., Jansen, J., and van Rossum, G. "Experiences with the Amoeba Distributed Operating System." *Communications of the ACM*, 33(12):46–63, December 1990b.

Tomlinson, R. "Selecting Sequence Numbers." In *Proceedings ACM SIGCOMM/SIGOPS Interprocess Communication Workshop*, pp. 11–23, 1975.

Tymes, L. "Routing and Flow Control in TYMNET." *IEEE Transactions on Communications*, COM-29(4), April 1981.

van der Goor, A. *Computer Architecture and Design*. Addison-Wesley, Reading, Mass., 1989.

Vetter, R., Spell, C., and Ward, C. "Mosaic and the World-Wide Web." *Computer*, 27(10):49–57, October 1994.

Watson, R. and Mamrak, S. "Gaining Efficiency in Transport Services by Appropriate Design and Implementation Choices." *ACM Transactions on Computer Systems*, 5(2):97–120, May 1987.

Watt, D. *Programming Language Syntax and Semantics*. Prentice-Hall, Englewood Cliffs, N.J., 1991.

Welsh, J. and McKeag, M. *Structured System Programming*. Prentice-Hall, Englewood Cliffs, N.J., 1980.

Wiederhold, G. *Database Design*. McGraw-Hill, New York, 2nd edition, 1983.

Wilkes, M. *Automatic Digital Computers*. Methuen, London, 1956.

Wirth, N. "The Programming Language Pascal." *Acta Informatica*, 1:35–63, 1971.

Wirth, N. *Systematic Programming*. Prentice-Hall, Englewood Cliffs, N.J., 1973.

Wirth, N. *Algorithms + Data Structures = Programs*. Prentice-Hall, Englewood Cliffs, N.J., 1976a.

Wirth, N. "Modula: A Language for Modular Multi-Programming." *Software – Practice & Experience*, 7:3–35, 1976b.

Wirth, N. *Programming in Modula-2*. Springer-Verlag, Berlin, 2nd edition, 1983.

Wright, G. and Stevens, W. *TCP/IP Illustrated, Volume 2: The Implementation*. Addison-Wesley, Reading, Mass., 1995.

Index

U

V

W

X